Tipu
Sultan

ADVANCE PRAISE FOR THE BOOK

'Stripping away the intermingling layers of deification and denigration in which Tipu Sultan has long been swaddled, Vikram Sampath seeks to demystify him, painting a searing portrait of this complex, mercurial, and vastly ambitious ruler and military commander who is many things to many people, Indian and British, historian and layperson, alike.

'It may well be impossible to resolve the contradiction between the visionary Indian resistance hero to British conquest, and the widely reviled murderer of thousands of Hindus and Christians. Nevertheless, Sampath gamely tries. Bemoaning Tipu's "socio-political weaponisation", he hopes to present the Tiger of Mysore as he was—warts and all—proving yet again that in history there are never just blacks and whites, for the past is steeped in varying hues of grey. Yet, at times, one feels that Sampath is holding an eighteenth-century warrior to the same standards a twenty-first-century citizen would hold his representative in a secular, liberal democracy.

'But what is indisputable is Sampath's prodigious scholarship—born of a blazing childhood passion for this epoch in Indian history—and the deftness with which he weaves five years of rigorous research into an engaging and remarkably written tome: one that, even after nine hundred pages, leaves you craving for more of the tumultuous-yet-thrilling era he brings to life. Even if one cannot always agree with all the conclusions he has drawn from the historical data in his arsenal, Vikram Sampath's *Tipu Sultan: The Saga of Mysore's Interregnum (1760–1799)* is an intellectually stimulating read. *Shabash!'*—**Shashi Tharoor, member of Parliament (Lok Sabha) for Thiruvananthapuram**

'Vikram Sampath has already made his mark as a historian who substantiates what he writes with extensive research. He now turns his lens to Tipu Sultan. Rarely are people objective about Tipu Sultan, preferring to fit him into a pre-conceived narrative. Vikram gives us the bare truth, so that we can make up our minds about the legacy of an individual who continues to be controversial'—**Bibek Debroy, author and economist**

'The eighteenth century was one of the darkest phases for India. It slid from prosperity and relative stability to a century of conflict and decline. The sheer complexity of the turbulence is both fascinating and disturbing. In this first volume of a study of Haider Ali and Tipu Sultan, Vikram Sampath has retold the story of how India lost its way and ended up losing its sovereignty to foreign powers. Apart from the richness of the events themselves, this book is an example of how narrative history should be written. It is a study where contrived romanticism of the past has been set aside in favour of the actual horrors that overwhelmed southern India'—**Swapan Dasgupta, writer on history and politics**

'The various histories of the life of Tipu has always, thus far, only illuminated one side of his rule. His other side has always been conveniently ignored. Vikram Sampath does the much-needed work of telling the true story of Tipu, from his fanatical views, to the mistakes he made that eroded the sizeable state his father built. I very much appreciate the effort to bring out this volume and hope readers see the true history of a falsely exalted personality'—**Yaduveer Krishnadatta Chamaraja Wadiyar, member of Parliament (Lok Sabha) for Mysore and Coorg, and scion of the Mysore royal family**

'Hyder Ali and Tipu Sultan were among the most colourful characters of eighteenth-century India—shameless opportunists who simultaneously opposed the East India Company as well as committed barbaric atrocities on several Indian communities. Yet again, Vikram Sampath has cut through the fog of time and legend to bring out the best available primary evidence. The public debate will continue but Vikram's excellent book will surely provide the basis of a more informed discussion'—**Sanjeev Sanyal, writer and economist**

Tipu Sultan

The Saga *of*
Mysore's
Interregnum
(1760–1799)

With a Foreword by
S.L. BHYRAPPA

VIKRAM SAMPATH

VINTAGE
An imprint of Penguin Random House

VINTAGE

Vintage is an imprint of the Penguin Random House group of
companies whose addresses can be found at global.penguinrandomhouse.com

Published by Penguin Random House India Pvt. Ltd
4th Floor, Capital Tower 1, MG Road,
Gurugram 122 002, Haryana, India

Penguin
Random House
India

First published in Vintage by Penguin Random House India 2024

10 9 8 7 6 5

The views and opinions expressed in this book are the author's own and the
facts are as reported by him which have been verified to the extent possible,
and the publishers are not in any way liable for the same.

Please note that no part of this book may be used or reproduced in any manner
for the purpose of training artificial intelligence technologies or systems.

ISBN 9780670094691

Typeset in Adobe Caslon Pro by MAP Systems, Bengaluru, India
Printed at Thomson Press India Ltd, New Delhi

www.penguin.co.in

MIX
Paper | Supporting
responsible forestry
FSC® C010615
FSC
www.fsc.org

*For my doting parents who have always been my inspiration,
and pillars of strength and the perennial wind beneath my wings*

Contents

Foreword

I have read a great deal of history on the 'legend' Tipu Sultan since my childhood. I am happy that I got an opportunity to read one more book on Tipu Sultan authored by historian Dr Vikram Sampath and to write the foreword for the same. Before I elaborate, I can only say that among the many books that I have read on the subject, this book is exceptional, for it is an exhaustive, intense and well-researched book with factual accounts and a captivating narrative style.

As I was reading this book, my memories went back to the articles I had written in a leading Kannada daily long ago when controversy erupted in Karnataka over the celebration of Tipu Sultan's birth anniversary (*jayanthi*). These articles give a critical view of Tipu Sultan's rule and legacy, covering religious persecution, forcible conversion and its impact on our culture.

During 1969–70, the Central government under Indira Gandhi, with a mission to integrate the nation through education, had established a committee under the chairmanship of G. Parthasarathy, a diplomat who was close to the Nehru–Gandhi family. At that time, I was a Reader in Philosophy of Education at NCERT and was selected as part of the five-member committee. In the first meeting, Mr Parthasarathy explained the purpose of the committee in his typical diplomatic polite language: 'It is our duty to remove thorns from the minds of the growing children, which will shape up as barriers for the national integration. Such thorns are mostly seen in history lessons. We can even find them occasionally in the lessons of language, social science and history. We have to weed out such thorns. We have to include only such thoughts that will inculcate the concept of national integration in the minds of our children. This committee has this great responsibility.'

When other members were nodding their heads respectfully, I politely questioned him: 'Sir, I cannot understand what you said. Will you please explain with some illustrations?'

He started saying, 'Ghazni Mohammed looted Somnath Temple, Aurangzeb built the mosques by demolishing the temples in Kashi and Mathura, he collected *jizya*, etc. How do such useless facts help build a strong India other than creating hatred in the minds?' When I said, 'But they are historical truths?', he replied, 'Plenty of truths are there. To use these truths with discrimination is the wisdom of the historians.'

I added, 'Sir, you gave examples of Kashi and Mathura. Even now, lakhs of people visit these places from nooks and corners of the country as pilgrims. They see huge mosques built using the same walls, pillars and columns of the demolished temples. Behind the mosque, they also see a cowshed-like structure built recently in a corner that represents our temple. The pilgrims are disturbed to witness such awful structures. They describe the plight of their temples to their relatives after they return home. Do you think such feelings can create national integration? One can hide the history in school texts. But can we hide such facts when the schoolchildren visit the place as part of the excursion? The researchers have listed more than 30,000 such ruined temples in India. Can we hide them all?'

Mr Parthasarthy interrupted me by asking, 'You are a professor of Philosophy. Please tell us what is the purpose of history?'

I explained, 'Nobody can define the purpose of history. We do not know how things will shape up in future because of the advancement in science and technology. Some Western thinkers might have called it the philosophy of history. But such thoughts are futile. Our discussion here should be: What is the purpose of teaching history? History is seeking the truth about our past events and learning about ancient human lives by studying the inscriptions, records, literary works, relics, artefacts and so on. Historical truths help us understand and learn the noble qualities that our ancestors adopted during their times . . .'

'Can we hurt the feelings of the minority? Can we divide the society? Can we sow the seeds of poison?' He stopped my explanation by asking such questions.

My line of argument was quite clear. Categorization on the lines of majority and minority would itself result in the division of society. It may be a strategy adopted to divide society for political gains. This idea of 'seeds of poison' is prejudiced. Why should the minority think of Ghazni Mohammed or Aurangzeb as their own people? Many kingdoms were destroyed by the religious bigotry of Aurangzeb. The Mughal Empire was at its pinnacle because of Akbar, who favoured religious harmony. We should teach such lessons to the children without offending or hiding the historical truths. These ideals of hiding history are due to political reasons. If education does not impart the intellectual power to face the truth and build emotional maturity, then such education is meaningless. I strongly reiterate: teaching history that is not based on truth is dangerous. (Since my stand irked the Chairman, the committee was restructured after some time, and my name was promptly deleted! Surprisingly, in my place, a lecturer in history with leftist ideals was included!).

It was unfortunate that history books for school students were once dominated by Marxist historians, and they always suppressed the truth. When reviewed, one can observe how members belonging to this group had schemes to invade the minds of growing children. For instance, students were not told how Muslim invaders destroyed the universities of Nalanda, Vikramasheela, Jagaddala, Odanthapura etc., and the brutal killings of the Buddhist monks—the worst catastrophe suffered by Buddhism in India.

The method adopted by the communists, who were unable to come out of the clutches of Marxism, the very basis of their identity, was to systematically appoint people in the universities who were loyal to their theories. They were expected to present their theories through newspapers, television and other media, get appreciative critiques for the books written by their 'favourite' authors, devise plans to dispel the writers from the opposite group. In addition, they would spread leftists views through frequent seminars and attract young minds, get teaching positions in universities. The communist parties' stand on truth became the gospel for its members. The best example that I can mention here is Russian books published by the communists and sold at cheaper rates in India and other countries.

* * *

During the freedom struggle, *laavani* singers, who were skilled in oral renditions but often lacked formal education, used to sing with an instrument called *damadi*, exaggerating Tipu Sultan. Some Muslim merchants encouraged these singers by giving them money. Tipu's reputation grew largely due to his opposition to British rule. He was painted as a patriot and dramas were performed to praise him. The audience believed this false narrative as true history. Marxists, politicians concerned with vote banks, Muslim artists, drama writers and directors, filmmakers portrayed him as a national leader in post-Independence India. True history lost its life. I have often written and lectured that authors of historical novels have the moral responsibility to present historical facts without distortions.

Followers of Tipu described the British as inhumane, highlighting their demand that Tipu surrender his children to them as hostages till he paid them their huge war indemnity. With this, it is claimed that a culture that entertained the surrendering of small kids as 'war prisoners' took birth! But what actually made Tipu surrender his children as war prisoners? The British demanded huge amount of money as their war expenditure. Since Tipu did not have money readily, he offered to keep his two young sons with the British. He promised that he would keep his two young sons, and he would get them back after he could arrange the cash. If Tipu was in the place of the British, he would have converted their children into Islam. But the British retained their original religion and were affectionate towards them.

It is not a new thing that many politicians address Tipu as a great son of Karnataka. During the rule of the Wadiyar dynasty, Kannada was the official language; but Tipu removed Kannada and changed the official language to Farsi (Persian). Since I belong to the family of *shanubhogas* (who were part of the revenue department of old Mysuru), I personally know the Kannada terminologies of that department. Tipu either added or changed Kannada terminologies to Farsi like; *khathe, khardi, pahani, khaneesumari, gudasta, takhte, thari, khushki, bagaytu, banjaru, jamabandi, ahavalu, khavandu, amaldar, shirastedar*, etc.

Tipu did not stop there. He even changed the original names of the places. So, Brahmapuri was changed as Sultanpet, Kozhikode of Kerala to Farrukhabad, Chitradurga to Farrukh Yab Hissar, Kodagu to Jafarabad, Devanahalli to Yusufkhan, Dindigal to Khaleelabad, Gutti to Faiz Hissar, Krishnagiri to Falk-il-Azam, Mysuru to Nazarabad, Penugonda to Fakrabad, Sankridurga to Muzifarabad, Sira to Rustumabad, Sakaleshpura to Manjarabad and so on. The question that revolves in our minds is whether all these actions of Tipu show his nationalism, loyalty to Kannada language and tolerance of other religions?

As I delved into the historical archives surrounding Tipu Sultan, I stumbled upon a fascinating collection that sheds new light on this controversial figure of Indian history. 'The Dreams of Tipu Sultan', a series of papers recovered by British Colonel William Kirkpatrick from the Srirangapatna Palace following Tipu's demise in the Fourth Anglo–Mysore War of 1799, offers an unfiltered glimpse into the mind of the Sultan himself.

These documents, penned in Farsi by Tipu, provide what I believe to be the most compelling and direct evidence of his religious fervour and political aspirations. Kirkpatrick's partial translations, alongside the original manuscripts, are now preserved in the India Office in London, serving as a testament to their historical significance. This collection offers readers a rare opportunity to hear Tipu Sultan's voice directly, unfiltered by the lens of either his admirers or detractors. It presents a complex picture of a ruler driven by religious zeal and expansionist dreams, compelling us to reassess our understanding of this ruler in Indian history.

What struck me most about these writings is the stark terminology Tipu employed. He consistently referred Hindus as '*kafirs*' or infidels and the British as 'Christians', revealing a theology and world view deeply rooted in religious distinctions. He had an unbridled zeal for converting non-Muslims to Muslims and non-Muslim states to Muslim states. In this entire book of his dreams, there is no mention or an iota of his thought of 'how to modernize India (or Mysore)'. Tipu's only mission was to throw out the British from India as he felt they were a major obstacle for him. It is unfortunate that 'secularists' portrayed Tipu as a great religiously tolerant person and as a freedom fighter. A man who took the support of the equally colonial and imperialist French, and invited Zaman Shah of Afghanistan, the Caliph of Turkey and the Shah of Persia to invade India and establish a Muslim Caliphate cannot be a freedom fighter.

Another aspect of Tipu Sultan's rule that warrants critical examination is his approach to education, often cited as evidence of his progressive stance. However, a closer look reveals a more complex picture. While Muslims in Malabar and Tamil Nadu have maintained their linguistic connections to Malayalam and Tamil, respectively, the Muslim population in Karnataka primarily speaks Urdu. This linguistic shift can be directly attributed to Tipu's policies, which mandated Farsi and Urdu as the sole permitted mediums of instruction.

When Tipu looted the Mysore Palace in 1796, he ordered to burn all the valuable and rare books and manuscripts, palm leaves that contained priceless handwritten notes to cook horse gram for his horses, and other files kept in the palace library. There are plenty of references in, for instance, the *Malabar Manual* by William Logan about the cruel military operations and Islamic atrocities of Tipu Sultan in Malabar—forcible mass circumcision and conversion, large-scale killings, looting and destruction of hundreds of Hindu temples, and other barbarities like gang-raping helpless women. There are hundreds of such incidents mentioned in various documents. It is impossible to reinforce nationalism based on the false picturization of History.

This extremely well-researched and interesting book by Vikram Sampath, *Tipu Sultan: The Tale of the Mysore Interregnum*, is the result of extensive historical research. The long list of references, variety of sources, citations and bibliography make it amply clear that he has stayed true to his craft and conscience as a historian. The book covers many known and hitherto unknown aspects of Tipu Sultan's legacy and stormy rule. Authors should enjoy complete liberty while writing serious historical books with ample reference to the inscriptions, records, relics, excavations and other evidences. Vikram has succeeded in this, just as he has in all his earlier books. He is an exception in the sense that while on the one hand he is loyal to the historical facts, he has also ably interpreted these historical evidences independently. And, more importantly, put this plethora of research findings in an interesting narrative that is sure to captivate every reader. I am sure this book will be a highly acclaimed and a definitive work on Tipu Sultan, and discerning readers will accept it as an authentic and unbiased version of Tipu's history. My warm blessings to Vikram to continue on his chosen path of fearlessly bringing to the fore honest and unbiased scholarship in Indian historiography.

15 August 2024

S.L. Bhyrappa
Mysuru

Prologue

After the storming of the fort of Srirangapatna in May 1799, which led to the annihilation of the most dreaded foe of the British—Tipu Sultan of Mysore—the victors found a rather curious toy in his chambers. 'The Musical Tiger', as it was called, was a near life-size figure of a tiger, carved and painted from wood, preying on a prostrate English soldier in uniform. It was designed in such a manner that by the turning of a handle, the animal's growls would mix with the shrieks of its distressed and dying victim. Tipu's favourite toy is supposed to have kept him busy in his waking hours and possibly fuelled and deepened his unbridled hatred for the British. The conquerors were amused by this contraption and shipped it to London, where it cast a spell on everyone who saw it after it was first displayed in the East India Company's museum in 1808. Once the Company was dissolved and its assets were all transferred to the British Crown, the toy seems to have shifted hands. For some strange reason, it was found to have made its way to the India Office Library. Tipu Sultan's restless spirit seemed to plague his foes even after his death. In the middle of an afternoon, when scholars were engrossed in their research, the contraption would suddenly start operating by itself, scaring the wits out of everyone in the room.[1] As the librarian A.J. Arberry recounted in *The Library of the India Office: A Historical Sketch*:

> But we almost forget our old friend, the tiger. Who has not seen and, what is more, heard him at the old India House? And who, having suffered under his unearthly sounds, can ever dismiss him from his memory? It seems that this horrid creature—we mean, of

course the figure representing it—was found among the treasures of Tippoo Sultan when he fell at the siege of Seringapatam [sic] . . . these shrieks and growls [of the victim and tiger respectively] were the constant plague of the student, busy at work in the library of the old India House, when the Leadenhall Street public, unremittingly, it appears, were bent on keeping up the performance of this barbarous machine. No doubt that a number of perverse lections have crept into the editions of our oriental works through the shock which the tiger caused to the nerves of the readers taken unawares. Luckily he is now removed from the library; but what is also lucky, a kind of fate has deprived him of his handle, and stopped up, we are happy to think, some of his internal organs; or, as an ignorant visitor would say, he is out of repair; and we do sincerely hope that he will remain so, to be seen and to be admired, if necessary, but to be heard no more.[2]

After it fell into disrepair, it was restored in a manner that left the apparatus without its auditory mechanism, but it remained a passive exhibit, admired by awestruck visitors. Like its owner, the toy too had been tamed and permanently silenced. It was among the items that were allotted to the Indian section of the South Kensington Museum, now called the Victoria and Albert Museum. One can see this muted toy in display even now at the V&A.

Much like the toy playing its act on unsuspecting readers in the library, the ghost of Tipu Sultan resurfaces every now and then, muddying and allowing contemporary politics in India to play out on either side of the debate. Be it controversies related to naming a university or the airport in Bengaluru after him, his problematic legacy towards faiths other than his own, his outlook towards the language of the state he ruled, Kannada, or the competitive politics constantly played out in his name by political parties and ideologues in Karnataka and the rest of the country.

In 2014, when the Congress Government in Karnataka decided to design a gigantic bust of Tipu Sultan brandishing his sword to represent the state in the national parade during the Republic Day, on Rajpath (now Kartavya Path), a giant war of words and acrimony broke out among politicians, media chatterati and social media users.[3] 'So, Karnataka is all about Tipu Sultan who killed thousands of Hindus??? Is this what secularism is all about??' screamed one post on X (then Twitter) while another questioned, 'If Tamil Nadu or West Bengal send a tableau of Robert Clive, will Centre accept it?' A decade earlier, when industrial baron Vijay Mallya bought Tipu's sword in an auction for Rs 1.5 crore, it created another storm. After his fortunes nosedived, Mallya was reported to have returned the sword in 2016, claiming that his family told him that 'it brought bad luck'.[4]

In 2015, the Congress government in Karnataka stirred the hornet's nest yet again by deciding to commemorate his birth anniversary as Tipu Jayanti, on 10 November, across the state. This led to a huge backlash, not only from the political opposition then, the Bharatiya Janata Party (BJP), but also several social organizations that had intergenerational memories of the trauma and tortures inflicted on their ancestors by Tipu Sultan. Along with the Sangh Parivar outfits that bitterly opposed this decision, several Mangalorean Catholic groups and institutions had their separate protests.[5] The Vishwa Hindu Parishad (VHP) held that they did not 'have an issue if a group of Tipu admirers celebrates his birthday. Our only issue is with the government spending the taxpayer's money to celebrate a ruler who was communal and had a history of killing and converting Hindus and Christians'.[6] The Mangalore based United Christian Association declared their opposition for the reason that Tipu's army 'demolished 27 churches, including Milagres Church (a 17th-century Catholic church) and took away 80,000 Catholic men, women and children. While some died, most were taken to Srirangapatna (Tipu's capital) and converted to Islam'.[7] The present-day Milagres Church was rebuilt much later, in 1911.

Things took an ugly turn when the protests in Kodagu (Coorg), where fierce opposition to Tipu Sultan for what he did to the brave Kodavas (Coorgis), sparked such a law and order issue that two people lost their lives too in Madikeri.[8] A Codava National Council

(CNC) that had been clamouring for separate statehood for two decades declared that 'Kodavas never forget and will never forgive Tipu Sultan for the excesses committed on them'.[9] The Dakshina Kannada and Udupi districts of Karnataka were also on boil as violent protests simmered across the coastal regions. The celebrations had to be held under the threat of Section 144 (that prohibited assembly of four or more people in any area) which was imposed in several districts of the state for about forty-eight hours around the Jayanti. It was only after the Government changed in Karnataka and the BJP was propelled into power in 2019 that a decision was taken to stop the Jayanti as a Government exercise.

The Kannada literary world too had always traditionally been deeply divided into pro and anti-Tipu camps, with the likes of Girish Karnad and U.R. Ananthamurthy, among others on one side and S.L. Bhyrappa and Chidananda Murthy, among others on the other. Karnad had to even apologize publicly for his demand to name the new airport in Bengaluru after Tipu Sultan, as Tipu was born there in Devanahalli, and not after the founder of the city Kempegowda.[10] Cautious about the backlash that it would receive from the community of Vokkaligas that Kempegowda came from, even the ruling Congress in the state left Karnad high and dry by disassociating themselves from his remarks.[11] Though most Bangaloreans, who have remained frustrated since 2008 when the new airport came up at Devanahalli, might want the political parties, governments and the intellectual class to envision a hi-speed multi-modal transport network to the far-flung airport, rather than bicker on meaningless naming controversies. But such is the allure of historical figures and controversial leaders that everyone seems intent on milking it for their advantage, one way or the other.

The theatre of the absurd continued in the run-up to the 2023 State elections in Karnataka. The BJP drummed up a story of Tipu Sultan having been killed not by the British but by two strongmen, Uri Gowda and Nanje Gowda, citing a book *Suvarna Mandya* by D. Javaregowda.[12] This again was with the idea of winning over the influential Vokkaliga vote bank in the state which the BJP was eyeing from their competitor then, the Janata Dal (Secular). For weeks thereafter, all that people in Karnataka did, especially in the media, was to engage in endless debates on these two chieftains—someone that no British or Mysorean chronicler had ever mentioned in their works. It was finally left to the religious heads of the community and the Vokkaligara Sangha to issue a sharp ultimatum to the BJP to stop 'peddling lies in the name of Vokkaligas', that this sordid controversy was laid to rest for now.[13]

Sadly, in all of this cacophonous surround sound, history becomes the real casualty. It hence becomes a historian's burden, nay, responsibility to lay bare the facts and documents out there and let the discerning reader judge for themselves as to which way their opinion veers. This is exactly what I have tried to do in this book—give the reader an unbiased and fact-based, objective assessment of this eighteenth century monarch of Mysore and his extremely troubled and polarizing legacy. To understand and contextualize Tipu Sultan, one needs to closely study his father Haidar Ali. Haidar was a typical Machiavellian ruler who ran with the hare and hunted with the hounds, raising his fortunes through sheer avarice and opportunism, usurping the very kingdom of the benefactor Wodeyar Maharaja of Mysore, who had paid a ransom to free him as a young boy. That he was destiny's chosen child and climbed the ladders of royalty in Mysore in just twelve years of his entry into public life is quite a story in itself. The first section of the book is hence dedicated entirely to the life and rise of Haidar Ali in the Mysorean polity, setting thereby also a clear contrast to the son who inherited all of this on a platter, only to squander it all away due to his short-sightedness and thereby usher utter ruin upon himself and his family. The several players in the absolutely chaotic eighteenth century in India—the Marathas, the Nizam, the Malabar chieftains, the Travancore Rajas, the Arcot Nawab, the waning Mughal dynasty and, of course, the European powers, particularly the British and French, become the chief dramatis personae who come and play their parts in this theatre of turmoil.

Quite ironically, I owe my literary career and sojourn into historical research to Tipu Sultan. I must have been a boy of twelve in the 1990s when the controversial tele-serial *The Sword of Tipu Sultan* was aired on the one and only channel we watched those days, Doordarshan. Produced and directed by Sanjay Khan, who also played the lead, the serial was based on an eponymous novel by Bhagwan S. Gidwani. The serial, however, raised several heckles in Karnataka as it did now during the Tipu Jayanti celebrations. The Bombay Malayalee Samajam posed fierce opposition to the serial for depicting Tipu as a messiah with a blemish-less halo and not showing the innumerable atrocities that were heaped in the Malabar regions of Kerala. A mass petition signed by over 500 citizens was sent to the Supreme Court of India where a public interest litigation had been filed 'against the distortion of history, and misuse of official media'.[14] Though this was dismissed, a writ petition followed in the Bombay High Court on 26 December 1989 by Dr Ravindra Ramdas, Shri R.G. Menon, Dr P.C.C. Raja and Shri Ravi Varma. But their case failed both at the Bombay High Court and later the appellate petition in the Supreme Court. A member of the Zamorin family in Calicut, Dr P.C.C. Raja then urged the Union Minister of Information and Broadcasting in his letter to him, dated 23 May 1990, to stop the telecast of the historical drama series as he could not 'allow history to be distorted, much less allow the serial to be telecast leaving out references to Tipu's atrocities and crimes which really outshine and outnumber his meagre achievements.'[15] But nothing seemed to stop the popular tele-serial from being aired. Historian Sitaram Goel wrote in anguish: 'One can conclude quite safely that Nehruvian Secularism is a magic formula for transmitting base metals into twenty-four carat gold. How else do we explain ... the fact of Aurangzeb becoming the benefactor of Hindu temples; or the fact of Sirajuddaula, Mir Qasim, Hyder Ali, Tipu Sultan and Bahadur Shah Zafar becoming the heroes of India's freedom struggle against British imperialism?'[16]

While people in Kerala felt affronted by the serial, opposition brewed even in Karnataka. A large part of Southern Karnataka, which was previously known as Mysore State before independence, was ruled by the Hindu monarchs of the Wodeyar dynasty. It was one of the longest reigning royal houses of India that maintained its hold over the region from 1399 when the dynasty was established, till 1947 when India won her freedom. There was only a brief forty year interregnum or an intermission period when their throne was usurped by Haidar Ali and his son Tipu Sultan. To boost the image of Tipu, the tele-serial portrayed the Mysore Royal Family in an extremely derisive manner. The ruler from whom Haidar usurped the throne, Immadi Krishnaraja Wodeyar, was shown as an obese retard who was effete and danced along with the court dancer. His wife, the sagacious queen of Mysore whose efforts eventually won back the kingdom for her family, Lakshmi Ammanni, was portrayed as a cunning and conniving vamp of sorts. This upset several common folks in the state who still hold the Wodeyar family in great regard and reverence for all the progressive measures that they took, especially the later rulers such as Chamaraja Wodeyar X, Nalwadi Krishnaraja Wodeyar and Jayachamaraja Wodeyar. When the studio caught fire and Sanjay Khan suffered a face burn, several people in Karnataka mumbled that it was the 'curse of the Wodeyar' that had caused this misfortune on the actor–director.

As a young boy who was watching all this drama unfold, I was seized by a mania to discover the real truth behind the false portrayal. Being a school student then who hated history for its puerile memorization of dates, wars and chronological successions of rulers, the study of Mysore's sovereigns came as a whiff of fresh air. It was a completely self-motivated exercise, undertaken without any duress. For a lower middle-class family like ours that barely managed to meet its ends then, it was a huge sacrifice on the part of my doting parents to fund this mania of their teenaged son. Every vacation meant going to Mysore, meeting members of the royal family, historians, archivists, old-timers and others to collect information about that one ruler and his wife who had been painted so badly in the tele-serial. Never was this done with an intention of writing a book, but with just the innocent joys of discovery and investigation. In the process, it became a family project of sorts with my parents and maternal grandmother joining forces in what would seem a meaningless exercise. Soon, the interest widened to the entire Wodeyar dynasty and compiling material around them.

All of this was going on as I prepared for my board exams, some entrance examinations and further study. The 'Mysore bug' kept me rivetted for almost a decade. It was later that I discovered that not a single book had been written in the modern times that covered the entire span of the Wodeyar history through the dimensions of political, social, economic and cultural history of the place and its contribution to the creation of a modern, progressive Karnataka. In the highly Delhi-centric view of Indian history, large swathes of the country remain underrepresented. But as Toni Morrison famously said, 'If there's a book that you want to read and it hasn't been written yet, then you must write it.' This was how, totally serendipitously, my childhood passion metamorphosed into my first book *Splendours of Royal Mysore: The Untold Story of the Wodeyars* in 2008. Haidar Ali and Tipu Sultan obviously found a section in this book.

I was thereafter invited for talks and lectures at several places and during one such exposition on the Interregnum period of Haidar and Tipu, when I began quoting verbatim some of the letters of Tipu, all hell broke loose in the hall. A section of the hitherto civilized audience broke up in sloganeering, hurling paper rockets at the podium and forcing the organizers to hurriedly terminate the session and usher me inside. Amidst the din, a man reached out to my bewildered and hassled father who sat among the audience with a terse message: 'He is your only son, advise him well if you wish to have him around you for long!' If this kerfuffle felt like a scene from a Bollywood film, it sadly was not, but was part of my father and my lived experience. The aggression of that evening stunned us, deeply impacting my mother's already precarious health. In our naivety, we believed that historiography meant telling the truth as it was. But its intense sociopolitical weaponization was something that we were both unaware of and yet to be confronted with.

A few months later, an article that I had written for a local newspaper with some references to Tipu, caused another huge furor. Lumpen fanatics gathered around the newspaper office, demanding my apology—something I stoutly refused because everything I had written was factual and well-documented. This incensed the hoodlums. My effigy and copies of the article were then burnt in the heart of the city by the protesters before they angrily departed shouting slogans and abuses. My harried mother made me vow that I'd never write or speak in public about Tipu thereafter, and to assuage her, I had grudgingly agreed. Now that she is no longer around in flesh and blood, I happily broke the promise made to her and decided to bring out a full-length, definitive biography of the man who intrudes our contemporary lives with such violent polarization. This idea of demystifying the man hovered in my mind for nearly the last twelve–fifteen years. Yet, it was only after my mother's sad and untimely demise in 2018 that I mustered the courage to take the idea that was gnawing my mind, to fruition. All of this with the fervent wish and prayer that from the heavens up there my mother would protect me against any such manufactured, bigoted and concocted outrage, if they were to befall on me for speaking the truth. These anecdotes are not just mine, but they could be of any historian who dares to wade through some of the no-go waters of Indian history or challenge supposed sacrosanct icons.

But at the end of the day, a historian's real shield is his or her faithful adherence to facts and facts alone. And thus, it is with this book too, as it has been in all my previous ones. I have always maintained a strict adherence to the archive and documents, as also to my conscience and craft, without prejudicing my writing either by contemporary viewpoints, the battlefield of politics of today or the straightjacket of ideology. When all of history is but an interim report, the onus is on successive generations to keep looking back and drawing from their experiences, inferences and research, retell the past. This book builds significantly on my earlier work on the history of Mysore, where the interregnum was but a short section. Drawing from diverse sources from primary ones in archives across India and outside, literature in several languages and oral histories, I zoom into those four decades of tumult that the region faced under the father–son duo. In this book, Tipu emerges for me as a complex character and a historian's enigma—one who defies easy compartmentalization. The good, the bad and the ugly in Tipu Sultan's legacy emerge. After all, in the Indic imagination, *Itihasa* (the Sanskrit word for history) translates literally to 'It thus happened'. Glossing over his cruelties and barbaric deeds, only to sound politically correct or labour under a sad misapprehension that whitewashing these crimes would somehow magically maintain social cohesion and national unity is being extremely treacherous and intellectually dishonest. At the same time, erasing some redeeming features of his character and life is also being disingenuous with history. The truths of history are sober and usually park themselves at the centre, amidst a large array of fuzzy grey that lies in between the strict boxes of white and black.

The bare truth, as I found it, has been presented in this book for the readers to absorb and assess for themselves about how they'd like to view Tipu's legacy. I sincerely hope the complexities and multiple layers in the contested character of Tipu and the numerous contemporary players in the chaotic Indian political theatre of his times evinces your interest and this book, which has truly been a labour of love and a consummation of a childhood passion, finds a resonance with you!

August 2024   Vikram Sampath
                                                          Bengaluru

1

The Ancestry of Haidar Ali Khan

Mir Hussain Ali Khan Kirmani, an Iranian émigré who served in the court of Tipu Sultan from 1781 to 1786, penned down an elaborate biographical study in Persian of his master's family in 1802. He wrote this treatise, titled *Nishan-i-Hydari*, while being held in captivity by the British in Vellore after the fall of Srirangapatna in 1799. Kirmani traces the lineage of Tipu Sultan and his father, Haidar Ali, and establishes that they were of Quraysh descent.[1] The Quraysh were a group of Arab clans that historically controlled and inhabited the city of Mecca and its Kaaba. Kirmani writes that during the reign of the Sultan of Bijapur, Muhammad Adil Shah (r. 1627–56 CE), a certain Wali Mohammad of this clan supposedly migrated from Delhi, coming down south to the town of Aland in Gulbarga. Given his religious predilection, Wali Mohammad's interest naturally gravitated towards the Banda Nawaz mausoleum there, of the fourteenth-century Sufi Banda Nawaz Gaisu Daraz. The adherents of the tomb not only received him with great respect but also made arrangements for a monthly allowance for his sustenance. Wali Mohammad had a son, Mohammad Ali, for whom he was looking for a worthy bride. From among the family of the adherents of the dargah, a suitable girl was selected for the young man.

However, it must be mentioned here that a slight variation of this ancestry, in terms of the names of the individuals, is found in one of the most celebrated accounts on the history of Mysore by Colonel Mark Wilks. A Manx soldier, historian and administrator in the East India Company, Wilks served as the Resident in Mysore

---

* Please refer to the corresponding illustration in the appendix.

from 1803 to 1808. This was when he became familiar with the affairs of the kingdom and made several Hindu and Muslim friends in the kingdom, through whom he gleaned important details for his magnum opus on Mysore's history. Wilks claims that the earliest ancestor of Haidar Ali of whom there has been some account was a religious, saintly man with an Afghani surname, named Mohammad Bhehlol, who was initially in the Punjab and later migrated to Aland along with his two sons, Mohammad Ali and Mohammad Wali.[2] He is said to have built a small mosque there and also a resting place for wandering fakirs who came by. He got his son Mohammad Ali married to the daughter of one of the adherents of a celebrated mausoleum in Gulbarga.

A lineage similar to the one adduced by Wilks is traced in the chronicle of Lewin Bentham Bowring, who had served as Chief Commissioner of Mysore between 1862 and 1870. Whatever be the minor discrepancies in tracing the ancestry, Bowring makes a compelling point about the need felt by the rulers and their court chroniclers to attribute descent from the highest social groups of the Islamic world, and sometimes from the Prophet himself, so as to legitimize their dynasty and its reign. This was possibly similar to the attempts of many Hindu rulers, too, who normally traced their ancestry to the solar or lunar family race of either Lord Rama or Lord Krishna. As Bowring states: 'In Hindustan, as elsewhere, when any man of vigour and energy has raised himself to a throne, it is not difficult to find for him a pedigree showing his noble descent, and it is not therefore surprising that native annalists should endeavour to prove that Haidar came from the famous race of the Koresh.'[3] A modern historian like Mohibbul Hasan, too, echoes the sentiment when he claims that 'it is also possible that the pedigree was manufactured to bolster up the dynastic prestige of Haidar and Tipu'.[4]

This newly migrated family lived in Gulbarga till the end of the reign of the successive sultan of Bijapur, Ali Adil Shah II (r. 1656–72 CE). After the death of the patriarch of the family, Mohammad Ali is said to have left for Bijapur to the residence of the seven brothers of his wife who were employed in the service of the sultan's army there. But as luck would have it, around this very time, in 1685, the Mughal invasion of Bijapur under Aurangzeb began and ended a year later with a resounding victory of the invading forces. In the bloody battle between the Mughals and the Bijapur sultanate, all the seven brothers-in-law of Mohammad Ali were killed. His grief-stricken wife was devastated by the demise of all her brothers and took to her bed, eschewing food, water and medicines, determining to end her life too. To save his family from the possible Mughal onslaught and for his wife's sake, Mohammad Ali migrated thereafter with his family to Kolar. Back then, Kolar was part of the *subah*, or province, of Sira (in today's Tumkur district of Karnataka), which was ruled by powerful *subahdars* (governors) of both the Bijapur sultans and then the Mughals. The Sira subah had seven *parganas*, or administrative units—Basavapattana, Sira, Budihal, Doddaballapura, Hoskote, Kolar and Penukonda. After the annihilation of the Deccan sultanates by the Mughals, Sira became an important headquarters of the imperial deputy. Aurangzeb appointed Qasim Khan as the subahdar of Sira in 1686. Qasim Khan's protégé Shah Muhammad Dakkhani was in charge of Kolar, and it was into his service that Mohammad Ali entered. He led a sedate life in Kolar by indulging in farming and renting fields and gardens.[5] His family, too, had grown by now, and he had four sons—Mohammad Ilyas, Mohammad, Mohammad Imam and Fatteh Mohammad.

The youngest son, Fatteh Mohammad, married Seydanee Saheba, the daughter of Burra Saheb, a religious man of Kolar, and she bore him three sons, Wali Sahab, Ali Sahab and Behelol Sahab.[6] All three sons were either killed in conflict or died early, without issue.[7] Around this very time, an Arab *nevayat* (newcomer), Mir Akbar Ali Khan, from a respectable family from the Konkan, was travelling across the peninsula towards Arcot with his wife, two daughters and son, Ibrahim. En route, the man was robbed and murdered by dacoits, and the harried family rushed towards Kolar, where, providentially, they met Fatteh Mohammad. Moved by the plight of the distraught family, he offered them financial assistance and also proposed to marry the elder daughter.

Following the death of Mohammad Ali in c. 1697, the four brothers dispersed to different places. Fatteh Mohammad left Kolar and joined the service of Nawab Saadatullah Khan of Arcot, who made him a *jamadar* in command of 200 foot and fifty horse.[8] Fortune smiled favourably on Fatteh Mohammad as he rose in rank to the command of 600 foot, fifty horse and fifty *juzail-burdar* (rocket men) in the Arcot service. For his valour in a skirmish at Jinjee, he was further presented with the honour of an elephant, a standard and a pair of *nagaras*, or kettledrums. For reasons unknown, despite a rising career graph in Arcot, he left the service there and briefly migrated to Mysore, perhaps at the suggestion of his paternal nephew Hydar Sahab (son of Mohammad Ilyas), who was employed in the Maharaja's government there. But this was a short-lived stint, and he left Mysore to enter the service of Nawab Dargah Quli Khan of Sira, who was appointed a subahdar there in 1714. He was made a commander of 400 foot and 100 horse, given the control of the fort of Doddaballapura and also of Budikota as a *jagir*, or appanage. Even as subahdars kept changing in Sura, Fatteh Mohammad's valour and dedication—which he displayed in several military campaigns, including the siege of Ganjikota near Doddaballapura— earned him the trust of his masters. He was richly rewarded with multiple promotions, including the title of 'Naik', which was affixed to his name.[9]

Even as his career seemed firmly saddled, the death of his second wife too, without an issue, left him depressed. That was when his mother-in-law offered her second daughter, Majeeda Begum, to him in marriage. Through this union was born another son, Shahabaz, in 1718, and Wali Mohammad, who died at the age of two. In 1721, at Budikota, the couple was blessed with a third son, whom they named Haidar Ali, literally meaning the lion. Interestingly, the astrologers whom the parents consulted regarding the fortunes of the newborn predicted a glorious political future, including the possibility of ruling over an entire kingdom. However, the boy was speculated to prove unlucky for his father and was destined to suffer the trauma of orphancy. Upon hearing this ominous prediction, many members of

Fatteh Mohammad's family strongly advised him to feed the child poisoned milk so that the father's life could be saved. But Fatteh Mohammad would have none of it, and refused all those entreaties and saved his son's life.[10]

The sudden and tragic turn of events in the political life of Fatteh Mohammad almost seemed like a perverse manifestation of the menacing prophecy. Dargah Quli Khan was killed in a battle, and his son Abdul Rasul Khan succeeded him. However, with the goodwill and support of the Nawab of Arcot, Saadatullah Khan, a rival claimant, Tahir Khan, secured his appointment to the subah of Sira. This led to a pitched battle between Abdul Rasul Khan—who was stoutly supported by Fatteh Mohammad—and Tahir Khan. In the ensuing armed conflict, both Abdul Rasul Khan and Fatteh Mohammad were brutally killed, in 1724.[11] Even as the beleaguered family of Fatteh Mohammad was coming to terms with his death, another catastrophe awaited them. Abbas Quli Khan, the son of their erstwhile benefactor Abdul Rasul Khan, who was left in possession of his father's jagir of Doddaballapura, asserted that the deceased Fatteh Mohammad had left behind debts that were due to Abbas Quli Khan and to local merchants. When he could not find a means to recover the financial dues, the entire property—including furniture, utensils, and the trinkets and jewels of the women of Fateh Mohammad's house—was plundered.[12] So consumed with hatred was he that Abbas Quli Khan seized the young sons of Fatteh Mohammad—Shahabaz, who was about eight years old, and Haidar Ali, who was three or four years old—confined them inside the hollow of a kettledrum and had it beaten upon to cause them immense distress.[13] The harried mother, Majeeda Begum, managed to escape and reached the gates of her husband's nephew Hydar Sahab, who was employed in the Mysore government in Bangalore. Hydar Sahab took her along to the capital of the Mysore kingdom, Srirangapatna, with an urgent appeal to the Maharaja of Mysore, Dodda Krishnaraja Wodeyar, through the office of his *dalavayi*, or Commander-in-Chief, Devarajayya. The Maharaja took pity on the plight of the young boys and wrote a letter to the Nawab of Sira, who in turn strongly reprimanded Abbas Quli Khan for his inhuman acts. The Maharaja very generously offered to clear the debt that was due to Fatteh Mohammad and assured that the young boys were to enter his service when they came of age. Till then, the boys were free to stay within his dominions, in the loving care of their paternal cousin Hydar Sahab, who was in Mysorean service. Little did the Maharaja know that this benevolent act of his would come back to bite his family decades later.

The kind act of the Maharaja of Mysore saved the young, fatherless kids during one of the worst calamities of their lives. Hydar Sahab looked after the two unfortunate boys like his own children, and, in due course, also taught them the use of arms and horsemanship. But this disturbing episode from his infancy had left an indelible scar on Haidar Ali's mind, as is evident in the ruthless manner in which he sought revenge from Abbas Quli Khan almost thirty-two years later, when he invaded Doddaballapura. Wilks mentions that this act carried all the 'virulence belonging to the memory of a recent injury',[14] implying that Haidar Ali perhaps never forgot the humiliation and torture that he had faced as a child and was burning with the fire of revenge. His troubled childhood left Haidar bereft of any interest in education, and he remained illiterate all his life. Bowring mentions that this was 'common enough in those days, when most chiefs were content with affixing to papers either their seal or some fanciful device in lieu of a signature'.[15] His growing-up years weren't pleasant either, and he seems to have been indolent and hedonistic in his pursuits. As Wilks states: 'When approaching maturity of age, he [Haidar Ali] had shewn [*sic: shown*] a greater disposition to the pursuit of pleasure and the sports of the chace [*sic: chase*] than to the restraints of a military life and would frequently absent himself for weeks together, secretly immersed in voluptuous riot, or passing with facility, as was the habit of his whole life, to the opposite extreme of abstinence and excessive exertion; wandering in the woods while pursuing, not without danger, his favourite amusements.'[16] Bowring substantiates this portrait of Haidar Ali in his teens and thereafter as someone of 'irregular habits, and addicted to low pursuits, but he was a keen sportsman, and full of dash and energy'.[17]

Years rolled by, and the boys grew up under the guidance and care of Hydar Sahab. When Shahabaz was old enough, he obtained a small position as a subordinate officer under Katti Gopalaraje Urs in Bangalore, with his younger brother shadowing him. Once they came of age, the brothers left Mysore for a brief while and entered the service of Abdul Wahhab Khan, the younger brother of Nawab Muhammad Ali of the Carnatic who held the jagir of Chittoor.[18] But they were soon recalled by Hydar Sahab, whose clout and prosperity in Mysore had grown considerably over the years. He took the brothers to Karachuri Nanjarajayya, the younger brother of Devarajayya and the powerful chief minister of the kingdom. Impressed by the young men, Nanjarajayya took them in the Mysorean service with a command of 300 foot and fifty horse.[19] When Hydar Sahab passed away, Shahabaz succeeded to the command of his detachment as well.

As for Haidar Ali, destiny had bigger plans for him. He had come a long way from the tortuous childhood episode of being imprisoned in a kettledrum that was beaten upon. From the obscure by-lanes of his early life, he was now going to be involuntarily posited right in the midst of the limelight on the highway of history, even as the political situation in southern India was marinating towards a slow potpourri of calamitous disaster.

2

Cataclysmic Convulsions

The Hindu Kingdom of Mysore

The Mysore kingdom that Haidar Ali and his brother had entered as young boys had a hoary history of its own. The Hindu dynasty that ruled there were known as the Wodeyars and they had come to establish their hold over the region in 1399. That was when Yaduraya, a young prince from Dwaraka in Gujarat, supposedly came down south, with his brother Krishnaraya, looking for better pastures. Destiny turned out to be in their favour. The principality had been left vulnerable to the machinations of a capricious minister who was seeking to usurp the kingdom after the death of its ruler. Yaduraya combated this upstart, saved the kingdom and also wedded the daughter of the deceased ruler, establishing the dynasty of the Wodeyars.

For almost two centuries thereafter, the Wodeyars were content being subsidiary chieftains of the mighty Vijayanagara Empire. Their sphere of influence did not go beyond a score of villages. But with the collapse of the Vijayanagara Empire in the Battle of Tallikota in 1565, several of the erstwhile Hindu vassal kingdoms, such as Mysore, Tiruchirappali, Thanjavur and Madurai, either asserted their independence or came under the control of the new powers, the Bijapur and Golconda sultanates, with the promise of payment of an annual tribute. As the empire's hold began to collapse post Tallikota, Raja Wodeyar (1578–1617 CE) of the dynasty broke free

---

* Please refer to the corresponding illustration in the appendix.

and established the independence of the Mysore kingdom in 1610 at the new capital city of Srirangapatna.

Srirangapatna—called variously as Seringapatam in colonial records or as Patan or, simply, Pattana—drew its name from its presiding deity: the giant, supine Lord Ranganathaswamy, resting on the majestic Adi Shesha serpent. It literally means the city of the holy Ranga. The ancient temple of this deity dates back to 1454, when Timmanna, a disciple of the celebrated Vaishnava saint and philosopher Sri Ramanujacharya, came to the Vijayanagara Empire and is said to have had this shrine constructed.[1] The city is situated at the upper end of an island surrounded by the Kaveri River. The river assumes force and magnitude here, with an extensive channel filled with rocks and fragments of granite. The island is about three miles long and one mile broad.[2] With Raja Wodeyar making this island city the new capital of the now-autonomous Wodeyar dynasty, Srirangapatna was to acquire a predominant position in South Indian politics for the next three centuries.

As the Wodeyar power began to be consolidated in the island city, they began confidently flexing their muscles against competitors and potential threats. Skirmishes with Bijapur, under its army general Randullah Khan and his deputy Shahaji Bhonsle, continued under one of Raja Wodeyar's chivalrous successors, Ranadhira Kanthirava Narasaraja Wodeyar (1638–59 CE). Fortunes kept swinging, with both sides alternating between victories and defeats. Ranadhira, however, managed to further cement the sovereignty of Mysore by minting his own coins and producing a royal seal with the emblem of Varahaswamy, the boar incarnation of Lord Vishnu.

Mysore's dream run continued during the reign of one of his successors, Chikkadevaraja Wodeyar (1673–1704 CE). He ushered in several administrative reforms, a postal system, a stringent taxation policy, which also led to repression, and an eighteen-department apparatus to run the government, called the Attara Kacheri. Mysore constantly had combats with the rising Maratha power under its newly coronated Chhatrapati Shivaji, who was keen on expanding his sphere of influence. On several occasions in 1682, while the Maratha armies ravaged Mysore, Chikkadevaraja put up stiff resistance, repulsed an attack on the capital Srirangapatna and killed the Maratha generals Dadaji, Jathaji and Nimbhaji, who had led this offensive. Aurangzeb, who was perennially irked by the emergent Maratha power, saw an advantageous development to befriend an enemy's enemy in the south. Kasim Khan, one of Aurangzeb's generals, had been sent in 1686 to South India after the fall of Bijapur, as the Nawab of Sira, to occupy as much territory below the Krishna River and induce the loyal chiefs there to accept the imperial power; he came in contact with Chikkadevaraja. A peaceful commercial transaction of Rs 3 lakh between them saw the transfer of Bangalore to the Wodeyars on purchase, after it had changed hands from the Marathas to Kasim Khan. 'The amicable arrangement,' writes Wilks, 'by which he [Chikkadevaraja] obtained possession of Bangalore would render it incumbent on Kasim Khan to represent Mysoor [*sic*] to Aurangzebe [*sic*] as a state which ought to be encouraged as a counterpoise in the south to the dangerous power of the Mahrattas; and although it is known that the conquest of Mysoor was in the direct contemplation of that emperor, it was obviously his interest to postpone it so long as the Raja could be of use by being placed on the flank and rear of his actual enemies'.[3] After Kasim Khan died in 1696 by taking poison and committing suicide, Chikkadevaraja felt an increasing need to establish direct contact through diplomatic channels with the emperor in Delhi. Under Karnik Lingappayya, a delegation was sent to the Mughal court in 1699, with costly gifts and presents to propitiate Aurangzeb and seek friendly terms. The delegation is said to have returned in 1700 with a signet ring of the emperor bearing the inscription 'Jagadevaraya', or king of the world, subtly implying the relative autonomy of Mysore and imperial permission to rule. Wilks, however, makes little of this delegation and regards it more as an image-building exercise by Chikkadevaraja against all his rival chieftains in the neighbourhood and, of course, the Marathas. 'The splendour of the embassy does not however appear to have made much impression at the imperial court . . . the Zemindar of Mysoor (as he is called) was not held to be a person of very high consideration,' he writes.[4] Mysore had thus become beholden to the

Mughal court as a vassal state, saving it from incursions by rivals or complete subjugation from Delhi; but it still opened the gates for repeated attacks on the pretext of revenue collection levied in exchange for its promised regional autonomy. The later stakeholders of the Mughal court, the Nizam or the Marathas, kept ravaging Mysore in the fulfilment of this very arrangement that had been agreed upon with Delhi. The Nizam considered Mysore as Mughal territory and hence believed it was his bounden right to levy taxes from there.

During the reign of weak rulers who succeeded Chikkadevaraja after his death in 1704, the chinks were exposed and the attacks only kept increasing, as time was to tell. For instance, in 1724, under the pretext of dereliction in payment of Mughal tax levies, a combined attack on Mysore was led by Saadatullah Khan, the Nawab of Arcot, the Ikkeri Nayaka, the Nawabs of Cudappah, Kurnool and Savanur, and the Ghorpade of Gutti, which shook Srirangapatna to its very foundations. Heavy cash indemnities of almost Rs 1 crore and jewels were offered to ward off the invaders rather than put up a defence. Saadatullah Khan distributed Rs 60 lakh among the allies, at Rs 12 lakh each, took the rest himself and then left Srirangapatna. Even as the polity in Mysore was recovering from this surgical strike, Peshwa Baji Rao I attacked Srirangaptna to collect arrears in 1726. Baji Rao was supposedly surprised by the heavy firing from the magazines of the fort and sustained considerable loss of men in his army. He is said to have remarked that 'it was a sheer impossibility to withstand the matchlockmen of Seringapatam which appeared to be nothing short of a city of cannons (*firangi-pattana*)'.[5] He was, of course, eventually bought off by Mysore, as was the case with all the attackers. However, expectedly, all these repeated buyouts thoroughly drained the already dwindling treasury of Mysore.

The Maratha Polity and Its Cesses

A little about the collection of tributes as Chauthai/Chauth (one-fourth) and Sardeshmukhi by the Marathas, a practice that predated

Chhatrapati Shivaji Maharaj. Around 1579, the Portuguese at Daman used to give a portion of the revenue to the Koli Raja of Ramnagar on the condition that he would levy no additional taxes nor make predatory attacks on Daman. During Shivaji Maharaj's time, this payment was made in exchange for the Maratha army being kept in another dominion for its protection. In the Maratha region, Deshmukhs (village or district officials) were traditionally appointed to collect land tax and receive a commission of 10 per cent for their services. A head Deshmukh who controlled a group of villages or one district was given the title of Sardeshmukh. Chhatrapati Shivaji rechristened himself as the supreme Sardeshmukh of the Maratha *swarajya*, or sovereign empire. The subordinate Deshmukhs were distributed *vatans*, or hereditary preserves, that remained unaffected by changes in government or political convulsions. Shivaji Maharaj's successors followed the same practice and assumed the function of Sardeshmukh of the Maratha Empire.

In the early decades of the eighteenth century, the new Chhatrapati, Shahu, conferred on his Brahmin confidant Balaji Vishwanath the office of Peshwa or prime minister as the latter had helped him consolidate his position against rival claims. While Shahu operated out of Satara, the Peshwa's sphere of influence was from Poona. With time, this set-up completely changed the Maratha polity, as also the character of its administration and government. The position of the Chhatrapati itself came to be eclipsed, and Poona and the Peshwa emerged as the nucleus of all political power of the Maratha Empire.

It was Peshwa Balaji Vishwanath who, in 1719, through deft diplomacy, managed to obtain a charter from the beleaguered Mughal emperor. This was quite a magna carta for the Marathas that validated their swarajya or sovereignty, and also conferred on them the right of collecting 25 per cent Chauth and 10 per cent Sardeshmukhi from all the six Mughal subahs of the Deccan. The total annual revenues roughly translated to about Rs 18 crore, of which 35 per cent was to now go to the Marathas.[6] In practice, the numbers fell much below these estimates. In return for these cesses, the Peshwa was to serve the Mughals with 15,000 soldiers and to help them maintain Mughal rule in the Deccan by quelling rebellions and dacoities.[7] A cash tribute of Rs 10 lakh was also to be paid to the Mughals by the Marathas. This opened up Maratha ambitions in north India, after they managed to humble the Mughal emperor, with whom they had endured a running feud since the time of Shivaji Maharaj. But the Nizam and other provincial governors seldom cared to honour these grants of 1719, citing that they were signed by the Mughal court under duress and the threat of military attack. Herein were sown the seeds of constant strife all through the eighteenth century, with the Marathas invading various parts of the country to collect the Chauth and the provinces resisting the payment of the same. About these cesses, Professor R.V. Oturkar explains:

> Marathas undertook to assist the Mughals in maintaining their sovereignty over the territory, without in any way being in a position to regulate their foreign policy. Whether the Mughals would adopt a policy of aggression or friendliness towards their neighbours, Marathas were, as it were, in duty bound to protect their dominions. Although they were not subordinate to the Mughals, they certainly consented to perform the task of their subordinate allies . . . the Marathas thus made themselves helpless instrument (s) of aggrandizement or indifferent copartners in the affairs of war whether for aggression or for protection. This is what made the Marathas unpopular both in the north as well as in the south as they were engaged in extending their sphere of influence all over India through Chauthai and Sardeshmukhi. In course of time, the right of collecting Chauth and Sardeshmukhi came to be assigned to some sardar as his Watan and therefore only helped to strengthen the position of the feudal lord in his aggressive designs. In later stages the different Maratha Sardars fought among themselves for seizing each other's rights of collecting Chauth and Sardeshmukhi with the result that Chauth and Sardeshmukhi became no more than tribute paid to the aggressor.[8]

It was Balaji Vishwanath's young son and successor, the heroic Baji Rao I, who managed to effectively enforce the terms of these grants. For this, he put together a group of young associates— Pawar, Holkar, Sindhia and others—who were then to become hereditary chieftains and de facto rulers of what is normally called the larger Maratha confederacy. This helped expand the Maratha influence beyond the six subahs of the Deccan, as was agreed upon in 1719. Each of these army chiefs carved out independent spheres of activity and influence—the Holkar in Indore, Sindhia in Gwalior, Ghorpade in the Karnatak regions south of the Krishna River, Bhonsle in Nagpur and Berar, Dabhadhe in Khandesh and parts of Gujarat. These multiple layers of power—the Chhatrapati, the Peshwa and then the independent *jagirdar*s or chieftains—worked well under strong leaders. But inherent in this multi-layer set-up was the inevitable formula for disaster when weaklings assumed the top positions, as time would tell in the case of the Marathas. For now, though, they basked in unhindered glory and expanded their sphere of influence through large parts of the subcontinent. Baji Rao managed to crush most opponents and reached the very gates of Delhi for the collection of Chauth.

Mysore's Period of Decline

As mentioned earlier, after Chikkadevaraja, several weak and ineffective rulers succeeded to the throne of Mysore. Chikkadevaraja's son, Kanthirava Maharaja, was born with a hearing and speech impairment, and was hence called 'Mooka Arasu'[9] (the dumb king). The affairs of state were largely carried out in sign language by the ruler. The devolution of power to subordinates meant its concentration in their hands during the reign of inept rulers. In particular, the office of the *dalavayi/dalavoy*, which had hitherto remained subservient to the king, began to subsume a lot of political power, in addition to the military clout that it always exercised. Right from the early years of the eighteenth century, it is notable that members of the family from Kalale began to exercise considerable hold over matters of state.

Matrimonial alliances with the royal family and the regular supply of a dalavayi to the Mysorean army, in conformity with a pact—over a century old—that Raja Wodeyar had with the Kalale family, became more pronounced between 1660 and 1704. This enhanced the referent power that they began to influence both on the king and the governance of the state. In May 1724, Devarajayya, who was in his fifties and the eldest son of Virarajayya, succeeded his father as the new dalavayi of Mysore. A cousin of his named Nanjarajayya of Bellur was made the sarvadhikari, or the chief executive officer, of the state. Along with a third entrant in the form of Devarajayya's younger brother Karachuri Nanjarajayya—'a brave, but violent, presumptuous, and improvident man of about thirty years of age'[10]—this triumvirate virtually controlled the affairs of Mysore during the time of Maharaja Dodda Krishnaraja Wodeyar (1714–32). The sarvadhikari was the de facto head of the departments of revenue and finance, and the dalavayi controlled the military. It was no secret how an organized system of embezzlement and fraud was set up by this trio. In the state administration, there was also an important position of a pradhan, privy councilor, who was to be in close contact with the Maharaja on matters of state. The trio had appointed, to this position, their trusted accomplice Venkatapathayya who readily played along with them in all their nefarious acts.

Things came to a terrible showdown when Dodda Krishnaraja's adopted son and successor, Chamaraja Wodeyar VII, began to realize the machinations of the trio and was determined to punish them. Devarajayya poisoned the ears of the dowager Rani Devajammanni against the king, who was her own adopted son. With the dowager rani on his side, Devarajayya plotted a major palace coup. While the king was in his durbar, Devarajayya had soldiers, who were on his payroll, virtually take the king hostage. When the harried courtiers tried to shut the palace doors and safeguard their ruler, Devarajayya had it stormed open with elephants. The king was unceremoniously deposed and then imprisoned in 1734. His six-year-old brother, Immadi Krishnaraja Wodeyar (or Krishnaraja Wodeyar II), was then crowned the new ruler the same year. With the dowager rani too oblivious to the evil intentions of the plotters, it was a free run for them during the time of the new king's infancy. As Wilks states: 'The profligacy of Nunjeraj [*sic*] made a shameless job of the revenue; appointing his own menial servants to the nominal office of Aumildar [*amildar*: a native collector of revenue in charge of a *taluq*, a division of a district], and still retaining them about his person; leaving to themselves or to the Perdhan [*sic*], to provide deputies, but prodigal at once and rapacious, exacting a certain proportion of the public plunder as a joint fund for himself and his brother.'[11] When the king came of age, Karachuri Nanjarajayya got his daughter Devajammanni married to him to further bring him under his control.

The Theatre of Strife: The Carnatic

Aurangzeb's invasion and defeat of Bijapur and Golconda brought about several changes in the dynamics of South India. He established feudatories as Nawabs, in Kurnool, Savanur, Cudappah, Arcot and Sira, and they came under the control of the Mughal Viceroy of the Deccan, initially stationed at Aurangabad. By early 1713, the man who filled this position was Asaf Jah, who had earlier been the subahdar of Oudh. One of Aurangzeb's successor emperors, Farrukhsiyar (1713–19) gave him the title of Nizam-ul-Mulk (or Nizam for short). As the Mughal Empire continued to unravel under the weight of its own contradictions and internal skirmishes, Nizam-ul-Mulk slowly broke away from the imperial clutches and declared his independence in 1724. The entire country south of the ghats virtually came under his control. This region below Hyderabad, which became his seat of power, was known as the Carnatic region. It was peninsular South India stretching for about 600 km across the coastline of the Bay of Bengal, upwards to the Eastern Ghats. It had three sub-regions: the Southern Carnatic, which lay to the south of the Coleroon River, from Cape Comorin, and passed through the towns of Thanjavur, Tiruchirapalli, Madurai, Tranquebar, Nagapattinam, Rameshwaram, Dindigul and Tinnevely; the Central Carnatic, which lay between the Coleroon and Pennar rivers and had Madras, Kanchipuram, Pondicherry, Arcot, Vellore, Cuddalore, Pulicat, Nellore and so on; and finally, the Northern Carnatic, which stretched from the Pennar to the south of the Krishna River, with Ongole as an important town. Mysore was not a part of this region but was its neighbouring independent kingdom.

Arcot: Among the Nawabs that Aurangzeb installed in this region, the Nawab of Arcot, who was, however, subservient to the Nizam, ranked higher. Aurangzeb appointed Zulfikar Ali (1690–1700) as the Nawab of Arcot and thereafter Daud Khan (1700–08). After Aurangzeb's death, a civil war broke out among his three sons who claimed the throne—Muazzam, who was the governor of Kabul; Muhammad Kam Baksh, the governor of Deccan; and Muhammad Azam Shah, the governor of Gujarat. To help resolve this strife, Daud Khan was recalled to Delhi. The civil war ended with the accession of Muazzam as the next ruler, with the title of Bahadur Shah I, also known as Shah Alam, in 1708. Saadatullah Khan, who belonged to the Navayat community of the Arabs, became Daud Khan's successor as the Nawab of Arcot from 1710 to 1732. He shifted the capital from Ginjee to Arcot and slowly began to establish the independence of Arcot, even as Mughal power kept waning in imperial Delhi with every successor being overthrown due to palace intrigues and internal strife. The intent of breaking away also meant defying the diktats of the Mughal Viceroy in the Deccan, the Nizam. Since he was childless, Saadatullah Khan adopted his nephew Dost Ali Khan, son of his brother Ghulam Ali Khan, as his successor by quietly obtaining the private consent of the weakened Mughal emperor and not keeping the Nizam in the loop. The Nizam's protestation or his refusal to accord legitimacy to the adoption and succession plan meant little to Saadatullah Khan, who had slowly begun to act as an independent ruler of the Arcot principality, which was ensconced in the central and southern Carnatic region.

Upon Saadatullah Khan's death in 1732, Dost Ali Khan succeeded him as the new Nawab of Arcot. In an early combat in his career, Dost Ali made a concerted attack on Mysore in August 1736, and sent his troops under Qasim Khan and Murad Khan. Surprisingly, Mysore put up strong resistance this time, and Dalavayi Devarajayya and Karachuri Nanjarajayya routed the Arcot army at Kalancha and returned to a triumphant welcome and public reception in Srirangapatna. This victory emboldened Mysore to dream of its southern expansion plans.

Keladi: Among the remnants of Vijayanagara were the Nayakas of Keladi, also known as the Ikkeri Nayakas or Bidanur Nayakas, who were based in today's Shimoga district of modern Karnataka. Like other feudatory chieftains, they too were aligned with the Rayas of Vijayanagara, who gave them provincial autonomy to rule over their small principalities, in return for money given to the imperial treasury as taxes and indemnities and military support in times of need. After the fall of the empire in Tallikota, they expanded their influence to the Malenadu region of the Western Ghats, coastal Karnataka, parts of Malabar and northern Kerala and the central plains along the Tungabhadra River. In the eighteenth century, its Nayakas, such as Hiriya Basappa Nayaka I (1697–1714) and Somashekhara Nayaka II (1714–39), had a hostile attitude towards Mysore, and skirmishes were common.

Marathas and Thanjavur: The Maratha power that had risen under Chhatrapati Shivaji managed to subsume all other minor remnants of Vijayanagara, such as Vellore, Ginjee and Kurnool, after 1677. Taking advantage of the jostling for power between the principalities of Madurai and Thanjavur Nayakas, who were actually related to each other, the Bijapur sultan sent his forces under Maratha general Ekoji (Venkoji), who was Shivaji's half-brother. Ekoji overthrew the Nayaka rule in Thanjavur in 1674 and established the Maratha dynasty there—which was to rule the region for nearly two centuries thereafter.

Madurai: The Nayaka rule continued in Madurai. But in 1732, when the Nayaka of Madurai, Vijayaranga Chokkanatha Nayaka, died, a war of claims to the throne erupted between his queen Meenakshi,

who succeeded him, and Bangaru Tirumala, a rival claimant. To
fish in troubled waters and to settle the matter, the then Nawab
of Arcot, Dost Ali Khan, sent his son-in-law Hussain Dost Khan,
popularly known as Chanda Sahib. Chanda Sahib managed to win
Rani Meenkashi's trust and also a huge sum of money that she
promised him to protect her against Bangaru Tirumala, who in turn
was forced to retreat down south, where he began to organize a small
army to regain what he claimed was his rightful succession. Chanda
Sahib, however, had no intention of being Meenakshi's saviour. He
had tricked her into a promise of loyalty by taking an oath of alliance
and friendship with her, on a fake Quran, which was actually a brick
covered with a cloth. She had fallen for this trick and entrusted all
her faith and money to him, against Bangaru. Chanda Sahib's eyes
were on the fertile lands of Tiruchirapalli in her domain, as its walled
city and the Rock Fort inside it were among the strongest citadels in
South India at that time. So while he managed to quell the uprising
of Bangaru and placed his own brothers Bade Sahib and Sadiq Sahib
in charge of Madurai and the nearby fort of Dindigul, he returned to
Tiruchirapalli to meet an exultant Meenakshi. Much to her shock,
though, her hitherto ally imprisoned her and took over the reins
of the kingdom. Kirmani also suggests that the avaricious Chanda
Sahib 'violated her person'.[12] So thoroughly shocked and disgusted
was Meenakshi by this sudden turn of events and the betrayal of her
'friend' that she ended her life in prison by taking poison in 1739.
This virtually ended the lineage of the Nayakas of Madurai.

In neighbouring Thanjavur, the Maratha rule had slowly
consolidated itself under Ekoji and later his sons, Shahaji II, Serfoji
and Tukoji. The fertile and well-irrigated lands with the Kaveri
River made the principality rich and prosperous in no time. When
Tukoji died in 1736, his son Shahaji III succeeded him. However,
his commander Sayyad Khan chose to depose him and place a
rival claimant, Sidhoji, as the successor. A harried Shahaji, who
was desperately seeking allies to regain his lost throne, approached
the French governor of Pondicherry, Benoit Dumas. In return for
the fertile eastern coast of Karaikal, Dumas pledged his support to
Shahaji. This brewing alliance scared Sayyad Khan, who happily

dropped Sidhoji and placed Shahaji back on the throne. With no reason left to seek support of the French, Shahaji obviously revoked the alliance. An enraged Dumas took the help of Chanda Sahib, who was perennially looking out to expand his sphere of influence in the Carnatic. They attacked Thanjavur and occupied Karaikal. Shahaji's woes did not end here. Chanda Sahib's rival in Arcot, Safdar Ali, who was the son of Nawab Dost Ali Khan, was watching, with a sense of alarm, the rising clout of his brother-in-law in the principalities of the south. To checkmate him in Thanjavur, Safdar Ali attacked the principality in 1739, defeated and deposed Shahaji, and installed instead another son of Tukoji, Pratapsinh (r. 1739–63 CE). Between themselves the two rivals of Arcot—Chanda Sahib and Safdar Ali—thus controlled sizeable regions in the Carnatic.

Around this time, the Persian ruler Nadir Shah invaded India and attacked Delhi in 1739. He defeated the weak Mughal Emperor Muhammad Shah near Karnal, and plundered Delhi to the last brick.

The Nizam in Hyderabad, meanwhile, had an obvious axe to grind against Arcot, which had been constantly defying his authority. So he tacitly encouraged and supported the Maratha plans to invade the Carnatic. In 1740, Maratha Emperor Shahu sent a huge army to the south under the leadership of his adopted son Fateh Sinh Bhonsle and commanded Raghuji Bhonsle of Nagpur to join the forces. They were mandated to liberate the Hindu principalities of Thanjavur and Madurai which had by now come under the Muslim influence of the two rivals of Arcot. On their way down south, the Maratha army easily vanquished the Nawabs of Kurnool and Cudappah, and headed towards Arcot. A distressed Dost Ali sent urgent summons to both his son and son-in-law, asking them to immediately return to the kingdom with their armies to defend against an imminent Maratha attack. For reasons best known to them, both Chanda Sahib and Safdar Ali took their own sweet time to rush back to Arcot even when they knew that the patriarch was in such a dire situation. By the time the replenishments reached Arcot, a massive Maratha army had gathered around the pass of Damalcheruvu, threatening to invade Arcot. Dost Ali refused to surrender and put up feeble resistance with his 700 mounted and 15,000 foot soldiers; he and his son Hasan Ali were killed in the battle. This unexpected defeat and the death of the Nawab sent shock waves through all the Muslim power centres in the Carnatic region. Chanda Sahib rushed to take shelter in the Tiruchirapalli Fort, while Safdar Ali retreated to the Vellore Fort. Their respective families and Dost Ali's widow, too, fled in fright, to Pondicherry around June 1740, where the French generously welcomed them and the vast amounts of treasures that they had brought with them. Eager to restore his father's throne to himself, Safdar Ali began secret negotiations with the Marathas, agreeing to pay Rs 1 crore in exchange for the Nawabship of Arcot to be returned to him as the legitimate successor. He even paid an advance of Rs 10 lakh. Safdar Ali managed to conduct these negotiations so secretively that Chanda Sahib did not get a whiff, even though the two met often while they visited their families in Pondicherry. The Marathas took the money, placed Safdar Ali as the new Nawab of Arcot and retreated from the Carnatic hastily, as the Peshwa, Baji Rao I, had died by then and his son Balaji Baji Rao, or Nanasaheb, was to succeed him.

Wars of Succession Begin

Stationed at Tiruchirapalli, Chanda Sahib refused to accept Safdar Ali as the new Nawab of Arcot. But before he could protest further, the Marathas were at the gates of his fort under the command of Raghuji Bhonsle. In haste, Chanda Sahib tried his best to avert a clash and offered to even pay a ransom of 22 lakh pagodas[13] to ward off the Marathas. But they were adamant and attacked the fort of Tiruchirapalli. Chanda Sahib's brothers, Bade Sahib and Sadiq Sahib, rushed to his help with their armies, but they were killed in the battle of Manaparai on 21 March 1741. Their corpses were sent to Chanda Sahib in a bedecked palanquin. All that was now left for the Marathas to do was storm the fort and take him captive. His entreaties and negotiations to save himself failed, and he was parcelled away as a war prisoner to Varhad, where he was lodged till

1744, before being sent away to Satara, having been ransomed for Rs 7.5 lakh. Safdar Ali's position as the Nawab of Arcot was thus strengthened, and as per the terms of the treaty with the Marathas, he was bound to pay tributes to Poona.

Murar Rao Ghorpade, who hailed from Gutti, was a military commander of the Maratha army that led this offensive against Chanda Sahib. He was a nephew of the celebrated warrior Santaji Ghorpade, who, along with Dhanaji Jadhav, had led valiant campaigns against the Mughals from 1689 to 1696. Murar Rao was left behind with 14,000 troops to manage the administration of the fort in Tiruchirapalli, restore the Hindu temples in the region that had suffered under the Nawab's rule and also remit a part of the Chauth or a quarter of the revenue collected as tribute to the Peshwa court, to which he had to pledge his loyalty. Appa Rao was stationed as the governor of Madurai. The Marathas tried their best to force the French in Pondicherry to hand over the family of Chanda Sahib that had sought shelter there, as also the vast treasures they had brought along. Interestingly, Dumas bribed his way out by supplying the best of French wine to Raghuji and his mistress. So enamoured were they of the delicacy of the wine that they ordered more and more of it and, in return, left the French to themselves and departed from the Deccan.

After defeating Dost Ali at Kalancha, Mysore began to rekindle its dreams that it had had since 1642, of occupying the fertile lands of Tiruchirapalli. When Chanda Sahib was defeated and taken prisoner by the Marathas, Mysore, in fact, fancied its chances in Tiruchirapalli and its merger into its own dominion. The Maharaja even wrote a letter to the Marathas on 5 December 1740 offering them Rs 50 lakh if they killed Chanda Sahib and resettled the Hindu kingdom in Tiruchirapalli.[14] However, the Maratha aim to retain the place under Murar Rao upset their plans, though Devarajayya kept a close watch on the rapidly changing developments there in this regard. In fact, he even made a preposterous offer of Rs 1 crore to the Nizam to take over Tiruchirapalli, knowing full well that repeated incursions, payouts and their own corrupt dealings had totally dried up the

Mysore treasury, and that there was no such money to be offered. Yet, the importance of Tiruchirapalli in the Mysorean scheme of things was noteworthy.

Meanwhile, trouble was brewing at the Nizam's court in Hyderabad as well. Nasir Jung, his son, had declared a rebellion against his father. He had done this while the latter was away in Delhi for about three years, with his elder son, Ghaziuddin, leaving behind Nasir Jung to officiate in Hyderabad in his absence. What stirred Nasir's courage to revolt against the powerful Nizam was a series of reverses that his father had been facing for some time. It had seemed to be an unending tale of woes for the Nizam. In an encounter with Peshwa Baji Rao I in 1738 in Bhopal, he was routed. A year later, when Nadir Shah plundered Delhi, he is said to have publicly humiliated Nizam-ul-Mulk by making him go to court seated on a donkey.[15] The father and son clashed in combat near the fort of Daulatabad on 23 July 1741. Mutawassil Khan, the son-in-law of the Nizam fighting on the latter's side, was about to shoot an arrow at Nasir Jung in this battle. But Mutawassil's son, Muzaffar Jung, who was riding with his father on the same elephant, implored him not to kill Nasir Jung, and his intervention saved Nasir's life on that fateful occasion. It was ironic that in the future Nasir Jung and Muzaffar Jung were to fight as rival claimants to the power in Hyderabad. His life might have been saved due to Muzaffar Jung, but Nasir's armies were completely routed by his father, and Nasir sheepishly sought forgiveness and reconciled with him.

Back in Arcot, it was not smooth sailing for Safdar Ali, who had been installed as the Nawab with the help of the Marathas. Even as he paid tributes to both the Marathas as well as his traditional overlord, the Nizam, little did he realize that his cousin Murtaza Ali was conspiring behind his back to usurp his place and even attempted, in vain, to poison Safdar Ali. But eventually Murtaza got Safdar Ali assassinated and declared himself as the new Nawab of Arcot. This angered the Marathas, under whose protection Safdar Ali had held office, and Murar Rao Ghorpade declared war against Murtaza. A frightened Murtaza escaped to Vellore, disguised as a woman. Safdar Ali's infant son was then placed on the throne of Arcot and given the title of Saadatullah Khan II.

Emboldened by his fresh success against his recalcitrant son, Nizam-ul-Mulk decided to stamp his authority amid the chaos that Arcot was witnessing. He was also uncomfortable with the increasing Maratha influence in what had traditionally been his domain. Seizing opportunity when both the Peshwa and Raghuji were away on their Bengal campaign against Nawab Alivardi Khan, the Nizam marched to Tiruchirapalli with a huge army to regain it from the Marathas in March 1743. Murar Rao held the fort for about six months, but in the absence of any strong replenishments from the main Maratha army, he finally decided to withdraw from Tiruchirapalli on 29 August 1743, for a payment of Rs 2 lakh and the fort of Penukonda. The Nizam appointed one of his loyalists, Anwaruddin—who belonged to the family of Qannauji Sheikhs and had shown great military mettle in campaigns since the time of Aurangzeb—as the regent of the infant Arcot Nawab. To secure his allegiance in Arcot, the Nizam took away Anwaruddin's third son, Muhammad Ali, as hostage to Hyderabad. Having assumed that he had put things in order in the Carnatic and stamped back his waning authority by displacing the Marathas, the Nizam retreated to Hyderabad.

But the arrangement he had secured at Arcot was to be short-lived as a power tussle began there soon after, at the instigation of Anwaruddin. In the ensuing chaos, the infant Nawab was stabbed to death, and Anwaruddin, who was already over seventy years old, staked his claim to the Nawabship of Arcot, laying the foundations for his Walajahi dynasty. With no one better placed for the position, the Nizam made him his representative as the 'Nawab of Carnatic' in July 1744. Anwaruddin's courage was to be tested a year later when the Marathas tried to regain Tiruchirapalli, which they had lost to the Nizam. Towards the end of 1744, the Peshwa dispatched Babuji Naik to wrest Tiruchirapalli back. But a formidable alliance awaited him. Anwaruddin and his son Muhammad Ali stitched up an alliance with the Nawabs of Cudappah, Kurnool, Savanaur and

Sira, and also the Wodeyars of Mysore and the Nayakas of Ikkeri to resist the Maratha incursion. Babuji Naik was completely routed and sent back in 1745.

Around this time, in 1749, Nanjarajayya led a campaign in Devanahalli in Bangalore district. With the help of the Marathas and the Nizam, the chief of Doddaballapura, Range Gowda, had taken possession of Devanahalli, and Mysore was determined to arrest the growing power of its rivals in its immediate vicinity. It was here that young Haidar Ali made his military debut as a volunteer horseman, along with his brother Shahabaz, who commanded 200 cavalry and 100 foot soldiers, joining him from Bangalore, where they were serving under Katti Gopalaraje Urs. Till then, Haidar was occasionally entrusted with the command of small parties of infantry in the trenches. It was observed that in perilous situations, he led the way skilfully and conducted himself with a certain coolness and confidence that is rare in a young novice soldier. In this campaign, the Mysore armies besieged Devanahalli for about nine months. They were aided by the forces of Nawab Anwaruddin and Dilawar Khan of Sira. The Marathas tried to send reinforcements to the beleaguered Range Gowda. But the Mysorean army was relentless, and even before the Maratha forces could reach, they stormed and captured the Devanahalli fort and took Gowda captive. Devanahalli was absorbed into Mysore, and Nanjarajayya returned triumphant to Srirangapatna. It was here that the heroics of the young Haidar in the campaign attracted the attention of Nanjarajayya. He rewarded Haidar with the command of fifty horse and 250 foot, with orders to recruit and augment the corps, and placed him in charge of one of the gates of this frontier fortress. This was the first step in the meteoric success of Haidar Ali Khan, who was to become destiny's chosen child in the years to come.

The French, meanwhile, were undertaking hectic parleys to ensure that Chanda Sahib, their favourite for the position of the Nawab of Arcot and through whom they could widen their sphere of influence in South India, could be released from Maratha custody, in which he had been languishing for years. The Marathas had fixed a ransom amount of Rs 7.5 lakh for the release of Chanda Sahib and his son Abid Sahib. In 1744, Chanda Sahib was internally shifted from Raghuji's custody to that of Maratha Emperor Shahu in Satara, even as the French seemed reluctant to pay for his freedom. Ever the calculative man, Chanda Sahib took full advantage of his move to the Maratha capital. He befriended Shahu's adopted son Fateh Sinh Bhonsle and won for himself some privileges and luxuries in his imprisonment. The French finally negotiated for a settlement of Rs 3 lakh to secure their protégé's release. This was to be paid in three instalments: a lakh in Satara; another when he was released and reached Cudappah; and the final instalment after he safely reached Arcot. Chanda Sahib's wife sent in all her jewels to secure her husband's release through the payment of this ransom money. The Peshwa agreed to release him on the condition that Hindu rule must not be interrupted in Tiruchirapalli.

The First Carnatic War

While wars of succession and chaos were the order of the day in South India, things were no different in distant Europe. In Austria, the Habsburg monarchy faced tumultuous times when Maria Theresa laid claim to succeed her father, Emperor Charles VI (1685–1740), upon his death, as the ruler. France, Prussia and Bavaria opposed her claim, while Britain, the Dutch Republic and Hanover (collectively known as 'Pragmatic Allies') supported her. Spain, Russia, Sweden, Sardinia and Saxony, too, entered the fray as the conflict widened. While the theatre of war was Europe, their participation on opposite sides in the Austrian War of Succession brought the British and the French in direct conflict across the world. It was also a battle to win the lucrative slave trade to the Americas and win territory in that new continent. This one-upmanship spilt over in India too, especially South India, where both these powers had been vying for trade and political benefits for long, and saw each other as threats. There was thus an already existing rivalry that just needed a spark to ignite. With the Carnatic having already become a hotbed of political flux, instability and wars of succession, the European script played out in South India too in the form of the Carnatic Wars.

The French East India Company (Compagnie française des Indes orientales), by then, had a new daring governor, Joseph François Dupleix, who had arrived in India in 1715. After having been a member of the Supreme Council in Pondicherry, he had been appointed as chief of the French factory in Chandernagore in Bengal. By his keen acumen, business sense and also knowledge of the locals, Dupleix not only amassed huge wealth for himself due to the coastal trade that he introduced there, but also transformed the sleepy, inconsequential town of Chandernagore on the banks of the Hooghly into a rich and prosperous colony. His success there led to his being appointed, on 4 January 1742, as governor of Pondicherry and ex-officio director of the affairs of the French East India Company, succeeding Dumas. He was seized by the zeal to expand the French sphere of influence beyond Pondicherry and some trading outposts on the Coromandel. On arriving in Pondicherry, he happened to meet Mahé de la Bourdonnais, a man whom he had known in his former years. They were almost of the same age, but very different in their dispositions and drives, and they had a history of competition and envy. Dupleix had bitterly criticized the appointment of La Bourdonnais as the governor of the Isle of France and Bourbon in 1735. 'The petulance and vivacity of the man make me fear it. The Company has been fascinated by the rigmaroles of this flighty spirit,'[16] wrote Dupleix about La Bourdonnais, whom he saw as a bitter rival to his own political advancement.

The flashpoint of the rivalry in Europe that had spilt over into India came about with the arrival of a naval squadron under La Bourdonnais, carrying troops to India all the way from France in September 1746 and attacking Madras, the main British settlement in the Carnatic. Madras then was weakly fortified and had a small defensive garrison that collapsed to the French might in a matter of just six days. The terms of settlement laid out by La Bourdonnais included payment of a cash ransom by the British East India Company, which the latter accepted and ratified. But these terms were unacceptable to Dupleix, who felt that they should levy a large sum from Madras, either before the assault or in case the French were too weak to hold it. He accused La Bourdonnais of having received a large sum of money from the British to conclude an unauthorized treaty for the ransom of Madras. Even as La Bourdonnais was trying to iron out his rivalry with Dupleix, ill luck struck him. His squadron was completely destroyed in a horrific cyclone, and he was thereafter forced to leave India. Dupleix conveniently reneged on the agreement with the British that La Bourdonnais had initiated.

Stepping up for their ally the British, the Nawab of Arcot Anwaruddin wrote harsh letters to Dupleix, admonishing the French for attacking Madras and threatening that they would now have to face the consequences in the form of an assault on Pondicherry. When the French set their eyes on the remaining British settlement in the Carnatic, Fort St David at Cuddalore, the combined forces of Nawab Anwaruddin and the British defeated them in December 1746. A British naval fleet under Admiral Edward Boscawen now arrived and threatened to attack Pondicherry by laying siege to it in 1748. Dupleix had strongly fortified the place, and so, despite their vast forces, the allies had to lift the siege after two months. The Treaty of Aix-la-Chapelle in October 1748 ended the Austrian succession and temporarily halted the hostilities, especially between Britain and France. One of the terms of the treaty was the return of Madras by the French, in exchange for Louisbourg in Canada. While the First Carnatic War ended with this, it sowed the seeds for the entanglement among the Indian powers of the time on the part of the two European rivals, and for their squabbles.

Political Flux Intensifies

Chanda Sahib was released in July 1748 from Maratha custody after all the ransom was paid to them. Raising a small army, he headed back southwards and, on the way, attacked the Nayaka in Keladi. After the battle that ensued, his son Abid Sahib and he himself were imprisoned once again. Somehow managing to extricate himself out of yet another prison stint, Chanda Sahib decided to then plunge head-on into a long-drawn succession battle that was to play out both in Hyderabad and Arcot.

On 19 June 1748, Nizam-ul-Mulk passed away, and this plunged Hyderabad into crisis, bringing the two claimants—Nasir Jung and Muzaffar Jung—into open conflict. Chanda Sahib allied with Muzaffar Jung in his claim, even as Dupleix sided them with 2000 French sepoys under his brother-in-law d'Auteuil. The allied forces marched menacingly towards Arcot. An alarmed Anwaruddin tried in vain to negotiate peace with the French, even as he sent word to his son Muhammad Ali to secure the fort of Tiruchirapalli. In the Battle of Ambur that followed on 16 July 1749, the superior French artillery was no match for Anwaruddin's forces; an arrow pierced Anwaruddin in the chest and killed him. It was a thumping victory for the allied forces of Muzaffar Jung, the French and Chanda Sahib. With Anwaruddin killed, Chanda Sahib was declared the Nawab of Arcot, and Muhammad Ali was ordered to hand over Tiruchirapalli.

Nasir Jung, who had been summoned to Delhi to face the second invasion of Ahmed Shah Abdali, the founder of the Durrani Empire of Afghanistan, was shocked to see his rival Muzaffar Jung making such rapid strides. He rushed back to the south, and was joined by the Maratha forces and some British troops under Major Lawrence. Mysore, too, sent troops to Nasir's aid, under Berki Venkat Rao, that joined him at Madhugiri. Shahabaz and Haidar Ali were part of this Mysorean military contingent. The strength of the allies kept swelling with time, and soon, Muhammad Ali too joined them with 6000 troops. This combined counter-alliance was determined to attack the earlier alliance that had occupied Arcot and was threatening Hyderabad. Seeing such a huge force advancing towards them, Muzaffar Jung and Chanda Sahib ran to Pondicherry to save their lives. An exasperated Dupleix wrote: 'How can such men think of ruling countries! They should not attempt more than they are fit for ... if a man trusts these dogs and acts with them, he will lose all sense of shame and bring dishonour upon himself.'[17] With two of his allies absconding, Dupleix could not match the combined opposition. By April 1750, Nasir Jung continued to have a victorious streak on the battleground and even managed to take his rival Muzaffar Jung as prisoner to Arcot, where he was kept imprisoned for a few months. When pressed to kill his rival, Nasir Jung is supposed to have said, 'I will never take the life of the man who saved mine,'[18] remembering how it was Muzaffar Jung's intervention in battle many years ago that had saved his life.

But the French soon overturned these reverses and managed to defeat the English in successive battles. Muhammad Ali, too, retired to Ginjee. At this point, Dupleix sent a young, able thirty-year-old man, Charles de Bussy, to occupy Ginjee. Bussy had played an important role even in the defence of Pondicherry in 1748 during the First Carnatic War. The Ginjee fort was one of the largest in India, comprising three main hills: Rajagiri, Krishnagiri and Chandragiri. This was the fort that had withstood Mughal siege for seven years in the 1690s. But with Bussy in command and the superior French artillery, it fell to their onslaught in a matter of a day, on 12 September 1750. Bussy was in total command of the fort and held on to it till the end of that year.

La Touche, the French commander of the forces at Ginjee, managed to gather intelligence about rumblings in rival Nasir Jung's camp—some of which they themselves had triggered—where the Marathas and the other Nawabs were getting increasingly disillusioned with him. So, it was decided to launch a surprise midnight attack on Nasir's camp. But somehow the information leaked to the other side, and the combatants met in the open field. Preparing himself for this battle, Nasir Jung looked at his own reflection in the mirror, addressing it thus: 'O! Meer Mohammad [his original name; Nasir Jung, or the Battle Victorious, was a title], the Almighty is thy protector!'[19] He went on to perform all the religious rituals and prayers of the day, and clothed in a simple muslin robe, instead of the usual armour that he would clad himself in from head to toe, proceeded to mount his elephant with no sense of urgency or anxiety. He somehow seemed resigned to his fate. Nasir Jung was joined by about 3000 horsemen and was perplexed to find his three allies—Himmat Bahadur Khan, the Nawab of Kurnool,

Abdul Nabi Khan, the Nawab of Cudappah, and Abdul Hakim Khan, the Nawab of Savanur—all ready and mounted on their elephants, but reluctant to join the battle. Moving closer towards Himmat Bahadur Khan, Nasir Jung greeted him with a salute, imploring him to join the battle. To his utter dismay, the Kurnool Nawab returned his ally's greeting with a volley of bullets that pierced Nasir's chest, and he fell down dead. His decapitated head was then sent as a gift to Muzaffar Jung in his prison cell.[20] Hearing about his ally's murder, a harried Muhammad Ali fled by night to Tiruchirapalli to save his life, with his rival Chanda Sahib in hot pursuit shortly thereafter.

Haidar Ali Makes Hay While the Sun Shines

In the huge chaos that followed the murder of Nasir Jung, Haidar Ali, with the aid of tribal Bedar peons, whom Wilks characterizes as 'brave and faithful thieves',[21] looted Nasir's army, gaining many camels laden with gold coins, 500 muskets and 300 horses.[22] Haidar had already prepared the means for availing for himself the benefits that such situations in battlefield accrued for him and had hence kept in his pay a body of these irregulars, some 300 or so in number, to help him in the loot amid the war. He began to use this loot money in wars to build his own small militia, which was to prove beneficial for him in the long run. That there was so much wealth available for looting is evidenced in the French account too, of how their spoils were so considerable 'that everyone from the councillor to the writer, from the captain to the private, had his share and officers who only joined the service later looked back with regret to the happy days when a mere ensign received 60,000 rupees. Never had so much gold been seen at Pondicherry. It was comparable with the solid gains of Plassey.'[23] This was possibly the first time that Haidar had an encounter with the French, and his high opinion of them, as against the British, might have been formed at this juncture.

Haidar triumphantly brought some of the spoils that his dacoits had looted as war trophies to Srirangapatna and submitted them to the Maharaja as tribute, thereby raising his own esteem in the ruler's eyes. A pleased Maharaja gifted three of the camels laden with gold coins as a reward for Haidar's daring and presence of mind in the midst of the disarray on the field. Haidar Ali had steadily but surely begun to make a definitive mark in the eyes of all the consequential elements of the Mysore polity, be it the Maharaja or Nanjarajayya, who began to repose the greatest trust in him. Before heading to the capital Srirangapatna, Haidar Ali stopped by in Pondicherry, and was hugely impressed with the discipline of the French troops and the skill of their engineer officers.[24] If at some point he wished to galvanize his own army, their expertise and help would be quintessential, he must have thought. All the loot that his Bedars were making in each military campaign was being assiduously used by Haidar to build his own private army. He began to use French sepoy deserters to train his own new recruits in the skills of European warfare tactics.

Tumultuous Twists

With Nasir Jung out of their way, the French were supremely satisfied with the turn of events. Their protégé Muzaffar Jung was now declared the new Nizam. Bussy was to be stationed at Hyderabad as a resident for the Nizam's protection, with 300 French troops and 2000 sepoys, in January 1751. With Muhammad Ali absconding, his rival Chanda Sahib was proclaimed the new Nawab of Carnatic at Arcot. This was the peak of Dupleix's military and diplomatic career. He received the title of Zafar Jung, and the jagir of Ginjee and several other places. Almost all of South India had fallen into the French lap.

However, Muzaffar Jung's glory was short-lived. Right on their way back to Hyderabad, the allied Nawabs of Kurnool, Cudappah and Savanur started squabbling about how they had received a raw deal and deserved better. Those who had hitherto been allies now met as enemies on the field, and Muzaffar Jung decided to take them on and be done with them. With the heroic assistance of Nizam Ali, a younger son of Asaf Jah, Jung actually got the Nawabs of Savanur and Kurnool killed, and their heads chopped off. But just when he was going to behead the Nawab of Cudappah, an arrow pierced his eye and left him mortally wounded. They won the battle, but it turned out to be a Pyrrhic victory. In a perverse tragedy, the victor Muzaffar Jung now lay dead. With both the claimants now gone, Hyderabad needed a new ruler. Ghaziuddin, Asaf Jah's eldest son, was away in Delhi. From among his younger sons who were there— Salabat Jung, Nizam Ali and Basalat Jung—Bussy had to quickly choose a successor to avoid further political chaos. The eldest of them, Salabat Jung, was proclaimed the new Nizam, while Basalat Jung was made the Nawab of Adoni. A grateful Salabat Jung made further generous grants of territory and treasures to his French overlords.

With Hyderabad slowly limping back to some semblance of political stability for now, the attention was fully drawn to Tiruchirapalli, which became the seat of drama, as it housed Muhammad Ali, who was desperately trying to regain Arcot from Chanda Sahib. Even as he was carrying out a pretence of a negotiation with Dupleix, Muhammad Ali was rallying his allies—the English, Murar Rao Ghorpade and the Maharaja of Mysore. Sheshagiri Pandit was sent to Mysore to negotiate with Krishnaraja Wodeyar II for his help in return for the prosperous and fertile lands of Tiruchirapalli and other territories they held till Cape Comorin. Pandit had found 'the Raja a pageant, the Dulwoy Deo Raj advanced in years and interfering but little in the active administration of public affairs, and the conduct of the government directed chiefly by Nunjeraj, the young Dulwoy as he was usually called'.[25] Much against the wishes of both the Maharaja and Devarajayya, Nanjarajayya, lured by the offer of gaining the fertile Tiruchirapalli, decided to march there with Haidar Ali and his 5000 cavalry and 10,000 infantry force. Detachments under Berki Venkat Rao and Veerannaraj left Dindigul and parked themselves in the vicinity of Tiruchirapalli. Mysore also provided financial assistance of Rs 80,000 to Muhammad Ali. The Mysorean troops kept waiting for a few months for the arrival of Murar Rao, and in the interim, Nanjarajayya kept his dialogue open with Dupleix as well, to figure out which deal worked best in Mysore's interest, especially for capturing Tiruchirapalli, which he had made his life's mission. In all the campaigns, Haidar was determined to leave his mark. His predatory light horse of irregulars, the *Kuzzaks*, under the command of his confidant Ghazi Khan Bede, often made surprise nocturnal attacks on the opponents, capturing arms, tents and cattle. In one such night attack, they even took two guns from the advanced guard of the French, earning some distinction for their actions.[26]

Muhammad Ali had tired Dupleix out with his prolonged negotiations that were going in circles. Running thin on his patience, Dupleix finally asked his brother-in-law to storm the fort of Tiruchirapalli in April 1751. It was here that the English hero Robert Clive made a daring mark. Clive began his career as a 'writer' (a term used for an office clerk at the time) for the East India Company in 1744, tallying books and arguing with errant suppliers while at Fort St George. But he showed his resilience during the French attack on Madras in 1746, refusing to take their oath of loyalty to the French emperor and instead escaping in disguise to Fort St David in Cuddalore, the British post. Here, Clive decided to enlist in the Company's army and avenge the insults his country had faced. During the subsequent siege of Pondicherry in 1748, Clive distinguished himself by defending a trench against a French sortie. When Muhammad Ali, one of the last major allies of the British, was put under duress in Tiruchirapalli, there was much consternation in the English camp. At that time, Clive, who had just returned from Bengal, insisted that he be sent to save the day for the British and their harried ally in Tiruchirapalli. With merely 200 Europeans, 300 sepoys and three small canons, Clive was sent to the scene of the siege. But instead of focusing on Tiruchirapalli, his contingent decided to occupy the fort of Arcot further north, diverting the enemy's attention. Chanda Sahib's son Raza Sahib was sent to besiege Arcot and liberate it from Clive. But by then the Maratha detachments from Murar Rao and the Mysorean troops had reached Clive in Arcot. After a fifty-day siege and suffering heavy losses, Raza Sahib and the French were forced to lift their siege of Arcot and retreat. The manner in which Clive had held the fort was widely appreciated, and Muhammad Ali bestowed the title of 'Sabit Jung', which translates to 'Proven Courageous in Battle', upon him. Clive continued his string of successes by taking the fort of Timiri by the end of 1751, and also Kanchipuram, by breaching the wall around its great temple. Thanjavur, too, was taken by the British.

The French were not prepared for these reverses after the series of victories that they had seen so far. They decided to threaten Madras, but Clive was quick to halt them before they reached Madras, at Kaveripakkam, ensuring a complete French rout. By March 1752, Clive now turned his attention to Tiruchirapalli, where the siege of the fort by Chanda Sahib and the French had gone on for almost a year, and where Muhammad Ali was hiding. Sensing the downturn in French fortunes, the British also sent the celebrated Major Stringer Lawrence, often called 'the Father of the Indian Army',[27] to command the forces. Chanda Sahib's health was declining, given the constant ravages of war and the decades-long imprisonment he had faced in his endless quest for power. He lifted the siege and retired to the temple town of Srirangam. When Chanda Sahib retreated, Muhammad Ali paid a visit to Nanjarajayya and, in a dramatic show of his keenness to honour the promise he had made to Mysore, handed over the keys of the fort of Tiruchirapalli to Nanjarajayya. However, being naively trustful of Muhammad Ali, Nanjarajayya told him that they would take possession of the fort only after Muhammad Ali had won his case decisively, for which all the allies were straining so much.

The French, too, found that this was turning into an unprofitable exercise, and the first signs of their retreat began with the French commander Jacques Law, who had replaced d'Auteuil, slowly posting himself away from Tiruchirapalli in the temple town and island of Srirangam. The gigantic Sri Ranganatha Swamy temple there had seven enclosures and high walls that went up to 25 feet; it was thereby the best place of retreat for the exhausted troops. But before the French realized that, Clive had encircled them there within Srirangam, cutting off all supplies and replenishments that were coming to their aid. With their situation becoming dangerously precarious, the French finally surrendered at Srirangam on 31 May 1752. After negotiations they were let off, but Chanda Sahib had to be handed over to the British, who kept him under their ally Manaji Appa, the general from Thanjavur. Murar Rao, too, was negotiating to secure the custody of Chanda Sahib that was also being sought by the Maharaja of Mysore. Sensing that his life was in danger, Chanda Sahib did what he did best—he made diplomatic overtures to bribe his opponent. He enticed Manaji with a hefty bribe if the latter let him off safely to Karaikal. Manaji agreed but had other plans. On their way to Karaikal, on 3 June 1752, when Chanda Sahib was in the middle of his prayers, Ashur Beg, a Pathan, with a Rajput accomplice, beheaded him.[28] Thus ended the troubled and stormy life of the unfortunate Chanda Sahib, whose unbridled ambitions since the time he entered Tiruchirapalli and betrayed Meenakshi in Madurai had wreaked complete havoc in the Carnatic. His dreams of becoming the Nawab of Arcot thus remained unfulfilled. His head was victoriously paraded, tied to the neck of a camel and carried around the fort, in front of Muhammad Ali and his allies, Murar Rao and Nanjarajayya, who were overjoyed and relieved. Spectators hurled the worst of invectives at it.[29] It was now the turn of Muhammad Ali, who had emerged victorious in this battle of nerves, with no special valour at his end, looking to live up to the promises he had made to his allies. The allies, however, were in for a rude shock.

Nanjarajayya's Tiruchirapalli Debacle

As the situation had now turned fully in Muhammad Ali's favour, Nanjarajayya implored the former to keep his promise of handing over Tiruchirapalli to Mysore. The plans of the Mysorean troops that had stayed on for such a long time, bearing great physical difficulties and incurring huge financial burdens, seemed to be coming to fruition, and their long-held dreams to occupy the fertile lands were finally materializing. Muhammad Ali asked Nanjarajayya to come over to the fort, inspect it and arrange for its garrisoning. As the select Mysorean retinue was entering the fort through its outer enclosure, Haidar Ali, who was accompanying Nanjarajayya, suspected some foul play and cautioned his master to tread cautiously and retrace his steps. Haidar's instincts were not misplaced. Even as the Mysore party was entering the fort, Muhammad Ali had the principal gates closed on them and began cannonading from above. If not for his mother, who reprimanded him for the ungrateful act of treachery towards his own allies, Muhammad Ali had intended to fire on them continuously and get done with the irritant altogether. Muhammad Ali's true intent was now laid bare to his erstwhile trusting ally.

A livid Nanjarajayya vowed to avenge this betrayal. Along with the forces of Mysore and Murar Rao, he laid a heavy siege to the fort even as Muhammad Ali was trapped inside. The besieging forces refused to march to Ginjee with the forces of Muhammad Ali and Major Lawrence until the demand for the handover of Tiruchirapalli to Mysore was complied with. Muhammad Ali tried various tricks to negotiate with them, procrastinating on the handover, but this time Nanjarajayya was firm on his demands. To salvage the situation for himself, Muhammad Ali then bribed Murar Rao, whom Nanjarajayya trusted immensely, with Rs 2 lakh and asked him to intercede. Through Murar Rao's mediation he managed to promise Nanjarajayya that the fort would be handed over within two months; and in the meantime, Mysore could station its *killedar* with 200 men in the fort as a symbolic occupation. Once this agreement was concluded, Muhammad Ali accompanied Murar Rao to meet Nanjarajayya. Many in the Mysorean side urged Nanjarajayya to seize this opportunity and have the treacherous Muhammad Ali arrested, as getting him to live up to his promises once he had made safe passage out was next to impossible. But so completely trusting of Murar Rao's faithfulness was Nanjarajayya that he disdainfully rejected all these proposals and exuded confidence in Rao's guarantee to the deal. Little did he know that Murar Rao was himself playing a dual game in this matter and was getting money from both sides, even as he posed as a trusted ally of Mysore. As per the terms of this deal, Katti Gopalaraje Urs and Pradhan Channappayya were to be stationed inside the fort with 200 sepoys and Srirangam was to be delivered to Nanjarajayya. Placing his brother-in-law Khair-ud-Din inside the fort, along with the English detachment under Captain John Dalton, Muhammad Ali secured his freedom and rushed to Fort St David with his and the English army, even as Nanjarajayya sat there believing that he had diplomatically struck the deal in Mysore's favour.

Nanjarajayya kept waiting for the promised period after which the fort would be delivered to Mysore. He even sent Seshagiri Pant and Berki Venkat Rao to Fort St David and Madras, respectively, to negotiate the settlement. They were asked to insist on paying Mysore the actual expenses that were incurred in the campaign as the next best alternative to the transfer of the fort itself. But Muhammad Ali, true to his track record, remained evasive and kept making vague promises. Even as Nanjarajayya remained poised to occupy the fort in what had now become an issue of acute prestige for him, some of the *palegars*, or chieftains, of Madurai and Dindigul, fanned by Pratapsinh of Thanjavur, rose in revolt against Mysore's attempts to intrude into the Carnatic. Back home from Srirangapatna, Devarajayya sent letters to his younger brother to abandon this wasteful campaign and return, but received a haughty reply saying that he would prefer 'to die rather than return with dishonour'.[30] Nanjarajayya was determined to somehow wrest either the fort or the commensurate expenses incurred, so that he could return to Srirangapatna with some modicum of self-respect. Sensing the danger at Tiruchirapalli with the brewing revolts, he moved to Srirangam and made it his base. His efforts to bribe Dalton and occupy the fort, too, were in vain. Dalton wrote rather disparagingly about the Mysorean army in his memoir: 'Such was the Mysorean army! An undisciplined rabble—a pack of rapacious wolves, eager for prey, but afraid to attack their enemy'.[31]

The Mysoreans who had entered the fort were feeling increasingly stifled by Khair-ud-Din and Dalton. They conspired to have the duo killed, but somehow this plan leaked out to the opposite camp. Katti Gopalaraje Urs was disarmed and detained within the fort like a virtual captive. Nanjarajayya protested loudly, with threats of renewing the siege and attacking Muhammad Ali, but basically, the threats achieved little and hardly managed to unnerve his opponents. To add to his woes, Nanjarajayya's erstwhile ally Murar Rao, at whose insistence the deal with Muhammad Ali had been signed and whose double dealing was unknown to him, happily switched sides to the French when Dupleix offered him a handsome payment of Rs 6 lakh. With his ally deserting him, Nanjarajayya's position was now precarious. Emboldened by this, Dalton and Khair-ud-Din made a surprise midnight attack on the Mysorean troops in January 1753 as the latter lay fast asleep in the enclosure of the Srirangam temple. The Mysore troops, under Hari Singh and Haidar Ali, put up a daring defence and drove the assailants away. Hari Singh, a Rajput jamadar, was both a rival and a personal enemy of Haidar; he considered the latter 'an upstart, indebted for his success in life more to fawning and flattery than to military merit; and would never condescend to address him, or speak of him, by any other designation than the *Naick*'.[32] A petrified Nanjarajayya rallied all his troops and decided to blockade Tiruchirapalli at the head of 6000 horses and 15,000 men. Conflicts between the two sides kept going on, with each side having a temporary upper hand at different times.

Exasperated, Nanjarajayya even wrote to Thomas Saunders, the British governor in Madras, to make good on the promise that was made to Mysore but he only received non-committal responses. Even in June 1752, when the news of Muhammad Ali's initial differences with Mysore came to light, Saunders had observed: 'The present dispute between the King of Mysore and the Nabob [Muhammad Ali] is an affair of the utmost consequence, in which we ought not to precipitate ourselves, as the effects may be dangerous, for, should we who receive a *jageer* for our alliance with the circar, be anyways instrumental in separating so large a district [as Trichinopoly] from the subaship, we might draw upon ourselves, the resentment of the Moors [Moghuls] in general, at the same time as the Mysore king supplies the Nabob with men and money, should he withdraw his assistance, it would greatly embarrass our affairs.'[33] So, they kept making promises to prevail upon their ally Muhammad Ali, so that he would live up to his word to Mysore, but never took these up seriously.

A *Despatch* report to the Court of Directors in London, dated
3 November 1752, summed up the position of the English at Fort
St George thus:

> The dispute between the Nabob and the King of Mysore
> continues. The latter has sent a Vakil to Madras with offers to
> support the Nabob if the English will guarantee the cession of
> Trichinopoly, but the Nabob declares that he has no power to
> execute his promise, which was made only out of dire necessity.
> Received a letter purporting to come from Salabat Jang, desiring
> the English to support Muhammad Ali and denying the latter's
> right to cede Trichinopoly. As the matter is intricate, have
> answered the King of Mysore that we are "merchants, allies of the
> circar and not the principals," that we cannot interfere in matters
> of this nature, but are willing to act as mediators. There is no
> doubt of the Nabob's having made the promise but both he and
> the King must have known that he could not fulfil it. The king is
> immensely rich and the acquisition of Trichinopoly would lead
> to his conquering Tanjore [where the English, and no less the
> French, had commercial settlements] and becoming overpowerful
> . . . in the South, Dupleix is negotiating with the Mysoreans and
> the Marathas.[34]

Despite suffering some reverses from Captain Dalton's onslaught,
the Mysorean troops maintained an iron-hold of a siege, blocking
food supplies from going inside and also preventing any army
replenishments. Muhammad Ali's forces and British contingents
from Madras under Major Stinger Lawrence came to Dalton's
aid, even as he was hemmed in from all sides by the Mysore army.
Nanjarajayya now turned to the French for their support. He had
been in talks with them for the longest time, but the negotiations
had not gone anywhere. Finally, by June 1753, with the offer of Rs
3 lakh, Dupleix dispatched 300 French soldiers, infantry and guns
to assist a beleaguered Nanjarajayya. This also brought the newly
acquired French ally, the ever-vacillating Murar Rao, back in the

support of Mysore's cause. His forces, along with the French under M. Astruc, joined Nanjarajayya against the combined attacks of Muhammad Ali and Major Lawrence. However, the Mysorean side and their allies faced terrible defeats; several of the French guns, mortars and wagons were seized by the opponents, and their infantry fled the field. Towards the end of November that year, with the new French commander Mainville and Murar Rao, Nanjarajayya planned to storm the fort by night and occupy it. Several Frenchmen even managed to enter the fort in the wee hours of the morning of 29 November 1753. But the British forces were alerted on time, and Captains Harrison and Kilpatrick opened fire and drove the assailants away, even killing several of them. Despite these reverses, an obdurate Nanjarajayya was unwilling to give up and continued to remain bullish about being able to wrest Tiruchirapalli. He had staked his entire life and reputation on this campaign's success. His personal honour and prestige were closely yoked to the accomplishment of this very objective. He ordered a fresh contingent of 2000 horse from Srirangapatna to aid the campaign.

On 13 February 1754, 12,000 Maratha and Mysore horse, 6000 sepoys and 400 French troops with seven guns managed to attack a British convoy that was making its way to Tiruchirapalli. It was the Rajput Jamadar of Mysore cavalry, Hari Singh, who led this charge. Once the operation was successful, Hari Singh found all the guns and tumbrils to be in the possession of Haidar, who had taken them away through his network of Bedars. Hari Singh made a huge show of protest; he had led the campaign and won the day, yet the spoils of the war were now with his most hated rival, Haidar. This was to become the template of his military career. After much negotiation, Haidar parted with just one gun and kept the rest with himself, claiming that they were his legitimate catch.

On 14 August 1754, a considerable British and Tanjorean detachment was sent to reinforce the British garrison in Tiruchirapalli. The French and Mysorean troops attacked it. Though it did not cause the other side much damage, it rattled some of the British troops. Haidar had kept a close watch and swooped down on the rear of the convoy, seizing thirty-five carts, some laden with arms and ammunition and others with baggage belonging to British officers.[35] Thus, at every junction, Haidar was not only learning the tactics and strategies of warfare but also building up his own treasures and military supplies through all the loot.

Even as the military campaigns were under way, the British tried the diplomatic channel and opened parallel negotiations with Mysore. Muhammad Ali seemed willing to mortgage districts belonging to Tiruchirapalli as security for the payment of the sum owed to Mysore; yet he was adamant on retaining the fort. In October 1753, Muhammad Ali authorized Saunders to negotiate amicable terms with Berki Venkat Rao in Madras. At Tiruchirapalli, Thomas Cooke, from the British side, negotiated with Nanjarajayya, with the intercession of Pratapsinh of Thanjavur. Mysore suggested a settlement of affairs for Rs 130 lakh on the security of the regions around Tiruchirapalli. But Pratapsinh's own apprehensions about the growing Mysorean clout with the handover of Tiruchirapalli, and his bargain to bring the amount to Rs 60 lakh, made Nanjarajayya livid. The negotiations broke down, both in Tiruchirapalli and in Madras. Saunders even contemplated sending a diplomat to Srirangapatna to directly negotiate with Krishnaraja Wodeyar II, as he suspected that Nanjarajayya was deliberately sabotaging all offers, possibly under French influence. Muhammad Ali was not too keen on ceding any more to Mysore. He merely wanted to detach Murar Rao from his opposing camp and also to maintain an amicable equation with Dupleix. Saunders, however, does seem to have sent a letter to 'the king of Mysore, begging him to drop the dispute [over claims on Tiruchirapalli] for the present and promising him the friendship of the English to assist in settling the matter later on'.[36]

A Thriftless Campaign

All through 1754, a lot of internal churn was witnessed in the English and Muhammad Ali camps; they were trying to iron out a peace treaty with Mysore, thinking of what its terms could be and how it would impact them strategically vis-à-vis the French. Some of the terms being considered for the treaty are mentioned by Wilks:

1. The Raja of Mysoor shall renounce the French connexion [*sic*] and aid in the establishment of Mohammed Ali. 2. He shall induce Morari Row to do the same. 3. Until Mohammed Ali be established, Nunjeraj shall defray the expenses of his own army, and that of Morari Row. 4. He shall give soucar security for the whole amount expended by the Company in the war of Trichinopoly, to be paid on the actual delivery of that place; which, however, shall pay the usual tribute to the Carnatic. 5. He shall pay ten lacs to Mohammed Ali, and shall cede to him a district and fort in Mysoor equal to two lacs a year . . . the other articles relate to exclusive trade with Mysoor; the time of delivering the fort of Trichinopoly; the arrangements regarding stores; an eventual invitation to the Raja of Tanjore to accede; and a reciprocal guarantee of the two Rajas, the English and Mohammed Ali.[37]

As luck could have it for Nanjarajayya, Dupleix's serial reverses since the advent of Clive had made him hugely unpopular back in France. In 1754, he was recalled to Paris, where he tried to sue the French East India Company for the money that he claimed they owed him. But he remained discredited thereafter and lived on in relative obscurity and lack of money, before eventually passing away in 1763. He was succeeded by Charles Godeheu, who actively pushed for a cessation of hostilities between the two European powers in India, for at least a period of eighteen months. Most French contingents were thereby recalled from their theatres of action, including the wasteful campaign in Tiruchirapalli that was being led only to assuage one man's ego. Barring 300 military and 1000 foot under M. Maissin, the French armies evacuated the Kaveri delta region, leaving Nanjarajayya to his fate. He complained bitterly to Godeheu, but his words fell on deaf ears. Nanjarajayya had already wasted around Rs 3–4 crore on this campaign. His persistence, even in the wake of this immense drain of Mysore's resources, was noted by Madras in a *Despatch* report:

Should the king of Mysore get Trichinopoly, he would become a dangerous neighbour, as both the French and the English have settlements in the kingdom of Tanjore . . . the king of Mysore is regarded as the richest and most powerful prince that pays tribute to the Moghal; but in spite of his extensive territory, ambition and avarice prompted him to his scheme on Trichinopoly. The king is young and all the power lies in the hands of the Dalaway, whose brother commands the Mysore troops at Srirangam. The expedition has cost great sums, but though the Mysoreans are reputed tenacious, they have been beaten so often and trust the French so little, that they would have withdrawn long ago but that the Dalaway's brother fears for his life should he acknowledge his defeat by withdrawal.[38]

In January 1755, Saunders sailed back to England and was succeeded in Madras by George Pigot. Berki Venkat Rao, who had virtually been held captive in Madras, was now released, free to head back to Srirangapatna. For Nanjarajayya, the enormity of the ignominious situation that he was in was considerable. Financially, it had stripped Mysore of its wealth. He still owed Rs 20–22 lakh to the French and Rs 10–12 lakh to Murar Rao. He had spent close to Rs 4 crore on the campaign so far and had achieved no tangible outcome. All the players were exhausted with his claims and were deserting him. The campaign was his brainchild, and he had staked his entire life's reputation on it. So, returning home empty-handed was not just discrediting his legacy but also meant a washout for whatever was left of his political career. The Maharaja had already been disgusted with the brothers; this episode only enhanced the growing rift between him and the duo, especially Nanjarajayya, who was also his father-in-law.

Fishing in troubled waters, Muhammad Ali instigated the troops of Mysore to demand their pay, which had fallen into arrears. So from early April 1755, they sat in a dharna outside Nanjarajayya's house. He fell back on Haidar Ali, who very deftly managed the crisis and dissuaded the troops by promising them half their dues within the next three months. 'So powerful indeed was the influence of his [Haidar's] personality over the military,' writes historian C. Hayavadana Rao, 'that they soon recognized him [Haidar] as their leader, went over to him and prepared to march back to Seringapatam [Srirangapatna] as if nothing had happened.'[39] Meanwhile, the French and Murar Rao, too, claimed their arrears, which Nanjarajayya had to settle. Nanjarajayya mortgaged Srirangam, Jambukeswaram and other places between the Kaveri and Coleroon rivers to the French, which yielded about Rs 4 lakh annually. So far from annexing new territory in the delta region, he ended up ceding whatever was already held.

While most of the Mysorean army was away in Tiruchirapalli, the Peshwa and the Nizam made several incursions, demanding stipulated payment of tributes. In 1751–52, the Peshwa put forth his claims for Chauth from Dalavayi Devarajayya. By March 1753, he managed to extract Rs 25–30 lakh from Srirangapatna, in return for a promise to not enter the already muddied waters of Tiruchirapalli. By March 1755, Salabat Jung had crossed the Krishna River along with Bussy, levying tributes from the Nawabs of Cudappah and Kurnool, before marching into Mysore. Encamping a few miles from Srirangapatna, he demanded the submission of *peshkash* (tributes) of Rs 3–5 crore. At this very time, the Peshwa's agents, led by Banaji Madhav Rao, were in Srirangapatna too, demanding the Chauth settlements. Soon, the Peshwa too crossed the Tungabhadra and halted outside Srirangapatna. Devarajayya was in dire straits. The funding of the Tiruchirapalli campaign had already dried up the treasury to a large extent. He tried buying time with both the Nizam and the Peshwa, explaining his difficulty in the wake of the campaign at Tiruchirapalli, and consequently, he could not meet their exorbitant demands. The French were requested in Pondicherry to help Mysore as an ally, and prevail upon Salabat Jung and Bussy to collect merely the normal tributes and not all the compounded arrears and expenses. Reluctant to intervene, the French governor wrote a letter to the Nizam and Bussy at a time when their combined forces were almost on the brink of capturing the fort. After prolonged negotiations, they settled for Rs 56 lakh. But so impoverished had Mysore become that only one-third of this amount could be paid in ready money. This, too, was arranged most shamefully from the treasury balances, as also by pawning valuables that belonged to the royal family, the palace and also the Sriranganatha Swamy temple, from which the capital drew its name. Such was the impact of the Devarajayya–Nanjarajayya hold on the Mysorean polity. For the remaining two-thirds, bills were issued on the security of local merchants, or *sowcars*, and their personal clerks (*gumastas*) pledged as hostages. It was only after these disgraceful payments were formalized that the Nizam's troops, along with Bussy, retired to Hyderabad. The Peshwa, who was operating around the Dharwar–Hubli–Kundgal region, was mollycoddled and persuaded by Bussy not to make demands of Mysore at this point, and was sent back.

It was a dire case of momentary survival for Mysore in each of these crises, to be able to live to tell the tale, but tragically not knowing when the next major blow might be struck, shaking it to its very foundation. Devarajayya could no longer afford to finance the vacuous campaign in Tiruchirapalli, and hence sternly ordered his brother to abandon it right there and return to Srirangapatna without further delay. At last, in April 1755, a thoroughly discredited, defeated and dispirited Nanjarajayya returned from the thriftless Tiruchirapalli campaign, which, over the four years that it had lasted, had impoverished the state completely, exposed all its weaknesses and handed to its protagonist a political debacle that he could barely recover from.

3

Before the Usurpation

While the Tiruchirapalli campaign brought great disgrace to Nanjarajayya and drained Mysore of all its wealth and prestige, if there was one man who benefited from the entire turn of events, it was Haidar Ali. He acquired his military skills mainly in those two and a half years, fighting at Tiruchirapalli with Nanjarajayya. At the fall of Chanda Sahib in June 1752, Haidar managed to purchase from that army several matchlocks for his men, at Rs 3–4 each.[1] These came in handy during the blockades that he helped create at Tiruchirapalli. Assimilating the traditional fighting methods of some of the Rajput chiefs in the Mysore army and the cavalry techniques of the Marathas, he also drew from the war strategies of the British and the French. One of his principal rivals in the Mysore army then was the Rajput chief Hari Singh, though they jointly led the charge at Srirangam in January 1753, seizing several firelocks there too. Though Hari Singh normally led cavalry charges and succeeded in them, given Haidar's large contingent of irregular Bedar peons, most of the guns and treasures usually fell in the latter's hands, much to Hari Singh's ire. Hari Singh was Devarajayya's man, and Devarajayya disapproved of his younger brother's increasing trust and reliance on Haidar Ali. 'Deo Raj [*sic*],' writes Wilks, 'had always opposed his brother's rapid advancement of Hyder, adopting the opinion of Herri Sing [*sic*] and all the old chiefs, who attributed that advancement more to his intrigues as a courtier, than his merit as a soldier. Herri Sing, in particular, made no scruple of avowing on

---

* Please refer to the corresponding illustration in the appendix.

all occasions his contempt for the Naick [Haidar]. Their hatred, in short, was mutual and open.'[2]

On his way back from the Tiruchirapalli campaign, Nanjarajayya dismissed several of his forces and placed the rest under Haidar's command, making him the *foujdar*, or military governor, of Dindigul and assigning to him the places below the ghats—Satyamangalam, Erode and Shankhagiri. He was now given honorifics and called 'Haidar Ali Khan Bahadur'. Haidar left for Dindigul at the head of 5000 infantry, 2500 horse, 2000 peons and six guns.[3] It was Berki Venkat Rao who had captured Dindigul for Mysore from the palegar of Uttamapalaiyam in 1745. The fort was situated on a rock, sixty-five miles south-west of Tiruchirapalli and about forty-five miles north-west of Madurai.

Just as his career was on the ascent, Haidar's personal life, too, was harmonious at this time. His brother Shahabaz had been married by now and had a son, Kadir Sahab, and two daughters. When Haidar turned nineteen, Shahabaz arranged for his marriage with the eldest daughter of Shah Miyan Sahib, a *peerzada*, or a pious man, in the custody of a Sufi mausoleum in Sira. In due course, she bore him a daughter, but shortly afterwards, his wife became afflicted with dropsy and was crippled for life.[4] His family urged him to remarry, but that was postponed due to the military campaigns that he had to go on with Nanjarajayya. Finally, his brother selected for him Fatima Begum (sometimes also referred to as Fakhr-un-nissa), daughter of Mir Muinuddin and sister of one Mir Ali Raza Khan, who had been the killedar of Gurramkonda and was living now at Baramahal. Though he took a second wife, Haidar was said to be extremely considerate to the first one and conferred on her the privilege of holding the principal sway in the household, regarding 'her as the ornament of his family, and placed all his family under her authority'.[5] His three brothers-in-law by the first wife—Saiyid Kamal, Makhdoom Sahib and Saiyid Ismail—as also several of his other relatives, found their way in the Mysore administration or army in some position or the other.

The Successor is Born

For three or four years after the second marriage, the couple had no children. It was then that they undertook a pilgrimage to the shrine of Tipu Mastan Oulia, a Sufi saint in Arcot, known to have miraculous powers. By the 'mediation of the transcendent merits of Tippoo Mustan Oulia, he [Haidar] obtained his wish, and in the hope of obtaining children, having taken refuge in the Almighty, and having offered up prayers and vows for the accomplishment of his desires . . . the tree of his hope blossomed and fructified.'[6]

Kirmani records that on the twentieth day of the month of Zil-Hijjah in the Islamic year 1163, corresponding to 20 November 1750 in the Gregorian calendar, Haidar Ali and his wife were blessed with a son in the town of Devanahalli, where they were residing. The child was born on the morning of that Saturday, 'shedding its light on the field of his father's wishes for progeny, dispelling the dark gloom obscuring his hopes and rejoicing the heart of both friend and stranger'.[7] For forty days thereafter, Haidar kept his house open for feasting and enjoyment, generously opening his treasury for friends and servants alike, to partake in gifts and merriment. *Nagaras*, or kettledrums, were beaten to announce the arrival of this son and to seek the blessings of well-wishers. Kirmani states that since the child was born 'owing to the secret aspirations and intercession of the Saint Tippoo Mustan, he was named Tippoo Sultan, and no care was omitted in his nurture and preservation'.[8, 9]

However, historian and independent researcher Nidhin George Olikara has recently shed more light on a plausible date of birth for Tipu.[10] He bases his claim on the *Fathul Mujahideen*, a military manual of Tipu in Persian, found in its original edition in the British Library in London. In the manual's fourth chapter, he argues that Tipu's commanders were given specific directives on when to fire gun salutes, and one such special date was supposedly the Sultan's birthday. This date, the fourteenth day of the Zakiri month for the Hijri year 1165, was based on the new Mauludi calendar that Tipu had started in Mysore, as against the Islamic lunar calendar or Hindu *panchanga* or almanac (more about this in a later chapter).

After much cross-tabulation with numerous calendars, Olikara infers that in Gregorian terms, this date translates to 1 December 1751, and that this date should be accepted as Tipu's actual date of birth.[11] However, the jury is out on the exact birthdate of the man; it oscillates between one of the two dates mentioned above.

The Dream Days in Dindigul

Buoyed by domestic bliss, Haidar subjugated the palegars of Palani, Virupakshi and Millemirangi, who were in and around his locus of influence in Dindigul, where he began to establish himself firmly. There were twenty-six *palayams*, or feudal estates, that came under his jurisdiction.[12] Their disunity was a boon for Haidar because had they all formed a confederacy against him, his doom would have been imminent. But Haidar managed to quell all of them and amass an exorbitant sum of Rs 20 lakh.[13] As mentioned earlier, right from his Tiruchurapalli days to his time in Dindigul, Haidar managed to use his irregular plunderers to amass as much as they could. As Wilks states: 'Nothing was unseasonable or unacceptable; from convoys of grain, down to the clothes, turbans and earrings of travelers, or villagers, whether men, women or children. Cattle and sheep were among the most profitable heads of plunder; muskets and horses were sometimes obtained in booty, sometimes by purchase.'[14] Wilks also narrates the shameful deceptions that Haidar practised with the Government of Mysore, sending to the latter a long list of men killed or wounded in military campaigns, for which they were to be given an allowance and compensation (called Zakham Patti). This amounted to about Rs 14 a month until the wounded were cured. On one occasion, for instance, which Wilks claims to have an eyewitness account of, there were about sixty-seven wounded men in a battle, but Haidar sent to Srirangapatna a list of people numbering 700. The rest of them were told to enact a charade of being grievously wounded, moan and groan in mock pain, and have their legs and arms bound with yellow turmeric bandages to convince the inspection officer who had come to ascertain if it was indeed that huge a casualty. Of the Rs 14, he gave only half to the actual wounded and pocketed the rest; and 'of the presents brought for the officers of the army he made a distribution equally skillful, while each officer was made to believe that he was the person most particularly favoured by'[15] Haidar.

Being unlettered, Haidar employed a shrewd and enterprising Marathi Brahmin *mutsaddi* (accountant), Khande Rao, as his aide. Besides being an adept bookkeeper, Khande Rao also served as Haidar's ambassador and campaigner back in the capital at Srirangapatna, painting fanciful tales and a larger-than-life image for his master in the corridors of power there. He readily helped Haidar fudge bills and accounts, and helped his master siphon funds, from which he was obviously receiving his own commission. He exaggerated to Nanjarajayya the disturbed state of the kingdom that necessitated an augmenting of troops for Haidar and for which, from time to time, more districts were to be added to his resources. On one occasion, Jehan Khan 'saw exhibited the maneuver which he calls a circular muster, by which ten thousand men were counted and passed as eighteen thousand'.[16] In the absence of any scrupulous centralized authority, it was thus a free-for-all, and Haidar merrily made hay while the sun shone.

Haidar began to win the goodwill of the local populace in Dindigul and also started consolidating his funds with all the legitimate and corrupt collections. The chiefs of Madura and Tinnevelly had been resisting the advances of Muhammad Ali and the British to occupy their positions and sought Haidar's help. They offered him the district of Sholavandam, which had a strategic pass and the only road that connected Madura and Tinnevelly. Haidar, however, was met with stiff resistance from Yusuf Khan, the general of Muhammad Ali, who, through his comparatively superior and disciplined army, routed Haidar and forced him back to Dindigul. This was a wake-up call for Haidar to modernize his army as quickly as he could. With his earlier introduction to the French, Haidar decided to obtain the services of the French artificers from Srirangam, Tiruchirapalli and Pondicherry, and began to organize a regular arsenal and artillery.

A lot of this needed expenditures that he could obviously not seek from an already impoverished Mysore treasury. He was therefore constantly on the lookout to augment his income whenever such an opportunity presented itself. And it did, with some differences that had arisen among the chiefs in Malabar.

Haidar's command extended to the boundaries of Palghat, whose Nair ruler, Komu Achan, was being hemmed in by the Zamorin (the Samudrin or Samoothiri ruler) of Calicut (Kozhikode) who had even attacked his territory and annexed a part of it. Komu Achan turned to Haidar for help, and the latter saw in this skirmish a good opportunity to replenish his treasury and strengthen his base. But before he could get involved directly in the crisis in Malabar, a bigger catastrophe was striking the door of the capital city of Srirangapatna, and it urgently needed his attention. He therefore dispatched his brother-in-law Makhdoom Sahib to Palghat, with 2000 horse, 5000 infantry and five guns.[17]

Palace Intrigues and Thereafter

Maharaja Krishnaraja Wodeyar II, who had just turned twenty-seven, had begun to despise the thralldom in which he had been held by the unscrupulous brothers. Despite Nanjarajayya being his father-in-law, there was little comfort that he could seek from him. After the wasteful Tiruchirapalli expedition, the Maharaja was emboldened to flex his might against their machinations. Ironically, he was supported by the dowager Rani Devajammanni, who had in the past conspired with the same Devarajayya to bring down the previous ruler, resulting in a painful and ignominious end for him. She advised the Maharaja to have Nanjarajayya arrested and appoint the current Pradhan Venkatapathayya in his place. Getting wind of this conspiracy, Nanjarajayya halted near Nanjangud, gathered his troops and marched to Srirangapatna in August 1755. So enraged was Nanjarajayya by these manoeuvres that he seized his erstwhile confidant Venkatapathayya, and his family and associates, put them in prisons at Manavallidurga and Kabbaladurga, and plundered their properties around October 1755. His ire now turned towards the Maharaja and, around October the same year, he even actively contemplated imprisoning him, killing him and placing the king's infant son on the throne.[18] This, despite his daughter being married to the king and being pregnant at the time. When his daughter heard about these vile plans, she made loud remonstrances to her father, beseeching righteousness and trying to invoke the fear of God in him. She also warned her husband to remain more cautious given the conspiracies that were brewing behind his back. The Maharaja immediately augmented his security with more than 4000 loyalists to guard his life. An ailing Devarajayya, who had earlier been the chief protagonist of many such unsavoury palace coups and intrigues, tried to act righteous and broker a rapprochement among all the parties, but in vain. Nanjarajayya's forces literally held the Maharaja under house arrest within the palace.

An increasingly stifled Krishnaraja Wodeyar II began sending out feelers to the Peshwa in Poona, seeking his assistance to rid himself of the vile brothers. On 3 August 1756, he even summoned Khande Rao and entrusted some 50,000 gold pieces to him and asked for the support of Haidar Ali to collect troops and attack the fort the following morning. When Devarajayya and Nanjarajayya got to know about this, they quickly ordered the fort gates to be shut, and troops to be garrisoned all over. Guns were mounted on the walls facing the palace and the residential quarters of the Maharaja; the infantry, Europeans and Topasses, who were hired at Tiruchirapalli, were all marshalled into action. It was a night to do or die. The plan was to have the Maharaja killed the next morning. It was all-out mayhem the following morning. The Maharaja, along with 300 members of the royal family, the priest, the nobility and other wealthy kinsmen, charged at the troops with drawn swords to resist the veritable siege that had been placed. Nanjarajayya ordered firing upon the assailants, and over a hundred men, women and servants of the royal family were killed. The brothers then stormed the palace, looking to behead the errant Maharaja. In a dramatic turn, the dowager rani who had brought up Krishnaraja Wodeyar clung to him and vowed that they should kill her first before attempting to hurt her adopted son. Even the Peshwa's vakil was aghast at the horrific scenes in the capital, protesting against such mistreatment and also writing to his master in Poona about all that was witnessed. About what transpired in the durbar on that unfortunate day, Wilks writes:

> The Raja was requested to seat himself in the usual hall of audience, while all the apartments were searched, and every male member produced. A certain number, on whose disposal he had not determined, were put in irons; and all the remainder had their noses and ears cut off in the Raja's presence, and in this state were turned out into the street. The creatures in his own pay, destined to replace the former attendants of the Raja, were then presented to him with an insulting mockery of respect; and after placing guards of his most confidential troops in the usual stations, he departed from the hall of audience, making the customary obeisance to the Raja, who had witnessed this extraordinary scene in an agony of silent terror and astonishment.[19]

Finally, the Maharaja, his wife, son and the dowager rani were all seized and put under a virtual house arrest under the careful watch of Nanjarajayya's loyalists.

After this distasteful episode, alarmed about his own safety, Devarajayya, who had been quite a participant in the entire matter along with his brother, decided to leave Srirangapatna in a huff and move to Satyamangalam, in Coimbatore district, along with 1000 horse, 3000 foot and the new Pradhan Channappayya in February 1757. This made Nanjarajayya the de facto ruler and master of the situation in Mysore. The Wodeyar, meanwhile, kept communication channels open with the Peshwa, even offering Rs 60 lakh for his support, as also with the French in Pondicherry, to help overthrow Nanjarajayya and liberate him. Things had deteriorated so badly between the two parties that regular rumours floated around that the Mysore king had been put to death. Nanjarajayya continued his blackmail with the Marathas that if the Peshwa dared to attack

Mysore, induced by the king's offer, he would not hesitate to have the Maharaja killed even before the troops reached Srirangapatna.

Peshwa Nanasaheb finally attacked Srirangapatna in March–April 1757, not as much to help the beleaguered Maharaja as, with Murar Rao, to extract the arrears and Chauth as per the agreement signed the previous year. A battery of thirty guns was opened by the Peshwa's brother Sadashiv Rao Bhau. Historian N.K. Sinha mentions that one of the shots even struck the top of the sacred Sriranganatha Swamy temple and a gun in the battery burst, killing several besiegers.[20] Fearing divine wrath, both parties tried to settle the terms. Initially, Nanjarajayya decided to buy them off through the payment of Rs 32 lakh—as cash tributes of Rs 5 lakh and offering the remainder through fourteen districts of the kingdom. Khande Rao, however, advised him to invite Haidar Ali to Srirangapatna and confer the matter with him.

On his arrival, Haidar Ali advised Nanjarajayya to procrastinate on the payment and promise to pay it over a time period, tire the Marathas out with the onset of the monsoon and make them return. Accordingly, Nanjarajayya paid a small amount to the Marathas, refused to pay the balance thereafter and also managed to drive away their forces from the allotted districts. He appreciated Haidar's wise counsel in the matter, and the latter's image was further enhanced in his estimation. This, however, opened the door for repeated Maratha incursions to collect what they claimed had been promised to them. The financial situation of the state was as precarious as the political flux. In such a scenario, the troops revolted, demanding a settlement of their arrears that had remained unpaid for long. They sat in dharna in front of Nanjarajayya's house, preventing him from even coming out.

Once again, Nanjarajayya reached out to his man Friday Haidar Ali, who quelled the revolt, got some of the assets of the kingdom disposed of, and paid the troops some of their dues and bought temporary peace. His role in resolving the crises, be it with the Peshwa or internal matters like the revolt of the troops, ironically won him both the attention and appreciation of the rivals—the Maharaja and Nanjarajayya, as also the Mysorean army. He was steadily climbing rung after rung on the ladder of political success. To further bolster his image, Haidar prevailed upon his mentor Nanjarajayya to make peace with his estranged brother Devarajayya, who had retired to Satyamangalam.

On his way to the capital from Dindigul, Haidar stopped at Satyamangalam and requested Devarajayya to join him for the reconciliation. When the latter refused, Haidar even fired a few shots at the fort in Satyamangalam, where Devarajayya was ensconced, much to the consternation of the old man and his officials. Left with few options, Devarajayya decided to give in and accompany Haidar to Srirangapatna. Both the brothers had the habit of addressing Haidar as Naik—in public durbars, addressing him in Kannada as 'Banni Nayakare!' (Please come hither, Naik!) Haidar somehow seemed to loathe this appellation, as he did not deem it respectful enough. In fact, he had got the Maharaja to have an injunction passed that whoever called him Naik would have his tongue cut off.[21] A poor man's tongue was actually cut off the very next day of the injunction being passed for addressing Haidar as Naik; the man was possibly genuinely ignorant about such a rule having come into existence.[22] Such was Haidar's deep class consciousness and sensitivity about how he was to be addressed. The elevation in title to 'Bahadur' by Nanjarajayya was seen as better suited and commensurate to his now-elevated status. Funnily enough, on their way back from Satyamangalam, either to spite the man he did not hold in too high a regard or out of forgetfulness, Devarajayya continued to address Haidar as Naik. At this, the latter remonstrated in a friendly manner and asked that Devarajayya correct himself henceforth. Excusing himself for what he claimed was a mistake caused by habit and not an intended insult, Devarajayya ordered that thenceforth all letters from him to Haidar would be addressed as 'Bahadur'.[23] The episode underscores how Haidar was acutely conscious of the class and position that he had come from, and how in his now-changed and elevated state he needed to be given appropriate respect by those who wielded power in Mysore.

Haidar also tried to broker a rapprochement of the brothers with the Maharaja, using the goodwill he had generated with the latter through his actions. After much persuasion, the brothers were finally united in June 1758 at a public durbar in Srirangapatna; they reconciled among themselves and also with the Maharaja, who only seemed too willing to forgive and forget all the horrors he had witnessed just recently through the actions of the two brothers.

However, shortly after this reconciliation, on his way back to Satyamangalam, Devarajayya, who had been ailing for a long time, died of dropsy on 23 June 1758. For all their recent rancour, the death of his elder brother and partner in crime shattered Nanjarajayya. The outcome was that he began to delegate a lot of responsibilities to his confidant Haidar Ali, either directly or through the latter's trusted aide Khande Rao, who was stationed in Srirangapatna. The issue of settling the arrears of the troops and assuaging their dissent was more or less Haidar's responsibility now. As N.K. Sinha states: 'In all these transactions, Haidar was all things to all men. Nanjaraj was grateful to him for his reconciliation with his brother before his death. The king looked upon him as his sole protector against Nanjaraj whose violence he could not possibly forget. The troops thought that they owed their payment entirely to his exertions.'[24]

But in the matter of the troops' payments, too, Haidar played his cards extremely well. He expressed his utter helplessness to both the Maharaja and Nanjarajayya that since there was no formal authority that had been vested in him, there was no real way in which he could effect a permanent cure to the problem of the troops' salaries. He therefore demanded that a *Karaar-Naame*, or deed, be issued in his name, investing him with absolute powers to punish and control anybody in the kingdom, except, of course, his superiors, the Maharaja and Nanjarajayya. So exasperated were both the Maharaja and Nanjarajayya with repeated dharnas from the troops who had recently even cut off supplies of food and water to the royal chambers, that they readily and unwittingly walked into the trap that Haidar had adroitly set up for them.

Accordingly, the deed was executed, and Haidar's representative, Khande Rao, was appointed as the chief executive officer, or *sarvadhikari*. Holding daily court in the palace, Khande Rao was to exercise 'his authority with a judicious combination of rigour and moderation, exacting presents and benevolences from the populace, amassing large sums of money and systematically quelling the rising of the military by paying off their arrears, by dismissing 4000 cavalry and plundering and enlisting in his own service, some of them, who remained unwieldy'.[25] Khande Rao began to retrench the existing troops that guarded the fort of Srirangapatna and instead had his own men posted at important positions in the fort.

About Haidar's meteoric rise in the politics of Mysore, historian N.K. Sinha writes: 'Haidar's rise, like that of many other great men, was as much due to his energy, enterprise and daring as to his opportunities. A detailed study of his career from 1750 to 1760 leads logically to the conclusion that he had a nicely calculated programme which unfolded itself stage by stage. But so much of his success he owed to external complications with their quick turns and sudden changes in the course of events that it is very difficult to say what he owed to his own foresight and how much to circumstances. Intrepid and swift, he was always ready to take advantage of his opportunities.'[26]

The Palghat campaign had, meanwhile, proceeded under Makhdoom Sahib's command. Haidar's forces were well organized and highly disciplined, and were trained under French commanders. The chiefs of Malabar were not accustomed to these modes of warfare, especially with a cavalry force. Unaccustomed to such measures, the forces of Calicut retreated and were hotly pursued by Makhdoom Sahib. The Zamorin understood early that Haidar's motive was not territorial expansion but to boost his coffers. He therefore negotiated a payment of Rs 12 lakh to Haidar and undertook to return to the raja of Palghat all the territories that had been wrested from him. Makhdoom received the first instalment and retreated from the region, leaving behind an agent to collect the balance. With the impending trouble off his back, the Zamorin, who obviously had no intentions of paying the balance, began to negotiate directly with Devarajayya, offering to pay the latter some money if he ordered the recall of the Muslim troops and had his own agents receive the money. Devarajayya, who was in any case opposed to Haidar and was sceptical of his increasing clout, decided to send his trusted aide

Hari Singh to the Malabar to complete the task. A miffed Haidar protested about the heavy expenses that he had already incurred in this campaign. Devarajayya got a draft of Rs 3 lakh issued for Haidar to cover his expenses, asked him to abandon the campaign there and hand over the charge from thereon to Hari Singh. But as luck would have it for Hari Singh, by the time he got to Calicut and could begin the transactions, news reached him of the sudden demise of his mentor Devarajayya. He abandoned the Malabar exercise and decided to head back to safeguard his own position, which he knew would be increasingly under threat with the death of his patron.

Expectedly, one of the first things that Haidar wanted to do with his enhanced power, with the relegation of Nanjarajayya to the background, was to fix for good his arch-rival Hari Singh. Haidar knew that if he had to ascend the ladder of political fortune, every perceived obstacle that came in his way had to be ruthlessly dealt with. On his way back to Srirangapatna, Hari Singh encamped in the open plains at Avanashi, in Coimbatore district, citing the outbreak of the south-west monsoon. However, he had secretly begun negotiating to find out if he could switch sides to the camp of the raja of Tanjore. On the pretext of sending his troops to Dindigul, Haidar detached Makhdoom Sahib with 1000 horse and 2000 infantry to attack Hari Singh by surprise. An unsuspecting Hari Singh was taken aback by this sudden ambush and in an unprepared state could barely manage to put up a stout defence. In the mayhem that followed, he and his principal officials and troops were all killed in the dead of the night. This was a dream scenario for the Zamorin of Calicut. He had escaped the payment of Rs 12 lakh that was promised to Makhdoom Sahib and had also managed to secure the withdrawal of Mysorean troops, both of Haidar as well as of Hari Singh, one of whom had been killed too now. The Zamorin also believed that the internal churn in the Mysore polity and the frequent attacks that it faced from the Marathas and the Nizam would keep them too embroiled to remember the Malabar dues, and that he could go back to heaving a sigh of relief. However, things were to turn out differently for him in due course.

In the meantime, Haidar's peons plundered Hari Singh's army in Avanashi, gathered 300 horses, 1000 muskets and three guns[27] that were brought triumphantly as trophies of war and laid at the feet of the Maharaja. Hari Singh was portrayed as a traitor who had both failed to collect the arrears from the Nairs of Calicut and had also been contemplating working for a rival kingdom, and hence his annihilation was justified. The three guns and fifteen beautiful horses were submitted to the Maharaja, while the rest went to Haidar's possession. A delighted Maharaja granted the city of Bangalore as a jagir to Haidar for these services. Haidar's military campaigns continued with his joining the French under M. Count de Lally in the latter's designs on Madura and Tinnevelly.

Climbing the Ladder

Continuing his goodwill with the Maharaja, Haidar also implored him to formalize the bonhomie with Nanjarajayya that had been interrupted by the death of the elder brother. Accordingly, on 24 October 1758, Krishnaraja Wodeyar concluded a 'Bhasha Patra' (Deed of Promise) with Nanjarajayya, whereby it was agreed that the government of Mysore was to firmly remain in the hands of the Wodeyars. Nanjarajayya and the members of his Kalale house were to retain the command of the Mysore army and enlist horses and men as required (these could be increased in times of need or war). He was assigned some ten taluks as jagirs that yielded a handsome income and could build a fort at Kalale. Till June 1759, Nanjarajayya, however, stayed on in Srirangapatna itself and only thereafter moved to Mysore.

It was now time for Haidar Ali to come face to face with the Marathas. Since the time of the invasion of Srirangapatna by the Peshwa in March–April 1757, it was a definite Maratha desire to control as much of southern India, as far as Rameshwaram. They detested the British efforts under George Pigot to negotiate a surrender of Tiruchirapalli to Mysore, as they eyed the place as a good southern base. The Peshwa had left behind several commanders in charge of prominent Maratha outposts in the south—Balwant Rao Mehendale, Visaji Krishna, Mukund Rao Sripat, Amrit Rao Shankar, Ragho Babaji and others—for levying contributions and collection of chauth arrears. Banaji Madhava Rao was at Srirangaptna as the Peshwa's representative to collect the arrears that were due to Poona. The promised period of repayment ended around September–October 1757, and Nanjarajayya was back to what he was best at—dilly-dallying and buying out time. A letter from Poona to Balwant Rao, dated 10 October 1757, clarifies that a tough stand was needed against Mysore: 'When the *khasa* [Peshwa] was here, the payment was promised. Now they have no money they say. Sweet words are of no use to us. They have wasted time. If you speak of money, is there any dearth of money in Nanjaraja's house?'[28] They tried to take Bangalore, but Balwant Rao managed to occupy just about thirteen to fourteen places around Bangalore, and there were no concerted attempts made by the Marathas. Berki Srinivasa Rao (mentioned as Srinivas Venkatesh Bangalorekar in Peshwa letters), son of Berki Venkat Rao, put up a spirited defence against the forces of Mukund Rao Sripat, pursuing him out of Bangalore, as far as Hoskote, wounding his men and capturing a few hundred horses. With some reinforcements from Srirangapatna, Berki Srinivasa Rao held on for a while, after which Mukund Rao Sripat managed to push back and have the former blockaded in Bangalore.

It was only around August 1758 that Gopal Rao Patwardhan and Malhar Rao Raste—who had been instructed by the Peshwa long back to head for Srirangapatna—made their way there with stern warnings to pay up within thirty-six hours or face a military onslaught.[29] With Mukund Rao Sripat having restricted Berki Srinivasa Rao to Bangalore in a veritable siege, the Maratha forces managed to take Kolar, Hoskote, Devanhalli, Maddur and Chennapatna, many of which lay midway between Bangalore and Srirangapatna. Some errors on the part of the Marathas, in the placement of guns, resulted in their failure to capture the Bangalore fort, which was still occupied by Berki Srinivasa Rao but whose position was getting increasingly precarious.

Banaji Madhava Rao was sent to Srirangapatna for the third time since 1755 along with Bhawanji Naik with a stern message demanding the settlement of arrears and biennial tribute for 1757–58 and 1758–59, failing which there would be dire consequences.[30] Mysore had to pay in the course of one year Rs 50 lakh in all, including Rs 30–32 lakh as arrears and Rs 20 lakh more as tribute for the current year. If Mysore consented to pay Rs 30 lakh each year, its territory was promised to be left unmolested. This could also be arranged as a Rs 15-lakh payment and the rest as ceding territory worth the balance amount that the Marathas were free to occupy.[31]

The Maratha forces seized Chennapatna, Maddur, Kankanhalli and Aprameyadurga. By September 1758, they renewed with added vigour their siege of Bangalore, where Berki Srinivasa Rao was holed up. He wrote desperate letters to the Maharaja, Nanjarajayya and his father, Berki Venkat Rao, requesting replenishments and help. Venkat Rao sent entreaties to Haidar Ali to save his son, and, having worked under him during the Tiruchirapalli campaign, Haidar was only too obliged to accede to the request. In consultation with Makhdoom Sahib and another trusted aide, Kabir Beg, Haidar planned the liberation of Chennapatna and Maddur as the preliminary steps to evacuate the Marathas from Bangalore. Using the services of a man who had held the place prior to the Maratha incursion, Haidar's men under Latif Ali Beg scaled the Maddur fort in the middle of the night using ladders. The Maratha side did not expect this nocturnal attack and, taken by surprise, they capitulated. In quick succession, both Maddur and Chennapatna were recaptured by Haidar, who now set out with substantial supplies for the relief of Bangalore. It was after a long time that Mysore had gathered enough courage to counter the Maratha incursion, and this was unexpected even for them. With great skill and military tactics, Haidar managed to salvage the situation in Bangalore, and by 20 October 1758, the siege of Bangalore was forcibly lifted by Gopal Rao. Haidar employed all that he had learnt during the Tiruchirapalli campaign to ensure a defeat of the Marathas. He had sufficient artillery, too, to strike them from a distance. He never faced them in battle on an open ground but led them through thick forests and vegetation, where he employed very similar tactics, of sudden attacks, that they had long employed under Chhatrapati Shivaji against the Mughals.

Gopal Rao Patwardhan gave hot pursuit to Haidar and his troops from Bangalore, but the latter drew him into the jungle tracts of Chennapatna, and for more than a month and a half, engaged in guerilla tactics and sudden attacks, harassing the invading forces and exhausting them. Gopal Rao was forced to settle for peace, and with Mysore having gained an upper hand in the combat, Haidar negotiated a payment of Rs 32 lakh—half of which was paid in cash immediately, while for the rest Haidar gave his personal security with the Maratha *sowcars*, or bankers, who seem to have readily reposed their faith in him. This, after liberating all the districts that had been pledged to the Marathas in 1757—districts that Haidar took under his control on the pretext of paying the arrears. As Wilks states: 'Such was Hyder's influence and credit, that he was enabled to make an arrangement with the *Soucars* (or bankers) of the enemy's camp; by which, on taking his personal security, they rendered themselves responsible for the remainder, on an understanding between all the parties interested in the transaction that Hyder was to have the direct management of the pledged districts, as the fund from which that remainder was to be liquidated.'[32] Peshwa Nanasaheb chided Gopal Rao Patwardhan and commented that Haidar had robbed him of his self-esteem.[33] However, this was just the beginning of a long rivalry between Gopal Rao Patwardhan and Haidar Ali, though the first round of it had undoubtedly gone decisively in the latter's favour. The Patwardhans were later assigned the specific responsibility of defending the territories north of the Tungabhadra River by the Peshwa.

Expectedly, this heroic act of driving the Marathas away and liberating Mysorean territories won Haidar great applause from his superiors. The delighted Maharaja welcomed him in a special darbar in December 1758, honoured him with costly presents and granted the title of 'Nawab' Fateh (victorious) Haidar Ali Khan Bahadur on him. That the title had the name of his father in it made it extra special for Haidar. A few months later, in April 1759, when Haidar told the Maharaja about the difficulties he faced in recruiting additional troops and also in fulfilling the claims of the Maratha bankers, he was readily assigned revenues from one half of the kingdom.[34] Thus, virtually, as circumstances unfolded, Haidar emerged as one of the most powerful persons in the polity of Mysore. It was just a matter of time before he was to formalize his authority and position.

Shadows in the Dark

However, unbeknownst to Haidar, his trusted lieutenant in Srirangapatna, Khande Rao, had plans of his own. Given his new position, Khande Rao had unbridled access to the palace and the royal family. Kirmani is brutal in his chastisement of Khande Rao's treachery (though completely silent on how Haidar treated Nanjarajayya!): 'He [Khande Rao] was like the base born silk worm, who when he invests himself with a silken robe of honour, loses himself. He did not reflect that treachery never fails to bring contempt and degradation in the end, but spread the net of his wiles, over the whole of the officers, and servants of the Mysore government, and associated them in his plans.'[35] Khande Rao particularly caught the attention of the old dowager rani Devajammanni, who had engineered many a coup and rebellions. She tried to gain the support of Khande Rao to permanently oust her bitter foe Nanjarajayya from public life, though the latter had already relegated himself to the margins. The public humiliation that the royal family and she herself had faced due to this man could not be assuaged by the mere pretence of a coerced reconciliation. The embers of discontent and insult were still alive and merely waiting to burst forth. Using the arrears for the troops as a ruse, she suggested that Nanjarajayya could be compelled somehow to retire for good from public life.

Dharnas by the troops were engineered, day after day, with great monotonous ferocity in front of Nanjarajayya's house before he finally, in exasperation, came out and pronounced his retirement from public life. But little did the dowager rani or Khande Rao realize that Haidar Ali himself was to now press for the ouster of Nanjarajayya, his one-time mentor and guide to whom he owed his entire ascent in politics. Having reached a certain degree of prominence and self-sufficiency, Haidar perhaps found his mentor to be an embarrassment—someone who had brought disrepute on himself and the royal family through his intemperate acts, thereby inviting public abhorrence as well. Following a mock interview with the Maharaja, he came out and made a demand that Nanjarajayya must surrender his office, retaining only the title of Sarvadhikari, have a jagir that yielded him a certain revenue and must leave the capital forthwith with about 1000 horse and 300 infantry. Caught totally unawares by this volte-face by his most trusted adherent, Nanjarajayya was forced to surrender. He left Srirangapatna in June 1759 towards Nanjangud to worship Lord Srikantheswara at the famous temple there. Citing illness, he then decided to halt in Mysore, but he extended his stay there. Haidar took exception to this and ordered him to proceed from Mysore without further delay. Nanjarajayya was livid with rage. 'I have made you what you are, and now you refuse me a place in which to hide my head. Do what you please; or what you can. I move not from Mysoor,'[36] he thundered.

In a shocking turn of events, Haidar then besieged the fort in Mysore and demanded that Nanjarajayya surrender the official seal, or *sannad*, of his office that the latter was unwilling to relinquish, as it had come down the generations to him. Haidar then opened fire, with all the arms, guns and muskets at his command, at the fort. Once friends, the duo now fought each other for nearly three months. A Portuguese contemporary account mentions that one of the reasons for the downfall of Nanjarajayya was Haidar's inducements to defection to Bento de Campos, the Portuguese commander of the White troops in Nanjarajayya's army. Though de Campos had pledged his unstinting support to Nanjarajayya over an 'image of our Lady the Virgin, which he used to keep probably as a secret Catholic',[37] the lure of money that Haidar offered superseded all divine vows. With all his troops, he shifted sides at the opportune moment. Eventually, lack of provisions and ammunition compelled Nanjarajayya to give up. He, along with his family, reached Haidar's camp as hostages. Haidar decided to let them live at Konanur, in the Hassan district and near the frontier of Coorg, and also gave them a jagir on the western frontier of Mysore. Nanjarajayya left for Konanur in utter disbelief and disgust at the surreal manner in which the tide had turned against him, cursing his own fate and himself for reposing trust in a man as ungrateful and untrustworthy as Haidar. The following year, with the death of Nanjarajayya's daughter and the wife of the Maharaja, Devajammanni, the relationship between him and the Maharaja further weakened. Around this time the Maharaja married a young lady, Lakshmi Ammanni (or Lakshmammanni), daughter of Katti Gopalaraje Urs, who had played an important role as Haidar's mentor in Bangalore and also in the Tiruchirapalli campaign. Rani Lakshmi Ammanni's importance in the annals of Mysore history was something that was going to unravel with time. For now, with Nanjarajayya's exit by the end of 1759, the Dalavayi regime that had lasted and wreaked havoc for Mysore since 1734 came to an end. But Mysore was gearing up for yet another tectonic shift in its polity soon enough.

Nanjarajayya's departure had made Haidar the undisputed new power centre in Mysore. He had established himself firmly at Dindigul by now, had taken possession of places like Polilur, Vaniyambadi and Krishnagiri, and the entire region below the ghats, which yielded a steady Rs 5 lakh revenue, was under his control. In early 1760, he asked the Maharaja to assign more territories to his command on the pretext of payment to troops and to repay the Maratha debts. Quite surprisingly for Haidar, his own confidant in Srirangapatna, Khande Rao, protested against such a move with the Maharaja. Politics might well be the pursuance of perennial self-interests, as Haidar had done vis-à-vis Nanjarajayya. But little did he imagine that the same game could be played against him as well by some of his aides, who might have their own political interests to pursue. The dowager rani, Devajammanni, was frustrated with the turn of events where an old, oppressive power centre, Nanjarajayya, was now replaced by a bigger and more odious one in the form of Haidar, whose sudden change towards his mentor was not something that even she had foreseen. She now teamed up with Khande Rao to dismantle this new irritant, whom she grossly undermined.

Out of the ten talukas (subdivision of a district, also called tehsil) that Haidar had demanded from the Maharaja, only four, namely, Shadamangala, Paramatti, Anantagiri and Namakkal, were granted to him, possibly due to the intervention of Khande Rao and the dowager rani. This brought about the first thaw in their relationship, and things were only going to head downhill between them thereafter.

The Palace Coup

Around May–June 1760, Haidar was away assisting the French, who were now embroiled in a new war of succession in Arcot with the two claimants, Raza Sahib, the son of Chanda Sahib, and Muhammad Ali. M. Lally sought Haidar's help in this crisis, in exchange for several places as jagirs and a payment of Rs 2 lakh a month for his troops. A certain bishop of Halicarnassus, 'a church militant prolate of doubtful history', negotiated an alliance between Haidar and the French.[38] However, Haidar had to return midway by July, as the Marathas under Visaji Pandit Binniwale had invaded again and were stationed at Doddaballapura, demanding the arrears of the previous years. Dispatching Makhdoom Sahib and Berki Venkat Rao with 3000 foot, horse and artillery to Pondicherry, Haidar rushed back to Srirangapatna with reduced troops. This was the perfect timing that Khande Rao and the dowager rani had always dreamt of—Haidar's presence in the capital with a reduced military strength. Feelers were sent out to the Marathas under Binniwale to join hands in their operation to expunge Haidar from the polity. They confabulated with the Maharaja and drew him in into their plot as well. The dowager rani impressed upon her adopted son that a man who could betray his mentor to whom he owed everything in life was the least trustworthy, and the day might not be far when he might overthrow the royal family too. If this opportunity was lost, then the Hindu royal house of Mysore might well be considered extinct, she prophesied. The Maharaja seemed convinced by the arguments that both of them put forth. Along with a select band of loyalists, like Kollegal Veeranna Shetty, Pradhan Venkatapathayya, Annayya Shastri and others, the three of them secretly congregated at the Sriranganatha Swamy temple in the capital. They all took an oath of fidelity to their cause and pledged to maintain utter secrecy regarding their plans, at the feet of the deity. In the inner recesses of that ancient temple, an elaborate plot was hatched to overthrow Haidar. A secret army, too, was appointed to assist the Maharaja in this, while Haidar was busily engaged with the Marathas. In the dead of the night, all the plans were drawn up elaborately, and the group dispersed with prayers for the success of their plot with daybreak.

On the fateful morning of 12 August 1760, Haidar, as usual, reached the fort after his pre-dawn exercises, but found that the gates would not be opened for him. To his dismay, some gunshots were fired from the top of the fort at the place where he stood; fortunately for him, the shots missed him narrowly. Suspecting foul play, he summoned his trusted aide, Khande Rao. To his horror, he was told that it was Khande Rao who was directing the fire from the ramparts. At once realizing Rao's treachery, Haidar rushed with a small band of troops who had accompanied him on the exercises and found cover in a hut that was out of reach of the ongoing firing. Using the boats that he found in the hut, he decided to set sail. The plan of Khande Rao and the rani was to invite the Marathas at this moment, when Haidar was at his most vulnerable, and to attack and imprison him. But as luck would have it for them, the arrival of the Marathas was delayed, thereby giving Haidar ample time to flee. Before leaving, he held out an olive branch to Khande Rao, reminding him that his present position and success were due to his benevolence, and that he had been a childhood friend and companion whom he had trusted deeply. But Rao was nonchalant. He coldly replied that all that was happening was as per the wishes of the Maharaja and his mother, and that he was merely an instrument in their hands and held no personal grudge against him. He reminded Haidar of his own ingratitude towards his mentor Nanjarajayya, and stated that the Maharaja now considered Haidar a nuisance and a threat, and wanted him to quit the Mysorean service and seek employment elsewhere. Haidar now realized that the conspiracy was much deeper than he had thought and that no amount of coaxing would sway Khande Rao from his position. If Khande Rao had so wanted, he could have well had Haidar killed at this point but perhaps desisted from doing so due to 'the remnant of virtuous feeling which could dictate a conduct so politically imprudent'[39] as to allow Haidar to escape. There was little time to waste for Haidar in meaningless talks and negotiations. He managed to get together a good deal of jewellery and money on 100 horses with six officers and two camels, and before daybreak fled the place for safety, much before the Marathas could make their presence known. It was a horribly botched exercise, and had the Maratha troops landed as planned, Haidar's life and career might have come to an abrupt and tragic halt. But he was destiny's favourite child and got a chance to rebuild his fortunes.

Khande Rao was astonished to find Haidar's residential apartments deserted. Haidar's family, which he had left behind, consisted of his wife, his nine-year-old son, Tipu, and his second son, Karim, who was prematurely born just the previous day 'in consequence of the fright'.[40] They were all imprisoned and placed in honourable confinement. Krishnaraja Wodeyar, meanwhile, hurriedly signed a peace treaty with the Marathas, granting them the biennial Chauth for 1758 and 1759, as agreed with Gopal Rao Patwardhan. He also sent emissaries to the British to aid him in liberating his kingdom from Haidar. But the British were not fully convinced of Mysore's fidelity, as they saw it as an ally of the French. Krishnaraja Wodeyar wrote to Captain Richard Smith, who was commanding at Karur in September 1760, explaining that Haidar had joined hands with the French against his wishes and orders, and that this was one of the reasons why he deserved to be punished. He promised military help from Mysore to the British against their ongoing conflict with the French. Khande Rao wrote similar letters to Lord Pigot in Madras. The British were highly enthusiastic about the prospect of an alliance with the Wodeyars in their efforts to quell Haidar, who had been a firm ally of their enemy, the French. They anxiously waited for a vakil from Mysore to come and negotiate the terms of the alliance. But for reasons best known to the royalist camp, several months passed, and the matter never moved ahead, much to the amazement of the British. Mysore was perhaps too sanguine about its alliance with the Marathas and did not think it important to team up with the British, too, at this juncture.

Khande Rao issued a red alert in the form of letters in the name of the Maharaja and in his own name, circulated all over the kingdom—it also reached the British in Madras and the neighbouring powers—proclaiming that Haidar had turned traitor. As an errant fugitive, Haidar had fled the capital, and a bounty was placed on his head, offering ample rewards to anyone aiding in his capture.

Haidar escaped to Anekal, where he was joined by his commander and brother-in-law, Ismail Ali. After the treachery of Khande Rao, who was the last person he ever suspected could do this to him, Haidar was apprehensive about everybody around him. He had been pushed against the wall by surprise and took every step cautiously. He sent Ismail Ali to Bangalore to ascertain if its commander, killedar Kabir Beg, was a loyalist. After assuring themselves of the same, Haidar moved to Bangalore. The garrison in the fort was chiefly composed of Hindu *piyadas*, or footmen, and only a smaller part of the regular infantry was Muslim. Haidar was apprehensive that the Hindu footmen would readily respond to the call of Khande Rao and hence excluded most of them from the fort. Just as he had surmised, Khande Rao's orders came, directing the piyadas to seize the killedar and preserve the fort for the Maharaja. But by the time these orders came in, Haidar had already entered the fort and had its gates securely fastened.

Haidar had been grounded and had to start rebuilding himself from scratch. The bulk of his treasures and his train of artillery and military stores were all lost. His revenues were under Khande Rao's control, and he only had Bangalore, Dindigul, Anekal and the fortress at Baramahal under his or his loyalists' command. He was himself holed up inside the Bangalore fort, with scarce troops and money. He took a loan of Rs 4 lakh from the sowcars of Bangalore and tried to reorganize his army. Noteworthily, he later repaid this amount, and it was this trait of a hyper-ambitious politician that kept Haidar in the good books of the business community and bankers.

But this was the most critical phase of his career. His entire life and its achievements thus far were at stake, and he was determined to win in what was a battle of nerves. Some of the smaller detachments, too, joined him, importantly, that of his favourite accomplice in Dindigul, Yaseen Khan, who had joined his service in 1757, after being disillusioned with Nawab Muhammad Ali of Arcot. Wilks states that Yaseen Khan, who was 'surnamed *Wunta Cooderi*, single or unique horseman . . . was, in his ordinary habits, of coarse and vulgar manners, and a master in the low slang . . . Hyder and Yaseen Khan were rivals in this obscene eloquence; and the former was in the habit of amusing himself with the foul-mouthed wit of Wunta Cooderie.'[41] So close was Yaseen to Haidar that in a conversation once, when Haidar was denunciating someone's ingratitude (*namak-harami*) and looked at Yaseen Khan, the latter snapped in a voice steeped in sarcasm: 'Why do you look at me? You had better consult Nunjeraj on the subject of *nemuc haramee!*'[42] Such a dreadful jest might have cost another man his head, but with Yaseen it was kosher, as he was so close to Haidar.

Haidar's other faithful accomplice, Makhdoom Sahib, tried to rush with his troops to Haidar's support in Bangalore from Pondicherry, where he had gone to aid the French. But they were stopped midway at Baramahal by the Maratha forces under Visaji Pandit and Gopal Hari and the Mysorean troops. Makhdoom rushed to the Anchetidurga fort for shelter. Haidar sent a small portion of his troops under Fazalullah Khan (also referred to as Faizullah Khan, he was the son-in-law of the Nawab of Sira, Dilawar Khan) and Kabir Beg to relieve Makhdoom. Makhdoom's position seemed as precarious as Haidar's own in Bangalore. Mysore troops of 4000 horse, 6000 sepoys, 500 soldiers and forty guns, too, were sent by Khande Rao to join forces with the Marathas. Along with the 10,000 horse of the Marathas under Visaji, Bangalore was blockaded for nearly two months, and Haidar's position hung precariously on a precipice. It seemed like a matter of time before he would be vanquished. This was the lowest ebb in Haidar's political life, after what he had suffered in childhood, and he stood at the threshold of defeat and total annihilation. But destiny seemed to favour him during every such crisis.

The Tide Turns

Just as he was being hemmed in from all sides by the Maratha forces, news trickled in of a massive blow to the Marathas in the debacle that they suffered in the Third Battle of Panipat in January 1761 against Afghan invader Ahmed Shah Abdali. The Peshwa recalled all Maratha detachments that were away on expeditions to Poona. Visaji tried to negotiate with Haidar to offer Baramahal and Rs 3 lakh to the Marathas to secure their exit from Mysore. When Haidar heard of the Maratha rout at Panipat, he refrained from offering Baramahal. Trying to cut their losses in the wake of the larger debacle, the Marathas took what they could, happily abandoned their ally Khande Rao and his master, the Maharaja, and exited from Mysore. Haidar was only too keen to cut this alliance against him by ensuring that the larger force of the Marathas was disengaged and things played out in exactly the same manner. Bangalore was finally relieved, as was Makhdoom Sahib in Anchetidurga; he immediately joined Haidar in Bangalore along with his troops. A French force of 200 cavalry and 100 infantry, too, joined him at Nanjangud, and he was determined to reclaim everything that he had lost. He crossed the Kaveri at Sosale but was halted here by the Mysorean troops.

Alarmed by his movements and the abrupt exit of the Marathas, Khande Rao launched an all-out offensive and managed to inflict a crushing defeat on Haidar at the Gejjalhatti Pass and put his troops to flight.[43] Haidar was terrified by this defeat in the very first encounter. Having been brought to his knees, Haidar set out to do the unthinkable—rush to his mentor, whom he had betrayed, and seek his help. Nanjarajayya, who was sulking in Konanur and licking his wounds following the treachery inflicted on him by his erstwhile protégé, was keeping a close watch on the dynamic developments in Mysore. But even he did not expect to see Haidar at his doorstep, literally grovelling at his feet, begging for pardon for his past acts and seeking support from him during a life-or-death situation for him. Berki Srinivasa Rao and others who were with Nanjarajayya advised him not to trust a man like Haidar and instead imprison him and hand him over to the Maharaja, thereby gaining his goodwill. But totally disregarding their wise counsel and reposing faith yet again in a man who had stabbed him in the back in the most unexpected way, Nanjarajayya threw in his lot with Haidar. He was welcomed and honoured with presents, his troops numbering 1500 and three guns[44] were put completely at Haidar's disposal, and new supplies and assistance were sought for his cause. So disgusted was Berki Srinivasa Rao by Nanjarajayya's actions that he left the scene and retired to Srirangapatna. Nanjarajayya also dispatched letters under the forged seal of the king, conveying the false information that he was being reinstated by the Maharaja as the Sarvadhikari and Haidar was to be his dalavayi. They also sent letters to Krishnaraja Wodeyar saying that if the latter handed Khande Rao to them, they would lay down their arms. But there was no positive response from the Maharaja. The Maharaja and Khande Rao tried to revive the earlier talks with the British that they themselves had aborted due to their over-reliance on the Marathas. But it was too late now, and the British were not as enthusiastic or trustful of the real motives.

Khande Rao was camping at Katte Malalavadi, about twenty-six miles south-west of Srirangapatna, and prepared to launch an attack on Nanjarajayya's possessions. Shortly after circulating the forged letters that proclaimed the appointment of Nanjarajayya as Sarvadhikari, Haidar got a new set of letters forged with the seal of Nanjarajayya on it. These declared Khande Rao as an offender to the throne of Mysore and called upon every patriotic Mysorean to contribute to his capture. These letters were distributed particularly among Khande Rao's army, which was now bewildered. They had just read about the purported change of guard and now the new power centre had called for the capture of Khande Rao. A contemporary Portuguese account also mentions that since the majority of Khande Rao's army comprised 'Moors' (Muslims), they were easily seduced with presents, promises and matters of common faith to desert their master and switch sides.[45]

'As Mercifully and Endearingly as My Own Parrot'

Hearing about the disarray and confusion in his own army, Khande
Rao fled to Srirangapatna in February 1761, with his own army
in hot pursuit. Haidar's troops, meanwhile, made surprise attacks
on the leaderless and disorganized army of Khande Rao. Haidar
descended from the ghats through the Gejjelhatti pass to reclaim
all the territories that he had lost to Khande Rao, receiving large
amounts as fine from Rao's allies. By May 1761, Haidar recovered
complete control over Satyamangalam, Kaveripuram, Namakkal,
Anantagiri, Shankhagiri and other forts, before reaching Chandgal
on the southern bank of the Kaveri, just opposite the central island
of Srirangapatna. Every evening, for eight days, on the pretext of a
parade, he crossed the river and made a sudden attack on Khande
Rao's already dispirited army, seizing his equipment and troops.
He even fired a few shots at the palace, some of which struck the
zenana and drew loud shrieks of fright from the women in the
royal house.[46] From Ganjam in Srirangapatna, he then sent a terse
message to the Maharaja. It read that Khande Rao was initially his
accomplice but since he was now under the Maharaja's service, he
must surrender him forthwith and also settle all the money that
was due to Haidar by the state. If these two conditions were met,
he would be more than happy to comply with the Maharaja's wish
of having him out of Mysorean service and that he would gladly
seek employment elsewhere. Haidar knew well that the financially
bankrupt state and an impoverished ruler were in no state to fulfil his
demands, especially with regard to the payment of balance. With no
other option available, Krishnaraja Wodeyar agreed to surrender his
faithful adherent Khande Rao.

The opportune date of 20 June 1761 arrived when much drama
was witnessed in the royal darbar. An agreement was formalized,
where Krishnaraja Wodeyar was assigned a territory yielding Rs 3
lakh to himself, and another yielding Rs 1 lakh to Nanjarajayya and
the management of the rest of the kingdom passed into the hands
of Haidar Ali. It effectively meant a complete usurpation of the
kingdom with Wodeyar being a mere nominal figurehead. Perhaps

seldom had the king of Mysore felt as helpless and embarrassed as Krishnaraja was in that darbar. The man that he and his family had attempted to eliminate through their supposedly astute plan was standing right in front of them, triumphant and defiant, dictating terms to them, and there was little that they could do about it. When Khande Rao was brought to the darbar in chains, there was loud sobbing and expressions of anguish from the women of the royal family, especially the dowager rani, who had orchestrated this whole episode. As Krishnaraja Wodeyar reluctantly signed the royal *firman* authorizing the transition of power into Haidar's hands, wails were heard from the women's quarters with the dowager rani and the king's wife Lakshmi Ammanni bursting into uncontrolled tears. But the Maharaja obviously did not enjoy that luxury, and hence, with a straight face, he went through the motions. This was a man (Haidar Ali) whom the Maharaja's father had saved from the direst of circumstances, and he was now usurping his ancestral throne from him. However, he had none but himself to blame for the sorry state of affairs that the kingdom had descended into under his weak leadership. If he had not capitulated to the machinations of his capricious dalavayis and used different office-bearers as pawns and buffers in the political game of chess, and rather asserted his own kingly power more authoritatively, he would not have had to see this day of ignominy.

There was much drama, though, before handing over Khande Rao to Haidar Ali. The man had betrayed his own patron to support the royal family in their attempts but could not be saved by his own new benefactors. The least they could do was to request Haidar to treat him well. Both the Maharaja and the dowager rani Devajammanni made Haidar promise not to take harsh action against Khande Rao. Haidar replied with a smirk that Khande Rao was his old accomplice and that he would do everything to look after him as mercifully and endearingly as he would look after his own parrot. But Haidar was a ruthless, vengeful and remorseless man. Khande Rao had broken his trust and brought him to the verge of destruction, and he could show no compassion to such an ingrate. The royal family felt relieved by the promise, but little did they imagine that Haidar would actually keep his word. Just like a parrot, Khande Rao was imprisoned in a huge iron cage in Bangalore and fed only milk and rice for the rest of his miserable life![47] It seems that the caged Khande Rao was kept in public view in Bangalore, adding to his misery and humiliation. An eyewitness, Francis Robson, who served in the East India Company's forces, records in his memoir on Haidar published in 1786 that 'the iron cage with his bones, are to be seen to this day, in the public bazzar of Bengalore'.[48]

N.K. Sinha sums up the story of the early life and rise of Haidar Ali thus:

As we study the history of the rise of Haidar Ali, he does not appear to have possessed the daring and generous spirit of the hero, who courts danger and fame, disdains artifice and boldly challenges the allegiance of others. He is more conspicuous for the steady pursuit of his aims, the flexibility of his means and the ability to submit his passions to the interest of his ambition. His career was marked by implacable vindictiveness and gross ingratitude, for revenge was profitable and gratitude expensive. Pride and virtue may recoil from many of his maneuvers but one cannot but admire his power of assigning to objectives their true priorities which, combined with his brilliant opportunism, led him from success to success. He very adroitly used the machinery of fraud and the machinery of force first to establish and then to consolidate his authority.[49]

4

Haidar's Rule

With the usurpation of Mysore being complete in 1761, Haidar set certain limits to various existing power centres. As far as possible, he did not want to come in direct conflict with the royal family of Mysore nor dispossess them entirely. It helped his cause to let a nominal Wodeyar ruler continue on the throne, even as he had grabbed all power and administration out of his hands. Orders were still issued in the Maharaja's name, though it was he who was drafting those orders. The trophies of war and victories were all placed at the feet of the Maharaja in a show of charade, though it was obvious to everyone as to who was pulling the strings. Given the popular goodwill that the royal family enjoyed with the people of Mysore, the majority of whom were Hindu and who might have detested the idea of a Muslim man whom their ruler had helped a few decades ago anointing himself as king, Haidar was reluctant to upset that apple cart. Moreover, it did not hurt his interests much to continue to allow the vestige of the Wodeyar to enjoy his nominal position on the throne, while everything in the kingdom was virtually in his hands. 'There is enough evidence to believe,' says Hayavadana Rao, 'that though by birth and faith he was a Muhammadan, Haidar treated the Hindus with goodwill and toleration; it might indeed be said that he was every inch a Hindu alike in temperament and training.'[1]

In fact, Hayavadana Rao quotes an interesting episode citing an account by Viscount Valentina in 1804. The annual procession of the presiding deity of the city, Sriranganatha Swamy, with all its

* Please refer to the corresponding illustration in the appendix.

accompanying music passed the Islamic seminary of a celebrated peerzada who resided in Srirangapatna with his pupils. So disgusted were the man and his pupils at this show of idolatry that went against the tenets of their faith, that they rushed forth, beat the devotees who were leading the procession and drove them away. The second day, the procession defiantly continued in front of the seminary. This time however, the Hindus were more in number and had come armed enough to hit back and drive away the Muslim assailants. An enraged peerzada and his pupils sought audience with Haidar and complained of the severe injuries they had all received. Hearing them patiently, Haidar remarked that they were the ones who violently attacked the procession party and so what else did they expect from the other side but retaliation. A flummoxed peerzada replied that the procession of an idol was an insult to Islam and ought not to be permitted under a Muslim government headed by a Muslim prince. To this, Haidar is said to have interrupted him and asked, 'Who told you that this was a Mussalman government, or that I was at the head of it?' The peerzada sought a private audience with Haidar, but when he realized that he could not change the latter's mind, he pompously declared that he was quitting the place. Haidar could care no less and asked him to go wherever he pleased. The peerzada retired briefly to Arcot but not liking the place as much as Srirangapatna, desired to return and live within the fort as before. Haidar supposedly denied him permission telling him that 'he had proved himself unworthy of doing so, but that he would give him a house anywhere else.' The angered peerzada went away to Madras, where he eventually died and was buried.[2]

Rao quotes Mirza Ikbal to state that Haidar never allowed any reduction in the allowances of Hindu temples and even allowed the conduct of the famed Dasara celebrations that Mysore was so famous for.[3] Citing the account of Dutch Governor Adrian Moens on Haidar, he states: 'Although he [Haidar] was a Moor [Muslim] and the kingdom of Mysore is a heathen country, in which, as is well-known cows are not eaten, much less killed, he gave out at once orders against the killing of cows and announced at the same time that everyone was free in the exercise of his religion and if he was obstructed in it, he might complain direct to himself and would obtain satisfaction.'4 Thus maintaining the goodwill of the Hindu majority of the kingdom, who would especially see him as a cunning usurper of the throne of their beloved king, seemed to be a top priority for Haidar.

The idea of creating a strong empire with centralized power had firmly taken root in his mind. Thus, territorial expansion, consolidation and frequent skirmishes with contemporary powers became the hallmarks of Haidar's rule. The English scuttling of the ongoing negotiations regarding Tiruchirapalli angered him as it did many Mysoreans who were part of that campaign, and this also seeded his hatred for them. The state of gloom and despair that had enveloped Mysore in the wake of that thriftless campaign, the subsequent political theatre of the absurd in the capital and the drying up of coffers and trade opportunities had all to be shirked off and the spirits revived with some grand military adventures.

The year 1761 itself was marked with numerous cataclysmic events in the history of India. While Mysore witnessed the usurpation of the throne by Haidar Ali, in the north the Marathas suffered a humiliating defeat at the hands of Afghan ruler Ahmed Shah Abdali in the Third Battle of Panipat. Peshwa Nanasaheb who lost his brother Sadashiv Rao Bhau and his son Vishwas Rao in the battle was a broken man after this debacle and died in June that year. Whatever vestiges were left of the Mughal Empire too were shattered post Panipat and the territory was splintered into several independent states. The ruler Shah Alam II's locus of authority virtually shrank from Delhi to Palam, a suburb. The Anglo–French War in South India, as a counterpart to the Seven Years' War in Europe, ended too with a total defeat for the French, the fall of Pondicherry and the destruction of their fortifications. Devoid of a home, the French looked for friendly alliances and rulers who would house them, and this situation was obviously utilized by Haidar to his advantage. Many of their troops joined his army and brought in numbers as well as European expertise in warfare.

Alliance with Basalat Jung

Matters were tumultuous yet again in Hyderabad. Salabat Jung had reduced himself to a mere puppet in the hands of his powerful brother Nizam Ali, who ousted another more enterprising brother Basalat Jung to Adoni. Salabat Jung was eventually imprisoned by Nizam Ali in July 1761 and, about fifteen months later, murdered in September 1763. At Adoni, Basalat Jung was getting increasingly restive; he wanted to expel his treacherous brother and also expand his sphere of influence towards the Maratha territories that bordered his. With the Marathas becoming dispirited after Panipat, Basalat Jung felt that this was the right time to strike at them. He decided to attack and annex Sira, Hoskote and other forts that were held by the Marathas. Sira turned out to be a tough nut to crack and he passed it by to Hoskote which was garrisoned by 700 peons under Mukund Rao Sripat. The siege went on for nearly two months and Basalat was tiring himself and his troops out. Haidar was keeping a close watch on the piteous plight of Basalat and the drama that was unfolding at Hoskote, which was a mere eighteen miles from his dominion in Bangalore. He sent Fazalullah Khan to Basalat's camp offering to help with Rs 3 lakh if he was invested with the office of the Nawab of Sira, 'an office, a country, and a capital, which was yet to be conquered!'[5] Little did he bother whether Basalat was indeed vested with the authority to make such a grant as he was not the official Nizam. But the *sannads* (deed of grant) were all drawn and Nawab Haidar Ali Khan Bahadur was designated as the new Nawab of Sira. Wilks narrates an interesting anecdote about the time when Haidar was negotiating with Basalat, when the latter, with a view to getting a larger sum of money as aid from Haidar, offered to honour him with a high-sounding Persian suffix 'Jung' to his name. The uneducated and non-elite however pronounced this word as '*Zung*', which was the tinkling circular bell that hung around the necks of cattle and camels. Being an unlettered man with uncouth manners, Haidar too retained this very pronunciation and so when this offer of Basalat was conveyed to him by Fazalullah, Haidar laughed boisterously, repeating the word '*Zung*' four or five times, sniping at him saying:

'Let me have nothing to do with your ornaments of a beast of burden, but if the great man insists on giving such a decoration, you may take it yourself!'[6] Fazalullah had a penchant for titles and so quickly took up his master's offer and began to style himself as 'Hybat Jung' or terror of war. An interesting picture emerges of Fazalullah Khan in the account of a Frenchman in Haidar's army Maistre de La Tour (M.D.L.T) as 'a man of very handsome figure and appearance, as fair as an [sic] European, very intelligent, of a most amiable and generous character, but more inclined to expense than his fortune allows.' This extravagance somehow seemed to have worked in his advantage as Haidar believed 'that they who love mirth and pleasure, are not the men who engage in conspiracies.'[7]

But the title and position of the Nawab of Sira seemed to have mattered more to Haidar as it was at Sira that his late father had served and had been killed, and where his brother and he were tortured and humiliated. By October 1761, Haidar's army besieged Hoskote and easily occupied it. It was with this very burning fire of revenge that Haidar proceeded thenceforth to Doddaballapura which was under Abbas Quli Khan, the same man who had tortured their family about thirty-two years ago. Basalat was not inclined to attack this place but Haidar made it clear to him that all the honours and deeds of grant were meaningless if he did not get a chance to seek his revenge and thus made this a precondition for his support. As Hayavadana Rao surmises: 'To Haidar, revenge seemed a kind of justice—may be, wild justice; still some kind of justice, which is as the balm to the pained heart. He studied revenge, and so kept his own wounds green.'[8] Abbas Quli Khan knew what was in store for him and even before Haidar reached Doddaballapura, he fled in fright to Madras, abandoning his ailing mother and family there. Doddaballapura was conquered without firing a single gunshot. But in a show of the kindness of human spirit, Haidar treated Quli Khan's family with utmost respect, unlike what the latter had done to him. While he appropriated all the property and treasures, he paid his respects to the old mother and assured her and the deserted family of sustenance and upkeep. Wilks terms this as 'among the very few examples in the history of his [Haidar's] life, of any remote tendency towards the amiable feelings of human nature.'[9]

The combined armies of Haidar Ali and Basalat Jung then laid siege at Sira, which had been the Maratha depot of provisions and military stores for the Carnatic campaigns under its killedar Triumbak Krishna. With his pack of artillery that was manned by Europeans, Haidar had little difficulty in taking Sira. He seized all that was found in Sira and, without his ally's knowledge, buried all the heavy artillery and stores that he wished to retain and merely threw out a few pieces of damaged artillery and old, useless stores that were presented to his unsuspecting ally as the only find from the place.[10] The befooled Basalat Jung then retired to Adoni in early 1762.

As the new master of Sira, Haidar now began to conquer all its dependencies. The palegar of Chikkaballapura, about fourteen miles to the east of Doddaballapura, was putting up a brave front of resistance. Haidar had been eyeing this place for a long time. Since the capture of Devanahalli in 1749, its chieftain had sought retirement in this town with his relative and they constantly plotted to regain their territory back from Mysore. Hence its occupation was important for Haidar. The palegar put up such a spirited defence and kept the enemy at bay that after two long months, Haidar could barely even commence his siege of the fort. The palegar was also expecting support from Murar Rao who sent Shiv Rao Ghorpade and Khande Rao Ghorpade with 2500 troops. But even before they could reach Chikkaballapura they were apprehended by the Mysorean detachment of 3000 foot and 1200 cavalry, badly beaten and sent back. But realizing that this was a long-drawn and wasteful campaign, Haidar negotiated peace with the palegar to settle for Rs 7 lakh to be paid in three instalments. With the first being paid, Haidar retired to Devanahalli. No sooner had he left than the palegar moved to the impregnable Nandidurga fortress and allowed Murar Rao's 500 strong Maratha force to occupy and defend his fort. Cheated by the palegar, an enraged Haidar now made a dash at Chikkaballapura and after a ten-day war claimed it. He did not attack Nandidurga but arranged for his garrisons at Chikkaballapura, Devanahalli and Bangalore to devastate the country and cut off all supplies. Murar Rao too had to be prevented from sending any further replenishments. A fierce battle between the two ensued in which, as Kirmani states, 'the troops of the Rao [Murar Rao] were scattered like grain shaken out of a slit bag, and they did not drink water until they arrived at the walls of Gooti [sic- Gutti].'[11] The Maratha dependencies of Penukonda and Madaksira were also taken from Murar Rao after this crushing defeat. These parts of Murar Rao's dominion amounted to almost 3 lakh pagodas annually and proved beneficial for Haidar's new acquisition of Sira. In the wake of such fierce defeats of his ally, the Chikkaballapura palegar was now forced to surrender. He was subjected to the worst of tortures and punishments for not only resisting Haidar but also for committing foul play. He was dispatched as a prisoner to Bangalore and his two sons were converted to Islam. One of them died later, but another who was renamed Safdar Khan was taken into the Mysorean troops.[12] Budruzzaman Khan was appointed the governor of the newly captured fort.

The palegars of Rayadurg and Harpanahalli (both in Bellary district) were the next to face Haidar's troops. They submitted readily without putting up any fight after seeing the plight that had befallen Chikkaballapura. The Nayaka of Chitradurga, Madakari Nayaka V, was however unwilling to surrender readily. He tried putting up some resistance but his well-wishers advised him not to antagonize Haidar and so he made peace with the submission of Rs 2 lakh and another lakh as a present.

The Conquest of Bidanur

Madakari Nayaka then made his way to Haidar's war camp with a visitor whom he wished to introduce him to. This was Chennabasavaiya, a seventeen-year-old man, who was introduced as the adopted son of Basavappa Nayaka, the Keladi chieftain of Bidanur (in today's Shivamogga district in Karnataka). Basavappa

Nayaka's death in 1754 led to the succession of his nephew whom he had adopted. But his widow Rani Veerammaji despised the heir and wanted her brother to become the ruler. Since the young boy was then merely nine years old, he was placed under the regency of his adopted mother. In addition to the Rani's dislike of the new ruler, a public scandal too had erupted in Bidanur with the Rani having a clandestine affair with her Dewan Nimbayya. The impudence of this affair had become the talk of the town and also of foreign travellers like the French Indologist Anquetil du Perron who passed through that region in 1757.[13] As the young heir grew up, he learnt of these unholy liaisons of his mother and was highly critical of her. This enraged the Rani and her lover who tried to get the boy murdered at the hands of a *jetti* (wrestler), whom they hired to have the boy killed by strangling him while shampooing him in his bath. The jetti meanwhile seems to have taken pity on the boy and saved his life through some clever tricks and instead ushered him to safety at Chitradurga. It was this young man whose case Madakari Nayaka came advocating with Haidar. In some quarters, this story was not believed and they considered the young man an imposter as the original prince had actually been murdered by the jetti in the bath. The veracity of these tales did not matter to Haidar; he just needed a convenient ruse to invade Bidanur. He hence readily agreed to help the young man in his claims to the throne of Bidanur against his conniving mother in return for Rs 40 lakh. Of course, he had other plans in his mind that he kept concealed for the moment.

The Canara region of Bidanur was in the beautiful and picturesque Western Ghats. Its fertile lands being a veritable granary, it was called as 'land of gold' by the Portuguese.[14] The Bidanur province extended in the east up to Holalakere, which was about twenty miles from Chitradurga and below the Sahyadri mountains on the sea coast; it extended from Mirjan to Mangalore. Kirmani paints a heavenly picture of Bidanur, the capital city of the Keladi Nayakas, situated in the scenic Western Ghat area

> from its beauty and verdure . . . equal to the Gardens of Paradise
> . . . if anyone burned with grief enters Bednore, were he even as a

bird roasting on the spit, he would regain his wings and feathers. In fact, that the fertility of the country was the envy of Kashmeer, for on it depended many cities, pleasant and rich, and its beautiful fields and meadows gave delight to the heart of the beholder; that moderate rains fell there for six months in every year, which gave life and verdure to the hearts of the withered vegetation and animal creation . . . the fruit trees were of all kinds . . . and the sandal trees filled the hearts . . . with fragrance . . . the rivers and streams of that flowery and ever blooming country are like the sea, ever flowing and the lakes and reservoirs ever full to the brim.[15]

Obviously a kingdom as coveted as that was always on Haidar's radar and an opportunity presented itself in the persona of Chennabasavayya who came to his camp seeking help.

Towards the end of January 1763, moving in four parallel columns via Sante Bidanur, Shimoga, Kumsi and finally through Anantapur, the Mysore troops made their way towards Bidanur. At Shimoga, that fell with little resistance, Haidar found a lakh of pagodas, a third of which he readily distributed among his troops to boost their morale for the long campaign. He began issuing proclamations in the name of Chennabasavayya, inviting the people of Bidanur to return to their original allegiance to their heir-apparent. But in private, he was mocked by the title of 'Ghyboo Raja' or the Raja of the Resurrection by Haidar and his men. But an overjoyed populace of Bidanur welcomed their young king with much fanfare. The people brought provisions voluntarily to the army that accompanied their legitimate sovereign. At Kumsi, Haidar was told that an old, faithful confidant of the deceased Raja, Linganna, had been imprisoned by the Rani. Haidar got the man released and out of gratitude, he shared all the information on secret routes to the fort with Haidar. On their way, at the small post of Aitoor, a garrison of hundred men who audaciously fired at his troops were all seized and their noses and ears cut off. They were then sent out to instil terror in the minds of the Rani and her confidants about what was coming their way if they defied Haidar. The Mysore army was at the gates of Bidanur by March 1763.

A flustered Rani tried to buy off Haidar at every step of his victorious march through her dominions. At one point, she even offered him 18 lakh pagodas. Haidar replied to her that he would return to Srirangapatna only if she handed over the kingdom to him, as compensation for which she would receive a residence at Srirangapatna. The Rani haughtily rejected the offer and resolved to defend her kingdom. The Nawab of Savanur Abdul Hakim Khan supported her by sending in 2000 horses and 4000 foot to her aid, and also encamping personally at some distance with a large force and heavy artillery. Haidar besieged the fort but the heroic Rani held it for a year. Fearing the onset of the monsoon, Haidar then ordered his troops to attack the fort as fiercely as possible and stream in. The troops did so and this time the Rani could not resist the attack. She set the palace on fire, lest it fall into her enemy's hands. With her paramour Nimbayya and a few other confidants, she then took flight to the fort of Kavaledurga, but was given hot pursuit by Haidar and his troops. He occupied several places en route that she had crossed—Basavarajdurg, Honnavar, Gokarna and Mangalore. Even at Kavaledurga, she bravely held the fort for over a month. Haidar sent messages to the Rani's troops mentioning that their master (Chennabasavayya) was with him and hence they should not take up arms against him. The people guarding the fort readily gave up defending the Rani and her entourage. Peixoto who served in Haidar's army was surprised by the ease with which Bidanur fell: 'If the place had been in the hands of someone who knows how to defend it, four such armies as these could not have taken it.'[16] The defenders of the place fled in fright and left one of the most opulent commercial towns of the coast with all its riches to the mercy of Haidar Ali.

Haidar captured Rani Veerammaji and Nimbayya and sent them to prison to the fort of Madhugiri. But as always, Haidar forgot his promise to Chennabasavayya. French historian J. Michaud mentions that the young man in his long years of living in secrecy had found his lady love in the valley in his childhood. The love had blossomed with time and the young lady accompanied him everywhere, including to the war camp of Haidar and later to Bidanur. Haidar 'young, boiling and impetuous'[17] saw the young, beautiful lady and his heart was instantly set on her. He demanded her as the price of his conquest. As Michaud explains: 'The young Raja still at an age when one prefers the heart of a woman to a kingdom, dared by his refusal, to expose himself to the danger of losing his crown again. Hyder, being angered, employed violence and carried away the young favourite of the Raja.'[18] The cruel injustice did not stop with this. Having possessed his lover by force, Haidar now decided to take over his kingdom too and conveniently packed off to Maddagiri prison even Chennabasavayya, whose cause he was so far claiming to fight. He immediately declared him to be an imposter, and not the original claimant, and hence needed to be packed off to prison. Ikkeri/Keladi was not merged with Mysore but created as a separate province. Haidar got a large booty from whatever was left after the palace was burnt down by Veerammaji—'two or three boxes of pearls and diamonds, two boxes of jewellery, two elephant housings richly embroidered and curiously wrought in gold and silver, a jewelled chain for the foot of an elephant, two sets of gold and silver bells for the necks of the royal elephants and two gold saddles'[19] were among the things that he carried back home. Wilks estimates the wealth that he gathered at Bidanur at about 12 million sterling.[20] Maistre de La Tour states that Haidar got 'pearls and precious stones to be measured in their sight with a corn measure; and that, having made two heaps of gold in ingots and trinkets, they surpassed the height of a man on horseback.'[21] Bidanur and the wealth that it accrued to him was to lay the foundations of Haidar's ambitions of building a strong empire and fortify Mysore's position of pre-eminence in the politics of the time.

He entered the fort victorious and for fifteen days there were grand festivities, lavish feasts, merrymaking, pomp and celebration marking this hard-earned victory. With his valiant army, he shared the costly spoils of the campaign: rich garments, gold bracelets, pearl necklaces, jewelled gorgets, splendid swords and also costly jagirs as per their ranks.[22] They were paid half a year's pay, not 'excepting those that were in garrison in different parts of his dominions.'[23] Haidar knew exactly how to keep his army happy and loyal to him. An old servant of his called Oojani (or Ujjanappa), of the Kuruba community of traditional sheep rearers, was given the name of Raja Ramachandra and appointed as the caretaker of the capital. Bidanur was renamed as Haidar Nagar, which in time, became known as Nagar. While everywhere else he had ruled as a representative of the Maharaja of Mysore, this was his first personal conquest, his 'swarajya' and hence proclaimed as his capital. He even struck his own coins here called Bahaduri Pagodas (or Haidari Pagodas). However, he remained extremely cautious and exhibited only the initial letter of his name and also associated several Hindu deities like Shiva and Parvati in the coinage. This was most probably done to assuage the masses who despised him for his treachery towards their prince and also the misbehaviour with the young lady who was forcibly taken away to the harem. This had led to several conspiracies against him.

Peixoto mentions that a detachment was sent under Lutf Ali Beg to Kumbla in around May 1763 where a combat with a local chieftain called Uda Purssu took place. His fort was besieged and his family, along with an army of 6000 Nairs, were holed in by Lutf Ali and Berki Venkat Rao, with their force of 3000 men, horses and foot. Uda Purssu sought help from the Raja of Nileswaram but the relief contingent was blocked by the Mysoreans. Haidar had given strict orders to capture the man alive as he wanted information about legendary treasures that were housed within their fort. Berki Venkat Rao used several tactics to try to make Uda Purssu surrender. When repeated enquiries from the Mysorean side failed and Uda Purssu kept evading, Haidar finally ordered him to be hanged on 7 October 1763.[24]

By then, the monsoons had commenced in June 1763 and Haidar was affected by a sudden attack of ague. It was at this time while he was lying in bed with high fever that his officers brought to him reports of investigations of the several conspiracies hatched by the old-timers of Bidanur. In prison, Veerammaji had conspired with some of her confidants and hatched an elaborate plot. In the palace of the old Rajas of Bidanur where Haidar stayed, there was a secret passage to an ancient temple outside, which was known to only the Rani and a few others. They planned to stock the passage with explosives and blow the palace up when Haidar was holding his midnight meeting with his officials.[25] Even in that state of ill-health, Haidar was keenly perceptive to listen to all the details and ordered the immediate hanging of the chief architects of the plot, right there in his presence. By the end of the day upwards of 300 people had been imprisoned on charges of sedition against him.[26] Several were found hanging from chief gateways of the city. As the entire exercise was completed, Haidar had ruthlessly put close to a thousand people to death.[27] Francis Robson mentions how 'their mangled limbs were found suspended on every tree in the environs of the city.'[28] He also details how Haidar ordered 'the chief persons of every town or village, of whom he had the least suspicion to be butchered in the like manner, besides many others, for the most trivial offences, had their noses or ears cut off. So that the inhabitants of the Biddenoor [sic] country, from the dread of his cruelty, were now reduced to the most servile obedience to his tyrannic will.'[29]

Venkappayya, who was in the Rani's service, had played an important role in helping Haidar manage the tumultuous aftermath of his Bidanur conquest and the conspiracies to assassinate Haidar. He strove for the next several years to restore the confidence of the local people in the new ruler.

Conquest of Other Principalities

In December 1763, Fazalullah Khan was dispatched on the conquest of Soonda, a principality to the north of Bidanur. It was ruled by a group of chieftains who had initially owed allegiance to Vijayanagara. Savaiveer Immadi Sadashiv Rajendra Wodeyar was the chieftain at this time. It was estimated in 1676 that the pepper country of the Raja of Soonda yielded a revenue of 30 lakh pagodas.[30] That was the wealth that this principality brought to the coffers. Upon hearing about the invasion by the Mysorean army, the ruler gathered his family and treasures and fled to Goa where he sought shelter from the Portuguese. They agreed to give him asylum in return for his

territories of Ponda, Sanguem, Canacona and Quepem. The whole
of his territory below the ghats came under Portuguese occupation
and they paid him a fixed stipend. He got a palace built at Ponda,
the Shivtirth palace, and settled down there. Thus, Soonda was
occupied by Haidar's forces with little effort, along with Shiveswar,
Sadashivgad and Ankola, and its vast treasures were confiscated.

In June 1763, Haidar and Fazalullah Khan attacked the Nawab
of Savanur, to avenge the latter's support to Veerammaji. The Nawab
fled in fright to the fort of Avari but was hotly pursued by Haidar's
men. A fierce siege followed and it was evident that Savanur would
fall. However, the Nawab's old mother visited Haidar's camp to
plead for her son and she was received with much respect.[31] Haidar
agreed to lift the siege if her son offered Rs 2 lakh and also aided
him in wresting Bankapur from the Marathas. Part of the payment
was made in kind in the form of elephants, camels, expensive
shawls embroidered in gold, silks, muslins, carpets, tents of velvet,
Burhampur cloths of great value, arms and ammunition, all of
which was estimated to several times more than what was actually
demanded of him. On the promise of helping him against the
Marathas in capturing Bankapur, the Nawab tried to procrastinate.
When Haidar sent his Brahmin emissary Bhima Rao to remind
him of the same, the Savanur troops opened fire. Enraged by the
treachery, Haidar threatened immediate assault on Savanur and the
Nawab came rushing to his camp. After making him wait for several
days, Haidar finally gave him an audience and chastised him that
he 'was not a worthy son of his mother and that for her sake he
had preserved him for that time.'[32] Bankapur fort was wrested from
the Maratha hold and Lala Miyan, Haidar's brother-in-law, was left
incharge of the place. Haidar marched back to Bidanur and stayed
there from September 1763 to March 1764.

The Malabar Affair

With the latest rounds of expansion, Haidar had stretched the
Mysore dominions on the north to the Maratha Empire, threatening

to intrude into their territory, and in the south to the boundaries of Malabar. Northern Kerala, between Cochin and South Canara, had at that time about five principalities of considerable importance. From the north downwards, these included Chirakkal (or Kolathiri or Koluthunad), Kottayam, Kadathanad (Vatakara), Calicut (Kozhikode) and Palghat. The Kolathiri, the ruling house of Koluthunad, were among the senior rulers of the region and the descendants of the Mushaka royal family, an ancient dynasty of Kerala. Their vassal, an Ali Raja Kunhi Amsa II of Cannanore (Kannur) of the Arakkal family of sea kings was constantly in strife with them. Being the only Muslim chieftain among them all, he saw in the rise of Haidar Ali, a great opportunity for himself. Ali Raja belonged to the Malabar Muslim community of the Mapillah (anglicized as Moplah and literally meaning son-in-law), claiming Arab descent, dating back to the times when Arab traders had landed on the coast of Kerala. A Nair minister of the Kolathiri king is supposed to have converted to Islam and thereby began the line of the Ali Rajas around the early twelfth century.[33] Wilks mentions the Mapillahs as the outcome of that 'intercourse between the females of that coast and their Arabian visitors; and in the process of time had formed a separate class in their community, which retained the religion of their Arabian progenitors, blended with many of the local customs of Malabar.'[34] Maistre de La Tour however says that the Mapillahs were 'lean, and of a short figure, not in the least resembling the other Arabs, who are large and handsome men, with black thick beards.'[35] The Mapillahs had taken control over a lot of commercial activity and earned wealth thereby, which, much against the principles of the Islamic faith, they lent out at exorbitant interest rates to the Nairs and Rajas 'upon pawns, and sometimes upon the harvests of pepper, cardamoms, and rice.'[36] This caused unrest among the two communities often and their wealth also attracted the envy of the Nairs. The Hindu Nairs were the military class of the Malabar and also formed part of the nobility in many of the Malabar principalities. They had different social customs, including that of polyandry, quite uncommon in other regions of the country then.

De La Tour talks of how Nair women were allowed to have four husbands and each and every house had as many doors as the lady of the house had husbands! There were fixed days when each husband could engage with his spouse. Upon his entry, each husband walked around the house 'striking with his sabre on his buckler[37]' and also left an attendant to guard against the entry of the other husbands while he was with the lady. On one day of the week, all the doors were left open and the lady dined with all her spouses. They followed a matrilinear system of succession and even the Zamorin of Calicut's heirs were the children of his sisters.

There was also a Raja of Nileswaram on the border of Bidanur, who was a branch of the Chirakkal/Kolathiri family. He kept having his feuds with the erstwhile Nayakas of Bidanur. On the western coast in Kerala were also European settlements and their jealousies and rivalries further complicated the already fractured system. The important ones were the English factory at Tellicherry, the French station at Mahe and the Dutch settlement at Cochin. The English and the Dutch also had a factory each at Calicut. The English factory at Tellicherry maintained close contact with the Kolathiris, and the rulers of Kottayam and Kadathanad. They also held the Dharma Pattanam island and vied for supremacy in the highly lucrative pepper trade in the region, which is what drew all the European powers here.

On capturing Bidanur, Haidar first wrote to the Raja of Nileswaram in May 1763 that some of the frontier fortresses that were claimed by the erstwhile Nayakas be made over to him. Upon his refusal, Haidar decided to wrest them by force and planned an incursion into the southern country. These plans made the Ali Raja of Cannanore feel overjoyed, as he wanted to be elevated to the same status as that of his master, the Kolathiri. He sent several emissaries to Haidar inviting him to invade the Malabar, offering his support in such an exercise.

The Marathas Strike

But even as Haidar was contemplating the Malabar campaign, his attention was diverted to the Maratha backlash from his expansionist

drives. He had got into their cross hairs by threatening to strike at
the very borders of their dominion. Taking complete advantage of
the demoralized Maratha side after the Panipat debacle and the
death of the Peshwa, Haidar flexed his might and tried to bring
the Maratha dependencies like Savanur, Kurnool and Sira under
his control and occupied Dharwar and Bankapur by September–
October 1763. Afzal Khan, brother of Fazalullah Khan, was put
in charge of Dharwar. Meghashyam Rao Patwardhan, a cousin of
Gopal Rao Patwardhan, who had been trying to resist Haidar's
expansion north of the Tungabhadra River and into the mainland of
the Maratha country, was imprisoned by Haidar. It was only Murar
Rao, from the Maratha side who was a thorn in his flesh and kept
fighting Haidar, even as the new Peshwa, sixteen-year-old Madhav
Rao, had taken over. Madhav Rao had a daunting task to rebuild
the broken fragments of the empire, consolidate his position and
expand further. On 10 August 1763, Madhav Rao and his forces
managed to comprehensively defeat the Nizam at Rakshasbhuwan.
This helped the Marathas immensely to boost their morale and
stamp their authority back. Now, the southern irritant, Haidar Ali
in Mysore, needed to be tackled. From her prison confines, Rani
Veerammaji in Bidanur too had sent secret emissaries to the new
Peshwa appealing for his help for her deliverance.

With all the preoccupations elsewhere, the march of the Peshwa
to the south was delayed and led to anxious entreaties from the
guardians of the forts and regions. For instance, on 9 February 1764,
the tormented killedar of the fort of Koppal wrote to Gopal Rao
Patwardhan: 'We are awaiting an army to punish Hyder for six
months now. He has captured all of Carnatic, and now besieged
Goa. He has won seaports. Soonda, Bidanur, Srirangapatnam are
all taken. He took Manoli (Manavalli). Koppal and Nargund are the
only two hill forts left. His shadow has fallen on the river Krishna! If
the master has given up on his possessions, how far can we hold out?
Like the pied cuckoo waits for the rains, we await the Shrimant's
[Peshwa] army!'[38]

The young Peshwa Madhav Rao was 'resolute, courageous and
dignified, always prompt and active, had the capacity of crushing the

enemy by paralyzing his will power. Wherever he was present, success always greeted the Marathas.'[39] He finally marched to Savanur where the Pathan Nawab joined him with about 2000 cavalry and 1000 infantry and proceeded towards the Tungabhadra River. Haidar too had reached Harihar with 35,000 troops, infantry, artillery and cavalry. Comparing the two armies, Wilks writes: 'The infantry and artillery of Madoo Row [sic: Madhav Rao] were superior in number to that of Hyder [sic] in about the same degree as his cavalry: his regular infantry was composed of a better description of men, but in point of discipline was inferior. Of his irregulars a large proportion of the matchlockmen were Arabs, and superior to the same description of troops in the service of his opponent; but the Mahratta pikemen were decidedly inferior to those of Chitteldroog [sic: Chitradurga], who (though as yet reluctantly) served in the army of Hyder.'[40]

The two sides clashed at Rattehalli, about thirty-six miles south of Savanur on 3 May 1764. The Marathas had laid a classic trap of deception for Haidar. Initially just Gopal Rao Patwardhan and Vithal Shivdev Vinchurkar made themselves visible to him with a very small force. Assuming that he could easily vanquish them, Haidar moved ahead with his army of 25,000 men, threw a few rockets at the opponents and pursued them, even as they kept drawing him in deeper and deeper into their zone. Suddenly, Haidar was alarmed to see a massive Maratha army of almost 50,000. Haidar sent an immediate message to Fazalullah Khan to join him with heavy artillery. He halted by the side of a dry rivulet but by then the Maratha gunfire had begun and continued unabated for about four and a half hours. Though Haidar had in his possession some forty guns, they were three or four pounders and no match for the onslaught he was facing. Suffering terribly, Fazalullah Khan did manage to tear through the Maratha cover and come to Haidar's relief, but that was almost closer to sunset. By then the Mysorean side had faced great casualties and upwards of a thousand were dead and another thousand grievously injured. Later, Haidar received an unexpected letter from Madhav Rao that said that 'he had heard his [Haidar's] name in Poona, where many of his heroic actions were related, and that he had come to seek him and fight him, for his father had advised him to cultivate friendship with all good soldiers and that was his own wish. But as he did not know whether all that was said was true, he had come himself to try him and he would expect the Nabob would quit his entrenchments tomorrow, come to his camp, where he would find him ready. If, on the contrary, this was not done, he would perceive that Haidar was no soldier and what was said of him was more than untruth. He would visit his camp and batteries the next day and tell him of the delight with which he left Poona to come and engage with him.'[41]

Haidar disregarded the request and marched to the entrenched fort at Anawatti. The hilly region there gave good cover to his troops and with the imminent onset of the monsoon, he did not foresee much harm from the Maratha side and anticipated their retreat. But Madhav Rao decided to stay on in Koppal, in the vicinity of Dharwar, during the monsoon and keep a close watch on Haidar. Dharwar had ample food and fodder and the Maratha army sustained itself there and also rejuvenated itself. Haidar anticipated his position worsening with each passing day and even sent desperate messages to the British Governor of Bombay in August 1764. He was willing to hand over the entire sandalwood and pepper trade of the coast to the British, as well as the lands north of the Tungabhadra to be made unto them.[42] Considering the Marathas as the bigger enemy, the British did send Haidar guns and ammunition.[43] Haidar wanted to firm up an alliance with the British and even met them at Honnavar, promising rich rewards and a grander alliance with them and the Nizam to act against the Marathas. But the British did not seem too enthused to ruffle feathers given the might of the Marathas, by forming a steady alliance.

Haidar then tried the same tactics of enticing the Marathas into pursuing him and descended on to Bankapur. His troops kept waiting from 7 a.m. till 3 p.m. but the Marathas never took the bait. He was forced to withdraw again to Anawatti. While the Marathas tried to take back Dharwar, Haidar, to divert them, tried to counter-attack Haveri which was in the possession of the Nawab of Savanur, but this was thwarted. Slowly, the Marathas advanced and managed to take back Dharwar by November 1764, before attacking Haidar in Anawatti by the end of that month. His strong battery and 3000

men, along with Portuguese commandant Joseph Menzes and
Fazalullah Khan, put up a stiff defence. Despite this, on 1 December
1764, a fierce battle took place where Haidar was totally defeated
and almost 1000–1500 of his troops were killed and six cannons
taken. Haidar even sustained a bullet injury. The Nizam who was
entertaining the idea of supporting Haidar in this difficult situation
thought it prudent to stay away after he saw the terrible defeat that
the latter suffered.

Haidar now sued for peace but the attempts did not move
ahead. Seeing the Marathas moving towards Bidanur, Haidar,
too, quickly changed his direction towards Shikarpur, where he
faced a few encounters with them. But soon he withdrew, first to
Anantapur and then to Bidanur. Madhav Rao seemed quite resolute
to conquer Bidanur too, but a sudden twist in the tale began at this
point. Around that time, Madhav Rao's paternal uncle Raghunath
Rao joined the Maratha camp towards the end of January 1765.
In what was a clear case of internal sabotage, much against the
wishes of several Maratha chiefs and also the Peshwa, Raghunath
Rao vehemently pressed for a termination of hostilities and the
conclusion of a peace treaty with Haidar. He thereby gave Haidar a
fresh lease of life from the dire straits that he had been pushed into.
Raghunath Rao had his own nefarious designs and had been eyeing
the position of the Peshwa, which he felt legitimately belonged to
him after his elder brother Peshwa Nanasaheb's death. He possibly
saw in Haidar a future ally who could help further his ambitions
and thus precipitated a cessation of hostilities.[44] As Wilks narrates:
'Naroo Shenker [sic: Naro Shankar] was the person sent by Ragonaut
Raw [sic: Raghunath Rao] to Hyder for the final adjustment of the
terms; and among them were without question some secret articles
which were the foundation of that good understanding which ever
afterwards subsisted between Hyder and Ragonaut Row.'[45] Madhav
Rao did not want to antagonize his uncle whose designs he seems to
have been wary of and therefore allowed him to dictate terms of an
agreement favourable to Haidar. Madhav Rao knew that his uncle
could team up with rivals like the Nizam and also Raghuji Bhonsle's

son Janoji who had strong political ambitions. Thus, he bought peace at the cost of a temporary setback, even as he kept doors open for a future invasion of Mysore by secretly allying with the Nizam and neutralizing the impact of Janoji.

Haidar had to pay Rs 28 lakh as an indemnity, another Rs 5 lakh as tributes and Rs 2 lakh towards war expenses. Half of the amounts were paid in cash and the remaining through bankers. He had to give up Bankapur and Harihar and also return the territories of Murar Rao and the Nawab of Savanur, in addition to releasing Meghashyam Rao Patwardhan. Since Murar Rao and the Nawab of Savanur were restored to their original positions as important border sentinels, the Maratha attacks on Haidar, below the Tungabhadra, could be resumed at any point of time. With this conclusion of peace in March 1765, in what is called the Treaty of Anantapur, Madhav Rao departed from the Carnatic, leaving Haidar terribly vanquished and putting a rude end to his victorious march till then.

Shortly after Madhav Rao crossed the Tungabhadra to head home, Haidar turned his attention first to the two hilly provinces of Balam (also called Aigur) and Coorg that lay to the south of Bidanur in order to secure them in the eventuality of a southern movement of his foes. Balam's chieftain Venkatadri Nayaka had even made minor incursions around Srirangapatna when Haidar was busily engaged with the Marathas, carrying away goods and cattle from the Mysore country. Haidar mounted an offensive on Balam, after which the Nayaka tried to flee with his family and property to Coorg to seek shelter under its ruler Chikkaveerappa. He was apprehended midway and a fierce battle ensued. Venkatadri Nayaka sued for peace and offered Haidar fifty camel-loads of money and precious ivory.[46]

Towards Coorg

The conquest and subjugation of Balam opened the doors to the attack on its contiguous principality, Coorg or Kodagu. It was a mountainous, richly forested area and the place where the Kaveri River originates at Thalacauvery in the Brahmagiri mountains of the Western Ghats section. It has always been a picturesque alpine region, with thick, dense woods, bound on the west by the majestic Ghats and looking down over the Malabar. Its sturdy, warlike race was known for its chivalry. The Coorgis claimed a hoary history dating back to the Puranic era. An offshoot of the Keladi Nayakas, the Haleri Rajas, who belonged to the Lingayat sect, brought the whole region under their command and became the rulers of Coorg, with Madikeri (Mercara) as capital. Skirmishes with Mysore and the Wodeyars were a common feature. From Chikkadevaraja Wodeyar, Coorg Raja Doddaveerappa managed to seize the coveted Yelu Saavira Seeme (literally meaning the land of seven thousand hamlets) region in 1690. He also assisted the Chirakkal Raja in the Malabar against the Bidanur Nayaka and thereby gained the district of Amara Sulya. Thus, the Coorg Rajas kept managing their territories through alliances and counter-alliances with warring political groups of the times.

For Haidar, the Heggala Pass in Coorg would give direct access to the Malabar region and so it was of strategic importance for him to conquer it at some point. Hence, after Balam, he left by both land and sea towards Coorg, transporting more of arms and material through boats than by land, given the difficult hilly terrain. He and Fazalullah Khan attacked Coorg from two directions and claimed the Yelu Savira Seeme region back. But Fazalullah Khan was routed by the valorous Coorgis, under their ruler Chikkaveerappa. Haidar did not wish to suffer more defeats at this stage and hence sued for peace, offering Ucchingi district that was to the north of Coorg for a payment of Rs 3 lakh. Half the amount was to be paid immediately and for the payment of the balance, Chikkaveerappa had to send a hostage from Coorg. Accordingly, the Raja of Coorg dispatched one of his able commanders Bonira Charmanna to Srirangapatna with the initial instalments.

But before the terms could be settled and Ucchingi could be occupied by the Coorgis, the ruler Chikkaveerappa died in 1766. He was succeeded jointly by Muddaraja and Muddaiah, who represented two distinct branches of the royal lineage—Haleri and Horamale respectively. Taking advantage of the change of guard, Haidar conveniently reneged on the promise of handing over Ucchingi, even after taking the initial payment from Coorg. Realizing that Haidar had not kept his word, the new rulers restarted negotiations which eventually failed and hostilities recommenced. Mudduraja's younger brother Lingaraja, assisted by his commanders Doddayya and Appachara Mandanna, attacked Fazalullah Khan and totally routed him. While Khan tried to flee to Mangalore, Lingaraja hotly pursued him and devastated him and his army. Khan's army, its treasures, ammunition and guns fell into Lingaraja possession. Doddayya and Mandanna were however martyred in this battle. The hostilities dragged on till 1768, after which Haidar once again brokered peace and this time, instead of Ucchingi, ceded the districts of Panje and Ballare to Coorg for a sum of Rs 75,000. The River Sarve was decided as the border between Mysore and Coorg.

The Malabar Invasion

Even before the actual invasion of the Malabar was carried out, Haidar had commenced astute diplomatic preparations for such an eventuality as early as October 1764. His diplomat Anant Rao was sent to Tellicherry to ascertain which direction the wind blew in vis-a-vis the English East India Company that had its factory there. The British had friendly relations with the rulers of Malabar, especially the Raja of Chirakkal. Haidar's intention was to sound out to the British his plans of invading Malabar and seeking British neutrality in the whole affair. Despite their long-standing association and intimate friendship with Chirakkal, the prospect of commercial losses ensured that the British conveyed their neutrality in the event that Mysore invaded Malabar. Anant Rao then met Ali Raja in Cannanore who had been openly advocating a Mysorean invasion.

Opportunity presented itself in the usual manner of a succession dispute in Chirakkal. The Chirakkal Raja was being opposed by one of the junior members of the family, Capu Thampan, who had the active support of Ali Raja in fostering the disturbance.

The Chirakkal Raja's forces defeated the combined troops of Ali
Raja and Capu Thampan, who then approached Haidar Ali for his
intervention. The Mapillah delegation under Ali Raja met Haidar
and pleaded with him to liberate Malabar. Ali Raja had several well-
equipped naval vessels that were ready to set sail and Haidar saw a
strategic advantage in allying with him if he wanted to conquer the
Malabar. He already had his eyes set on the Malabar and but for the
Maratha invasion, he would have made it the object of his attacks
immediately after Bidanur. He had to wipe off the ignominy of his
recent humiliating defeat to the Marathas and also the botched-up
campaign in Coorg. Haidar made Ali Raja his high admiral and the
latter's brother Sheik Ali 'intendant of the marine, of the ports, and of
the maritime commerce of his dominions.'[47] Significant money was
also given to them to purchase or build new naval vessels. Ali Raja in
fact formed his fleet and, under Haidar's banners, attacked Maldives,
took its king prisoner and even gouged out his eyes. Maistre de La
Tour however mentions that when Ali Raja went to Bidanur to pay
tribute to Haidar and present the blinded king, for this barbarity,
Haidar 'whose character is far from cruel,'[48] dispossessed Ali Raja of
the admiralship and handed it over to an English renegade, Stanet.
Haidar's conduct in war being no less cruel, one wonders why he
admonished Ali Raja for his inhuman treatment of the Maldives
king, whom Haidar tried to mollify through his profuse apologies
and the grant of a luxurious palace in Bidanur. However, through
this, the title of the king of the twelve thousand islands of the sea
became one of Haidar's titles, boosting his image further.[49]

Using the cause of Capu Thampan and also the earlier arrears
of 12 lakh that were owed to Mysore by the Zamorin of Calicut,
Haidar crossed the borders from Mangalore in February 1766 with
about 40,000 men, 10,000 cavalry and four pieces of cannon.[50]
Realizing that it was to be a long haul, he carried along provisions
that were to last for nearly four months. A powerful fleet too was
kept on standby along the coast under Stanet. Piexoto mentions
that in addition to the army proceeding by land, the naval fleet itself
consisted of 'upwards of 80 vessels by sea.'[51] These helped transport

heavy war materials and also enabled the crossing of numerous rivers in the region that made military engagements on the western coast difficult.

The first clash took place at Baliapatanam, where nearly 500 Nairs put up a brave resistance. But they were all killed indiscriminately with heavy artillery firing and the whole region was 'disturbed by robbing, setting the houses on fire . . . the inhabitants ran away to the woods and some to Travancore.'[52] Chirakkal surrendered after this without any serious attempt at resistance and the Raja fled to take shelter in the English settlement. Haidar protested against the support of the British to the Chirakkal Raja against what they had promised Anant Rao, but to no avail. The Chirakkal Raja had several sons who were made prisoners, one of whom Haidar grew fond of. He was forcibly converted to Islam and renamed Ayaz Khan.[53] This man was to play a larger role in the history of the region as time was to tell.

Haidar then marched southwards to Kottayam. After a frail attempt at resistance, Kottayam too surrendered to Haidar's might. The Nairs fled to the English and French settlements at Tellicherry and Mahe respectively. From Kottayam, Haidar marched ahead towards Kadathanad, expecting it to fall too as a pack of cards like the previous two principalities. As Haidar attempted to cross the Mahe River that separated Kadathanad from Kottayam, he was given a strong resistance by a powerful Nair force on the other side of the river that tried to prevent him from crossing over. It took immense effort on the part of the Mysorean infantry and artillery to try and push back and cross. Angered by this stiff resistance that the Kadathanad Nairs had put up, Haidar ordered a merciless counter-attack on them. De La Tour documents what happened with the Nairs there:

> This order being executed with the utmost strictness nothing was to be seen in the roads for the distance of four leagues round but scattered limbs and mutilated bodies. The country of the Nayars [Nairs] was thrown into general consternation which was

much increased by the cruelty of the Mapileys [Mapillahs], who
followed the cavalry, massacred all who had escaped, without
sparing women and children; so that the army advancing under
the conduct of this enraged multitude, instead of meeting with
resistance, found the villages, fortresses, temples and in general
every habitable place forsaken and deserted.[54]

After this victorious bloodbath, the Mysore troops entered Calicut.

The Zamorin Maanavikrama met Haidar in his camp in
Kurumbranad on 11 April 1766 and was received with all courtesies
and honours that befitted him. The terms of submission were
discussed and agreed upon that the Zamorin was to accept Mysore's
suzerainty and pay up a tribute of 4 lakh Venetian sequins (gold
coins of Venice). The duo then proceeded towards Calicut from
the war camp, but by then a detachment of the Mysore army had
already attacked the Zamorin's fort and driven away its garrison.
The Zamorin was aghast at what he believed was a breach of the
agreement they had just reached. But Haidar justified his behaviour
on the basis of past experience with the Zamorin, who too had
conveniently forgotten his promise of tributes to Mysore. A nephew
and heir-apparent of the ageing Zamorin had parked himself away
from Calicut and was determined to offer stiff resistance to Haidar,
despite his uncle's remonstrances. In such a condition, Haidar
was doubly untrusting of the Zamorin's intentions to pay him the
stipulated amount and thereby imposed tight restrictions on him in
a veritable siege of sorts till he paid up the money. Historian K.M.
Panikkar mentions that even in these dire situations, the Zamorin
negotiated with Haidar to send him rice that was sufficient for
feeding 1200 Brahmins whom he fed daily at the palace. Haidar
agreed initially, but as days passed, possibly suspecting some foul
play in the stocking of provisions, the amount of rice sent in kept
diminishing daily, till they finally stopped.[55] This immensely hurt the
pride of the old Zamorin as his religious duties were being impinged
upon. Fearing further humiliation and a possible forcible conversion,
he took an extreme and a tragic step to save his honour. Locking
himself up in his room in the palace, he set himself on fire along

with the palace. Wilks mentions that 'several of the Raja's personal attendants who were accidentally excluded when he closed the door, afterwards threw themselves into the flames, and perished with their master.'[56] The rest of the Zamorin's family and some of the Brahmin dependents however managed to escape to Travancore by sea.

The problem of Calicut had thus sorted itself out for Haidar, in the most tragic manner, and he ended up becoming its master. In a matter of just four months, four ancient kingdoms of Malabar— Chirakkal, Kottayam, Kadathanad and Calicut—had fallen to Haidar with minimal efforts. After Bidanur, he had annexed another rich and fertile region up to the borders of Cochin, now giving Mysore a coastline, as well as free access to French and English ports. The Dutch agents met him at Calicut and sought peace with him. To the south of Kerala were the kingdoms of Cochin and Travancore that he now eyed. The Cochin Raja paid Rs 4 lakh and eight elephants and readily became a feudatory of Mysore.

But Travancore was not an easy target. It had just emerged as a powerful kingdom under its ruler Martanda Varma (1706–58) who had suppressed all internal rebellions within his kingdom, unified the warring principalities, annexed Quilon and Elayada Swaroopam principalities and, most importantly, had dealt a crushing blow to the Dutch East India Company in the Battle of Colachel in 1741, establishing his unquestioned supremacy from Kanyakumari to Comorin. After defeating the Dutch, their military commander, a Flemish officer named De Lannoy was inducted into the Travancore army to modernize it on European lines in artillery and weaponry. De Lannoy, famous as *Valia Kappithan* or the Great Captain helped create a special regiment of sepoys within the Travancore army that became famous for its heroic achievements in times to come. In 1753, Martanda Varma had sought Mysore help against the Cochin Raja who tried to instigate a coordinated coup against him, but this had fizzled out.

After Martanda Varma's death in 1758, his nephew Rama Varma succeeded him and it was from him that Haidar demanded a tribute of 15 lakh and twenty elephants if he were to be left free to rule. Rama Varma refused to comply citing his allegiance to the British and Nawab of Arcot Muhammad Ali and offered to pay a reasonable sum if Haidar reinstated the Zamorin in Calicut and the Kolathiri Raja—this despite them being his rivals. He perhaps wanted a buffer state between his domain and Mysore, which had now almost reached his boundaries. But even before Haidar could contemplate an invasion of Travancore, his urgent presence was required back at Mysore and so he left the Malabar, putting the whole region to the north of Cochin under the governorship of Madanna, who had been an experienced revenue officer, and with a Mapillah contingent. He gave the Travancore Raja time to reconsider his proposal and said that he would return soon to settle his scores with him. Rama Varma decided to start fortifications on the northern frontiers under General De Lannoy and his Dewan Subba Iyen. The Travancore State Manual mentions that this commenced at 'Yellumgayree to the eastward of which the hills, were supposed to afford some defence: they then extended twenty-four miles to the westward and terminated at Jacotay . . . the whole measuring at the highest part above fifteen feet . . . the ditch was . . . about half that depth, or two or three feet broad.'[57] The long and extensive fortifications called Travancore Lines or *Netum Kotta* were to prove beneficial for the kingdom in the future. The Travancore Lines stretched in an almost straight line from the shore of the Cochin backwaters, opposite the town of Cranganore, to the foot of the Ghats. Haidar tried to take necessary precautions against Travancore's resistance against his advance by trying to win over the British in Madras. He confirmed to them their former privileges and also allowed them to open a factory at Honnavar. But he grossly miscalculated the gathering of forces against him that was gradually building up.

But by then an emergency had come up in Mysore caused by the sudden demise of the Maharaja Krishnaraja Wodeyar II on 25 April 1766. The deceased Raja's son through Devajammani (the daughter of Nanjarajayya), Nanjaraja Wodeyar, aged about eighteen then, was placed on the throne as his successor. Haidar, on his arrival at the capital, went through the charade and motions of offering public respects to the new monarch. However, the young man had begun to show signs of wanting to exercise his freedom and Haidar was quite determined to crush those feelings before they began to gain strength. The personal stipend that was allotted to the royal family was continued to the new ruler too, but a significant part of the palace treasures, its cash and valuables except what the women of the household wore, were merrily plundered by Haidar's men. His spies were stationed within the palace at all important positions to keep a close watch on the new ruler and his associates.

The Nair Uprising

Within a few months of his departure from the Malabar in the smug hope that he had conquered the region, Haidar was pulled back there in July 1766. During the torrential monsoons that were so common in the region, most rivers swelled and overflooded. The valorous Nairs, who were smarting under the humiliating defeat that was handed down to them, decided to take advantage of the monsoons and their own familiarity with the terrain to harass and expel the Mysore army. The harsh measures adopted by Madanna to increase his resources in the region also added to their angst. It was believed that the king of Travancore and the nephew of the deceased Zamorin had instigated this uprising. By the end of June, the Nairs of Kottayam and Kadathanad had risen in rebellion, attacking all of Haidar's blockhouses (called then as *Lakkadi-Kotta*) in the region. With most rivers overflowing, quick relief and communication too was a challenge for the Mysoreans who were not familiar with the terrain. They then managed to invade Calicut and Ponnani and that was when Raza Sahib (son of Chanda Sahib who was with Haidar) was alerted. His troops suffered terrible reverses at the hands of the brave Nairs. Many died of starvation as provisions could not be dispatched and also the weather brought its share of sicknesses. De La Tour speaks about how the Nairs 'cut off five French soldiers, deserters from Mahe . . . they ripped up two women who accompanied these unfortunate soldiers.'[58] A small garrison of about 200 men stationed at Pudiyangadi too was massacred by the Nairs.[59] Raza Sahib was himself entrapped by them from all sides near the confluence of two rivers and sent emergency messages to Haidar who was camped in Coimbatore. An enraged Haidar stormed into Malabar to relieve Raza Sahib with a force of 10,000 infantry, 3000 cavalry, twelve pieces of cannon, some 300 newly recruited Europeans from Pondicherry and sufficient provisions to last for a while. The troops were asked to march with minimal clothes on them, barring light drawers and shoes. They faced great difficulty in crossing the narrow, mountainous terrains and overflowing rivers, with the torrential rains beating down on them incessantly, braving storms, cloudbursts and lightning.

Haidar clashed with the Nairs at Vettat Puthiyangadi where the Nairs had taken up a fortified position. Four thousand of his best sepoys formed a right wing that was commanded by a Portuguese lieutenant colonel who had recently joined from Goa; they were charged with attacking the village. Topasses commanded by an English officer comprised the left wing and Haidar himself formed the main body with a large contingent of French troops. A fierce battle ensued where the Nairs returned fire with considerable deftness and made things rather difficult for the Mysore forces. One of Haidar's commanders, Asof Khan, was beheaded and for a brief while, the rebels managed to liberate Calicut. It was almost a lost cause for Haidar till the French troops in his army took things head on and launched a massive frontal attack on the Nairs and drove them away. So impressed was Haidar that the French commander was instantly rewarded with the title of Bahadur and was made a *mansabdar* of 10,000 horses.

Haidar followed this with a merciless revenge against the Nairs who had dared to challenge his might. De La Tour mentions what followed thereafter:

> Wherever he turned, he found no opponent, nor even any human creature; every inhabited place was forsaken: and the poor inhabitants, who fled to the woods and mountains in the most inclement season, had the anguish to behold their houses in flames, their fruit-trees cut down, their cattle destroyed and their temples burned. The perfidy of the Nayres [Nairs] had been too great for

them to trust the offers of pardon made by Hyder, by means of Brahmins he despatched into the woods and mountains to recall these unhappy people; who were hanged without mercy, and their wives and children reduced to slavery; whenever they were found in the woods by the troops of Hyder; severity and mildness being both equally ineffectual in making them return to their homes.[60]

Peixoto too paints a gruesome picture of the Malabar after this conquest:

The entire Nair country was plundered; their homes were burnt and a universal massacre of the Nair caste was ordered. The Nairs were hunted down and butchered. Hyder gave 'Rupees 5 to anyone who brought him the head of a Nair that was able to fight; if it was an old man, he gave four, and if of a boy he gave three rupees.' A price of three rupees was also paid for every Nair woman captured alive. Many women were thus captured and transported to distant places as presents to governors and chiefs.[61]

Before leaving Malabar, Haidar passed an edict that deprived the Nairs of all their privileges. They were hitherto considered the second important caste after the Brahmins, but were downgraded to the lowest of the caste hierarchies, requiring them to even salute the lowest of the castes and the untouchables. They were forbidden from possessing arms, while all other castes were allowed to have them and also kill any Nair they found bearing arms, creating thereby a sense of fear and insecurity in the Nairs.[62] As de La Tour states: 'By this rigorous edict Hyder expected to make all the other castes enemies of the Nayres [Nairs]; and that they would rejoice in the occasion of revenging themselves for the tyrannic oppression this nobility had till then exerted over them.'[63] Those Nairs who agreed to convert to Islam were reinstated with all their past privileges.[64] While some of them succumbed and converted, most of the Nairs remained defiant and held on to their faith, dispersing instead to seek refuge in the safe havens of Travancore. With Manjeri as his base, Haidar ordered a systematic hunt of the Nairs who had fled to the mountains and those who were caught were mercilessly hanged or beheaded. Later as their numbers kept increasing, Haidar devised a plan to collect the Nairs he had captured, put them in concentration camps and transport them to Mysore. Wilks states that the tortuous manner in which they were transported back, subjected to physical and mental strains, diseases and hunger resulted in just 200 of the 15,000 transportees surviving the ordeal.[65] As trouble was brewing with the Marathas and the Nizam, Haidar had to head back, leaving behind a wailing Malabar amidst a trail of untold misery and destruction.

The Treaty of Paris and Thereafter

Meanwhile, a development in distant Europe was to reconfigure politics in India. The Seven Years' War that Britain and France engaged in concluded with the signing of the Treaty of Paris on 10 February 1763. The treaty also marked the beginning of the rise of the British as a global power beyond Europe. In India, it transformed the British from being a mere trading company to a veritable political entity that had a locus in the internal affairs of several kingdoms. Even during the Tiruchirapalli fiasco, the British had conveniently positioned themselves as mere 'allies to the Circar, not principals.'[66] This was one luxury that they could no longer afford. The Eleventh Article of the Treaty pertained to India and stipulated a return to the status that existed in South India in 1749. Britain was to 'restore to France, in the condition they are now in the different factories, which that crown possessed, as well as the coast of Coromandel and Orixa [Orissa], as on that of Malabar, as also in Bengal, at the beginning of the year 1749.'[67] France was to renounce all its acquisitions on the Coromandel Coast and Orissa since 1749, and not erect fortifications or keep troops in any part of the Mughal Subedari of Bengal. To restore tranquillity in the Deccan, the Article formally recognized Muhammad Ali Walajah as the lawful Nawab of the Carnatic and, funnily enough, Salabat Jung (who had by then been unlawfully deposed by his brother Nizam Ali in June 1762) as the lawful Subahdar of the Deccan (i.e., the Nizam). Both parties were to renounce all demands and charges against each other or their Indian allies for the pillage and depredations of war in the preceding years. On the changing role of the British and the French in Indian politics, Hayavadana Rao explains: 'Two European nations had for the first time assumed to themselves the right of not only deciding for themselves . . . on political and territorial claims, over which so far they had not established any actual authority but also the right of conferring official appointments to high territorial office—including the Nizamships and Nawabships—and thus by virtue of their military power to determine the interior arrangements of the Mughal Empire itself, of which they had so far pretended to be but auxiliaries and allies in a subordinate capacity.'[68]

The treaty was political suicide for the French who had unwittingly surrendered their territories on the eastern coast. During the Seven Years' War, the British had managed to capture Pondicherry in 1761, which they returned after the Treaty. The decline of French fortunes was further accentuated by the defeat of the ally of the French, Nawab Siraj ud Daula of Bengal in the Battle of Palashi (Plassey) in 1757. This conquest gave the British control over the rich province of Bengal and thereby laid the foundations of what was an accidental empire in India, which was at that time driven by the necessity of military and trading security against their rivals, both the French and Indian players. It was only by the time the British entered the scene of war in Mysore later that decade—a series of battles that went on for a quarter of a century, that a more clear, strategic and long-term vision seems to have developed in them to eliminate their rivals and establish the foundations of a political hegemony.

The treaty evidently had several repercussions among the players in South India. It awakened in Muhammad Ali great ambitions of expansion and also of deposing the Nizam in Hyderabad and routing Haidar Ali in Mysore and overrunning Travancore. Whether he had the means and the wherewithal to fulfil these mighty ambitions was beyond his scrutiny. But the treaty had effectively emboldened him to stand against his hitherto masters, the titular Mughal and his deputy in the Deccan, the Nizam. It also strengthened him against his brother, Mahfuz Khan, who was desperately waiting to overthrow him and take over the throne and was in the good books of Haidar.

For Nizam Ali, it was a massive betrayal of promises made to him as the brother he had deposed almost a year and half ago had been now recognized as the lawful Nizam. Being pushed to the wall, Nizam Ali went berserk. He hastened his intentions to eventually have his imprisoned brother Salabat Jung murdered in September 1763, within seven months of the signing of the Treaty of Paris. In 1763, he tried to ally with Janoji Bhonsle to uproot the Peshwa himself, but Janoji's defection at a crucial time in the war extinguished all his hopes in that matter. Both Madhav Rao and Nizam Ali were nursing their angst against Janoji for his treachery and awaiting revenge against him in their own ways. In 1765, in a successful campaign south of the Krishna River, Nizam Ali subjugated his other brother, Basalat Jung (who had allied with Haidar) as well. This double victory against both his brothers, who were contenders to his throne, emboldened Nizam Ali to flex his muscles in South India against Haidar and Muhammad Ali. In an unthinkable turn of events, the hitherto foes Madhav Rao and Nizam Ali entered into a secret treaty in early 1766 and marched against Janoji, compelling him to surrender three-fourths of the territories he had gained. But Madhav Rao was to discover later that Nizam Ali was the most undependable ally.

The British meanwhile had been pressing Nizam Ali to hand over the lease of the prized Northern Circars that he had earlier awarded to Muhammad Ali. The Northern Circars were comprised of five prominent districts of the Deccan Subah (Srikakulam, Rajamundhry, Ellore, Kondapalli and Guntur) and was a narrow strip of rich territories on the western edge of the Bay of Bengal. The British were even willing to pay six times the amount to obtain the lease as the Court of Directors of the English East India Company was apprehensive of any French expansion in these areas. Robert Clive, who had already got the diwani of Bengal after the victorious Battle of Palashi from the Mughal Emperor, convinced the latter to also hand over the Northern Circars to the Company. Thus, despite Nizam Ali's reluctance, the British wrested the territory and victoriously sent an embassy to his court, asking him to gift the area as a tributary dependency. Accordingly, on 12 November 1766, a treaty was concluded at Hyderabad by General Calliaud which stipulated the stationing of an auxiliary force there at Nizam Ali's disposal to help him against any predatory attacks by the Marathas or Mysore. With this masterstroke, Hyderabad, that had been a firm base of the French since the times of Bussy, now became a British protectorate. Colonel Joseph Smith, who had played an important role in the Tiruchirapalli campaign against D'Auteuil was selected to proceed to Hyderabad to execute the terms of the agreement and to command the British troops stationed there. These counter-moves by Nizam Ali with the British must have alarmed Madhav Rao who had allied with him to subjugate Janoji. He anyway had an unfinished agenda in Mysore and without waiting for his so-called ally decided to cross the Krishna River in January 1767 to invade Mysore.

Interestingly, his advance was requested by the young, newly installed Maharaja Nanjaraja Wodeyar who was feeling increasingly alarmed by the rapid expansion of Haidar and sought to clip his wings with the help of the Marathas. His grandmother, the Dowager Rani Devajammanni, and his stepmother, Rani Lakshmi Ammanni, were further provoking him to assert his authority. He finally sent emissaries to Madhav Rao seeking his support to liberate the royal family from Haidar's clutches. Sadly for them, Haidar's spy network was extensive enough to catch this transaction. While he tried to ignore the young Maharaja's mischief, he quickly dispatched his diplomat Mohabat Ali to Poona to negotiate with the Peshwa and avert any clash. But the Peshwa, who was still hurting under the wasted opportunity of the previous Mysore invasion due to his uncle's collusion with Haidar, 'professed nothing short of the entire subversion of Hyder's usurped authority'[69] and decided to invade Mysore the second time.

The Marathas Invade Mysore Again

Madhav Rao marched towards Sira and was joined by his loyalists on the way, the Nawab of Savanur and Murar Rao from Gutti. Others who were disgruntled with Haidar due to his conquests against them, like the Chitradurga Nayaka, also met the Peshwa. Mir Ali Raza Khan, Haidar's brother-in-law, was in charge of Sira with 4000 horses and 6000 infantry and, for a brief while, gave a stout defence to the Maratha attack. But Raza Khan turned treacherous and after a fortnight or so, handed over the keys of the fort to Madhav Rao and made peace. From here, Madhav Rao proceeded to Maddagiri where, as per his promise to her, he liberated the erstwhile Bidanur Rani Veerammaji and her associates who had been held captive by Haidar. The Rani was promised asylum in Poona, but unfortunately, she died during the long journey to Poona. Next, Chennarayadurga that was held by Sardar Khan too fell after a brief resistance, following which Madhav Rao managed to capture Hoskote, Chikkaballapura, Doddaballapura, Kolar, Mulbagal and Gurramkonda. It was a sizeable accession of all the new territories that Haidar had captured since the time he had usurped the throne. For his treachery, Mir Ali Raza Khan was rewarded with the fort of Gurramkonda as a jagir by the Peshwa. One is unsure though as to why Mir Ali Raza defected to the Maratha side. It could possibly be because of the wrath of his brother-in-law for his failure in holding the bastion against the foes. But how ill at ease he was in the Maratha camp was evident when at Chennarayadurga, some of the irregulars of the Maratha army, the *pindaris* and the *gardis,* went to the camp of Murar Rao and, with some people there, looted the camp of Mir Ali Raza, including getting into his zenana. It is said that when the Peshwa heard of this, 'he looked like God Siva when angry. Forty or fifty of these looters had their hands chopped off.'[70] The Peshwa personally went to the camp of Mir Raza and assuaged him with dresses, utensils, sweets, horses, jewellery and even cash of 1 lakh as compensation. Mir Ali Raza was not on good terms with Murar Rao and it was suspected that the latter had engineered this attack, though the investigations into the matter were inconclusive.

Bolstered by the string of successes, the Maratha army made an attack on Srirangapatna next. Haidar decided to follow the scorched-earth policy to counter the Maratha attack, whereby he ordered to 'break down all the embankments of the reservoirs of water on the approach of the Mahratta army; to poison the wells with milk hedge; to burn all the forage, even to the thatch of the houses; to bury the grain . . . and the cattle to the woods; and to leave the Mahrattas neither forage, water, nor food.'[71] Surprise night attacks were also made on the Maratha army and their possessions looted. Madhav Rao retreated towards Ambajidurga thereafter, after he had overrun all of eastern Mysore.

Fearing a possible menacing movement of Nizam Ali, too, on Srirangapatna, Haidar quickly sued peace with the Marathas through his interlocutors, Karim Khan and an extremely witty and skillful diplomat, Appaji Ram. Wilks narrates how during the negotiations when the Maratha side berated Haidar for usurping Bidanur and imprisoning its sovereign, Appaji Ram replied in a tone of repentant humility that indeed this was the case, but that they, in Mysore, had learnt this respectfully from the better side. This seemed to insinuate that the Peshwa himself had virtually taken over the authority from the Chhatrapati in Satara and thus had little moral authority to grandstand on usurpation. Appaji Ram concluded that they would gladly follow the moral doctrines that the other side both preach and profess on political conduct. At this, Wilks states that Madhav Rao 'hung down his head, the whole assembly refrained with difficulty from a burst of laughter, and the ground was quickly cleared for actual business.'[72] Appaji Ram managed to purchase the Maratha retreat for Rs 35 lakh, half of which was paid right there in April 1767. The initial demand had been 70 lakh and that then came down to 40 lakh by March.[73] Madhav Rao managed to secure possession of all the districts of Mysore south-eastward of Sira; the rest was returned while Kolar remained in pledge till the balance was paid. The original demand was to return all the territories of the Marathas and their dependencies, along with the state of Soonda. But the Nizam's uncertain polices vis-à-vis Mysore removed quite a bit of the sting off the Maratha offensive and Madhav Rao accordingly left Mysore on 11 May 1767.

Tipu's Early Life

Even as Haidar was involved in one military campaign after another in quick succession, his son Tipu was growing up to become a fine soldier. But surprisingly, there is so little known about Tipu's early life, right from the time of his birth to his first burst on the battlefield as a spirited teenager. The first account on him is during the flight of Haidar from Srirangapatna at the height of the treachery and machinations of Khande Rao, when he left behind his family that included a nine-year-old Tipu and a prematurely born (due to the fright that the situation had caused) younger son, a timid boy named Karim. Khande Rao had moved them from their palace to a mosque inside the fort of Srirangapatna, but treated the family with dignity. Undoubtedly, an incident such as this, where his father was so brutally targeted and his very existence was at stake, must have left a deep imprint on young Tipu. Some chroniclers including Kirmani and Peixoto suggest that the appellation 'Sultan' was given to Tipu at birth. While others such as Michaud state that being unsatisfied with the position of a mere regent of the Maharaja (as Haidar was), Tipu gave himself the title of Sultan after succeeding his father.[74] However in contemporary literature, he is referred to as 'Tipu Sahib' in his early years.

Though himself illiterate, Haidar strove to get his sons educated. However, Haidar was deeply disappointed by the quality of education that was being imparted to his son, as he was to discover accidentally. Hayavadana Rao writes about this episode:

> Haidar, who lamented more deeply than we will ever be able to discern or measure, the lack of education in himself, not only encouraged Mullahs for teaching the elements of Persian and Hindustani, but also, what is more interesting, entrusted the care of Tipu, his son and successor, to a duly qualified Muslim teacher. His attempt at educating Tipu in the traditional mode is a chapter of history by itself. It is said that Tipu's teacher was never questioned by Haidar as to the progress made by the boy for many years, at the end of which period, he one day conducted a public examination of Tipu. This showed that the boy had not obtained the training required for a soldier's son; instead, he had everything that would be requisite to turn him into a good Moulvie. Haidar's displeasure knew no bounds and he exclaimed, much in the strain of Aurangzib, that his boy had not been taught the things that would make him a great and good ruler. He had not been taught; he thundered forth, the modes of warfare he should know, the

manner of conquering countries or conducting diplomacy with
the surrounding nations, or even the duties of kingship. Instead,
Haidar protested, everything requisite for converting him into a
religious zealot had been done and his mind filled with notions
and fancies which had made him hate everything not connected
with Islam. Everything indeed had been done, concluded Haidar
in his anger, to ruin his family and his kingdom and nothing to
advance either.[75]

Haidar had chastised the teacher for filling his son's mind with
such religious bigotry that would ensure a total destruction of his
kingdom.[76] The seeds of religious intolerance had thus been sown
at an early age in Tipu's mind. It was then that one of the best
officers and confidants of Haidar's army, Ghazi Khan, was made
Tipu's military preceptor who taught him the various elements of
warfare, from riding and shooting to fencing and techniques of
European combat. Kirmani mentions that Haidar 'took great pains
in the training and education of his sons, and appointed men of his
court to the duties of tutors and servants to them, who made him
[Tipu] acquainted with every particular relating to their manners
and conversation; and sentinels, from the Nawaub's guard, were
placed around their houses or tents.'[77]

It seems that Haidar had moved Tipu to Bangalore and later
after its conquest, to the safety of Bidanur or Nagar.[78] When Haidar
invaded Malabar in 1766, Tipu was asked to accompany him to
get some practical experience of warfare. During the subsequent
conquest of Balam in 1765, Tipu played an important role in this
campaign. With about 2000–3000 troops, he had managed to
penetrate through the thick forests of the region where the chieftain
had tried to flee and take refuge. His attack forced the chieftain
to surrender.[79] About Haidar's delegation of power to his son on
each of his campaigns during his veritable probation as a military
commander, Kirmani states:

Whenever Tippoo was commissioned to repel enemies, or to
attack forts, to whatever quarter he might be sent, he was first
summoned to the presence; and the Nawaub [Haidar]with

his own lips told him that he had selected him for this service, because he found him worthy in all matters to be employed; that he committed a force of so many horse and foot, so many guns, and a treasury of so much money to his orders; and that he must take great care no neglect occurred, and using great prudence and caution, return successful. He then dismissed him. The officers and men, who were placed under Tippoo on this occasion, were also sent for and strictly enjoined that, as the prince was young, they should never allow him to be separate from them, or peril himself by inconsiderate rashness; but, on the contrary, consider his safety at all times as placed at their responsibility by their faith and agreement. When fortunate and victorious, the prince returned to the presence, from his expedition, he was again placed under surveillance, as above related . . . the young Princes had permission to sleep in their *Zunanas* or women's apartments, only every fourth night.[80]

Tipu was to distinguish himself as an independent warrior of considerable repute in the campaign that Haidar had mounted against the British, which was commonly known as the First Anglo–Mysore War from 1767 to 1769. This was a veritable baptism by fire for the young teenager and, to his merit, he made his presence felt during this campaign.

5

The First Anglo–Mysore War

New Alliances

During the Maratha invasion of Mysore, the Peshwa had expected his 'ally', the mercurial Nizam Ali to support the campaign. But the Nizam seemed to deliberately delay joining Madhav Rao along with his troops. His brother Basalat Jung and a detachment of English troops under Colonel Joseph Smith marched towards Srirangapatna only by April 1767. By then Haidar had managed to secure the return of Madhav Rao, and Nizam Ali was left encamping between Chennapatna and Srirangapatna. Haidar, too, was anxious to ensure that his rivals were all isolated from one another. Peace with the Marathas was bought for now. He then decided to separate Nizam Ali from the British, with whom he had established communication earlier itself through Mahfuz Khan, the brother and rival of the Nawab of Arcot Muhammad Ali. Rukn-ud-daula, the dewan of Nizam Ali, mediated with Haidar and a secret alliance was stitched together on the payment of Rs 30 lakh by Mysore. Nizam Ali saw Muhammad Ali as a potential threat to his authority and anyone who helped uproot the latter was a friend. For Haidar, Muhammad Ali brought back memories of the humiliating Tiruchirapalli deceit that rankled in the heart of every brave Mysorean, including himself as he had been an integral part of that campaign. He also viewed Muhammad Ali as a peril to his own southern expansionist plans. He had even sent emissaries to Muhammad Ali in 1766 to honour the past commitments and hand over Tiruchirapalli to Mysore to secure

---

* Please refer to the corresponding illustration in the appendix.

permanent peace in the region, but the latter had haughtily ignored the entreaties. Haidar had also sent his diplomat Vinnaji Pant to the British Governor in Madras asking them not to help Muhammad Ali who, according to him, had vitiated the peace of the south by his devious ways. But the British refused and decided to stick with their old ally. They were themselves, like other powers in South India, feeling threatened by the expansionist drive of Haidar and his consecutive annexations of so many territories after becoming the supreme dictator of Mysore. Hence, this brewing alliance of Haidar and Nizam Ali and the other players seemed like a perfect and logical coming together of parties with similar goals and interests. The Nizam had wished to meet Haidar in Chennapatna where he was ensconced, but the latter decided to send instead his son Tipu, who was barely seventeen years old then, along with Makhdoom Sahib, Ghazi Khan, Meer Ismail Sahib and others on 11 June 1767.[1] De La Tour details how Haidar was extremely apprehensive about trusting the Nizam and sending his son Tipu to his camp:

> Hyder, at the moment of parting with his son, was in the greatest perplexity and concern, and expressed it to his friends. 'I am afraid,' said he, 'of the perfidious and cruel Nizam; he has assassinated his own brother, will he spare my son? Or, at least, have I not reason to conclude that he will detain him, and compel me, by the apprehension of my son's danger, either to pay him a large sum or to make great concessions to him? For, in short, I trust my son in the hands of a wretch to whom nothing is sacred.' This discourse and many other actions of his, prove that one of the greatest weaknesses of Hyder is his extreme affection for his children and all his relations. However, on the assurances made by Raja Saeb and Meer Fesoulla Khan (who were charged to accompany his son, and who protested they would themselves perish before the least accident should happen to the young prince), he suffered him to depart, being likewise much encouraged by reflecting on the bravery of the troops and the nobility that attended him.[2]

Haidar's fears were evidently misplaced as Kirmani's eloquent account narrates:

> When the Prince [Tipu] arrived near the Nizam's tent, the crash of the drums and kettle drums of his body guard struck fear to the ears of the Nizam, who ascending a balcony on his tent, saw and admired (nevertheless) the pomp and parade of Tippoo's cavalry escort; and the discipline and order of his troops. The Nizam, after that, received him with great liberality and kindness, and, having gained his heart, by honied words and phrases, addressed him by the title of *Nuseebuddowla* [The fortune of the State], and casting his plans and schemes aside, consulted him on the feasibility of chastising Muhammad Ali Khan, the Soubadar of Arkat [Arcot], and the English; and then dismissed him, with the present of a Khillaut, and the shawls the Nizam himself wore.[3]

To further cement the ties among co-religionists, matrimonial links too were explored. It was decided that Tipu would marry Mahfuz Khan's daughter and lay claim to the Nawabship of Arcot, which Mahfuz Khan was expected to give up in favour of his son-in-law. Nizam Ali, being the lawful Subahdar of the Deccan, was to formally confer the rights of Arcot on Tipu after the signing of this agreement. It was also decided that the combined forces would invade Arcot and reduce Muhammad Ali completely. Haidar was to pay Rs 6 lakh per month to Nizam Ali and have the sole right to put up garrisons in the numerous forts of Arcot, all of which was to be handed to the command of Makhdoom Sahib, Haidar's brother-in-law, who would govern on behalf of his nephew Tipu and Mahfuz Khan. Raza Sahib, the son of the deceased Chanda Sahib, whose cause all these players were claiming to espouse thus far, was to eschew all his claims on Arcot to Tipu. In return, he would be given the lordship of Tanjore, which was to be a vassal of Arcot. This was the elaborate plan that all the players agreed upon to cement a political and familial alliance. They decided to take the

French in Pondicherry into confidence and sought their help in the case of necessity.[4]

The unscrupulous Nizam Ali had tried to fool the Marathas that he was on their side by tardily proceeding towards Srirangapatna to their aid with the British. Even Col Smith was unsure why their combined forces were just resting their heels while the Peshwa was engaged in a pitched battle in Mysore. Madhav Rao was too shrewd to not notice this duplicity and hence chartered his own independent course of action, took what he could from Mysore and even withdrew from them without, for once, consulting or informing his allies—the Nizam and the British. He even scoffed at their suggestions of sharing the spoils of war with them—one in which they had no role to play. Nizam Ali then used this as an excuse to berate the Marathas to Smith and the British, of how unilaterally and unwittingly Madhav Rao had withdrawn his troops, with scant respect for his alliance partners.

Even as the British entered Mysore, the monsoons broke, forcing them to take refuge in Devanahalli, near Bangalore. Nizam Ali kept promising to help them with transport but that remained a mere promise. To Smith's dismay, he saw the Nizam being accorded a friendly welcome in Mysore, as they had already had backroom negotiations to seal a secret alliance. Nizam Ali once again conned Smith by promising unswerving friendship and even egged him on to attack Bangalore as the monsoons had subsided slightly. As Smith's troops marched towards Bangalore, he was horrified to see Nizam Ali moving away in the opposite direction, with not even a word of explanation. Smith sent several reports to the British Governor in Madras, Charles Bourchier, about the Nizam's deceit and that they had better watch out for an ugly turn of events, but the latter felt that they could still somehow manage to prevail upon him. Even as the British sat there wondering what was going on, unbeknownst to them, Nizam Ali had sealed the deal with Haidar and of course the other players like Mahfuz Khan and Raza Sahib. To guard himself against any eventualities, Nizam Ali also kept the British in good humour, constantly fooling them with assurances and dramatic proclamations of his loyalty and they too seemed to imprudently trust his theatrics. Such a master politician was Nizam Ali, capable of playing both sides with equal finesse, and so adroitly was the entire operation conducted that it missed the prying British ears. Smith and his troops did not know, that right under their noses their partner had happily switched sides, until three days before the combined forces of Nizam Ali and Haidar actually attacked Muhammad Ali. A desperate Smith wrote to his friend Lord Clive: 'Although it was as plain as noon day to every person (except the Council) that they (Nizam Ali and Haidar) were preparing to enter the Carnatic jointly, no measures were taken to establish magazines of provisions in proper places, nor any steps to supply our army in time of need.' This was the extent of British naivete and their lack of preparedness that they were actually supplying provisions and arms to their enemy till even three days before the attack on their ally. But it was a royal coup that Haidar and Nizam Ali had pulled off and for the former, it meant isolating the British from the tripartite alliance that was threatening to be formed against him.

The Fate of Nanjarajayya

Before proceeding on the expedition, Haidar had a task to complete at home. His spies had conveyed to him some information about his former mentor, Nanjarajayya, to whom he had rushed when faced with Khande Rao's treachery and with whose help he reversed the difficult situation he was placed in and, as was his nature, conveniently dumped him thereafter. A restive Nanjarajayya had been sending emissaries to Madhav Rao and Nizam Ali to have Haidar murdered. He had also tried to meddle in the succession to the throne after the death of Krishnaraja Wodeyar II by advocating the cause of the younger son, Bettada Chamaraja Wodeyar, rather than the elder, Nanjaraja Wodeyar, whom Haidar eventually selected. Haidar did not want to leave the capital for long, which he anticipated he would have to, with the new battle with the British and Muhammad Ali, without settling the problem in the form of Nanjarajayya. He was

invited to Srirangapatna to come and encamp there with his little
army. But Nanjarajayya was extremely wary of his untrustworthy
hitherto protégé and ignored all the invitations. Haidar paid a
visit to Nanjarajayya's house in Mysore, in all humility and show
of courtesy, executing an agreement (*kararnama*) with him that
Nanjarajayya would be assigned a territory worth Rs. 3 lakh and also
agreeing to host a lavish wedding for his son Virarajayya. He was also
promised the command of the Mysore Gate and the eastern gate of
the Srirangapatna fort. Though old and feeble now, Nanjarajayya's
political instincts were still agile and he saw through the game plan
and knew that accepting this invite to go to Srirangapatna would
be nothing short of suicide. Playing on the Muslim sentiments of
Haidar, he preconditioned his departure to Srirangapatna on the
oath that Haidar would take on the Quran that no harm would befall
Nanjarajayya. Haidar did take the oath, but quite like how Chanda
Sahib had tricked Rani Meenakshi of Madurai, the book on which
he swore was an ordinary one with just the splendid outer cover of
the Quran in which it was draped. Not imagining this fraudulent
move, Nanjarajayya felt relieved and made his way to Srirangapatna.

On reaching the capital, Nanjarajayya's small army was encircled
by Haidar's troops on the pretext of arranging a grand reception
for the old man. Perceiving this, Nanjarajayya, under the pretext of
enquiring about some medicinal drugs from Pondicherry, approached
Mir Sahib, the Persian writer to Haidar's French officer and offered
him Rs 8 lakh worth in gold, silver, precious stones and elephants if
they assisted him in assassinating Haidar. When this information
leaked to Haidar, this was the last straw on the proverbial camel's
back. De La Tour mentions what fate befell Nanjarajayya thereafter:

> On the day appointed, Nand Raj [Nanjarajayya] without
> any mistrust, made a pompous entrance into Seringapatam
> [Srirangapatna], at the head of his little army, the cannon firing
> and the troops beating to arms and saluting him. Being arrived at
> his palace, his attention was taken up by the compliments of the
> great men of the city, who were admitted by few at a time, on the

pretended account of not making too great a crowd. Mughdoom [Makhdoom Sahib] then entered the city, followed by a number of officers and made a sign to the troops, not to pay him any honours: he went directly to the palace of Nand Raj, where everyone supposed he was going to pay his respects; and dismounting, he caused the first company of his battalions of sepoys who guarded the gate to follow him. As soon as he came into the presence of Nand Raj, who came to meet him, he acquainted him, that Hyder, being informed that he was surrounded by people who gave him bad advice, had sent him to remove them from about him: at the same time, he commanded all present to leave the palace, which was done without uttering a word; the grenadiers followed them; and Mughdoom remaining with Nand Raj, his two sons and some officers, the conversation was carried on with the greatest politeness. Mughdoom acquainted the two princes that they were to make the campaign; and that instead of one father they would find two in Hyder and himself. During this short conversation, the women and all the family of Mughdoom were announced. Mughdoom took his leave, carrying the two princes with him, to whom he represented, that it became their dignity to wait upon the Nabob [Haidar] and give him an account of all that had passed. These young noblemen departed, accompanied by many of Mughdoom's officers; neither they nor Nand Raj expressing the least astonishment or chagrin. After their departure, Mughdoom spoke a word to Nand Raj's general, who ordered his troops to ground their arms, which was done with great silence. All the gates and windows of Nand Raj's palace that looked towards the street, were afterwards walled up, except the principal entrance.[5]

Thus, in the most silent, cold and calculative manner, Haidar neutralized the old man. To Nanjarajayya's utter shock and dismay, Haidar had betrayed him a second time, as he found himself a prisoner in his own palace, his guards captured and Haidar's sentinels placed in command. His accomplices, including one Mallu Anna, were heavily fined, while those among his coterie who had helped

Haidar, such as Obalayya and Kalappa, got important positions in the treasury office (*Toshe Khane Daftar*). Haidar paid the arrears that were due to Nanjarajayya's troops and confiscated his jagir worth Rs 4 lakh. Half of this was assigned to the old man, along with his ancestral principality of Kalale for his own maintenance. The remaining half was assigned to his sons, who happily followed Haidar in his campaign against Muhammad Ali and the British. The Mysore records speak no more of the wily Nanjarajayya who had wreaked so much havoc on the polity with his incessant machinations and of course the wasteful Tiruchirapalli campaign. He remained imprisoned in his misery, cursing his fate and his lack of wisdom for trusting someone as ungrateful as Haidar, before he eventually died in captivity in 1773, as a thoroughly disillusioned man. Haidar then confiscated Kalale and made provisions for bare necessities for the family in Srirangapatna. When he decided to show some compassion towards the son, Virarajayya, the latter was indifferent and hence an enraged Haidar imprisoned him too in 1779. With that the last vestiges of the infamous Dalavayi family and all that went with it, came to a rude and abrupt end.

The War Begins

After sorting the domestic mess, Haidar, along with the combined forces of nearly 50,000 men and 100 guns, burst into the battlefield against Muhammad Ali and the British.[6] The confederates made a quick round-up and took over Vaniyambadi, Changama, Tirupattoor and Kaveripatnam, laying siege to the rock fortress in Krishnagiri. Heading the cavalry, Haidar entered the Carnatic on 25 August 1767 through one of the passes near Krishnagiri. Simultaneously, a section of the Mysore troops, under Tipu and Berki Srinivasa Rao, raided Arcot. It was only after all this action that Muhammad Ali and the British under Col Smith finally took the field against Haidar. Haidar initially contented himself with cutting off all supplies to the British forces. He kept sending fresh detachments of horses and was determined to follow this strategy but was compelled by the haughty

Nizam to not carry on with this tedious method and instead attack Smith near the fort of Changama. Haidar had planned to cut down the relatively small British army into pieces near Changama. As the British were marching forth, Haidar planned to check them frontally, while attacking the rear with his rockets, musketry and cavalry. Though the surrounding hills were all occupied by the confederate forces, Smith managed to drive through and take possession of the ground that was an important post to facilitate their forward march. Fierce resistance followed, especially from Haidar, in which he was also badly wounded in his leg and had to be carried away from the field. Haidar lost nearly 1000 of his best men in this battle[7] which nearly went in the British favour. But despite this, Haidar pursued the opponent and, his guns still blazing, he plundered the supplies and killed several of the English forces. Smith was forced to retreat to Tiruvannamalai, about twenty miles to the south-east, where a hard contest ensued on 26 September 1767. He was joined by forces from Tiruchirapalli led by Col John Wood.

At Tiruvannamalai, the confederate army took a strong position on the other side of the hills. They finally marched with nineteen pieces of heavy cannon and eighteen and twenty-four pounders towards the British camp. Smith's guns were inferior, and he found it difficult to reply to the constant Mysorean cannonade. He however misled the confederates into believing that the British were retreating but made a rear attack to drive the former away. Through the course of both the battles, the conduct and participation of Nizam Ali left much to be desired and always attempted to dominate over Haidar's calculated military decisions. To add to the confusion, one of Nizam Ali's favourite wives, who always travelled with him, tried to prevail on directing the movement of elephants in the line of sight of the enemy's firing, causing immense loss of men and elephants thereby.[8] Despite loud proclamations that he would prefer a death on the battlefield like Nasir Jung to a dishonourable flight, Nizam Ali was seen rushing away at the greatest speed with a select body of his cavalry towards Singarapettah, leaving his minister and Commander-in-Chief Rukn-ud-daula to direct the retreat of the rest of his troops. Being abandoned in this manner, Haidar began to focus on protecting his own troops. Haidar was beginning to realize that the alliance with Nizam Ali was more of a liability than an advantage and some change in military strategy was necessary if they had to win. Kirmani too speaks derisively of the Nizam's army, quoting approvingly of English commanders that 'they did not estimate the Moghul [Nizam] army at the value of a grain of barley.'[9] He also states that the Nizam 'was firing away with his guns, without aim or object' and his army was 'like a herd of timid deer standing about without order . . . His troops, who had never been engaged in a hard fought or well-contested battle, left their master to his fate, and like a flock of sheep at the sight of a wolf, were so scattered, that even round the elephant of the Nizam, scarcely two thousand horse remained.'[10]

Col Smith saw the confusion that was gripping the opposite side and made vain attempts to loot them at night with Major Thomas Fitzgerald. But it was Haidar's spies who were actually advising him in this and they thus thwarted the entire exercise. However, forty-one pieces of Nizam Ali's heavy artillery fell into British hands, his great elephant was killed and the howdah plundered and looted of its ornaments. The loss of the English army was about 150 men wounded and killed, but those of the confederates exceeded 4000, 'with 64 guns, chiefly 18 and 16 pounders, with their tumbrils, and a large quantity of stores of every description, excepting rice, a small supply of which at this moment would have exceeded in value all the trophies of the day.'[11]

Tipu, who was raiding the Arcot countryside along with his military preceptor Ghazi Khan, almost reached Madras where they 'robbed, destroyed and broke all that was possible'.[12] When he heard of the reverses that were suffered at Tiruvannamalai, he rushed to join his father, who was then 'freed from all thought and apprehension'.[13] The fear that Tipu had perhaps broken into Madras and taken it spread like wildfire and travelled all the way to Europe, through frantic messages sent from Pondicherry, Tranquebar and other European settlements in India. 'The caravans,' writes De La Tour, 'and every possible conveyance, distributed this news with pleasure;

for the jealousy and hatred that other nations have conceived against the English, smothered the account that they themselves have given of their victory at Tirnmale [Tiruvannamalai].'[14] So much so, that this rumour actually caused the price of the Company's stock at London to fall at once from 275 to 222.[15] Such was the horror that the father–son duo of Mysore instilled in British hearts. And this, despite the British actually having marked significant victories against the confederates. The British side under Major Fitzgerald and Col Tod tried to intercept Tipu during his return from the mount, but he was too quick for them. After reverses in the battle of Changama, the battle of Tiruvannamalai, too, thus ended in a severe defeat for the confederate forces.

Concerned about the reverses her son had faced in battle, Haidar's mother decided to make the long journey from Bidanur where she was residing to the war camp to meet him and boost his morale. His entire army went into a parade to welcome her. Haidar and his sons received the palanquin in which she arrived there, covered in muslin. Her retinue consisted of about 200 women, mounted on horses, and enveloped in thick muslin so that not a part of their clothes or bodies could be seen. There were eight carriages drawn by large Persian oxen, ten elephants and several camels and other beasts of burden that came along with her palanquin. When she was led inside the tent, Haidar asked his mother what had compelled her to make this long, arduous journey in such trying and risky circumstances to meet him. The mother replied that she wished to see how he had managed to take the reverses that she had heard he had suffered. In reply, Haidar mentioned that the same God who handed those reverses also supported him in facing them. This relieved his mother and she blessed him abundantly and departed. De La Tour who records this episode mentions that merely two days later, Haidar's fortunes in the war suddenly seemed to look up.[16]

The Uneasy Alliance

The two battles had exposed the weaknesses in the confederate army and both parties were blaming each other for the sorry state of affairs. Nizam Ali invited his ally for a feast in his camp. Haidar, along with Tipu and a few select officers, paid a visit and presented several gifts to his ally. The Nizam seated Haidar on a throne of gold, with cushions of cloth of gold, that he gifted to him by the end of the meeting and also honoured him with the title of 'Haidar Jung.' Haidar returned the compliment by inviting his ally to his camp where he made him sit on a throne made of 'bags of coined silver, amounting to a lakh of rupees, covered with cushions of embroidered silver',[17] all of which he too gifted to Nizam Ali. Seeing the Nizam despondent about his own conduct in the war, Haidar mollified him with soothing words that 'victory and defeat came from God; that similar mischances had often befallen kings and princes of great renown, who, nevertheless had attained the very highest ranks of fame for strength of mind and courage . . . that he should not allow the rust of doubt and despondency to rest on the clear mirror of his heart, nor permit the dust of shame or regret to stick to the skirt of his intentions and projects.'[18] All this show of fake courtesy and camaraderie was to finally convey the message to Nizam Ali that if they had to win this battle, they would have no option but to fight from two separate fronts against their enemy.

The Nizam agreed and, in November 1767, marched with his troops towards Hoskote and then towards Kaveripatnam, while Haidar, with his troops, advanced into the Baramahal valley. Here, taking advantage of the British contingents having gone into their cantonments across three places—Kanchipuram, Wandiwash and Tiruchirapalli that were at considerable distance from each other, Haidar burst forth and easily took the mud forts of Tirupattur and Vaniyambadi by 15 November 1767. He then besieged Ambur that was a strong place, located on the summit of a granite mountain, accessible only on one side and about 110 miles from Madras.

He initially tried to befriend the killedar of Ambur, Maklis Khan, who was willing to surrender it. But the British found out and imprisoned Maklis Khan, necessitating a pitched battle for Haidar at Ambur. Captain Calvert, who was commanding the fort, sent urgent messages to the Governor in Madras to send him military replenishments. Heavy firing from Haidar literally brought Calvert to his knees, but after nearly a month of siege, and after seeing a British reinforcement joining Calvert from Vellore, Haidar decided to raise the siege and move up the valley. Among the people whose loss Haidar lamented during this siege was his relative, Khaki Shah, who had been one of his emissaries who had tricked Nanjarajayya into believing that Haidar had taken oath on the Quran with a false book. Many adherents of the faith believed that this was akin to profaning the holy book and hence such people met their just ends in misery in no time and so had Khaki Shah as well.[19]

Col Smith had entered the scene by now and decided to pursue Haidar, who divided his combined army between Tipu and Rukn-ud-daula, who had stayed on from the Nizam's side. As the intensity of the attack increased, expectedly the latter retreated in a cowardly manner. But Tipu continued the charge spiritedly, putting their guard to flight and also imprisoning several of their officers and soldiers, with their horses and palanquins. Rukn-ud-daula was given an earful by Haidar for not putting up any defence and told that he should leave and join his master, because his presence would ensure that Haidar 'could never expect to see the face of victory.'[20] But Rukn-ud-daula insisted that he would stay on, upon which it was agreed that he would always encamp at least two miles away from Haidar's army and not even enter their camp and use messengers if needed to convey any information. Such was the chemistry between the so-called allies.

The British counter-attack however continued and Smith even managed to fell Monsieur Aumont, the commandant of the Europeans in Haidar's army, forcing Haidar to retreat to Kaveripatnam where the Nizam had encamped. By mid-December 1767 though, in the midst of all these sudden turns on the battlefield, Haidar heard the news that the Nairs in Malabar, taking advantage of the distraction of the Mysorean forces in the battle with the British, had once again risen up in rebellion to liberate themselves. The British on the western coast had been advised to encourage these revolts in a bid to also distract Haidar from the Carnatic. From Bombay, the British troops were assembling in the harbours of Canara and Mangalore. Haidar therefore decided to send a part of his army, with heavy guns and baggage, along with Tipu, Ghazi Khan and Lutf Ali Beg to quell these disturbances.

But Haidar had more reasons to worry as Nizam Ali was panic-stricken by now. A detachment of British troops from Bengal under Col Peach had made a powerful diversion by sea, landing in the Northern Circars and advanced to Warangal, close to his capital, Hyderabad. In utter fright, Nizam Ali did what he was best at—double-dealing. He opened secret negotiations with Col Smith to avoid an attack on Hyderabad. Haidar had in 'every estimate of the conduct of Nizam Ali, remembered that he was the murderer of his own brother; and held his character in as much contempt as was consistent with the incessant fear of being overreached by some unsuspected treachery.'[21] Rukn-ud-daula had secret plans to raid his ally's army, even though outwardly he was expressing unswerving loyalty. On his master's advice, Rukn-ud-daula had also begun negotiations with Muhammad Ali, which went on for a few months and by the end of it, he gladly confirmed the Nawabship of the Carnatic to him and his own cession of the Northern Circars to the British. Guntur was to be left in the possession of Basalat Jung, Nizam Ali's brother. As De la Tour laments: 'Thus it was that Suba [Nizam], who twenty years before held the destiny of India in his hands, became a kind of beggar among the powers, and daily lost that credit and consideration which gave him his superb titles.'[22] Thus, by end-February 1768, Nizam Ali's defection was complete; he smugly marched back to Hyderabad with the confederate alliance in tatters.

Trouble on the Western Front

Even as Haidar was coming to terms with the treachery of the Nizam, he realized that the British had managed significant successes on the western coast. Between February and April 1768, they had reduced the Mysorean ports in Canara of Honavar, Mangalore and Basavarajadurga and were now threatening to advance towards Bidanur. Haidar himself rushed towards the Canara region, abandoning the Carnatic campaign. At Bidanur, he collected nearly 20,000 peasants from the countryside and armed them with wooden muskets of ebony and standards of coloured cloth, marched down to Mangalore with this huge force by early May 1768, tricking the British of the presence of a large battalion and scared them. Tipu managed to make a daring attack on the British batteries and emerged victorious. This was followed by a heavy cannonade from the Mysorean side that helped liberate Mangalore from British capture. The rout of the English side was complete, with the whole army consisting of the general, forty-six officers, 680 English troops and 6000 sepoys, along with their arms and baggage being in shambles. As Robson writes: 'On his [Haidar's] approach to Mangalore, the Bombay detachment were intimidated, and most shamefully abandoned their conquests; the greater part of them were made prisoners, many guns and stores, and the money they had taken for the use of the detachment was also taken. This infamous behaviour of theirs greatly encouraged Hyder's troops, and left him at liberty to return to defend his country on this side.'[23] Haidar is said to have been so overjoyed with his son's valour in Mangalore that he wept with joy while embracing him in the war tent.[24] The Portuguese merchants and some Christian priests belonging to three churches in Mangalore who were suspected of hobnobbing with the British to assist them in their campaign were rounded up and taken as prisoners.[25]

Honnavar and Basavarajadurga were to revert to Mysore next. Haidar also skillfully made peace with the Nairs in Malabar through Madanna, his governor there, by allowing them a semblance of autonomy on the condition that they reimbursed his military expenses. This was a trap he was laying for them, but lulled by false confidence, they unwittingly fell for it. In Bidanur, the landholders had been drained by Haidar's stern exaction measures and had assisted the British expedition by supplying them provisions and other conveniences. Having kept a track of these developments,

Haidar summoned them on the pretext of wanting to meet them to settle the following year's revenue figures. When they came to meet him, he nonchalantly declared to them that their treachery was known and if their lives mattered to them, they would need to pay heavy fines.[26] The British diversion on the western coast was thus a complete failure and Haidar returned to Bangalore, a much relieved man by the end of July 1768.

The War Continues

During the time Haidar was thus preoccupied on the western front, Muhammad Ali and the British aspired to regain ground in the Carnatic and occupy all the fertile territories adjacent to the Carnatic–Payeenghat (low-lying areas, as against Balaghat, which means higher ground or hills). They hoped to capture territories from Vaniyambadi on the north to Dindigul on the south-east and Palghat on the south-west, following which, they would penetrate into Mysore, first at Bangalore and then the capital city of Srirangapatna—the two important nuclei of the Mysore kingdom. N.K. Sinha describes the Bangalore fort thus:

> It was admirably constructed, fitted with all the necessaries of war and provisions for 12 months. The walls were of stone. The well-built bastions were turfed, the ramparts wide, the ditch deep, the glacis and esplanade excellent. There were batteries on the salient angles and redoubts without; 3000 of Haidar's best sepoys were within the walls and more than 7000 other troops. Haidar himself, with 1000 sepoys, 7000 horse and 20,000 Poligar troops, was outside, ready to come to its relief. All this could not have been vanquished by the threats of a half-starved, ill-recruited, ill-supplied, ill-paid, harassed [British and their allies] army.[27]

The British army was broken up into two divisions, the northern one under Col Smith and the southern one under Col Wood, to give effect to the designs. A host of places fell to the combined British troops under these two men—Dharmapuri, Salem, Attur, Namakkal, Erode, Satyamangalam, Coimbatore, Ratnagiri, Sulagiri, Dindigul and so on, as well as secured their positions in the important passes of Gajjalahatti, Talamalai and Kaveripuram that connected them directly to the heart of the Mysore kingdom. But from a military strategy perspective, it was grossly unwise of the British to spread themselves thin over such a vast territory when their forces were not large enough to sustain the occupation.

By then, the Governor of Madras and the Council there decided that two Field Deputies, Col John Call and George Mackay, along with Muhammad Ali who would finance the conquests and also provide intelligence on the enemy moves, were to be dispatched to assist Col Smith. But so imperfect and unreliable was Muhammad Ali's gathering of intelligence that they came to know of Haidar's march to Bidanur only three months after his actual departure there. Their plans to foil Haidar's efforts to relieve the western coast were thus ruined but they carried on with the military campaign in the Carnatic region. Captain Richard Mathews, a daring officer, took a string of forts, along with Col Donald Campbell. Masti, Mulbagal, Kolar, Anekal, Denkanikote and others fell in quick succession by July 1768. Murar Rao, too, joined hands with the British and his general Yoonas Khan joined the British army at Hosur with 300 men. The combined forces were eyeing the capture of Bangalore that would mean a big jolt to Haidar. They marched towards Hoskote by August, where Murar Rao joined them with 3000 horse and 2000 irregular infantry. Prior to their designs of taking Bangalore, they decided to besiege Chikkaballapura.

By August 1768, Haidar being back from the western coast, rushed to save Bangalore and decided to reduce his long-time foe Murar Rao's forces in Hoskote that were encamped in a manner that there was hardly any communication with the British line. Haidar is said to have been determined to get the head of Murar Rao, which was to be 'the great object of the enterprise.'[28] But the confusion in the camp and Murar Rao's own deft moves ruined Haidar's plans and though Murar Rao was wounded and Yoonas Khan had his right arm literally cut through by a sabre, not much loss could be inflicted on them. Hoskote was recaptured. Alarmed by this turn of events, Muhammad Ali lifted the siege of Chikkaballapura and fled to the security of Kolar with a strong escort in early September 1768, citing ill health. An immense quantity of artillery and ammunition intended for the capture of Bangalore was left there, up for grabs for Haidar.

Haidar moved towards Gurramkonda next which had been granted as a jagir or fiefdom by the Peshwa to his brother-in-law Mir Ali Raza Khan (or Mir Sahib) since 1767 when he switched sides. Haidar's wife had rebuked him for this treachery and he was even offered more jagirs if he moved back to the family fold. But the wrath of Haidar kept Mir Sahib sceptical of a reconciliation. Now, virtually friendless and facing both the British and Muhammad Ali's forces, and an inimical Nizam Ali and Peshwa who were ever eager to swoop on his domains, Haidar urged a rapprochement. Besides, Mir Sahib was a good soldier and it helped to have him on his side. Leaving behind Mir Sahib's nephew, Saiyid Sahib, in Gurramkonda, Haidar took the former along on his campaign. Almost half of his domain and strategic positions had all passed into the hands of the enemy and Bangalore was still under their threat. The astute politician that he was, Haidar did not want to expose the chinks in his own warfare and those of the Mysore army, and sued for peace with Muhammad Ali and the British. He was willing to cede the Baramahal province and pay Rs 10 lakh. But puffed by their string of successes, the British field deputies and Muhammad Ali put a range of unreasonable and extreme demands to Haidar's vakil who came to negotiate the terms of peace. They sought, in addition to Baramahal, Coimbatore, Krishnagiri, Shankaridurga and Dindigul, a payment of upwards of Rs 70 lakh, trade and other concessions on the Malabar coast, payments of tributes to Nizam Ali and some cessions to Murar Rao. As Malleson notes: 'Rarely have rapacity and extortion met with a prompter punishment. Driven to bay, the wild and untutored genius asserted itself.'[29] A miffed Haidar called off the peace talks as there was no way that he could agree to such humiliating and unilateral terms—something that the British would repent for a long time. With the failure of the talks in September 1768, the field for conflict was left open yet again.

The Strike-Back

As a first counter-attack, the very next month Haidar managed to skilfully take back Mulbagal, despite stiff opposition provided by Col Wood. Haidar kept playing hide and seek with the British and 'would come almost within cannon shot of the English army and then move off with ease.'[30] Drawing the opponent deep inside the country, Haidar then alarmed the field deputies and Muhammad Ali with a heavy cannonade in Kolar in November 1768. Robson reminisces that 'During this engagement, Hyder's artillery was managed with equal skill, and fired as briskly as those of the English, a circumstance never experienced before from any of the country powers . . . many of the English sepoys had deserted to Hyder on account of the scarcity of provisions, amongst whom were some of those artillery sepoys, and were the very men that managed his guns in the late engagement.'[31]

The Madras Council, however, was getting restive about the dance that Haidar was making their armies perform. Smith, unable to terminate the war conclusively in their favour despite his best efforts, was recalled to Madras, and succeeded by Wood. The field deputies who tried to dictate terms to Smith and never gave him a free hand in the operations blamed him for all their 'own idle, vain and indigested plans.'[32] These field deputies and Muhammad Ali, too, were ordered by the Council to suspend plans to besiege Bangalore and move instead to the Carnatic.

Meanwhile, Haidar, who was on a mission to regain all the lost territories, laid siege to Hosur. He then moved towards Bagalur, about ten miles away from Hosur, which had a small fort that was garrisoned by the British army under Captain Alexander and serving Muhammad Ali. A walled town or *pettah* was connected to the fort and, on one side, lived the inhabitants, who were mainly farmers and traders. Alexander's forces, upon seeing Haidar approach, retreated quickly into the fort and closed its doors. Enraged at not finding a ready entrance to the fort, he stormed the pettah, resulting in terrible carnage of nearly 2000–3000 men, women and children, then took possession of it, along with the stores, baggage, the two eighteen pounders and more than 2000 draught and carriage cattle.[33] Historian Shama Rao describes the scene at Bagalur: 'The heavier and the more active animals pressed forward on the weaker, until they were piled on one another in a mass of dead and dying, of which the human beings formed too large a proportion and the perils which the retreating garrison encountered in clearing this dreadful scene were not inferior to those which they sustained from the pursuing enemy.'[34] Haidar's heavy cannonade wounded several British officers, including Captain Cosby, and killed several others. For this gross misjudgment of the situation leading to a terrible dishonour for the Company, Col Wood was not only recalled but also court-martialled. He was even dismissed from service with penalties slapped on him. He was tried for nine charges, including appropriating for his own use, stores, grains and plunder and also misconduct on field.[35] Col Lang succeeded him in early December 1768.

Haidar created alarm and panic in the enemy troops by spreading rumours that Nawab Muhammad Ali had run away from the battle and that the British commanders were being recalled or sacked due to their incompetence. His own cavalry was divided into three units, two of which were given to his brothers-in-law, Makhdoom Sahib and Mir Ali Raza, while he commanded one. The grenadiers too were similarly bifurcated. Fazalullah Khan provided a stout defence at the pass of Gajjalahatti from where the British were trying to penetrate into Mysore and attack Srirangapatna. Haidar, leaving the main army under Tipu, then descended into the Baramahal area and, in quick succession and with great ease, without firing a shot, took the forts of Dharmapuri, Tingrecotta, Omalur, Attur, Salem and Namakkal in December 1768. Erode and Karur too fell to his might next. At this juncture, had Haidar decided not to turn towards Karur but to Tiruchirapalli which was as vulnerable; he would most likely have managed to annex it easily, thereby fulfilling a long cherished Mysorean dream to own the place.

However, within just six weeks, Haidar managed to recover all the lost territories within his dominion and, by January 1769, burst forth into the Carnatic, threatening to invade the very seat of British power, Madras. Fazalullah Khan was stationed at Dindigul to carry on the war southwards in the Madura and Tinnevelly regions. In Haidar's victorious march through the lower Carnatic, he subjugated the Raja of Tanjore to pay Rs 4 lakh and, passing through Cuddalore, turned even towards Pondicherry.

Overtures for Peace

Alarmed by his rapid resurgence from near defeat, the British, who had arrogantly rebuffed his overtures for peace, tried to rekindle peace talks. Accordingly, in January 1769, they dispatched Captain Brooke to interview Haidar and understand him better. Haidar bluntly told them that he had made every effort to establish amity with the British and, for many years, had even kept an envoy at Fort St George for this purpose. But the British were being willingly manipulated by the wily Muhammad Ali who had been constantly trying to drive a wedge between the two of them. He conveyed that he was sincerely desirous of promoting the goodwill of the British and their commercial establishments on the west coast or their trade in pepper, sandalwood and other products from Mysore, which he had always been happy to support, in exchange for the products manufactured in Europe. Despite this, Muhammad Ali's pernicious influence had coloured the British outlook towards him and Mysore thus far and therefore his elimination in the Anglo–Mysore equation was necessary to him. He then spoke in confidence to Brooke that he had specific information that the Peshwa was planning an invasion of the Carnatic and in such an eventuality, whether the British desired Mysore to side with them or with the Marathas depended completely on what decision Madras took in this matter. Haidar wanted an authorized and competent person from the British side like Col Smith, and not emissaries like Brooke who had no powers to finalize anything, to be in discussion with him to finalize a lasting settlement. When asked if he wished to send a vakil to Madras to negotiate, Haidar declined, saying that he knew well by now that at Madras, every effort would be made, and also encouraged by Muhammad Ali, to thwart all such attempts and instead keep the British engaged in a perennial state of war so that he could maintain his own relevance and also plead their support. Knowingly or otherwise, the British had nurtured this attitude for long now and hence he saw no logic in wasting time on such diplomatic channels. He was willing to talk to Col Smith or some gentleman of rank who was vested with the requisite authority to take decisions in such matters, independent of all other players in the region.

Brooke diligently carried back the message from Haidar to Madras who then dispatched Mr Andrews to carry forward the negotiations with him, even as they reappointed Col Smith to lead the military charge, if the need arose, along with Major Fitzgerald and Col Lang. Andrews, aged forty-five, was a hard negotiator and a politically astute diplomat. About two decades ago when he was barely in his twenties, he had managed to seal a deal with the Ganjam chiefs in favour of the British for easy transit of the Company's letters between Madras and Bengal. That success had brought him much fame and he had been commissioned to several important assignments thereafter. He had kept a close watch on the activities of Nizam Salabat Jung and Bussy and provided valuable guidance to the Council on how to deal with those situations. He had served on the Council at Madras when Pigot was the Governor.

After a lot of back and forth on where the negotiations were to be held, Haidar met Andrews at Tyagadurg on 22 February 1769. Haidar repeated the demands he had made and after much haggling, Andrews carried these back to Madras where the Council rejected them summarily. Haidar independently even sent his vakil to Col Smith, whom he seemed to greatly admire and respect, with the message that he was sincerely desirous of lasting peace with the British. But these meetings of his vakil, too, did not bear fruit.

Once the peace proposals were rejected by the Council, it was time to renew hostilities and March 1769 saw the resumption of war. By then, Haidar had specific intelligence that the Marathas were keenly contemplating a third invasion of Mysore. He was thus restive to conclude this long drawn hostility with the British that had yielded so little thus far. Moreover, with a capable officer like Col Smith now back in command, he was deeply apprehensive of keeping up the momentum of his war-fatigued troops. He therefore thought of a rash, bold move that could turn the entire situation to his advantage, forcing the British into complete submission.

Haidar at the Gates of Madras

Haidar laid waste to the territories close to Madras, 'the Black Town' (the township of the natives that grew around Fort St George, as Chennapattanam) and its suburbs. 'The Black Town,' writes De La Tour, 'contains a great number of inhabitants, not less than four hundred thousands according to the English calculation; and their number was vastly augmented by the fugitives from the country. Though it bears the name of the Black Town, it is inhabited by great numbers of Europeans of all nations, who have warehouses furnished with the richest products of every country. Among others, there is a large colony of very rich Armenians, possessed of immense riches; and great numbers of Guzerats, or wealthy bankers, dealers in pearls, precious stones and coral; in short, this town is always one of the richest emporiums in the world.'[36]

Tipu and Mir Ali Raza Khan retook in swift succession all the places garrisoned by the British in the Carnatic Balaghat. They then descended to the outskirts of Madras and raided Tirumal Kheni (Triplicane) and Muthyalpet (localities in modern Chennai), alarming Muhammad Ali. Haidar threatened to set fire to Black Town and arrived at the very gates of Madras. Smith and Col Lang tried to encircle and intercept all connection to Haidar's forces from Mysore, at Wandiwash and Tyagadurg respectively. But giving them all a slip at each effort to intercept him and making them go around in circles, by 29 March 1769, Haidar and his troops were standing at St Thomas Mount, merely seven miles west of Madras. He had covered close to 130 miles on horseback in barely three and a half days. The British were outwitted and terrified and were now willing to listen to Haidar.

Haidar meanwhile wrote a letter directly to Governor Charles Bourchier, demanding that Josias Du Pré, a member of Council who was due to succeed him as governor, be sent if he wished peace. He had an upper hand now in the military domain and could afford to demand his terms. Bourchier realized that calling for peace was the only way to save the British forces from an embarrassing defeat. An immediate cessation of hostilities from Smith and Lang was ordered. Du Pré and George Bourchier, the governor's brother, met Haidar's vakil, Vinnaji Pant. On 3 April 1769, a treaty was executed between the Company and Haidar where it was agreed that there should be perpetual peace and friendship between the two parties and that they would assist the other when attacked. For commercial understanding on the west coast, a separate conversation was to be held with Company agents in Bombay, ensuring absolute liberty of commerce. Prisoners on both sides were to be released and all forts and places occupied to be mutually restored, except Karur that was originally a Mysore territory but had been forcibly taken by Muhammad Ali. The Company also promised to present Haidar a fifty-gun ship (which they did in 1772–73).[37] They engaged to supply 12,000 Europeans to serve in his army as often as he should demand it. The two sides presented valuable gifts to each other to seal their new-found bonhomie.

Another treaty was executed between Haidar and Muhammad Ali under which the latter was to immediately evacuate from Hoskote and deliver to Mysore, not only all the artillery, arms and ammunition but also an annual tribute of Rs 6 lakh. Both the Nawabs, as they were to be designated, would maintain their respective status quo ante and the British were not to interfere in their affairs except when Haidar himself was the aggressor. With the terms being thus settled, much to Mysore's advantage, Haidar victoriously returned to Bangalore by the end of the month.

In a private letter, Du Pré writes about his reflections on the conclusion of the war that badly hit British prestige in India:

> We have at length concluded a peace with Hyder such as will do us no honour; yet it was necessary, and there was no alternative but that or worse. The reason it seems so disgraceful is that it [the war] was begun with ideas of conquest on our part, and it is said this is the first time a country enemy has gained an advantage over us. The latter part of this war, which probably will be thought the most disgraceful, is in reality nothing more than we have always thought the country liable to. An army of Moratta [sic: Maratha] horse we always dreaded, because we always knew that it was not their business to fight, but to plunder, burn and destroy. The difference has only been in name: it was Hyder [sic] instead of Moratta, and I think there can be no doubt but that, whilst our force consists of infantry only, any power with a large body of horse may plunder and ruin the country; and if we have nothing to support our armies in the field or in garrison but the current revenues of the country, the failure of these must bring ruin to us . . . what then must have been our condition had the war continued! We had but provision for 15 days in the Black Town when the peace was concluded. Nothing could have prevented him in that part more than in the south from burning and destroying all the grain in stock in the villages, and on the ground. A famine would have ensued; and as it is, grain is scarce, and there certainly will be greater distress before the next crop. Although it was clear that peace, such as it is, was better for the Company than the continuance of the War, yet my mortifications are not small, and I cannot avoid thinking myself unfortunate in coming to India just in time to share disgrace, and to have, from henceforth, affairs to manage which are so encumbered and entangled that I can see no course we can take without being exposed to new embarrassments.[38]

Peixoto, who had left Haidar's service in the middle of the war, was in Madras when the British signed the treaty with Mysore to make peace. When he congratulated the governor and the councillors for the termination of hostilities, they rather sheepishly requested him not to make them feel more ashamed of themselves. 'Others said,' he writes, 'that it seemed to them that the time was arrived in which the English nation was to decline since experience shewed it, that all knew that it was much declined in their time.'[39]

De La Tour's graphic account of the caricature that Haidar had ordered to be made depicts the morale of the two powers:

There was fixed to the gate of Fort St George, called the Royal Gate, a design, in which was seen Hyder Ali Khan seated under a canopy, upon a pile of cannon; Mr Dupré and the other ambassador being on their knees before him. Hyder held in his right hand the nose (this gentleman is dignified with the nose of an enormous magnitude) of Mr Dupré, drawn in the form of an elephant's trunk, which he shook for the purpose of making him vomit guineas and pagodas, that were seen issuing from the mouth of this plenipotentiary. In the back ground appeared Fort St George; and on one of the bastions, the Governor and council were drawn on their knees, holding out their hands to the Nabob. On one side of the council, was a large mastiff growling at Hyder, the letters J.C. (for John Call) being marked on his collar[40] and behind the mastiff stood a little French dog, busily employed licking his posteriors. This last animal was adorned with a star, such as the Chevalier de Christ, Colonel Call's confidant, wore. At a distance were seen the English camp, and General Smith holding the treaty of peace in his hand, and breaking his sword. By this peace, Hyder Ali Khan Bahadoor gloriously finished a war, which all India supposed would terminate in his ruin.[41]

The Court of Directors in their significant and noteworthy assessment of this war wrote:

The several powers of India, whose dread of our name and arm have contributed, in a great measure, to our prosperity and security, have seen terms of peace, dictated to our Governor of

Fort St George, by a country power, at the gates of Madras. The Company's interest and influence in India have suffered such diminution and discredit that the most consummate abilities, persevering assiduity, unshaken fidelity and intrepid courage in our future servants, may perhaps be proved insufficient in many years to restore the English East India Company to a proper degree of credit and dignity in the eyes of the nations and inhabitants of Indostan [sic]. It is our opinion that you have so untruly made us principals in the quarrel with Haidar, the said war has been very improperly conducted and most disadvantageously concluded.[42]

Haidar, however, had great regard for Col Smith, whom he called his preceptor in the science of war, whom he wished to befriend after the conclusion of peace.[43] He was keen to have an interview with him and that was one reason he even suggested his name as the interlocutor when Captain Brooke and Andrews came to negotiate peace. But this never materialized even after the Treaty of Madras was signed between the parties. He then requested a portrait of Col Smith to be presented to him, which was duly complied with. This portrait was found in 1799 during the fall of Srirangapatna by the British.[44]

Assessment of the War and Peace

In the earlier battles in India that the British engaged in, be it at Plassey or Buxar, the numerical strength of the Indian side hardly came of use. The opponent's discipline, swiftness, fire control and military techniques often took the Indian side by surprise and they capitulated. The First Anglo–Mysore War was a classic instance that shattered the myth of the infallibility of European powers against an Indian force. There was no longer that element of surprise, as rulers like Haidar had begun training their troops under Europeans in their techniques of combat. Haidar had advantages over the British in terms of cavalry so he could afford to make ravages, cut off the envoys, incapacitate their intelligence networks and also quickly retreat in the wake of defeat. The pursuit of the enemy was the second most important factor after vanquishing it. Here too, the British immobility to move fast hit them hard. Smith's utter weakness when it came to cavalry limited his options in warfare and constrained his choice of the theatre of war to the mountainous regions. On the other hand, Haidar's superior cavalry was much more mobile, swift and daring than the British. What also seriously impaired the British campaign in this war was the constant meddling in day-to-day operations by the Madras Council and its obdurate field deputies whose gigantic egos clashed with those of first-rate officers such as Col Smith. Even after Wood was routed in Mulbagal, the Council continued to repose its faith in him and even recalled Smith to replace him with Wood, until the Bagalur fiasco ensued. Smith found it difficult even to secure oxen for the conveyance of baggage, artillery and ammunition because of the interference and corrupt practices of the Council.[45] As Michaud summarizes: 'Hyder had often been victorious, but even in defeats he had learnt the art of success. He had perfected the discipline of his troops; he had found officers and he had trained soldiers. But of all the gains from this war, what touched the heart of Hyder was that he saw the young Tippoo Saheb grow up under his eyes in the school of victory. He distinguished himself in numerous exploits, and he announced himself to the people as the worthy inheritor of the glory and projects of his father.'[46]

Even British chroniclers such as Wilks had words of praise for Haidar for his adroit control in the war and for turning reverses into successes. Wilks states that Haidar 'committed not one political mistake, and that of his military errors more ought to be ascribed to his just diffidence in the talents and discipline of his officers and troops, than to the misconception of what might be achieved with better instruments.'[47] He also chastises the Company's faulty decision-making for their humiliating defeat: 'The strange combination of vicious arrangements, corrupt influence, and political incapacity, which directed the general measures of the Government of Madras have been too constantly traced to demand recapitulation.'[48]

Haidar's main motive in concluding the treaty was his long-nourished anxiety about the coming together of all his opponents—the British, the Nizam and the Marathas. He thus wanted to isolate them and had tried to do so by temporarily buying peace with the Marathas prior to the war and by that disastrous alliance with an untrustworthy, mercurial Nizam Ali. Now befriending the British, he thought, would bring lasting peace, wean away Muhammad Ali from them and thereby prevent his own isolation in the south. He showed too much eagerness to conclude the treaty, as there was also a ticking danger of a possible Maratha invasion. In this, he did not quite pay adequate attention to the wordings of the clauses, especially the defensive alliance with the British in case a third party attacked Mysore. Whether this clause would stand the test of the events of the future, time would tell.

But undoubtedly, the victory in the First Anglo–Mysore War and Haidar's virtual dictation of the terms of peace to conclude it, at the gates of the British seat of power in Madras, had enhanced his prestige and image among all the contemporary players of the time. But this was to be short-lived as within the womb of the terms of the Treaty itself lay the seeds of future conflict and discord, and it was just a matter of time before hostilities among the major players were to erupt in manifold ways.

6

Period of Unrest

The Marathas Attack Again

There was hardly any respite for a battle-weary Haidar. Despite his commanding position in the final stages of the First Anglo–Mysore War and his ability to dictate the terms of peace to the British at the very gates of their power in Madras, he hardly got a chance to even savour this hard-won victory. The Marathas were knocking at the door yet again. Under Mahimaji Sindhia, the Maratha foujdar of Chikkaballapura, a force of 400 horses and an alliance of neighbouring palegars, the Marathas had invaded the southern country and attempted to capture Gurramkonda. Haidar dispatched a strong force of 5000 horse, 4000 foot and 4000 irregulars to combat them under Berki Srinivasa Rao and Mir Ali Raza Khan. The two sides clashed in July 1769, when the Maratha army was so comprehensively routed that Mahimaji retreated in despair. The secret treaty between Haidar and Nizam Ali in 1767 had brought Cudappah, Kurnool and other places that lay between the Tungabhadra River and the northern borders of Mysore into the nominal control of Haidar. To consolidate his hold over these regions, Haidar began a swift tour to levy tributes on the chieftains in Kotikonda, Kupgal and other places. Talpul, which was held by Rakhmaji Bhonsle, was taken over by Haidar. He invited Rakhmaji for talks but treacherously seized him and his men and put them to death. However, in Bellary, Haidar was pushed back with considerable loss.

---

* Please refer to the corresponding illustration in the appendix.

Gopal Rao Patwardhan protested against this aggression of Haidar and the latter replied: 'It was agreed between us that within four months Sira, Hoskote and Ballapur taluk would be returned to me, but even after the lapse of two years with a man of your worth as the go-between this has not been done. Please request the Peshwa to right this wrong. Mahimaji Sindhia, *qiladar* of Ballapur, was taking into his service some of our dissatisfied men and was fomenting trouble in our own territory. Hence, I drove him out.'[1] Haidar similarly spread his wings across the entire frontier, exacting tributes from Chitradurga, Harpanahalli, Harihar, Savanur and Gutti. The territories of his old foe Murar Rao were all taken over with just the fort of Gutti left for him. Haidar even summoned him to his camp like a subordinate, causing much consternation to the Maratha side. Murar Rao was directed to pay Rs 50,000 as an annual indemnity to Srirangapatna.

That Haidar had come so menacingly close to the very borders of the Maratha Empire, and his newly acquired stature after the Treaty of Madras, sent obvious alarm bells ringing in the Peshwa court in Poona. Madhav Rao could simply not digest the fact that his previous two campaigns to subjugate Haidar totally had been abortive, despite his bravery and statesmanship—once due to the intrigues of his uncle Raghunath Rao who had a secret understanding with Haidar and the second time, due to the vacillations of his treacherous ally, Nizam Ali. That Haidar was quietly instigating the Peshwa's opponents, be it his secret dalliance with Raghunath Rao or by stirring up Janoji Bhonsle against the Peshwa in 1769, even after their rapprochement, was added reason for Madhav Rao's irritation. Principally, questioning Haidar's right to levy contributions on the palegars who, he claimed, came under his suzerainty, Madhav Rao used that as a ruse to make his third invasion of Mysore in December 1769 with an army of nearly 75,000. Haidar marked a quick retreat from the northern borders near the Maratha territories on his favourite elephant, Imam Baksh, towards the forest of Udagani. About 25,000 troops were kept under Tipu, Mir Raza, Berki Venkata Rao and Makhdoom Ali at the borders of Bidanur. About 20,000 troops were scattered across the kingdom and nearly 35,000 were with him at all times. He had fortified Bangalore and Srirangapatna where he was hopeful of being able to hold out for four to six months till the monsoons arrived.

But Madhav Rao, who was determined to fight to the finish this time, hotly pursued him, along with the palegar of Chitradurga, Madakari Nayaka, who had an old axe to grind with Haidar, and the long-standing foe, Murar Rao. They marched towards Srirangapatna, by the way of Penukonda, overrunning all the Mysorean territories on the way, till Nagamangala. They virtually encircled Haidar—the Peshwa encamping near Srirangapatna and Gopal Rao Patwardhan near Savanur. The Maratha forces under Gopal Rao Patwardhan, his cousins Parshuram Bhau Patwardhan and Nilkanth Rao Patwardhan and another force under Anand Rao Raste kept a close watch on Haidar's movements. They planned a twofold attack on Haidar if he emerged from the forest. In trying to stop the Peshwa's advance, Haidar ordered 'all straw and wood that could be gathered, to be set on fire, to fill up wells and ponds and send word to people in the villages to retire into the capital city.'[2]

Not wishing to take on another battle so close on the heels of a long conflict in the Carnatic, Haidar sent Raza Sahib (Chanda Sahib's son) and Appaji Ram as emissaries to discuss peace with Madhav Rao. The Peshwa put forward audacious demands of Rs 1 crore for the crime of collecting heavy levies from his subordinate palegars and also the submission of two years' due that was payable by Mysore, at Rs 12 lakh per annum. Haidar submitted that he was a soldier of fortune and had no treasure but his sword. Thus, there was no way he would be able to satisfy these exorbitant and inflated demands, especially since the kingdom had been war ravaged and its treasury running dry. If the 12 lakh levy were to satisfy the Peshwa, he offered to arrange for the same. The talks failed and, in the process, Haidar also lost Raza Sahib, who had long served under him. Raza Sahib, enterprising and cunning like his father Chanda Sahib, stealthily used the contacts that he developed in the Peshwa's court during the brief course of the negotiations to defect to the Maratha side. Haidar's promise to elevate Raza Sahib and

Mahfuz Khan, along with Tipu himself to the Nawabship of Arcot, as decided by the treaty with Nizam Ali, had come a cropper after the confederate alliance broke. Haidar's attempts to keep him on their side by engaging Raza Sahib in a matrimonial alliance with his daughter did not interest the latter as much as the conferment of the throne of Tanjore that was assured to him. This daughter of Haidar was the only one who had survived under the care of 'Modin Saib in spite of his [Haidar's] custom of killing his daughters as soon as they were born.'[3] Knowing that the Maratha side was strong and resolute under Madhav Rao, he deemed this as the opportune moment to switch sides.

The two sides clashed thereafter. The Peshwa marched forth to occupy Kadur, Banavar, Budihal, Kandikere, Chikkanayakanahalli and other places. Haidar had expected that as per the Treaty of Madras, in the event of an aggression on his territories, the British would come forth for help. It was based on this misplaced trust that he had confidently strutted around on the Maratha borders and tried to subjugate their palegars. But to his dismay, he realized that the British were far from eager to lend their support—this barely a few months after the treaty they had signed. He knew that once again, he was all alone in this battle. Tipu was sent to Bangalore and then to Srirangapatna, with 3000 horses to check the Maratha advance. But he was pursued by the Marathas and took shelter in the fort of Magadi which they besieged. Haidar was forced to move out from Udagani towards Channagiri. On 10 February 1770, he attacked Chikkanayakanahalli that the Marathas had occupied. Around 300 Marathas were killed there and many taken prisoner. Those who were left had their noses and ears cut off. Seeing the fright that set in the Maratha camps, the Peshwa ordered Narasing Rao Dhaigude, Shahji Bhonsle of Akkalkot and Mahimaji Sindhia to go to Chikkanayakanahalli with about 3000 cavalry. Mir Raza played an important role in checking all Maratha advances, and repeated attempts by the Peshwa to have him captured failed.

Haidar knew that any forward movement by him would be keenly observed and that the Marathas would crush him from both ends. He had to eliminate one front and decided to neutralize Gopal Rao Patwardhan's offensive. He created a false impression among the Marathas that he was slowly retreating to Srirangapatna and that some of his belongings were being sent back daily. The group that had kept a close watch on his moves thus felt relieved that the enemy was retreating and slackened their guard. At that time, Haidar planned his offensive. On the dark, new moon night of 25 February 1770 when the Maratha army under Gopal Rao Patwardhan, Daulat Rao Bhonsle and others was camping near Masur, Haidar made a surprise night attack. Despite a Muslim *gardi* informant from Haidar's camp giving Gopal Rao information that Haidar was contemplating such a move, the Maratha side took it lightly. The gardi told them that he had served under Peshwa Nanasaheb and had been a loyalist and hence had come to warn them and, if found false, they could put him under a guard and also cut off his arms and legs. Still, the Maratha side either did not believe him or were too complacent. Before they realized it, Haidar's guns were blazing and his rockets came on their tents in showers. Piexoto, who was part of this campaign, recounts:

> With about 2000 horse, 600 foot, 8 field pieces, 700 rocket boys, with flambeaus ready to be lighted, 16 pieces of hand artillery, the attack was launched. As soon as those who were to begin the attack were perceived by the enemy, they beat to arms but did nothing to endeavour to retreat, leaving their camp and tent and many of their worst horses behind them and waited for daylight to see whether they could recover anything . . . the Nabob gave orders for the whole of the artillery to fire with a high elevation . . . the enemy's camp was plundered . . . we took two colours from the Marathas, and also took some horses alive, with many tents and utensils. Abouts 200 horses were killed, but few people. On our side the loss was only three men.[4]

The noses and ears of the men in the Maratha ranks were also cut off.[5]

But Peshwa Madhav Rao was undeterred by these reverses and he carried forth to occupy all the major posts in the districts of Hassan and Belur. He reduced Nandidurga, Chikkaballapura, Doddaballapura, Kolar and Mulbagal and a vast part of the eastern territories of Mysore. Gopal Rao Patwardhan advised him to direct his attention to Bidanur instead, thereby diverting Haidar and also his strong positions in both Bangalore and Srirangapatna. But the Peshwa did not heed this advice. Tipu and Mir Raza kept up their attacks on the Marathas from various points and when outnumbered, would retreat into the forests whose topography they were well acquainted with. Haidar knew that in the past invasions, too, the Marathas seldom stayed on in the areas they conquered and the campaigns they undertook were more akin to raids. So, he was hopeful of being able to retrieve the losses of places once they left. And for them to leave, the onset of the monsoons was what he was desperately waiting for. But it was still the month of March and the rains were a few months ahead of his plans.

The Peshwa's advance was halted in mid-April 1770 by the obscure fort of Nijagal, which was about thirty miles north-west of Bangalore. Its killedar Sardar Khan provided stiff resistance, was well-stocked and had nearly 3000 men under his command there, even as the Marathas besieged him. For almost three months, he foiled numerous attempts by the Marathas to storm the fort. While directing the operations, the Peshwa's younger brother, Narayan Rao, too was wounded. Piqued at the unexpected obstacle coming his way, Madhav Rao ordered an instant storming of the fort, but failed again. In spite of a breach being effected in the wall of the fort, nearly six attempts to storm it were in vain. The Peshwa even offered to allow the garrison to leave the fort unharmed, if they surrendered. But this was ignored and the defence of the fort carried on. With the help of Madakari Nayaka of Chitradurga, Madhav Rao then decided to lead the assault himself. Finally on 1 May 1770, he managed to take the place after a strenuous campaign. Following the terrible custom of the Mysoreans, Madhav Rao, too, had the noses and ears of the garrison cut off. When Sardar Khan was being led for a similar treatment, the Peshwa noticed that despite the defeat, the man was a true soldier who held his head high and his body language exuded quiet confidence and dignity. When asked if he did not fear similar mutilation as his garrison had faced, Sardar Khan courageously replied that the mutilation might be his, but the disgrace would be the Peshwa's. Madhav Rao was quite stunned by the reply and he immediately ordered his unconditional release.

With the impending monsoons and also his own health battered after a deadly attack of consumption (tuberculosis), Madhav Rao decided to retreat from Mysore and left for Poona on 12 May 1770. Trimbak Rao Pethe, or Trimbak Mama as he was fondly called by all due to his family relations with the Peshwa, was left behind in the Carnatic as the chief of the army. Though Madhav Rao did not manage to crush Haidar as he had planned, he succeeded in conquering several forts and regions belonging to the latter. This was just the start of a longer offensive between the two, once the monsoons retreated.

Domestic Tumult

In the midst of the Maratha campaign, Haidar made a visit to Srirangapatna and made his usual courtesy call on the titular Maharaja Nanjaraja Wodeyar. Peixoto gives an account of the meeting in his characteristic style:

> The Nabob [Haidar] . . . was received by the King with attention in the customary form, which is, the King remains sitting, and the Nabob to throw himself at his feet. The King wanted to exempt the Nabob from this humble ceremony, but the Nabob did it instantly. The King then ordered him to sit down, which he did, after saying he could not sit in his presence. There was with the king, his mother, who, it is said, is a lady of good judgment, and daughter of the Rajah Nande Rajah [Nanjarajayya] . . . and after the compliments were over, during which the Queen mother looked very grave, the Nabob told the King that the Marrata [Maratha Peshwa] was come [sic] with great power to contribute that kingdom, and that he was asked a very great sum which seemed to him too much, wherefore he would rather fight

and shew him that this kingdom dreaded not his power, that he hath been in the field on that account and hath already shown his intentions . . . that he, the Marrata, did not stand to give battle, but only took satisfaction to ruin the country as much as possible, breaking, burning, and totally ruining the inhabitants, which he could not hinder him from, as the Marrata force did consist in cavalry, and his own in foot. Wherefore he acquainted him, that he might order him what he thought proper in this particular. The King answered him, 'I and this whole kingdom do not dread any invasion of the Marrata, nor any other enemy, as long as God preserves your life. All what (you) do for the utility, conservation and ease of the people, are precious enamels with which you augment your name. The security and defence of the kingdom is [sic] in your hand, and in me the confidence that you will prosper in everything.' The Nabob remained mute without answering the king, and without any farther long stay, took his leave and came to his Palace.[6]

This eyewitness account from Peixoto gives an important insight into the charade that the Wodeyar–Haidar equation was. Haidar had wilfully nurtured the false pretensions of being a humble servant who would not be ashamed of falling at the titular's feet in the public gaze, attempting to seek his counsel on important matters of state or warfare and submit the trophies of war to his feet. Everyone, including the Maharaja, knew that this was a farce being enacted, but they all carried on with it as it also gave Haidar the legitimacy and support of the people and the court that still held the royal family in great esteem. But Haidar knew that the young man who was now nearing adulthood was slowly getting restive about his own limitations and veritable captivity. He had been flexing his muscles through manipulations and representations sent to Haidar's adversaries seeking their help. All this had not gone unnoticed by Haidar, who knew that once the young man came into his own, he would prove to be a threat to his authority. The baser instincts eventually got the better of Haidar.

The young Maharaja who had just turned twenty-two was healthy as one of his age should be. One night, after his dinner, he was sent a cup of milk to drink. Little did Nanjaraja Wodeyar realize that it was to be his last drink. Shortly afterwards, by about 2 a.m., on 2 August 1770, he died mysteriously. The royal family was to realize to its horror later that the cup of milk had been sent by none other than Haidar. Peixoto confirms this in his account where he says: 'In the night he [the Maharaja] drank after supper a cup of milk which Hyder had sent him. Hyder pretended to be sorry and sent for the surgeon who replied that he left the king the previous night in sound health. For this, he was put into prison and condemned to pay a great sum into the Royal treasury . . . during the burial, even the silver vessels belonging to the royal family had to be brought from Hyder's palace.'[7] There was no way Haidar wanted to brook another insurgence from the royal family, as it had in the past threatened his very existence. If the life of a young man had to be snuffed out mercilessly for this, the tyranny in Haidar was rife enough to commit such remorseless acts. Wilks however mentions that since Nanjaraja Wodeyar had made vain attempts to open channels of communication with the Marathas, Haidar 'ordered him without hesitation to be strangled in the bath.'[8]

Hayavadana Rao reflects on this gruesome episode:

In the midst of his savage purpose, Haidar was, we have to concede, a man. He was not a mere monster, who mechanically perpetrated cold-blooded deeds. Despite the tendencies of the times and his own baser instincts, to which he fell a prey sometimes, there is enough in him to show that he was a humanized being. It is this humanizing touch in him that helped to individualize him and make him convincing as man among men. That explains to some small extent the great hold he had upon the imagination of the men of his time . . . we have seen in him thus far the play of at least three conflicting motives and passions—his love for money as means to an end, the end being political mastery; his hatred for everyone who comes in the way of attaining that mastery; and worse than either of these, his personal animosity against Nanjaraja [Wodeyar], whom he dreaded far more for his cunning than ever for the power that he might, perchance, wield against him to his discomfiture at a moment when he least expected it . . . when his personal feelings, however rise, as now and then they certainly do, superior to these animal instincts in him, then Haidar becomes for the moment a far different person and a truly impressive figure. His directions carry moral weight; his doings assume a mighty purpose; his fights lift him above the sordid and brutal ideas to which he seems to have been born heir to; in a word, he becomes a sort of symbol, despite his birth, religion and up-bringing, of the national fight that Mysore put up to avert the awful tragedy that the 18th century witnessed in Southern India.[9]

A fortnight later, Nanjaraja Wodeyar's eleven-year-old younger brother, Bettada Chamaraja Wodeyar VIII (and grandson of Nanjarajayya), was named the new Maharaja. With all perceived domestic threats to his authority having thus evanesced, Haidar could rest assured till the time the new incumbent attained majority, if at all he survived that age and did not start thinking for himself and acting independently. For now, having settled the domestic affair in cold blood, he could focus his energies on the next wave of the Maratha attacks that were waiting to happen.

Maratha Attacks Resume

With the monsoon behind them, the Marathas planned their next attack, though unfortunately for them, the Peshwa's continuing ill health kept him away from the campaign. But he dispatched 10,000 troops and ten cannons under Appaji Balwant and Malhar Rao Panse to join Trimbak Mama. Trimbak besieged Gurramkonda towards the end of September 1770, which was commanded by Saiyid Sahib, nephew of Mir Ali Raza. Saiyid Sahib gave a stout defence for nearly two months and eventually capitulated after the intercession of Murar Rao. Gopal Rao Patwardhan meanwhile defeated three Mysorean generals, Chandroji Jadhav, Balaji Pant and Syed Muhammad, who were totally taken by surprise by him at Punganuru. Gopal Rao Patwardhan then encamped between Kolar and Mulbagal. His health then rapidly declined after which Gopal Rao Patwardhan retreated to Miraj, where he eventually died in early 1771, though he was barely fifty years old then. He had been one of the chief defenders of the Maratha empire against Haidar Ali and a steadfast loyalist of Peshwa Madhav Rao.

Gopal Rao's eldest brother, Vaman Rao, though himself afflicted by a chest ailment, was asked to join Trimbak Rao with his troops. He reached the Kanakagiri camp and thereafter Devadurga that was quickly captured. The Mysorean detachments that were sent to counter the Marathas were all vanquished completely by Trimbak Rao. With a force of 12,000 horse, 15,000 regular infantry, 1000 peons or irregular infantry, armed with matchlocks, and forty field-guns, Haidar set off from Srirangapatna. But the opposing force was almost double his with 40,000 horse and 10,000 infantry. Haidar hoped to deceive Trimbak Rao by tying torches to the horns of 2000 bullocks that were to be let loose in the direction of the Maratha army. He assumed that the Marathas would assume this to be the direction of the opponent and set forth and, at that point, he would make a rear attack on them. However, Trimbak Rao was too smart for Haidar and saw through this game plan. He pursued Haidar, who in his usual nimble way, managed to escape through the Magadi forests and eventually took shelter in the Melukote hills towards the end of February 1771. Trimbak Rao then collected all his detachments and moved to the siege of Melukote. Sakharam Hari Gupte cut off all supplies coming to Haidar from the capital city of Srirangapatna.

Melukote was an ancient temple-town with a hoary history and had been blessed by the presence of the tenth-century philosopher, social reformer and exponent of Srivaishnavism, Sri Ramanujacharya. Melukote (or Thirunarayanapura) had emerged as an important citadel of Sri Vaishnava philosophy and traditions thereafter. It was to these hills and the fort there that Haidar escaped, hotly pursued and besieged by the Marathas. With his entire infantry and artillery,

Haidar opened constant fire and musketry to drive them away, but they continued to surround the fort from a distance. He was held in this position for nearly eight days, after which his provisions began to dwindle. By 5 March 1771, he decided to quietly retreat to Srirangapatna which was about twenty-two miles away through the route of the hills of Chinkurli. By night, Haidar, after cutting down the jungle behind the hills and already having sent Mir Ali Raza Khan with all the artillery, set off with his horse and regular foot. After midnight, they began beating of the *noubats* or customary music to give a false impression to the enemy that the headquarters were still active. Tipu was given the task of ensuring that the baggage was set in motion. But the terrain was extremely rocky and uneven and they could all barely cross seven to eight miles by sunrise. By then, the Maratha scouts noticed the movements and informed Trimbak Rao about Haidar's flight. Trimbak Rao ordered his troops to follow them and bring their artillery. The baggage that Haidar had commissioned to Tipu to bring forth was however lost somewhere in the woods and there was no sight of it.

Haidar had apparently been drinking a lot the previous evening before their unexpected flight. Wilks mentions that he was normally addicted to drinking, though the matter would be strictly concealed and managed within his inner circle, possibly for religious reasons. It was not known if he used strong liquors for sensual indulgence or to induce sleep, but he resorted to them on most nights before retiring to bed. All the battles and tumult seemed to have naturally taken their toll on Haidar's peace of mind and turned him into an insomniac. Once in a war tent he had commented to his close associate Ghulam Ali that the state of a yogi was much better than his envied monarchy as the former sees no conspirators when awake, and no assassins when asleep.[10] Through the night of trudging through the jungle, Haidar could naturally not catch a wink of sleep. The insomnia and the acute embarrassment of being discovered by the enemy, combined with the effect of alcohol the previous evening, made Haidar extremely irritated and livid. When he did not find Tipu readily at the helm, he summoned him, hurled the vilest of invectives on him and, in a fit of drunken rage, seized a large cane from the hand of one of his attendants and in full public view, flogged him mercilessly.[11] Tipu was aghast at the treatment his father had meted out to him and, withdrawing from his presence, dashed his turban and sword to the ground and declared, in the name of Allah and his Prophet, that his father could now fight this battle himself and he would not draw his sword for the day. He kept his word and the division was commanded by Yaseen Khan Wunti Kudri.

The Battle of Chinkurli

Haidar of course galloped away towards Srirangapatna while ordering his troops '*Chellaou, Chellaou*' or get on, keep going. He managed to reach Chinkurli, about eleven miles from Srirangapatna. The Maratha cavalry had surrounded them in every direction and even captured one of Haidar's guns and used that to start firing from the banks of the Moti Talab or the Pearl Tank (now called Tonnuru Kere). But there was no cohesion and direction within the Maratha camp and each commander was left to his own measures. By then, the sun had come up and in a lot of cross-firing, Trimbak Rao was also slightly wounded when a bullet shot past his ear. He and Balwant Rao beat a hasty retreat, Nilkanth Rao Patwardhan was killed by a musket ball and it seemed as if the Marathas might lose. But then a shot from one of the Maratha cannons struck a few rockets on the Mysorean side. They were laden on camels and when they exploded, they caused immense disarray among the animals that started running helter-skelter. The fire soon spread to the ammunition boxes and blew them all up. Seeing the confusion in the enemy camp, with the soldiers running amok in distress, the Marathas decided to make a frontal attack.

What followed was a scene of abject plunder and slaughter at the hands of the Maratha irregulars, the Pindaris, who looted Haidar's army. Twenty-five guns of large size, thirteen elephants, fifty camels, three howdahs or silver castles and two chests containing jewels, two camel loads of rich vests and several kettledrums and banners, oxen, bullocks and nearly 7000–8000 horses were captured by the

Marathas.[12] Among those who fell in the disaster were fifty Europeans and Mysorean officers such as Narayana Rao, Srinivasa Jivaji and Lala Mian, the son-in-law of Haidar's elder brother, Shahabaz. Mir Ali Raza Khan, Ali Zaman Khan, Abdul Muhammad Mirdhe and Yaseen Khan Wunti Kudri among Haidar's chief officers were taken prisoners. In fact, Yaseen Khan Wunti Kudri, who had a likeness to his master, was actually mistaken for Haidar by the Marathas who were jubilant that they had succeeded in capturing their hated enemy. Yaseen Khan was lying unconscious on the ground, having been severely wounded in the explosion, and was picked up by the Marathas, but treated with respect as a state prisoner as they thought that he was Haidar. Fazalullah Khan was the only one who managed to display some sagacity and, with his followers, managed to cut through the Maratha ranks when they were intending to plunder. Though his army was devastated in this entire episode, known as the 'Chinkurli disaster,' Haidar somehow managed to flee to Srirangapatna in utter fright with Ghazi Khan and others. He took advantage of the Marathas slackening under the mistaken notion of having captured him after they got Yaseen Khan. In a comedy of errors, Yaseen Khan too played the imposter role to perfection, lulling the Marathas into believing that they had indeed captured their dreaded foe. It took them nearly eight to ten days to realize the true identity of Yaseen Khan, by which time Haidar quickly stripped his clothes off and fled the field to regroup.

Meanwhile, Tipu had gone missing after the tantrum he had thrown and Haidar, now repentant for his rude outburst, prayed for his son at the tomb of Khadar Wali in Srirangapatna after reaching the capital. Wilks mentions that Haidar had lost all hopes of his son being alive: 'Hyder, having in the meanwhile given him up as lost, long continued passionately to exclaim, in terms which indicated more resignation than his manner evinced, "God gave him, and God hath taken him away," himself remaining at a small mosque to the north of the river, and refusing to enter the capital.'[13]

Tipu had, by then, been surrounded by enemy forces from all sides. He thereafter disguised himself as a mendicant (*fakir*), along with Syed Muhammad, and they slipped away, literally begging their way through the Maratha ranks. He joined his father at the tomb where the latter was praying for his well-being. Kirmani writes in his characteristic hyperbole that Haidar 'threw open the door of his treasury of gold and jewels, to every horseman or foot soldier who had escaped from that disastrous battle. He gave his two handsful [sic] of gold, and to every man who returned with his horse and arms, he gave besides an honorary dress, a present of five handsful [sic] of gold.'[14] Haidar obviously knew the value of what it meant to come back alive from that carnage of a battle. It had been a day of unmitigated disaster for him and was the most shocking and embarrassing defeat the Mysore army had faced in recent times. All of Haidar's military equipment was plundered and trampled beneath the hoofs of the Maratha horses. His store department and artillery had fallen into their hands; several of his officers were killed, wounded or taken prisoner. But as Wilks rightly surmises that while 'the day was lost by Hyder, it was not won by the Mahrattas.'[15]

Interestingly, a curious document entitled 'An Agreement' was discovered decades later in the palace of Srirangapatna after its fall to the British. It was a narrow slip, about 12 inches long, and had eight articles in it and lay deposited in a basket among several other articles belonging to the time of Haidar Ali. It bore the signature of 'Tippoo Sultan,' had the royal signet or ring-seal and the date of 1184 Hijri (roughly around this period of 1770 CE). The eight articles read as follows:

1. I will not do [any] one thing without the pleasure of your blessed Majesty, Lord of Benefits [or my bountiful Lord]: if I do, let me be punished, in whatever manner may seem fitting to your auspicious mind.
2. If, in the affairs of the *Sircar*, I should commit theft, or be guilty of fraud, great or small, let me, as the due punishment thereof, be strangled.
3. If I be guilty of prevarication, or misrepresentation, or of deceit, the due punishment thereof is this same strangulation.
4. Without the orders of the Presence, I will not receive from anyone *Nuzzers*; neither will I take things from any one

[meaning perhaps forcibly]: if I do, let my nose be cut off, and let me be driven out from the city.

5. If, excepting on the affairs of the *Sircar*, I should hold conversation [probably cabal or intrigue] with any person, or be guilty of deceit, let me, in punishment thereof, be stretched on a cross.

6. Whenever a country shall be committed to my charge by the *Sircar*, and an army be placed under my command, I will carry on all business regarding the same, with the advice, and through the medium of such confidential persons as may be appointed [for the purpose] by the Sircar; and if I transact such affairs through any other channel than this, let me be strangled.

7. If there should be any occasion for correspondence by writing, or to buy or give [away] anything, or any letter should arrive from any place, I will do nothing [in such matters] without the concurrence and advice of the person appointed by the *Sircar*.

8. I have written and delivered these few articles of my own free will, keeping the contents whereof in my heart's remembrance, I will act in each article accordingly. If I forget this, and act in any other [or different] manner, let me be punished, agreeably to the foregoing writing.[16]

This bewildering document was discovered by William Kirkpatrick who was assigned the task of cataloguing and making sense of the heap of papers that were found in the palace at Srirangapatna in 1799. As Kirkpatrick notes: 'The place in which it was discovered, joined to the seal and internal evidence furnished by its extraordinary tenor, sufficiently establishes its genuineness; but whether the engagement it contains was voluntarily entered into by the Sultan, or exacted by Hyder, does not appear. The latter however, is not unlikely to have been the case, notwithstanding what the writer himself declares in the eighth article.'[17] Given the accounts of chroniclers like Kirmani, Piexoto and De La Tour, who had an insider's view into the affairs in Mysore then and were witness to the rapport between the father

and son that they have reported on several occasions, including
Tipu's successful campaigns during the First Anglo–Mysore War
and Haidar's joy over it, this 'agreement' from the son to the
father is mystifying. At what point the relationship or the trust
that Haidar seemed to repose in his son soured, necessitating that
such a document be signed thereafter, is completely unknown. All
we know from the account of Wilks is the annoyance with which
Haidar caned his son during the Chinkurli episode and the latter's
angry outburst at being so humiliated in public. Was that episode
a catalyst to him demanding such an undertaking from his son, or
did Tipu voluntarily decide to mollify his father by committing
himself to such extreme clauses, we will possibly never know. But
the mention of crimes—petty ones to graver—theft, fraud, deceit,
misrepresentation, intrigue and so on, and the punishments for each
thereof, suggests, if proactively initiated by Haidar, that all was not
well between the duo and that he held his son in little esteem possibly
due to some past misdemeanours and transgressions. Kirkpatrick
also conjectures that such extreme corporal punishments from his
father possibly contributed to Tipu, too, being as cruel and heartless
with anyone who disobeyed him or was accused of malfeasance.[18]

The Maratha Campaign Continues

Returning to the conflict with the Marathas that Haidar faced, the
former was overjoyed by the loot that they had captured at Chinkurli.
They spent several days plundering and desolating the country, rather
than striking at Haider when he was militarily and psychologically
at his ebb. Unwittingly, and in possible complacency, they allowed
Haidar about ten days to regroup himself. As mentioned earlier,
they were in a world of make-believe that they had captured Haidar
already, while in reality it was Yaseen Khan. As Kirmani writes:
'Yaseen Khan being a prudent man, who, merely from gratitude,
endeavoured to shield his master from injury . . . laughed in his
sleeve at the soft flattering words of Trimuk [Trimbak], but gave
him no answer. When however, in the course of about eight or ten

days, Trimuk was informed, that the Nawaub [Haidar] was safe, and that he was assembling troops, collecting stores, and mounting guns, to strengthen the fort, he became aware that his prisoner was one of the Nawaub's faithful and devoted servants, and was ashamed of his own want of discernment; and he marched forthwith to attack the fort.'[19]

By then, Haidar had strengthened the Srirangapatna fort on all sides, erected new works and mounted guns on important posts. Trimbak Rao belatedly marched towards Srirangapatna and laid siege to it for nearly a month and three days—this, much against the wishes of the Peshwa who had advised him to take Bidanur, instead, as both Srirangapatna and Bangalore were strong bastions. Haidar managed to lure away the battle-weary Maratha soldiers, enticing them with gifts and money. Haidar even dispatched his commander Mohammad Ali, on the latter's incessant request, to stealthily go by night and capture the Maratha battery when they were asleep. The Marathas were smug enough to not even realize that it was an enemy unit that was coming up to the rear of their battery. A huge carnage of the Maratha soldiers followed. Kirmani recounts: 'He [Mohammad Ali] without hesitation marched into the battery and instantly gave his orders to his men to attack, and throwing their hand grenades on the heads of these worshippers of pride, they raised out of them the black smoke of destruction, and with the merciless sword cut off the heads of the soldiers, pioneers and men lying in the battery and trenches, and laid them up in heaps. They then buried all the larger guns, but the light guns, being more useful and available, were sent off to the presence [Haidar].'[20] During the return though, when many of his soldiers were wounded by the Maratha counter-attack, Mohammad Ali committed the most barbaric act of butchering his own wounded men, so that their wailings did not communicate the news of his flight to the opponent.[21] On his victorious arrival at the Srirangapatna fort, Mohammad Ali was welcomed and addressed by the honorific of 'son' by Haidar.

Eventually, the Marathas diluted the siege by dividing the army into two units—one that stayed on in Srirangapatna and another that descended through the Gajjalahatti Pass, with the intent of attacking the Mysorean districts of Coimbatore, Palghat and Dindigul. Trimbak Rao sent emissaries to Muhammad Ali, the British and the French seeking from each their help against Mysore. But none of them were forthcoming and Trimbak Rao's gains in Chinkurli were fast fading into a potential disaster.

On a festive occasion, Trimbak Rao and his army decided to bathe in the holy Sangam or confluence of two rivers in Srirangapatna and offer their prayers. The army, which had been so fatigued after so many months of war, decided to enjoy some amusements and frolicked and swam around in the waters. Haidar had received information about this movement and dispatched both Tipu as well as Mohammad Ali under the command of Ghazi Khan, with 4000 matchlockmen, 400 Pindaris and four guns. Kirmani narrates:

> The commandant now suddenly charged them, and with the fire of guns and musketry broke their ranks and sent a great many of them to their eternal abodes. In this skirmish two or three chiefs of the Mahrattas were killed and the elephant which carried the flag and kettle-drums was also killed. Ghazi Khan and Haidar's son [implying Mohammad Ali perhaps] esteeming this a most favourable opportunity, galloped their horse at once into the midst of the fugitives; and as long as they had strength, withdrew not their hands from spoil and slaughter; following the fugitives half a fursung, taking four or five thousand horses, and two thousand prisoners . . . and a great quantity of plunder. The face of Trimuk [sic: Trimbak], on his hearing this intelligence, became yellow, and in the greatest haste and trepidation, with his clothes wet and his lips dry, he returned and encamped near the Mooti Talaub or Tank.[22]

Trimbak then sought an auspicious date to begin cannonading the fort. But by then, Haidar had managed to raise his forces to about 10,000, had completely scorched the earth around the capital, causing great distress for food and supplies among the Maratha army. Even fodder for the animals was not easily available for them and their morale was obviously dipping by the day. Sensing their discomfiture, Haidar sent a peace proposal promising to pay 45 lakh over three years in return for restoration of all the conquered territories. The Marathas refused to accept these terms and Haidar, who was now in a position of relative control, refused to climb down. With few options left, Trimbak Rao withdrew the siege and moved again towards Moti Talab.

These isolated incidents of success by the Mysorean forces did not dampen the spirits of the Marathas though. Negotiations through Appaji Ram, too, continued in parallel, even as the skirmishes were underway. Trimbak Rao demanded Rs 60 lakh and Haidar's support in attacking Arcot. He was willing to hand over areas around Srirangapatna that had been occupied but for other places like Chikkaballapura, Nandigad and so on, he wanted Haidar to confer with the Peshwa. The negotiations ended abruptly as neither party was agreeable.

Trimbak Rao then received a distress message from the Raja of Tanjore that he had been besieged by Muhammad Ali of Arcot and sought his help. Leaving Vaman Rao at the helm of the Mysore campaign, Trimbak rushed to Tanjore, by which time, Muhammad Ali had lifted the siege. He collected Rs 4 lakh from the Raja and also from Muhammad Ali, then entered Baramahal, and looted Coimbatore and other possessions of Haidar between September 1771 and February 1772. While Trimbak was in the Carnatic, Tipu inflicted a crushing defeat on him near Dharmapuri, while Mohammad Ali managed to vanquish the Maratha troops at Kaveripatnam and secured the release of many prisoners of Chinkurli.

The Marathas were being thus continuously harassed and attacked at regular intervals by Mysorean detachments. On one occasion, at Chennarayapatna, Tipu, with about 5000–6000 regular and irregular foot, attacked by night a huge Maratha replenishment that was coming in from Poona. The contingent had 8000 regular horses, 10,000 regular infantry and an immense supply of stores, provisions and treasures carried on thirty elephants, 100 camels and fifty mules. There was a large cache of gold and silver items, as well as ammunition. Kirmani records: 'Tippoo at once assailed them in suchwise [sic] that he did not allow one among them to escape in safety or fail to take every article of the least value belonging to the Mahrattas including their treasure, and this done, he sent them off to the capital Puttun [Srirangapatna] or rather to his illustrious father, while he himself marched toward Nuggur [Nagar/Bidanur].'[23]

Trimbak encamped at Bangalore and was contemplating an attack of Bidanur, when he received news from the Peshwa that his health had deteriorated terminally and hence all detachments were needed to report back in Poona. After two months of back and forth, peace was finally sealed between the Marathas and Haidar. The Marathas were to retain Sira, Doddaballapura, Hoskote and Kolar, in addition to Gurramkonda, Chennarayadurga and Maddagiri. Haidar's northern frontiers were thus reduced now to lesser than they were under the Mysore royal house. The rest of whatever was left of the territories conquered was restored to Haidar, who had to pay Rs 50 lakh and an additional Rs 10 lakh as darbar charges of compensation to Trimbak Rao and his sardars. Haidar paid Rs 24 lakh in cash, another five in kind and the rest was on banker security. The negotiations and the Maratha campaign ended in July 1772.

It must be mentioned here that the repeated attacks of the Marathas, especially Madhav Rao's protracted campaign from 1770 to 1772, left several areas in Mysore completely ravaged. Even the holy town of Melukote was not spared. Francis Buchanan, a Scottish physician who had made significant contributions as a geographer, botanist and zoologist, travelled extensively through India, including South India. After the fall of Tipu Sultan in 1799, he undertook a survey of the entire southern country from Madras to Mysore and Malabar, documenting in fine detail the lives of common Indians, their occupations, the varied flora and fauna, festivals, oral histories and traditions of the times. Writing on 29 August 1800, he describes the greatness of Melukote [Mail-cotay as he calls it] that he visited as a seat of Sri Vaishnava philosophy and Sanskrit learning. Buchanan states:

Soon after this period, the Maratthas gained a victory over Hyder, and encamped for some time on the south side of the hill. The Brahmans here were too cunning to be caught, and the place was entirely deserted; but even the temples of their gods did not escape Marattah rapacity. For the sake of the iron-work and to get at it easily, they burned the immense wooden *Raths*, or chariots on which the idols are carried in procession; and the fire spread to the religious buildings, some of which were entirely consumed. A sufficient number, however, still remain . . . the town has never recovered itself since the first Mahrattah invasion. Hyder, indeed, allowed to the Brahmans the full enjoyment of their revenues; but his son first reduced their lands to 6000 Pagodas a year; then to four; then to two; and at length to one thousand; finally, he entirely took away their land, and gave them an annual pension of 1000 Pagodas.[24]

Buchanan's account is full of several such locations in Mysore that had never recovered from the excesses of Maratha ravages. About Chinya in Mandya, he writes on 28 August 1800 that: 'It was formerly of some note; but about 30 years ago [implying this latest mentioned campaign] it was destroyed by the Marattah army, then attacking Hyder, and it has never since recovered.'[25] About Katte Malavady too, Buchanan records on 9 September 1800: 'About thirty years ago it was fully inhabited, and had a large suburb (*Petta*); while the cultivation all around was complete. At that period a Marattah army, commanded by Badji Row [sic], laid everything waste, and most of the inhabitants perished of hunger. So complete was the destruction, that even the excellent government of Hyder did not restore to the district more than half of its former cultivation. The town never regained its inhabitants, and was occupied by forty or fifty houses of Brahmans, who lived scattered amid the ruins.'[26] About Satyagala, he states that 'a party of Marattah plunderers ravaged all this neighbourhood; and they were followed by a dreadful famine, in which 400 families in Satteagala perished of hunger.'[27] Several more such towns are mentioned by Buchanan in Chitradurga, Hassan,

Coorg, Davanagere, Chamarajanagara and other districts in modern Karnataka that simply could not resurrect themselves, even three decades after the pillage and plunder. Thus, the impact of these invasions was borne by common Mysoreans, perhaps several times more than the ruling class. However, in the battles of those times, these possibly were unavoidable collateral damage that common people of any dominion faced when an oppressive invading army entered its territories.

This campaign exposed Haidar's weaknesses completely, bringing him immense disgrace, and wore the sheen off his spectacular victory against the British at the gates of Madras in 1769. It also brought about a complete change in Haidar's attitude towards the British who had remained coyly non-committal throughout this period, despite their treaty obligations to help Mysore in the eventuality of external aggression. This brought about in Haidar a distinctive hatred for British duplicity and he realized that their alleged friendship was not something that he could count on. N.K. Sinha summarizes this change in Haidar:

> This campaign, so inglorious in Haidar's career, was largely responsible for the strong anti-British turn of later Mysore foreign policy. Haidar's caustic reply to a query of Srinivas Rao, the British vakil, in July 1782 explains what opinion he formed of the value of the alliance with the British after the experience of these months. He said: 'When the Marathas had entered my country, I wrote them in a variety of ways, desiring them to send succour. In reply they at first told me that they would send them, and after some time they said they had written to Europe and expected orders from thence. To this I urged that it would be a year and six months before their orders could be obtained from Europe and of what use would their succour be then. The Governor's answer was that without orders from Europe they could do nothing and yet at length after a long time had elapsed, they pretended that till then they had received no directions.' Trimbak Rao contributed materially to bringing about this estrangement. Haidar could not

easily forget these months of stress and strife . . . the British did not join him [Trimbak] against Haidar, nor Haidar against the British. But in Haidar's eyes the value of British friendship stood clearly revealed.[28]

Turmoil in Poona

Meanwhile, catastrophe awaited the Marathas in Poona. After a prolonged illness, as he was suffering from tuberculosis, the young and dynamic Peshwa Madhav Rao passed away on 18 November 1772 at the young age of twenty-eight. He had succeeded in bringing the Maratha empire out of the shadows of the devastation of Panipat. It might be no exaggeration to state that had Madhav Rao lived longer, the history of India might have taken a different turn and it might not have been that easy for the British to subjugate the country. He was succeeded by his young and tactless brother, Narayan Rao, with his uncle Raghunath Rao (or Raghoba as he was called) as the regent. As mentioned earlier, Raghoba had always coveted the position of the Peshwa and he was miffed that he had missed the opportunity twice—once when his brother Nanasaheb had died and he had assumed that he would succeed him and now, to Narayan Rao. His outspoken wife Anandi Bai's scornful jibes and taunts deepened his ambitions. Narayan Rao realized that there was trouble brewing and began to send feelers to both Nizam Ali and Haidar, seeking to imprison Raghoba. He was finally arrested, and in prison, Raghoba conspired with the gardis, a pindari-like tribe who were in charge of the prison. Raghoba gave them a letter that proved to be decisive. For an exchange of 5 lakh and three forts, he issued a forged document to the gardis led by Sumer Singh and Muhammad Isaf, with the message 'Capture the Peshwa.' The letter however conveniently found its way to the apartments of Anandi Bai for her perusal. So angered was she by the shabby treatment meted to her husband that she appended the message with the phrase 'put him to death' (*dharave* or capture, in Marathi, was changed to *maarave* or kill).

On 30 August 1773, Narayan Rao was resting in the courtyard after lunch when the gardis barged in and demanded their arrears. On Narayan Rao's reprimand, they unsheathed their swords and got ready to strike, even as the harried Peshwa ran helter-skelter in his palace, seeking protection. He was eventually caught and mercilessly hacked to death by Sumer Singh Gardi. Raghoba was released from prison and fulfilled his ambition of becoming the Peshwa the very following day. This was chiefly because of his military might at that time; also there was no other member of the Peshwa family available for succession. The murdered Peshwa's wife was pregnant and was expecting a child very soon. Garnering support for his claim to the position which he knew he had taken over illegitimately, Raghoba even concluded a peace treaty in Kalyandurg with Haidar with whom he had a long-standing equation of bonhomie in anticipation of this very occasion. It was agreed that the entire area north of Srirangapatna, up to the banks of the Krishna River, extending to Badami, Jalahalli, Sira, Maddagiri, Hoskote, Doddaballapura and Chennarayadurga would be restored to Haidar. A reduced subsidy of Rs 6 lakh was to be paid to Raghoba.

When Raghoba's half-brother Baji Rao Barve, along with Haidar's men, reached Sira, the killedar there, Bapuji Sindhia, the son of Mahimaji Sindhia, refused to honour the words of Raghoba whom he did not recognize as the legitimate Peshwa. Haidar then sent Tipu to conquer Sira, which he did after a spirited resistance from Sindhia for three months. Bapuji was taken prisoner and sent to Srirangapatna. Maddagiri and Chennarayadurga too fell in quick succession. The other areas too including Hoskote, Doddaballapura and Gurramkonda had to be wrested back forcefully as the Marathas were refusing to honour any word that Raghoba had given to Haidar. But, as Wilks writes, 'in one short campaign, from September 1773 till February 1774, he [Haidar] . . . completely reconquered every place that had been wrested from him by the Mahrattas.'[29]

Meanwhile, Nana Phadnis and the other nobles and chieftains of the Peshwa court who detested the turn of events formed the *Barbhai* or union of twelve chiefs and ministers to oust Raghoba from the position that he had treacherously occupied. The wise statesman Balaji Janardhan 'Nana' Phadnis belonged to a hereditary family that had been serving the Peshwas on financial and administrative matters for three generations. Nana Phadnis had been a close associate of Peshwa Madhav Rao and honed his administrative skills under him. He became quite the custodian of the moral compass of the Maratha Empire, after the shocking assassination of Peshwa Narayana Rao.

Around this time, Narayana Rao's widow Ganga Bai gave birth to a boy who was named Madhav Rao II. The Barbhai tied the Mohur of the Peshwaship to the child in his cradle and named him 'Srimant Peshwa Sawai Madhav Rao' with Nana Phadnis as his regent and guardian. A strict internal investigation by Ramshastri Prabhune, the chief judge of the Peshwa period, proclaimed Raghoba as guilty of the murder of his nephew and severely castigated him. A civil war broke out within the Maratha establishment in 1773, taking advantage of which the British managed to grab the island of Salsette, adjacent to Bombay. The Chhatrapati in Satara thereafter stripped Raghoba of his office in February 1774 and he was declared a state offender. Anticipating trouble for himself, Raghoba fled to Bombay and on 6 March 1775, signed the Treaty of Surat with the British to help him regain the Peshwaship. This triggered the first Anglo–Maratha war. Subsequent to his signing the treaty, Raghoba addressed a letter to Haidar, through Baji Rao Barve, asking the latter 'to take possession of the whole of the Mahratta territory up to the right bank of the Kitsna [Krishna River]; and be ready from that advanced position to assist Ragoba in the execution of his designs, with military as well as pecuniary aid.'[30] Haidar accordingly even sent Rs 16 lakh for the assistance of Raghoba.

The Government in Calcutta, under the powers vested in them by the Regulating Act of 1773, however dropped the cause of Raghoba after concluding the treaty with him in Surat, on the pretext that it was signed without taking due permissions. They instead began negotiating with the Barbhai group in Poona and even concluded the Treaty of Purandhar with them in March 1776. Raghoba, who had taken flight from home and was banking on British support, was now literally left in the lurch. At this juncture, he even contemplated taking asylum in Haidar's court as he counted on him as an ally.[31] The British however renewed their treaty with Raghoba only in 1778, by which time he had grown quite apprehensive about their true designs.

For Mysore and Haidar, the tumultuous situation in Poona came like a godsend. It enhanced his own bargaining power with Poona and he demanded the confirmation of territories ceded to him by Raghoba. The Marathas were too embroiled in their own internal squabbles to bother to invade or trouble Mysore as they had been doing so catastrophically in the last couple of years. This gave Haidar the opportunity to establish some semblance of peace in his kingdom, quell all rebellions in his dominion and outside, punish those who had betrayed him and also regain the territories he had lost in earlier battles. The palegars of Chitradurga and Harpanahalli were attacked for supporting the Marathas during their campaign and heavy fines were levied on them.

Malabar and Coorg Expedition

The brewing revolts of the Nairs in Malabar had been temporarily quelled during the peak of the First Anglo–Mysore War when Haidar had somehow managed to buy peace. But given Haidar's diversion in wars with the British and the Marathas, the Zamorin happily forgot to pay his tributes and the Nair unrest was once again catching momentum in 1773. Haidar sent his agents Rangappa Nayaka and Ramagiri Channarajayya to demand arrears, but they were treacherously slain by the Nairs. Incensed by this, Haidar dispatched a detachment of 40,000 men under Berki Srinivasa Rao and Saiyid Sahib. On hearing about this force leaving Mysore for his dominion, the Zamorin quickly concluded a treaty with the French at Mahe on 12 January 1774, becoming their vassal and seeking their protection. M. Dupart, the French Governor, immediately sent a detachment to Calicut to aid the Zamorin and also sent messages to Srinivasa Rao that he desist from attacking as the place was now their protectorate. But disregarding their warnings, Berki Srinivasa Rao continued his march and forced Calicut to surrender. The French conveniently withdrew to Mahe without offering any support, and the Zamorin himself fled in fright to Travancore. The Nairs were castigated for repeatedly creating unrest. Srinivasa Rao was then stationed as the faujdar of the place to maintain peace and control over the region.

Haidar also realized that if he had to keep Malabar under control, the interjacent principality of Coorg needed to be subdued. With this intent, he entered Coorg in March 1774. He had an axe to grind with the Raja of Coorg as well, as the latter had not allowed free passage for the Mysore convoys during the Maratha invasion of 1771. When Mohammad Ali had marched through Periapatna against Trimbak Rao, the Raja had treacherously got the heads of the Mysorean garrison, that was stationed at the fort of Madikeri, cut off, thus harming the campaign.

There was also a succession war in Coorg. The joint rulers Muddaraja and Muddaiah had both died in quick succession by 1770. Mudduraja's younger brother, Lingaraja, who had, in an earlier campaign against Mysore, even beaten Fazalullah Khan demanded the throne for himself as he had earlier let his brothers rule Coorg jointly. But Malliaiah, the son of Muddaiah, one of the deceased Rajas, insisted that his son Devapparaja was the rightful heir. This split the royal house of Coorg right in the middle, much to the delight of Haidar. Lingaraja then fled from Coorg and ironically sought shelter in Mysore along with his nephews and kept prevailing upon Haidar to support his claim. But at that time, Haidar was caught in a life and death situation with the Maratha invasion and the Chinkurli disaster and could obviously not divert his attention to Coorg. Lingaraja encouraged Haidar that an invasion of bounteous Coorg would immensely help Mysore which had been ravaged by famine after the Maratha invasions. Lingaraja facilitated the entry of Haidar into Coorg in 1773 and organized his supporters there to rally behind the Mysorean army.

Haidar's invasion of Coorg was totally unexpected. He assembled on a woody hill and declared a reward of Rs 5 for each head of a Coorgi (Kodava) that was submitted to him. He sat there ghoulishly superintending the submissions and dispensing the reward money as heads began to pile up. Nearly 700 had been thus paid for, when a peon came forth and deposited two heads of handsome men.[32] Suddenly, Haidar seems to have been beset with pity and humane feelings and reprimanded the peon if he felt no compunction in decapitating such comely heads. Had it not been for the 'beauty' of the heads, the barbarity might have still continued. But he ordered this to stop and have the prisoners brought in. The conquest was thus completed with little effort. Madikeri, Patteri Nadu, Bale Nadu and other places in Coorg easily fell to his might and the Raja, Devapparaja, ran away from the scene. Haidar's main aim was to quell any revolts here and to gain direct and easy access to Malabar. He erected the fort of Madikeri in a central location, confirmed the land holders of their possessions at a slightly increased revenue and returned to Srirangapatna victoriously by June 1774. Devapparaja had fled initially to Kottayam where he was plundered. He then escaped to the Maratha territories in disguise but was captured by Haidar's men in Harihar and sent to Srirangapatna, where he was put to death along with his children in 1774. This brought to an end the Horamale branch of the royal family. Coorg was restored to Lingaraja on the promise of an annual tribute of Rs 24,000 and the surrender of Suliya, Yelu Savira Seeme and two other districts to Mysore. He was however permitted to take a portion of Waynad.

But shortly after his departure from Coorg, an insurrection began to brew there. This was largely fuelled by the locals who resented the foreign yoke of Mysore interfering in their daily lives and also the high rate of revenues that were levied on them. The highest revenue they had ever paid was a tenth of the produce, which had now been substantially hiked by Haidar. Protesting against these excesses, they destroyed all the minor establishments that had sprung up all over Coorg for collecting revenues and also surrounded the new capital of Madikeri to reduce it by famine. Haidar could not afford another rebellion here and so he decided to deal with the situation very firmly and suppress it with a single, mighty blow. His entire infantry in several columns was pushed into Coorg and every man who was suspected as being above the class of an ordinary soldier was ruthlessly hanged. A series of blockhouses were erected in every part of the region to interconnect them and also to intimidate the locals. All of this was completed by early 1775.

Opponents Combine

Haidar's old foes, Murar Rao in Gutti and Basalat Jung in Adoni, were meanwhile confabulating with the courts in Poona and Hyderabad to contemplate a combined incursion into Mysore. Nizam Ali was convinced by them to send his Commander-in-Chief Ibrahim Khan Dhoonsa with a large force, artillery and stores. They directed their attention to Bellary, which had repulsed Haidar in 1769, but had thence reverted to his control. Basalat's commander Safdar Jung, Devichand Kirtiwant, the Dewan of Adoni, and the French troops of 200 under Lally besieged Bellary. After several months, Haidar finally decided to rush to Bellary's aid by November 1775, along with his daring commander Mohammad Ali. His troops attacked the camp of Basalat Jung from every side, discharging rockets, matchlocks, arrows and camel swivels. It was a total rout and Kirtiwant, too, was killed and the French fled leaving behind their baggage, tents and standards for Mysorean looters. Haidar then marched to Adoni and extracted from Basalat Jung Rs 10 lakh towards two months of salary for his military and also reimbursed himself a lakh of pagodas on the condition that Jung would not plunder his jagirs henceforth. Haidar was determined to punish Dhoonsa too, but he had retreated by then to Hyderabad after the news of the fall of Bellary. Haidar was now determined to face Murar Rao who had been a thorn in the flesh of Mysore since the times of the shameful Tiruchirapalli campaign.

Haidar tried to befriend Murar Rao with cordial messages, informing him about his arrival at the latter's house, that for old times' sake he was willing to forgive his excesses if Murar Rao gave up the hill-fort of Gutti and its dependencies, the spoils of Chinkurli and also Rs 1 lakh in lieu of grain and forage for his horses. Murar

Rao however chose to reply with rude and obstinate retorts, referring to Haidar as starting off his career as a mere Naik, while he had been a Senapati of the Maratha Empire. An angered Haidar decided to siege the place. Murar Rao sought urgent help from both Poona and Hyderabad, but none came to his rescue. The Barbhai were dealing with too many internal issues to be able to concern themselves much with what was happening with their old friend. The fort of Gutti was strong and impregnable and, but for treachery and famine, it was tough to reduce it. Towards the end of January 1776, after a siege of about five weeks, Haidar took the town and the lower fort by assault, along with a large booty of 2000 horse, several elephants, large amounts of property, equipment, field guns and stores.

The siege of the upper fort carried on for the next two months. By March 1776, Murar Rao sued for peace. He settled to pay Rs 12 lakh, 8 lakh in cash or valuables and for the remainder, a hostage. But Murar Rao's deception on complying with the terms angered Haidar and he renewed the siege. All supplies of water to the fort were cut off and Murar Rao's men were dying of thirst. In distress, Murar Rao sent his minister, Pali Khan, to Haidar, seeking forgiveness for playing truant. Haidar replied that there was abundant water below and Murar Rao and his men could come down to quench their thirst themselves, provided they came unarmed. He assured them of the safety of their life and property. Murar Rao, his son and the unarmed garrison descended from the top of the hill in a palanquin and submitted themselves to Haidar's clemency. Haidar's forces then went atop and plundered the belongings and palace of Murar Rao. All his people were taken prisoners and Haidar's men, Balaji Rao and Roshan Khan, were appointed as the Subedar and Killedar of Gutti respectively. All of Murar Rao's territories were duly annexed to Mysore. Haidar refused to even accede to Murar Rao's requests for a meeting, citing that he had no time to spare. They were all packed off to the dreadful prison of Kabbaladurg, where eventually Murar Rao was put to death on Haidar's orders in May 1779. Many of his family members survived for nearly fifteen years, till Tipu ordered a general massacre of all prisoners in 1791. Thus ended the story of

Murar Rao Ghorpade of Gutti who had played such a vital role in the politics of South India since the times of the Carnatic Wars.

This was followed by an annexation of the territories of the Nawab of Savanur and the Chief of Anegondi. Haidar had successfully made the Mysore kingdom coterminous with the Krishna River in the north and effectively reversed all the losses he had faced during the earlier Maratha incursion. However, there was little respite for Haidar as the succeeding years were to bring in more conflicts, more turmoil and battles that he had to brace himself for.

7

Towards a New Churn

A Succession Farce

In the midst of all the conquests that Haidar was embroiled in, back home in Srirangapatna, the titular Maharaja Bettada Chamaraja Wodeyar VIII died mysteriously on 16 September 1776, when he was only seventeen. The reason for his death was unknown. But as Hayavadana Rao surmises, there is evidence to believe that, like his predecessor, he too was 'poisoned by Haidar, who, in the zenith of his power as the sarvadhikari [dictator] of Mysore, would not evidently brook any ruling king attaining his majority.'[1] Haidar had had no qualms about displaying the puppet ruler to his masses or for the latter to conduct the most important annual ritual of Mysore, Dasara, 'exhibiting the pageant, seated on his ivory throne, in the balcony of state; himself [Haidar] occupying the place of minister and commander-in-chief.'[2] With both the young sons of Krishnaraja Wodeyar II now dead, there was no direct lineal heir to the throne. Krishnaraja's widow, Maharani Lakshmi Ammanni, made it amply clear to Haidar that she wanted to see someone of the nearest familial line succeeding to the throne. Her choice centred on two young men belonging to two noble households connected with the royal family—her younger sister's son, Narasarajayya, and her co-wife's grandson, Siddarajayya. Her contention was that the succession of either of these young men was strictly in accordance with the Hindu customs and traditions of Kshatriya royal houses. Both the men had

* Please refer to the corresponding illustration in the appendix.

a direct connect with her deceased husband and thus had a rightful claim on the throne, she surmised.

Haidar was cautious in proclaiming his decision. He knew that if he consented to the candidature of either of the two men that the Queen Mother was suggesting, they would be on her side and their combined might could spell possible disaster for him, as it had done in the past. He declared that the claim was going to be open to all young men in the nobility and not restricted to only the two preferred candidates of the Rani. To assuage her, he conducted an interview of sorts with her two preferred boys. He dismissed one of them as being too lame to ascend the throne, while the other was shelved as being dull-witted and afflicted with leprosy. He instead decided to conduct a farcical mockery of an exercise to choose the new ruler. Children collected from different branches of the royal house were all gathered in a room that was filled with a wide variety of items—fruits, sweets, flowers, books, ornaments, bags of money, weapons and instruments of manly pursuits and so on. The children were left to themselves to pick what they wished, of course under the watchful hawk-eye of Haidar. As the children walked around the room joyfully, picking up items that caught their fancy, one of them, a bright bonny child aged three, the son of Arikuthara Devaraja Urs and Honnajamma, picked up a dagger in one hand and a mirror in the other. Gleefully pointing at him, Haidar exclaimed to one and all present there: 'There you go! He is our next Maharaja!' His skewed rationale was that the child had shown an equanimity of mind of being interested in both warfare, as well as pleasurable activities and that is what a good ruler needed to have. Haidar's word was final and there was no appeal possible. The unsuspecting little boy was quickly garlanded, presented betel leaves, grand clothes and ornaments and escorted towards the throne. Orders were sent that Maharani Lakshmi Ammanni should be duly informed of all that transpired and needless to say, she was to give her consent to the choice he made. She was later compelled to formally adopt the boy with all due religious rituals and have him installed on the throne as '*Khasa*' Chamaraja Wodeyar IX (Khasa, literally meaning legitimate) on

27 September 1776. The infant, aged three, was obviously a passport for Haidar's own independent rule, till the time he would come of age. The outraged Rani knew that given the unenviable position that she was in, as one of the senior surviving members of the royal family, she had little choice but to kowtow to the dictator's wishes. This incident however furthered her long-standing resolve to do all that she could under her limited command to throw away the yoke of Haidar and his family that she believed had eclipsed her own and that of the kingdom.

New Rumblings

Haidar had barely completed his farce in Srirangapatna than the news reached him of a brewing confederacy of the Nizam and the government in Poona, along with the support of the Nayaka of Chitradurga, planning an invasion of the northern territories of Mysore. Just after his conquest of Gutti, Haidar had marched towards Savanur and occupied more than half of the territories of Savanur's Pathan Nawab Abdul Hakim Khan. The monsoon had forced him to retreat temporarily to Srirangapatna, though he had left behind select corps at Bankapur. Savanur had been a Maratha subordinate and hence the government in Poona wanted to liberate it from Haidar's command. Hence a section of the Maratha army under Haripant and three other sardars advanced on Savanur towards the end of 1776 to dislodge Haidar's troops from Savanur, before the combined armies could invade. Parshuram Bhau, by now the acknowledged head of the Patwardhan clan, joined the force. Haidar was determined to repel this attack and sent his gallant commander, Mohammad Ali, for this. He was assisted by Raghoba's troops led by Baji Rao Barve. A fierce clash followed where Mohammad Ali and Barve brought the Maratha army under the fire of the Mysore guns and created great confusion in their ranks. They managed to rout the opponent and captured two out of the four chiefs, several subordinate officers and nearly 3000 horses. This was not the kind of start that the confederates had expected against Haidar. Hearing about the rout of the advance army, Parshuram Bhau, the Maratha general in command of the main army with about 30,000 men, retreated to Miraj and thought it prudent not to march further. He reported to Poona that strong reinforcements were necessary if Haidar was to be defeated. Nizam Ali's troops of 40,000 under Ibrahim Khan Dhoonsa too fell back behind the Tungabhadra River.

By then, the floods in the rivers had helped create significant barriers for the invaders and Haidar was, at least for the present, relieved from the dangers of the confederate attack. He decided to use this time to punish the errant Madakari Nayaka of Chitradurga who had always played an inimical role towards Mysore during the Maratha invasions. He had even allowed Shivram Bhau, the nephew of Murar Rao, to escape from Madaksira to Poona by way of Chitradurga. In the latest instant, Nayaka had invited the Marathas to invade Mysore. All of his actions were sufficient for Haidar to nurse a grouse against him, in addition to, of course, coveting the celebrated and impregnable fort of Chitradurga that he always wished to possess. Haidar found an ally in Krishnappa, a minister of the Chief of Rayadurg, who had been insulted by Madakari Nayaka and was seeking revenge. Krishnappa further instigated Haidar to attack Chitradurga and offered his support as well.

Departing from Gutti in June 1777, Haidar marched towards Chitradurga, even as he dispatched Fazalullah Khan to attack the palegar of Harpanahalli who had treacherously murdered a Mysorean officer. Fazalullah Khan besieged the forts of Ujjini and Kittur, forcing the palegar to pay Rs 70,000 as a fine for his offences. Haidar tried to mediate with Madakari Nayaka to hand over his capital to Mysore and accept in return a jagir yielding Rs 50,000 as revenue. Madakari Nayaka shot down the offer, forcing Haidar to lay siege in July. The siege went on for nearly three months with both sides unrelenting. Finally, Madakari Nayaka offered a ransom amount and promised to join Haidar's standard, when summoned next. Haidar was content to lift the siege and accept these terms for the time being, as he knew he had to face the Maratha army again. This could also be a possible test of Chitradurga's loyalty that he had professed.

The Maratha army, under its Commander-in-Chief Haripant, along with Manaji Phadke, was approaching from Poona with an army of 60,000 horses and commensurate infantry and guns, crossing the Tungabhadra by way of Shirahatti and Lakshmeshwar. Haidar was trying to use the offices of Raghoba's agent in his court, Baji Rao Barve, to create discord among the Maratha chiefs. Manaji was secretly bought off by Haidar with a bribe of Rs 6 lakh to separate his forces from those of Haripant. A depleted army now waited in vain both for reinforcements from Poona and the usual prevaricating ally, Nizam Ali, to join his forces, but that never happened. Finally, Haripant crossed the Tungabhadra and encamped at Raravi, to advance into Mysore. When the two armies met in combat, Haidar noticed some indecision on Manaji's part and therefore suspected treason from the latter. He made visible demonstrations of communication towards his supposed ally, that induced considerable suspicions in the mind of Haripant himself about the fidelity of Manaji towards the cause. Manaji was thereby attacked by Haripant and thrown off the field, forcing the former to re-cross the Tungabhadra again with his troops. During these operations, Ibrahim Khan Dhoonsa had remained strategically aloof, as he too had been lured by Haidar's gold. With little options left, Haripant beat a hasty retreat in December 1777.

Haidar now followed up the pursuit of fulfilling the terms of the agreement he had signed with Raghoba and seized large parts of the territories between the Tungabhadra and Krishna Rivers. Pursuing the retreating army and driving them away, he dispatched Sardar Khan for the siege of Dharwar. In April 1778, he reduced the strongholds of Kopal and Bahadurbanda along with others like Gajendragadh, Badami, Jalihal and others. Dharwar was a prolonged campaign but it eventually capitulated. The Maratha chiefs, known as the Deshayees, who ruled this part of the region submitted themselves by consenting readily to offer *peshkash* or tributes, with further sums as a gift. Thus, as 1778 ended, Haidar had significantly expanded his kingdom and fixed the Krishna River as its northern boundary.

Haidar had also noted with disdain that the chief of Cudappah and the Nayaka of Chitradurga had not maintained their promise of offering support during this campaign. It was now time to teach them a decisive lesson, as he had emerged stronger from this campaign. He detached Mir Ali Raza to Cudappah and himself marched towards Chitradurga for the second assault.

The Siege of Chitradurga

Taking advantage of Haidar's prolonged military campaigns, the Nayaka had defied his authority and plundered some of the border areas of Mysore. Haidar had already dispatched Tipu to besiege the fort and joined him shortly thereafter. The palegar (Nayaka) held out for nearly three months; several of his trustworthy chiefs and next of kin were killed or wounded during this time in the sallies that were made. In one such sally, the palegar himself and his brother Parashuramappa Nayaka were wounded badly by a bullet shot from the Mysorean garrison and the fort was on the verge of collapse. It got a lifeline with a timely reinforcement of 10,000 horses each from Shivram Bhau (Murar Rao's nephew) and Pandurang Tatya (brother of Gopal Rao Patwardhan) and another led by Parshuram Bhau. Haidar then tightened the siege and sent his commandant, Mohammad Ali, and his Risaldar, Shripat Rao, to fight the Maratha reinforcements that were coming for the assistance of the Nayaka. They fought at Sirsi and the Maratha armies were routed, Shivram and Pandurang themselves being taken prisoners.

Kirmani makes this a battle between the 'infidels armed to the teeth' and 'the bravest and noblest of the Ghazies, or Mussalman soldiers.'[3] Despite such a protracted siege, the fort stoutly held on. Its five strong gateways made it impregnable. Each of the gateways led through a stone wall, proceeding up the hill. In fact, Chitradurga was famed for its rock fort given its inaccessibility and its commanding position on account of its point of vantage for defence. Haidar's patience was running out. He decided to create a mock withdrawal of the siege, so that the palegar would be less cautious and possibly step out, upon which, hiding from the trenches, he and his army could follow him from behind and put him to death. There were several

Muslim officers and soldiers in the Nayaka's army and Haidar also tried to use the lure of religion to seduce them.[4]

Around this time, providentially for Haidar, the Nayaka's father-in-law, the chief of Jarimale, arrived near his camp. He had been within the fort during the siege and now assuming that the siege had been lifted, he had taken leave of his son-in-law to proceed downwards to a shrine at the foot of the hill—quite close to where Haidar was encamped. But Haidar ensured that this was presented to Madakari Nayaka in a distorted manner that his own father-in-law and brothers-in-law were conspiring with Haidar for his downfall. The enraged Nayaka then ordered that his innocent father-in-law be pursued and eventually beheaded. This caused an uproar among the dead man's sons who vowed revenge and joined hands with Haidar, promising to give him all the details and secrets of the impregnable fort. There was a temple of Goddess Kali on the summit of the fort whom the Bedars propitiated daily to ensure the invincibility of the fort. The Bedars were the same community that the Chitradurga palegar belonged to, those who lived by hunting and tending cattle and sheep. On Mondays, there was a ritual that involved a sortie of sorts, leading to human sacrifice. A chain of heads was then offered to the shrine of the goddess. In fact, after the fall of the place, 'heads were found ranged in rows of small pyramids, in front of the temple of the Goddess, to the number of about two thousand.'[5]

The sons of the beheaded Jarimale chief showed Haidar's men a secret path that led to the inside of the fort, such a path 'as the eyes of fancy never figured, or the imagination of the learned ever conceived.'[6] It was a narrow, winding tunnel that allowed only one soldier at a time to enter. It was called the *Onake Kandi Bagilu* or a passage that allowed for just a pestle to be thrust through it. In single file, they decided to wriggle through this passage and storm the fort from within thereafter. It is here that local folklore talks about the story of a courageous common woman, Obavva, whose defiance temporarily shook the ground from under the feet of Haidar's exalted army.

Obavva, the wife of a bugler who had just returned home from duty for his supper, had come out to fetch drinking water from a freshwater pond that flowed near this passage. To her horror, she noticed mysterious movements near the passage and realized that in single file the enemy's soldiers were entering the fort. Not wanting to disturb her husband who was in the middle of his meal, she picked up a domestic pestle (*onake* in Kannada) that was there nearby and hid in the darkness around the secret entrance. As each soldier of the Mysorean army tried to wriggle his way out of the passage and enter the fort, she smashed his skull with her pestle and dragged his corpse away, waiting for her next victim to emerge. In this manner, Obavva slew several soldiers and a heap of bodies accumulated near the passage by the time her husband stepped out looking for his wife who had promised to return with some water to drink. He was horrified by the scene that he saw there; his wife had become the very incarnation of the goddess atop the fort who the Bedars propitiated with human sacrifice. He sounded the bugle alarm and the troops sallied out to defend the fort against the besiegers. Some of the besiegers took their revenge by stabbing Obavva from behind and her story was thus immortalized in local folklore and popular culture as 'Onake Obavva' or the lady with the pestle. A documented account of this popular and heroic folktale is found in the writings of S. Srikantaiya:

> The story of *Vanike kandi* connected with the second attack of Haider on Chitaldurg [Chitradurga] is interesting and is a remarkable testimony to the prowess of a lady, Obavva. Haider's forces were unable to affect an entry into the fort and to storm it was next to impossible. Crevices in the walls where a woman was carrying curds to the fortress was discovered and the invading army attempted to march through in single file there. Nearby this passage was a fresh water pond half way up the hill. One day, when a bugler went to dine, Obavva, his wife, who went to get water from the pond, noticed the enemy marching in single file near this entrance. It was dark and hiding herself behind the entrance, she killed soldier after soldier with her *vanake* (pestle) as he marched through the entrance, till her husband returned. Needless to add, in spite of this heroism, thanks to the treachery of Mussalman

employees of the Nayakas and the army of Jaramale, Haider was ultimately successful in 1779.[7]

Despite Obavva's heroics, the besiegers trooped in. As Kirmani recounts: 'After a little fighting, the bonds which united the garrison of the fort were broken asunder, and, like falling leaves in autumn, they were dispersed and scattered on all sides, while the besiegers, now fearlessly mounting the hills, beat their drums, in token of victory, and watered the swords and spears of their resentment in the blood of the infidels, and beat the black dust of existence out of the bodies of the unfortunate garrison.'[8] The palegar discovered that his faithful lieutenant Hombalappa had been slain. Unluckily for him, that very day, the ritual sortie too had failed and thus his superstitious beliefs were aroused that the goddess was no longer propitiated and that the Nayaka's fall was thus imminent. Realizing that it was meaningless to fight now with all his trusted commanders killed, the Nayaka mounted a palanquin, descended from the fort and surrendered himself to Haidar by early March 1779. He and his entire family were imprisoned and packed off to Srirangapatna. Kirmani however notes that an anonymous author mentions that the unfortunate palegar was taken to the top of a precipice and then thrown down from there to be dashed to pieces.[9] Sheikh Ayaz, the Nair boy whom Haidar had converted to Islam, was left there to look after Chitradurga. The fort and his belongings in cash, ornaments, treasures accounting to about Rs 5 lakh were ruthlessly plundered. The mighty and legendary fort of Chitradurga thus capitulated to the might of Haidar.

The Cudappah Campaign

As mentioned earlier, Mir Ali Raza had been dispatched to Cudappah by the end of 1778 to punish its errant Nawab. But the nephews of the Nawab, Hussain Miyan and Saiyid Miyan, managed to put up such a stout resistance that Mir Ali could make little progress. Finally, after the Chitradurga conquest, Haidar himself decided to join the campaign at Cudappah. Being unaware of Haidar's joining the detachment, the Pathans of the Nawab's army tried to encircle Mir Ali Raza, but were in turn surrounded by Haidar and his troops, forcing them to retreat. But they were hemmed in from all sides by the augmented Mysorean troops at Balsanahalli. Despite this, as Kirmani notes, 'every individual Afghan [Pathan] gave such proofs of his skill in the use of the sword, that their prowess is still recorded in the page of memorable events; and the young lads, mounted on their elephants, plied their arrows with both hands so fast, and gave such proofs of courage, that two thousand brave and experienced men of the Nawaub's [Haidar's] army were slain by them.'[10] Eventually the Pathans surrendered and about 300 of them were made prisoners, while all their horses, elephants and military stores were captured by Haidar's men. In April 1779, Haidar then entered and took Cudappah at the very first assault. Abdul Halim Khan, the Nawab, had fled away to Sidhout, to the north-east of Cudappah.

Haidar was keen to enlist some of the Pathans, numbering about eighty who could not provide any security for themselves, into his own army. Haidar's men attempted to disarm them, which they deeply resented and took as an affront. In the hope of finding sureties for them they were all placed in a tent opposite Haidar's. Incensed by the treatment meted out to them, by midnight, the Pathans slew some of the guards of their tent and tiptoed towards Haidar's tent with the intent of murdering him in his sleep. Haidar was awake even in the wee hours of the night and could hear a distinctive commotion coming in and guessed that something was fishy. His reflexes were swift and he quickly leapt out of his bed, placing a long pillow in the place where he had been sleeping and covering it with a quilt. Cutting a passage for himself from the tent with his sword, he escaped. Two of the Pathans stormed into his tent and made a decisive cut at the figure they thought was Haidar on the bed. Much to their disappointment, they realized that it was a pillow and that Haidar had already escaped. An attendant who always slept beside Haidar's bed with a lance in his hand was awakened by this noise and he quickly caught the two intruders and raised an alarm. In no time, the rest of the accomplices were all rounded up. An enraged Haidar gave orders 'to cut off the hands and feet of the Afghan [Pathan] prisoners at the joints with axes and saws . . . and these men, with the blood streaming from their legs and arms, were carried through the streets and lanes of the town, and were then left outside the walls.'[11] This was done to instil a sense of terror among anyone else in the town or within his army to prevent them from contemplating such bravado in the future. Some of the unfortunate Pathans were dragged around the camp, tied by a short, loose cord to the feet of elephants.[12]

Abdul Halim Khan, who had taken shelter at Sidhout, heard of the tragedy that had befallen his erstwhile Pathan warriors and was alarmed enough to ask the inhabitants of Cudappah to take shelter in the hills. But Haidar's predatory horsemen or Kuzzaks fell on these unfortunate people while they were on their way, looted their possessions, violated their women and killed several of them.[13] The Nawab knew that his options were running out and he tried to compromise, but could not afford to pay Rs 10 lakh and also surrender the fort of Ganjikota as Haidar was demanding. Haidar directed Mir Ali Raza to reduce Ganjikota and by 27 May 1779, the Nawab meekly surrendered to Haidar. He and his family were made prisoners and packed off unceremoniously to Srirangapatna, to be held in captivity in the suburb of Ganjam. Shortly thereafter the Nawab was secretly massacred after there were murmurs of new assassination attempts that his relatives were making. Mir Ali Raza was offered Cudappah as a jagir for his services in reducing it. Haidar also took to his harem the Nawab's sister who was famous for her legendary beauty. She had threatened to commit suicide if she was taken away as a concubine and hence, he married her through a proper *nikah* ceremony.[14]

Malabar Malaise

The south-western corner of Mysore, the Malabar region, was a constant source of bother for Haidar as it simply did not accept his stranglehold, and discontent kept brewing. As mentioned earlier, while the northern kingdoms and principalities of Malabar had all been subjugated, Cochin and Travancore had maintained their autonomy. Cochin had of course agreed to pay regular tributes. In 1773, Berki Srinivasa Rao demanded Rs 4 lakh from the Raja of Cochin for military expenses and he had readily done that to buy peace. In 1776, a dispute arose over a territory known as Talpatti Mel Vettam that was part of the Zamorin's territories and had been occupied by Cochin in the aftermath of the disarray resulting from the Mysorean invasion. Srinivasa Rao demanded its surrender and a payment of arrears of its revenue that Cochin had collected. The Raja of Cochin made evasive promises and tried to skirt the matter. However, Haidar dispatched Sardar Khan to Trichur and occupied it. Sardar Khan felt that this was the appropriate occasion to finally annex Cochin, but in panic the Raja sent emissaries, Komi Achan and Iswar Pattar, to Srirangapatna, assuring Haidar of his complete cooperation, including the surrender of the disputed tract, payment of Rs 4 lakh, four elephants and annual tributes of Rs 1 lakh and a fifth. The ruler of Cranganore, which was situated on the borders of Cochin and Travancore, was also being constantly harassed by Mysore to pay up tributes or face military action. As part of the same treaty with the Raja of Cochin, Cranganore too agreed to pay Rs 1 lakh and a fifth and one-fifth later as annual tributes.

Sardar Khan then marched northwards, but his eyes were fixed on southern Kerala, namely, Travancore and Cochin, and he found a way to advance there. He sent emissaries to the Dutch commander of Cochin, requesting free passage through Dutch-held domains up to Travancore. The Dutch still held possession of their fort at Cranganore that effectually protected the western flank of the Travancore Lines, and also commanded the natural water communications between north and south Kerala. The Dutch Company was in an awkward situation as Cochin and Travancore were its allies, but at the same time it did not want to antagonize a powerful kingdom like Mysore. So, they sent in their usual reply that such decisions needed ratification from Batavia, but this was unacceptable to the

Mysoreans. Sardar Khan marched in August 1776 at the head of an army of 10,000 men to demand the surrender of Chetwa and Cranganore, as they belonged to the erstwhile Zamorin's territories. In vain, the Dutch protested against these unwarranted hostilities with their Governor Moens offering mediation between Haidar and the Rajas of Travancore and Cochin. But none of this came through and by October 1776, Haidar's troops advanced on Cranganore and surprised it. To prevent the further advance of Mysore into the southern regions, the Dutch got the island of Vypeen, called Aykotta, fortified, had the troops from Travancore stationed there along with a battleship *Verwagting*. The Raja of Travancore meanwhile tried to enlist the support of Muhammad Ali of Arcot and the British in Madras against the predatory attempts of Mysore.

While Haidar's troops retreated from Aykotta, they pressed on to the territories from Chetwa to Cranganore. The fort of Chetwa could not hold out for longer and by November 1776, capitulated to Mysore, on the condition that the Dutch garrison stationed there should be safely allowed passage to Cranganore. But Sardar Khan violated the agreement and took them all prisoners and packed them off to Srirangapatna. As William Logan states: 'The prisoners were plundered of everything, even to their clothes, and with the women, children and slaves, were sent to Calicut. From thence the military were dispatched, loaded with chains to Seringapatam, where all took service with Hyder, excepting the Commandant of Chetwai [Chetwa] and the Resident.'[15]

Though the Dutch wanted to retaliate, the Raja of Travancore advised Moens not to precipitate the matter at present. A charade of friendship was maintained between Haidar and the Dutch, though the latter waited for an opportunity to revert to status quo. Gifts and presents from Batavia were sent to Haidar to placate him and get him to release their prisoners. But the Dutch avoided any alliance with him as that would cease their neutrality with both the British and Travancore, who were both opposed to Haidar. The Dutch Council also tried to instruct the Raja of Travancore not to be too friendly with the British in his zeal to protect himself from Mysore, and kept inducing him to believe that he had nothing to fear from Haidar.

In early January 1778, the Dutch finally undertook an expedition against the Mysoreans, starting from Cranganore, driving away about 400 of their troops from the palace of the king there. They then marched to the fort of Chetwa and laid siege to it. However, the Mysorean force held it stubbornly. Haidar finally decide to invade Cranganore in March 1778 with about 3000 infantry, 150 cavalry and artillery men with four cannons. The Dutch were overpowered and they retreated. Governor Moens tried his best to have peace between the Company and Haidar but the latter treated these overtures with contemptuous disdain. Haidar kept his eyes on Travancore and was eager to force the Dutch to conclude an offensive and defensive alliance with him. By 1780, Haidar had thus, with Calicut as his base in the Malabar, extended his sway over the territories between Chetwa and Cranganore; Chetwa was well-garrisoned and he was within reach of Travancore, too, with Aykotta shielding that kingdom.

To manage the Malabar better, from 1775 Haidar followed a slightly different approach in some areas. Having his nominees as governors with direct rule from Mysore seemed untenable as it had only contributed to flaming passions among the fiercely independent Nairs. He therefore tried to use the princes of the Malabar itself as proxies and agents to run his government there. Ali Raja of Cannanore had failed to pay tributes and hence the Regent of Koluthunad was nominated to his ancestral domains in Chirakkal, with a Mysorean officer stationed there to administer revenue. At times, this policy of using the local princes was extended to the whole coast, but done very cautiously depending on the nature of risks involved. Between 1775 and 1778, this was possibly one of the reasons for the establishment of some semblance of relative peace in the region. But it was impossible to crush the zeal of the Nairs who felt perpetually stifled by Mysore's dominance and once again broke out in rebellion in 1778.

The Rajas of Calicut, Kadathanad and Kottayam joined forces to throw out the yoke of Mysore from the Malabar, aided of course by the various European Companies operating there. It was a strange equation, where aided by Mysore, while the Chirakkal Regent supported the French, he also supplied pepper to the competitive

British factory at Tellicherry. The French bitterly complained about their pepper trade being sabotaged by the handiwork of the Regent and the treaties that he was signing. Around this time, war had once again broken out between the British and the French after a long period of peace, with the latter recognizing the declaration of American independence on 13 March 1778. The British therefore wanted to drive the French out of Mahe. For Haidar, Mahe was his gateway to Europe. He was getting his guns, ammunition and French reinforcements from here, and hence, naturally did not wish to cede it to British hands. Even as he was busy consolidating his position between the Tungabhadra and Krishna rivers, the news reached Haidar that the British had laid siege to Pondicherry and by October 1778, it had fallen to their might. He therefore did not want to risk losing access to Mahe and ordered the Raja of Chirakkal to help the French, his allies, against possible British aggression. The Regent of Chirakkal moved at the head of 1500 of his Nair force to help the French garrison in Mahe, along with Haidar's own contingent of 2000 men that joined in from Coorg. The other princes in the Malabar were unwilling to be drawn into this conflict, though initially they provided lukewarm assurances to Haidar of supporting the French.

The British realized the strategic and commercial interests that Kerala offered and hence wanted to stamp their authority and show of strength to intimidate the local players there. Accordingly, a very large naval force was stationed on the coast under Captain Walker in 1779. In March 1779, Col Braithwaite landed on the coast with another large battalion and in three weeks, a significant reinforcement came in with three companies of artillery under Major Clifton in the *Royal Charlotte*. Her Majesty's ships *Sea Horse* and *Coventry*, with the *Resolution* in convoy, also landed on the shores of Kerala. This British show of strength gave a sense of succour to the Raja of Kottayam and the Zamorin who were suffocated under Haidar's thralldom. They professed open support to the British and in return received arms and ammunition from them to hold out against Chirakkal that had tried to blockade Tellicherry and help the French. The Regent of

Chirakkal was forced to retreat and Mahe fell to the British by 19 March 1779.

Quite unscrupulously, after this objective was completed, the British deserted the Zamorin and the Kottayam Raja, leaving them to face the ire of Haidar. The two were left in an unenviable position with the British stating that going beyond a point in supporting them meant jeopardizing the Company's interests vis-à-vis Mysore—something that they did not wish to undertake now. The Raja of Chirakkal was the only ally for Haidar and he, along with Balwant Rao from the Mysore army, managed to crush all insurrection on the part of the Kottayam Raja who had to eventually flee from his kingdom. The Raja of Kadathanad, too, was deposed and a younger prince who was favourably inclined to Mysore was made incharge.

The Malabar was thus an expensive campaign for Haidar, where the incoming revenues were outweighed by the expenditures involved in just maintaining the territories and tranquillity there. The Nairs had opted for desertion of their lands rather than submission to the conqueror. But all the churn was leading its way towards yet another major conflict that was brewing and would erupt soon among all the major players in the region.

Domestic Matters

Haidar protested with the British about the capture of Mahe which impeded his interests. The Madras Government and the Governor, Sir Thomas Rumboldt, thought it prudent to conciliate him and sent a most unlikely person—a missionary named Frederick Schwartz—to Srirangapatna to negotiate with Haidar. Schwartz was a German by birth and belonged to the Danish Mission Society that had been established in Tanjore. He was a learned man with pleasing manners and an affable demeanour and possessed some knowledge of India and her languages. Schwartz arrived in Srirangapatna on 25 August 1779 and had interviews with Haidar. His memoirs give an interesting first-person, ringside account of

Haidar, his establishment and his personality at the time, and is hence reproduced here at some length:

> Haidar's palace is a fine building in the Indian style. Opposite to it is an open place. On both sides are ranges of open buildings where the military and civil servants have their offices and constantly attend and Haidar Naik can overlook them from his balcony . . . Although Haidar sometimes rewards his servants the principal motive is fear. Two hundred people with whips stand always ready to use them. Not a day passes on which numbers are not flogged. Haidar applies the same cat to all transgressors alike, gentlemen and horse-keepers, tax-gatherers and his own sons and when he has inflicted such a public scourging upon the greatest gentlemen, he does not dismiss them. No! they remain in the same office and bear the marks of stripes on their backs as public warnings. For he seems to think that almost all people who seek to enrich themselves are devoid of all principles of honour . . . the most dreadful punishments were daily inflicted. Many who read it may think the account exaggerated, but the poor man was tied up, two men came with their whips and cut him dreadfully and with sharp nails was his flesh torn asunder and then scourged afresh, his shrieks rending the air. Although the punishments are so dreadful, yet there are people enough who seek employments and outbid each other and the Brahmins are by far the worst in this traffic.
>
> When I came to Haidar, he desired me to sit down alongside of him. The floor was covered with the most exquisite tapestry. He received me very politely, listened in a friendly manner and seeming pleasure to all what I had to say. He spoke very openly and without reserve and said that the Europeans had broken their solemn engagements and promises but nevertheless he was willing to live in peace with them . . .
>
> When I sat near Haidar Naik, I particularly observed in what a regular succession and with what rapid dispatch his affairs proceeded one after the other. Whenever he made a pause in speaking, an account was read to him of the districts and letters

received. He heard them and ordered the answers immediately. The writers ran, wrote the letters, read them and Haidar affixed his seal. Thus, one evening a great many letters were expedited. Haidar can neither read nor write but his memory is excellent. He orders one man to write a letter and read it to him. Then he calls another to read it again. If the writer has in the least deviated from his orders, his head pays for it.

What religion people profess or whether they profess any at all, that is perfectly indifferent to him. He has none himself and leaves everyone to his choice.

His army is under the care of four chief officers called Bakshis. One might call them paymasters. But they have to do not only with the pay but also with the recruiting services and other things which belong to an army. There are also judges that settle differences. With these men I had frequent discourses. Some spoke Persian, others only Hindustani, but all were Mahomedans. They asked what the right prayer was and to whom we ought to pray. I declared to them how we being sinful men and therefore deserving God's curse and eternal death could not come before God but in the name of our mediator Jesus Christ. I explained to them also the Lord's prayer. To persons who understood Tamil, I explained the doctrines in Tamil, to the others in Hindustani language. As the ministers of Haidar's court are mainly Brahmins, I had many conversations with them. Some answered with modesty and others did not choose to talk on so great a subject and only hinted that their noble pagodas [temples] were not built in vain. I said the edifices may indeed serve for some use but not the idols which they adored. Without the fort were some hundred Europeans commanded by a Frenchman and a squadron of Hussars under the command of Captain Budene, a German. Part of these troops were German, others Frenchmen. I found also some Malabar Christians. Every Sunday I performed Divine Service in German and in Malayalam without asking anybody's leave . . . we sang, preached and prayed and nobody presumed to hinder us . . .

In Haidar Naik's palace the high and low come to me and asked what our doctrine was, so that I could speak as long as I had strength. Haidar's youngest son saw and saluted me in the Durbar or hall of audience. He sent to request me to come into his apartment. I sent him word that I would gladly come if his father permitted it; without his father's leave I might hurt both him and myself. Of this, he was perfectly sensible. The most intimate friends dare not speak their sentiments freely. Haidar has his spies everywhere. But I knew that I might speak of religion night and day without giving him the least offence.

I sat often with Haidar in a hall that is open on the garden side. In the garden, trees were grafted and bore two sorts of fruit. He had also fine cypress trees, fountains, etc. I observed a number of young boys bringing some earth into the garden. On enquiry I was informed that Haidar had raised a battalion of orphans who have nobody else to provide for them and whom he educates at his expense, for he allowed no orphan to be neglected in all his dominions. He feeds and clothes them and gives little wooden firelocks with which they exercise . . .

On the last evening when I took my leave from Haidar, he requested me to speak Persian as I had done with his people. I did so and explained the motive of my journey to him: 'You may perhaps wonder,' said I, 'what could have induced me, a priest, who has nothing to do with political concerns to come to you and that on an errand which does not belong to my sacerdotal functions. But as I was plainly told that the sole object of my journey was the preservation and confirmation of peace, and having witnessed more than once, the misery and horrors attending on war, I thought within my own mind, how happy I should deem myself if I could be of service in cementing a durable friendship between the two Governments and thus securing the blessings of peace to this devoted country and its inhabitants . . .' He said with great cordiality: 'Very well, very well. I am of the same opinion with you and wish that the English may be as studious of peace as you are. If they offer me the hand of peace and concord, I shall not withdraw mine.'

I then took my leave of him. On reaching my palanquin, I found that Haidar had sent three hundred rupees for my travelling expenses . . .[16]

The account of Schwartz gives us a good peep into the atmosphere that prevailed in Srirangapatna under Haidar. While there seems to be a general cloud of fear, suspicion, surveillance and inhuman punishments, there was also freedom to talk about any religious beliefs as he did not seem to have cared much for it. His courtesy and concern, even in quietly and without ostentation sending Schwartz money for expense on the return journey, do portray a humane picture of Haidar, whose life had till then been ravaged by the scourge of constant wars and bloodshed. The orphans that Schwartz mentions are most possibly what were known as the *chela* (meaning slave or disciple) battalions. Young boys from captured territories were often brought back to Srirangapatna, converted to Islam, trained in arms and a militia of them created. Wilks states that after the conquest of Chitradurga, about 20,000 such boys had been taken away, converted and recruited as the first regular chela corps, in imitation of the Turkish Janissaries.[17] Bowring states that the kind-hearted but simple missionary, Schwartz, was led to believe that they were destitute orphans whom Haidar had taken under his protection.[18]

Haidar sent through Schwartz to the Madras Government a letter that chided them for their utter disregard for treaty obligations and promises made. The refusal of the British to come to his aid when Madhav Rao invaded Mysore immediately after the First Anglo–Mysore War and the conclusion of peace seems to have been a permanent sore for Haidar and he brought this up again in his letter. He went back to the days of the siege of Tiruchirapalli and how Mysore had been duped into supporting their ally, Muhammad Ali, and got nothing in return but ignominy and a huge drain of its resources. He protested against their hostilities in Mahe and their attempts to support rebellions in the Malabar against his authority. He added: 'I have not yet taken revenge—it is no matter. But if you henceforth forgetting all treaties and engagements of the Company still are intent on breaking with me, what advantage can attend writing to you? When such improper conduct is pursued, what engagements will remain inviolate? I leave you to judge on whose part the engagements and promises have been broken. You are acquainted with everything. It is right to act in all things with prudence and foresight.'[19]

The British too seemed well aware of how Haidar had utter contempt for them and found them thoroughly untrustworthy of the promises they made. In a communiqué, the President and Council of Fort St George wrote: 'Haidar has long solicited and even importuned this Government to enter into a close union with him but the consideration of temporary inconvenience arising from the terms of such a union, which could only be founded upon agreements of mutual assistance and support, has hitherto obstructed the measure and Haidar has been consequently left in difficulty and distress to seek aid of foreign nations, particularly the French. The reluctance on our part to accept the repeated offers made by Haidar at a time when our assistance might have been useful to him will no doubt render it more difficult to obtain assistance or at least a neutral conduct on his part.'[20]

At the conclusion of the First Anglo–Mysore War, another treaty was concluded between Mysore and the British in 1770 for the settlement of the western coast. The British were given permission to have a factory at Honnavar for pepper and sandalwood and an exclusive right to purchase the entire quantity of these items in return for supplies of guns, saltpetre, lead and cash. Haidar made repeated entreaties to the British to honour their part of the commitment, but he was jolted to hear that in 1772, the Court of Directors disapproved of the treaty itself. This naturally forced Haidar to turn to the French for his supplies. When, in 1773, the British helped Muhammad Ali to seize Tanjore and later seized the island of Salsette, both actions that were bound to embitter them with the

Marathas, Haidar thought of capitalizing on this to his advantage by befriending the foes of his most important foe, the Marathas. He sent overtures to the British and even Muhammad Ali to reconcile, but the latter's obstinacy derailed all such efforts. He kept Haidar's emissaries hanging uncertainly, frustrating them thereby.

Both the French and Dutch had their residents in Haidar's court and the British hoped that he might at least permit that allowance to them as well. However, they needed to bring their ally Muhammad Ali of Arcot, too, on board for this and the latter was perpetually apprehensive and spiteful of Haidar. His sense of envy and insecurity proved an obstacle in any meaningful rapprochement between Mysore and the British.

Haidar's Officers

As Schwartz had mentioned, there were several Brahmins who formed part of Haidar's bureaucracy. He left most of the fiscal institutions that had been long-established by Chikkadevaraja Wodeyar as they were. But he added to the established revenues whatever had been secretly levied by an Amil, resulting in a marked increase in complaints and disputes, along with augmented coffers. Hayavadana Rao describes his polity as 'unbridled autocracy of the Cromwellian type, dominated by the civil and military elements and entirely subservient to his personal will.'[21] In 1775, he bifurcated the *Mahalat Kacheri* (the Revenue/Finance department) into the Balaghat Kacheri and the Payanghat Kacheri. The former was placed under Nazim-ud-din of Arcot as Dewan, with Jadir Rama Rao as Chief Accountant (*Munshi*) and Puttayya, Singayya, Appaji Rao, Keshava Rao, Koneri Rao and Lala Lingo Pant managing the records (*Daftar*). The Payanghat Kacheri was placed under Mir Ali Hakim and his younger brother Mohammad Ghouse, with Kadim Shamaiya as Chief Accountant and Kacheri Krishnaiya, Subba Rao and Kushal Chand managing the records. But grave irregularities prevailed in the operations of these offices, with serious charges of embezzlement of funds being rampant. On receiving intelligence of these malpractices, in 1779 Haidar abolished the new offices and instead re-amalgamated them and placed them under an able officer, Shamaiya. He had been a part of the intelligence and post office (*Anche*) and was hence popularly known as Anche Shamaiya.

A devout Sri Vaishnava Brahmin, Anche Shamaiya belonged to Sulakunte in Kolar and had known Haidar since his youth. He slowly began to wield a lot of power over the affairs of state. Venkatapathayya was made the incharge of the daftar and the Dewanship of the Kacheri was given to Mir Muhammad Sadak, son of Mir Ali Hakim. On Shamaiya's advice, the police, finance and espionage departments were all merged and given supreme powers. A special commission was formed to investigate all charges of embezzlement; it went into finding documentary evidence of all the frauds—often, imagined ones that never occurred. Popular in court parlance as *sullu-patti*s or false affidavits, they were the proverbial Damocles' sword that hung on the heads of all the rivals of Shamaiya and those he despised. Instead of calling him the *Anche-walla* or postman, most people in the kingdom referred to him rather as the *patti-walla* or the one who drafted the statements. Shamaiya misused the powers vested in him to unleash a reign of terror amongst such people against whom he had an axe to grind. For instance, Harikara Nayaka Shamaiya, one of his rivals, was heavily taxed, flogged and imprisoned, and his brothers Singaiya and Sheshaiya were severely tortured. Salayat Khan and Mohammad Ghouse of the erstwhile Payanghat Kacheri too were not spared and the former in fact died of the wounds inflicted on him during flogging. Even the high-ranking diplomat Appaji Ram, the famed interlocutor who was known for his wit and his several diplomatic successes with the enemy camps, did not escape Shamaiya's dangerous net. A huge bill of payables, more than half of which he had not even used, was slapped on him with warnings of dire consequences if unpaid. He eventually had to borrow money from his family and friends to avoid getting into the cross hairs of Anche Shamaiya. Many amildars and officers were similarly punished—tied to elephants' legs, flogged to death or pierced with needles.

Another officer who got into the bad books of Anche Shamaiya was a Madhwa Brahmin named Purnaiya. Born in 1746 at Thirukambur in Tiruchirapalli district, Purnaiya had lost his father at the tender age of ten. His mother, Lakshiamma, worked really hard to bring up her two sons, Purnaiya and Venkat Rao. A trader, Ranga Setty, noticed Purnaiya's innate talents in numbers and calculations and appointed him as his *gumasta* or clerk. The family then migrated to Satyamangalam in 1760 where Ranga Setty's friend, Annadana Setty, who was a chief supplier to Haidar's palace, took young Purnaiya to Srirangapatna and introduced him to the establishment there. The boy was soon recruited as a junior accountant in the *daftar*. Maharashtrian Brahmin Krishna Rao, who headed the Toshikhane or treasury, had an officer Venkataramanayya who dealt with Annadana Setty's dealings with Haidar's establishment. Purnaiya often settled these accounts and once, when a major discrepancy arose in the tallying of the accounts, Purnaiya's smart intervention in resolving the matter instantly caught Haidar's attention.

Slowly, he became a confidant of Haidar and began to rise up the ranks. It is said that Haidar often quizzed his officers on several topics of his interest and anyone who gave an intelligent and witty response was amply rewarded. Once, sometime in 1770, Purnaiya had managed to give a convincing reply to Haidar's query as to why a huge log of timber floated on water, while a small stone sank. So impressed was Haidar by Purnaiya's rationale for this that he decided to make him the head of the Toshikhane *daftar*, to keep the accounts in Kannada, which had hitherto been maintained in Marathi under Krishna Rao. Purnaiya's steady rise must have most probably created tensions between him and Anche Shamaiya. A sum of 1,11,000 Varahas [a currency measure] were exacted from him on false allegations that were levelled and he was subjected to immense torture. He would have even been put to death but for the timely intervention of Bacche Rao, who prevailed upon Berki Srinivasa Rao to represent to Haidar to commute the death sentence and keep him under guard if needed. After suffering prison, Purnaiya was released on security through the intervention of Mustafa Ali Khan, Annadana Setty and Narasa Setty and, over time, reinstated to his office. Such were the excesses of Anche Shamaiya and the civil establishment that he ran with little trepidation, as Haidar remained away from the capital most of the year on his extensive military campaigns.

Yet, Haidar had great regard for Shamaiya and honoured him with an umbrella, medal, pearl necklace, palanquin, a cash reward of 5000 Varahas, an allowance of 1000 Varahas and costly shawls. His elder brother, Rangaiya, was also granted additional allowance of thirty Varahas and the younger one, Aprameya was placed in charge of the Toshikhane records, as also of the cavalry, infantry and other departments. The whole family had thus entrenched themselves deeply within the polity.

Among Haidar's gallant military officers was Fazalullah Khan whose contributions have been spoken of earlier. He had supported Haidar when the latter was at the nadir of his career in 1760 with the tide turning against him in the aftermath of Khande Rao's treachery. Fazalullah Khan had been honoured with several titles and also had the singular distinction of sitting on the same throne as Haidar, with attendants behind him to fan him. All of this changed with the arrival of the *nevayats* from Arcot who were deeply envious of Fazalullah Khan's exalted status. They kept filling Haidar's ears against him and, over time, managed to sunder their intimate bond. Things came to such a pass that Haidar even sent Fazalullah Khan a demand that he submit eight lakh Pagodas that he was told he owed to the state. The latter literally pawned and sold all his valuables to make the payment, reducing himself to a state of penury; he eventually died with the same sense of disenchantment and betrayal that he felt the ungrateful Haidar had meted out to him.

In 1779, Haidar also dispatched a grand embassy to Delhi to secure for himself the imperial grants of the subahdari of the two Carnatics of Bijapur and Hyderabad. The motive, as Wilks states, seems to be 'in order that an exterior dignity which still commanded some respect, might accompany the possession of an authority, which he had now an early prospect of conferring on himself.'[22] His dreams, however, remained just dreams.

Haidar's Navy

After his conquest of Bidanur in 1763 and Soonda in 1764, the ports of Onore (Honnavar), Mangalore, Bhatkal and Piro (Sadashivgad) came into Haidar's possession. This gave Haidar the desire to build a navy of his own as he had seen how the might of the British and Maratha power, and earlier that of the Portuguese, rested on their respective maritime supremacies. He knew that without such an arrangement, he would be at the mercies of those naval powers, both militarily and also for maritime trade. With the conquests in Malabar, more sea ports came under his sway. Ali Raja of Cannanore and his Mapillahs were great navigators and they formed an excellent crew to man the ships that Haidar was getting built.

With Haidar's rising power, the Portuguese thought it appropriate to send a short biography of his, along with a letter dated 26 January 1764, to Lisbon. Here, though they talk about his conquest of the Canara region, they do not mention anything about his naval power. But around 23 September 1765, one of their letters says the following:

> The whole of this part of Asia (now) enjoys the benefit of a peace (which is) insecure, on account of the unbridled ambition of the potentates who rule this area: Our neighbours, the Marathas and Aidar Aly Can concluded it in the last winter, and the freedom in which the latter is, permits him to augment a fleet which has already begun to cause us some anxiety, and if at present we fear him as a pirate, we have reason to apprehend that time and luck may give him the power to ruin us. We know that his fleet now consists of thirty vessels of war and a large number of transport ships. It is commanded by an Englishman with some European officers.[23]

Thus, in 1763 after conquering Bidanur, within a mere span of two years, Haidar seems to have put together a naval fleet of some sorts and much like other regional powers, used European officers to modernize and also command them. But whether this naval fleet was of any major use to him or aided his military strength is something that is doubtful. In the accounts of Charles Rathbone Low, British officer of the Indian Navy, we get to know that in 1768, during the First Anglo–Mysore War, the British in Bombay launched an expedition to attack Haidar's seaports in the Malabar with a squadron of ships, 400 European troops and a large body of their sepoys. As Low states:

> The expedition first made its appearance off Onore, or Honawur [sic], where Hyder Ally, the great ruler of Mysore . . . had begun to prepare a fleet. He had, however, alienated from his interests the captains of his ships by appointing as his admiral Ali Bey [Lutf Ali Beg], an officer of cavalry, who of course, was totally ignorant of nautical matters. The consequence was that, when the expedition appeared off Onore, Hyder's fleet consisting of two ships, two grabs, [*ghurabs*] and ten *galivats*,[24] sailed and joined the English. Onore, and Fortified Island, at the mouth of the Onore River, were captured and thence the expedition sailed to Mangalore.[25]

The deserting Englishman being referred above was Stannett whom Haidar had inducted to command his fleet after displacing Ali Raja following his atrocity on the king of Maldives. Stannett and Lutf Ali Beg did not get along and so the former used the earliest opportunity to defect. This also seemed to be a common feature where European officers of other nationalities deserted Maratha chief Daulat Rao Sindhia during the Second Maratha War. Another Portuguese letter, dated 28 December 1778, states that Haidar was again building a large number of men of war and that a Dutchman Joe Azelars was employed to boost the port of Bhatkal. Haidar had always maintained a friendly and non-confrontationist stance with the Dutch and often approached them for help with carpenters and blacksmiths to build him ships in Calicut. Innes Munro, a captain in the late 73rd or Lord Macleod's Regiment of Highlanders, states in his accounts:

As all great acquisitions in this country are made by force of arms, the first object with Hyder Ally was to establish a good army; and experience taught him, in the course of his frequent conflicts with the English, that European discipline was absolutely essential to that end. He therefore endeavoured, by every possible means, to allure to his standard military adventures of all nations and tribes, but particularly the European artificers and sepoys, that had been trained up in the Company's service, to whom he held out the most tempting rewards . . . by this means he soon brought his established forces to a perfection in European discipline never before known amongst the black powers in India; and his progress in tactics has been a matter of astonishment and terror to all those who have ventured to encounter him in the field. But what at once shew the extended ideas and ambition of this prince, are his surprising endeavours to become formidable at sea. No art has been left untried to entice into his pay our ship-carpenters and dockyard-men from Bombay and other places; and in this attempt the French and other European powers have been induced to assist him; so that the progress which he has already made in constructing docks and equipping a naval force is almost incredible.[26]

A Portuguese letter of 28 December 1778 states:

I should particularly inform you that the Nabob Aidar Ali, aspiring to make himself as respectable on the sea as he is formidable on land has ordered the construction of many sailing ships in all the places of the south coast (which are) big enough for this great work. He has hitherto in the sea or in stocks eight three-masted ships which carry 28 to 40 pieces (of artillery) and a similar number of *Palas*,[27] also in the sea or in stocks, of lesser tonnage. For making a great progress in the work and to provide necessary accommodation for building and preserving the most powerful fleet in Asia, he began this month to build a stockade above the water line in the gulf of Batical [Bhatkal], which is situated near Onore on the firm land to the south, and is very near the island of Angediva, with

the intention of constructing a huge mole which will enclose a
port, where (at the full tide) it is said, a large fleet can anchor.
The projected work also includes fortification for the defence of
the port. It is being at present outlined according to its circuit
inland; it will have an enclosure big enough for a large borough
for the residence of numerous merchants of all nationalities who
are expected to be attracted by the gift of convenient plots of the
neighbouring lands and the loan of capital, which will ensure their
establishment in that place where large warehouses for storing
goods, articles and ammunition for a big marine, and factories for
the work of a busy arsenal have been so well-planned.[28]

The Portuguese had kept a close watch on this ambitious project
that quite threatened them. Much to their delight and to Haidar's
own ill luck, the enterprise did not proceed satisfactorily and was
plagued with all kinds of impediments. They note this cheerfully in
their letter correspondences, dated 11 May 1779, that it experienced
'opposition from the Brahmans who assist him as inspectors or
overseers of that work.'[29] The grand naval projects of Haidar were
to receive further blows during his forthcoming skirmish with
the British. Though it was an aborted and unsuccessful attempt,
Haidar's move to build a navy in right earnest were surely proof
of his foresight and strategic thinking. His European advisers
obviously did not share the zeal or patriotic sentiments that he
brought to the enterprise. Added to this, his own ignorance of
maritime matters and constant warfare diverted his attention from
a task as important as this. As Buchanan states: 'The attempt is,
however, no impeachment on the sagacity of Haidar, who having
been educated in a place remote from every kind of navigation,
could have no idea of what boats could perform, nor of what
obstacles would prevent their utility.'[30] On some of the unique
features of Haidar's military power, Innes Munro writes:

Hyder Ally also employs some thousands of men for throwing
rockets. This is a missive weapon, and made in the same form as

those used by schoolboys, with this difference, that the stalk is a thick bamboo, eight or ten feet long, which has a tube of iron, from six to twelve pounds weight, fixed to the end of it, in which the fuse and powder are placed. In wet weather, or marshy grounds, these are set off flying in the air, and will reach to the distance of a mile and a half; but upon dry grounds they are pointed horizontally, and bound in a very uncertain direction, often creating great damage, particularly amongst cavalry and ammunition tumbrils. Hyder's train of artillery is chiefly composed of French and Danish guns of different calibers, but most commonly heavy metal, which are doubly yoked with trained bullocks; and are as well and expeditiously served as ours.[31]

Discontent Within

Even as Haidar was busy strengthening his military and naval strength, there was a brewing discontent that had the potential to totally derail him. This came from the most unlikely of quarters, from within the zenana of the displaced royal family of Mysore. Maharani Lakshmi Ammanni, the widow of Krishnaraja Wodeyar II, was a woman with a mission. Seeing that Haidar's hold on the polity was increasing by the day, she burned with the desire to rid her family and the kingdom of this eclipse. Born in 1742 to Katti Gopalaraja Urs, under whom Haidar had worked along with his brother during their early years in Bangalore, Lakshmi Ammanni had been widowed at twenty-four. Haidar's high-handed approach when it came to appointing rulers of his choice, disregarding her nominees, created a natural disgust in her mind. Her annoyance was furthered when Haidar appointed Muddu Malamma, her late husband's illegitimate wife, as the regent of the young king, Bettada Chamaraja Wodeyar. As G.R. Josyer puts it, 'while yet looking forward to a long career of womanly and queenly happiness, Lakshmammanni was left a dowerless widow, without offspring, without husband, without kingdom, with princely orphans to maintain and a powerful usurper to fight against! If she had been the Miss Mayo type of Indian woman, she would have lost heart and cowered before her responsibility.'[32] But she certainly was made of stronger stuff.

As early as 1765, emissaries had been sent to Lord Pigot, the Governor of Madras, through Rayadurga Srinivasa Rao. Pigot had responded favourably, but said that vanquishing a powerful man like Haidar would require a permanent and trusted envoy of the royal family to be stationed in Madras and inform the British regularly about the happenings in Mysore. But the tumult of that decade somehow kept the British too preoccupied to respond to the Rani's overtures.

The Rani deeply trusted the community of the Sri Vaishnavas or the Iyengars who had been loyally associated with the royal family for long. Known as the community of Mandyam Iyengars, they traced their origins to Mahavidwan U. Ve. Anandalvan or Anantaraya Swami (1053–1154), born in Siruputtur. He was a contemporary of the great Sri Vaishnava philosopher and the proponent of the Vishistadwaita school, Bhagwad Ramanujacharya. Anantaraya was a devoted disciple of the saint and they belonged to the Bharadwaja *gotra* or lineage. His descendants came to be known as the Mandyam Anandampillai (M.A.) family. Even during the Vijayanagara era, this community had an important position in the sociocultural, political and intellectual milieu. Under Chikkadevaraja Wodeyar, who was a staunch Vaishnava, their importance and role was greatly enhanced. Apart from royal patronage, they also occupied positions in the administration either as gurus of the kings or as senior officials, as mentioned.

In fact, it was a member of this family, Govindarajayya, who had solemnized the marriage of Rani Lakshmi Ammanni with Maharaja Krishnaraja Wodeyar. Haidar had always seen them with immense suspicion given this close association. In 1765, he had even ordered a raid on the house of Govindarajayya on the charges that he had secretly buried treasures whose location he refused to disclose. The frustrated raider had attacked and even strangled him to death.[33] His sons, Tirumala Rao and Narayana Rao,[34] were incensed by this inhuman act and vowed to avenge their father's death by teaming up with Rani Lakshmi Ammanni, and offering their services to her as her Pradhans. Incidentally, they were nephews of Anche Shamaiya.

Given her restrictions and limitations, the Rani used the duo, famously known as the Mysore Pradhans, as her emissaries with several powers of the time, seeking support against Haidar. Through them, messages were carried to Poona to Madhav Rao to request Maratha support, which did come. But, as mentioned earlier, Haidar had cleverly made peace and bought them off. Since he did not want to take any harsh measures against the royal family, and more so a woman member of it, Haidar's ire fell on Tirumala Rao whom he suspected to be instrumental in these negotiations with the Peshwa. He got Tirumala Rao arrested and when he later went on his conquest of Bellary and Gutti, took him along, lest the latter carry out any conspiracies in the capital in his absence. Tirumala Rao was then packed off to Cudappah. Rani Lakshmi Ammanni's requests reached him even in Cudappah. The British had helped the native ruler of Tanjore to occupy his lawful throne. Emboldened by this, she saw hope in the British as being able to help her family too. But she needed an able negotiator who could convey her messages and offers to the Company. Therefore, in 1776, she prevailed upon Tirumala Rao to carry her offer to Lord Pigot and, in return, offered the position of Dewan of Mysore in perpetuity to the Pradhan family once the kingdom passed back to the Wodeyar family. He was also promised an annual salary that was 10 per cent of the state revenue. This was an assignment fraught with danger, as Haidar's strict surveillance system had the Pradhans on its radar all the time. Yet, both their admiration for the royal family and of course the generous rewards being offered in lieu of their support made the brothers accept the Rani's offer.

But as luck could have it for the Rani and her Pradhans, a controversy had broken out in Madras about Pigot's involvement in the Tanjore affair and he was arrested by his opponents. Despite this, the Pradhans managed to communicate with Pigot who advised them to stay at Tanjore, where he promised to meet them after a year when he was confident of being relieved of all the false charges and reinstated as governor. The brothers accordingly took shelter in Tanjore. But to their immense disappointment, within a few months, the news reached them that Pigot had died in Madras. There were all kinds of rumours that it was Muhammad Ali of Arcot who had been involved in the death of Pigot through a mysterious black magic ritual that he had got a Brahmin, Achena Pandit, to perform. A cobra hung from its tail to the roof of a building, with proper incense and a fire lit below, was ritualistically sacrificed in the belief that it would bring about the death of an opponent.[35]

The Pradhans however were now caught in a no man's land and did not know where to proceed. However, the Raja of Tanjore and the British Resident there, John Sullivan, was sympathetic to their cause and offered them shelter. By then Haidar got wind of these activities and issued a red alert in their name, ordering an arrest or killing of the Pradhans. They patiently bided their time in Tanjore, waiting for the next earliest opportunity to carry forward the negotiations. That opportunity was to present itself to them soon enough.

Though she remained in seclusion in the zenana, Maharani Lakshmi Ammanni remained undaunted as some of her letters to the well-wishers of her family demonstrate her quiet faith in the mercy of providence to relieve the misfortune that had befallen her family. The night shall pass and the sun will eventually rise, was her constant refrain. 'May Lord Ranga help us!' was how she signed off most of her letters, writing them under a pseudonym of 'Sri Ranga'— in reverence to the Lord Ranganatha Swamy of Srirangapatna. The locals and the subjects held her in the highest esteem and fondly called her 'Mahamathrushree,' the maternal figure. Even as Haidar was virulently involved in his numerous campaigns, his enemy within was secretly showing the doorway to his most hated foe, the British, and trying to strike at the very roots of his establishment and shaking his foundations, brick by brick.

Political and Matrimonial Alliances

After several long conquests, Haidar finally returned to Srirangapatna in 1779 for some well-earned respite. But even while he was with his family, politics did not seem to have left his mind. While the Pathan Nawab of Cudappah had been reduced, the one in Savanur was still inimical. So, Haidar decided to establish matrimonial relationships with the Nawab through his children. He offered the hand of his daughter in marriage to the Nawab's eldest son, Abdul Khire Khan (or Khira Miyan), and in return sought the Nawab's daughter for his second son, Karim Sahib. Karim, the second son, who was born prematurely the day before Haidar's sudden flight from Srirangapatna after Khande Rao's treachery, was born to him and the daughter of Mehdi Beg, a commander of 200 horse at Arcot. The mother had died shortly after the birth of Karim and another daughter and the children were brought up by one of Haidar's favourite dancing girls, Zohreh. Haidar sent his vakils to Savanur to negotiate the alliances with the Nawab, informing him that 'acting together, they might wage war with greater effect on the infidels, and that as a result of their union, the whole body of the Mussulman people, and the high and low of all tribes, might repose happily on the couch of comfort and safety, and continually offer up prayers for the lasting prosperity of their government.'[36]

The Nawab, who had seen the threatening menace of Haidar in Chitradurga and Cudappah recently, was gratified that peace could be established with Mysore through these alliances. He readily sent in his affirmative and was soon welcomed in Srirangapatna with much fanfare. It was also agreed that half of Savanur that had remained with Haidar after the Maratha conquests was to be returned to the Nawab, along with Bankapur, as a gift. The Nawab had to maintain at Haidar's service 2000 select Pathan horses to be commanded by two of his sons. With all the agreements in place, the two marriages were then celebrated at Srirangapatna with great pomp and merrymaking. Haidar's select high officials Anche Shamaiya, Purnaiya, Krishna Rao, Mir Sadak and Mustafa Ali Khan were the notables who assembled to witness the celebrations.

Even as Haidar was enjoying the celebrations of his children's marriages, there came to Srirangapatna from Poona an envoy of the Barbhai group and the new Peshwa Sawai Madhav Rao, ostensibly to convey the good wishes of the group of ministers there. Ganesh Rao was however sent to negotiate with Haidar and influence him to join an emerging alliance of the Marathas and the Nizam with the objective of driving the British out of India. It was a well-thought of strategy of uniting all the Indian forces against the European power and was possibly the brainchild of Nana Phadnis. Nizam Ali, the capricious ally, was dissatisfied with the British as the latter had discontinued the tributes that were due for the Northern Circars and for leasing Guntur to Muhammad Ali of Arcot, rather than Basalat Jung who had hitherto enjoyed the jagirs of Adoni, Guntur and so on. Given Basalat Jung's increasing closeness to the French, the British were always apprehensive of him and wanted to cut the influence of the French in his polity by forcibly finding their foothold in his jagirs. In their zeal to foil the French, the British kindled the jealousies and insecurities of both Nizam Ali and Haidar as these new moves threatened both their territories.

Haidar therefore lent a sympathetic ear to these talks as he had grown to increasingly distrust the British, especially after they failed to keep their promises in the Treaty of Madras of 1769, by not following up with any help to Mysore when Madhav Rao invaded shortly afterwards. Haidar had thereafter made overtures to the French and their Governor M. Bellicombe had willingly supplied stores and ammunition to Mysore with a promise of military assistance. French General M. Lally even moved over to Haidar's side with 100 European infantry, fifty European cavalry, 1000 native infantry and two guns. Haidar's military strategy was to have an efficient army that was trained by a European power, commensurate to that of the British in order to extract his revenge from them.

Ganesh Rao represented to Haidar that were he to give up his support to the fugitive and murderer Raghoba and, in return, the grants that Raghoba had made of the territory between the Tungabhadra and Krishna Rivers would be confirmed by the new dispensation in Poona. All past demands of Rs 25 lakh balance payments due since the time of Trimbak Rao were to be written off and a more modest annual payment of Rs 11 lakh was fixed. Nizam Ali was to invade the Northern Circars, the Marathas of Berar, Malwa and north India to attack Bengal and Bihar, while those in

Poona would attack Bombay. Haidar was to direct his force against the Carnatic and Madras. It was an all-out attempt to expel the British completely from India.

The stage was now being set for another major and decisive conflict that Haidar was to be involved in—one that would also be among his last.

8

The Second Anglo–Mysore War

It was no coincidence that the idea of a united front against the British originated from Poona. The Maratha state was a confederacy of several principalities that were loosely held together and extended their sway over a vast part of the subcontinent, coming thereby in direct conflict with the British, not just in the Deccan but in the rest of the country too, be it Bengal, Madras or Bombay. By 1778, Nana Phadnis's authority had been consolidated in Poona, though the British preferred a more pliant representative there like Raghoba. In lieu of their support to his claim of the Peshwa position, Raghoba had even offered the British the entire Konkan, command over one of the ghats and also the right of sardeshmukhi from Maratha jagirs. But hatred and revulsion for Raghoba among the nobility in Poona, especially after the murder of the Peshwa, was at an all-time high and the British knew this only too well. The first British Governor General Warren Hastings also realized this and he had his own favourite, Mudhoji Bhonsle, in Nagpur whom he wanted to plant as a puppet Peshwa. Nana Phadnis was aware of this threat that the British posed of wanting to control the Maratha Empire through subterfuge. The British had not honoured any clause of the Treaty of Purandhar that they had signed with the ministers of Poona; they had continued to shelter the fugitive Raghoba and had fomented dissension in the infant Peshwa's dominions. A clash between the combined troops of Raghoba and the British against Poona took place, where the former was vanquished and Raghoba gave himself up to Mahadji Sindhia. As he had done in the past, too, Raghoba

* Please refer to the corresponding illustration in the appendix.

214

however managed to escape from Mahadji's clutches and sought shelter in Surat with Col Goddard.

With a rapprochement with the British seeming unlikely, the Marathas did not want to open two war fronts and hence thought of truce with their old foe, Haidar Ali. So keen was Nana Phadnis for an alliance with Haidar that several of his demands were conceded. The Maratha envoy at Srirangapatna noted: 'This agreement is not a small thing. We have together embarked on the same venture. Such a friendship and such understanding could not be established in the days of the deceased Peshwa (Madhav Rao).'[1]

Emboldened by this emerging alliance, there was a definite change in Haidar's stance towards the British, whom he, as it is, despised for several reasons. While he had cordially treated the earlier envoy Rev. Schwartz whom the Madras Government had sent to Srirangapatna, the same courtesy was not extended to George Gray, formerly of the Bengal Civil Service, whom the British sent for talks. On his arrival in Srirangapatna in February 1780, Gray was assigned a dingy, miserable shed that was filled with artillery ropes. Gray delivered a letter from the Madras Government along with a Hogskin saddle and a gun as presents to Haidar. Much to his dismay, these were returned the next morning as not being befitting the receiver or the giver.[2] Haidar gave no personal interview or attention to Gray; only his agent, Muhammad Usman, held talks with Gray. Through his coldness and through Usman's strong words, Haidar conveyed amply that he no longer cared for an alliance with the British. Gray waited for nearly a month in Srirangapatna but by March 1780, was unceremoniously asked by Haidar to leave the capital forthwith. As Gray reports:

> I took occasion at the same time to express to the Nabob [Haidar] the sentiments of regard and friendship which the Government of Fort St George and the English nation in general entertained towards His Highness, but I am sorry to say my professions on that subject . . . were answered with reproaches of expected breaches of treaties and the British nation was charged with a positive breach

of treaty. Notwithstanding the unpleasant manifestation of the Nabob's sentiments, I continued in Seringapatam [Srirangapatna] in hopes of finding some favourable opportunity of an explanation but I was completely disappointed; for he never permitted me to visit him again till the 19th March, when he sent me purposely to give me an audience of leave. I have to observe that my reception at the court was neither friendly nor respectful, a few instances of politeness were overbalanced by many more of inattention and slight and I will venture to say that the latter had the appearance of being evidently marked.[3]

The Invasion of the Carnatic

Haidar's intentions were thus as clear as daylight. His Brahmin astrologers advised him to commence hostilities on the auspicious date of 28 May 1780 and accordingly Haidar marched out of Srirangapatna with an unprecedented large force of nearly a lakh. It was undeniably one of the largest armies ever assembled in southern India. To keep his movement secretive, it was declared that he was heading towards Kolar, where his father lay buried, to perform some rituals at his tomb. But prayers for the success of the military expedition were ordered to be offered from mosques and the *japam* to be conducted in Hindu temples. With 45,000 cavalry, thirty battalions of sepoys, seventy pieces of cannon, with an immense quantity of military stores of every kind, along with some 50,000 troops, Haidar's army was daunting. The French had sent him 300 Europeans under the command of Lally. Tipu, whom Innes Munro mentions as 'a prince possessed of all his father's military genius, with no less abilities; and who is always deemed a formidable second to Hyder in every enterprise'[4] was obviously an integral part of the expedition. Several killedars of forts on the route from Mysore, belonging to Muhammad Ali of Arcot were bought out by him and his spies obtained employment in the British army as guides. Muhammad Ali kept warning the British of an impending attack by Haidar, but the latter were now too used to his false alarms bordering on a hysterical paranoia for Haidar that they barely gave it much credence. Muhammad Ali of course made no commitments of either money or troops to the British to carry out his defence against the latest Mysore invasion. Haidar had sent Muhammad Ali another warning asking the latter to honour the old commitment made to Mysore of ceding Tiruchirapalli, but he remained indifferent.

Descending on the plains through Baramahal and the Changama Pass, Haidar swept down like an avalanche, beginning his march of pillage and burning of villages on the route to the Carnatic. From Masulipatnam in the north to Arcot, Chingleput, Vellore, Pondicherry, Kumbakonam, Tanjore, Tiruchirapalli, Madurai and Rameshwaram in the south, the whole Carnatic region was raided. Balavant Rao was dispatched with 500 horses to Karur to intercept the British forces before they reached Tiruchirapalli and Sardar Khan to Calicut to guard Tellicherry. A detachment under his second son, Karim Sahib, plundered the seaport town of Porto Novo (Mahmood Bundar), south of Pondicherry, in June. Kirmani states that Karim 'plundered the houses of all the wealthy merchants, bankers and traders, of bales and bales of merchandise, and bags on bags of gold and jewels . . . cloths of great value, and dresses of honour from the countries of Bengal, Bunaras, China, Kashmeer, Boorhanpoor, Mutchliputtun. All these articles were taken, and laden on elephants, camels, bullocks and carts; and with the merchant to whom they had belonged, and his dependents, as prisoners were sent to the Nawaub.'[5] Information of all these movements were sent to Madras, but the government there hardly paid any attention to it.

With the intention of completely isolating Fort St George and preventing any help from coming, both from the north and the west, Haidar laid waste to the entire country that stretched in between. He took the hill-fort of Tiruvannamalai and Chetput. Tipu was dispatched to reduce Arni and Timri, which he readily took along with smaller forts of Tiruvatoor, Gulwa and Kaveripak. Edmund Burke, the statesman and orator in England, recounts:

He [Haidar] became at length so confident of his force, so collected in his might, that he made no secret whatsoever of his dreadful resolution. Having terminated his disputes with every enemy, and every rival, who buried their mutual animosities in their common detestation against the creditors of the Nabob of Arcot, he drew from every quarter whatever a savage ferocity could add to his new rudiments in the arts of destruction; and compounding all the materials of fury, havoc, and desolation, into one black cloud, he hung for a while on the declivities of the mountains. Whilst the authors of all these evils were idly and stupidly gazing on this menacing meteor, which blackened all their horizon, it suddenly burst, and poured down the whole of its contents upon the plains of the Carnatic. Then ensued a scene of woe, the like of which no eye had seen, no heart conceived, and which no tongue can adequately tell. All the horrors of war before known or heard of, were mercy to that new havoc. A storm of universal fire blasted every field, consumed every house, destroyed every temple. The miserable inhabitants flying from their flaming villages, in part were slaughtered; others, without regard to sex, to age, to the respect of rank, or sacredness of function; fathers torn from children, husbands from wives, enveloped in a whirlwind of cavalry, and amidst the goading spears of drivers, and the trampling of pursuing horses, were swept into captivity, in an unknown and hostile land. Those who were able to evade this tempest, fled to the walled cities. But escaping from fire, sword, and exile, they fell into the jaws of famine.[6]

Innes Munro, an eyewitness and a captain in the late 73rd or Lord Macleod's Regiment of Highlanders, records the horrors that this invasion of the Carnatic by Haidar brought in its wake:

All the villages blazing on every quarter within view of this garrison, and as many of the inhabitants as could escape with their lives flying towards us in immense droves from all parts of the country, whose cries and lamentations were distinctly heard a full mile off, being closely pursued by those inhuman barbarians, who brandished their bloody swords in triumph as they galloped along . . . aged parents borne . . . upon the bleeding shoulders of their offspring, who were wantonly mutilated; mothers bewailing the loss of their helpless infants that had fallen a sacrifice to the fury of the enemy on the first surprise; and innocent virgins clinging for protection to the arms of their lacerated brothers. This was indeed a melancholy spectacle, which made the deepest impression upon our sympathizing minds, as yet unaccustomed to such scenes of brutality and horror; but which a poor soldier must not only learn to behold, but participate in, with calmness and indifference. Such was the extreme terror of those inoffensive and unhappy people, that they never once slackened their pace until they found themselves immersed in the ditch of Pondmalee.[7]

The Battle of Polilur

By 21 August 1780, Haidar turned his victorious march towards Arcot to lay siege to it. It was only when the smoke of the pillage was visibly seen from St Thomas Mount that the British realized what had hit them. It was too sudden and a surprise attack and the Madras Government was taken unawares though they knew of the confabulations between Mysore, Hyderabad and Poona. The Madras Government had no cavalry of its own and depended on Muhammad Ali for this. He however had not been able to pay salaries to his cavalry and several of them had consequently deserted him and defected to Haidar. The spy system of the British too was poorly organized and was not able to catch the intent and extent of the invasion that Haidar had planned. Innes Munro states that the poor spies who usually managed to get them some intelligence into Haidar's movements 'generally did it at the expense of their ears and noses, and some even of their lives; a risk which at last no man would venture to run for any pecuniary reward whatever.'[8] Finally, when they did manage to get their act together, they dispatched Lieutenant Colonel (Lt Col) Baillie, who was in command of a detachment in Guntur, to proceed southwards with 200 European infantry, two companies of artillery, five battalions of sepoys and ten field pieces. Simultaneously, Col Braithwaite was dispatched from

Pondicherry with 200 European foot, 100 European artillery, ten guns, four battalions of sepoys and a regiment of Arcot's cavalry. Col Cosby joined in from Tiruchirapalli. A field army was also put together at Kanchipuram under Major General Sir Hector Munro, the Commander-in-Chief of the Madras army, and a force of 3000 men from Madras under Lord Macleod. The harsh, scorching sun and the sultry weather added to the woes of the Europeans with nearly 'two hundred of the best men in the corps dropping down upon the road, quite exhausted and overpowered by his (sun's) vertical and scorching rays.'[9] Haidar who had besieged Arcot had kept himself fully appraised of the movement of the English troops through his spies. To avoid the junction of Baillie and Munro, he stationed himself at an advantageous position between the two and directed Tipu to intercept the former with his force of nearly 20,000 horse and foot with twelve guns.

Baillie however camped on the wrong side of the river and with the rains beating down, the river was fully swollen, impeding his further movement. It was only by the evening of 5 September 1780, battling torrential rains, that Baillie finally managed to arrive at Perambakam, about fourteen miles from Kanchipuram. Immediately he faced an onslaught from Tipu who was waiting for his prey. John Lindsay recounts that on 6 September 'a long, heavy and uninterrupted cannonade of six hours was heard.'[10] Baillie sent urgent requests to Munro, who was in Kanchipuram, seeking help. He wrote: 'On the fifth I crossed the river and on the sixth I commenced my march to join; in the morning I was attacked by a formidable army, consisting of horse, infantry and guns, commanded by Tippoo Saib, and after a severe action I entirely defeated him; he is now near me—I cannot come on. I am in want of everything, and expect you with anxiety!'[11] Haidar had conveniently stationed himself just two miles away between Baillie and Munro. Munro had his entire stockade in the temple of Kanchipuram, but hesitated to come out and openly attack Haidar for fear that if he left his station and set out, Haidar would pounce on it from another side, take possession of the town and also his supplies. To avoid the interception,

Munro dispatched Lt Col Fletcher with a strong detachment commanded by Lieutenant John Lindsay, Captains Baird, Phillips, Ferrier, Rumley and Gowdie to take a wide detour and aid Baillie who was hemmed in. Fletcher managed to reach by 8 September and emboldened by the reinforcement, Baillie foolishly attempted to march forth towards Kanchipuram with 3700 men. He had barely crossed five miles than Tipu's strong attacks commenced. Soon, being assured of Munro's reluctance to step out, Haidar too decided to join his son from the other end in furthering Baillie's misery. They kept such a close patrol of cavalry between the two camps that it was impossible for the British to counteract their vigilance. Innes Munro recounts that 'Hyder's means of intelligence were so multiplied and superior to ours, that nothing went on in either of our camps which he was not immediately informed of.'[12]

The Mysorean guns went all blazing against Baillie's army that had reached a village named Pullalur (Polilur). A section of Tipu's cavalry attacked Baillie's forces causing huge stampedes and disorders in the latter. Three of Baillie's ammunition tumbrils exploded, causing more confusion and disarray in his ranks. As Francis Robson gives a first-hand account: 'Tippoo Saib . . . took immediate advantage thereof, and with his cavalry made a rapid charge, penetrated their broken square, and being followed by the French corps, and the infantry of his first line, completed the overthrow of this gallant little band'.[13] Biccaji Sindhia, a high-ranking officer in the Mysore cavalry, decided to take advantage of this confusion in the enemy troops. Haidar had admonished Sindhia for not being cautious enough and for allowing Fletcher to join Baillie. Sindhia now wanted to repair his reputation and charged at the enemy, but was killed in the ambush, along with fifteen of his family members. Finally, Baillie displayed his white handkerchief as a token of surrender. Col Lally headed the French contingent of Haidar's army in this war. Col Baillie, David Baird and several other British officers were all taken prisoners. Of eighty-six British officers, thirty-six were killed or died of their wounds, thirty-four were wounded and taken, while sixteen were not wounded but taken prisoner.[14]

The defeat at Polilur was a serious blow to British prestige which had already suffered immensely in the First Anglo–Mysore War. It was one of the first and most serious setbacks that the British suffered in India. The whole detachment was either killed or taken prisoner. This defeat caused obvious consternation in Madras and in the Supreme Government in Calcutta. Sir Hector Munro, the hero of Buxar, who prided himself in having defeated three rulers—Mughal Emperor Shah Alam, Nawab of Awadh Shuja-ud-daula and Nawab of Bengal Mir Qasim, ran for his life to Madras, throwing all his cannons into the tank at Kanchipuram. Though Lally advised Haidar to pursue Munro, Haidar's inactivity gave Munro the opportunity to slip away. Had he followed him up to the gates of Madras as he had done more than a decade ago at the conclusion of the First Anglo–Mysore War, the fall of the Madras Government would have become inevitable. To that extent, it was a huge lost opportunity and miscalculation on Haidar's part, despite Lally's counsel. But that was the precipice on which British fortunes were precariously perched at this time of their history in India. Munro's strategy and Baillie's warfare had failed miserably and boomeranged on them badly.

It is said that when Baillie was taken to Haidar, the latter expressed regret at the fate that had befallen the British officer and gave him Rs 1000, so that he and his fellow-prisoners could 'eat, drink, sleep and be happy.'[15] The French, especially Lally and Pimorin, managed to convince Haidar to provide medical aid to their fellow-Europeans who were severely injured. Haidar, whom Lindsay saw as being dressed in a blue silk jacket and a red turban, appeared very pleased and often burst out into fits of laughter while conversing with Lally.[16] Heads of the slain opponents were being routinely brought to Haidar, who was enjoying the sight with great pleasure.[17] Haidar's young soldiers too amused themselves by fleshing their swords through the already wounded and beaten opponents, not sparing even women and children, plundering everyone till the last remnant of clothing too.[18] Eyewitness accounts of Innes Munro paint a dreary picture of the travails that the prisoners from his side had to face during their surrender and long march thereafter to Srirangapatna, where they were lodged in prison:

Some had been dragged to Hyder's camp, so mangled, so besmeared with blood, and covered with dust, that not a feature was to be recognized; some had dropped speechless upon the road from the cruel treatment of their conductors, who refused them even a drink of water to quench their burning thirst. Even the gentle little offices of humanity, which those less maimed might have shewn to their fellows, were cruelly interdicted; their savage guards buffeting and beating them with ends of their firelocks on the slightest symptom of tenderness which melting nature might discover . . . under this load of sorrow, of apprehension, and of suffering they remained for some days in the enemy's camp, when they were removed to Arcot and Arne. From thence, the whole were soon afterwards marched in an ignominious manner to Seringapatnam, Bangalore and other remote garrisons in the Misore [Mysore] country, escorted by a strong guard, who led them round every little village on the road, as a public testimony of their heroic exploits. In the course of this march, they were dreadfully exposed from their naked condition, to the violence of the sun . . . to complete their miseries, upon their arrival at the prisons appointed for them, their legs and arms were loaded with heavy irons and they were immured in horrid dungeons, where, during a wretched captivity, the treatment which they had to anticipate was such as hardly to be paralleled in the black annals of Asiatic cruelty.[19]

Among the prisoners was the young son of the commander of Vellore, Col Ross Lang. He was serving as a volunteer in the British army. Haidar sent for the boy and ordered him to write a letter to his father asking him to hand over the place he was commanding or face his son's death. On the boy's refusal, he was threatened and coerced till he burst out into tears and addressed Haidar: 'If you consider me base enough to write such a letter; on what ground can you think so meanly of my father? It is in your power to present me before the ramparts of Vellore and cut me into a thousand pieces in my father's presence; but it is out of your power to make him a traitor.'[20] When further threats and coercion did not work, the brave little boy was remanded to prison.

John Lindsay, who was around nineteen years of age then, kept a journal of his march of about 240 miles, along with his fellow-prisoners, to Srirangapatna that began on 22 September 1780, giving a graphic portrait of all that they endured en route and in the capital. They halted in each place where they were placed in the scorching heat for the onlookers and villagers to stare at for several hours. Nights were usually spent in cowsheds without a mat to lie on. But even in these situations of extreme torture, tiny glimmers of humanity shone in some of their opponents, which Lindsay documents. While there were many whom he trusted to help him as he lay in anguish but they stole his paltry possessions, he talks of one Mysorean sepoy who took pity on him when he came down with dysentery and high fever. He offered to make him a medicine if he so desired. On his affirmative, the sepoy made a decoction of green pomegranate juice and sour milk, after drinking which Lindsay fell into deep slumber. Much to his relief, he woke up pretty cured of the malady. The sepoy whose earnings were a mere Rs 6 a month, also offered one rupee to Lindsay, which the latter declined to take. 'This generous behaviour,' wrote Lindsay, 'so different from what I had hitherto experienced, drew tears from my eyes, and I thanked him for his generosity, but would not take his money.'[21] On 6 November 1780, the prisoners managed to finally reach Srirangapatna and stayed imprisoned in miserable conditions till 1784 with the conclusion of the war. Baillie however died in the interim.

When Lord Macleod reached Madras and sent a messenger to Haidar, seeking the restitution of some important papers that had been confiscated from his baggage during the retreat from Kanchipuram, Haidar scoffed saying: 'In so small an army as the British, such a thing might be done; but how was it possible for the commander of one hundred thousand men, to attend to such trifles?'[22] Bowring writes that this 'disaster was the most fatal that had ever overtaken the British arms in India.'[23] Obviously, both Haidar and Tipu were supremely proud of their achievements in the battle of Polilur. So much so that a painting was commissioned on the western wall of their Daria Dowlat Bagh palace in Srirangapatna to depict the happenings of this battle, known as *'Lally–Baillie*

Yuddha.' Baillie is depicted sitting in a palanquin gnawing his thumb with annoyance. Haidar is seen on an elephant amidst his troops, marching forth in the battle. There are swordsmen on horseback and footmen with spears. A second panel depicts Tipu riding on a horse and proceeding to this battle. The third panel shows the victory of Mysore at the battle. Haidar and Tipu guide their troops and the Mysore cavalry is shown charging at the red-coated British soldiers from both directions. A ball from the French gunners is seen exploding the British ammunition, indicating the certainty of their defeat. As historian N.K. Sinha writes:

> This victory revealed Haidar's best qualities as a general—his accurate intelligence, his correct estimate of the mental qualities of the enemy, his readiness to run a considerable risk to win a great success. The defeat of a British army was a rare achievement in Indian wars and a French officer of Haidar wrote, 'There is not in India an example of a similar defeat.' It is true that the armies were not evenly matched. In numbers, in cavalry (of which the British had none), and in artillery Haidar had a great superiority, and it was the mistakes of the British and the inactivity of Munro that caused the disaster. Nevertheless, Haidar had seized his opportunity and used it brilliantly.[24]

The War Continues

After the victory in Polilur, Haidar returned to Arcot to continue the siege on 19 September 1780. He ordered a simultaneous assault by two columns under Tipu and Maha Mirza Khan each. In the battle that ensued, Haidar's son-in-law, Saiyid Hafiz Ali Khan, was killed by a cannon ball. By the end of November 1780, the place surrendered to him and Muhammad Ali's governor there Achanna Pandit and others in the fort like Arshad Beg Khan, Chistiyar Khan and Saiyid Hamid were taken prisoners but treated with consideration. Mir Sadak was appointed the Subahdar of the city of Arcot. Arcot was made the headquarters for Haidar's subsequent attacks in the Carnatic. The whole territory was overrun and plundered, and the hapless inhabitants faced the invader's fury and pillage. Several of them ran away to seek shelter in Tanjore. Haidar, in the intoxication of his stupendous success, even declared Tipu as the Nawab of the Carnatic.

With the fall of Arcot, Haidar turned his attention to reduce the Carnatic Payanghat all through December 1780, penetrating deep into the south as far as Tanjore and taking possession of several places and forts in the region. Achanna was restored to his position on the condition of the payment of an annual tribute. By early January 1781, Haidar had resumed his ambush with the siege of five places that were commanded by English officers—Ambur, Vellore, Wandiwash, Permacoil and Chingleput. Ambur was an important centre in the Carnatic and it held out for over a month, under Captain Keating, before falling to the ammunition of Tipu and Lally by 13 January.

The news of the disaster for the British in the Carnatic and the failure of Sir Hector Munro in preventing this, set alarm bells ringing in the Supreme Government at Calcutta. The Governor-General Warren Hastings resolved to retrieve the situation and deputed Sir Eyre Coote, a man of reputation who was serving as Commander-in-Chief in India and a member of the Supreme Council. He was one of the key architects of the British victory in the Battle of Plassey. Though he was sixty years old by then, Coote's mental faculties were sharp as ever, though physically he was not as strong as he was earlier. He was cheered as being 'the distinguished favourite of heaven if he succeeds'[25] amidst a situation of total gloom and doom in the British camp. Eyre Coote arrived at Madras in November 1780 with a large contingent of troops and Rs 15 lakh. The Governor of Madras Whitehill was suspended for his lackadaisical attitude and lack of foresight and strategy that were deemed as the causes for this failure. Sir Charles Smith, a Senior Member of Council, replaced him. Heads had to roll. Such was the earth-shattering impact that the Mysorean attack had on the British establishment.

Hastings also tried to break the confederacy of Mysore, Hyderabad and Poona, which in real terms had done precious little to help Haidar, who was left much to his own resources to handle the situation. The weakest link in the confederacy, as always, was Nizam Ali. He was bought over by Hastings by the restitution of Guntur, which was his main grouse.

As Haidar advanced towards Wandiwash, Eyre Coote deputed Lieutenant Flint to the place to assist Muhammad Ali's killedar there. The killedar however had been bought over by Haidar and was readying to surrender the fort. Flint got wind of the treachery and, evading the Mysore cavalry, reached Wandiwash. He spoke affably with the killedar, though the latter tried to ward him off, asking him to return. He sought an audience with the killedar, stating that he had a letter from the Nawab of Arcot to deliver to him. In his presence however, Flint confessed that he had no such letter and that he was instead carrying the message of the Madras Government that was acting on behalf of the Nawab. The killedar laughed derisively and asked Flint to leave the place right away. However, Flint's men tightly caught hold of the killedar and asked him to mend his ways, be in titular command and leave the work of defending the place to the British. The daring of the young Flint shocked one and all and the killedar had no option but to acquiesce, even as Flint took complete charge of the fort. He had no artillery men with him, but he sought out all the goldsmiths and trained them to be gunners. He contacted the headmen of the nearby villages and got their assurance of regular supplies and provisions, so that he need not raid them. Meer Sahib had laid siege to Wandiwash with a powerful train of artillery, 11,000 foot and 22,000 horses. However, Flint held on to his position despite several attempts to ambush him. Tipu meanwhile opened his campaign with the siege of Ambur, which soon surrendered to his might.

Coote began his campaign in mid-January 1781 to relieve Chingleput, Wandiwash and Permacoil. Sir Hector Munro and Lord Macleod accompanied him. At this time, news came of a French fleet under the Chevalier Monsieur d'Ovres being sighted off Madras. This was a reaction of the French to the successive defeats of the British; their Governor in Mauritius, Francois de Souillac, had dispatched a squadron of seven ships of the line and five frigates under d'Ovres on a roving expedition to India. They attempted to cut off Coote's supplies from Bengal that came via the sea route. While Coote had initially thought of retracing his steps to Madras, he decided to move down the coast to Pondicherry and Cuddalore, destroying the surf boats that might be of use were the French fleet to arrive there. But by February, in Cuddalore, his supplies had been fully exhausted. His army needed a minimum of 4,50,000 bags of rice to feed his men, but had received only 1,25,000. Though the situation improved slightly with time, rice supplies remained extremely limited with just 90,000 extra bags being received.[26] Haidar had pursued Coote and was encamped barely ten miles away. Haidar was confident that with his troops and the French fleet, he would be able to hem in Coote, too, and his surrender seemed just a matter of time. Coote's army was on the verge of starvation at this critical juncture. In Coote's own words: 'I cannot command rice enough to move either to the northward or the southward. I offered him (Haidar) battle yesterday, but I no sooner shewed myself, than he moved off, and has taken possession of and strengthened all the roads leading to the southward. I have written to Nagore in the most pressing terms for supplies—I depend upon every effort in your power—everything must be risked to assist me—my difficulties are great indeed. I need say no more to induce you to take such steps as will speedily enable me to act as becomes a soldier.'[27]

However, from 8 February to 16 June, the British troops stayed on here stressfully, in expectation of supplies from Madras and Masulipatnam. There was not much movement from the Mysorean end too, barring their conquest of Tiruvadi and Tyagadurg, along with Udaiyarpalayam, Ariyalur and Palamcotta. Admiral Sir Edward Hughes opened a new western front for Haidar by reducing the French fort of Mahe and destroying Haidar's infant navy in his own ports of Calicut and Mangalore. This forced the French fleet to change directions and navigate back to Mauritius, opening up the lines for the much needed supplies for Coote. At the brink of definite collapse, destiny suddenly seemed to have smiled on Coote. Haidar retreated from Cuddalore to Porto Novo, leaving behind Mir Ali

Raza Khan, Sidi Hilal and Ghazi Khan to intercept all supplies to the British. He reduced and occupied all the intermediate posts between the English army and the southern provinces and then marched to Porto Novo. From here, detachments were sent into the interior to Tanjore, which was totally ravaged. The idea was to draw Coote out from Cuddalore through all these acts in the southern end. Weavers and their families were forcibly gathered from Tanjore and packed off to Srirangapatna. Wilks states that 'captive boys destined to the exterior honour of Islam, were driven to the same place with equal numbers of females, the associates of the present, and the mothers of a future race of military slaves.'[28] Robson mentions the plunder of Hindu temples in Tanjore:

> Hyder entered the Tanjore country, plundering and burning every village in their way; spreading desolation everywhere; even the Gentoo [Hindu] temples, which hitherto were held sacred by all castes, were plundered of their *swamies*, or idols, by his people of the Moorish [Muslim] sect. About this time a Gentoo *subidar* or captain in his service, requested his permission to bear a Gentoo flag, with the figure of the Swamie Annamoontoo [possibly Hanumanta?] on it. On which, Hyder desired to know who this Annamoontoo was; in the course of the subidar's narration, he said Annamoontoo was born of a man; Hyder then observed his father was certainly the devil, to which the subidar assenting, Hyder ordered a flag to be made, with the figure of a devil evacuating Annamoontoo from behind, which he shrewdly observed, was the only aperture he could escape at; and obliged that subidar's company to bear it. The same flag was afterwards taken from them by the English, near Negapatam [Nagapattinam].[29]

Kirmani proudly recounts the manner in which Tanjore was ravaged by the forces of Tipu:

> Prince Tippoo with seven thousand horse, four thousand regular and irregular foot and five guns, [marched] towards Tujawur

[Tanjore] and Nuthurnuggur [Tiruchirapalli]. With this force, the
Prince Tippoo boldly advanced into the country of Tujawur. His
soldiers, brave as Roostum, in obedience of his orders, plundered
and destroyed the environs of that town, which in population
and fertility, may be called equal to Kashmere . . . the habitations
and idol temples of that country, which threw shame on the best
paintings of China, and resembled the beauties of Paradise, they
levelled with the ground, and setting fire to most of the houses,
shops and bazaars, they laid waste the whole of the country. They
set the country in a blaze, they took the lock or latch, and set fire
to the door. By the hoofs of the Islam horse, plains and mountains
were rendered indistinguishable. Sacks upon sacks of corn, herd
upon herd of cattle, flocks of sheep and goats, with other articles
considered worthy the notice of Hydur were sent to him . . .
and plundered Seerung [Srirangam?] and Jhumgiri [?], ancient
temples, seated between the waters of the Kaveri and Kaverum
held in great veneration by the Hindoos, and the gaze and delight
of the world . . . the young men, fond of beauty and enjoyment,
obtained lovely virgins and slave girls, of the Brahmun caste, and
Bayaderes, beautiful as the moon, arrayed with ornaments of
gold and jewels, to their hearts desire, and warmed themselves
thoroughly in the arms of beauty. Of the whole of the plunder
taken, one fourth was returned to the Sirkar.[30]

Both Tipu and Haidar, along with his irregulars (Kuzzaks), then
sieged the fort of Tiruchirapalli in June 1781. Heads of slain
men were sent to the British inside the fort, packed in twenty
large baskets, to terrorize them and to force them to give up their
possessions. Col Nixon Hall and other British officers had no more
than 200–300 men inside the fort. Preparations seemed afoot for a
night attack on the fort and its capture—a long-cherished dream of
Mysore since the days of Nanjarajayya. But Tiruchirapalli seemed
evasive as always. On receiving intelligence of the imminent fall of
Tiruchirapalli, with a view to diverting Haidar from there, Coote
finally left Cuddalore and attacked Chidambaram about twenty-six
miles to its south. The large and ancient holy shrine of Lord Shiva

there had been used by Haidar to prevent the enemy's progress and also to stock his ammunitions, provisions and supplies. It was a strategically important place for him and if it fell into Coote's hands, it would be disastrous. Even as he received messages from Jehan Khan, his commandant at Chidambaram, Haidar retreated from Tiruchirapalli towards Chidambaram by 18 June 1780. In a valiant manner, the Mysore army ensured that Coote was repulsed and nearly 200 of his men were killed. Coote retreated quickly to Porto Novo, with Haidar in pursuit.

Battle of Porto Novo

The two finally met in battle on 1 July 1781 at Porto Novo in a combat that lasted for eight hours. Haidar's army was nearly eight times that of Coote's, with twenty-five battalions of infantry, 400 Europeans, 40,000 horse, about 1,00,000 matchlock men and peons and forty-seven pieces of cannon. But after a severe engagement, Haidar was completely vanquished. Haidar's detachment was engaged by the first line of the British army, while another under Lally was repulsed by General Stuart. Haidar's defeat was complete and he ordered the withdrawal of the guns and the retreat of his troops to the plains. In the severe ambush from the British side, a shot from a cannon aboard one of the ships struck Mir Ali Raza Khan, Haidar's brother-in-law and trusted commander, and he was killed. His son, Sidi Halal, was also slain in combat, as were nearly 4000 of Haidar's men. Haidar himself, who was watching the operations from a *chowkee* or post, was almost on the verge of being taken captive too, before a loyal attendant whisked him away at the right time. Lally too was seriously injured and a Portuguese officer defected to the British side. Coote however erred here in not commanding his troops for a hot pursuit at a time when the opponent was militarily vanquished and his morale was low. Innes Munro too rues:

> Upon the conclusion of this hard-contested business, how mortifying was it to find that no other advantage had been gained by us after such extreme fatigue than the simple possession of the

field?—a compensation very inadequate to the loss of so many gallant soldiers. This might have been one of the most glorious and decisive victories ever obtained, had the General [Coote] permitted the line to advance at an earlier period of the day. There cannot be a doubt but it would have finally terminated the war, as most of the enemy's guns must have inevitably fallen into our hands . . . it was also a matter of surprise to many in the army that the British cavalry were not ordered to pursue the fugitives.[31]

The victory was not a great one for Coote, but definitely a morale booster, especially after Polilur. Robson alludes to this when he says that this battle was so important for the British 'as their fate in India totally depended' on it and had they lost, 'we [British] should have been deprived of all our possessions in that country.'[32] Haidar's army was still huge and active and ready to strike back. The defeat was not crushing enough for him to be dismantled, in addition to the tactical errors that Innes Munro talks about. The British recovered a bit of their prestige after the disastrous affair in Polilur. Haidar's army hastily retreated to Chidambaram, while Tipu was sent to resume the siege of Wandiwash. Eyre Coote was joined at Pulicat with a Bengal detachment of 5000 men that came in under Col Pierce. Saiyid Sahib was dispatched to reattempt the conquest of Tanjore and Tiruchirapalli. As August 1781 drew to an end, Haidar, despite the reverse in Porto Novo, was virtually in possession of the whole Carnatic Payanghat region, with the exception of Masulipatnam, Nellore, Madras, Chingleput, Vellore, Nagar, Wandiwash, Porto Novo, Tanjore, Tiruchirapalli and Madurai. Active campaigns by the Mysoreans were still underway in many of the above places. Haidar and Tipu had stormed and taken Permacoil, and Lally, Saiyid Hamid and Shaikh Oonsur were sent in a vain attempt to once again take Wandiwash.

Battles at Polilur and Sholinghur and After

Coote meanwhile added immensely to his strength with the reinforcement that came in from Bengal. Expecting to find stores at Tripasore, which was guarded by a Mysore garrison, he laid siege to it and took it before Haidar's forces could appear there. When he suggested that the Mysore garrison he had imprisoned be exchanged with the prisoners Haidar had earlier taken, the latter haughtily replied to him that the men he had captured at Tripasore were all worthless and untrustworthy for him and that they were his prisoners whom he recommended that Coote put to death within six days. He resolved to meet Haidar in the battlefield a second time and they clashed at the same place where the British had earlier been decimated, in what is known as the second battle of Polilur on 27 August 1781. In fact, it was Haidar who drew him to battle there, driven by the superstition that Polilur had proved so lucky for him earlier and that it would repeat its benevolence. But in the action that lasted all day, Haidar's troops were driven out from all their posts and forced to retreat, even as Coote maintained complete possession of the field of battle. Haidar's troops, as estimated by Coote, were around 1,50,000 men that day with eighty pieces of cannon, and of this he lost about 2000 men. The Mysorean accounts maintain that while Porto Novo was a severe defeat, Polilur was not a debacle for Mysore. It was a drawn battle, where both sides minimized their losses.[33] For many British officers and soldiers, it was a melancholic moment at Polilur as the putrid and decaying bodies of their friends in the army and some kith and kin who had participated in the previous encounter under Baillie at the same spot were still there for them to behold. 'One poor soldier, with the tear of affection glistening in his eye,' writes Innes Munro, 'picked up the decaying spatterdash of his valued brother, with the name yet entire upon it, which the tinge of blood and effect of weather had kindly spared!—another discovered the club or plaited hair of his bosom friend, which he himself had helped to form, and knew by the tie and still remaining colour! A third mournfully recognized the feather which had decorated the cap of his inseparable companion.'[34] The unfortunate side effects of these bloody battles which tore asunder the lives of many common people.

On 27 September 1781, the two armies clashed again at the Sholinghur pass, where Haidar was trying to block the British advance

to Vellore for its relief. There was heavy cannonading on both sides
and by evening, victory was declared for the British, even as Haidar's
troops beat a hasty retreat from the field towards Kaveripak. Haidar
lost anywhere between 2000–5000 men in this battle. The palegars
of Kalahasti, Venkatagiri and Bomraj, emboldened by the British
victory, sought shelter and lent their support to them. Enraged by
this, Haidar sent his corps to burn the villages in their dominions
and lay waste their country.

There had been a change in guard in Madras with Lord
Macartney taking over from Charles Smith as Governor and being
in direct control of the war strategy. There was much criticism of the
mismanagement and slothful attitude of the Madras Government.
Innes Munro too reflects on 'the unfortunate check which was
invariably given to the ardour of General Coote in all his exploits.
He never was once provided with a sufficient quantity of provisions
to render any one action decisive; for a victory was no sooner gained
than he was forced to retire to Madras for a fresh supply of grain; a
necessity which rendered battles fruitless, and the successful support
of a war impossible.'[35] After the battle of Sholinghur, Coote was
reduced to a further pitiable condition and denied any substantial
support from Madras, which itself had been reduced to extremities
to be able to stand by him. But it was to Coote's perseverance and tact
that even in such testing times, where his government proved itself
singularly incapable of supporting him, he won over the support of
local palegars like Bomraj and others who sustained the British army
with grains.

Lord Macartney was keen to change this situation and also
relieve Vellore. Accordingly, Coote sent a strong force under
Lt Col Owen to the place on 16 October 1781. The garrison in
Vellore was in distress as Haidar had kept a flying party hovering
about it and cutting off all communications. The siege in Vellore
had been vigorously pursued by Haidar under the skilful supervision
of French engineers and owing to the failing supplies there, its
surrender seemed imminent. The British troops, under Owen,
attempted in vain to block supplies from Chittoor to Haidar to

cause him distress. But Haidar made a sudden attack with all his regular infantry and the best of cavalry on Owen's detachment on 23 October from the Timory plains where he had encamped, forcing Owen to retreat with heavy losses to Madowaddy. It was only by 3 November that the distress of the Vellore garrison could be addressed as the British accidentally discovered a huge quantity of rice that was hidden underground and this was secretly dispatched to Vellore without catching Haidar's attention.

Lord Macartney, since the time of his arrival in Madras, issued directions for the capture of all the Dutch factories on the coast and a siege of their principal settlement in South India, of Nagapattinam. He wanted to thereby cut off the Dutch support to Haidar and attacked their forts at Sadras and Pulicat in June–July 1781. Around this time, Macartney also sent a letter to Haidar to find out if a termination of war with negotiations were a possibility. With the concurrence of Eyre Coote and Edward Hughes, Macartney sent this olive branch, despite it being outside his remit to conduct treaties, which strictly came under the purview of the Supreme Council in Calcutta. Haidar gave a patient hearing to the British envoy but wrote back to Macartney thus:

> The Governor and Sirdars who enter into treaties, after one or two years return to Europe, and their acts and deeds become of no effect; and fresh Governors and Sirdars introduce new conversations. Prior to your coming, when the governor and Council of Madras had departed from their treaty of alliance and friendship, I sent my vakeel to confer with them and to ask the reason for such breach of faith; the answer given was, that they who made the conditions were gone to Europe. You write that you have come with the sanction of the King and Company to settle all matters; which gives me great happiness. You, Sir, are a man of wisdom and comprehend all things. Whatever you may judge most proper and best, that you will do. You mention that troops have arrived and are daily arriving from Europe; of this I have not a doubt; I depend upon the favour of God for my succours.[36]

This vague and non-committal response from Haidar, though it reflected his genuine and reasonable grouse, was deemed as being hostile and inimical to conciliation. Hence it was decided that the hostilities be continued and the Dutch be reduced. Coote was however not in favour of opening another war front, but Macartney prevailed. Sir Hector Munro undertook the siege, along with Col Braithwaite and the fleet of Admiral Sir Edward Hughes. The Dutch then concluded a defensive treaty with Haidar on 4 September 1781 as per which the English district of Nagore and other places were to be ceded to the Dutch, who in turn would provide all support to Mysore in its current war against the British. The garrison of Nagapattinam was a large and powerful one, composed of 8000 men, made up of 500 European regular troops, 700 Malays, 4500 sepoys and 2300 of Haidar Ali's best troops, a thousand of which were cavalry. The chief engineer was a Frenchman and there were several German officers with the infantry. After a pitched battle between both sides, the British prevailed and managed to take Nagapattinam by 12 November, despite the best efforts of the Dutch–Mysore combine. Many naval stores fell into British hands, as also three Dutch ships in the harbour and a huge treasure. Several German and Swiss soldiers in the garrison joined the British side. The reduction of the place and its occupation by the British helped them get to Tanjore and the southern provinces of Tiruchirapalli and Madurai. However, the year ended with Haidar managing to take back Chittoor that the British had wrested. Tripasore was besieged by Tipu, though Coote managed to relieve it.

But, despite all the military successes, the condition of the British army under Coote continued to be desperate for supplies and provisions. In anguish, Coote wrote on 29 November 1781 to the Supreme Council at Fort William, Calcutta:

> Such was the distress to which the army was reduced for provisions that in the march from Chittore to the relief of Tripassore, one half was three successive days alternative without rice. The followers of the army from the last time of their leaving Madras until they

came back to Tripassore had had two *seers* (4 lb.) of paddy served out to them. Numbers have died by hunger and the inclemency of the weather, from which causes in the course of two march we lost nearly a hundred cavalry, likewise bullocks, elephants and camels, both public and private. In short, the scene exhibited was more like a field of battle than a line of march.[37]

All of this, in addition to the terrible heat of southern India took its toll on Eyre Coote who suffered a physical breakdown and had to be literally carried around in a palanquin around December 1781. Wilks mentions that one important issue that pervaded all of Coote's official correspondences to the governments in Calcutta or Madras was the 'duplicity and iniquity'[38] of Muhammad Ali of Arcot. Practically, the British had been fighting this war to defend and safeguard his possessions against the aggression of Haidar. But singularly lacking was any modicum of support from Muhammad Ali's side to the war either in procuring supplies or in contributing men or money. Lord Macartney exhausted all his diplomatic skills that he prided himself on, trying to din some sense into Muhammad Ali to rectify his conduct. But being both obstinate and wily, Muhammad Ali instead attempted to create disaffection between Macartney and Coote by displaying fake letters to the former of how he had made ample supplies all through the war, which Coote might have used for his personal gains. Coote had constantly advised Warren Hastings that the Madras Government should take over the direct management of Arcot from Muhammad Ali as he had misgoverned the place and proved to be both an ineffective and untrustworthy ally. Finally, towards the end of 1781, after strict orders from Hastings, the Nawab of Arcot consented to assign the revenues of his country to the Company for a period of five years, reserving one-sixth of it for his personal use, and to all the revenues being carefully administered by a selected Board of Revenue Commissioners.

It was ironical that Haidar and the British had been fighting each other at such enormous costs to both sides due to this man, Muhammad Ali, who was the source of the trouble between them.

Perhaps the realization of this futility was dawning on the British, as much as it seemed to be on Haidar too. Wilks records that Purnaiya had narrated to him a conversation between him and Haidar, when the latter in a moment of rare introspection, candour and rumination had spoken his heart out to him in the war camp. Haidar is supposed to have told Purnaiya:

> I have committed a great error. I have purchased a draught of *seandee* [*sendi*, fermented juice of the wild date tree], at the price of a lakh of pagodas. I shall pay dearly for my arrogance: between me and the English there was perhaps mutual grounds of dissatisfaction, but no sufficient cause for war, and I might have made them my friends in spite of Mahommed Ali, the most treacherous of men. The defeat of many Baillies and Braithwaites will not destroy them. I can ruin their resources by land, but I cannot dry up the sea; and I must be first weary of a war in which I can gain nothing by fighting. I ought to have reflected that no man of common sense will trust a Mahratta, and that they themselves do not expect to be trusted. I have been amused by idle expectations of a French force from Europe, but supposing it to arrive, and to be successful here, I must go alone against the Mahrattas, and incur the reproach of the French for distrusting them; for I dare not admit them in force to Mysoor.[39]

Whether it was the weariness of the long-drawn war whose fortunes kept oscillating or a genuine reflection of the blunders committed in diplomacy, it was too late to rescind. The war had caused immense losses to both sides and the futility of it all seemed to be dawning upon them. But all parties had hardened positions and there was no looking back.

Around December 1781, Haidar also seems to have been consumed by alarm for his own safety. He got enclosures erected of coconut and palmyra stumps, with the enclosure being filled with pieces of wood and the entire structure called *lakadi-kote* intended to act as a bulwark against cannonading. In Arcot, he summoned all his principal officers, along with Tipu, for a consultation on how to combat the British, who he saw as an obstacle to his dream of becoming the paramount power in South India. Tipu is said to have brashly commented in the meeting that it was Haidar who should consider himself responsible for making the British so powerful. Obviously, that was not something Haidar wanted to hear from his son, and that too in the presence of all his officers. He chided Tipu and narrated his series of conquests where he had defeated the British. But each time he vanquished them, they were getting reinforcements from Bengal and Bombay and also relief all the way from England. He wondered how his son would be capable of being his successor, if perchance he (Haidar) was shot dead in combat in the near future, if he did not understand this basic element of diplomacy and statecraft. Given that Haidar's rage was on the ascent, all the officers intervened to calm him down and forgive Tipu for his intemperate remarks. Before dispersing the meeting, Haidar told them that in his view, the only way to keep the British at bay was to somehow manage to keep them at war with the French in the Indian subcontinent, set up the people of Iran and Kandahar against them in Bengal, prevail upon the Marathas to keep them busy in Bombay and for Mysore itself to utilize French support to cut off supplies and harass them in Madras.[40]

Malabar Rumblings and Thereafter

Since November 1781, the Mysorean army under Sardar Khan, with the support of their trusted ally, the Chirakkal Raja, had laid siege to Tellicherry, the only British possession on the west coast. The position of the British there was precarious with an inadequate number of troops. But a timely reinforcement from Bombay and the steadfast support from the Raja of Kottayam resurrected them. The Raja of Kottayam attacked Sardar Khan from the rear and Major Abingdon, with his troops, further attacked and managed to crush the besieging Mysorean forces. Sardar Khan was taken prisoner, with 1200 men. When his desire to be sent back to Srirangapatna was denied, to avoid the disgrace of detention, he committed suicide. Major Abingdon remained in command of the western coast till the arrival of Lt Col Humberston Mackenzie on 18 February 1782 at Calicut. Calicut had, by then, been captured by Abingdon. This had a huge morale-boosting effect on the Nairs, who had perpetual hatred for the Mysore subjugation, and they rose in a violent revolt all over the Malabar region. The tinderbox that the Malabar was, needed just a spark to be ablaze. Haidar's garrisons and storehouses were destroyed. In the short span of just a fortnight or so, the power of Mysore had been reduced all over Kerala, except Palghat. Haidar, who already was in the midst of a difficult situation in the Carnatic, now had another problem to address.

The British followed up with their capture of the western coast by taking more forts from the already vanquished Dutch—Trincomalee, Tuticorin and so on. Trincomalee provided a safe harbour in which the British fleet could find shelter throughout the year, instead of seeking security at Bombay in the winter. But by October the same year, the French managed to wrest this port from the British. With the British in command now on both the western and eastern coasts, attacks on Madras or any of the other British strongholds was unfeasible for Haidar. All he could do now was to harass and wear out the enemy through surprise attacks on detachments and convoys, and on isolated outposts and forts. His strategy was to limit the British power to the coast and not let it be extended into the plains. Though Coote remained invincible on the field and had never been defeated thus far by Haidar, his forces were never large enough, as compared to Haidar, to effect a complete crushing defeat. In addition, the already mentioned problems with supplies and stores handicapped his campaign severely, as did the sluggish pace of his army due to the heavy baggage. Haidar, on the other hand, had a nimble, mobile army that was faster and could both attack and retreat quickly.

After a series of reverses, the Mysore side finally had a sliver of victory on 17–18 February 1782, when, upon receiving intelligence of Col Braithwaite encamping at Anagundi, six miles north-east of Kumbakonam, they attacked him from all sides. Tipu and Lally conducted this campaign with aplomb. With a force of 10,000 cavalry, twenty cannons and some infantry and 400 Europeans, they destroyed the British force of 1600 soldiers. The British tried to retreat to Tanjore, but that seemed an impossibility and hence a battle ensued. In this, Lt Sampson distinguished himself by making daring attacks on the *kushoons* or infantry brigades of Haidar. The combat that lasted for about twenty-six hours resulted in a total defeat of the British detachment, followed by a loot of their supplies and baggage and a deadly carnage in their ranks. Col Braithwaite surrendered and was packed off as a prisoner to Srirangapatna. Of twenty officers belonging to the detachment, twelve had been killed. This defeat undid for the British all the advantages accrued in Porto Novo. The southern army of the British was extremely weakened after this loss and it took them quite some time to recover. They could no longer get grain and cattle from the rich plains of Tanjore.

The Changing Course of the War

But despite these successes, Haidar knew that the prospects for the future were not that bright. When he had agreed to the overtures of the Marathas to get into an alliance, he had hoped that a grand tripartite army of the Marathas, the Nizam and Mysore would ambush the British and drive them away from India. The hopes were that such a large confederate army would ensure that the British could possibly not hold on beyond a few months. But the weakest link in the alliance, the Nizam, got bought over by the British early on. Haidar still hoped that the Nizam would carry out his undertaking to subdue the Circars on the eastern coast. But following his pact with Hastings, Nizam Ali contributed neither men, material nor money for the campaign to Haidar. Moreover, the British alarmed him with rumours that the Mughal emperor was considering conferring the Viceroyalty of the Deccan, which the Nizam held, to Haidar, arousing his insecurities.

The Marathas, though, being the progenitors of the alliance, hardly took part with Haidar in the war and were handling their own isolated campaigns against the British. Mudhoji Bhonsle had remained lukewarm in his support. Hastings now detached him from the Maratha confederacy by attacking his dominions in the centre of the peninsula from the side of Bengal. Haidar heard that Warren Hastings had concluded a treaty with Mahadji Sindhia on 13 October 1781. His mediation was being sought to bring about peace between the British and Haidar and also with Poona. When Haidar's vakil in Poona, Noor-ud-din, got wind of the treaty that Mahadji had signed, he warned Haidar that the Marathas might conclude peace with the British and combine with them to have Mysore evacuate the territories between the Tungabhadra and Krishna that were allotted to it since the time of Raghoba's grant. There really was no strong common cause between Mysore and the Marathas and both sides, after a bitter acrimonious past, had done precious little to earn each other's trust.

Haidar had been vanquished in every combat with Sir Eyre Coote. He had counted on the French support and its fleet to neutralize the British sea power. But after making dramatic guest appearances on and off the coast, the French fleet did nothing to bolster Haidar's power and navigated away to Mauritius. Bussy had kept promising to come to their aid but had not turned up for months. Added to this, the brewing rebellion of the Nairs in Malabar had instigated similar uprisings in neighbouring Coorg and Balam, which detested Haidar's autocratic rule. Haidar was reflecting deeply on how things stood for now and it was not a promising prospect evidently. He thought it was prudent to abandon the conquest of the Coromandel coast and instead direct his focus and undivided attention on expelling the British from the western coast, preserving his core dominions in Mysore and seeing how matters unfold. He mined the fortifications in Arcot and was just about resigned to his fate when a large French fleet, under one of the ablest admirals that France had ever sent to the East, Vice Admiral Pierre Andre de Suffren, appeared off the Coromandel Coast, raising Haidar's hopes.

A combine of about 2000 French troops that landed in April at Porto Novo under sailor Duchemin and Mysorean detachment under Tipu proceeded to Cuddalore. Without firing a shot, it was captured from the British. Suffren began to intercept supply convoys from Bengal for the British troops, seizing some 1000 tons of rice, and even captured the British frigate *Coventry*. Emboldened by these successes, Haidar also moved in and soon by May 1782, Permacoil and Tyagadurg were taken and he was advancing towards Wandiwash. Coote set forth to check his advance. Karim Sahib had been sent to Madras to attack it and cause alarm to the British, and also obstruct the passage of troops proceeding to join the main English army of Coote. But seeing reinforced enemy troops, he quickly retreated, inviting Haidar's ire. Evidently, Karim was not 'born for pre-eminence as a soldier.'[41] Coote's troubles as usual with supplies and provisions and serious differences that had cropped up between him and Macartney were other slivers of hope for Haidar. Despite Suffren's presence, not many benefits accrued to the Mysore–French combine. Pradeep Barua lists the reasons for the same:

> Despite several engagements at Sadras, Providien, Negapatam, and Trincomali, Suffren failed to destroy the British squadron. Although the rival squadrons were well-matched in numbers, Suffren's tactical abilities enabled him to best Admiral Hughes, the British commander, on several occasions. However, his inability to communicate his plans effectively to his ship captains often resulted in confusion, and a decisive and annihilating victory over the British squadron could not be achieved. This failure ensured a stalemate that ultimately favoured the British. The French had very limited resources in India, a fact reinforced by their loss of Pondicherry. This meant that their ability to repair, provision and replenish the crew of their ships was significantly inferior to that of the British, who retreated to either Bombay or Calcutta to re-supply with equipment and manpower. Never again would the French be able to gain an opportunity to completely cut the vital sea links between Madras and Bengal.[42]

Coote now decided to proceed to Arni, which was the chief depot from where Haidar procured his supplies and ammunition. He calculated that an attack here would divert his opponent who would rush to its defence from his entrenched safe position at Kellinur. But Haidar got to know of this and dispatched Tipu to strengthen Arni and himself joined the following day. On 30 May 1782, Haidar's forces defeated an elite unit of Coote's army known as 'The Grand Guard', killing some 166 men and taking two cannons. The two armies once again clashed on 2 June 1782 in what is known as the Battle of Arni. Haidar divided the Mysore forces into four parts—the largest led by him and his faithful palegars, and the rest by Lally, Commandant Muhammad Ali and Tipu—to attack the British from all sides. It was a day for the British that Wilks states was 'of severe fatigue and varied cannonade, rather than of battle, and a succession of skillful manoeuvres, to combine with the essential protection of baggage, the means of closing with the enemy'. Despite Coote's best efforts, the British suffered considerable losses in Arni and were forced to beat a retreat to Vellore. Nearly 2000 of their soldiers were taken prisoners after a night attack and cavalry charge that Haidar managed. This was the last time Haidar and Coote were to clash and the odds had ended in the former's favour.

Even as the war raged on in the Carnatic, Haidar heard about the Marathas having settled peace with the British through the Treaty of Salbai on 17 May 1782. The British retained control of Salsette and Broach and also finally gave up their support to Raghoba and recognized Sawai Madhav Rao as the legitimate Peshwa. The treaty also stipulated that within six months, Haidar would have to relinquish to the British and their allies all the territories taken from them since his truce with the late Madhav Rao in February 1767. Haidar was also to evacuate the Carnatic, failing which both the parties would unite to expel him from there. It was a complete reversal of all the agreements that the Marathas had made with Haidar, but this was only to be expected. The British and Muhammad Ali however tried to sue for peace with Haidar by sending to his camp two officers of the rank of colonel to negotiate terms. Haidar however was stern and clear that he valued no commitment from Muhammad Ali as the latter had not kept a single promise right since he had committed to cede Tiruchirapalli to his former master, Nanjarajayya. He demanded the immediate cession of Tiruchirapalli under the old agreement and a reimbursement of all the dues to Mysore for its participation in that thriftless campaign. The negotiations went on for over a month and ended in failure by July 1782.

Attempts at Restoration

Even as Haidar sat lamenting the betrayal of the grand alliance by his supposed allies, unbeknownst to him, other formations were being activated against him. The Mysore Pradhans of Maharani Lakshmi Ammanni who had taken refuge in Tanjore used the good offices of Rev. Schwartz and William Burke to get in touch with the British Resident of Tanjore John Sullivan. In their formal letter to him, the brothers apprised Sullivan that they had been living in Tanjore under the protection of Tuljamaharajah for over six years now, spending about 35,000 pagodas of their private funds. Given that the Rani was in virtual captivity in Srirangapatna, there was not much they could expect from her in the form of help. In addition to seeking the Company's support for vanquishing Haidar Ali and reinstating the Wodeyar family's nominee as chosen by the Rani, the Pradhans also insisted that the treaty help in the recovery 'of all our expenses, the grant of a commission of 10 per cent on the revenues of the State and the conferring of the Ministership upon us and our descendants in perpetuity.'[43]

Sullivan in turn introduced them to Lord Macartney who took over as the Governor of Madras on 22 June 1781. Macartney was only too pleased to know about this revolt that was brewing from within Mysore. 'After looking into the papers and documents produced by the Vakeels [pradhans], satisfied that the Ranee and her partisans would assist the British in their undertaking to confer peace upon the country usurped by Hyder,'[44] Macartney offered his total support to the efforts of the Rani. In the representations, interestingly,

Rani Lakshmi Ammanni is referred to in the masculine as 'Rana'.
Tirumala Rao and Narayana Rao, in their communication, stated:

> Hyder Naig has usurped all our master's country, destroyed him
> and his two sons and still keeps his widow, our Rana, in prison
> at Seringapatam. The English know that Hyder Naig was a
> servant of our master's when he did these things. The English
> Company are well-acquainted with the usurpation of Hyder Ali
> and the misfortunes which he has brought upon the family of
> the Rajah of Mysore . . . they are willing to assist with their
> troops in reducing Hyder Ali, and in re-establishing the Rajah
> in his hereditary dominions . . . If the English, who are great
> and powerful, will punish this usurper, and deliver to our master
> the countries Hyder has taken from him, we will enter into the
> following conditions.[45]

The Rana Treaty, as it was called, was signed on 28 October 1782
by John Sullivan and Tirumala Rao, in the presence of Schwartz,
and its objective was stated as 'restoration of the Hindoo dynasty
of Mysore.'[46] The treaty had fifteen articles. A successive scale of
payment of money on the Rani's part was suggested for all the favours
that were expected of the Company. Some of the undertakings and
conditions set forth by the Rani as part of the Treaty are as under:

> We will pay to the Company 3 Lakhs of Kandirayen Pagodas
> [Canteroi Pagodas: measure of currency] as soon as their troops
> shall have driven the enemy out of the Coimbatour [sic] etc.,
> countries on this side of the mountains. As soon as the English
> troops shall have ascended the Balaghat and possessed themselves
> of the forts of Ardmelli or Viseyburam we will pay the further sum
> of one lakh of pagodas. Upon the surrender of the fort of Mysore,
> and the government of the country being given to our Rana, or
> whoever she may adopt, we will pay another lakh of Pagodas and
> upon the fall of Seringapatam, we will pay Five Lakhs of Pagodas,
> that is to say, in all the sum of Ten Lakhs of Pagodas. We will
> engage further that from the day our Rana or whoever she may
> adopt shall be proclaimed in Seringapatam, the sum of Five Lakhs

of Pagodas shall be paid annually to the Company by monthly instalments, and moreover that a *jaghire* [sic] to the annual value of one Lakh of Pagodas shall be assigned to the Company, in whatever part of the said dominions they may think proper . . . The Company will undertake to protect the government of Mysore, and will maintain an army in that country; but as the number of troops that may be required for that purpose cannot be determined, the government of Mysore must engage to pay whatever the charges of such an army may exceed the sum of five lakhs of pagodas . . . the Company shall take the protection of all our country into their own hands, and that for this purpose they shall keep an army of sepoys, of European soldiers, and of European artillery, with all the officers, guns, stores etc., field and garrison equipage usually attached to such an army, in the same manner as given to the Rajah of Tanjore . . . the Company shall not interfere in the management of the country nor in the arrangements for the *peshcush* and *chout*; that the *killadars, amuldar,* and other officers who may be appointed by the Rana for the management of the country shall be employed, and none others, in the collections . . . the Company shall not interfere in the business of the polygars . . . the amount of the former *peshcush* from Mysore to the Mogul as well as the amount of the former *chout* to the Mahrattas, must be regularly paid into the Company's treasury, to be by them accounted for to the Mogul's officer and to the Mahrattas. If by their influence and friendly offices the Company should prevail with the Mahrattas and the Mogul to exempt Mysore from the future payment of *peshcush* and *chout*, the amount of those charges will be held by the Company as a fund for defraying any extraordinary expenses, which may be incurred either in future wars, in the building and repairing of forts, or in the augmentation of the military force for the defence and protection of Mysore . . . the Company will order to deliver over to us whatever jewels, treasure, elephants, horses, military stores and effects of every kind, belonging to Hyder Naig and his officers, that may be found in the different forts, towns etc., or that may be taken in the field . . . Hyder Naig and all prisoners of every rank who may be taken in the field in the different forts, towns etc., shall be delivered over to the Rana's officers . . . Seringapatam being a place of religious worship, no troops shall be stationed within the walls of that place except in time of actual war . . . should it happen that the Company may not be able to reduce Hyder Naig, but on the contrary that they should be obliged to make peace with him, in that event the Company must take us and all the people who may join with us under their protection, and continue the same to us and our family forever. And further they must engage to pay back whatever money may be advanced them on account of our Rana for the purposes before mentioned. The Governor and Council of Madras must procure a *Sunnud* from the Company in England to confirm to our Rana and her successors the full possession and government of all the countries that may be taken as before mentioned from Hyder Naig for ever and ever, upon the conditions hereinbefore expressed.[47]

It was agreed that if the British took over Mysore after defeating Haidar, the kingdom would be restored to the Rani's chosen successor and she was to provide for the military expenses of the campaign and also the stationed force in Mysore thereafter. If peace was broached with Haidar, the Company undertook to protect all those within Mysore who supported them in the campaign. If their efforts failed to dislodge Haidar, they committed to reimbursing the Rani her expenses for the war. To cement this friendship, Lord Macartney also wrote a letter to Maharani Lakshmi Ammanni:

To Her Highness the Maharanee,

God Bless you! I received the letter you sent with Narayan Row and have noted its contents with pleasure. I have been always anxious to serve your interests. The ingratitude and injustice of Hyder to your Royal family are publicly known to everybody. It has become a matter of necessity not only for us, but for others also, to punish him for his misdeeds. I write this in accordance with the treaty with you. If God blesses the efforts of the Company, it will be seen how your rights will be respected. We also count much upon the services of Tirumal Row and other such intelligent noblemen on your behalf. And hence you may rest assured your Kingdom will be restored to you. Hyder has declared war against us and our allies through enmity. We shall therefore necessarily invade his territories from all quarters. And by the grace of God, we will restore the rightful owners those territories which Hyder has occupied by fraud and force. The English and the Company will see to this with special care. And we shall always do what is just and upright. The Ranee and her partisans should join the Company in this noble work. And there is no doubt that good will result in every way.[48]

Thus, the efforts to extricate Mysore from the hold of Haidar and restore it to the original Hindu dynasty was being relentlessly carried out.

Malabar Unrest

With the outbreak of the Nair revolt in the Malabar in the aftermath of Sardar Khan's death, Haidar dispatched his brother-in-law, Saiyid Makhdoom, to restore peace there. To quell similar uprisings in neighbouring Balam and Coorg, he sent Woffadar, one of his *chela* brigades, and Sheikh Ayaz to Balam from Bidanur where the latter was governor. Makhdoom marched to Kerala, towards Calicut, through the Palghat pass with a large force of 7000. By early April 1782, Col Humberston Mackenzie from Bombay succeeded Major Abingdon as the commander in the west coast. He had with him forces under General Meadows and Commodore Johnson. Joining the rebelling Nairs, Humberstone moved southwards and met Makhdoom's forces at Tirur Angadi. Makhdoom had taken a disadvantageous position with a deep river in the rear. The British and Nair forces managed to attack vigorously and drove the vast Mysorean forces from their pitch. Retreat too was made difficult for them and Makhdoom, along with several of his men, was killed.

Bolstered by this success, Humberstone now attempted to reduce Palghat, which was the main impregnable fortress for Mysore in the

Malabar region. He was reinforced by troops sent in from Bombay and the king of Travancore. Leaving behind his battering train and heavy equipment under the protection of his sepoys, Humberstone marched ahead with his six six-pounders and two nine-pounders. He knew it would not be an easy task to reclaim Palghat and personally gathered intelligence about the region, the terrain and the fort. He realized that the fort was not easy to storm and could resist a long-drawn siege. The Mysore forces had intercepted his movements and attacked him from the rear as he was heading back to his headquarters after the reconnoitring expedition, forcing Humberstone to abandon all his provisions and flee back.

The defeat and death of Makhdoom alarmed Haidar, who had already been wearied in battle to the perilous situation that prevailed in the Malabar. He therefore decided to immediately dispatch a much larger and stronger force, this time under Tipu himself, with Lally to accompany him as his advisor. The force was kept concealed in neighbouring Coimbatore on the pretext of readying it for an eastern campaign, but the plan was to silently swoop over Kerala and recapture all the troubled areas. This strong army made a sudden appearance on Humberstone's rear and, afraid to face such a determined force, he beat a hasty retreat inward, despite the flooded rivers after the monsoon. He somehow managed to reach the coast and handed over charge to Col McLeod at Paniani. Sir Eyre Coote had sent McLeod to assume command of the Malabar campaign and he had reached there by 19 November 1782. Tipu had encamped himself with his vast army barely two miles outside the town. The hostile forces remained in this position for a week and it was only on 29 November 1782 that Tipu launched his first attack on the opponent in four columns, one of them headed by Lally. But the extreme vigilance, discipline and defiance of the numerically smaller English troops resulted in total confusion for the Mysorean side, with Tipu himself being wounded in his thigh and his troops dispersed. After this failed attempt, he retraced his steps, waiting for the arrival of heavy equipment from the main army that was camped with Haidar. But a news of a different kind was to reach him then that was to alter the political landscape of both Mysore and the whole of South India.

Haidar's End

Right after the battle of Arni, Haidar had noticed a strange boil that had erupted on his back. He initially attributed it to an accidental scratch but the abscess soon began to increase and he consulted his physician regarding this. He was told that this was merely an impact of a disorderly stomach and that it could be remedied with purgative medicines. But none of this gave him any relief and the abscess kept increasing in size with every passing day, consuming Haidar with immense pain and physical discomfort. The disease was finally diagnosed as *surtan* or cancer of the back. The royal physician suggested that the best remedy for the disease was the application of sheep's liver, along with vapours of stimulating medicines that also cleansed the blood. But Haidar came to increasingly realize that his end was possibly nearing. Even as he was engaged in the numerous campaigns of the Second Anglo–Mysore war, the malignancy of the tumour kept increasing, thereby completely impairing his movements and strength. He was in the war camp at Narasingarayanapet, near Chittoor at this time. His ministers kept insisting that Tipu, who had been dispatched to the Malabar be recalled, but Haidar refused to accede. He called for his secretary and ordered him to write a letter to Tipu which was to convey to him 'to make all necessary arrangements in that quarter (where he was stationed) as quickly as possible, and then return; that he was deeply to consider the result of all the necessary relations and connections of the government small and great; and that if troops were necessary to his aid, he should send for them; for that, in matters of state, he had given him power to act at discretion or as he pleased; and that he was not to neglect or forget his duties to the government for a moment.'[49]

Purnaiya, who had become Haidar's trusted associate, was at the helm of affairs in the war camp. News of Haidar's illness was concealed completely from the army, as well as the general public, lest it create confusion and also embolden the enemy. Other than Purnaiya, it was only the close inner circle of Commandant Muhammad Ali, Anche Shamaiah, Toshikhane Krishna Rao, Mir Muhammad Sadak, Badar-u-Zumaun Khan, Maha Mirza Khan, Ghazi Khan and Abu Muhammad Mirdha who knew of the precarious health of their ruler. Rumours were agog that Purnaiya had murdered Haidar and so on, but the latter came down heavily on such mischief-mongers. To instil confidence in the troops, bugles and drums were played outside Haidar's tent, to convey an image of business as usual.

Haidar threw open the doors of his treasury and amply rewarded all his loyal soldiers and officers with a month's pay as a gift. On the last day of Mohurrum il Huram, he asked his attendants to bathe him, though he had been advised not to. Putting on fresh clothes, he sat down to pray, drank some hot broth and laid down to rest. That very night, on 7 December 1782, Haidar Ali, the man who rose from rags to riches and changed not only his own, but the fate of all of South India, with his daring and relentless exploits, breathed his last at the age of sixty. Thus ended the life of one of Mysore's and India's great warriors, a man blessed with an insurmountable spirit coupled with a cunning and shrewd intellect, a savagery that few possessed and a courage to face the challenges that life posed, thereby turning the tables against destiny itself.

Shama Rao pithily reflects on what this episode meant in the larger annals of the times:

> It will be no exaggeration if we say that Haidar's death at the time at which it occurred may be regarded not as a mere episode in the general history of India but as an important event which tended to establish the British power in India sooner than it would have been otherwise possible. The English and the French were contending for supremacy and their rivalry helped many of the Indian princes to further their own ambitions. On account of the weakness that had overtaken the Mughal court, there was really no paramount power to keep the turbulent chiefs and adventurers under proper control. While the English and the French were loyal to their countries, the Indians on the other hand, whether chiefs

or ordinary adventurers, played each for his own hand, and ideas of patriotism or maintenance of other larger interests never seem to have crossed their minds. While in 1773, the Regulating Act passed by the Parliament in England introduced unity of rule in the Presidencies of Bengal, Madras and Bombay by placing at their head a governor–general and subordinating Madras and Bombay to him, the Peshwas, Scindias, Holkars, Nawabs and Palegars not only fought among themselves but even when they formed a confederacy, they could not sustain it for any length of time.[50]

9

The Man and His Legacy

Haidar Ali was an astute and ruthless politician, a powerful autocrat and a man driven by an overzealous ambition. He, however, was not an innovative ruler in terms of bringing about too many changes or reforms in the polity or administration. A big reason for that was possibly the fact that the majority of his active public life was consumed by the ravages of war and he hardly had the luxury of time spans of peace where he could afford to focus on civilian matters. Alongside, as mentioned earlier, since he did not wish to convey to the public at large that he had dispossessed the Hindu royal family that was revered, he let several institutions and organs of government continue as it were during their times, with minimal changes to suit his interests.

Administration and Revenue

The state itself was broadly divided into the sovereign part (of the *Kartaar*, the Wodeyar) and what came under Haidar's personal control. The whole of the Mysore kingdom with all new additions of territory, up to the Krishna River on one side and Fort St George on the other, fell in the former bracket, while Bidanur that he had annexed and named Haidar Nagar (or just Nagar) was under the latter category. One is not sure if he made any distinctions between the revenues derived from the two regions. The state was divided into several *subahs* (provinces), though their exact number is not mentioned anywhere. It was under a Subahdar, assisted by a Dewan or Finance Minister and a Faujdar or local militia. The Subahdar controlled civil and criminal subjects in the administration and also headed a court of justice. Kazis administered civil law among Muslims, while Panchayats were for the Hindus. Kotwals carried on police duties and ensured local law and order. The local chief executive officer in the districts was the Amildar to whom the district was leased and who collected revenues. In each taluk, two Brahmin official reporters, termed as Harikaras, were stationed to hear all complaints and report them to the Revenue Department at the headquarters of the Government. They also reported on all the wastelands within their areas. In Bidanur, after the landholders ganged up in a conspiracy against him, he disarmed them and began a thorough land assessment process. The traditional palegars whom he subjugated were often reinstated on the condition of paying fixed annual tributes.

Mysore, under Haidar Ali, is defined in an inscription of 1790 as being a three-crore country—referring therein to the revenue derived from it.[1] In the 'Political Survey of the Northern Circars' of 1784, James Grant estimates that Haidar owned territory of about 75,000 square miles and his yearly effective revenue could not exceed two crore and twenty lakh. 'A saving might have been made in times of peace,' he states, 'to support the extraordinariness of mediated ambitious war of one krore [sic] of rupees annually.'[2] Given the regular loot of treasures from several wars and conquests, an exact estimate of the income from wars too becomes difficult. But the increase in revenue after Haidar's usurpation was a whopping 155 per cent rise over what it was under the Wodeyar and Dalavayi regime.[3]

The two broad divisions of the kingdom geographically were the Payanghat (the provinces below the ghats, including the Baramahals or the land of twelve fortresses, Salem and Erode, in addition to Arcot taken in 1782) and Balaghat (above the ghats, including Mysore, Srirangapatna, Bangalore, Kolar, Bidanur, Chitradurga etc.). There is scanty documentation about the taxes, revenue and resources of the Mysore kingdom under Haidar Ali. The Attara Kacheri system of eighteen departments that Chikkadevaraja Wodeyar had established for streamlining administration and taxation was continued by him. These were:

1. *Nirupa Chavadi*: Recording petitions from officials.
2. *Ayakattu Chavadi:* Civil and military accounts in all administrative units, central exchequer, royal household etc.
3. *Mysuru Hobali Vicharada Chavadi:* Administration of Mysore.
4. *Patnada Hobali Vicharada Chavadi:* Administration of Srirangapatna.
5. *Simeya Kandachar:* Accounts of civil and military establishments in units, arms, ammunitions, stores, provisions, etc.
6. *Bagila Kandachar:* Accounts of troops stationed at headquarters.
7. *Sunkada Chavadi:* Duties, road tolls, import–export duties and customs.
8. *Pom Chavadi:* A tax called *Pom* was levied in addition to the *sunka* (toll) on commodities purchased or disposed by certain classes of people such as Brahmins and officers.
9. *Tundeya/Thodaya Chavadi:* Tax-collecting department where a quarter of the first duty was collected at the capital city.
10. *Mysuru Hobali Vichara Chavadi:* Central office to which all correspondence related to administration, accounts etc. of provinces under the jurisdiction of Mysore were sent.
11. *Patnada Hobali Vichara Chavadi:* A similar one as above for those that came under the jurisdiction of Srirangapatna.
12. *Benne Chavadi:* Animal husbandry, breeding of cows for milk, butter, etc.
13. *Patnada Chavadi:* Repairs of forts, palaces, public places.
14. *Behina Chavadi:* Public information, department of post and espionage responsible for speedy delivery of couriers (*anche harikaras*) and petitions (*nirupas*).
15. *Sammukhada Chavadi:* Palace officers, domestic and personal servants.
16. *Devasthanada Chavadi:* Grants to temple, priests, repairs, charitable activities.

17. *Kabbinada Chavadi:* Purchase of raw iron ore, manufacture of iron.

18. *Hogesoppina Chavadi:* Tobacco department.

The heads of revenue were generally land tax, *panchabab* (five items of toddy, arrack, ganja, betel and tobacco) and *bajebab* (other taxes). In the Malabar, export duties called *adlami* were imposed. During 1770–79, the English had the advantage of paying customs revenue at the rate of 1½ per cent.[4] There were close to 1,93, 959 temples and *agraharas* (Brahmin colonies) and 20,000 mutts during the period.[5] *Inam* grants of villages, houses, residential colonies given to Brahmins and priests continued; in addition, similar *khairati* grants were issued for Muslims. Haidar rationalized the rents that were collected from several of the purchased agaraharas. In the Malabar, the Namboodiri Brahmins and the Nairs were the landholders or Jenmkars and they leased out their estates to farmers called Kanumkars. Haidar fixed a systematic land tax in the Malabar. The landholders got 3/20th, the Kanumkars 11/20th and 6/20th to the government.

Trade, Coinage and Army

Monopolies of the state in iron, tobacco and sandalwood continued. A sixth of the lawful share of crop was levied along with other taxes on homes, looms, transit, caste heads and so on. Old weights and measures continued. The coinage that Haidar minted was also conservative and low-key. His earliest coin was the Bahaduri Pagoda, copied the way the Bidanur rulers minted theirs. It was in Bidanur that Haidar began the minting and circulation of his coins, Haidari Pagodas and gold fanams. He did so however with extreme caution, for none of his coins exhibit more than the initials of his name 'He' in Persian, inscribed on the obverse. In many coins, the images of Hindu deities were allowed to continue in the manner that they did. A Muhammad Shahi pagoda struck at Gutti was a copy of the Mughal coin, which even Murar Rao issued. In 1780–81, he struck copper paisas (*duddu*) at Srirangapatna, with the elephant on the obverse. There are some coins with Kannada numerals too.[6] The mint towns that were active during his time were Srirangapatna, Bangalore, Gutti and Bidanur. Financial transactions with neighbours were, as before, through the agency of financiers, who were rich bankers or Sowcars. They were either of local origin or from outside the kingdom, belonging to Gujarat and Sindh. The name Gujerati was attached to them in popular parlance and their integrity, credit and skill in business was rated very highly.

A new trading centre was established on the island of Srirangapatna called Shahar Ganjam. Bangalore was an important trading centre for the Nizam's territories and Arcot, while Periapatna for trade with the western coast. Kandahalli, Kaveripuram and Sirsi were other important entrepots for trade with neighbouring regions. Royal palaces and garden retreats like Lal Bagh and Daria Daulat Bagh were constructed at Bangalore and Srirangapatna. Haidar seems to have been fascinated by the palace and garden of Dilawar Khan of Sira and modelled his palaces in both the cities in the same fashion. Plants for the gardens were imported from Delhi, Lahore and Multan.

Just before Haidar's death, an embassy from Louis XVI is supposed to have arrived in Mysore with regard to both political and commercial alliance with the kingdom. Since Haidar was away in the war camp, they waited on him. French accounts mention that a portrait of Louis XVI was presented to Haidar, which he received, though no such portrait was found in the collection of paintings in Srirangapatna or elsewhere.[7] It was of course left to his son Tipu to further the long-standing relationship that Mysore had built with the French, as we shall see later.

For the kingdom's defence, there was a well-disciplined, standing army of 1,80,000 men. In addition, there were troops numbering 1,62,500 under several denominations: stable horse, pindari horse, silledars or men enlisted with their horses and arms, workmen as masons and bricklayers, barr or regular infantry, bodyguards, garrisons and detachments across the kingdom, Africans, harkars/runners and spies, pioneers, servants, blacksmiths and carpenters.[8]

During the peak of the Maratha campaign of Mysore in 1771–72, Peixoto states: 'The Nawab's force . . . then consisted of 15,000 fire-arms, 12,000 horse, 2000 rocket boys, and 50,000 matchlocks with which it was necessary to garrison the forts. The custom of the troops was moreover to fight behind the walls or in woods. The Mahrata [sic] force on the other hand was mostly cavalry and numbered 3,00,000 horse, besides the considerable number of troops on foot, who were all well-disciplined.'[9] In addition to the Chela batallions, he also had more than 1,10,000 Kandachar peons. These were the irregular troops who were variously armed, but generally with matchlocks and pikes. On his military legacy, N.K. Sinha writes:

> As a soldier, Haidar suffered repeated defeats. But he never despaired. He did not show any conspicuous ability as a tactician but he showed a great ability as an organizer and his general plan of a campaign was always sound. His army, compared with that of the British, was inferior in leadership as also in the fighting qualities of the soldiers. In numbers, supplies and equipment it was always superior . . . Haidar's ability to stand the shocks of war was superb. He was always animated by his difficulties.[10]

Personal Characteristics

Haidar Ali, the man who captured the popular imagination with his meteoric rise from humble origins, and who stayed at the top through a unique blend of leadership, intellect, avarice and manipulation, has been an object of much interest and study by his contemporaries and historians alike. These accounts paint a picture of the man behind the ruthless monarch, his motivations and his shortcomings.

De La Tour mentions him as being about five feet six inches tall with coarse features and brown complexion, 'very lusty, though active, and capable of bearing fatigue as well as on foot as on horseback.'.[11] His nose was small and turned up and he had a rather thick lower lip. Unlike the normal customs among Muslims, he was clean-shaven and sported neither moustache nor beard. He loved wearing white muslin garments with neatly fit sleeves, drawn close by strings, and wore a turban of the same fabric. The garment he wore was usually long and in ample folds, so that when he walked 'a page supports their train from their first stepping off the carpet to their entering into their carriages.'[12] This was the attire in the palace or in durbars, but obviously he wore a different attire during his numerous military campaigns which are what his stormy life was made up of. The military uniform had a vest of white satin, with gold flowers, faced with yellow and attached by cords or strings of the same colour and drawers too of the same materials. His boots were usually of yellow velvet, were long and had pointed tips. Haidar wore a scarf of white silk around his waist and a bright red or yellow coloured turban, usually of Burhanpur manufacture. While on foot, he commonly used a gold-headed cane, and on horseback a sabre that hung by a belt of velvet embroidered with gold and fastened over his shoulder with a clasp of gold, enriched with several precious stones. He never had much fascination for jewellery and his turban and clothes remained largely unadorned by them. He never used necklaces or bracelets and instead preferred simplicity. Though not deemed as particularly handsome, his visage inspired confidence and a raw energy.

During his interactions with people, he tended to be reserved initially with strangers, but once the ice was broken, he was given to great ribaldry and coarse language that he was famous for. He had the skill of being able to hold a conversation on any topic. He was easily accessible to his officers and the public alike. Interestingly, the fakirs or Islamic religious mendicants, were the ones whom he did not give ready audience to unlike most other Muslim kings who held these men as holy and venerated them. Instead, they would be sent across to an officer who would look after their needs, if any, but Haidar's time was not to be trifled with indulging them. Religious matters did not seem to be too high on Haidar's daily agenda, as several eyewitnesses had pointed out.

Despite all the parties of pleasure that he generously indulged in, he normally retired to bed every day a little after midnight and rose with the sun, at around 6 a.m. Immediately after he rose, the majors of the army, who were on duty the previous day and those who were to relieve them, entered and received orders that had to be given to the officers and army generals. As he washed his face, his messengers and spies stood around and conveyed any important intelligence that they might have gathered over the previous evening. Couriers that had arrived were placed at his feet for his perusal. In times of leisure and certainly not in the midst of a military campaign, his toilet normally took him over two to three hours. This was chiefly taken over by his favourite barbers who took the utmost care in grooming him and plucking off all the hairs from his night-grown stubble. Tuesdays and Fridays were stipulated for extra grooming and shaves and no one dared to disturb him during this indulgence. For some strange reason, after the usurpation of the kingdom, he chose to be totally hairless. The shave would begin with a tonsure or shaving of his facial hair—beard, moustache, eyelashes and even eyebrows. This caused his sharp features to seem all the more prominent. In fact, Haidar's confidant, Yaseen Khan Wunti Kudri who had a slight physical resemblance to him, quickly shaved off his beard and whiskers and folded a turban around his head like his master, to be caught by the Marathas under Trimbak Mama during the Chinkurli disaster, mistaking him for Haidar.

Between 8 a.m. and 9 a.m. he departed from his palace and gave audience to his secretaries in an assembly hall, passing on letters that were meant for them, along with advice on replies. He also met his sons, friends and relatives here, and enjoyed refreshments with them all. Appearing on a balcony next, he received the salute of his elephants and horses. Next, tigers passed by, led by the hand, and were fed by him with sweets. These tigers were covered 'with a mantle of green and gold hanging to the ground and a bonnet on their head, of cloth embroidered with gold, with which their eyes can be immediately covered, if they should chance to prove mischievous.'[13]

By around 10.30 a.m. he normally entered his durbar or hall of audience with a wider range of people. He sat on a grand sofa, beneath a canopy and often on some balcony that opened out to a courtyard where people assembled to greet him. His trusted friends, officers or relatives normally sat on either side of him. No one dared to converse or even whisper in his presence in his durbars. All requests and petitions by those who wished a redress of their concerns were at this point placed before him for his consideration. Some thirty to forty secretaries normally sat on the wall to his left, constantly taking down notes and orders that he kept pronouncing. New animals or cannons purchased were also inspected at this time. Couriers would arrive here almost every few minutes and their business would be conducted noisily. These would be read out to him and also instant replies composed in most cases. Haidar, having been completely illiterate all his life, had the only intellectual achievement of having learnt, with much difficulty, to write the first letter of his name 'Hai.' This was affixed in an inverted form whenever any paper required his signature. The royal seal, of which his principal secretary was the guardian, would then be affixed on the signed letters. The impression on his seal was the following verse: 'Futteh Hydur was manifested or born, to conquer the world. There is no man equal to Ali and no sword like his!'[14] Sometimes Haidar himself carried a private seal with him or wore it as a ring on his finger.

He spoke Kannada, Marathi, Telugu and Tamil with fluency, but had no knowledge of Persian or Arabic. Despite his illiteracy, he was blessed with an elephant-like memory and is said to have been able to recollect every word and incident for several years. Even if he had met someone decades before, he had the ability to instantly recognize the person, even if the latter had aged or dressed differently. It was said that he also had the talent of distinguishing and comprehending different voices. People credited him with being a veritable face-reader of sorts, a skill that he had probably picked up out of insecurities born out of suspicions in the wake of so many insurrections. He seldom met visitors from unknown lands and if he did, it was only after they were subjected to extensive cross-examinations regarding their motives. While he had a cheerful disposition, and made witty conversations and cracked lewd, bawdy jokes, people were petrified of his short temper. On such occasions when he would lose his temper, he would burst forth with the worst of invectives and cause his hapless victim to shiver under the impact of his uncontrollable wrath. Wilks attributes the anger in Haidar not to 'some mental disturbance, but of the alleged necessity of ruling with a spectre of iron; and keeping forever present the terror of his power.'[15] His favourite cuss word seems to have been '*lowndika*' or son of a slave girl, which he sometimes even used in endearment.[16]

In these morning durbars of people, justice would be instantly administered in many cases that did not need much adjudication. De La Tour mentions an instance in 1767: while in Coimbatore, Haidar was taking an evening ride in his horse carriage when an old woman interrupted his path and cried out aloud for justice. Haidar immediately ordered the carriage to be stopped and heard her tale of woe. She replied that one of his former ushers, Agha Mohammad, had ravaged her beautiful daughter on whom he had his eyes set for long. She complained that she had sent many requests to catch Haidar's attention through one of his chief ushers, Hyder Sha, but received no answers. Haidar was incensed and stormed into his palace, even as his other officers feared the punishment that might befall both the errant officers. They tried to intercede with him seeking their pardon. 'I cannot grant your request,' he said, 'there is no greater crime than that of interrupting the communication between a sovereign and his subjects. It is the duty of the powerful to see that the weak have justice. The sovereign is the only protector God has given them; and the prince who suffers oppression to pass unpunished among his subjects, is deservedly deprived of their affection and confidence, and at last compels them to revolt against him.'[17] Hyder Sha was his favourite usher who always preceded him in the durbar and wore a rich and large collar of gold as a sign of his eminence. Yet, he was ordered to be punished with 200 lashings. Agha Mohammad was also summoned and punished.

It was only by 3 p.m. that this elaborate durbar would conclude and Haidar would retire to his apartments for a siesta. He returned to the hall by 5.30 p.m. to witness the exercise of the troops and cavalry. An hour later, a procession of bearers of flambeaux appeared in the courtyard and saluted him. He was fond of show and parade on great occasions and at such times was attended by a thousand spearmen, preceded by bards who sang of his exploits in the Kannada language. By sunset, his apartments were completely illuminated with tapers in chandeliers of exquisite workmanship, ornamented with festoons of fragrant and delicate flowers. The apartments were normally covered with white muslin, spread upon the most exquisite and beautiful Persian carpets. White seemed to be Haidar's favourite colour and most of his furniture were draped in cloths of the colour. Private gatherings followed with family, friends and close officers. The young nobility, too, in all their finery and swords, moved around busily, talking merrily to one another as the evening moved to one of entertainment. Drinks and dinner were served to all present, even as a comedy show or a dance or music performance of courtesans went on. If the woman was a Hindu, she was to wear a white dress, and if she were Muslim, a dress embroidered with gold.[18] In the song and dance, she was not allowed to laugh or smile or display wanton gestures or steps. She was to perform slowly and softly. And as many men as there might be in the gathering, they were not allowed to ogle at the beauty of the woman, but instead keep their eyes fixated at him and admire his beauty alone. If any of the men even by chance happened to look at the dancing girls, he would coarsely abuse them saying 'Look! Look! Well! For your mother (meaning the dancing girl), has left her house and is occupied in dancing in the midst of her husbands!'[19] In fact, Peixoto mentions how, when a certain concubine casually lifted her eyes at a servant, Haidar killed her with his own hand and the hapless servant was ruthlessly skinned.[20] If he was in the company of intimate friends, however, he was more civil.

Both the comics and the artists who performed in these soirees were naturally women, who were under a lady directress who often purchased these young girls at the tender ages of four or five, taught them various art forms and also how to seduce the nobility. 'They have,' notes De La Tour, 'the most delicate features, large dark eyes, beautiful eye-brows, small mouth and the finest teeth; their cheeks are dimpled and their black hair hangs in flowing tresses to the ground; their complexion is a clear brown ... their habit is always a fine gauze, very richly embroidered with gold; and they are covered with jewels; their head, their neck, their ears, their breasts, their arms, fingers, legs and toes have their jewels; and even their nose is ornamented with a small diamond that gives them an arch look, which is far from being unpleasing.'[21] Haidar never concentrated too much on any of these soirees much as he was perpetually active, mentally. He sometimes passed silently into a side chamber to discuss matters of secrecy or urgent importance. At the end of every performance, flowers were brought to him, which he used for himself and also distributed among his favourite officers. If he wished to honour someone, he normally made a collar of the fragrant Mysore jasmine flowers with his own hands, as he conversed, knotted them with silk and put that around the neck of the fortunate recipient of his affection. This was his normal practice with the Europeans, particularly the French. Anyone who received this esteem was hugely complimented by the other men of the durbar as he had been chosen to be the apple of the Nawab's eye.

At around 11 p.m. or by midnight, the revelry would end and everyone would retire, except those who stayed on to sup with Haidar. Wilks states that Haidar 'was addicted to drinking, but these excesses were so prudently managed, as to be known to few; the time was soon before his usual hour of retiring to rest, and he slept off the after effects. Whether the use of strong liquours at the time of retiring to rest, was intended exclusively as a sensual indulgence, or partly as a soporific, is a question on which his old associates are not agreed.'[22] Thus, contrary to the diktats of his religion, he 'drank largely, but secretly, of European liquors,'[23] before he retired for the day. This was this normal routine when he was not involved in the military campaigns—which was only too seldom. During his military camps, he normally went for a chase in the forests twice a week, hunting stags, roebucks, antelopes and tigers.

Haidar had very plain dietary habits and was not too fond of delicacies, or too particular about what he ate. Whatever was placed on his table, he ate, showing no preference for sweet, salty or sour dishes. During his campaigns, he sustained on parched grams, almonds, and dry bread made of jowar, rice or ragi. His lifestyle was thus more like that of a soldier, perpetually on the field, rather than that of a flamboyant monarch.

The employees of his kingdom received their salaries through a system called *patta*. This had two broad categories—Shamsi and Khamri, which corresponded to the solar and lunar months of the Muslim calendar. The wages were seldom paid for a whole month; months in the Muslim calendar with fewer days earned them lower wages. On an annual basis, employees got their salary for just nine to ten months of a traditional twelve-month year. But they got a few gifts in kind, such as the loot money after successful expeditions or on rare occasions when Haidar was generous enough to give them a gift or bonus. They had to wait patiently for these to be sanctioned. His natural suspicion also ensured that Haidar resorted to various means, including severest tortures for the extraction of information. Those who were killed in the battle fighting for him were never given a burial.[24] Mirza Ikbal notes how he was an extremely difficult man to please:

> If anyone was sent in command of an expedition, and was delayed or unsuccessful, he was on his return sent for to the presence, and severely reproached by Hydur himself. If, on the contrary, he did his work soon and was successful, still, on his return, he was abused for having (as Hydur said), sacrificed the lives of his best men in rash, and profitless attacks. In fact, in his life, he was never known to praise anyone. In all his measures, he availed himself of the aid of threats and violence, to instill fear into men's minds.[25]

He had a special interest in and knowledge about horses, their varieties, temperaments, purchase, training, upkeep and safety. Horse dealers were paid liberally and treated with great hospitality and were showered with gifts and delicacies. He normally inspected the animals himself before buying them. Since he never gave leave to his servants to visit their native towns, most of them pining to return, would often disguise themselves as mendicants and escape with the horse dealers.[26]

The Autocrat

Hayavadana Rao mentions that 'his humble and agreeable manners attracted from all parts many adventurers to his service . . . even in public, he assumed no distinction between himself and one of his private troopers, nor were any deductions made from the pay of the soldiery in his employ. Whatever changes may have come over him in his later years, in the earlier part of his career—when he was still on the first steps of the ladder of fortune, he was simple, unostentatious and inviting to a degree.'[27]

About his reputation of being a ruthless man, given to exactions and tortures, Wilks makes an interesting observation that despite this, people from across the country were attracted to his court and his standard, as it offered them excellent opportunities in advancing their wealth and careers. 'A person once engaged in his service,' he writes, 'and deemed to be worth keeping, was a prisoner for life: he would hear of no home but his own, and suffered no return; but the summary severity, cruelty, and injustice of his character were directed, rather to the instruments than the objects of his rule; official men had cause to tremble; but the mass of the population felt that the vigour of the Government compensated for many ills, and rendered their condition comparatively safe.'[28]

Mirza Ikbal, however, has a different take on Haidar's lack of compassion for any of the people who worked for him or even died for him. He writes:

Notwithstanding the great riches which God from his hidden treasures had granted to him, he was at times so avaricious that even the pen is ashamed to write an account of his meanness. Sometimes, however on the reverse, he became very generous; but in fact, amassing wealth appeared to him as the renovation of his faculties. Indeed, many men followed him to the field, and lost their lives there, to whom or to whose children or relations, he never gave a single farthing. He never gave his dancing girls, who every day danced before him, anything beyond their yearly allowance, except, perhaps a trifle on very rare occasions. On those days, when before the balcony of the palace a lion net was suspended, and a man and a lion were placed in the arena, to fight together, if the lion killed the man, nothing was given; but if the man killed the lion, he received the present of a golden chain, or necklace. In general, he was so good a marksman with his matchlock that he did not suffer the lion to kill the man.[29]

Severe curbs were imposed on the freedom of the subjects of the kingdom as he constantly feared treachery or mobilization against him. People could not gather in large groups or talk loudly in public gatherings. They had to obtain the permission of his office for events such as a wedding in their family. In fact, he had a vast body of spies who had an uncanny flair for mingling freely and constantly with the general public, assessing their mood. People would often comment that even walls and doors in Mysore could have been planted with ears by the Nawab, and hence one was always on one's guard. The spies even loitered around wedding celebrations, sometimes pinching away some goodies from either the bride or bridegroom's side, even as they gathered intelligence from the casual conversations at such get-togethers. Whoever entered the dominions of Mysore was no longer free to do what they wished and stayed on or left only on Haidar's pleasure and with his consent. Mirza Ikbal states that 'by his power, mankind were [sic] held in fear and trembling; and from his severity, God's creatures day and night were thrown into apprehension and terror. Cutting off the nose and ears of any person in his territories, was the commonest thing imaginable; and the killing a man there, was thought no more of than treading on an ant. No person of respectability ever left his house with an expectation to return safe to it.'[30]

If people were caught embezzling funds from the revenues allocated for them or there was a deficit in the collection, they were given the harshest of punishments. As Schwartz, too, had noted in his memoirs how on a daily basis the severest of tortures were organized for errant officials who literally trembled at the very thought of being apprehended. Mirza Ikbal elaborates:

> He [errant] was seized and tied with ropes, like a horse, before and behind, and having been stripped naked, an order was given to flog him with a whip . . . beat him cruelly over the back and loins, after which salt was thrown upon his wounds. If he complained, he was beaten on the mouth with a shoe; and if he cried, red pepper, dried and pounded, was thrown in his eyes; and he was tortured in this way every day for a month, if he did not agree to pay the money. Besides this, every two or three days, iron spits or rods were made red hot, and he was burned or branded all over him. This was in addition to imprisonment, starvation, and chains. As soon as the delinquent had paid the money, Hydur's rage was softened and he presented him with shawls, and golden chains, and again offered the same office to the poor man who had just escaped from death. But if he refused to take it, the fire of Hydur's wrath was rekindled. His cruelty, however, was still greater, when exerted in extorting money from the Hindoos.[31]

Man of Pleasures

The Kannada work *Haidar-Namah* written in 1784 as his memoir by an anonymous Hindu admirer praises Haidar to the skies and terms him as a man who was the epitome of perfection in all qualities (*sakala gunabhirama*). But he mentions that were some defects in him that were intricately a part of his nature, like poison mixed with milk. 'One such is noteworthy,' he states, 'namely, the capture by force of beautiful damsels wherever they might be found. A second one was that he was treacherous, broke promises, and teased and punished men summarily without due enquiry. Had he only been free from these defects, there is no doubt that he would have been considered the noblest of men in this world (*satpurusha*). But, alas, just as a thousand paintings are marred by a blot of ink, the regime of Haidar could not last long.'[32]

About the first defect mentioned above, it was said that the towns and villages of Mysore abounded with nomadic women playing the *dolu* (drum) and singing melodiously to entertain people. A regular feature of Mysorean weddings and get-togethers, these women were actually under Haidar's pay and secretly gathered information for him about not only the *vox populi* of the kingdom, but about beautiful women who lived in the countryside. Haidar's men would then go to the suggested house and either through coercion or wilful surrender, bring those beauties to Haidar's harem in Srirangapatna. Soon, families began to be petrified by the voice of the dolu woman—the woman who was believed to usher in good fortune now became the harbinger of doom for the young women in any household. The captive women were classified into four groups in the harem and distinguished by the colour of their dress—red, green, blue and white. Each group was assigned different chores under the supervision of a female head, who finally reported to Haidar's principal wife, Fatima Begum. Not all were subjected to Haidar's lust, some of them he seldom even spoke to. Sometimes he even sent them back to their parents after using them or partitioned them amongst his followers.[33] The unfortunate girls ended up being domestic slaves and also added a touch of glamour to the royal household and in the *nataka shala* or centre for performing arts where those women who had any talents in music or dance were packed off to. They were trained there and utilized for his entertainments and soirees.[34] He however seems to be extremely possessive of his concubines and if any of them were suspected of infidelity, they had to pay a heavy price, as was mentioned by Peixoto earlier.

Other than his three wives, Haidar had upwards of 4000 concubines, distributed all over the kingdom, though principally in Srirangapatna, Bangalore and Bidanur. They were of all castes and even included some European mistresses. When he was overcome with the desire to indulge in intercourse, he would take a slow walk in the garden, where the concubines would assemble in two rows. They would hold a nose ring in their hands and he would pick the ring of those he wanted, giving 'the sign for them to go to him that night.'[35] Peixoto states that besides these concubines, he 'would amuse himself with others who were brought to him by force on pain of death.'[36]

Tipu's mother was Haidar's favourite wife and each time he entered her apartments, he would bring along the costliest of jewels and valuables as gifts. The entire harem of captive females would wait on him and fan or caress him. On the day he visited the women's apartments, every chief lady had her division of women, dressed in a different colour—red, green, violet, yellow, orange, purple, white, gold, sandal and rose—and standing apart from each other. They sat down near him but he seldom even looked at them or spoke to them; he had his eyes only for his darling wife. But despite all this love for her, he was also extremely scared of her as she was blessed with the most caustic tongue and verbally abused him in the coarsest manner. A man who could withstand the mightiest foe in the battlefield would be found meekly submitting in silence to the 'virago's torrent of hot words coolly.'[37] He knew that in her actions she was kind and cared for him, but it was just that her words were scathing and sarcastic. He just began to take it as 'her familiar mode of greeting him as he entered her apartment'[38] and normally avoided any confrontation or verbal duel. When the monologue of abuses crossed a certain decibel level for his comfort, he would make a hurried exit, citing some excuse, and muttering, 'It is from the fear of your tongue that I have given up entering the women's apartments.'[39] He would then join his friends such as Ghulam Ali Khan, Bahadur and Ali Zumaun Khan for a drink, lamenting all along that his wife's acid tongue was far worse than encountering the British in a battle.[40] Most often therefore his dinner and sleep at night was always outside the women's apartments, for fear of the wife.

Even Tipu seemed to be fully under the sway of his mother. After the First Anglo–Mysore war, Haidar had, on his return from

Madras via Arcot, selected a bride for Tipu. But his wife and Tipu himself had other plans, preferring instead the daughter of Lala Amin, one of the heroes of the Chinkurli episode. They went ahead and selected the pretty girl, angering Haidar initially, but later on he gave in to his wife's strong demands. Tipu wedded on the same day, as per Islamic laws, a woman of his choice and also the one that his father had selected for him.

One of Haidar's close friends, Khaki Shah, was the man who had participated in the task of defrauding Nanjarajayya by making Haidar take an oath on a brick that was presented as the Quran. Khaki Shah was reckoned as one of the wittiest men of his times and the two friends enjoyed each other's ribaldry. He was related to many in the harem of Haidar and often sent messages to the women in the harem in Haidar's name, causing conflicts between them or disappointments to some others. These pranks that broke the hearts of some of the inmates of the harem were then the subject of mirth and boisterous laughter over drinks for the two men. It was another matter that such pranks cost the duo heavily. Once, Haidar too sent a fake message to his friend's wife that her husband had been killed in battle. The lady was so attached to her husband that she could not bear the news of his death and swallowed poison to end her life. When Khaki Shah heard of his beloved wife's passing away as a result of a harmless joke, he was devastated and vowed to renounce the world. After long and much coercion from Haidar, he rejoined service, only to be killed later in the battle, which many faithful attributed to his profaning the Quran as a means to defraud another man.

Haidar's Religious Policy

About Haidar's attitude towards religion, Wilks states the following:

> Hyder was of all Mahommedan princes the most tolerant, if, indeed, he is to be considered as a Mussulman. He neither practiced, nor had ever been instructed how to practice, the usual

forms of prayer, the fasts and other observances. He had a small rosary, on which he had been taught to enumerate a few of the attributes of God, and this was the whole of his exterior religion. It was his avowed and public opinion, that all religions proceed from God, and are all equal in the sight of God; and it is certain, that the mediatory power represented by Runga Sawmey [Sri Ranganatha Swamy], the great idol in the temple of Seringapatam, had as much, if not more, of his respect, than all the Inaums, with Mahommed as their head.[41]

Even Rev. Schwartz, who had come to his palace as an emissary, had testified on similar lines, when he wrote: 'What religion people profess, or whether they profess any at all, that is perfectly indifferent to him. He has none himself and leaves everyone to his choice.'[42] Schwartz, as mentioned earlier, freely went around conducting sermons and prayers and preaching the Bible to those interested, during his short stay in Srirangapatna, and none seemed to mind it.

The famed festival of Mysore, the Dasara, which had hoary roots back to the Vijayanagara times and those of Raja Wodeyar, starting 1610, were allowed to be carried out unabated. The deposed Maharaja sat on his ancestral throne and celebrated the festival with the same pomp and glory as his ancestors might have. This was also partly because all through his career, Haidar carefully calibrated his image of not assuming any external visages of royalty or denying the claims of the Hindu dynasty. It was another thing that through subterfuge, he eliminated the king himself or interfered in the succession lines. But overtly, there was no affront to the family, as he very well knew that the population, being a Hindu majority one that looked up to the dynasty with reverence, would brook no disrespect and he would be condemned as an ungrateful usurper. Haidar happily participated in the Dasara festivities and the durbars, and mounted on his elephant, followed the Maharaja on his royal procession on the tenth day of Vijayadashami to the Banni Mantap. The procession also had several units of his army and cavalry, including Europeans, 500 men mounted on camels, bedecked elephants, regiments of handsome

Abyssinian horses wearing plumes of red–black ostrich feathers and carrying steel-headed lances. The infantry, nobility, principal officers—all richly dressed and bejewelled, were part of this merry jamboree.[43] Kirmani of course states that these customs, being those of infidels, were something Haidar was averse to follow, 'but still with a view to please and gain the affections of the Mysoreans, that is the descendants of Jug Kishen Raj Oodere [Krishnaraja Wodeyar II], and his ministers . . . and because the service or agency of infidels is not infidelity, he held a banquet of ten days.'[44]

There are also letters of his that were written to the Jagadguru Shankaracharya, the pontiff of the sacred *mutt* in Sringeri that was established by Adi Shankaracharya as one of the four cardinal centres for Advaita Vedanta. Sringeri was an important centre for Vedic learning, Sanskrit and traditional knowledge, with goddess Sharadamba as the presiding deity. The mutt itself came to be known as Dakshinamanya Sri Sharada Peetham, with its counterparts in Badrikashram Jyotirpeeth (north India), Sharada Peeth in Dwarka (western India) and Govardhan Peeth in Puri (eastern India). Interestingly, even during the heights of political turmoil, all the rivals of the South—Mysore, Marathas, Nizam and even the British—held the lineage of the Jagadguru of Sringeri in the highest esteem. Sri Narasimha Bharati Swami VII (1767–70) and Sri Sacchidananda Bharati Swami III (1770–1814) were the pontiffs during the times of Haidar Ali, and later Tipu Sultan. One letter, dated 29 April 1769, details Haidar sending to the Jagadguru an elephant, five horses, a palanquin, five camels, a sari for the deity of goddess Sharadamba, two shawls, two pairs of dhotis and Rs 10,500, as the latter was undertaking a trip to Poona.[45] He addressed him as 'a great and holy personage' and added that 'it is nothing but natural for anyone to cherish a desire to pay respects to you.'[46] Another letter, written somewhere between 1768 and 1770, assured the Jagadguru of maintaining the time-honoured *inams* or grants to the mutt, requested him to accept the gifts sent in his honour and also acknowledged the Swami's benedictory letter.[47] In another letter dated 23 August 1777, Haidar expresses his delight on coming

to know of the Swamiji's return from Poona and his observing the
chaturmasya or four-month holy period of penance and austerities in
Harkeri on the banks of the Tungabhadra River. He wished the safe
return of the Jagadguru to Sringeri after his penance and requested
him to observe similar worship in Sringeri for the prosperity of the
kingdom. The Jagadguru seems to have sent him clothes that were
blessed by him, which Haidar gratefully acknowledges and sends
back two shawls as his token of respect.[48] Just before launching
on his offensive in the Second Anglo–Mysore War, there is a royal
proclamation too that Haidar issued on 8 February 1780 to killedars
and officers not to impede or obstruct any of the time-tested
traditions and rituals in the mutt.[49]

Once, when seasonal rains had failed, Haidar called the zamindars
and asked them to request the Brahmins to perform a *japam* or
chants for bringing down rain.[50] A letter in Fort St George talks
about his gifting an elephant and a palanquin to the holy temple
in Tirupati in 1779.[51] In 1774, when the house of one Kadimuddin
that was adjacent to the temple of Sri Ranganatha Swamy caught
fire, the blaze spread to the temple too and damaged a portion of it.
Haidar is said to have instructed an immediate repair of the temple,
which was carried out within a month. His principal officers and
confidants, too, were both Hindu and Muslim—Abu Muhammad
Mirda, Mir Muhammad Sadak, Purnaiya, Shamaiya and Krishna
Rao. His revenue officers and vakils (diplomats), too, were largely
Brahmins, the chief among them being Appaji Ram. But important
positions of forts and armies were given to Muslims, and more so to
family members whom he seemed to trust more against any acts of
possible treachery.

How much of these gestures were out of genuine respect towards
another faith and how much was necessitated by realpolitik, as
Kirmani suggests, for keeping Mysoreans happy, is something that
we will never know. In his campaigns outside Mysore, it has already
been seen how holy places were desecrated or captives circumcised
and converted. This was possibly more to do with humiliation and
cultural subjugation of a vanquished community, than completely

theologically driven. One cannot, however, deny the theological
sanction for such acts, which were committed in addition to the
normal pillage and plunder that all wars and protagonists of the time
casually involved themselves in when it came to enemy territory.

An interesting incident is narrated by Kirmani about a huge
conflict that arose between the Shia and Sunni sects in Srirangapatna,
with the two coming to blows from initial verbal duels. They were
summoned to Haidar's presence individually and questioned. The
Sunni submitted that the other was extremely disrespectful in his
words towards the successors of the Prophet and even used abusive
language against them that made him feel as if 'a thorn had been
broken in his heart.'[52] Haidar next summoned the Shia and asked
him for an explanation. The latter said the first Caliph Abu Bakr
had committed some excesses against Murtaza Ali and the second
Caliph Omar frequently ill-treated Fatima, and several other tales.
Hence, as descendants of Hussain, he, being a Shia, was within his
rights to speak disrespectfully about them all. At this, Haidar coolly
asked him if the people he mentioned or reproached were still alive.
On hearing a 'no' from the other side, Haidar lost his temper and
shouted at him: 'He is a man who declares his opinion of the good
or evil of another before his face, not behind his back. Do you know
that back-biting is unlawful? And I should think that as you act in
this manner, you must also be base born. If you ever again waste and
destroy your time and that of the Sirkar in such an irreverent, wicked
dispute, you may rely on it, a camel bag and a mallet will be ready
for you![53]'

On another occasion, in his court, a fable was being narrated
by a group of both Shias and Sunnis who had assembled there. The
tale of a traveller on horseback, whose horse suddenly got stuck in a
quagmire and sunk to the ground. The man dismounted and ordered
the horse to get up in the name of the Caliph Abu Bakr and the horse
made no movement. He then invoked Caliph Omar and Osman
and others, but the poor animal was stuck in its position. When he
finally invoked the name of Murtaza Ali, the horse sprung from the
quicksand and was ready to gallop. At this, the man got enraged

and calling the horse a heretic that was no longer of use to him cut off its legs with a single stroke of his sword. Haidar heard this fable patiently and then laughed aloud saying, 'What a wonderful fool this man must have been! Did he not know that he who was the strongest brought the horse out of the mire!'[54] The image that one conceives of Haidar from these several recorded anecdotes is that of a man given to a rational and practical approach towards religion, where even faith was tempered by statecraft and diplomacy and not merely by rigid dogmas and biases.

It was mentioned earlier how Haidar had exacted an agreement from Tipu around or after the time of what transpired at Chinkurli. It seems that he had disagreements with his son even on the latter's attitude towards faiths other than their own. Wilks describes this dissimilarity between the duo:

Hyder, from the earliest youth of Tippoo, made no secret of lamenting, that his [Tipu's] intellect was of an inferior order, and his disposition wantonly cruel, deceitful, vicious and intractable. Among the pranks which he [Tipu] practiced about this period, two gave particular offence to his father. 1st. In taking his exercise on horseback, it was his particular delight to hunt the sacred bulls of the Hindoo temples, wounding them, and sometimes destroying them with his lance (indeed after his own accession he made no scruple of recommending this divine animal to his associates as the best beef). Hyder was shocked at these wanton and unprofitable outrages, on the feelings of the great mass of his subjects. 2nd. An English soldier who had been made a prisoner during Colonel Smith's war, had remained in Mysoor, on the liberation of his associates. Tippoo one day took the opportunity of having him suddenly seized, and causing the outward and visible sign of Islam to be inflicted in his presence [circumcision]. Hyder was at the time particularly anxious to conciliate the English; he abused his son in the grossest terms, put him in solitary confinement, and when released, forbade his courtiers to speak with him; an interdiction which was frequently repeated, as the consequence of subsequent offences. On this occasion, as on many others, he predicted that this worthless successor, would lose the empire which he had created; he observed, that in order to indulge a silly prejudice, he had insulted and injured the soldier, in a manner which could answer no rational purpose, and might one day bring the vengeance of the English nation on his house . . . Tippoo never returned from a detachment, without attempting secret embezzlement of the plunder. Hyder on such occasions would lose all patience, and in plain terms call him a thief, and a blockhead; observing that he had not the common sense to perceive that he was stealing from himself: for unhappily, said he, you will be my successor; would that I had begotten Ayaz [Sheikh Ayaz] instead of you![55]

It is perhaps for all these above reasons that Bowring states that despite the terror that he inspired, Haidar's name 'is always mentioned in Mysore with respect, if not with admiration. While the cruelties which he sometimes practiced are forgotten, his prowess and success have an abiding place in the memory of the people.'[56] The general impression that was formed of Haidar Ali in the annals of history was as of a great enemy of the British in India. N.K. Sinha narrates an interesting anecdote about what impression Haidar had left even on an average schoolboy, back in England, who knew little or nothing of India:

In October 1781, when John Malcolm, a candidate for writership, was taken to the India House and was on a fair way to be rejected, one of the directors said to him, 'Why my little man, what would you do if you were to meet Haidar Ali?', 'Do Sir? I would out with my sword and cut off his head!' 'You will do' was the rejoinder. 'Let him pass!' was the comment . . . He [Haidar] brought them almost on the verge of destruction in India. But the adoption of an anti-British policy was not due to passion, prejudice, malice or insolence. It was inevitable in the existing situation.[57]

An appropriate concluding assessment of Haidar Ali, his stormy life and his legacy is in the words of historian Hayavadana Rao:

> Haidar may have been illiterate but he was not unintelligent. On the other hand, he was shrewd, carefully calculating, hard thinking, always with an eye to turning transactions to his own profit. He was also deep-seated, cunning, with a thorough understanding of mundane matters, never yielding to mere sentiment, appeal or importunity. He could be in turn kind, friendly, dissimulating and cruel. He could enjoy a joke and indulge in one too. He was, in a word, perfectly human, with an understanding of men and things that surprised those around him and made them fear him and his artful ways and sudden turns of disposition. To describe him either in uniform black paint as a hard, rapacious person bent on plundering his neighbours or to represent him in so dazzling a light that he becomes almost indistinguishable is hardly correct. He was extraordinary in the sense that history, ancient or modern, affords no exact parallel to him. If to the people of the eighteenth century he was a terror and his name was associated always with war—indicated popularly throughout the whole of Southern India by such phrases as *Haidarana Haavali* [the terror of Haidar] and *Haidar Kalaapam* [Haidar's exploits]—to the people of the twentieth-century, he is still continuing to be something of a marvel. That is where he is interesting, yet as a unique historical personage.[58]

10

Passing on the Mantle

As Haidar's health continued to deteriorate in the war camp and his recovery seemed impossible, the man who took charge of the precarious situation was his confidant, Purnaiya. Purnaiya decided that in the event of his master's passing away, the state of affairs should be kept totally hidden from the army and the people at large, lest it incite rebellions and enthuse the opponents. Other than a close coterie of Commandant Muhammad Ali, Anche Shamaiah, Toshikhane Krishna Rao, Mir Muhammad Sadak, Badar-u-Zumaun Khan, Maha Mirza Khan, Ghazi Khan and Abu Muhammad Mirdha, no one knew that Haidar was sinking and it was only a matter of time before he passed on to the other realm on 7 December 1782. Even after Haidar's passing, his body was shifted out of the camp secretly on 9 December 1782, in a large chest filled with aromatics, making it appear to the soldiers and onlookers as if it was valuable plunder from the war that was being sent away after being shown to Haidar. The casket carrying his corpse was taken away to Kolar to be buried there in the tomb of Haidar's father. The usual buzz around Haidar's camp, the letters being ferried in and out, envoys, horses being led for display, beating of drums and all other formalities were carried out in a stoic and business-as-usual manner, without letting anyone know that their ruler had died. Surgeons and doctors kept visiting his camp twice a day, as also the chiefs and others who made diurnal visits. It was truly a testament of Purnaiya's sagacity and presence of mind that he managed this difficult situation with such ease. At the same time, multiple couriers

* Please refer to the corresponding illustration in the appendix.

were dispatched to Tipu, who was away in the Malabar campaign, to return at the earliest opportunity.

Despite the entire affair being shrouded in such secrecy, the army knew that their ruler was grievously unwell. This itself was enough to set into motion the wheels of rebellion. This was sparked by Muhammad Amin, the son of Ibrahim Sahib, Haidar's cousin. He was a chief in the army and commanded 4000 horses. Anticipating his uncle's death, Amin ganged up with Shums-ud-din, the Bakshi, to favour Haidar's injudicious second son, Karim, as his successor. They knew that with a weak ruler their fortunes could be bolstered. This was also a way to bring in discord between the brothers, Tipu and Karim, and spark off rivalry and wars of succession. They joined hands with a French officer, Bouthenot, who commanded 100 French cavalry, to execute their plans. However, on receiving intelligence of foul play, Purnaiya summoned these men on the pretext of being called for discussions by Haidar to his tent. Upon their entry, they were interrogated and after they confessed to their evil intentions, they were put in irons and packed off to the dungeons in Srirangapatna for the crime of conspiring to overthrow the government. Bouthenot too was arrested for treason and sent to the capital to prevent him from corresponding with Madras to incite Tipu's officers.

The letter from Narasingarayanapet, informing him of his father's death, reached Tipu on 11 December. He was crestfallen to hear the news and immediately abandoned the Malabar campaign to rush back to Kolar where his father's body lay, waiting for the son to perform the obsequies. On the way, in Coimbatore, Tipu appointed Sayyid Muhammad Mahdavi, Commandant of Srirangapatna, in place of Muhammad Shitab. Sayyid had saved Tipu's life in Chinkurli but had earned the wrath of Haidar who had relegated him to the position of a mere horseman in Tipu's personal guard. It is quite revealing that the first appointment made by a son grieving for his father was of a man whom his deceased father did not favour much or think too highly of. Tipu ordered Arshad Beg Khan to take charge of Malabar and be on the defensive at Palghat. By then, the Mysore army had left Narasingarayanpet and a palanquin, purportedly carrying Haidar in it and covered with all the honours of war, also headed out by 21 December. In order not to disturb the supposed patient who lay inside, drums and other instruments were beaten in a muted manner. Tipu managed to reach the camp that had been set up about two miles away from the main army by the evening of 28 December. Refusing to be received with any pomp and show, he entered the camp in a quiet, private manner after sunset. He seated himself on the ground on a plain carpet, as a mark of respect and grief for his deceased father, 'declining to ascend the *musnud* [throne] from an affectation of grief.'[1] The funeral prayers and other rituals were then conducted for Haidar. The customary mourning rituals were observed at Srirangapatna, too, 'but the people seemed not to regret the loss of their ruler.'[2] Later, Tipu ordered for the body to be removed from Kolar and moved to Srirangapatna where he had a grand mausoleum, the Gumbaz in Lal Bagh, erected in Haidar's memory in March 1783.

The next morning, Tipu called for his brother and all the principal officers who had ensured secrecy of affairs and thereby demonstrated their patriotism and loyalty towards the kingdom and him by quelling all rumours and rumblings, and expressed his immense gratitude. British accounts talk of Tipu contemplating making preparations to storm his brother's camp and imprison him, lest he lay claim to the throne.[3] But being of inferior intellect and prowess, Karim willingly surrendered rather than defend his rights. Whatever might be the truth here, it was certainly a peaceful and bloodless succession after Haidar's sudden demise.

On the evening of 29 December 1782 (Hayavadana Rao mentions this date as 2 January 1783),[4] Tipu ascended the throne of his father as the new Sarvadhikari or Supreme Dictator of Mysore, as the head of an army of 88,000 men, a treasury consisting of Rs 3 crore in cash, besides an immense amount of jewels and other valuables. As Innes Munro states, 'without a single opponent, or the least symptom of the commotion usual upon such an occasion, he [Tipu] . . . (was) proclaimed Nabob of Misore [sic], and Generalissimo of their armies.'[5] Even a British prisoner of war, James Bristow, who was languishing in the dungeons in Srirangapatna, recounts how smooth the transition was and credits Tipu's 'abilities as a politician as well as a soldier; such authority, at least did his known character carry with it, that no open attempts were made to oppose his accession, or divide and circumscribe his power.'[6]

It was after this ceremony that he began to be addressed as Tipu Sultan. Several European writers had till then called him 'Tippoo Saib' and therefore, as Hayavadana Rao deduces, 'the affix "Sultan" cannot thus be taken as part and parcel of a proper name.'[7] Even a favourable French biographer, Joseph Michaud, notes: 'Tippoo Saheb had more of vanity than of real greatness in his character. The modest title of regent did not satisfy his ambition, and he assumed the title of Sultan. The ghost of Hyder Ali, who appeared still to be the ruler of the realm of Mysore, and the love of the people towards the young Prince, caused the new denomination to be approved, but they did not give him the power to sustain the splendour. One could say in general of Tippoo Saheb, that he occupied himself too much with the means of displaying his power and not enough with those of consolidating it and of rendering his power legitimate in the eyes of his subjects.'[8]

As a gesture of goodwill, he paid off all the arrears of the troops and made liberal gifts of money and promises of favour to commanders of forts, army chiefs, revenue collectors, farmers and others. In an effusive and gushy manner, Kirmani notes: 'In that assembly, melodious poets and eloquent orators, from the clouds of their invention, showered the orient pearls of prose and verse on the head of the young king, and were liberally rewarded from the table of his bounty.'[9] Though no other contemporary sources mention this, Michaud talks of an emotional letter, almost in the form of a will, that Haidar had left behind for his son:

My son, I leave you an Empire which I have not received from my ancestors. A sceptre acquired by violence is always fragile; meanwhile you will not find any obstacles in your family; you have no rivals among the Chiefs of the army. I do not leave you any enemies among my subjects. You have nothing to fear as regards the internal affairs of your state. But it is necessary to carry your

vision very far. India since the death of Aurangazeb has lost her
rank among the Empires of Asia. This fair land is parceled out into
provinces which make war, one against the other; and the people
divided into multitude of sects, have lost their love of country.
The Hindus mollified by their pacific maxims are little able to
defend their country which has become the prey of strangers.
The Mussalmans are more united and more enterprising than the
feeble Hindus. It is to them that should belong the glory of saving
Hindustan. My son, combine all your efforts to make the Koran
triumph. If God helps this noble endeavour the day is not far,
perhaps when the sword of Mahomet will place you on the throne
of Tamarlane. The greatest obstacle you have to conquer is the
jealousy of the Europeans. The English are today all powerful in
India. It is necessary to weaken them by war. The resources of
Hindustan do not suffice to expel them from the lands they have
invaded. Put the nations of Europe one against the other. It is by
the aid of the French that you could conquer the British armies
which are better trained than the Indian. The Europeans have
super tactics; always use against them their own weapons. If God
had allowed me a longer career, you need only have enjoyed the
success of my enterprises. But I leave you for achieving them, rich
provinces, a population of twelve million souls, troops, treasures
and immense resources. I need not awaken your courage. I have
seen you often fight by my side, and you shall be the inheritor of
my glory. Remember, above all, that valour can elevate us to a
throne, but it sufficeth not always to reserve an Empire. While
we may seize a crown owing to the timidity of the people, it can
escape us if we do not make haste to entrust it to their love.[10]

If the letter is authentic and not a poor French attempt to make
their own position indispensable for Mysore in its quest to vanquish
the British, it offers a clear road map for what the Sultan needed to
have in mind for his reign. Why this letter seems suspect is that the
British records talk about Haidar instructing Tipu and Purnaiya not
to rely too much on the French and, instead of bringing disgrace

upon himself, Tipu must attempt peace with the British on whatever optimal terms were possible and return to Srirangapatna.[11]

The Second Anglo–Mysore War Continues

The war with the British had temporarily halted in view of the Malabar affairs and of course Haidar's death. By then, numerous changes had occurred in the Madras Government with Lord Macartney becoming the Governor on 22 June 1781. The Madras Government was increasingly getting annoyed with Muhammad Ali, the Nawab of Arcot, who kept promising to assign to them a portion of his revenues as cost of the war with Haidar and Mysore, which the British were for all practical purposes fighting on his behalf. But his vacillation and duplicity were increasingly becoming stumbling blocks in an amicable relationship between the two parties. On his end, Muhammad Ali hatched a larger plot. He decided to overlook the Madras Government and deal directly with the Governor-General and the Supreme Government in Calcutta. He dispatched his dewan, Saiyid Khwaja Hashim Khan, along with a Madras civil servant, Richard Joseph, to call upon Governor-General Warren Hastings. Totally circumventing the Governor of Madras, Hastings and Muhammad Ali entered into an agreement on 2 April 1781. According to this, Sullivan was to remain a resident at the Nawab's court as an agent of Hastings. Muhammad Ali was to be declared as the undisputed and legitimate, hereditary sovereign of the Carnatic. This was a blatant attempt to supersede Macartney who naturally protested and asked the Supreme Government to have the agreement cancelled. Eventually Calcutta gave in, and a rapprochement was attempted between Muhammad Ali and Macartney in December 1781. The Nawab had to assign all his revenues, except one-sixth that he reserved for his personal expenditure to the Company for a period of five years. Macartney got the entire control over the collection of revenues and Muhammad Ali was virtually reduced to becoming a titular Nawab. A carefully selected Board of Governors, that was put together by Macartney, was to manage the revenue administration.

After humbling his petulant and untrustworthy ally, Macartney was keen to prevent Tipu's re-entry into the Carnatic. Around the time when Haidar passed away, his chief opponent, Sir Eyre Coote, too died and was succeeded by Major General James Stuart as the Commander-in-Chief. After assuming position, the first act that Tipu did was to seek peace with Macartney. Around 12 February 1783, the agent of the Raja of Tanjore, Sambhaji, was sent by Macartney to ascertain Tipu's motives. From Mysore, Srinivasa Rao was sent to negotiate terms of reconciliation. Tipu wanted a handover of a few districts such as Pudukottai and Polypady and other smaller posts in the Carnatic that lay adjacent to his domains. Of course, the old issue of Tiruchirapalli and its handover, too, came up. Through the Treaty of Salbai, the Peshwa had earlier undertaken to prevail upon Haidar to release all the British prisoners of war who were languishing in different Mysorean jails under great duress. This was naturally a top priority for the Madras Government, too, in these new negotiations. Macartney also suggested that Mysore needed to detach itself from the French connection if it wanted to secure lasting peace with the British. The negotiations ended with Srinivasa Rao urging Macartney to send an authorized person on behalf of the Company to discuss the finer details. The strain of war had caused the Madras army immense hardships and the acute shortage of supplies plagued them perennially. The constant bickering between the civil and military authorities at Madras had also hindered the war in the earlier phases. While Macartney was willing to concede and conclude the war and even had the support of the Court of Directors, the Supreme Government in Calcutta and Governor-General Hastings, who despised Macartney, put a spanner in the works. Hastings refused to empower Macartney to unilaterally sign any such treaty and said that he would grant three million sterling to Madras to continue the hostilities. Thus, the negotiations reached a point of no return and had to be shelved, and the hostilities thereafter resumed with Tipu marching on with his army towards Kaveripak.

By then, the rains had abated and Tipu camped at Arni, where a French contingent of over 1000 troops joined him from Cuddalore towards the end of January 1783. The British forces were plagued by lack of provisions and rice as before and many were starving or ill as a result. Thus, Stuart postponed his advance even after hearing about Haidar's death and the urge to take immediate advantage of a Mysore that he assumed was in the flux of transition. Instead of organizing himself and his troops, Stuart wasted the opportunity in squabbles and arguments with every officer, be they civil, military or navy. It was only after 5 February 1783 that he was able to move towards Wandiwash to attack Tipu, who had by then already moved in the same direction with the French troops under Cossigny. The two troops, separated by the Palar River, prepared for a clash, a week later, by the 13th. After an entire day of mutual exchanges of firing, the British retraced their steps towards Wandiwash, only to be hotly pursued by the Mysorean troops. The Mysore horse and rocket-men 'killed and wounded near two hundred'[12] of the British troops. Stuart even blew up the fortifications of Wandiwash and Karunguli, lest they fall into the Sultan's hands. But Tipu could not take full advantage of the panic that he had set amongst the British as he heard disturbing news from the western front where British forces, under General Matthews, had plans of invading the Malabar, forcing his retreat from the Carnatic.

Even when Tipu was at Paniani, the Bombay Government had sent its Commander-in-Chief Brigadier-General Richard Matthews to attack the western possessions of Haidar and to divert the Mysore army from the Carnatic. Accordingly, Matthews had occupied several places, including Mangalore and the port of Honnavar that had five warships of Mysore. On hearing about Haidar's death, the Bombay Government directed Matthews to relinquish his operations and directly attack Mysore territories and capture Bidanur. By early January 1783, Matthews marched on towards Kundapura, capturing Rajahmandurg. Kundapura was the point of the coast closest to Bidanur that the British now wanted to take badly. Being a rich and fertile area, Bidanur held the promise of furnishing a regular supply of provisions and other requirements for the British army via the coast.

Also, given how emotionally attached Haidar had been to Bidanur, its occupation would definitely deal a huge moral blow to Tipu.

At around this time, a curious situation arose with respect to Sheikh Ayaz, Haidar's favourite chela from the Malabar conquest and adopted son, who had been entrusted with the governorship of Chitradurga. Ayaz and Tipu shared a tempestuous relationship since their youth. Ayaz's daring and independent character had always been publicly praised by Haidar, who often contrasted him to his own son, thereby creating deep-rooted resentment for Ayaz in Tipu's mind. A British soldier who was taken captive, John Scurry, too mentions this equation between the two men thus:

> As he [Sheikh Ayaz] approached towards manhood, he was much distinguished for his obedience, punctual discharge of duty, and gratitude to his benefactor. Tippoo, on the contrary, when young, was remarkable for his stubborn and untractable [sic] disposition. Hyder perceived the difference between the natural character of these lads; and frequently, when Tippoo had behaved in an undutiful manner, in his father's presence, Iyard Cawn [Sheikh Ayaz] was ordered to chastise him. This circumstance implanted in the bosom of Tippoo, the seeds of hatred against Iyard, which were never ever eradicated.[13]

It was believed that Haidar had wanted Tipu and Karim to divide the kingdom amongst them and Sheikh Ayaz was to retain his elevated rank as Governor of Bidanur and Chitradurga.[14] The death of his benefactor and adopted father, Haidar, obviously stirred insecurity and fear in Ayaz, who obstinately refused to owe any allegiance to the new sovereign. It turned out that Ayaz's fears were not totally misplaced. He had managed a suitable system of espionage to ensure that several of Tipu's letters and declarations found their way to his camp and every detail of it was read out to him and scrutinized, as he was illiterate. The letters were often read out to him in an isolated place with no one else being around to know their contents. Around 24 January 1783, one such intercepted letter from Tipu sent shivers down Ayaz's spine. It contained Tipu's orders to his commander, Lutf Ali Beg, to proceed with a light corps of cavalry towards Coorg and thereafter to Bidanur to put Ayaz to death, if he resisted, and take over as the Commander there. The unfortunate Brahmin clerk who innocently opened the bundle of intercepted letters and read out this one to his master was put to instant death to prevent discovery.[15] The presence of Matthews in the vicinity gave Ayaz hope amidst these turbulent times. He decided that aligning with Matthews would be the safest bulwark against Tipu's malevolent designs.

By 29 January 1783, as Matthews marched towards Bidanur, he was pleasantly surprised to note that Sheikh Ayaz had released a British prisoner, Captain Donald Campbell, with a message of goodwill and his readiness to surrender the place. Finding it hard to believe this, Matthews moved forward towards the Bidanur fort and was again surprised to see the fort gates open in welcome. Sheikh Ayaz had firmly decided to surrender to the forces of Matthews and in return negotiate that his own private property be secured and that he continue to remain in his state of dignity and position under British protection. The British were thus in complete occupation of the strategically important Bidanur, without firing a single shot or signing any treaty agreements. Twenty-four chests filled with invaluable treasures found their way to the British possession, and yet a lot more remained. Such was the affluence of Bidanur.

The British forces then moved towards Anantapur (modern day Anandapura in Shimoga district) and readily occupied the place by 14 February 1783 after breaching the fort. What followed in Anantapur was unmitigated and wanton cruelties inflicted by the British forces. A contemporary anonymous British officer notes in his memoirs:

We are sorry to say, that as slaughter, cruelty, rapine and avarice had disgraced this expedition in its commencement at Onore [Honnavar], so the same detestable maxims and vices continued to stain its whole progress . . . accounts of this slaughter have been suppressed . . . the spectacle which was there [at Anantpur] exhibited of four hundred beautiful women, all bleeding with wounds from the bayonet and either already dead or expiring in each other's arms! While the common soldiers casting off all obedience to their officers, were stripping off their jewels and committing every outrage on their bodies. Many of the women rather than be torn from their relations threw themselves into large tanks and were drowned.[16]

Another account talks of how 'all the inhabitants [were] wantonly and inhumanly put to death, and their bodies thrown into several tanks.'[17] After inflicting such horrific tortures on the innocent people of Anantapur, Matthews left Colonel John Campbell in charge of Mangalore, returning triumphantly to Bidanur. By now, practically all of the western dominions of Mysore were firmly under his control.

Lutf Ali Beg's march towards Bidanur proved futile and he was waiting for reinforcements. At this time, he received directions from Tipu to proceed towards Mangalore as he himself was going to march towards Bidanur to punish Ayaz for his treachery. Tipu had an axe to grind with Ayaz and did not want to forego the chance. Leaving the command in the Carnatic under Saiyid Sahib, Tipu marched through the Changama pass, Devanahalli, Maddagiri, Sira and Chitradurga, reaching the outskirts of Bidanur by the end of March. On hearing of Tipu's arrival in the vicinity, Ayaz fled in fright to Bombay, leaving Matthews behind to safeguard Bidanur. By 7 April 1783, Tipu reached Bidanur and divided his army into two columns, one which took the southern route of Kavaledurga and Haidargarh that fell to his might without any resistance. The other column went northwards and easily reoccupied Anantapur. He now encircled Bidanur completely and besieged Matthews. Thirteen batteries were erected, and their firing caused considerable damage to the fort and its buildings and killed or wounded several in the British garrison. The Mysore troops also blocked all supplies from coming in. The siege lasted eighteen days in which the British plight was horrific with the scarcity of water, provisions and ammunition.

A fever too raged, with more than 350 people within the fort sick and lying exposed to the sun. Captain Fetherson, who had been sent to aid Matthews, was killed. Matthews himself was by then facing serious allegations of corruption and unfair distribution of the war plunder from his fellow officers. The Government of Bombay even decided to supersede him with Col Macleod who was promoted to the rank of Brigadier-General. With his condition become untenable with each passing day, by the end of April 1783, Matthews sent out a flag of truce to Tipu, proposing to surrender.

A treaty was concluded with Matthews whereby the British relinquished the forts of Bidanur, Kavaledurga and Anantapur. In return, they were to be given a free exit to Bombay, via Goa. Wilks's mention of the very first article of this treaty, as stated by Tipu's royal chronicler, is interesting: 'When the English garrison shall march out, the holy warriors of Islam shall not ridicule them, nor call them by abusive names, nor throw stones at them, nor spit at them.'[18] While surrendering, Matthews ordered his soldiers to draw as much money as they wanted from the Paymaster-General.[19] The British therefore left the fort, trying to stuff themselves with every little bit of treasure that was still left in the fort. When a group of British soldiers were being driven out of the fort, a small bag that belonged to one of them burst open and out came tumbling several pieces of gold. This alerted Tipu's men and when they searched the entire party, every knapsack was found lined with gold. Scurry mentions that gold coins were even 'thrust down the throats of dogs and goats, and even the crops of fowls were crammed with the precious morsels.'[20] About 40,000 pagodas were recovered from the soldiers themselves.

Tipu was determined to teach Matthews a lesson for the kind of atrocities that he had committed and for the pillage of the treasury in Bidanur. No sooner had he and his troops surrendered their arms and were leaving Bidanur than the Mysore troops surrounded them from all sides and captured them. They were marched off in iron chains to different prisons in Srirangapatna, Chitradurga, Bangalore, Kabbaladurga, Gutti and other places. Tipu thereafter had complete control over Bidanur and, for the first time after his accession to the throne, gave a public durbar, seated on a throne in the place that had changed his father's political fortunes. Salutes were fired for this first victory that he had secured for himself after his accession. Wasting no time, Tipu marched towards the Malabar coast, to reduce all the places that had been garrisoned by the British. His next focus was on the recovery of Mangalore that was under Colonel John Campbell. Mangalore had been an important part of Haidar's kingdom and had nurtured all his hopes of building a naval power for Mysore, in addition to its commercial importance as a major port of trade.

The Mangalore Campaign

With an army of 60,000 cavalry, 30,000 sepoys, 600 French infantry under Colonel Cossigny and Lally's corps, a regiment from the isle of France or Mauritius, 100 pieces of artillery and 1,40,000 fighting men, Tipu attacked Mangalore on 19 May 1783. Accompanied by his brother Karim and Haidar's trusted commandant, Muhammad Ali, Tipu led the offensive and laid siege to the fort there. Fortifications were dismantled in stages, breaches effected, and by the end of July 1783, preparations were made to assault the fort. Tipu writes about this campaign:

> The worthless Nazerene [Christians] who commanded the fort had erected a battery of heavy guns on an eminence near the fort in which were placed about three hundred Nazerenes and a thousand other troops . . . the gunners of the Hydery army [Mysorean], served the batteries in such a manner, that ten guns of the fort were dismounted and shattered to pieces, and a great number of the Nazerenes sent to hell. In the end the Nazerenes abandoned all their guns. And were no longer able to appear on the walls; while I had two or three batteries erected, in which placing six mortars, I caused large stones to be thrown from them. Hereupon the Nazerenes without religion dug trenches within the fort, into which they slunk (for shelter).[21]

By then, the British garrison in the fort had been stricken by disease, despair and deprivation of provisions. But, after nearly fifty-six days of conflict, as the morale of the besieged British forces was steadily dipping, news reached them that right from their mother countries itself, the French and the British had decided on a cessation of their hostilities worldwide. Consequently, Cossigny was asked to withdraw around 22 July 1783 from the scene of conflict, leaving Tipu flabbergasted and thoroughly enraged at what he considered as French treachery. He held out conditions that Campbell be evacuated from Mangalore and he retire to Tellicherry with all the honours of war—something that the British rejected. Wilks berates what he terms as the 'dark stupidity' and 'strange political suicide' of the Sultan to continue the operations in Mangalore at a time when even the French had withdrawn from active hostilities. He explains the cause of this as being the 'miserable pride' of Tipu to show that he could achieve an exploit himself which the French troops could not accomplish.[22]

However, with French mediation and the efforts of Monsieur Piveron de Morlat, the envoy from the Court of France in Tipu's durbar, an armistice was signed on 2 August 1783, as per which Campbell was to remain in possession of the fort of Mangalore, while Tipu was to control the trenches and batteries erected in front of the fort. Neither side was to extend their lines but were to maintain their positions as they were on the day the armistice was signed. Tipu could not erect any fresh batteries and the British could not repair the breaches and damages to the fortification or receive help from outside. After the armistice was signed, Tipu expressed a desire to see Campbell and the two met in the former's camp on 13 August 1783. Campbell's memoirs record that he was received in the most polite and generous manner by Tipu who complimented him for his bravery. He even presented Campbell and his associates rich shawls as gifts and later sent for them a fine horse as a gift.[23]

As per the armistice, the British could buy provisions from a bazaar that was specially to be set up for their replenishments. Determined to break the British stronghold, Tipu however began a systematic violation of the armistice. While the bazaar to provide the provisions was made available, every commodity there was so overpriced that they were most often out of reach for purchase by the British. Hayavadana Rao states how 'a fowl sold from nine to twelve rupees, a seer of rice for four, a seer of salt for three and a frog for six pence.'[24] Seven boats from Bombay that came in with replenishments for the garrison were all seized and sold at the same bazaar. Tipu was revelling in the British discomfiture. Again, in breach of the armistice, he erected a new work on the southern harbour. All this, even as communication was opened with Campbell and General Norman Macleod who had landed in Mangalore on 20 August as the chief commander of Malabar and Kanara.

In an elaborate account of the interview between Tipu and Macleod on 20–21 August 1783, the latter wrote to the Select Committee at Bombay describing the details. Tipu is said to have told him: 'I am sincere in my desire for peace with the English. I respect them and if they act fairly with me, I will be their friend. I should be glad if the General would go to the King of England from me and tell him about me. I want to be a friend to him and his people and will send presents through the General [Macleod] to the King. I will be glad to see the General at my darbar tomorrow and to hear all he has to say. I will open my heart to him and he must act fairly with me, and I have a great opinion of him and Lieutenant-Colonel Campbell. They have shewed themselves [as] good warriors and I wish to raise their name.'[25] The subsequent communication between Tipu and Macleod harped back to Mysore's old demands for handover and reparations for the wasteful campaign of Tiruchirapalli, along with remonstrances about how Muhammad Ali of Arcot had poisoned British minds against Haidar and Tipu due to which these wars were being fought purposelessly. Like Haidar, he appealed for lasting peace between Mysore and the British. He offered to take Macleod along with him to Srirangapatna and release all the British prisoners lodged there.

But by October 1783, the British stores started reducing considerably. Incidents like the arrival of Macleod with reinforcements were clear breaches of the terms of the armistice by the British who were keen to retain the important fort of Mangalore. By November, Macleod reappeared in Mangalore, demanding that he be allowed to send in 4000 bales of rice into the fort. Tipu stoutly refused as he believed that the agreed quota, as per the armistice, had already been sent in and he suspected that the British were hoarding supplies to prepare themselves for a long haul against him, merely citing deficiency of provisions. The armistice terms clearly stated that not more than ten to twelve days' provisions could be sent inside the fort. A middle ground was reached with Tipu allowing 1000 bales of rice to be sent in first and only after their consumption, an additional 1000 to be sent in. But the aggression with which Macleod put forth his demands vitiated whatever semblance of peace the armistice had even vaguely tried to achieve. Hence Tipu too broke the terms of the armistice and began repairing his old works and erecting new batteries in every direction, thereby effectively converting the siege to a blockade. The plight of the soldiers inside the fort held under siege was getting precarious by the day and after eight months, their patience was on the wane. With hunger, sickness and frustration building up, the outbreak of a mutiny too was not being ruled out. Twelve to fifteen men were dying every day; scurvy was raging inside the fort and hospitals were filled with almost two-thirds of the garrison and the rest barely had any strength to even hold their arms.[26] Campbell himself was grievously unwell and in the last stages of consumption, and 'was so emaciated and enfeebled . . . that what he spoke was in a low tone of voice, only to be heard by advancing . . . ears close to his lips.'[27] The quality of provisions, including the beef and pork being sent in, was putrid or often of such inferior quality that it added to the sickness of the garrison.[28] Such extreme starvation was endured by the besieged that 'animals and reptiles not usually eaten were sold at prices beyond all credibility'.[29] Of course, for all of this, the British had only themselves to blame.

Macleod sailed away to Tellicherry and then to Cannanore to relieve the garrison that had been reduced to just twenty days' stock, even as Campbell held on against all odds. But he had other plans there and, in early December 1783, attacked Cannanore. He justified this aggression to the fact that on 30 November, 300 of his men, who were coming to Tellicherry from Karwar, were imprisoned by the queen, the Bibi of Cannanore Junumabe II Sultana, an ally of Tipu. She was the sister of Ali Raja Kunhi Amsa. Both Tipu's armies and the Bibi's forces had put them all in irons and refused to release them, due to which Macleod was forced to attack Cannanore, which was an equally prized and lucrative fortress that the British wanted to own. In a short campaign of six days, from 9 to 14 December 1783, the Mapillahs in Cannanore put up a brave defence but were vanquished. Bibi's side suffered heavy casualties and she herself was taken prisoner with her family and adherents. They were released on the conditions of a treaty thereafter, preceded however by an immense loot by the British of the treasures, provisions and properties of the Arakkal family.[30]

The Southern Attack and the Royal Rebellion

Earlier in the year, when the Bidanur campaign and the subsequent Mangalore siege began, Lord Macartney had planned two strategies to divert Tipu's attention. The Malabar detachment under Macleod and Humberston was further reinforced with a considerable force from the Northern Circars under General Jones. At the same time, Col Fullarton was dispatched to penetrate deep into the southern pockets of the Mysore kingdom with an eye on capturing Srirangapatna itself. With a large battalion from Tanjore, Tiruchirapalli and Tinnevelly, Fullarton occupied several border areas to the southern side of the Mysore kingdom. Between October and November 1783, Fullarton successfully captured Palghat and Coimbatore, with which a direct access was now made possible to Srirangapatna for the British. The occupation of a post like Palghat, one of the strongest forts in India, which was right between Malabar and Coimbatore, was strategically important for the British. The Zamorin and his Nairs generously contributed provisions that the British always lacked. The Rajas of Cochin and Travancore too were willing to be co-opted. The mountains that bounded the pass which Palghat commanded were strengthened by thick forests and surrounding woods, enabling a small body of infantry to defend the territory against a larger army. The British plan was to exert pressure on Tipu from other sides so that he would give up his siege of Mangalore. But these invasions of Mysore by the British were as much their violations of the armistice as Tipu had disregarded the terms. Tipu's commander, Roshan Khan, was constantly opposing these invasions but the British haughtily disregarded them all. Macartney kept sending Fullarton two sets of contradictory orders, only to fool the Mysoreans. Those sent through Tipu's officers advised him to restrain from hostilities, while those sent to him directly ordered aggressive attacks.[31]

Meanwhile, steady help had been coming in for the British from the displaced royal family and Maharani Lakshmi Ammanni's adherents, as per the 'Rana treaty' that she had signed with them in October 1782. Fullarton reopened the talks with the adherents of the royal family and they continued to supply grains and ensure the repair of carriages. Fullarton records in his memoirs that the British 'had every reason to rely on the Gentoo [Hindu] or Canara race forming a great mass of inhabitants in Mysore, who had unequivocal proofs of my earnest zeal to support their interests and favourite family [the Wodeyars]; while every circumstance of present situation or of future prospect seemed to mark this interesting moment as the crisis of the war.'[32]

This 'interesting moment' and 'crisis' that Fullarton mentioned was the acute trouble that was brewing for the Sultan in his own capital city. An account of a British prisoner in Srirangapatna mentions that 'how dangerous so-ever this conspiracy might appear to be, yet every member at first appeared steady and undaunted.'[33] The chief architect of this revolution of sorts that had taken up momentum was Anche Shamaiya, the terror kingpin during Haidar's times. He was ostensibly with Tipu in Mangalore, but was secretly commanding his partners in crime back in Srirangapatna. His brother Rangaiya and Narasinga Rao, the town mayor, were co-actors in this plot that included Subbaraja Urs of the displaced royal family. Singaiya (or Singaraiyengar), the provincial head of the department at Coimbatore, was also in the capital and he was roped in, too, as were two subahdars and nine headmen, as well as both Hindu and Muslim commandants of corps. They felt that the time was most propitious to conduct a coup of sorts to displace for good the influence of the house of Haidar on Mysore, and to restore the dispossessed Hindu dynasty of the Wodeyars. With Haidar's death and Tipu still not being totally in command, and being generally disliked even by his own father on certain occasions,[34] this caucus felt that the iron was hot enough for them to strike. Added to this was the disgruntlement of several palegars who had sustained indignities and loss of territories right from the times of Haidar. All the conspirators met numerous times in secrecy and swore their allegiance to the plot. They seem to have conjured a very planned and calculated attempt to stage their coup at the opportune time when the British would be at the gates of Srirangapatna. The authority of the commandant of the fort in Srirangapatna was to be usurped and the idea was to let the British occupy it and permanently prevent Tipu's return to the capital. The Mysore Pradhans Tirumala Rao and Narayana Rao were to assist Col Lang and guide his way to the gates of Srirangapatna, which they did with their own small army of 300 horse from 2 April 1783. They had marched through Karur, Vijayamangalam and Dindigul, conquering them. Midway, Col Lang resigned and Fullarton was sent to succeed to the command. He managed to take Dharapuram and then of course finally Palghat and Coimbatore fell. His army was a weak one though and was mainly aimed at keeping the pressure off the British in Bidanur and Mangalore, and could have hardly been the force that invaded Srirangapatna as the plotters had wished. Fullarton kept moving in and out of the campaign, being called in by Stuart midway to assist him in Cuddalore. However, 'the Hindoo colours of Mysoor were hoisted on the ramparts'[35] of the forts thus occupied, signifying a liberation from usurpation by the house of Haidar. The management of some of these districts was handed over to Tirumala Rao.

The titular Wodeyar ruler was to then be vested with complete authority and Shamaiya, Rangaiya and Narasinga Rao were to form the new administration. The killedar, the head-major and Asad Khan, the Commandant, were all to be captured and put to death. All the British prisoners lodged in the dungeons in Srirangapatna were to be released and put under the command of General Matthews. The Marathas and the people in Coorg who nursed a grudge against the forcible Mysorean occupation were also brought into the ambit of this insurrection.

Narasinga Rao was in charge of executing the plot and he chose 9 a.m. of 24 July 1783 as the moment to strike. This was when Asad Khan distributed payslips to the troops, who normally assembled unarmed in the court to collect their salaries. *Jetties* or professional athletes/wrestlers were paid to grab the soldiers and the commandant then and slay them, and prepare the ground for the British arrival. Everything seemed to be going perfectly well for the conspirators.

On the eve of the execution of the plot, when the Governor of Srirangapatna Saiyid Muhammad Mahdavi was returning to his home from duty, he was silently accosted by a subahdar who commanded a hundred men and was a part of the conspiracy. Unfortunately for the plotters, the subahdar disclosed all the plans to Saiyid Muhammad Khan who immediately swung into emergency action. Guards were ordered and the whole party was seized and thrown into prison. With the hope of getting a royal pardon, Narasinga Rao sang like a canary, spilling all the details of the conspiracy. To instil fear in the hearts of anyone who nursed such nefarious plans, immediate measures were taken to strip the conspirators naked and execute them by 'the horrible process of being loosely tied to an elephant's foot, and dragged in that state through the streets of the town.'[36] Tipu's orders were sought from Mangalore for executing the principal perpetrators and once those were received, Narasinga Rao, Subbaraja Urs, the commandants of the corps, and the jetties were all executed. Anche Shamaiya was sent in heavy iron chains from Mangalore and, with his brother, Rangaiya, was imprisoned in separate iron cages, fed low diets, publicly flogged and their backs 'rubbed with chilleys [sic] or cayenne pepper,'[37] even as they kept denying their involvement in the plot till the very end. Kirmani states that Tipu dispatched his trusted commandant, Muhammad Ali, to restore order in the capital and punish the mischief-makers. Muhammad Ali, along with the killedar and his deputies, then stormed the houses of Anche Shamaiah and his associates 'and before they could open their eyes from the sleep of neglect and folly, they were dragged out of their beds and put in prison. The next morning, with the sanction of the Sultan's mother, some of the rebels were blown from a gun; the companions of Shamia [Shamaiya] impaled, and he himself loaded with irons and confined in an iron cage—a fit punishment for his villainy.'[38] Destiny seemed to have come full circle for Shamaiya who had earlier meted out such horrific punishments on others, including Purnaiya. Strict curfew orders were imposed in Srirangapatna and citizens told not to assemble in groups or in the dark of the night on the threat of similar punishments.

Though the scheme backfired badly, it was remarkable that it kept Maharani Lakshmi Ammanni outside its ambit of suspicion. Even Wilks, who wrote his chronicles after interviews with the Maharani, was unable to ascertain if she had any knowledge or role in such a massive coup that was planned. He writes:

> Neither evidence, nor the unlimited use of torture, had directed, the slightest suspicion towards the imprisoned Ranee; it is just possible, that she might afterwards have been induced by the political rivalry . . . to assume a disguise in her confidential conversations with the late Sir Barry Close, and with the author; but the absence even of suspicion, when so strongly excited by circumstances, added to her uniform and consistent assurances, convinced them both, of her entire ignorance of every part of the correspondence conducted in her name. But that conviction must not be understood to impugn the reality of Tremalrow's [Tirumala Rao] projects for the subversion of the actual government. Long before the usurpation of Hyder, the Hindoo prince had been kept in ignorance of acts purporting to be his own, as profound as was

the ignorance of the imprisoned Ranee in 1783; and simulated authority had been familiar habit of the court.[39]

Pradhan Narayana Rao, Tirumala Rao's brother, was also captured and imprisoned, but he later managed to escape and join his brother. To teach a lasting lesson to the Mysore Pradhans and their families not to ever attempt such an insurrection again, Tipu ordered nearly 700 families of Iyengars, Sri Vaishnavite Brahmins who shared the same gotra of Bharadwaja with those of the Pradhans, to be captured and thrust into the dungeons of Srirangapatna. A worse fate awaited them when Tipu returned to the capital from Mangalore later that year. It was the time of Deepawali and all of Mysore was agog with festivities and celebrations. In order to give them a sense of false assurance, these unfortunate families were let out for a day to have a feast around the precincts of the Lakshmi Narasimha temple in Srirangapatna, adjacent to the shrine of the presiding deity, Lord Ranganathaswami. While they were gathered for their festival meal on the night of Naraka Chaturdashi, the night before the new moon of Deepawali, the place was locked in from the outside and armed soldiers and elephants were let in, resulting in a huge commotion and a stampede. Many of them— men, women and children—were trampled or suffocated to death and those who tried to escape were apprehended and mercilessly hacked. The properties and jagirs assigned to these families were confiscated. Such is the intergenerational trauma and memory of this episode that has otherwise gone unrecorded in written history and survives as oral narrative that to this day the Anandampillai or the Mandyam Iyengars of the Bharadwaja gotra who reside in Mysore, Srirangapatna, Melukote, Mandya and other places do not celebrate the festival of Deepawali on the day that the rest of the country does. They commemorate this as a day of mourning and quiet contemplation of the misfortune and inhuman massacre that befell so many of their ancestors, for virtually no fault of theirs.[40] But it is intriguing however that Wilks, Hayavadana Rao and other chroniclers have not made a detailed mention of this episode, though

they have all alluded to several hundreds of the caste members of
Tirumala Rao being put to death by Tipu.[41]

Back in Mangalore

Even though Tipu had nipped in the bud a major insurrection
back home that threatened to overthrow his power, his position
in Mangalore was not too advantageous ever since he had signed
the armistice in August 1783. Without the French support, he had
not been able to effect a breach in the fort there and each time he
tried, Campbell managed to push back. His army, especially the
cavalry, was getting increasingly worn out, especially with the raging
monsoon. His failure in Mangalore had emboldened the spirits of the
Coorg Raja to assert his suzerainty, and the latter had even defeated
a section of the Mysorean troops at Periapatna, barely few miles
away from Srirangapatna. All the rulers of Kerala had also grouped
against him, and the British were attacking from the Cudappah side,
led by Gen. Jones, and the southern side by Fullarton.

All of these, in addition to possibly the tumultuous incidents back
home, must have had a deleterious effect on Tipu's mind. His rash
and thoughtless behaviour that was to now follow alludes to this. He
suspected Rustum Ali Beg, the killedar of Mangalore, of treachery
for not having defended the fort enough. The fact that it was taking
him months to occupy the fort now, while it was so easily taken by
Matthews in March 1783, made him suspect that perhaps Rustum,
too, had gone the Sheikh Ayaz way. A committee of investigation was
set up and Rustum even sent in an apology for any inadvertent acts of
omission that he might have committed. But Tipu was unconvinced
and towards the end of November 1783, he ordered Rustum's
execution for treachery. His case was stoutly defended by the loyalist
Commandant Muhammad Ali, as Rustum was his close friend.
Keen to save his friend, Muhammad Ali rescued the imprisoned
Rustum and openly declared that he would not let him suffer execution,
crying out for justice in the name of God. Whilst Muhammad Ali
was talking to Rustum, several hundred soldiers gathered around
them in solidarity. On hearing this, Tipu got paranoid that perhaps

they were instigating the army to revolt. Hence, in a shocking turn of events, an incensed Tipu ordered that Muhammad Ali be packed off in irons to Srirangapatna. So devastated and humiliated did Muhammad Ali feel about this treatment meted out to him, despite decades of loyalty, that he strangled himself to death using the common groom's cord for leading a horse. Strangely again, Tipu was so overcome with grief on hearing about Muhammad Ali's death that he ordered the strict confinement of Shaikh Hamid, the man whom Tipu himself had appointed to take Muhammad Ali to Srirangapatna in chains. Such was the vacillation of a man who had just taken on the reins of power. That Tipu could contemplate such action against Muhammad Ali, who had been his close associate, is bewildering. In fact, Hayavadana Rao mentions that in 1780, just before the outbreak of the Second Anglo–Mysore War and Haidar's invasion of the Carnatic, Muhammad Ali had teamed up with Tipu to help the latter for 'the dethronement of his father.'[42] Their plans had not fructified as the events of the war overtook them.

The British accounts, however, have a completely different picture of Muhammad Ali and the circumstances that led to his end. Major-General Keith M'Alister, in his account based on an interview with Campbell in his dying days, mentions that Muhammad Ali had been in contact with Campbell, promising to hand over Tipu to the British. But Campbell did not trust Muhammad Ali and thought it was a ploy on the part of the opponents to sabotage. But Tipu got wind of this affair and hence ordered seventy to eighty conspirators, including Muhammad Ali, to be hanged instantly on three gibbets. When his turn was to come, Muhammad Ali loudly called out to the French surgeon who was nearby to witness this gory spectacle to feel his pulse and see if he saw any sense of fear or alarm; that Tipu could kill him, but to frighten him was beyond his power. This bravado seemed to have had its impact on the Sultan who then pardoned him and sent him off to Srirangapatna for confinement, and he was never heard of again. M'Alister states that Muhammad Ali had been a favourite of Haidar and had enjoyed his confidence, 'which it is said that his son Tippoo had withdrawn from him; this he keenly and strongly felt . . . which probably led him to plan the capture and ruin, and overthrow of his master.'[43] Innes Munro states that these 'commotions' arose in Tipu's army, incited by Tipu's brother, Karim Sahib, and his adherents, 'which terminated in the death of Mahomed Ally his principal general, and many of the conspirators.'[44]

Negotiations for Peace

After the aborted attempt in February 1783 at restoring peace, another opportunity came up after the armistice. In September, Mysorean diplomats Appaji Ram and Srinivasa Rao arrived in Madras to explore opportunities to conclude the war and negotiate terms of peace. Tipu now demanded a mutual restitution of all conquered territories, the possession of Vellore, Tiagar and a few other places in the Carnatic as a jagir, a mutual release of prisoners, including Sheikh Ayaz who had fled to Bombay and then to Tellicherry, ostensibly under British protection and that of the Raja of Travancore. They also sought an offensive and defensive alliance between Tipu and the British. The British rejected most of the proposals. They stated that Ayaz was contractually someone they had promised protection to and they did not know about his current whereabouts to hand him over. The offensive and defensive clause was what had irked Haidar after the First Anglo–Mysore War and had led to this current conflict. Hence, this too was ruled out, as also handing over jagirs to Tipu. The Company stipulated instead that if either party was in a conflict with any Indian or European power, other than the Rajas of Tanjore and Travancore and the Nawab of Arcot, neither side would support the enemies. But this too was shot down by the Supreme Government in Calcutta on the premise that it would offend the Marathas, who had to be brought into the ambit, as also the Nizam. Tipu was averse to link peace with the British to any precondition with powers such as the Marathas with whom Mysore had lot of claims and counterclaims to settle. Hence, he wanted a direct peace treaty between Mysore and Madras, rather than under the rubric of the treaty of Salbai and the shadow of the Poona Court. The negotiations broke down on this front and the vakils departed empty-handed from Madras.

But as the siege continued in Mangalore and the constant struggle for provisions, further complicated by a looming famine in north India that made export of grains to the southern campaign difficult, made Hastings budge from his intransigence. By early November 1783, Anthony Sadlier, second-in-Council, and George Leonard Staunton, Private Secretary to Macartney, were appointed Commissioners and, with a guard of cavalry under Captain Thomas Dallas, they set out from Madras to negotiate peace with Tipu Sultan. In Kanchipuram, they met Sayyid Sahib who was empowered by Tipu to carry out the talks. It was suggested that Tipu first vacate completely from the Carnatic and only after that the British would leave Tipu's territories that were occupied. Mangalore and other possessions, however, were to be vacated only after Tipu released all the imprisoned British soldiers. Sayyid Sahib turned the offer down immediately. Appaji Ram intervened to suggest a middle path where the departure from Carnatic could happen first, but the British needed to vacate Mangalore before demanding a release of prisoners. This clause caused considerable disputes and differences among the commissioners themselves who did not share too great a rapport with each other. Thereafter, a third member, John Huddleston, was sent in to temper down the differences between the other two members. Several rounds of hard negotiations and bargains continued between the two sides at Arni and Malavalli, with neither willing to climb down. The Commissioners' demands to visit Srirangapatna and meet the British prisoners of war were also turned down, causing much consternation. They had to take a long, circuitous route to reach Mangalore. Tipu feared that allowing them into Srirangapatna would enable them to gain access to the secrets of the fort and its military installations that he could not afford to risk, close on the heels of an insurrection back home.

The Commissioners then sought an interview with the Sultan himself, which he haughtily declined. But to spite them, he continued his acts of hostility, 'erecting gibbets opposite to the tent doors of each of the Commissioners, carrying by surprise a post dependent on Honnavar, cutting up a subaltern detachment from Col Fullarton's army.'[45] To make matters worse, several British officers in prison were put to death. Among them was also Gen. Matthews. At the time of Matthews's death, he was tied up in irons and had not changed his linens in twenty days. He had refused to eat anything as he had received intelligence that the food might be poisoned. Some of the guards took pity on him and shared a bit of their meal with sometimes. But he could not hold off for long. Matthews finally ate the 'poisoned food and drank too, whether to quench the rage of inflamed thirst, or to drown the torments of his soul in utter insensibility, of the poisoned cup. Within six hours after this fatal repast, he was found dead.'[46] All of Tipu's actions were clearly done to revel in the helplessness and discomfiture of the British, as their woes increased by the day. Mohibbul Hasan, however, argues against any ill-treatment or attempts to intimidate the Commissioners; he says that they were fairly treated and all of this were 'stories fabricated by Macleod and others . . . taken to be true by Englishmen both in India and in England.'[47] A similar argument is put forth by historian H.H. Dodwell in his account: "There is no reason to suppose that the commissioners were treated with worse than the contemptuous pride which was to have been expected. Tipu believed himself to have won the war and behaved accordingly.'[48]

But the Supreme Government in Calcutta was getting increasingly restive at the suicidal actions of Macartney's southern campaign. Hastings had almost concluded a treaty by the middle of January 1784, with the Peshwa and Mahadji Sindhia, to effect a combined attack on Tipu. He was not in favour of peace which Macartney was pushing for and wanted to extend the hostilities now with Maratha support. Alarmed by the developments, Tipu finally, by February 1784, thought it prudent to end the war from a position of strength, rather than vacillate towards a disadvantageous circumstance.

Campbell finally surrendered due to intense sickness and desperation which had engulfed the British garrison in Mangalore. The siege of Mangalore was lifted on 29 January 1784. So exhausted was Campbell at the end of this ordeal that he quit service on 15 February and a month later, on 23 March 1784, he died. After having led the hapless Commissioners from place to place and spiting their authority at every stage, Tipu finally gave them an audience and decided to sign the terms of peace that had been hard negotiated by both sides. The Second Anglo–Mysore War that had begun way back in 1780 under Haidar, more as a direct conflict between Mysore and Arcot, transformed thereafter to one between Mysore and the British and which, being carried on under Tipu, ended on 11 March 1784 with the signing of the Treaty of Mangalore.

The Treaty of Mangalore

This became an important document in the history of India as perhaps the last occasion when an Indian power dictated terms to the British, who were reduced to the state of being humble supplicants for peace. In fact, so desperate were they for peace that they readily coaxed Fullarton to relinquish all that he had captured in the Carnatic to encourage reciprocation. The treaty was truly a diplomatic victory for Tipu Sultan. He had honourably concluded a long-drawn war. He frustrated the Maratha designs to seize his northern possessions. Concluded over ten articles, the treaty had the following principal provisions:[49]

1. Peace and friendship to be immediately established between the Company and Nawab Tipu Sultan Bahaddur and their respective friends and allies, including the Rajas of Tanjore and Travancore and the Carnatic–Payanghat on the English side, and the Bibi of Cannanore and the Rajas and Zamindars of the Malabar coast on the Nawab's side. The British were not to attack Tipu directly or indirectly, nor assist his enemies or wage wars against his allies.
2. Tipu had to completely evacuate his troops from the Carnatic and release all prisoners-of-war—a measure to be reciprocated by the British.
3. The British had to give up Honawar, Karwar, Sadashivgarh and adjoining forts to their original masters, as also Karur, Aravakurichi, Dindigul and Dharapuram districts to Mysore.

4. Cannanore was to be restored to its queen, Ali Raja Bibi; Tipu was to relinquish claims over Amburgarh and Satgarh forts in the Carnatic.
5. Tipu had to give up all earlier claims on the Carnatic region.
6. Prisoners were to be reunited with their families.
7. Tipu was to maintain peace with the Rajas and Zamindars of the Coromandel Coast and not punish them for assisting the British.
8. Tipu was to restore the factory and privileges of the British in Calicut and Tellicherry, as they were in 1779, before Sardar Khan took them over.
9. Mysore had to renew and confirm the commercial privileges and immunities extended to the British Company by the late Haidar Ali and honour the treaty signed between the two on 8 August 1770.

That the treaty omitted his name completely, and thereby challenged his status as the sovereign of the Carnatic, piqued Nawab Muhammad Ali of Arcot. He bitterly complained to Hastings who tried to get a modification to the treaty done with his name inserted as the sovereign of the Carnatic, which had been so extensively discussed in the treaty. But Macartney refused to comply and pass on the amended treaty to Tipu, lest it arouse suspicions in him and spoil the negotiations that had finally been concluded. This widened the breach further between Hastings and Macartney, with the former even contemplating in vain, strict disciplinary action and suspension from governorship of Madras against the latter. But Macartney seemed to have influential friends in England and Hastings's proposal was rejected by the Councillors back home.[50] Muhammad Ali was left to his plight, as he had anyway proved to be a worthless ally.

The contents of the treaty and the manner in which it was concluded was heavily denounced both in England and the Company in India. Hastings thought of it as a humiliating pacification, appealing to the King of England and the Parliament to punish the

Madras Government, saying that the British nation's honour and faith had both been violated.[51] From the day the treaty was signed, the British possibly determined themselves to subvert and diminish Tipu's power for good. In an elaborate reflection on the war and what the British believed was a humiliating treaty, as well as a future road map, Innes Munro states:

It is to be hoped that the treaty of peace, which the Company have lately concluded with Tippoo Sahib, is only meant to be temporary. Such, I am certain, must be the wish of every Briton actuated by sentiments of patriotism, and capable of feeling the indignities which have been uniformly heaped upon the British name. Can any Englishman read of the sufferings of his unfortunate countrymen, in the different prisons of Misore [sic], without dropping a tear of sympathy?—or can he peruse the account of the repeated indignity and contempt with which his nation has been treated by the present usurper of Misore, without being filled with indignation, and burning with sentiments of retaliation and revenge? . . . To retrieve our sinking reputation in India must be the united effort of labour and wisdom . . . no measure would be more likely to effect this desirable purpose than to crush the object of our just revenge, the present usurper of the Misore throne . . . in my humble opinion, the fairest opportunity that ever can offer of accomplishing this great end was lost by concluding a peace with the Misorians, at a period that seemed pregnant with every advantage to our arms . . . four such armies advancing boldly and at the same time to one great object, viz. Seringapatam [sic], with a view of placing the rightful heir upon the throne, could not possibly have failed of success . . . prudence and policy will clearly dictate, that the deposing [of] Tippoo Sahib, in attempting which little is to be dreaded, and establishing the lawful sovereign upon the throne of Misore, are objects of the most essential consequence to the interests of the India Company in the Carnatic. By such means the Marrattas [sic] would be kept as much in awe as at present; and the Company, in the king of Misore, would most likely secure a peaceable neighbour and a powerful ally.[52]

Treatment of English Prisoners

One of the constant peeves of the Company, during the course of
the Second Anglo–Mysore War, was what they termed the extreme
tortures that were meted out to their soldiers who were captured
by both Haidar Ali and later Tipu Sultan, and thrown away into
several dungeons across Mysore. Hence most of the negotiations and
accounts of the time deal with the urgency with which the Company
sought a release of their soldiers from the prisons of hell in Mysore.
There are heart-wrenching memoirs of several of these captives.
Of the prisoners who were caught during the Battle of Polilur in
1780, three batches were formed. Colonel Baillie, Captain Baird
and a few other officers were commanded to remain with Haidar's
camp. About twenty-three officers, who were not wounded, were
dispatched to Bangalore and other places, while another twenty-
seven wounded ones were packed off to Arni in country carts and
dhoolies. The first batch traversed a distance of nearly 240 miles and
reached Srirangapatna by 6 November 1780. The dungeon there
was an oblong square, seventy feet in length, with a kind of shed
inside inwards and open in the middle. A guard was stationed at an
end which was also allotted for cooking. There were four rooms with
no windows and mats laid out on the floor as beds. The prisoners
were given a little over four annas a day for their daily needs and
sometimes, a little arrack. A French surgeon attended to dressing
their open wounds, while a few Indian servants hovered around to
get them provisions from the bazaars and also served as their window
to the rest of the world. They remained in this state till 23 December
1780, when a second batch of twenty-five prisoners joined them.

By 10 May 1781, all the prisoners woke up to the clanging thuds
of irons and were told by the killedar that Haidar had ordered all
of them to be put in irons. Baird had a bullet wound on his thigh
that was still raw. Captain Lucas's protests to not endanger Baird's
life by putting him in irons were considered and he was the only
one left unchained. Baillie, Captain Rumney, Lieutenants Fraser and
Sampson were all in leg irons. The throats of the last three were later
cut at Mysore.[53] Baillie died towards end of 1782, and one is not sure

if he was actually poisoned. Towards the second half of 1782, Haidar's officers made an offer to some of the prisoners to enter their master's services for which they would receive three times their current pay, and as many horses, palanquins and wives that they chose. But the prisoners unanimously rejected the proposals.[54]

James Scurry, a British sailor, was taken prisoner by the French and was among the 500 British prisoners of war handed over to Haidar by the French Admiral Suffrein in June 1782. Scurry was barely sixteen years old then. After being lodged in Bangalore for a few months, he and several of his batch of prisoners were packed off to Srirangapatna. Here, after shaving off their heads, the unfortunate prisoners were to learn that Haidar had ordered for their forced circumcision and thereby a conversion to Islam.[55] Scurry writes: 'A mat, and a kind of sheet, was provided for each of us, we were ordered to arrange ourselves in two rows, and then lie down on our mats. This being done, the guards, barbers . . . came among us, and seizing the youngest, Randal Cadman, a midshipman, they placed him on a cudgeree pot, when four of these stout men held his legs and arms, while the barber performed his office [circumcised him]. In this manner, they went through the operation, and in two hours, the "pious" work was finished, and we were laid on our separate mats.'[56] Even as they lay writhing in pain and being fed a strong opiate, *majum*, priests were ushered in to instruct the 'converts' on the theology of their new faith and its tenets. The converted were then drafted into Haidar's chela (slave) battalion. Their ears were pierced and a slave's mark put on each of them. They were normally given excruciating tasks and many kept fainting while they did these. The chelas were bundled together in dank, dingy rooms, with little place to even breathe and surrounded by mounds of filth that was seldom cleaned. All of this led to the outbreak of numerous diseases and fatal epidemics.[57] Scurry managed to escape only in 1791 and reached a small fort that was under Maratha control and thereafter joined a British detachment operating with the Maratha army near Dharwad.

Another prisoner of war James Bristow recounts the horrific ritual of forcible conversion and circumcision that took place in September

1781 at the behest of one Sergeant Dempster whose name repeatedly occurs in all accounts as the collaborator conducting this act:

> This incident spread general terror amongst the rest of the prisoners, everyone apprehending that he might be the next victim devoted to Mahometism; nor were our fears groundless, for early in January 1782, the same persons entered our prison, accompanied by Sergeant Dempster, and made a second selection of fourteen, in which number I had the misfortune to be included. As Dempster was suspected of a share in this horrid business, at least so far as pointing out the objects on whom the choice ought to fall; every one of us were highly exasperated against him, and it was fortunate for him that he was protected by his guards. The treatment the first victim had undergone, served in some degree to apprise us of the inutility of resistance. With horror and indignation, we swallowed the narcotic potion, and those whom the dose had no effect upon, were forcibly seized and pinioned by stout coffres whilst the operation [circumcision] was performed (having previously shaved us in the customary manner). After the operation, our right ears were perforated and small silver rings with round knobs fixed in them, this being the mark of slavery amongst the Mahometans. As soon as we had recovered from this diabolical ceremony, we were transferred to what is termed the tyrant's *Chaylah* battalions (that is, slaves), these are composed of such of his own subjects as have been condemned to perpetual slavery, and such unfortunate captives as he takes in war . . . after we had been made what was termed Musselmen, we neglected no opportunity of evincing our contempt for the religion of our tormentors, and the cruel force they had employed against us, by catching dogs and bandicoots and circumcising them publicly.[58]

The English prisoners also noted in their memoirs that they observed large numbers of Hindu boys and girls, too, being carried away from their homes and against the wishes of their parents, forcibly converted and married off at the whims of their captors. Recounting his experience from the dungeons in Srirangapatna on 10 March 1781, Captain Lindsay writes: 'The greatest part of the houses and choultries [resting places for travellers] around us, we found, were full of multitudes of inhabitants of the Carnatic, all of whom Haidar had made embrace the Mahometan religion; about three-thousand of these unwilling proselytes, most of them being young men, were formed into different battalions, and were now exercised mornings and evenings upon the parade, upon the instructions of two or three Frenchmen . . . on another part of the parade there was about an equal number of women and girls, under the same description, confined together, and who we were informed, were reserved to be married to the boys, when they were grown up.'[59]

Another British officer, who notes anonymously in his account, records many such details of forced conversion and circumcision of several English prisoners, as well as Hindu citizens, whom he calls the 'Carnatic slave boys,'[60] possibly captured in war. He notes that on 30 October 1781, 'Duncan Macintosh and Donald Steward, privates, both of the 73rd Regiment, were forcibly taken out and circumcised.'[61] On 19 June 1782, he records: 'Arrived prisoners, fourteen European children, eight boys and six girls. It is reported that they were taken at Cuddalore.'[62] Likewise, on 13 July 1782, 'Arrived prisoners, five hundred Carnatic boys, in order to be made slaves, and to be entered into Haidar's slave battalions.'[63] Some of the youngest and handsomest boys were also selected and lodged at Haidar's palace; some serving as dancing boys, others castrated as eunuchs.[64] There are numerous such entries in this account, more like a diary, that records the making of slaves and forced conversions, right from Haidar's time.

The prisoners had evinced some ray of hope after Haidar's death that their lot might now improve, through 'the mildness of Tippoo's temper, who had hitherto borne a character of humanity.'[65] But their conditions remained more or less the same, or worsened in some cases, after Tipu's accession. As Bristow recounts that while Tipu might not have surpassed his father's cruelty, he certainly equalled it in terms of his hatred for Europeans, that 'his character had not hitherto appeared in a true light, but that now, when he found it no longer necessary to dissemble or conciliate the affections of his father's subjects, he threw aside the mask, and showed himself in his genuine colours.'[66] After the Bidanur conquest, several English soldiers were sent away to different prisons across Mysore. Captain Henry Oakes, Adjutant General to the Army under Matthews's command, was imprisoned in the Chitradurga fort, with heavy irons put around his feet. Thirty of them, along with 'two black girls, and seven servants were confined in a room about thirty feet square, with a yard of about ten feet, upon two pice a day and a seer of rice.'[67] Oakes states that 'when an officer was declared dead, they used, without the least ceremony, to drag him out by the heels and throw him over the walls of the prison, where we have often heard the tigers at night devouring them.'[68]

Bristow writes about an incident that took place immediately after the Bidanur conquest:

> A singular species of cruelty that had no other object in view than wanton malice, and the barbarous delight our villains constantly took in tormenting and insulting the English prisoners, occurred about this time. Four European women, with their husbands, belonging to the Bedanore garrison, were brought to Seringapatam [sic], where they were torn from the men, whom the villains sent to Chittledroog [Chitradurga], and afterwards allotted the women to four of the black slaves. Two became the property of the natives of Mysore, and the other two became the property of a couple of abominable Abyssinians, with whom they were compelled to live. I saw these women myself, they were good-looking females, but pity was all the assistance I was able to afford them.[69]

It was only after the Treaty of Mangalore was signed in March 1784 that many of the prisoners finally found their freedom. The news was received by the prisoners with great exultation and with an emotional catharsis. Those who had been converted to Islam were however retained.[70] Although their irons were knocked off, it is said that it took them some time to use their limbs to walk around freely.[71]

The Plight of the Christians of Mangalore

The Roman Catholics who form part of the Mangalore Diocese and speak Konkani are the Canara or Mangalore Christians. The history of the Syrian Christians, who form a major community in South India, especially Kerala, dates back to the first century of the Common Era, and owes its existence to St Thomas. The spread of Christianity however gathered momentum with the arrival of the Portuguese in 1498. Many of those who are today known as the Mangalore Christians were Goan Catholic settlers who migrated to coastal Karnataka in several waves to escape the persecution meted out during the Goan Inquisition. When the Portuguese had their conflicts with the Adil Shahis of Bijapur and later the Marathas, several of them again migrated to the Canara region. Francis Buchanan mentions that the Nayakas of Ikkeri allowed these migrants to settle down honourably in their dominions in the Tuluva region. They were prized as efficient agriculturists and hence the Nayaka was in favour of settling them in his domains.[72] Historian George M. Moraes states that the Christians managed to negotiate extremely favourable living conditions from the Nayaka. Disputes arising amongst them or with other Hindu subjects were to be settled by the Portuguese Factor and the Vicar or other priests of their faith, but not the Nayaka's local governors. Christians were to be exempt from imprisonment for debts and were not allowed to cohabit with Hindu subjects. If a Christian was found to have cohabited with a Hindu, their priest was empowered to deport the culprit to Goa for strict punishments. Portuguese were to be allowed to erect churches at their will, punish the members of their faith as per their strictures and not those of the Nayaka and also remain exempt from tax for any luggage carried, except on goods for sale. Moraes mentions that the Christians had thus come to occupy an 'autonomous position, very nearly forming a "state within a state."'[73] These immigrants retained

their Konkani language, dress and mannerisms. They soon came
to establish twenty-seven churches in the Tulu land, each under a
vicar and overall, under a vicar-general, subject to the authority of
the archbishop of Goa.[74] When Haidar conquered Canara from the
Ikkeri Nayakas in 1765, there were about 58,000 Catholics who had
settled there.[75] He however confirmed the perpetuation of the time-
honoured privileges that the Christians there enjoyed. He recognized
the jurisdiction of the clergy over its subjects as well.

Things soured between the Christians and Haidar during the
First Anglo–Mysore War when the Government of Bombay sent
Admiral Watson and Major Garvin to seize Mangalore. Haidar
and his forces had expected that given their patronage to them, the
Portuguese factor Francisco Alexandre da Cunha Gusmao and the
Christians in Mangalore would stand by them against the British.
But surprisingly, they sided with the enemy and this incensed Haidar.
The Portuguese factor was however later shocked to discover that
the British, whom he had sided with, felt no gratitude and in fact
deprived him of his guards and lowered the Portuguese flag. Gusmao
had to sail away to Goa after this. Haidar with 3000 veterans and 1200
cavalry, and Tipu with 3000 cavalry, then marched from Mangalore
and by May 1768, they had taken the city of Mangalore. On the
occupation of Mangalore, Haidar did not put the Portuguese and the
Christians to death, as per the normal Portuguese punishment for
treachery, but decided instead to be lenient and imprisoned several
of them. Father Sebastian de Faria, the Vicar Vara of Honnavar,
was taken prisoner to Haidar Nagar along with two more priests.[76]
With the conclusion of the war and with the Marathas threatening
to invade again, Haidar was keen to restore peace in the Canara and
also to assuage the Portuguese. He therefore negotiated with them
and the Portuguese factory was restored of all its rights and the vicars
who had been arrested were released. Relations with Goa, too, were
normalized with the signing of the treaty on 13 June 1771. The
Portuguese were allowed to continue their factory at Mangalore, and
sandalwood, rice, pepper and other spices were to be freely available to
them. Parish priests would have the freedom as before to administer

justice among the Christians. No obstacle would be placed by the Mysore Sarcar to any Hindu converting to Christianity.[77]

The bonhomie lasted till about 1776 when Haidar decided to imprison the Portuguese Factor of Mangalore and dismantled their fortifications. By then, Haidar had grown in stature and power and he saw no need to grant so many concessions to the Portuguese. He demanded that they help him with six hundred European troopers every year to serve in his military campaigns. The Portuguese were reluctant to comply and negotiations followed for several years, culminating in a second treaty between the two sides. Haidar agreed to permit the Portuguese to levy tributes and collect customs as they had been doing earlier. They could continue to keep their factory in Mangalore, but had to promise to aid in the defence of the town against enemies. Religious freedom to follow their faith was sanctioned to the Christians there.

Under Tipu's rule, during the Second Anglo–Mysore War, he was initially pleased with the Portuguese when the latter refused to grant asylum to Sheikh Ayaz in Goa. But as the battle intensified with Mangalore as its locus, Tipu's apprehensions that the Christians there would betray him in favour of the British started gaining momentum. Major John Campbell informed the President in Bombay in May 1783: 'There are a number of native Christians here who had been formerly attached to the Artillery; 34 of them are taken in the same service here, and Francis Pinto, late an ensign in the "Bombay Natives," whom General Matthews had promised to employ and give Ensign's pay and *batta*, I have appointed to take charge of them with the same rank, pay and allowance as he had formerly.'[78] Father Don Joaquim de Miranda, the head of the Mount Marion Jesuit mission, who had shared an affable relationship with Haidar, had supposedly even supplied the British garrison with 1000 bags of rice.[79]

In addition to actively helping the British army either as spies or regulars, there was pecuniary support too that some of the Christians in Mangalore had provided to the British. In fact, a note that was recovered from Matthews's prison, after he was killed in captivity by poisoning, mentions that 'he [Matthews] had borrowed 330,000 rupees from the Malabar Christians, for the support of his army.'[80] Malabar here meant the larger western coast that included Canara. Matthews had requested anyone who had happened to read it to make it known to the President and Council in any of the Presidencies. Right from his younger days, unlike his father, Tipu had viewed the Christians in Mangalore with immense suspicion, especially after their support to the British during the First Anglo–Mysore War.[81] The revelations that now came tumbling out, about the active connivance in the hostilities against him, became a legitimate reason for Tipu to inflict the harshest treatment possible in order to teach them a lesson. He waited till the war ended in Mangalore and soon after the treaty was signed, Tipu sought his revenge. He fined the priests Rs 3 lakh and had them expelled from his dominions.[82] Tipu decided to make an example of the community by charging them with sedition and inflicting inhuman tortures on them. Just as in Srirangapatna a few months prior, when he had initiated a mass massacre of the Mandyam Iyengars, the entire community always ended up paying the price for the alleged treachery of a few members amongst them. Tipu had no consideration for such nuances; the persecution always had to be large-scale to instil a sense of horror in the hearts of everyone so they never attempted such bravado again.

The news of Tipu's possible retributive actions leaked out to the Christian clergy. Precious items were all removed from the churches and taken to places of safety like the island of Anjediva, three miles off Karwar, that was under Portuguese jurisdiction. Even the Hindus and Hindu temples are said to have deposited their treasures here, fearing a massive backlash from Tipu.[83] Father Miranda was banished to Tellicherry and the twenty seminarians at Feringpet, who were studying under him for the priesthood, were all sent away. The other priests and their possessions too were dismantled. The Christian community was thus left leaderless, with no spiritual guides to advise them on their future course of action. After this, Tipu's attention fell on the hapless Christians in Canara.

Lists were drawn up of the names of the Christian residents and distributed amongst all the principal officers to the effect that on

the night of Ash Wednesday, 24 February 1784, all of them should
be seized and assembled in certain villages. The day chosen for the
persecution was also sacred to the communities concerned, be it the
Naraka Chaturdashi night before Diwali for the Mandyam Iyengars
and Ash Wednesday, the first day of Lent marking six weeks of
penitence before Easter. From this day was to begin for the Canara
Christians a long period of sufferings and torture, extending to nearly
fifteen years, in an alien land, under hostile rule with their lives and
properties destroyed and 'young girls and women lost forever in the
harems of the Sultan's officers and minions.'[84] Tipu's orders to his
subordinates were clear: 'You shall seize all Padres and Cullistauns
[Christians] that are found within your District and send them
under guard to the Huzur, and you shall inquire and ascertain what
zindigie [property], grain, cattle, land, plantations, etc. they possess
and shall sequestrate the whole thereof for the Government; and
you shall deliver over the lands and plantations to other ryots, whom
you shall encourage to cultivate them, as in case they are not kept
in cultivation, you shall be required to make good what they should
have produced. In future, if any person of the caste of Cullistaun
shall take up his abode in your District, you shall, according to the
above directions, seize him with his family and children and send
him and them to the Huzur.'[85] Tipu's own account corroborates the
Diocese's record stated above on what fate befell the Christians of
Mangalore. In the *Tarikh-i-Khudadadi,* Tipu writes:

> The port of Kurial [Mangalore] fell into our hands; on which
> occasion the odious proceedings of the accursed Padres becoming
> fully known to us, and causing our zeal for the faith to boil over,
> we instantly directed the Diwan of the Huzoor Kuchery to prepare
> a list of all houses occupied by the Christians, taking care not to
> omit a single habitation. The officers of the Kuchery, accordingly,
> employing the Mutsaddies [civil officers] of Sode, Nagar, Kurial
> etc. for this purpose, soon prepared and delivered to us a detailed
> report on the subject. After this, we caused an officer and some
> soldiers to be stationed in every place inhabited by the Christians,
> signifying to them, that, at the end of a certain time, they should

receive further orders, which they were then to carry into full effect. These men and officers being all arrived at their respective posts, the following orders were transmitted to them, viz. 'On such a day of the week and the month, and at the hour of the morning prayer, let all the Christians, whatever their number may be, together with their women and children, be made prisoners and dispatched to our presence.' And on the sealed cover, on superscription, of each of these dispatches, we specified the week and the month on which it was to be opened and read. Accordingly our orders were everywhere opened at the same moment; and at the same hour (namely, that of morning prayer) were the whole of the Christians, male and female, without the exception of a single individual, to the number of sixty thousand, made prisoners and dispatched to our Presence; from whence we caused them, after furnishing them duly with provisions, to be conveyed, under proper guards, to Seringapatam; to the Talukdars of which place we sent orders, directing that (the said Christians) should be divided into Risalas, or corps, of five hundred men, and a person of reputable and upright character placed, as Risaldar, at the head of each. Of these Risalas, four (together with their women and children) were directed to be stationed at each of the following places, where they were duly fed and clothed, and ultimately admitted to the honour of Islamism; and the appellation of Ahmady was bestowed upon the collective body.[86]

There are varied numbers to describe how many captives were taken from Mangalore. Tipu's own account above, as also those of Abbé Dubois, Sir Thomas Munro, Hamilton and the *Imperial Gazetteer*, mentions it as 60,000.[87] However, the accounts of Buchanan, historian Saldanha and an old Kannada manuscript written by a Catholic, the Barcoor manuscript, peg this figure at 80,000. Wilks and Bowring mention it as 30,000. The *Imperial Gazetteer* Volume XIV states:

When in 1784, Tippu succeeded in driving the English out of Kanara, he was determined on both political and religious grounds to convert the native Christians of Kanara to Islam. After taking a secret census, he despatched troops who arrested 60,000 or according to other accounts 30,000 out of 80,000 Christians found. The churches were dismantled and every trace of the Christian religion disappeared. Except infirm women and children, the prisoners were marched under strong military escort to Seringapatam . . . the men were circumcised, the unmarried girls were carried as concubines and many of the married women were badly treated.[88]

Only about 7000 Christians were left behind in Mangalore as they went into hiding when these combing operations to arrest them were underway. Some extant families have even earned their new surnames, courtesy their innovative and brave methods to circumvent Tipu and his forces. For instance, some of them have the name *Koleogar* or Kholiyegars as they hid under a heap of *kole* (dried leaves in Konkani) that were found aplenty in the long, dry months leading to summer.[89]

After comparing several accounts, author Severine Silva concludes that 'to all intents and purposes, the number of Canara Christians taken captive to Seringapatam is not more than 40,000 and possibly not less than 20,000; possibly it was about 30,000 and not more.'[90]

The Barcoor manuscript suggests that there were about 60,000 Christians from South Canara and 20,000 from North Canara who were holed up and made to march on foot from there to Srirangapatna. They were made to walk tortuous routes inside the dense forests of the Western Ghats, climbing nearly 4000 ft along two routes. One was from Bantwal via Virajapet and Coorg to Mysore and another along the Gersoppa falls in Shimoga. Those captives who were rebellious and protested were indiscriminately hacked or thrown off the cliffs. The Nettrekere town en route derives its name, as per popular oral history, from the large pool of blood that was caused by the killings of Christians on their march to Srirangapatna.[91]

Most of the people who were bundled off from Mangalore were labourers and cultivators; they were sent in two batches. All the camps were under martial law orders where the commanding officer's orders were final. Any disobedience meant instant death. The officers' whims determined the marches and halts. On the way, when pregnant women, who were also forced to walk on this tortuous march, developed labour pains, many of them had to deliver their babies on the side of the roads and resume their march thereafter. For a brief while, the babies were allowed to be tied to cloth cradles suspended from the branches of trees.[92] If children were a burden, the only alternative was to abandon them on the way. Those who died were buried on the way. Most often the corpses would be buried in a small hollow in the sand, scooped out with bare hands by the family members, only to be fed on later by dogs and jackals. Thieves stole away any decent clothes that covered the remains of the dead who were consigned to the earth.[93] To avoid all this, the family sometimes threw the body into a well or lake on the way. The journey by foot was long, varying from 240 to 320 km by foot through rugged, inhospitable terrain. The tortuous march was rendered more miserable, on account of thorny paths, where the victims suffered immensely.

The Barcoor manuscript talks of how, by the time the captives reached Shahar Ganjam, a suburb of Srirangapatna, several diseases such as smallpox, dysentery, fever, cholera and so on broke out. These diseases, and the sheer exhaustion of the long journey, resulted in about one-third of the group dying.[94] Given the large numbers of deaths, even proper burials of these unfortunate victims was rendered difficult. In many cases, the corpses were left for the jackals to feast on.[95] Severe punishments like cutting off of lips and noses and being paraded through the streets of Srirangapatna on donkeys was commonplace.[96] One such victim, Moblé Antony, is supposed to have confronted the Sultan: 'You have disfigured my features by cutting off my nose and ears. You have forgotten the favours done to you. May God behold this.'[97] Then raising his eyes to the heavens, he is said to have made a fervent prayer and dropped down dead. He was hailed as a brave martyr for the faith by his unfortunate co-religionists. Several of them who refused to convert were hanged or ordered to be tied to the feet of elephants, dragged around and trampled upon in the most barbaric manner.[98] Many of the survivors were circumcised and converted to Islam. The Barcoor manuscript records how, out of every Risala formed, routinely twenty-five men were selected and circumcised, proclaiming their conversion thereby to Islam. About 200 young and robust girls were selected for the royal harem.[99] Mohibbul Hasan however downplays these incidents, attributing them to colonial exaggeration to demonize Tipu and argues that several of these captives converted to Islam 'voluntarily in order to escape the boredom of prison life. After they were released, they were given responsible posts in the palace and in the army'.[100] But contemporary accounts paint a different picture of the treatment meted out to these unfortunate captives.

James Scurry, the British prisoner in Srirangapatna, in his account mentions 30,000 unfortunate Malabar Christians who were marched off to the capital city. He recounts:

> The sufferings of these poor creatures were most excruciating . . . all who were fit to carry arms were circumcised, and forced into four battalions . . . when recovered [from circumcision], they were armed and drilled and ordered to Mysore, nine miles from the capital, but for what purpose we never could learn. Their daughters were many of them beautiful girls, and Tippoo was determined to have them for his seraglio; but this they refused; and Mysore was invested by his orders, and the four battalions were disarmed and brought prisoners to Seringapatam. This being done, the officers tied their hands behind them . . . their noses, ears, and upper lips were cut off; they were then mounted on asses, their faces towards the tail, and led through Patam [Srirangapatna], with a wretch before them proclaiming their crime. One fell from his beast, and expired on the spot through loss of blood. Such a mangled and bloody scene excited the compassion of numbers, and our hearts were ready to burst at the inhuman sight. It was reported that Tippoo relented in this case, and I rather think it is true as he never gave any further orders respecting their women. The twenty-six

that survived were sent to his different arsenals, where, after the lapse of a few years, I saw several of them lingering out a most miserable existence.[101]

A Roman Catholic French priest, Abbé Jean-Antoine Dubois, who came to India in 1792 and returned to France after thirty-two years, in 1823, also records the travails of the Christians of Canara. He mentions:

> When the late Tippoo Sultan sought to extend his own religious creed all over his dominions, and make by little and little all the inhabitants in Mysore converts to Islamism, he wished to begin this fanatical undertaking with the native Christians living in his country, at the most odious to him, on the score their religion. In consequence, in the year 1784, he gave secret orders to his officers in the different districts, to make the most diligent inquiries after the places where the Christians were to be found, and to cause the whole of them to be seized on the same day, and conducted under strong escorts to Seringapatam. This order was punctually carried into execution; very few of them escaped and I have it from good authority that the aggregated number of the persons seized in this manner, amounted to more than 60,000. Sometime after their arrival at Seringapatam, Tippoo ordered the whole to undergo the rites of circumcision, and be made converts to Mahometanism. The Christians were put together during the several days after the ceremony lasted . . . after the fall of the late Tippoo Sultan most of these apostates came back to be reconciled to their former religion, saying that their apostasy had only been external, and they always kept in their hearts the true faith in Christ. Almost 2000 of them fell in my way and nearly 20,000 returned to the Mangalore district, from whence they had been carried away, and rebuilt there their former places of worship.[102]

Dubois was however deeply critical of these captives for what he considered their meek submission to the oppressor's attempts to convert them and none of them standing up to be a martyr for their faith, rather than turning apostate.

In their works, A.L.P. D'Souza and Kranti Farias document the destruction of all the twenty-seven churches in Canara by Tipu Sultan during this period in Mangalore, Bantwal, Moolki, Barcoor, Kundapura, Honnavar and Sunkery.[103] This included the old and historic Milagres Church that was built in 1680. The Sultan Battery fortification and watch tower was built in Boloor to prevent the entry of British warships and the stones for this too came from several destroyed churches. It is estimated that property of the value of five lakh that belonged to the community was confiscated and parcelled out among the Muslims and others sold at competitive bids.[104]

The scourge and painful memories of what the community went through during those dark years of Tipu's reign remains a raw nerve for the Christians in Mangalore. The historic episodes have also found a lot of resonance in oral history and literature. Konkani litterateur V.J.P. Saldanha's works of historical fiction such as *Belthangaddicho Balthazar, Devache Krupen, Sardarachi Sinol* and *Infernachi Daram* are heart-wrenching accounts of the travails of the Christian captives and their sufferings in the dungeons of Srirangapatna, thus immortalizing this dark chapter of their past.

11

Sarkar-e-Khudadad

The Treaty of Mangalore, the victorious conclusion of the Second Anglo–Mysore War and the successful suppression of several rebellions that threatened to uproot his rule strengthened and legitimized Tipu's accession to the throne of Mysore. With the Treaty of Mangalore having been signed on 11 March 1784, Tipu was imbued with renewed confidence about his supremacy. It is said that he consolidated his position only on his return to Srirangapatna, fresh from the victory of this war.[1] Tipu's coins too begin to appear from this year onwards, indicating his coming out of the shadows of his illustrious father and stamping his own individuality. Mysore under him was to be called *Sarkar-e-Khudadad* or the God-given kingdom. The kingdom was indeed destiny's blessing to the house of Haidar, not an inheritance that had come down from their ancestors, and Tipu was acutely aware of this.

After the conclusion of peace in Mangalore, Tipu ascended the ghats and began a march through Balam. The principality had been witnessing rebellious acts for long, and Tipu, fresh from victory, decided to assert his authority there by quelling these revolts. A new fortress was erected there and named Munzirabad. According to the Sultan's own account, this was built on the site of the one which had been raised about twenty-five years ago, around 1764, by Fazalullah Khan, Haidar's trusted officer; it had been demolished subsequently by the Raja of Balam.[2] Tipu states: 'I directed that it should be constructed with nine sides, than which there is no better figure for a fortification.'[3] The name Munzirabad was supposedly

* Please refer to the corresponding illustration in the appendix.

chosen on numerological considerations—adding the place values of the alphabets, as assigned by Tipu, is supposed to indicate the Hijri year of its occupation, 1198.[4]

The Coorg Conundrum

Proceeding thereafter from Balam, through the hills and forests, Tipu made his way to Coorg. The principality had seen simmering discontent all along as they resented the interference of Mysore and Haidar Ali in their affairs. When Lingaraja, the Raja whom Haidar had placed on the throne in lieu of his support to quell the succession feud, died in 1780, Haidar had taken his seventeen-year-old son and heir, Virarajendra, his other sons Appajiraja and Lingarajendra, and the royal family as hostages under house arrest in Haleri and later in the dingy, old fort of Gorur. A Brahmin named Subarasayya, who was earlier the treasurer of the Coorg Raja, was appointed as the Commissioner of Coorg. Angered by the imprisonment of their princes and the appointment of a Brahmin to command them, the valiant people of Coorg burnt with an intense spirit of revenge against the overlord of Mysore.[5] Since then, the struggle for liberation from the yoke of Mysore became more intense among the brave warrior class of the Kodavas. An open rebellion broke out in June 1782.

In 1782, Haidar had sent Woffadar, one of his chela brigades, to quell the rebellion in Balam and Coorg. Woffadar had crushed the revolt and also constructed an imposing fort there, Madikeri, to overawe the locals. Making his way to Coorg via Periapatna, the Mysorean army divided itself into two divisions, and rapidly marched to the residence of the governor of the district where all the rebels had holed up. Several of them were taken prisoners here. Katti Naik, the leader of the rebels, managed to flee with his family through the dense forests and glens of Coorg. From thence, he managed to escape to Tellicherry, where he died soon after, while his family was captured by Tipu. In his memoirs, Tipu derisively called him 'Kutty Naik', meaning a dog. The rebels had demolished the fort of Madikeri, which Tipu ordered to be rebuilt. He appointed a loyalist,

Zain-ul-abidin Mehdvi, as foujdar or military governor of the district and renamed Madikeri as Zuffurabad (the abode of victory).

The social custom of polyandry that existed among the Kodavas had morally repulsed Haidar and he had sought to abolish it. But even during Tipu's entry into Coorg, the practice had continued.[6] Calling together the people of Coorg, Tipu gave them a long haranguing sermon on their political and moral sins and said that they had better watch out in future if they did not wish to incur his wrath. Written copies of the same were also distributed among the community. Addressing them in the most humiliating and abusive manner, he said:

> It is the custom with you, for the eldest of five brothers to marry and for the wife of such brother to be common to all five; hence there cannot be the slightest or remotest doubt of your being all bastards and whoresons. This is about the seventh time that you have acted treasonably towards the sircar, and plundered our armies. I have now [therefore] vowed to the true God, that if you ever again conduct yourselves traitorously or wickedly, I will not revile or molest a single individual among you, but making Ahmedies [i.e. Muslims] of the whole of you, transplant you all from this country to some other; by which means, from being illegitimate, your progeny or descendants may become legitimate, and the epithet of whoresons (born of sinful mothers) may no longer belong to your tribe.[7]

After restoring a semblance of peace in Coorg, or at least as he assumed that he had, Tipu marched back to Srirangapatna towards the end of 1784. No sooner had Tipu headed back to his capital than troubles began to erupt once more in Coorg. Puffed by his closeness to the Sultan, Mehdvi, the new foujdar, had become a debauched autocrat in a short span of time. He had forcibly abducted the sister of one Momuti Nair, a minister of the local chief.[8] These excesses had naturally inflamed passions among the Kodavas, particularly Momuti and his colleague Ranga Nair. Soon the discontent spread among all the peasantry who were bearing the brunt of Mysore's

exploitation and heavy taxation, and now the additional scourge
of their women being brazenly molested by Mehdvi. Kirmani too
corroborates these excesses committed by Mehdvi:

> When Zein ool Abidin Mehdivi, the Foujdar of Koorg, from
> his intimacy with the Sultan, and the confidence he reposed in
> him was placed in uncontrolled authority there, he filled all parts
> of the kingdom with rebellion, and regulated the affairs of the
> government according merely to his caprice and folly; in so much
> that from the inherent vices of his disposition, he extended the
> hand of lust to the women of the peasantry, and compelled the
> handsomest among them to submit to his will and pleasure. In
> consequence of this tyrannical conduct, the whole of the people of
> Koorg advanced into the field of enmity and defiance.[9]

Gathering in large numbers, the rebels besieged Zuffurabad. Mehdivi
had become so complacent that he had not even anticipated such an
eventuality and made preparations for the stocking of provisions and
ammunition. The inmates were reduced to such a pitiable condition
due to the onslaught of the siege that they were fearful of even
stepping out of the fort, even during daytime. Urgent messages were
then dispatched to the Sultan in Srirangapatna seeking his support.

Meanwhile, the young Coorg Raja, Virarajendra, who had been a
witness to the crusades that his father had fought all his life to liberate
his land and his people, continued to languish in Gorur. It became
a matter of loyalty and duty for several brave Kodava soldiers like
Kuletira Ponnanna and his brother Machayya to free Virarajendra
and the entire royal family from Tipu's captivity. Getting wind of
these plans, Tipu had the royal family shifted to prison in Periapatna.
He appointed one of his lieutenants, Ismail Khan, to assist Hombale
Nayaka in keeping a close watch on the rebellious royals. But none
of this stopped the rebellious activities in Coorg.

By September 1785, with a determination to punish the Kodavas
for what they had been doing, Tipu ordered the commander or
sipahadar of one of his *kushoons* (infantry brigades of five thousand
men), Zain-ul-abidin Shoostri to invade Coorg and terminate

the insurgency. In his later dated 17 September 1785 to Shoostri, Tipu writes:

> It has lately been represented to us, that the Koorgs have committed some excesses at Zuferabad. We have, in consequence, written to the *Buktshy* [Bakshi] of the *Jyshe* [army], to dispatch you with two guns and your kushoon to that place. He is also ordered to advance you Two Thousand Behadury pagodas, on account of the pay of your kushoon, as well as a thousand rupees, to be applied in compensations to the wounded . . . you will proceed, as directed above, to Zuferabad; to the Foujdar of which place, Zynul Aabideen, we have addressed another letter, which is enclosed. You are, in conjunction with him, to make a general attack on the Koorgs; when having put to the sword, or made prisoners of the whole of them, **both the slain and the prisoners are to be made Musulmans** *[emphasis mine].* In short, you must so manage matters, as to prevent them from exciting any further sedition or disturbance.[10]

The horrifying aspect of the above directive to Shoostri was the clear mandate to the Sultan's commanders to not only convert the prisoners they caught, but even the slain were not spared. Even the dead were to be circumcised and converted to Islam by his military commanders.

Shoostri was a theologian, and also a man of letters who had authored a seminal military manual and treatise called *Fathul Mujahideen* or the Victory of the Holy Warriors. It was his prescription that determined the manner in which Tipu had organized his army. From the regular infantry, about five thousand men were selected to form a kushoon or brigade, under a sipahadar. In each kushoon, there were four *Risalas* or regiments of infantry and one of cavalry under a risaladar or colonel. He commanded over ten *jowkdars* or captains, the heads of a group of 100 men that formed a *jowk*. Every jowk or company included two *sur kheils*, ten *jemadars*, and ten *duffadars*. In those regiments of troop or regular horse that were modelled on European lines, the Major was called *teepadar* or *youzdar*; while the adjutant was the *soubadar* or *nakib*.[11] A section of this treatise was dedicated to the mode of warfare and strategy in dense, woody areas and hence Tipu perhaps believed that Shoostri would be the right man to undertake this exercise. He was sent with an abundance of stores and about 2000 irregular foot (*ahasham*). Shoostri marched quickly towards the ghats that led to Coorg, entering the place via Ulugulli. But he soon found himself being attacked from all sides by the rebels with their arrows and muskets. A terrified Shoostri found himself completely outwitted by the sturdy rebels and feigning fever and stomach pain he made a quick retreat to the pass of Siddhapura. There was obviously a big mismatch between his theoretical prescriptions of warfare strategy and their practical applications on ground, for which the Sultan mocked and admonished him. 'Truly, how can the hard duties of soldiers be expected from luxurious and effeminate men!'[12] was the jibe directed at Shoostri.

By late October 1785, Tipu decided to attack Coorg in two columns himself at the head of 20,000 regular infantry, 12,000 irregular foot, 10,000 horses and twenty-one field-pieces. Leaving his horse at the pass of Siddhapura, Periapatna and Munzirabad, along with his kushoons, Tipu began destroying the countryside, burning fields and lands in the verdant Coorg. Then entering the woods of Coorg through the Turkul ghat, he began assaulting the stockade gate and besieging the hideouts of the rebels. The French contingent under Lally and Tipu's chela regiments that he had named Asad Ilahi, managed to attack and kill several insurgents. Despite the heavy onslaught of the Mysorean and French forces, the brave Kodavas managed to hold on to their ground. After a protracted battle, the invading forces managed to dislocate the natives and compelled them to flee, even as they were hotly pursued.

Tipu dispatched several risalas with a large supply of stores and provisions to relieve the hapless victims inside the Zuffurabad fort. The Kodavas, being unable to counter such an ambush, dispersed themselves inside the hilly terrain that they were so familiar with and decided to remain low-profile. But the troops under Lally proceeded towards the Cardamom Ghats, while those under Shoostri and Hussain Ali Khan Bakshi marched towards Kurumbanad. The rest of the sipahadars marched forward to the Talakaveri and Kushalpur areas, while Tipu encamped himself firmly in the centre. Their strategy was to encircle the insurgents from all over and diminish their chances of escaping or regrouping. They caused a massive destruction of the region, the woods and towns, capturing a large number of people from the area. By December 1785, Tipu had managed to conclusively settle peace at Zuffurabad and moved forward towards Talakaveri.

The combined Mysorean and French troops relentlessly pursued the rebels and launched an all-out combing operation against them. Realizing the valour and numerical strength of the Kodavas, Tipu resorted to foul play. Through lies and blandishments, proposing reconciliation, he invited them all for talks. The unsuspecting Kodavas assembled at Bhagamandala to meet Tipu who had encamped at Devati Paramb on the fateful day of 12 December 1785. While both sides agreed to disarm themselves for the talks and a charade of goodwill and security was used to lull them, the Kodavas found to their utter horror that a section of the Mysorean troops remained armed, fell upon them stealthily and seized them all. The entire body of prisoners was then mercilessly brutalized and packed off like a 'herd of cattle.'[13] Rev. Hermann Moegling, a German missionary from the Basel mission, who came to Coorg in 1853, mentions in his *Coorg Memoirs*:

> After fifteen days, he [Tipu] went to Talakaveri. He encamped at Devatiparambu. At first, he negotiated. When the Coorgs felt secure, he seized them suddenly with their families and carried them to Mysore. There he separated them and forced them to become Musulmans. They were received as Sheiks, Syeds, Mogals and Patans. In course he sent Mohammadans of the four classes into Coorg and gave to them the lands and slaves of the rulers. Besides, he transplanted large numbers of farmers from Adwani [Adoni] in the Bellary district into Coorg as labourers on the estates of the new Musulman rulers. Nagappaya, the nephew of Subarasaya, was charged with the Government of the country.[14]

Nagappayya, who had been nominated as the Coorg incharge, soon fell out of favour. He was convicted of embezzlement and corruption and condemned to the gallows. He however fled from Coorg to save his life and sought shelter with the Kote Raja in Malabar.

To the Sheik and Syed converts whom he transplanted into a depopulated, barren Coorg, Tipu gave a cruel task:

> The country is given to you in Jaghir, improve it and be happy; the extermination of those mountaineers being determined on you, you are required as an imperious duty, to search for and to slay all who may have escaped our just vengeance; their wives and children will become your slaves.[15]

The converted Kodavas who managed to escape or returned to their homelands began calling themselves Kodava Mapillhas. They were ostracized as outcastes by the surviving locals as they had already been converted and there was no process of reconversions. Several of these families are still extant in Coorg and share the same family names as the natives. Muslim family names similar to the Kodavas of the region, such as Kuvalera, Italtanda, Mitaltanda, Kuppodanda and Kappanjeera are prevalent among these Mapillhas.[16] Some even escaped from Mysore to the Nilgiri hills and reside there now as the Badaga community and speak a unique dialect of their own. The community has memories of their ancestors escaping to these hills to save themselves from the cruelty and oppression of the Sultan of Mysore.[17] These instances serve as rude reminders of Tipu's atrocities in Coorg and his attempts to alter the demographics, faith and culture of the Kodavas.

Folklore in Coorg is rife with stories about this traumatic episode of betrayal, subterfuge and torture that their ancestors were subjected to by Tipu. The *Pattole Palame*, a precious compilation of the oral histories and heritage of the Kodavas, was compiled and published by Nadikerianda Chinnappa in 1924. It has been hailed as one of the earliest and most expansive archives of folklore in any Indian language. This book too bewails the Devati Paramb deception that the Kodavas endured. Contemporary Kodava writers such as Addanda Karyappa, in his Kannada book *Tippu Matthu Kodavaru* and I.M. Muthanna in *Tipu X-rayed* also mention a large-scale massacre of Kodavas who had assembled that day at Devati Paramb. The rest were packed off to Srirangapatna for tortures and conversion. There is no way to ascertain the exact number of people massacred on this occasion.

Some of the temples of the Kodavas, like the Bhagavathy temple near Kotakeri was demolished and the Biddatanda Ainmane was burnt down by Tipu.[18] However, several temples and their deities were secretly translocated by the Kodavas and the Brahmin priests to be hidden in safety and escape the wrath of Tipu's marauding forces.[19] The Omkareshwara temple was replaced with a tomb.[20] It is believed that several of these shrines, including that of the famous Bhagandeshwara temple, remained in disuse or ruins and the idols hidden in several secret locations, only to be reinstalled and worshipped later, once the Coorg Raja's power was re-established.[21] The Bhagandeshwara temple was made into a fortress and renamed as Afzalabad.[22]

During his expedition, Tipu also went to Periapatna fort to meet the royal family that he had imprisoned there. The three sons of Lingaraja, namely Virarajendra, Appajiraja and Lingarajendra, were among the detainees. Gloating in the string of successes that he had chartered in Coorg, he is supposed to have treated the royals with the least of dignity, addressing Virarajendra too insultingly as a petty vassal. He demanded that Virarajendra and his brothers embrace Islam and spread it among the people of their domain to which the twenty-one-year-old raja sternly replied, 'We would all rather die than give up our religion.'[23] Sensing the utter dismay and uneasiness even among his Hindu officers like Hombale Nayaka at this preposterous suggestion to the royal family, Tipu retreated and did not pursue the matter further. However, his eyes fell on Virarajendra's beautiful sister, Neelammaji, and cousin Devammaji. Both were picked up for his *zenana* in Srirangapatna—the former's name being changed to Mehtab (half-moon) and the latter to Aftab (sun). These actions severely alienated the Hindus, both Kodavas and Mysoreans, who were present there to officiate for Tipu, like Hombale Nayaka who nursed a secret passion himself for the pretty princess, Neelammaji.[24] But, at the height of his political and military success, Tipu was least perturbed about what people thought of his actions.

In a self-congratulatory account of the successful Coorg expedition, Tipu writes to the Nawab of Kurnool, Ranmast Khan, in a letter dated 5 January 1786:

> Some time ago . . . the exciters of sedition in the Koorg country . . . raised their heads, one and all, in tumult. Immediately, on our hearing of this circumstance, we proceeded with the utmost speed, and at once, made prisoners of forty thousand sedition-exciting Koorgs, who, alarmed at the approach of our victorious army, had slunk into woods, and concealed themselves in lofty mountains, inaccessible even to birds. Then carrying them away from their native country we raised them to the honour of Islam, and incorporated them with our Ahmadi corps. As these happy tidings are calculated, at once, to convey a warning to hypocrites, and to afford delight to friends, [but more especially] to the chiefs of the true believers, then pen of amity has here recited them [for your information].[25]

In another letter to Meer Muinudeen, dated 13 January 1786, Tipu once again corroborates the act of transporting and converting the captives from Coorg: 'By the favour of the Almighty and the assistance of the Prophet, we have arranged and adjusted the affairs of the taluk of Zufeerabad in the most suitable manner; the tribe of Koorgs to the number of fifty thousand men and women, having been made captives, and incorporated with the Ahmadi class . . . this being an event calculated to give strength to the people of Islam, we wish that brother [all co-religionists] all joy on this auspicious occasion.'[26]

A large part of the population of Coorg was made prisoner. The number of prisoners and converts varies from Tipu's own letters to those of the several chroniclers. In the letter above to Meer Muinudeen, Tipu gloats about 50,000 Kodavas being made captives, converted to Islam and incorporated into the Ahmadi class. In the letter to Ranmast Khan above, Tipu is gloating about 50,000 prisoners whom he converted. In his account, Kirmani states that 'in the course of seven months and a few days, eighty thousand men, women and children were made prisoners . . . the prisoners . . . had been all made Musulmans and were styled Ahmudees, were formed into eight *risalas* or regiments and veteran officers were appointed to train and discipline them.'[27] Momuti Nair and Ranga Nair were captured by Lally on the Cardamom ghats. While the former died, Ranga Nair was circumcised and made a Muslim, named Shaikh Ahmed and appointed as a *risaldar*.[28] Though Kirmani states that the Sultan took Shaikh Ahmed as a son, it did not mean he literally considered him so, as all the men whom he made slaves were also called his sons, just as Haidar had his chela brigade of 'orphans.'

Rev. Georg Richter, another German missionary of the Basel Mission who Moegling had brought in to Coorg around 1856, records how Tipu captured '85,000 souls, sent them to Seringapatam and, carrying out his former threat, had them forcibly circumcised.'[29] Wilks pegs this number at 70,000. He writes: ' . . . [Tipu] closed in on the great mass of the population, male and female, amounting to about 70,000, and drove them off like a herd of cattle to Seringapatam, where the Sultaun's threats were but too effectually executed.'[30] He mentions that on the same 'auspicious' day of the circumcision (meaning thereby their conversion) of 'the great mass of the Coorgs' in Srirangapatna, Tipu ascended his throne with all pomp and regalty.[31] Several of these unfortunate Kodavas languished in the jails in Srirangapatna or were enlisted into the Ahmadi corps of converted soldiers. In the Mysore and Coorg gazetteer, Lewis Rice talks about nearly 12,000 of these imprisoned converts escaping from the prison in February 1792 when Srirangapatna was attacked by the British under Lord Cornwallis.[32] Notwithstanding these varied numbers of prisoners, ranging from 40,000 to 85,000, it does seem likely that a virtual exodus of Kodavas was undertaken during this campaign by Tipu.

However, some historians like Mohibbul Hasan have found these figures to be 'preposterous' as 'the whole population of Coorg, at that time did not amount to these figures.' He quotes the *Imperial Gazetteer* of 1885 that mentions that the population of Coorg 'was returned at 65,437' in 1836.[33] He surmises therefore that in 1785, so many Kodavas could not even have been present. But these assertions are comprehensively debunked by another historian, Gajanan Bhaskar Mehendale, who calls Hasan's information as being 'incomplete and misleading.'[34] Mehendale quotes the entire passage of the *Imperial Gazetteer* that Hasan only partially references to make his point. It mentions that the first census, conducted in 1871, indicated a population of 1,68,312 in Coorg. The second census of 1881 showed the population having increased to 1,78,302, implying thereby an increase of 6 per cent in the decade. The figure of 65,437 in 1836 was thus merely an estimate by the British that had annexed Coorg just two years earlier, in 1834. Drawing a parallel with Poland, Mehendale states that the Jewish population in Poland was three million in 1939 and is now than less than a hundred thousand. From the current numbers, one cannot deduce that 3 million did not exist in 1939 when the Jews there suffered Hitler's holocaust. Natural and man-made calamities must be factored in while retrospectively extrapolating or working back the population for a previous era. In the case of Coorg, Mehendale works back the figures, decade-by-decade, from the census of 1871 with a population of 1,68,270, assuming a natural growth rate of 6 per cent and absence of natural or man-made calamities, to arrive at an estimate of 1,02,500 as Coorg's population during Tipu's barbaric invasion of 1785.[35] That many of these were killed at Devati Paramb on that fateful day and a large number, over and above 40,000, were converted and transported to Srirangapatna, this seems like a reasonable estimate in terms of figures. This, even if one discounts all the exaggerated numbers provided more as bravado and gloating about their own successes, by both Tipu in his letters and the Muslim chroniclers of his times.

Around the middle of January 1786, after making all arrangements for the security of the place and constructing several wooden or stockaded forts (*lakadi kote*), Tipu returned to

Srirangapatna. Upon his return, an auspicious moment was chosen by astrologers when in a public show of strength, the infidels from Coorg were to be 'converted to the true faith.'[36] All the Muslims of the capital were invited to the Lal Bagh Mosque in Srirangapatna to witness this grand spectacle whose intent was kept unknown to everyone, including the officiating priest, till the last moment. In a departure from earlier traditions of opening prayers with benedictions to Mughal Emperor Shah Alam, much to the astonishment of the gatherers, the prayers began with salutations to the might of Tipu Sultan. In Tipu's own words, Shah Alam deserved no respect as he was 'the prisoner of Sindea [Mahadji] and none but an idiot could consider him as a sovereign.'[37] The success in Mangalore and then Coorg had made Tipu emboldened enough to consider himself as a powerful autonomous sovereign and a counterpart to the Mughal Emperor.

Conflict with the Marathas

An uneasy calm had been settled between Mysore and its long-lasting foes, the Marathas, after Nana Phadnis and Haidar entered into a tactical arrangement before the outbreak of the Second Anglo–Mysore War. But the Maratha attitude changed markedly after they signed the Treaty of Salbai with the British on 17 May 1782. Hastings and the Maratha representative, Mahadji Sindhia, had concluded these terms after protracted negotiations. It was a complete reversal of all the agreements that the Marathas had made with Haidar, causing considerable and justified discontent in Mysore. After Haidar's death, Nana continued to press upon Tipu to abide by the terms of the Treaty of Salbai or face Maratha invasion. Through his vakil, Nur Muhammad Khan, Tipu informed Nana Phadnis that Mysore had suffered hugely on account of the Marathas and expressed his discontent on their reneging on the terms of the alliance. But the talks went nowhere. On 28 October 1783, Mahadji Sindhia, representing the Peshwa, and David Anderson, on behalf of the British, signed a treaty whereby the Peshwa was to call upon Tipu to release all the British prisoners of war and restore the Carnatic, failing which the Marathas would join the British in an attack on Mysore. Of course, this treaty did not yield much result because of 'Nana's jealousy of Sindhia's assumption of authority . . . in which Sindhia and the English would have borne parts so prominent.'[38]

When Tipu and the British finalized the Treaty of Mangalore, much to the former's satisfaction, there was a complete absence of any allusion to the Treaty of Salbai or the honouring of those terms by Tipu. Hastings did try to assuage the feelings of the Marathas who felt thoroughly slighted that 'any Treaty could be settled [by the British] without their concurrence, and declared that such an agreement would be a violation'[39] of the Treaty of Salbai. Nana's inclusion in the peace negotiations between Mysore and the British and his prevailing upon Tipu to bury the hatchet with the British would have obviously enhanced his prestige both within and outside Poona. But such an opportunity had sadly passed for Nana, with Tipu's victory in the Second Anglo–Mysore War and the favourable Treaty of Mangalore. An army from Poona, under Haripant Phadke, was already being readied by Nana to invade Mysore, when he received the disappointing news of the Treaty of Mangalore.[40] In his first missive against Mysore, Nana sent his demands to Tipu that the latter must clear the arrears of Chauth and Sardeshmukhi that had accumulated over the past four years. Tipu responded to this with utmost politeness, saying he very much intended to do so, but was not in a position right then as he had just concluded an expensive war against the British.[41] He also bitterly lamented about the Maratha breach of faith during the Second Anglo–Mysore War.[42]

Determined to avenge the disadvantageous situation vis-à-vis Mysore, Nana called upon Tukoji Holkar to support the efforts to subjugate Tipu. Simultaneously, he also parleyed with the Nizam to form a joint alliance against Tipu. The two sides met secretly in May 1784 ostensibly to resolve some of their differences, especially on payments of Chauth and Sardeshmukhi arrears from Hyderabad. But in reality, they met at Yadgir later in June 1784, amidst great fanfare from both sides, to firm up an offensive alliance against Tipu to recover territories that both sides had lost to Mysore.[43] Right from Haidar's times, the Nizam shared a very tenuous relationship with Mysore. The latter had refused to accept the Nizam's suzerainty and had even brought areas such as Kurnool, Cudappah etc., that were under Hyderabad, under their control. The Nizam had always been demanding in vain *peshkush* or tributes for the Carnatic Balaghat that Tipu had taken.

When he heard about the parleys at Yadgir, Tipu wrote to the Nizam, demanding the subahdari of Bijapur and saying that he was the master of the whole country south of the Krishna River. This was enough to terrorize the Nizam, who had scarcely reached his capital, with paranoia of a possible attack by Tipu of his kingdom. He immediately shot off letters to his new-found ally, Nana, seeking his help against a possible Mysorean invasion. At the same time, he also dispatched an envoy to Mysore to placate Tipu. But all of these were merely hallucinations of the Nizam as Tipu had no intention then to attack the former's territories and was merely flexing his might. Nana too was unable to send any help to his ally at that time as he was completely preoccupied in resolving internal troubles that had arisen with a conspiracy to depose Sawai Madhav Rao and elevate Baji Rao, the son of Raghunath Rao, who had just died, as Peshwa.[44]

The Nargund Flashpoint

In 1778, during his invasion of Dharwar, Haidar had occupied Nargund, a small principality south of the Malaprabha River, that was a feudatory of the Peshwa. The Brahmin Desayees who held sway over the region had submitted to Haidar's might and agreed to pay moderate annual tributes to Mysore. In his agreement with Haidar before the Second Anglo–Mysore War, Nana too had confirmed this arrangement and also recognized Haidar's control over territories south of the Krishna River, that included principalities like Nargund and Kittur. But the Desayee of Nargund, Venkat Rao Bhave, and his minister, Kalo Pant Pethe, nursed a deep grouse against Mysore for this humiliating capitulation and regarded the Peshwa as their true master. Pethe even wrote to Chintaman Rao, the senior chief of the Patwardhans, in January 1783, apprising him of the death of Haidar and the flux in the kingdom of Mysore, which the Peshwas could use to their advantage to defeat Tipu forever and re-annex all lost territories.[45] But the situation in Poona itself was so volatile then due to the internal political churn that they could not handle an invasion on Mysore. This left the Desayee deeply disappointed and he began negotiating with the British, offering his cooperation in any attack on Mysore. But the Treaty of Mangalore and the peace which the British had signed with Tipu dashed the hopes of the Desayee. Along with these secret parleys that Nargund was conducting with both Nana and the British, they also attacked the fort of Sode, a dependency of Gurramkonda, plundering the towns belonging to it and stirring up revolts, in alliance with the chief of Madanapalli. Their tributes to Mysore too had lapsed for two years.

Enraged by these excesses, Tipu increased the demands of tributes from Nargund, which they found it impossible to comply with. The Desayee complained bitterly to Nana, urging him to intervene in their favour. Nana accordingly wrote to Tipu that jagirdars on the transfer of districts were 'liable to no additional payments; and that the rights of the *Suwusthanees* [Brahmins who possessed old traditional jagir] who had been guilty of no treason against the state to which they owed allegiance, had been invariably respected.'[46] Tipu shot back that the Desayee was indeed guilty of treason as he had wished his downfall, that Nana had no locus standi in the issue as Nargund was now part of Mysore and, as its sovereign, he [Tipu] had every right to levy whatever tribute he desired, rather than be dictated from Poona about their erstwhile arrangements with the same principality. Elaborating his stand to Muhammad Ghias Khan and Noor Muhammad Khan, who were his diplomatic agents or vakils stationed at the Poona court, Tipu writes:

Representations of the contumacious conduct of the Zemindar of Nergund were frequently transmitted [by us], in the course of last year to Noor Mohammed Khan, who, no doubt communicated the same to all the chiefs there [Poona]. If a petty zemindar, and a subject of our government, like this, may not be punished, how shall our authority be maintained? . . . thus the chastisement of this zemindar becomes necessary. If he is brought to reason from thence [the Peshwa court] it will be well; otherwise, he will be exterminated . . . if the chiefs of that place [Poona], forgetting our past favours, should dispatch an army to the assistance of the zemindar of Nergund, what will it signify? We have, under the divine blessing, sent a strong force to reduce Nergund, and are in no fear of its suffering any misfortune from their army.[47]

Tipu was determined to discipline the Desayee and strengthen Nargund, which was an important frontier of his kingdom, in the looming inevitability of a confederate attack on him by Poona and Hyderabad. He sent Saiyid Ghafoor to Nargund to negotiate with Venkat Rao and his minister Kalo Pant to pay arrears and remain loyal. Ghafoor reported that the Desayee seemed more aligned to the Peshwa and was emboldened due to his family relations with Parshuram Bhau, one of the principal Patwardhan chieftains, who was in Miraj. Finally, by February 1785, Tipu sent his *sipahasalar* (Commander-in-Chief), also his cousin and brother-in-law, Burhan-ud-din at the head of 5000 horse and three kushoons. He was soon joined on the way by Saiyid Ghafoor, the sipahadar, near Dharwar, and Saiyid Hamid. Messages were sent to the Desayee to surrender. But he and Kalo Pant were fully confident of help coming in from the Peshwa and so decided to defy the orders of Tipu's army. With 2000 cavalry and 2000 infantry, and a few guns, Kalo Pant advanced to counter Burhan-ud-din outside the walls of Nargund. But he was defeated and forced to retreat. Burhan then directed his entire artillery force against the town. But Nargund was not going to give up so easily. Kalo Pant led several sorties, attacking the batteries of the opponent and killing many on the other side. One night, a small force of Nargund managed a surprise attack on Burhan's army stationed at the foot of the mountain, killing the Bakshi Salabat Khan and about 200 horses. Despite all their efforts, the Mysorean army was unable to capture the fort.

Soon, with the advent of scorching summer, they were beset with problems of water shortage. Carriers were brought in, to bring water from the river below, mounted on camels and bullocks. But even this was not sufficient. Battling all these odds, Burhan and his army managed to persist and soon carried on their batteries to the very foot of the fort walls.

All along Kalo Pant had managed to put up a brave front on the assurances that Parshuram Bhau Patwardhan had been giving him about the eventual help from Poona. But Nana, dogged by the internal conflicts in the Peshwa court, as also Haripant Phadke, had ignored all of Bhau's requests. When Burhan's armies reached the very walls of the Nargund fort and occupied the town, Parshuram Bhau made urgent requests to Nana to act decisively. Tipu's vakils in Poona had all along been assuring him that their master would not occupy Nargund and that the siege would be lifted. With the crisis now having become acute, Nana could no longer afford to procrastinate and continue being tardy. He ordered Parshuram Bhau to march for the relief of Venkat Rao and also dispatched Ganesh Pant Behre with 5000 troops to join him. Parshuram Bhau had been frustrated by Nana's dilatory nature and inaction. But now, immediately after receiving the green signal from Poona, he swung into action, collected his armies and divided them into three divisions. Under Janoba Subedar, 5000 cavalries were placed to safeguard the communications that went through Manoli. Raghunath Rao Kurundwadkar, at the command of 10,000 cavalry, was to march to Nargund, via Ramdurg. With 7000 troops as reserve, he was stationed at Mudhol and was to assist the other divisions as and when the need arose.

Observing the relief army coming to the rescue of Nargund, Burhan decided to take the fort by storm before the divisions approached. Situated atop a steep hill, the fort was strong enough to sustain them for another six months. With its 2000 strong garrison, provisions and ammunition, it was comfortably placed and was hopeful of bolstering its strength once the Maratha armies joined them. Burhan's two attempts to assault the fort went in vain.

Even as the battle was on, the siege was temporarily lifted to enable negotiations. Nana instructed Bhau not to precipitate matters till the end of the monsoon and to evacuate Venkat Rao and Kalo Pant from the fort. But they refused to be evacuated and insisted on staying on to provide resistance. Bhau was already annoyed with Nana's pacifism and this new instruction was met with further irritation. Ganesh Pant Behre and he disregarded Nana's advice and attacked the Mysoreans, only to be repulsed with the loss of twenty men and an elephant. They were severely reprimanded by Nana for disobeying his orders and going ahead with an offensive when negotiations were going on. Tipu's vakils in Poona bargained hard, agreeing to pay the two-year arrears of the tributes on the precondition of being able to deal with Nargund in the manner that they wished. Nana had planned to collect the arrears and then drag matters on till after the monsoon, when a strong attack could repulse the Mysoreans and Nargund could be liberated from them for good. But even as he kept humouring Tipu's vakils and buying time, he had been preparing for a long-drawn war, sealing alliances with the British, the Nizam and other chiefs of the Maratha confederacy, such as Tukoji Holkar.

Bhau's attack on the Mysore army gave Tipu a good excuse to commence defence operations from his end. He sent his cousin, Kumr-ud-din, with 4000 horses to join Burhan and to checkmate the Maratha forces. Around mid-April 1785, Kumr-ud-din managed to reach the vicinity of the Nargund fort. The combined Mysorean forces managed to reduce the strategic fort of Ramdurg on 5 May and then the town of Manoli (in Belgaum district) that gave them a distinct advantage in the Nargund campaign. Nargund was effectively cordoned off from any external assistance by this capture by the Mysorean armies. The personal rivalries between Tipu's two cousins, Burhan and Kumr-ud-din, however 'resulted in prolonging the operations in consequence of divided counsels and reciprocal complaints to Tipu.'[48] Tipu, in one of his letters dated 25 June 1785, also expresses his annoyance at the delay that was going on due to the possible ego clashes between the two men. 'We have repeatedly written before now,' admonished Tipu, 'desiring you to advance your batteries close to the walls of the fort; to destroy these effectually; to fill the ditch; and [finally] with the concurrence and advice of the Sipahdars, to proceed to the assault of the place. Such being the case, it is astonishing that you should wait, and continually apply to us for fresh orders for storming.'[49] Interestingly, Tipu often sent the same letters or directives to several officers and commanders in the army, superiors and juniors. Kirkpatrick surmises that this habit of the Sultan of corresponding separately with superior officers of his army, even as he corresponded with the chief commanders, was because the former 'acted as so many spies' upon the latter. 'Such a wretched system,' he states, 'would be naturally enough suggested by the characteristic jealousy and distrust of the Sultan.'[50]

Tipu decided to offer the Desayees the option of a capitulation. In his letter to Kumr-ud-din dated 21 June 1785, he states:

> Let a capitulation be granted to the besieged, allowing them to depart with their arms and accoutrements. Kala Pandit, with his family and kindred, and the principal bankers, must also be induced by engagements, to descend from the fort, upon doing which they may be placed under a guard, and Ten lakhs of pagodas to be demanded of them, for the ravages committed in our territories. If they pay this sum, it will be well; otherwise, they must be kept in confinement. In short, you are, by finesse, to get the aforesaid Pundit, together with his kindred and the bankers, out of the fort, and then to secure their persons. When your batteries are erected close to the walls of the fort, and the ditch is completely filled, you will, if the measure be approved of by the *Sipahdars*, advance to the assault: otherwise, the attempt will not be proper, inasmuch as this is a hill-fort affair.[51]

Accordingly, Burhan sent emissaries to Kalo Pant to surrender and seek pardon from the Sultan, which would ensure that his life and property would be saved, but the latter stoutly refused and conveyed his confidence to continue with the resistance. The combined armies of Burhan and Kumr-ud-din followed this up with incessant cannonading of the fort and cutting off supplies, including water. The situation within Nargund fort became precarious. Even as the attacks on the fort continued, Tipu sent several letters to the two men leading these attacks, clearly directing their strategy and also the barbarity that needed to be inflicted on the hapless inmates once the fort surrendered. To Burhan on 16 July 1785, Tipu writes:

> We have learned, by a letter from the *Sipahdar;* Mahomed Ali, that he has carried his approaches to the edge of the ditch; that the walls and batteries on his side are levelled to the ground; and that the ditch only remains to be filled. That, then, is a trifling affair. Let the ditch be filled, and with the consent and concurrence of all, let the place be stormed and taken. If, however, the garrison will capitulate, it will be all well: and [in this case] with the exception of Kala Pundit, the rest may be allowed their lives and arms; but the Pundit's person must be secured. In the event however, of [your being obliged to proceed to] the assault of the place, **every living creature in it, whether man or woman, old or young, child, dog, cat, or anything else, must be put to the sword** *(emphasis mine)*, with the single exception of Kala Pandit. What more?[52]

In a subsequent letter, he advises both the men that they 'must temporize, and employ every means, fair or foul, which may induce the besieged to surrender the fort.'[53] His letters display the natural impatience that had set in Tipu to storm and occupy the fort as early as possible, given the long, protracted campaign. By the end of July 1785, the fort could no longer hold on and finally capitulated. About 1650 men marched out of the fort on 29 July. The Desayee demanded for his security the sanction of oaths or the signing of a *Kowl-nama* or agreement between both parties. Tipu found this suggestion ridiculous. 'Where is the necessity for oaths and the affair, in an affair of this kind?' he thundered. He instead advised Burhan and Kumr-ud-din to employ 'every possible artifice and deception, [to] get the garrison to quit the place.'[54] They assured the Desayee of a guarantee that he desired if he evacuated the fort. But once he descended with an escort of his select guard, he was detained under several pretenses, as per the Sultan's express orders to his commanders. Four of the most opulent bankers and distinguished commanders of cavalry, and also other classes and departments, were all to be placed under guard. The rest were to be released and contrary to his earlier directive, no mass carnage of every living being was conducted.

After several months of negotiations, finally, on 6 October 1785, Kala Pandit and his entire family was placed under a guard and dispatched in irons to Srirangapatna first and then moved to the dreaded dungeons of Kabbaladurga, where he eventually met his end. James Duff states that the Pandit's 'daughter was reserved for the Sultan's seraglio.'[55] He further adds: 'To crown these acts, as if he designed to render himself as odious as possible to the Mahrattas, Tippoo forcibly circumcised many of the Hindoo inhabitants of the territory south of the Kitsna [Krishna River], and two thousand Brahmins, disciples of Shunkeracharya, destroyed themselves to avoid the detested violation.'[56]

The conquest of Nargund was closely followed by the Mysore armies occupying the nearby Kittur, in the Belgaum district, that was under another Desayee chieftain Mallasarja. The Desayee here, too, had shown signs of revolting against Mysorean occupation, and his tributes of Rs 5.5 lakh had fallen into arrears. Seeing the vast Mysore army heading towards his fort and having seen the fate that had befallen Nargund, the Desayee readily surrendered without a fight. His minister Gurupant was also imprisoned by the invading forces. In a letter to Burhan dated 3 February 1786, Tipu directs him to dispatch the Desayee of Kittur and his family in irons, to his presence in Srirangapatna and that all 'the gold, silver, jewels, horses, elephants' belonging to the Desayee be confiscated.[57] Through November–December 1785, Burhan managed to occupy several other Maratha territories such as Dodvad, Khanapur, Sada, Hoskote, Padshahpur and Jamboti.

However, rivalry had broken out between Burhan and Kumr-ud-din with the former being jealous that Nargund had fallen only after the latter's arrival. Burhan was also suspicious that Kumr-ud-din was possibly turning traitor and opening secret negotiations with the Nizam. Tipu immediately recalled Kumr-ud-din back to Srirangapatna and placed him in confinement. His troops were incorporated into Tipu's army. Wilks accounts however that Kumr-ud-din also spread malicious rumours about the Sultan's death, just before the Coorg campaign in October 1785 that gathered wide momentum all over India. Tipu had actually ordered a grand funeral for an eminent officer of Mysore, Sirajuddin Muhammad Khan, whose remains were being carried in a stately procession in a palanquin. At this juncture, Kumr-ud-din allegedly circulated the rumours that the palanquin actually carried the Sultan's remains, causing great disarray and confusion in the Mysorean ranks. When the suspicion against him was confirmed, Kumr-ud-din was placed in detention for two years and fell from the Sultan's grace, albeit temporarily.[58]

The Offensive Alliance

Alarmed by the advances of Tipu and his conquests of Nargund, Kittur and other territories, Nana Phadnis resumed his attempts to form a coalition against Mysore. He sent messages to the British Governor of Bombay Rawson Hart Boddam, offering the Company any two of Tipu's seaports on the Malabar coast if they supported an invasion of Mysore. Boddam directed Nana to the Supreme Government and Sir John Macpherson who had succeeded Hastings as the new Governor-General in February 1785. To carry on specific negotiations with the Government in Calcutta, Nana had to rely on the man he did not quite like, Mahadji Sindhia. Nana and Mahadji never got along and were suspicious of one another, 'with the result that a kind of double government [of the Marathas] came into being between the north and the south'[59] that Mahadji and Nana respectively controlled. In his anxiety to obtain British support and also thwart Mahadji, Nana insisted on the British sending a

Resident at the Peshwa durbar in Poona. Finally, Charles Malet was appointed to the position. This aroused further jealousies in Mahadji and, to assuage him, Malet was instructed to send his dispatches to the Supreme government 'for the purpose of being submitted for Sindia's information and obtaining his opinions.'[60]

Macpherson was non-committal about any firm alliance with the Marathas, citing the Treaty of Mangalore also as an impediment for such a teaming up against Tipu. He, however, assured Sindhia that in case of any reverses, the British would not let the Marathas be overpowered by Tipu and would jump in for their support. Nana seemed to exert more and more on the British to give up their laconic stance and participate in an offensive alliance against Tipu. He even brought to the British notice the possibility of a new treaty that was concluded between the French and Tipu, bringing the two powers closer than before. Yet, Macpherson did not bite the bullet and stuck to his stand of entering a war if the need arose—which was a cause of despair for the Marathas.

Keen to firm up terms with a vacillatory Nizam, Nana sent his vakil, Krishna Rao Ballal, to the latter's court to follow up on their Yadgir meeting. Nana also gathered the support of several Maratha chieftains and confederates in this brewing alliance. He decided to bury his differences and angst against Mudhoji Bhonsle of Nagpur, who had supported the British against the Peshwa in the First Anglo–Maratha War. Tukoji Holkar was always a ready ally. Even Parshuram Bhau who detested Nana's tactics, more so after the debacle at Nargund, also decided to bury the hatchet with him. The Nizam meanwhile sought Rs 25 lakh as war expenses and also the restoration of Bijapur and Ahmednagar to him. To secure his consent, Krishna Rao Ballal unilaterally assured him of these terms, without even consulting Nana. Pleased with his assurances, the Nizam decided to proceed again by the end of November 1785 to Yadgir to meet the Maratha confederates. Nana, Haripant Phadke, Parshuram Bhau, Raghunath Rao Kurundwadkar and others too joined in this meeting that lasted for over a month. The Nizam's court writer mentions that, 'The whole of their proceedings are in a most confused state, and what they determine one day is objected to on the next.'[61] Finally, they decided that the allies should first direct all their energies at conquering the Maratha districts between the rivers Tungabhadra and Krishna. Collections of Chauth from the Nizam were all adjusted. Tipu's conquered territories were to be then divided among the allies, the Nizam, the Peshwa, Sindhia and Holkar.[62] Nana however reneged on the claims of the Nizam over Bijapur and Ahmednagar, stating that Krishna Rao Ballal was not authorized even to confirm such terms. This caused some irritation to the Nizam and he decided to return to Hyderabad in a huff. But he however honoured the alliance and left behind 25,000 troops under the command of Tahawwar Jung, who was to take orders from Haripant. The stage was now set for an invasion of Mysore by the confederates.

Tipu tried to negotiate peace with the confederates. On his return from Coorg in January 1786, he sent a vakil to Hyderabad and another to Tukoji Holkar with a secret offer to the latter of Rs 5 lakh if he left the confederacy. Not much came of these efforts though.

Tipu was deeply aware of the latent hostility that was lurking amongst the Marathas against him. Consequently, Muhammad Ghiyas and Noor Mohammad Khan who were his vakils or agents in the Poona court had been told to leave the place by Tipu as early as July 1785. 'The hostile intentions of the chiefs in that quarter [Poona] are evident,' wrote Tipu on 21 July 1785, ' . . . therefore, both set out for our presence, with the whole of your retinue. This order is accordingly to be considered by you of equal force with a hundred orders. You must not wait for any other; but, immediately on receipt of our present commands, proceed with Noor Mohammed Khan, and all the people attached to you; to the Presence. We shall write no more on this subject.'[63] But despite such a strong order, the two continued to remain in Poona till almost May 1786. They kept writing to him that Nana was not allowing them permission to depart and seemed to be buying time, which Tipu noticed and even mildly reprimanded them. In a letter dated 14 August 1785, he wrote: 'You may pass twenty days or a month longer there, in an evasive or procrastinating way, but at the end of that time, you must, in whatever manner may be [necessary], set out for our Presence, since your remaining there is incompatible with our dignity.'[64]

Tipu occasionally sent chastising letters to the duo, but eventually seemed to have allowed them to linger on in Poona. They too kept sending letters of complaints to Tipu about how Brahmins in their embassy were secretly conspiring against them, in connivance with their co-religionists in the Peshwa court. Tipu found this astonishing and ordered the traitors to be flogged or severely punished.[65] Interestingly, Tipu was getting to know about these intrigues from the Maratha vakil in his court, Lakshman Rao Raste. On another occasion, on 2 December 1785, Tipu reprimanded his agents in Poona for their lethargy that they allowed their 'people should act in this improper manner, and that you, instead of punishing them for so doing, should complain of them to us, is to be attributed to your great age, and to the climate of that place [Poona]. Communicate to us the names of the several persons who have been guilty of this shameful conduct.'[66]

Their presence however came handy now when Tipu wanted to open negotiations with Nana. Through them he sent twelve elephants and Rs 3 lakh worth jewellery as gifts to Nana, to persuade him not to open hostilities. Ghiyas conveyed to Nana in an interview with him that was arranged through the intercession of Lakshman Rao Raste that Haidar Ali had always supported the cause of the young Peshwa when his life was in danger. Even Tipu had maintained the same policy of friendship and supported the Peshwa's cause in the wake of the turmoil in Poona. It was the Marathas who violated the agreements that were formed by the two forces, leading to the outbreak of the Second Anglo–Mysore War. They had unilaterally signed peace with the British and dumped their ally, Mysore, to carry on an expensive and protracted war with the latter. But Nana was resolute. He demanded a clearance of arrears for hostilities to be suspended. The talks went nowhere and the vakils returned empty-handed.

Tipu had all along anticipated such an attack on Mysore from the confederates, especially after the failure of negotiations.

Right from February 1786, Tipu's letters to Burhan-ud-din warned him of such an imminent invasion. 'We have heard,' he wrote, 'the enemy has detached a large force for the purpose of falling suddenly upon your army: we therefore write, to desire that you will, immediately on the receipt of this letter, take up a position at Dharwar, and dispatching the whole of your baggage into the country of Nugr [Bidanur], remain youself with your army unencumbered. You must, on this point, employ the strictest precautions. Let it not be (God forbid!) that the enemy should surprise you.'[67] Tipu kept apprising Burhan of all the activities on the opposing front that the state intelligence system was able to gather.

On 3 May 1786, Tipu issued his famous proclamation or manifesto that was then circulated to all the principal officers, who were then to distribute copies of this among the faithful. The manifesto was like an article of faith of his Sarkar-e-Khudadad, its policy towards believers and infidels and how each category needed to be treated. It seems like a manifesto both for war as well as peacetimes, including for Muslims living in kingdoms ruled by infidels. Declaring a holy war or *jihad* against the infidels, Tipu proclaimed at length, quoting verses generously from the Quran:

Whereas in conformity with the commands of God and the
Prophet [which say]:

'Fight with those who do not believe in God, and in the last day; and who do not consider those things as unlawful, which God and his Prophet have prohibited, and profess not the true religion; and [fight] with those, unto whom the scriptures have been given, until they pay tribute by right of subjection, and be reduced low,[68]

it is our constant object and sincere intention, that those worthless and stiff-necked infidels, who have turned aside their heads from obedience to the true-believers, and openly raised the standards of infidelity, should be chastised by the hands of the faithful, or made either to acknowledge the true religion or to pay tribute, particularly at this time, when owing to the imbecility of the princes of Hind, that insolent race having conceived the futile opinion, that the true believers are become weak, mean and contemptible; and not satisfied even with this, but preparing for war, have over-run and laid waste the territories of the Moslems, and extended the hand of violence and injustice on the property and honour of the faithful.

Wherefore, we, trusting to the Divine power and aid, and supported by our holy religion [according to the passage]:

'Oh! True Believers! Shall I show you a merchandize, which shall deliver you from a painful torment [hereafter]? Believe in God and his Apostle, and defend God's true religion with your substance and in your persons. This [will be] better for you, if you knew it. He will forgive you your sins, and introduce you into gardens, through which rivers flow, and agreeable habitations in places of perpetual abode. This [will be] great felicity; and [ye shall obtain] other things which you desire, [namely] assistance from God and a speedy victory.[69]

Having come to the resolution of prosecuting a holy war [against them], deem it expedient [agreeably to the text]

Command them to do what is lawful [proper], and prohibit their doing that which is unlawful; and observe the ordinances of God,

To make known what is the pure Mahomedan law, to all and every class of Musulmans, both far and near, and thereby to extract the cotton of negligence from the ears of their understanding; and more specially those persons who, unmindful of the meaning of the sacred text:

Do not obey the unbelievers and hypocrites, for certainly God is omniscient and all-wise.

Having yielded obedience to the infidels, and engaged in the service of those miserable tribes. It is therefore written to all those who reside in the dominions of the infidels,

They seek to deceive God and those who do not believe; but they
deceive themselves only, and are not sensible thereof. There is an
infirmity in their hearts. May God increase their infirmity!
They shall suffer a grievous punishment, because they have been
guilty of falsehood.[70]

And to whose situation the [above] verse may be justly
applied, that considering it to be their indispensable duty to
quit the territories of the unbelievers, they should repair, with
confident hearts and assured minds to these parts, where, by the
Divine blessing, they shall be still provided for than they
are at present, and their lives, honour, and property, remain
under the protection of God; while such as we are without
the means of subsistence there, shall have a suitable allowance
made to them here.

We have accordingly issued preemptory orders throughout
our dominions to this effect: 'Receive into your protection all
persons seeking refuge [in our territories] and report to the
Presence the particulars of their situation, in order that, if it
please God the Aider, due provision may be made for them.

Whosoever shall refuse to give ear to these words, shall
contravene their promulgation, shall be considered as destitute
of [every particle of] honour [or zeal], as a stranger to [or no
participator in] the bliss derived from [a steady]faith, and as
deserving to be banished from the presence of God, to be
excluded from the circle of the faithful and to be accounted as
one of the accursed infidels.

Verse from Hafiz:
If you place your foot in the path of law and of religion, Hafiz,
In reward for your zeal, the Chief of Nujuf [Ali] will
become your Protector

Let them not say of anything [or on any occasion] I will do so;
but if please God [it shall be done]. Grace be to him who follows
this direction.[71]

The Mysore Invasion

In early May 1786, the confederates attacked Badami on the northern
frontier of Mysore, with a strong force. It was a well-fortified town
under the commandant Haidar Bakhsh, with a garrison of about
3000 men. The fort was besieged and heavily attacked. The inmates
offered a stiff resistance though, rolling down heavy stones from the
walls and a relentless fire of musketry, causing the death of nearly
800 each of the Maratha and Nizam forces. It finally fell to the might
of the assailants on 20 May. Haidar Bakhsh was told to surrender
unconditionally, with the assurance that the lives of his garrison
would be protected. Though Parshuram Bhau suggested that he be
imprisoned, Nana and Haripant refused to heed his words as they
had promised amnesty.

After the fall of Badami, Nana, Mudhoji Bhosle and Parshuram
Bhau returned to their respective places, leaving Haripant in sole
command of the confederate forces. In June 1786, Haripant marched
to Gajendragadh, whose commander Rajjab Khan had refused to
surrender. Mysorean forces sent to relieve him were intercepted by
Haripant and, with no replenishment coming his way, Khan finally
surrendered. The confederate troops were then marshalled to reduce
Dharwar, Julihul, Navalgunda, Nargund and other places. Haripant
also managed to conquer Bahadur Benda while Raghunath Rao
Patwardhan besieged Koppal. Sensing an opportunity, the palegars of
Sirahatti, Damul, Kanakagiri and Anegondi switched their allegiance
to the Marathas. The northern frontiers of his kingdom seemed to
be slipping out of Tipu's hands. Forces under Burhan's father-in-
law, Badr-u-zaman Khan, joined him from Bidanur. Though not
effective enough for an offensive attack, Burhan managed to keep
the advancing Maratha armies in check.

Nana had dispatched Tukoji Holkar in February to counter Burhan. With Ganesh Pant Behre, Tukoji had managed to occupy several areas in the Kittur district, except its main fort. There was meanwhile trouble brewing for Tipu at Savanur. Though Haidar had made all attempts to establish cordial relations with the Nawab of Savanur and had also planned a double matrimonial alliance, after his death, relations progressively soured. The Nawab was stipulated to pay tributes to Mysore, which had fallen into arrears of nearly Rs 21 lakh. The Marathas had been instigating him to defy the agreements with Mysore and promised to come to his aid. While the Nawab had grudgingly paid half the tributes, he was procrastinating on the remaining part. Tipu sent his bankers, under Raghavendra Naik, with some troops to recover the remainder. On getting intelligence of this, Holkar and Behre attacked the banker midway and also exacted a ransom of Rs 2 lakh from them. Burhan, who had been closely watching their moves, marched towards Savanur to combat them. But he was defeated by the combined forces of the Marathas and the Nawab of Savanur.

Buoyed by this success, Tukoji Holkar marched towards Kittur with 15,000 troops, even as he left behind Ganesh Pant Behre at Bankapur with another 15,000 men to protect the Nawab of Savanur. Bapu Holkar was given the task of establishing Maratha supremacy in the Dharwar area. Behre managed to capture most of the territories in the Lakshmeshwar region, which originally belonged to the Patwardhans and had moved to Mysore. Soon Old Hubli too fell to their might. Though reinforced with forces from Bidanur under his father-in-law, the Mysorean forces under Burhan were hugely outnumbered by the confederate army. Barring the stronghold forts of Kittur and Dharwar that stoutly resisted all assaults, all the other places in the region fell like pins to the Maratha onslaught and Burhan could only watch helplessly.

Tipu Enters the Fray

Finally, in June 1786, when Tipu heard of the unending victories of the Marathas and their steady advance on the north of the Tungabhadra, he departed from Bangalore with six brigades of regular infantry, three regiments of regular cavalry, 10,000 irregular foot, 30,000 horse and twenty-two heavy guns. While the confederates were expecting him to rush to the relief of Burhan, Tipu surprised them with his sudden strategy. Gathering the support of the local palegars of Rayadurga, Harapanahalli and other places, he stormed the fort of Adoni, one of the Nizam's important frontier posts. It was under the command of Mahabat Jung, the son of Basalat Jung and the nephew of Nizam Ali. Tipu's strategy was clear—diverting the confederates from their attack on his northern borders and, if they persisted there, annex Adoni. The confederates could not afford to let the Nizam's kin suffer and also lose a frontier post.

Mahabat Jung was petrified at the sight of the advancing Mysore troops. He tried to buy out the invading troops and dispatched his minister, Asad Ali Khan, to Tipu, imploring him not to cause harm to him. Even Jung's widowed mother was urged to write a letter to Tipu to be kind to her son. Tipu replied to all these overtures sternly that he had no option in the wake of the alliance that Nizam Ali had finalized with Nana, and that Mahabat Jung could save himself if he joined Tipu's side against the confederates. Jung refused the offer and decided to open hostilities. Tipu thereafter opened up the trenches against Adoni and began military operations. The town was attacked and easily taken. Continuous cannonading from the Mysore side was intended to take the strongly built, too, and also prevent the confederates from rushing to the relief of Mahabat Jung. But the inmates of the fort offered stiff resistance to Tipu's actions. The Mysorean side suffered heavy losses in the process. By then, the Nizam and Nana had returned to their capitals, and the allied armies under Mughal Ali, younger brother of Nizam Ali, Mushir-ul-Mulk, Tej Jung, Tahawwar Jung, Ganesh Pant, Appa Balvant, Yashvant Rao Holkar, Parshuram Bhau, Haripant and others arrived with an army of about 60,000 men at the other side of the Tungabhadra in order to relieve Adoni. Tipu had little option but to finally lift the siege on 25 June, about ten days after the commencement of operations, and he stationed himself some distance away.

The confederates thereafter reached Adoni and decided to evacuate all the inmates to safety. There was a severe lack of supplies and the confederates were not sure that they could hold on for longer if Tipu laid siege again. Parshuram Bhau strongly opposed the move that he considered cowardly and pusillanimous, but there were few options left to them. The Nizam too had, as always, participated in a very half-hearted manner. But the confederates were in such haste and alarm that they left behind 'the whole of the wearing apparel of the females, and every article of household furniture belonging to them. In this naked condition, carrying the women along with them, they took at midnight the road of flight; and made a shameful retreat.'[72] As James Duff states: 'The retreat was judiciously executed; but the unpardonable oversight of leaving the fort, guns, ammunition and stores, without an attempt to render them unserviceable to their enemy, cancelled any merit the commanders might have otherwise claimed.'[73]

Mahabat Jung and his family were moved to the safety of Raichur fort. Tipu then sent Mir Sadak to take possession of the deserted fort of Adoni. He pursued the confederates across the Tungabhadra but not beyond a point as the river had by then swollen after the monsoon. Tipu merely managed to take some of his opponents as prisoners and seized a few of their possessions. The guns and stores in the Adoni fort were shifted to Gutti and Bellary. To prevent any future surrender of the place, the fortifications were demolished and Adoni was placed under the charge of Qutub-ud-din Khan Daulat Zai.

Attack on Savanur and After

Seeing the confederates comfortably camping on the other side of the river, Tipu decided to change his tactic. Braving the swollen Tungabhadra River, he and the Mysorean army attempted to cross it in pursuit of their opponents. Haripant had complacently ignored the warnings from the Nawab of Savanur that his spies were bringing in reports of Tipu attempting such daredevilry. Haripant meanwhile had been joined by Tukoji Holkar from Hubli and Raghunath Rao

Patwardhan from Koppal. As historian G.S. Sardesai notes: 'This was an occasion on which most of the Maratha chiefs and commanders except Mahadji Sindia were present in the camp which totaled some 75 thousand. They saw how powerful Tipu was on account of his disciplined infantry and efficient artillery. The Marathas depended solely on their old-fashioned guerilla tactics. The present occasion supplied a realistic demonstration of the comparative merits of the two methods of war on which depended the defence of national freedom, and which now came to be employed extensively on the large plain of Savanur.'[74]

Tipu made a few surprise nocturnal attacks but his designs were spoiled as the Marathas got wind of the plan ahead of time. The Marathas meanwhile slowly made their progress towards Savanur by October 1786, with Tipu in hot pursuit. Burhan and Badr-uz-Zaman Khan too joined him, along with a large tranche of provisions from Bidanur. Tipu was also joined by some irregulars under Ghazi Khan, his earliest military preceptor and one who was deeply respected by Haidar Ali as the best partisan in his army. In the middle of the night, four columns of the Mysorean army under Maha Mirza Khan, Burhan, Mir Moin-ud-din and the last one led by Tipu himself was to attack the Maratha camp from all sides. Tipu had lulled the Marathas by making mock demonstrations of attacks and then retreating. Though the dark, stormy night with incessant rains made sure that all the columns, except that of Tipu, lost their way, the Mysore forces opened heavy fire. This resulted in heavy losses for the Marathas, and Haripant ordered a quick retreat with all the troops, away from Savanur. This totally alarmed the Nawab of Savanur who had risked his family ties with Tipu to antagonize him. He knew that with the Marathas in flight, his life was at risk if he came under Tipu's attack. Leaving his son, Abdul Khire Khan (Khira Miyan), in the capital, the Nawab of Savanur, Abdul Hakim, fled from the place on 29 October. The Marathas sent him to Miraj to take refuge there. Tipu then easily took possession of Savanur. The Patwardhans openly confessed: 'Our tactics don't work before the enemy's heavy artillery.'[75] Tipu's triumph in Savanur was complete. The enormous

wealth and treasures that were accumulated there were looted to the
last brick. Mir Sadak and Madhi Khan Bakshi were sent to overlook
the capture and loot of Savanur. As Kirmani records:

> The officers sent, agreeably to their orders, without opposition
> from anyone, took and dispatched to the presence whatever they
> found of gold, silver, carpets, or tents, vessels, arms, etc. as for
> instance in Abdul Hakim's wardrobe, they found fifty turbans
> of different colours of the Boorhanpoor chintz kind, hung upon
> pegs in the wall, and honorary dresses of great splendour and
> value, of the same colour corresponding to the turbans, under
> cloth covers or in packages; but, besides these articles of great
> value brought from all countries laid about in heaps, and these
> with lists of all of them were sent to the Sultan, and after being
> inspected by him were deposited in the *Tosha Khana* [treasury
> in Srirangapatna]. The light guns were all added to the Sultan's
> artillery and one gun composed of five metals, twelve legal *guz*
> in length, was broken up and sent to the mint to be coined into
> half pence. In fact, all the valuables, among which were carpets
> of the most elegant pattern with gold and silver flowers, each the
> load of four or five camels, and the *Kaleechas* and *Surrinjas* (other
> kinds of carpets), of which each was the load of an elephant,
> were all seized by the Sultan's servants.[76]

Khira Miyan submitted himself to the Sultan and apologized for his
father's treachery. Tipu put him under strict surveillance, but given
the close relationship they shared, he spared his life.

After conquering Savanur, Tipu marched northwards, encamping
at Bankapur. Here, he distributed his army into four divisions, each
consisting of four kushoons, 5000 irregular foot, 5000 Sillahadar
horse and fifteen guns. They were placed under the command of
Mir Moin-ud-din (Saiyid Sahib), Burhan-ud-din, Maha Mirza
Khan and Husain Ali Khan. Tipu himself was at the command
of two kushoons (the Asad Ilahi and Ahmadi), three *mokubs* or
regiments of horse, 4000 *kuzzaks*, eight *dustas* (a *dusta* was about
1200) of the *paigah* or household horse and 10,000 *ahasham* infantry.

The first three divisions were directed against the dependencies of Hyderabad, conquest of those at Poona and for the maintenance of order in Raichur, Kittur and other places. The last division was to proceed to Srirangapatna to protect the capital and its adjoining areas. Tipu himself was to attack the Marathas. Mir Moin-ud-din made a surprise attack and occupied the hill fort of Mondergi Durg that was garrisoned by the Marathas. Burhan, too, took Bankapur and Misrikote that the Marathas held.

At this juncture of war, Tipu sent a letter to Tukoji Holkar:

> You have obtained experience in feats of arms, and are distinguished among the chiefs of superior valour. Now that war has commenced its destructive career, and thousands are doomed to fall, why should we longer witness the causeless effusion of human blood? It is better that you and I should singly descend into the field of combat; let the Almighty determine who is the conqueror and who the vanquished, and let that result terminate the contest. Or, if you have not sufficient confidence in your own single arm, take to your aid from one to ten men of your own selection, and I will meet you with equal numbers. Such was the practice in the days of our Prophet, and though long discontinued, I desire to renew that species of warfare. But if prudence should dictate your declining the second proposition also, let the two armies be drawn out, select your weapons, and let us, chief opposed to chief, horseman opposed to horseman, and foot-soldier opposed to foot-soldier, engage in a pitched battle, and let the vanquished become the subject of the victors.[77]

Tipu's proposition caused, according to Wilks, Holkar 'to tremble for his life, not a very consistent effect on an individual distinguished for rash fearlessness.'[78] His followers recommended war and Holkar hesitatingly agreed to face the enemy in battle, though something else was cooking in the background.

Tipu was also resorting to bribery of some of the Maratha chiefs, 'with assurances of a pacific nature to the confederates at large.'[79] Even as these attempts were underway, Tipu assembled his four divisions on the banks of the Gandaki River for a night attack on 2 December 1786. Arranging all his kushoons, he himself mounted an elephant and ordered the men of his household cavalry or paigah to march forth. The Marathas retaliated, and heavy action followed that went on for a day. But Tipu managed to completely overpower the opponent. He managed to get possession, among other booty, of the splendid camp equipage and stores of Tahawwar Jung and nearly 500 camels. Kirmani recounts how the fire of rockets and musketry from Tipu's army came blazing so close to Holkar's eyes that he 'immediately ran away leaving his favourite wife asleep in the tent.'[80] The Nizam and Mudhoji Bhonsle were the most affected by this raid. Their tents were pillaged and 'eighteen women, the wives of the Mahratta chiefs, with their gold and jewels taken.'[81] Kirmani states that Tipu let off these women after making them promise that they would convince their husbands to abandon the wasteful battle and sue for peace. The women on their return were however shunned by their husbands who apprehended that they had been violated by the Muslim camp. The women then loudly reproached their husbands for their 'illiberality . . . (and) want of shame'[82] and prevailed upon them to make peace with Tipu.

Recounting the Maratha debacle, Charles Malet, the British Resident in the Peshwa durbar, reports in his letter dated 12 December 1786 to Sir Archibald Campbell, the Governor of Madras:

> About 10 days ago Tippoo made a very serious night attack on the Mahratta Camp which fell more severely on the Bhonsla and Nizam's quarters, the bazaars and baggage of which was plundered by the enemy. Hurry Punt's quarters being less encumbered escaped better, but the whole army was thrown into great confusion, and Tippoo after remaining on the Mahratta ground all night, and finding in the morning that the enemy had retreated seven coss further, returned to his tents. This has been a severe blow on the Mahrattas and will I apprehend be found so in its consequences. The plunder acquired by it will in some measure reconcile Tippoo's troops to their bad payment, while the Mahrattas (who) used to

commit depredations on others will be greatly disconcerted on finding the tables turned.[83]

Malet also alluded to the fact that this night attack on the Marathas happened with the active connivance of Holkar with whom Tipu had been having secret dealings. There were reports of emissaries from Tipu's side moving in and out of Holkar's camps. Malet writes that 'he [Holkar] bore no part in the loss of the attack. He cannot be supposed from past events to have any personal affection for Nana or any desire to raise his glory. Politically he is certainly interested in the existence of a southern power to employ the attention of the Poona ministry. He has long complained of inattention to his pecuniary wants and has long been employed much against his inclination at a distance from his own *Jaghire* which has suffered great dilapidations in his absence.'[84] There was also talk about the other chief, Gangadhar Rao Raste, of the influential Brahmin family that had matrimonial ties with the Peshwa's family and estates in Bundelkhand, Nasik, Satara, Khandesh and other areas, too turning against the confederates in this campaign.[85] As Sardesai analyses: 'Tipu succeeded on account of his superior tactics, sudden movements, quick perception of the enemy's weak points and the readiness to take advantage of them. He deluded the Marathas by constantly keeping up a show of negotiations for peace. Holkar and some others were secretly seduced, the reports of which were freely discussed in the camp. Months were wasted by the Marathas in a desultory warfare. Haripant found it difficult to carry on the war.'[86] Tipu's well-disciplined forces with their superiority in infantry and artillery and his own strategic planning of the war contributed to his success. The other side, despite their numerical superiority, suffered from lack of vision and tact, indiscipline, infighting and jealousies among the chiefs, and the liability of the Nizam being part of the alliance.

After this victory, Tipu marched towards Koppal and Bahadur Benda. The strong fort of Bahadur Benda that Haripant had occupied was besieged by Tipu. After continued attacks for about nine to ten days, the fort fell to Tipu on 13 January 1787. Yvon, Malet's newsagent, wrote to him on 15 January, 'It is amazing such a strong fort as this was taken in seven or eight days and the Mahratta army between 4 or 5 leagues distance.'[87] The Hindu match-lock men in Bahadur Benda, who were formerly in Tipu's garrison and had shifted their allegiance to the Marathas, were severely punished with their noses and ears cut off, and Hanumant Naik, their chief, had both his legs amputated.[88] Tipu's further actions, especially his surprise nocturnal attacks, turned out to be unfavourable for the confederates, especially the Nizam whose troops were ill-organized.[89] The attacks continued till February 10 when a cessation of hostilities was finally announced.

Towards Peace

With the repeated reverses that their side faced, the internal rivalries and distrust among the Maratha chiefs and the tardy participation of the Nizam, Nana Phadnis saw little merit in continuing the wasteful battle. His hopes were dashed further when the new Governor-General Lord Charles Cornwallis, who had come to India in September 1786, bluntly refused to participate in any wars other than defensive ones. Negotiations then began from both sides to conclude the long-drawn battle and sue for peace. Badr-uz-Zaman Khan and Ali Raza Khan, two officers of the highest rank in the Mysore army, were sent for negotiations. From the Maratha side, Tukoji Holkar and Gangadhar Rao Raste conducted the talks that finally concluded on 14 February 1787. Interestingly, so terrorized were the Marathas by the surprise attacks at night conducted by Tipu that they apprehended through their spies that the delegation he sent too might be the Sultan's ploy to undertake a sudden ambush. The agents spent enough time assuring the Maratha chiefs that there was no malevolent intent on their part and that they had come there in good faith. Such was the terror that Tipu had inflicted on the Maratha chiefs.

It was thereafter agreed after lot of amendments, by April 1787, with the signing of the Treaty of Gajendragadh that Tipu, the Peshwa and the Nizam were to remain united and in possession of their former territories. If any fourth person made a hostile attempt on any of the allies' dominions, the others would join in repelling such moves. Tipu agreed to pay the arrears due to the Marathas on the condition of 'being acknowledged as the undisputed master of everything south of the Krishna River, from sea to sea.'[90] Of the Rs 65 lakh that was due from his side, Rs 12 lakh annually was to be paid and Rs 3 lakh towards the durbar expenses. Kittur and Nargund, that were the original cause of the war, were to be surrendered to the Peshwa, who was also granted possession of Badami. Gajendragadh and Dharwar were to remain with Tipu, as also Kanakagiri and Anegondi. Adoni was to be restored to Mahabat Jung. Savanur was to be restored to the Nawab only after he cleared his dues to Tipu. The Nizam had not even been made a party to the treaty initially due to the annoyance of the Marathas about his ineffective participation in the war. Only after his protests was his name included in the treaty and Tipu agreed to return some of the Nizam's frontier posts that he had captured. Writing about the treaty, Tipu recounts:

It was not my intention, in the beginning to have gone to war with the Mahrattas; but when they, thinking proper to requite the favours they had received from us, by a conduct entirely the contrary [to what I had a right to expect], had advanced [into my country], I consequently judged it necessary to repel their aggression, by just so much chastisement as should suffice to satisfy them, and make them solicit peace. Having brought the business accordingly to this point, I agreed to an accommodation, and to give them twelve lakhs of rupees. The treaty being concluded, I wrote [a letter] to Lewai Madhee Rao [Sawai Madhav Rao—Tipu address the Peshwa in the feminine as Madhee], which I sent to him, together with a *kulgy* and *surpaish* of precious stones and an elephant. I also sent an elephant, with a dress and jewels, to Tukojee Holkar;

and the same to Rao Rasta and to Hurry Pundit. These presents
I forwarded by the hands of confidential *vakeels*.[91]

While several of these terms were concluded, the point of debate and
disagreement came on an unexpected condition that Tipu put forth—
of 'being acknowledged and styled the *Bawdsha* of the Deccan, and
wants the Mahratta government to sign the present treaty to him as
such.'[92] The Peshwa, apparently to undermine Tipu, used to address
him often as Futteh Ali Khan, his childhood name. Tipu, in his
constant yearning for legitimacy and respectability among his peers,
hence made this title of 'Badshah' an important aspect of the treaty.
Haripant stoutly refused to accede to this demand, upon which
Holkar interceded, urging him to compromise as it was a relatively
trifling matter. They finally decided that Tipu would henceforth
be addressed as 'Tipu Sultan Bahadur Futteh Ali Khan.' As Malet
notes in his journal, 'the appellation of *Behadur* was the only word of
additional dignity to be used in the Paishwa's future address to this
prince, who is not even styled *Nabob* by this Durbar.'[93]

    After concluding peace, on the way back to Srirangapatna,
Tipu subjugated Harapanahalli and Rayadurga. The palegars
Venkatapati of Rayadurga and Basappa Naik of Harapanahalli had
earlier pledged their loyalty to Haidar Ali but hardly lived up to it.
They constantly joined hands with the enemies of Mysore. During
the current Mysore–Maratha War, they had leaked secrets to the
other side, especially while Tipu was at Savanur, and also made
unsuccessful attempts to assassinate him. In the midst of the war,
Tipu did not want to punish them. But now that peace had been
concluded, he sent about 2000 men to storm the forts and take it
by force. The palegars were imprisoned and sent away as prisoners
in irons to Bangalore and then to Kabbaladurga, where they faced a
miserable death.

'Padshah' Tipu Sultan Bahaddur's Sultanat

For Tipu, it was a victorious return to Srirangapatna. In merely five
years after his sudden succession following the death of his father,

he had humbled the British and made them sign a humiliating treaty, overpowered the Marathas and thwarted their attempts to upstage him, established his supremacy over the territories south of the Krishna River, subjugated rebellious palegars and chieftains including rebellions in Coorg, as also palace coup attempts of internal sabotage. He had every reason to feel puffed by the string of successes that had come his way. After his Coorg expedition, while he styled himself as an emperor like Shah Alam, this time around there were legitimate reasons to elevate his stature. It was a constant embarrassment for Tipu that there was no legal sanction or title that he held that stamped his authority as the legitimate ruler of Mysore. Though the Mughal emperor's position had been thoroughly weakened after the death of Aurangzeb, still it was his imperial authority that granted various powers in the subcontinent to hold territories, wield power or collect revenue and taxes. In the past, the Wodeyars, too, under Chikkadevaraja Wodeyar, had obtained this right from the Mughal emperor. The Marathas, the Nizam and the Nawab of Arcot possessed legal authority sanctioned by the Mughal court. The Nizam was the legitimate Viceroy of the Mughals in the Deccan. The Arcot Nawab too had wrested his title 'Walajah' and the authority to rule the Carnatic, as technically a dependent state of the Nizam. Even the East India Company sought *sannads* (legal claims) and titles from the same power, even though it was a figurehead, a weakened one. This practice carried on till 1858, till the overthrow of Bahadur Shah Zafar.

Legally speaking, Haidar had a claim on his authority as it was granted formally to him by Immadi Krishnaraja Wodeyar who had appointed him. Of course, that did not make him a part of the big league and he was often referred to as just as a powerful zamindar of the Maharaja of Mysore. But even that position was not a hereditary one. Tipu, having deposed the Wodeyar and assuming independent charge, was hence always looked down upon, insulted and chastised as being a mere upstart and usurper, and not a legal claimant. Hence, his burning desire to remedy this situation at the earliest by seeking the validation of his authority from his peers and the superior, the Mughal. This explains why he insisted on the titles from the Peshwa

too during the conclusion of the treaty in 1787, but that was not to
come. Without this stamp of approval, all his victories and military
successes had little meaning, as he was not respected as a legitimate
sovereign in the country.

Acutely aware of this position, in 1783, he had tried to obtain
the sannad of Arcot and a rank of 7000 through Mukunda Rao, his
vakil in Delhi. He even offered to pay the peshkush or tributes and
a large sum of money to the emperor. Tipu even asked the French to
intercede on his behalf and convince the emperor regarding this. The
French representative in Delhi, Montigny, managed to lobby hard
for Tipu's case and even won over several of the emperor's nobility
to his side. The Emperor Shah Alam at that time was considering
an alliance with the French against the British, whose rising power
he was increasingly threatened by. So Tipu strongly believed that he
had a good chance to get this task done through the French, under
Colonel Demonte. But all these efforts were thwarted by Major
Brown, the British representative in Delhi, and Majdud-ud-daulah,
the emperor's favourite minister who was in favour of aligning with
the East India Company. Possibly to safeguard their allies in the
Deccan, the Nizam and the Nawab of Arcot, who detested Tipu and
felt threatened by him, the British prevailed upon Shah Alam not
to confer any such sannads on Tipu granting him legal legitimacy
to rule Mysore. The court intrigues had the better of him and the
emperor finally refused Tipu's offer. He instead merely granted Tipu
an impressive title to mollify him—Umdat-ul-Mulk Mubarak-ud-
Daulat Tipu Sultan Fath Ali Khan Bahadur Hizbar Jang Fadwi
Shah Alam Badshah Ghazi.[94]

In a letter expressing his servility and respect for the emperor,
Tipu wrote to Shah Alam on 23 June 1785:

Upon receipt of the Imperial Mandate, [my] glorified head
touched the summit of honour. The special gifts of ennobling
quality, which your Majesty, in your boundless favour, graciously
bestowed [on me], by the hands of Rao Bal Mukn Doss, also
arrived in the most auspicious conjuncture, and put [me] in

possession of the wealth of distinction and pre-eminence. In acknowledgement of this magnificent donation, I respectfully offer my most humble obeisance. This steadfast believer, with a view to the support of the firm religion of Mahommed, undertook [some time since] the chastisement of the Nazarene tribe [the British, Christians in general]; who unable to maintain the war I waged against them, solicited peace [of me] in the most abject manner. This is so notorious a fact, as not to require to be enlarged on. With the divine aid and blessing of God, it is now again my steady determination to set about the total extirpation and destruction of the enemies of the faith. In token of my sincere attachment to your Majesty, I send, by way of *Nuzr*, a hundred and twenty-one gold *Mohrs* to your resplendent presence; let them be honoured by Your Majesty's acceptance. I am humbly hopeful that I may continue to be honoured and distinguished by the receipt of your ennobling commands, More would exceed the bounds of respect.[95]

It was thus Tipu's first salvo against Shah Alam where, after his Coorg expedition, he issued orders that the *khutba* or Friday sermons be made in his name and not that of the emperor's as was the common practice in mosques all over the country. The religious heads in Mysore, the *ulama*, do not seem to have opposed this decision and readily acquiesced to his demand. It was a religious sanction, more than a royal or legal one, that he conferred on himself. That this was paramount on his mind becomes clear when he made this an important clause of negotiation with the Marathas at the conclusion of the long war in 1787. While the confederates might not have bestowed on him his coveted title of Padshah, there was nothing that could stop him from assuming the same for himself. The sweet allure and intoxication of victory is a heady feeling for any soldier, and Tipu was no different.

On a chosen Friday, the announcements were made all over the capital of the new title and the prayers were read in the name, and for the well-being, of Padshah Tipu Sultan Bahaddur. This was a direct challenge to Shah Alam and was possible because of the totally enfeebled and weakened position of the figurehead emperor in Delhi. Tipu could call himself whatever he wished to, but obviously the writ ran only within the dominion of Mysore where he was the dictator. No one outside legitimized this and it is possible that they scoffed at his attempts, causing him more angst about his inferior status.

In an assertion of his authority, he struck new silver coins and rupees called Imami. On one side of it was written: 'The religion of Ahmed enlightened the world from the victories of Hydur' and on the obverse, 'He is the sole or only just king.'[96] The higher denomination coins in gold and silver carried a *julus* or reign year, 'a very public declaration of kingship.'[97] Unlike other Indian rulers and their coins, none of his coins referenced the Mughal emperor or his reign year. They had insignias of an elephant, again as a royal indicator. In all, Tipu struggled hard to assert his claim and independence despite the lack of support from anywhere.

In another show of imperial might, a grand royal mosque was planned to be built in Srirangapatna from 1783–84. Over two years and at an expense of Rs 3 lakh, 'the prayers of Eedi Fitr, in the year 1204 Hijri [1789–90 CE] were the first said in that mosque, and it was named by the Sultan [as] Masjid-e-Ala.'[98] Kirmani states that the site of the construction of this mosque too had a backstory. During the treachery of Khande Rao, when Haidar Ali was forced to abandon his family and flee to Bangalore, Rao had confined Haidar's family in a house near the Gunjam gate of the fort. Just before this house stood an ancient Hindu temple, which had a large courtyard where Hindu children played. Tipu, who was a young boy of six or seven then, would often leave his house and stand there watching in amusement the kids at play. On one such occasion, a fakir who was passing by saw young Tipu and predicted a glorious, kingly future for him. Kirmani writes:

[The Fakir said:] 'Fortunate child, at a future time thou wilt be the king of this country, and when time comes, remember my words: take this temple and destroy it, and build a Musjid in its place, and for ages it will remain a memorial of thee.' The Sultan smiled and in reply told him, 'That whenever, by his blessing, he should become a Padishah, or king, he would do as he [the fakir] directed.' When, therefore, after a short time his father became a prince, the possessor of wealth and territory, he remembered his promise, and after his return from the Nuggur and Gorial Bunder [Mangalore], he purchased the temple from the adorers of the image in it (which after all was nothing but the figure of a bull, made of brick and mortar) and with their goodwill and the Brahmins, therefore taking away their image, placed it in the Deorai Peenth [Gunjam gate], and the temple was pulled down, and the foundations of a new Musjid raised on the site, agreeably to a plan of the mosque, built by Ali Adil Shah, at Beejapoor, and brought from thence.[99]

To imprint his stamp on every aspect of governance, driven by this very insecurity, Tipu began attempting several measures. He divided his Sarkar-e-Khudadad or God-given kingdom into three distinct parts. The coastal region was termed Suba Yum (the sea), the cities and towns in the hilly and woody areas were terms Suba Turun and the open, level country as Suba Ghubra (the earth). In a kingdom where Kannada was widely spoken, these measures to name regions in Persian were obviously not in sync with the aspirations of the people. The chief officers of *parganas* or administrative units were called Asof. Around every city, town and fort, at the distance of one *fursung* (4½ miles), a strong stockade was built with four gates. These were manned regularly by guards, and no one could cross them without the permission of the guards. He even stockaded the frontier between the limits of Mysore and the districts of the Carnatic–Payanghat, preventing anyone from entering Mysore from the Payanghat or from leaving the Balaghat region. In a typical assertion of his royal stature, he began issuing *hukumnamahs* or declarations of rules and regulations related to various departments of government, such as revenue, treasury, armoury, granary, kitchen, hospital and so on. Tipu's manufactories were called Tara Mandal (literally, constellation) and established in Srirangapatna, Bangalore, Chitradurga and Bidanur.

Tipu also seemed most eager to obliterate every trace of the previous Wodeyars from whom his father had usurped the kingdom. Old palaces, forts, bridges and buildings that were built over centuries by the Hindu rulers were all ruthlessly brought down and in their very place, new monuments erected. The city of Mysore too became a victim to this zealous effort. As Wilks states: 'The town and fort of Mysoor, the ancient residence of the rajas [Wodeyars], and the capital from which the whole country derived its name, was an offensive memorial of the deposed family, and he determined that the existence, and if possible, the remembrance of such a place, should be extinguished. The fort was levelled with the ground, and the materials were employed in the erection of another fortress on a neighbouring height . . . the town was utterly destroyed and the inhabitants were ordered to remove at their option, to Gunj-aum [Ganjam] on the island of Seringapatam, or to the *Agrar* [Agrahara: Brahmin village] of Bumboor, now to be named Sultaun-pet, a little to the southward of that island.'[100] Names of places were all Islamized. Mysore city, after its destruction, was renamed Nazarbad or the place visited by the eye of the Almighty.

Another area where he wished to leave his imprint was in the calendar system. He devised his own calendar called Mauludi. The normal Hijri calendar that the Muslims used worldwide had the twelve months based on the moon cycles. It fell short of the solar calendar by about eleven days. This also impacted decisions related to land revenue and taxation for the governments if they used the Hijri calendar as progressively, the number of days/months in the lunar system would be lesser. Even as he wanted to impose the Muslim calendar on Mysore, Tipu realized this drawback. Sometime between January and June 1784 is when he is supposed to have innovated this new system of the Mauludi calendar. This new era that he sought to begin had twelve luni–solar years of twelve lunar months. The shortage of eleven days was regularized by adopting the intercalary months from the Hindu Panchanga (calendar) that was prevalent in Mysore. Like the Hindu calendar, the Mauludi too was divided into cycles of sixty years each with a different name and then repeating thereafter. The years and months were all given new names by him: Chaitra month was called Ahmedy, Vaishakha as Behary, Jyeshta as Jaffury, Ashadha as Daraey, Shravana as Hashimy, Bhadrapada as Wassaey, Ashwija as Zuburjudy, Kartika as Haidari, Margashira as Tulooey, Pushya as Yoosufy, Magha as Eezidy and Phalguna as Byazy. The digits of the four numerals that constituted the year in this system were to be read right to left, unlike the Hijri's left to right. The new year began, like it did for the Hindus on Ugadi, and the days were mere equivalents of the *tithis* or the lunar days in the Panchang. The power of each letter depended on its place in the alphabet. Thus, the numerical letters composing the name of every year when added indicated the place-value of that year in the cycle. Months too were ordered in a manner that the first letter of each showed its place-value in the year as in the alphabet. The calendar though was hardly popular and lasted as long as Tipu was alive. After him, the calendar too vanished.

As Josyer writes:

Regulations military, naval, commercial, fiscal; police, judicature, and ethics were embraced by the code of this Minos: and his reformation of the Calendar and of the system of weights and measures, was to class him with those philosophical statesmen and sovereigns of whose useful labours his secretary had obtained some obscure intelligence. It may be briefly stated regarding the whole, that the name of every object was changed: of cycles, years, months; weights, measures, coins, forts, towns, offices—military and civil, the official designations of all persons and things without exception—a single parody of what was transpiring in France. The administration itself was called Sarkar Khodadad or God-Given Government. Persian was introduced for military commands and official use. Exports and imports were prohibited, for the protection of domestic trade; liquor shops were abolished. Lands and grants of Hindu temples, and the service Inams of Patels were confiscated. The revenue regulations of Chikkadevaraja Wodeyar, however, remained unaltered, but were re-published as ordinances of the Sultan. He strove, in short, to obliterate every trace of the previous rulers. For this purpose, even the fine irrigation works, centuries old, of the Hindu Rajas were to be destroyed and reconstructed in his own name.[101]

Tipu's Foreign Embassies

In this quest for legitimacy and acceptance, Tipu decided to approach a higher authority, after being rebuffed by the Mughal emperor. The Muslim world, the *ummah,* and its interconnectedness through the authority of the Caliph, was Tipu's next refuge. In the past, right from the slave dynasty of Iltutmish to the Tughlaqs, Lodhis and other nawabs, several Muslim rulers had sought royal status from the Caliph. It was only the Mughals who considered themselves as sovereigns of their kingdom and did not seek the approval from the Caliph. So Tipu too decided to turn westward to the Ottoman Caliph in Constantinople after being rebuffed within the subcontinent. He also wanted to seek the Caliph's support in terms of money and soldiers to fight the British and their allies. Even Haidar Ali had obtained a body of 1000 men from Shiraz in Persia in 1775.[102]

Tipu played to the religious sentiments of the Caliph by informing him that the British had occupied dominions of the Mughal emperor in Bengal, Carnatic and other places and had been steadily converting Muslims to Christianity and hence it was the Caliph's religious duty to intervene and save fellow-Muslims.[103] To the Caliph for instance, he writes in a hukumnamah dated 17 November 1785: 'When the dominance of infidelity reached its acme, the ardour for Islam was enflamed, and our master [Haidar Ali] launched an attack on the faithless Christians, sent thousands of them to the lowest hell and made many of them captives and prisoners . . . You, who are a great King of Muslims, should strive by all means to strengthen the True Religion. Whatever is required from the Government of our master [Tipu] will be furnished . . . the faithless Christians need to receive chastisement from the King of Muslims. Whatever forces the Ruler of Turkey would send abroad ships, whatever expenditure is incurred on them will be paid by us . . . Whenever [the Ottoman emperor] asks for the return of his army, it will be sent back on the ships of our Government.'[104] In his letters to his envoys though, the kings of England and France are referred to as rajas, and the Sultan of Turkey is not called Caliph but as 'Khundkar' or Sultan and at certain places as *Qaiser-i-Rum* (Sultan of Turkey) and *Padshah-i-Ahl-i-Islam* or the king of all Muslims.[105]

An initial embassy was sent in 1784 under Othman Khan, formerly Tipu's valet, more as a roving expedition to gather a sense of the mood in Constantinople. A permanent vakil from Mysore was stationed in Muscat, which was an important emporium of trade between India, the Red Sea and the Persian Gulf. A factory too was established in Muscat in 1785. After Othman Khan's return, in quick succession, on 17 November 1785, a large contingent from Mysore headed to the port of Tadri on the Malabar coast, under the leadership of Ghulam Ali Khan. He was one of Tipu's trusted officers and had entered the Mysorean service from Arcot in 1780 when Haidar Ali had captured the fort there. He was accompanied by Lutf Ali Khan, Shah Nurullah and Muhammad Haneef. Nurullah was a Sayyid of Persian origin and Haidar Ali had earlier sent him to Shiraz in 1770 to obtain military help from Mohammad Karim Khan-i-Zand, the founder of the Zand dynasty that held sway over most of Persia (Iran), except for Khorasan. Karim Khan had offered Bandar Abbas to Haidar but he was unable to take complete advantage of this.[106]

In four ships named *Ghurab-i-Surati*, *Fakhr-ul-Marakib*, *Fath-i-Shahi* and *Nabi Baksh*, more than 900 men, which included secretaries, vakils, interpreters, sweepers, cooks and soldiers, carried with them several precious gifts, sandalwood products, spices, rich garments, jewellery, ivory and four elephants. They were to call upon the Caliph, the Ottoman Sultan Abdul Hamid I, in Istanbul. Along with seeking the Caliph's grant of legal sanction to rule Mysore, Tipu's entreaty to him had several other points. Mysore and the Ottoman Caliphate were to remain cordial friends at all times and the latter was to send to Mysore a body of skilled troops that Tipu would maintain at his expense. They would be sent back at Tipu's

expense if the Caliph so needed them. Mysore also sought from the
Ottomans skilled technicians who could make muskets, guns, glass,
chinaware and so on. Mysore was also to be given trading facilities
in the Ottoman Empire and in reciprocation he would offer similar
privileges to them in his kingdom. The port of Mangalore was to
be gifted to the Caliph in return for the port of Basra, the chief
port of Iraq. They also sought permission to erect a commercial
factory at Basra with exclusive privileges. The embassy was also
tasked with promoting the trade of Mysore in Muscat, Persia and
the Ottoman Empire. Mysore already had an agent and warehouse
in Muscat and this embassy was to provide a further fillip to these
commercial aspirations. The items they were carrying on board
the ships were both presents for the Caliph and his nobility, and
also served as advertisements of Mysorean products in important
ports of the Middle East. The original plan was that the embassy
was to proceed from Constantinople to France and then England,
too, on this mission. The idea here seems to be that in the wake of
the French betrayal in the Second Anglo–Mysore War, of pulling
out abruptly, whether Mysore could try out the support of a new
country like Turkey, more so since they were co-religionists. If this
plan failed, the idea seems to have been to pursue France to forge a
common and well-defined alliance with Mysore against the British
and entice them with a share of the British possessions in India. If
all of these failed, the final resort was to attempt an alliance with
the British themselves, provided they handed over Tiruchirapalli to
Mysore from their ally, the Nawab of Arcot.

Even before the embassy left, Tipu had made it abundantly clear
to them that they needed to keep their eyes and ears open about
everything that they encountered and document everything down:

> The particulars of every stage of journey and leading officials of each
> of the three States [Turkey, France and England], with indications
> of the status of the said leading officials and descriptions of their
> affairs as discovered [by you] and the industries and rarities of each
> city and territory and the account of the affairs of the cities, should
> be written down in front of each of you, in the hand of both the

said munshis and by the Persian-writing *mutasaddi* [official], each in a separate book.[107]

He also ordered them to bring back stone-coal (*sang-i-angisht*) from Turkey in ships as ballast.[108] They were to also get from Turkey 'better craftsmen to manufacture muskets, cannon pieces, clocks (*gharial*), glass, chinaware and mirrors'.[109] Good carpenters and ironsmiths for the construction of ships and those craftsmen unavailable in India were to be brought along from both Turkey and France.[110] Silkworms and those who cultivated them were also recommended to be brought in, as were twelve eunuchs (*khoja*) aged nine or ten, belonging preferably to the Abyssinian (*habshi*) race.[111] Tipu also asked his envoys to bring back for him five or six fair-faced girls from amongst Turks, Arabs or Mughals after paying whatever needed to be, for their purchase.[112] In his letters and *hukumnamahs* to the embassy, Tipu gave them clear and detailed instructions on what to do, what all to stock in their ships, what dresses to wear and how to reach Constantinople, in the same manner that Othman Khan had. For instance, he wrote on 1 March 1786:

It is our wish to obtain the possession of the port of Bussorah (Basra) in farm. Consequently, we are for several reasons, well-pleased at your going to that place. Proceeding thither, accordingly, you will examine into the state of things there, and make every [necessary] enquiry respecting the port, where you will, at the same time, dispose of your merchandize. From thence you must repair straight to Nujuf [the sacred place of the Karbala plains where the battle between the sons of Ali and Yezeed took place], the most noble, where presenting[113] our very humble duty, you will represent in the most respectful and submissive manner, that if it be agreeable [to the priests in charge of the holy shrine] to have an aqueduct brought to Nujuf the most noble [from the Euphrates], and they will signify their pleasure to that effect, we will, in the following year, send the necessary people and money for its construction.[114]

It was rather presumptuous of Tipu to assume that he would be permitted to dig a canal to bring the waters of the Euphrates to the holy shrine of Nejef. This was his attempt to also pit himself as a global pan-Islamic philanthropist. As Kirkpatrick analyses: 'The Sultan's project of acquiring possession of Bussorah was, probably, as extravagant as any he ever entertained. By what means he could hope to attain such an object, it would be difficult to conceive . . . it has been said that that the ambassadors were empowered to offer Mangalore in exchange for it. But it is unlikely that a prince of the Sultan's characteristic jealousy and distrust should have consented to such an arrangement: and the letter before us . . . [is] not containing the most distant allusion to an exchange, it distinctly speaks of his wish "to farm" the port in question.'

The diary of the embassy, *Waqai-i-Manazil-i-Rum*, maintained by the secretary Khwaja Abdul Qadir, has graphic details of the journey undertaken, the places visited and the people they met. It was in accordance with Tipu's instructions to the embassy to document everything related to their journey. From the Malabar, they sailed to Muscat by 8 April 1786, and to Bushire, Kharag, Khor Basra and then Basra by 22 August 1786. They met several influential people in all the destinations, seeking commercial relations with Mysore. Sulaiman Pasha, the Governor of Basra on the Persian Gulf, received them hospitably. But the delegation was detained in Basra for several months before obtaining permission to sail to Constantinople. During this detention, the envoys made their religious pilgrimage to the holy shrines of Nejef and Karbala.

It was only by 5 November 1787, close to two years since they sailed from the Malabar coast, that they finally met the Caliph and the Grand Vizier. The elephants had sadly died on the way, even before they reached Basra. The Caliph received them with high honours and invested them with sable furs and the two secretaries with ermine furs. Importantly for Tipu, the envoy managed to obtain from the Caliph the permission to assume the title of an independent king of Mysore, strike coins and also have the khutba read in his name. Letters professing friendship, a sword and a shield studded with precious stones were presented to Tipu by the Caliph and the Grand Vizier. However, none of the commercial concessions or military assistance was agreed upon by the Ottoman empire.

Wilks narrates the fiasco that the conversation with the Grand Vizier, his Reis Effendi, the Ottoman Minister of foreign affairs, the Ratib or interpreter and the embassy turned out to be:

> Vizeer: Open your business.
>
> Gholaum Ali: Our master is anxious for the establishment of a direct intercourse between the two countries, and offers as a *nezer*, the fort and territory of Mangalore.
>
> Vizeer: It shall be considered, proceed!
>
> Gholaum Ali: He wishes in return, to be favoured with the port and territory of Bussora.
>
> Ratib (Before translating to his superior): Bethink yourselves of where you are, and whom you are addressing and speak with discretion.
>
> Shah Noor Ullah: Why, what mighty affair is a sea-port? When I was on an embassy to Persia, Kurreem Khan, the king, offered me two sea-ports as a personal interest.
>
> Reis Effendi (after hearing the interpretation): And pray, Sir, who may you be? And where have you left your senses? Who is your king Kurreem Khan? And before whom do you speak? Kurreem Khan was a black guard.

Gholaum Ali, finding that matters were going wrong, interposed to explain away the proposition, into a request for the Sultaun's ships being hospitably received at the port of Bussora.[115]

When the request to dig the canal to the Nejef was suggested to the Grand Vizier, who was already annoyed, he smiled and mockingly replied in Turkish to the embassy that 'if the thing was proper, it would be effected without the aid of the mighty Tipu Sultan'.[116] In fact, when they had made the proposal to Sulaiman Pasha, the Governor of Basra, in his characteristic wit and mocking tone, he had told them that 'the suggestion had once been made in days of yore, but had been forbidden in the dream or revelation of a saint, and that without some communication of assent from the invisible world, the project could not be resumed!'[117] That the diplomats were anything but diplomatic seemed to become evident in their conversations with the high-ranking officials of the empire.

Tipu seemed to be extremely annoyed with the embassy for their delayed journey and possible tardiness. In a letter to Ghulam Ali Khan, Lutf Ali Khan and Shah Nurullah, he angrily writes:

> It is astonishing, that notwithstanding the written instructions [which you have received on this head], you should instead of writing to us in detail, refer us to a letter from Shah Noorullah. It appears by this, that you never look at your instructions; agreeably to the saying, 'the epistles of lovers [are hung or placed] upon deer's horns.' Do not lose your wits in this manner, but act according to your instructions . . . we have invested you with full powers; you should therefore, act in all matters, according as you may think best suited to the circumstances of the moment, and not wait for our orders . . . we have learned from report that one of the elephants which you took with you died on your way to Muscat. It is astonishing that you should not have mentioned this circumstance.[118]

The conduct of some of the members of the embassy too does not seem to have been very appropriate. The *Waqai* journal notes:

> Lutf Ali Khan, sitting in a palanquin, wandered about the lanes and bazars of Basra. Setting down his palanquin at this place and that, he engaged in buying small cornelian stones, etc., thus throwing to the wind all respect for his status of a chief, his palanquin and the good name of this Government. Previously too, he twice went about in lane and bazar, visiting every shop, and arguing with each shop-keeper and grocer over every copper coin.[119]

The embassy came at a huge cost for the Mysore kingdom. In addition to the enormous expenditure involved, there was immense loss of life and suffering that the travellers underwent. As luck would have it, while they were in Constantinople, the plague broke out there, killing several members of the delegation, who suffered in addition to fever, cold and dysentery. By the end of January 1788, only seventy members of the group survived and just a handful managed to return to their homes. Three of the four ships they had sailed in were wrecked or destroyed. Politically too, the situation was extremely unlucky for the embassy. The alliance between Russian Empress Catherine II and Austrian Emperor Joseph II to partition the European provinces of the Ottoman empire and place Catherine's grandson, Constantine, on the throne had sparked off great turmoil in the entire region. Consequently, Turkey had declared war on Russia, just months before the embassy reached there. The outbreak of the Russo–Turkish War (1787–92) and the Austro–Turkish War (1788–91) had plunged the region into great chaos. At such a politically volatile time, Turkey was looking for allies and support in the European world. While France initially remained lukewarm, the British were more than keen to support Turkey's cause and restore the balance of power. In such circumstances, Tipu seeking an alliance with the Ottoman Caliph against the British or Turkey's help to oust the British from India which hardly featured on the radar of the Caliph, did not make much sense to the Ottomans. The embassy returned with not much to celebrate about and also after having suffered immensely in the course of this long sojourn. On the sad turn of fortunes for the unlucky embassy on their return to Srirangapatna, Hayavadana Rao writes:

> The cost of the embassy was estimated at Rupees Twenty Lakhs, and besides return presents of ornamented sword and shield and friendly and congratulatory letters from the Viziers, the only value received in turn, as was slily observed, was a *firman* from the Sultan of Constantinople, and sixty-five half quires of journal worth about five rupees! But Tipu, attributing no part of this result to his own folly and ignorance, ascribed the whole to the unskillfulness or dishonesty of Ghulam Ali Khan, who was soon divested of all his

employment and ordered to confine himself to his house. During
the investigation that preceded this result, Tipu one evening
directed one of the officers-in-waiting to call the *man-eaters*. The
officer stared; and Tipu explained by desiring him 'to call the men
who had lately returned from Room (Constantinople) after eating
their companions.' This joke became current as long as its novelty
lasted, the ambassadors were distinguished by the nick-name of
the *man-eaters!*[120]

Thus ended the sad tale of the unfortunate embassy to Constantinople
and its ambassadors. However, Tipu's position seemed to be
bolstered by the sanction he obtained from the Caliph to rule as
an independent sovereign. On the advice of his loyalists, Tipu then
'collected all the treasures of the state, or rather assumed the pomp
and splendour of royalty, and directed the formation of a throne
of gold, ornamented with jewels of great value in the shape of a
tiger.'[121] The motif of the tiger and its growling visage became
a personification of the Sultan and his power. Tiger stripes were
adopted in the uniform of the infantry, in the insignia of royalty, as a
distinctive ornament in palaces and in casting guns. In his residence
too, outside the court of entrance, royal tigers were found chained
to symbolize the might of the Sarkar-e-Khudadad. The golden
throne that he got commissioned took a while to be built. It had an
octagonal wooden platform that was raised about 4 feet from the
ground. The eight supports to this platform were in the form of
tiger's legs. Above each support was a small, jewelled tiger head,
while the front had a full life-size tiger head as a support. It was made
of solid gold and glittered with the most precious of stones making
up its eyes and teeth. One ascended the throne by a stairway of silver
steps which were secured with silver nails on either side. Above the
richly ornamented canopy was suspended a beautiful, dazzling and
fluttering *humma*, the mythical bird of paradise, made of beautiful
precious stones like diamonds, rubies and emeralds. This was in
conformation with the Islamic belief that the head on which the
shadow of this bird falls is destined to wear a royal crown. The entire

height of the throne, including the canopy, was about eight to nine feet. It was another matter that Tipu never got an opportunity to sit on this throne as future events were to unfortunately prove for him.

Embassy to France

Frustrated with his embassy to Constantinople that was initially envisaged to visit France and England too, Tipu decided to send another special embassy to France. But surprisingly, in his reprimanding letters to Ghulam Ali Khan, he never revoked the earlier embassy or revealed to them the formation of a new embassy to France, Instead, he kept informing them that their visit to France was still on the cards, though perhaps at a later time. The reason was perhaps because the new embassy was on its way to Pondicherry then and there was a likelihood of its detention there for some time before they could set sail. In fact, that embassy took off from the French Presidency only by the middle of 1787.

Tipu had not been particularly happy with the French conduct in the Second Anglo–Mysore War. They had not helped him as much as they had promised and had midway advocated peace and cessation of hostilities with the British, given their international commitments with England. The French were aware of having rubbed Tipu the wrong way and wished to make amends. The Governor-General of the French establishments in the East, Vicomte de Souillac, wrote to him on 19 August 1785, urging Tipu to let bygones be bygones and saying that the two allies must plan a comprehensive strategy to oust the British from India. Souillac's agent, Rama Rao, even came to Mysore with several promises on how the partnership between the two could be strengthened. The French did not want to antagonize any of the major Indian powers by aligning with one against another. Souillac's idea was to create a larger Indian confederacy that included Tipu, Nana and the Nizam, under their leadership, that could thwart British designs in India. But Souillac did not have a very favourable opinion of Tipu and considered him to be 'proud, vain, imperious and undependable' and felt that it would be good if he 'were beaten and humiliated [by the British], for then he would throw himself into the arms of the French.'[122]

However, David Charpentier de Cossigny, the Governor of Pondicherry, differed with Souillac's views and considered Tipu the most important power that they must ally with to drive the British out. Cossigny kept warning Nana that if the major powers did not unite against the British, their positions would be reduced to what had happened to the Nawabs in Bengal and Awadh. Even during the confederates' invasion of Mysore, Cossigny played an active role in trying to mediate peace with Mysore and convincing the Marathas and the Nizam about the futility of the war. He even favoured an alliance and military support to Tipu. But the sixteenth article of the Treaty of Versailles, signed in 1783, forbade the English and the French from participating in the wars of the Indian powers. So, unless the British joined the Marathas to attack Tipu, there was no way that the French could ally with him.

The French also sought a larger establishment on the Malabar coast as Mahe had been destroyed by the British in the previous war. But Tipu was wary of them this time and kept his promises evasive. Instead of talking to the officials here, Tipu was mulling on the idea of negotiating directly with the King of France, Louis XVI, and his ministers. Meanwhile, back in France there was growing interest in reviving trade opportunities with India that had been on the wane. Under the finance minister, Charles Alexandre de Calonne, who headed a court capitalists' group that was close to Queen Marie-Antoinette, there were plans to run the French East India Company as a purely for-profit business venture, rather than letting it be subservient to the changing political interests of the Crown.

In the interim, Tipu's stellar successes in the war against the confederates and the French failure to manage any inroads into the courts of Poona and Hyderabad that were vigorously guarded by the British Residents there, changed Souillac's policy and attitude towards Mysore. He began to look more favourably, as Cossigny had suggested, at aligning with Tipu. Tipu had also very graciously forgiven the dues of Rs 17 lakh that Haidar had loaned to the French during the Second Anglo–Mysore War. This showed that he was genuinely keen on pursuing a friendship with France. Souillac and

Cossigny were now on the same page in terms of allowing Tipu to send an embassy to Louis XVI to negotiate a lasting alliance between Mysore and France. Since the embassy to Constantinople was in no position to further its journey to Paris, a new embassy had to be sent. But the expenses of this new embassy from Mysore to Paris were to be borne by the French government, as a measure of goodwill. The boat that was to carry the envoys, *Roi l'aurore*, was gifted by Souillac to Tipu. The boat could fly Tipu's flag all along till it reached French shores. He could carry an Indian crew and a Muslim captain, though the real captain was Pierre Monneron, a French East India Company diplomat. Monneron was authorized by Louis XVI to meet Tipu Sultan in Mysore and re-establish relations. Though from the king's point of view, he was envisaging this primarily as a commercial partnership. After having made peace with the British at Versailles and mounting debts from the American Revolution, Louis XVI did not want to embroil himself in any political skirmishes, least of all in faraway India. Even before the embassy reached Paris, Louis XVI had taken a decision to withdraw the remaining French troops from Pondicherry and relocate them to Mauritius, thereby tacitly accepting Britain's supremacy in India and being loathe to be drawn into further military conquests with them. However, Louis XVI was advised to accord a grand welcome to this embassy from Mysore, more so for the optics of it all, to unsettle his European rivals and play a charade of the Mysore–France relationship seeming to be 'more important than it actually is'.[123]

Tipu, on his part, was contemplating this mission solely for the purposes of political alignment and military partnership. He did see the mission enhancing commercial interests by making Mysore an economic hub for cotton and silk textiles, sandalwood, ivory, pearls and other goods from his kingdom that could be traded in France. In the earlier Constantinople delegation that was tasked with going to France, Tipu had made it clear that from the French he expected about 10,000 European soldiers to be sent for his aid in the battles with the British. In his letter to Louis XVI, Tipu put forth his demand that he 'should first give us a written agreement and we will give you a similar written agreement thereafter to the effect, that, first, a war of ten years should be undertaken against the enemy [British and their allies]. During this period whatever happens by accident of fate, no peace would still be concluded [with the enemy].'[124] Further, he enticed the French with the prospect of an occupation of the strategic port of Chennapattan [Madras] that was the British stronghold, once their allied forces defeated them. All other seaports on the Eastern coast were also promised to be handed over to the French. In the course of the suggested ten-year war to humble the British completely, armies were promised to be organized between Mysore and the French to attack and occupy Bombay, Bengal, Gujarat and other places that the British held.[125]

Muhammad Darwesh Khan, Akbar Ali Khan and Osman Khan were the envoys who were sent in the delegation. In all, some forty-five persons set sail for Paris from Pondicherry on 22 July 1787. After ten months and seventeen days, the *l'aurore* that carried the embassy touched the shores of Toulon in France on 9 June 1788.

The embassy stayed in Paris for three months and were shown all the prominent places in the city. They became quite an object of oriental fascination for Parisians who had never seen anything from Mysore or India up close. The royal gardens of Saint-Cloud have gouache depictions of the Mysorean embassy by Charles-Eloi Asselin, dating 8 August 1788, and the awe with which they were accosted everywhere. Historian Meredith Martin traces this oriental fascination, especially with Mysore, to the earlier depictions of French artists such as Antoine Borel of Haidar Ali 'spanking a British officer with a bundle of twigs that a French soldier has supplied.'[126] Martin explains, from several other images in France at that time, that this phenomenon was termed as 'Indomania' by archaeologist–historian Jean-Marie Lafont. It was an obsession in France of the country's status in India, with a burning desire to enhance it, most often at the expense of the British. Most French accounts portray Haidar Ali and Tipu Sultan in glowing terms, unlike the British representation of them as despots. The sight of these eastern ambassadors in all their traditional wear attracted Paris's artists, fashion experts and commercial establishments alike. The embassy also visited some of France's silk manufactories at Lyon and other places—theatres, operas, military reviews and fireworks displays.

Finally, on 10 August 1788, Louis XVI received the envoys at the Versailles palace, with great pomp and splendour, in an overcrowded, enthusiastic public reception. Darwesh Khan presented the king with gold, diamonds, pearls, silks and muslins that they had brought from Mysore. He also delivered an address to the king that updated him of the history and background of the Anglo–Mysorean strife, the contributions and the several lapses by the French, especially Bussy, Duchemin and Cossigny's withdrawal at the height of the war. He also made a request from his king Tipu for technicians, workers, doctors and also seeds of flowers and various kinds of plants for the gardens in Mysore.

The French interestingly threw Bussy under the bus. He had already died in 1784 and putting the blame on him for the lapses in the Mysore–French relationship was an easy task. The message from Louis XVI to Tipu said:

> His Imperial Majesty has given particular attention to what is written. He has seen with great regret the manner in which M. de Bussy who was asked to command the troops in India behaved during the time of the last peace. His intention should not have been to separate from such a faithful ally as Tipu Sultan without informing him about the negotiations which had begun in Europe about the cease-fire. But the distance of these places, the advanced age, the infirmity of the French General [Bussy], would surely make you understand that the General had not comprehended the instructions which had been sent to him and he did not definitely adhere to them.[127]

But as mentioned earlier, Louis XVI had no intention of firming up any military or diplomatic alliance with Mysore, especially against the British, with whom they had signed a peace treaty after much strife. In addition, the situation in France itself was one of deep turmoil given that it was sitting on the cusp of the French Revolution and the popular disenchantment with the monarchy. The internal tumult further constrained Louis XVI from being able to offer anything substantial to the embassy or to Tipu in return, except some vague assurances, homilies on how they wished for peace among all princes of Asia, along with sundry gifts and porcelain hookahs. The clothes and jewels too from Mysore did not particularly catch the attention of the monarchy or the business community to elicit any commercial understanding. They were looking forward to grander, more exotic and opulent items from the East. Queen Marie-Antoinette had by then become very unpopular in France and her name was embroiled in several financial scandals and profligacy at a time of economic recession that she kept herself absent from all the public ceremonies with regard to the Mysore embassy. Some of the easier requests for workers and technicians and plants and seeds were more readily conceded.

The embassy tried to outlive its hospitality as it seemed so fascinated by France and its many sights. They were finally told politely to leave, before the cold weather became an impediment to their return. They had spent all the money amounting to Rs 1,00,000 that Tipu had sent them for expenses, and also got into a further debt of 49,414 livres on account of their luxury purchases.[128] In addition, they had been 'captivated by the beauty of female infidels . . . even accepting presents of forbidden liquors, and . . . were accordingly disgraced.'[129] The envoys finally left on 17 November 1788 and reached Pondicherry by 11 May 1789. The disgraced and unsuccessful envoys were received with great indignation by Tipu. He was enraged when the envoys, in their deposition before him in court, painted a grand and beautiful picture of the luxuries and pomp of France. He was least interested in these and was looking for an offensive and defensive alliance with the French against the British. 'Tippoo Saheb,' writes Michaud, 'had the pretension of being one of the greatest monarchs of the world. He did not like to hear that there existed in the western world, and especially among the Christians, a kingdom richer and more flourishing than his own. He forbade his ambassadors to talk of France in this manner. His orders were not followed strictly, and the description of the prosperity of France was a favourite topic among the great and small.'[130] In his rage and frustration, Tipu is said to have got Akbar Ali Khan and Osman Khan killed when they were walking alone in a garden, on the pretext that they had been treasonous.[131] Thus ended the miserable tale of the second foreign embassy from Mysore.

While these embassies might have ended with little or no benefits for Mysore, they certainly demonstrated a larger vision that Tipu had for the political, diplomatic, commercial and strategic interests of his Sarkar-e-Khudadad, along with a broad world view of global politics.

12

Southern Terror

The string of victories in battles, the several foreign embassies and the numerous innovations that he undertook for his Sarkar-e-Khudadad filled Tipu with unbridled confidence, bordering on hubris. The southern borders of his kingdom, Coorg, Balam and Malabar, had always been irritants, right from the time of Haidar Ali's annexation. Every now and then a rebellion would be thrown up by new players, all of whom detested the autocracy of Mysore and its forcible occupation. Malabar, in particular, had always been a thorn in his side. Tipu was keen to find a permanent settlement to this recurring problem. Buoyed by his own enhanced stature, he knew that the time had now come to stamp his royal authority against all insurgents.

After the Treaty of Mangalore in 1784, the Rajas of Kerala who had all revolted earlier against Mysore at the encouragement of the British were literally left to themselves. The first article of the treaty ironically declared all the zamindars and Rajas of Kerala coast to be friends and allies of Tipu. Though British factors themselves, in Tellicherry, protested against this abandonment of their traditional, loyal allies, the British hands were virtually tied at the end of the Second Anglo–Mysore War. Shortly before his death, Haidar had appointed Arshad Beg Khan as the civil and military governor of Malabar. Wilks describes him as a 'Mussulman of rare talents, humanity and probity,'[1] who made genuine attempts to restore a semblance of peace on the Malabar coast. He introduced regular revenue laws to assess the lands favourably. Based on an estimate of

---

* Please refer to the corresponding illustration in the appendix.

the produce, he fixed average taxes for every tree. For instance, for every coconut tree, there was a tax of half a fanam (⅕th of a rupee). Young and very old trees were exempted from taxes. The average yield of a tree was 1⅛th of a fanam and thus the assessment was about ⅔th. Through this system, Arshad Beg managed to bring a lot of land back under cultivation.

But Tipu decided to separate the civil and military functions in the Malabar. He brought in Mir Ibrahim, a relative of Zain-ul-abidin Shoostri, as the military governor there. Mir Ibrahim, relatively new, inexperienced and headstrong, undid in just a few months all the good work that Arshad Beg had managed in years. Breaking earlier written engagements or *kowles* with the local princes and landlords, he imposed new revenue exactions that angered most of the Nair chiefs. Tipu of course strictly told Mir Ibrahim to confine himself to the collection of revenue and fiscal matters and not 'form the design of chastising either the Nairs or Moplahs,'[2] as that was the business of the foujdar or military governor, Arshad Beg.

A Moplah notable, Mancheri Kurukkal, had managed to galvanize the anger of the Nairs and other chiefs in Calicut into a brewing revolt. On 21 May 1786, Tipu wrote to Arshad Beg: 'Getting possession of the villain, Goorkul [Kurukkal], and of his wife and children, you must forcibly make Musulmans of them, and then dispatch the whole under a guard to Patan [Srirangapatna].'[3] Eventually, Arshad Beg had to prevail upon one of the Rajas of the Zamorin's family, Ravi Varma, to unite forces against Kurukkal, who fled. In Tipu's own letter to the sipahadar in Calicut, Abdul Karim, on 13 June 1786, he details the unfortunate fate that befell on Kurukkal. 'The villain Goorkul,' writes Tipu, 'being wounded, had thrown himself, together with his wife and children, into a fire [kindled for the purpose] which had consumed them all . . . the mapillahs have taken to flight.'[4]

Despite the success in crushing the rebellion, Arshad Beg felt deeply hurt for being forced to share power with a complete newcomer and a novice, Mir Ibrahim, and expressed his desire to retire. In 1786, he conveyed to Tipu his desire to make a pilgrimage to Mecca. However, in the letters of Tipu to his officers, a different picture emerges. In his terse directive to Arshad Beg, Tipu writes on 28 December 1786 to 'abandon your vain idea of proceeding [on a pilgrimage] to the Holy Temple, and apply yourself, according to custom, to the affairs of the Sircar. This the most advisable thing you can do.'[5] In another letter to the dewans in Calicut, Tipu strictly asks them to dissuade Arshad Beg from leaving for Mecca, urging them to persuade him and, if that failed, confine him. 'You must,' he writes, 'likewise, imprison the courtesan who had been the cause of this affair.'[6] In his observations regarding the letters, Kirkpatrick states that a love affair brewed between Arshad Beg and a courtesan, something that the Sultan detested and asked him to renounce. In protest, the love-struck Beg made hollow protestations of heading to Mecca, which he eventually did not pursue, especially after his female interest was banished from Calicut by Tipu.[7] Arshad Beg seems to have continued in service for a while, as evidenced by future correspondence with the Sultan. Arshad Beg however wrote to his sovereign to avert the destruction of the Malabar due to the high-handedness of Mir Ibrahim and urged the Sultan to visit the region. In due course, Tipu removed and disgraced both Mir Ibrahim and Arshad Beg from service. But by then, Malabar had already touched the precipice of another brewing rebellion.

In January 1788, Tipu proceeded to the Malabar at the head of a large army, via the pass of Tamarasseri. He easily reached Calicut without any opposition. He conducted a thorough inquiry lasting over three months, into all aspects of administration, revenue collection and also the social and religious customs of the Malabar. The designation of a religious figure called Shaikh-ul-Islam was also created to morally reform what Tipu thought were degenerate social customs in Malabar. Quoting Tipu's memoirs, Wilks writes:

> The country of Calicut is situated on the coast of the ocean, and is named Malabar: its breadth does not exceed twenty-three coss [one coss= 2¼ miles] and its length is nearly two hundred. The Mahommedan inhabitants are called Pilla [Mapilla] and the infidels Naimars; and the rainy season lasts six months, and mud

continues throughout the year, the roads are excessively difficult, and the inhabitants prone to resistance, dividing their time between agriculture and arms. Such is the excess of infidelity, that if a Mussulman touch the exterior wall of a house, the dwelling can only be purified by setting it on fire. From the origin of Islam in Hind, to the present day, no person had interfered with these practices, except the revered [Haidar Ali] who is in paradise, after the conquest of the country . . . and during the twenty-five years that the country of Calicut had belonged to this dynasty, in as much as twenty thousand troops were maintained for its occupation, and the revenues never equaled their monthly pay; the balance, to a large amount, was uniformly discharged from the general treasury. Notwithstanding all this, the actual circumstances of the country were never properly investigated, until his Majesty, the shadow of God, directed his propitious steps and remained three months in that country. He observed that the cultivators (instead of being collected in villages as in other parts of India) have each his separate dwelling and garden adjoining his field; these solitary dwellings he classed into groups of forty houses, with a local chief and an accountant to each an establishment which was to watch over the morals and realize the revenue; and a Sheikh-ul-Islam to each district for religious purposes alone; and addressed to the principal inhabitants a proclamation to the following effect: 'From the period of the conquest until this day, during twenty-four years, you have been a turbulent and refractory people, and in the wars waged during your rainy season, you have caused numbers of our warriors to taste the draught of martyrdom. Be it so. What is past is past. Hereafter, you must proceed in an opposite manner; dwell quietly, and pay your dues like good subjects; and since it is a practice with you, for one woman to associate with ten men, and you leave your mothers and sisters unconstrained in their obscene practices, and are thence born in adultery, and are more shameless in your connections than the beasts of the field; I hereby require you to forsake these sinful practices and live like the rest of mankind. And if you are disobedient to these commands, I have made repeated vows, to honour the whole of you with Islam, and to march all the chief persons to the seat of empire. Other moral inferences and religious instruction, applicable to spiritual and temporal concerns, were also written with his own hand and graciously bestowed upon them.[8]

As he had in Coorg, Tipu assumed on himself the moral responsibility of what he termed as reforming the people of Malabar. It was also an indictment of the matriarchal system that prevailed in Kerala for centuries. He considered it his divinely ordained duty to civilize the 'barbaric' and 'obscene' customs in Malabar. Just as he had done in Mysore, Tipu ordered the complete destruction of Calicut and its fort. In its place, a few miles away, a new fortress was built and the place was renamed as Farookhi/Feroke. By then the monsoon had set in and Tipu marched through swamps and floods with incessant torrential rains lashing through, to reach Coimbatore. When he was advised not to embark on a journey during such inclement weather, Tipu is said to have remarked that he would 'order the clouds to cease discharging their waters, until he should have passed.'[9] Wilks surmises that it is tough to comprehend whether he said this in jest or whether it was a 'blasphemous pretension', as during this period, puffed up by his own power and pride, Tipu supposedly often compared himself even with Prophet Mohammed. As Wilks states: 'He frequently placed his own exploits in the cause of religion, particularly in the number of his converts, above those of Mahommed . . . and that Mahommed was but such a man as Tippoo Sultaun . . . pretensions of this nature gave great offence to the orthodox . . . drunk with flattery, and uncontrolled dominion, he would have openly claimed the apostolic character, and as his followers believe, a still more impious assumption.'[10] The band of sycophants that he seemed to have surrounded himself with contributed to this bloated self-image that was bordering on megalomania. Of course, the clouds expectedly did not listen to his orders and his army suffered great hardships by the time they reached Coimbatore.

Meanwhile, in Malabar, the Kolathiri prince of Chirakkal (Koluthunad) had been a staunch ally of Tipu and was held high in his favour. This created sufficient insecurities and fears in the Kolathiri's perennial rival, the Bibi of Cannanore, who had been advised by Tipu to make peace with Chirakkal and antagonize the British instead. She had hoped that as under Haidar Ali, the position of the governor of Koluthunad would be conferred on her family by Tipu, but was disappointed by his evasive responses. She hence reached out to the British factors in Tellicherry to take her under their protection. Empowered by Tipu's patronage, the Kolathiri prince sent his emissaries to Tellicherry on 27 May 1788, demanding immediate settlement of arrears of Rs 1 lakh, while he himself owed the Company about Rs 4 lakh. The factors decided to ignore his bravado, but they were in for a shock when they realized that, in early June 1788, the Kolathiri intended to attack and capture the Dharmapattanam island which had been the undisputed possession of the Company since 1733. The British realized that the agent provocateur here was Tipu who was firing his guns on them from the Kolathiri prince's shoulders. Their apprehensions were validated when they heard that the prince was accorded a grand and hospitable welcome in Coimbatore by Tipu, almost in appreciation for his aggressive stand on Dharmapattanam. There were reports of the Kolathiri planning an attack on Muicara, to the south of Tellicherry. The factors however heaved a sigh of relief because after his return from Coimbatore, the Kolathiri prince fell ill and died on 19 June at Palghat. His brother who succeeded him did not make such aggressive grandstanding against the Company, though he kept pressing for clearance of dues.

By July 1788, the Company had decided to send messages to Madras and Calcutta about the tense situation that had been caused in the region due to the Kolathiri prince's invasions into their territories. These messages were normally dispatched through Brahmins who had free access across borders by virtue of their social status. *Malabar Manual* records that 'the factors now learnt that the Brahman messengers were no longer safe; a Brahman selected to convey the message refused to go; and assigned as his reason that there was a "report prevailing that the Nabob [Tipu] had issued orders for all the Brahmans on the coast to be seized and sent up to Seringapatam." And on the 20th [of July 1788], confirmation of the fact was received from Calicut, where "200 Brahmans had been seized and confined, made Mussulmen, and forced to eat beef and other things contrary to their caste."[11] By the end of August that year, identical reports started pouring in from the Kottayam and Kadathanad Rajas, beseeching the Company 'to take the Brahmans, the poor, and the whole kingdom under their protection'[12] and against the wrath of Tipu's forces. These actions were perhaps also driven by Tipu's reformist zeal as he had commanded his officers in Calicut to undertake the 'moral' upliftment of the people of Malabar. Not only were the Brahmins victimized, the Kshatriya Raja of Parappanad and Tichera Terupar, a prominent Nair of Nelumboor, and several others were forcibly carried away to Coimbatore, circumcised and forced to eat beef.[13]

Malabar and Coorg Erupt Again

The peace in Malabar was thus short-lived and within just a few months after Tipu's return to Srirangapatna, another massive revolt was threatening to rock the coast. In utter desperation, in the wake of the forced conversions and barbarities, the Nairs rose in rebellion. The Mapillahs in Malabar, though Muslim, were also disgruntled with Mysore for the oppressive taxes and decided to support this uprising. This, even as the Bibi of Cannanore, the chief to whom the Mapillahs swore allegiance, was trying to cozy up to the British. Ravi Varma of the Zamorin's family[14] became the face of the revolution. The Tellicherry merchants who were under the Company's protection also supplied the insurgents with gunpowder, money and other support. By November 1788, Ravi Varma was victorious in the open country and was threatening to invade Calicut. The Malabar rebels were joined by the Coorgis (Kodavas) who anyway had an old axe to grind against Tipu.

The Kodavas meanwhile had been relentless in trying to free their imprisoned king from Periapatna where Tipu had confined him and his family. Two prominent Kodava chiefs Pattacheravanda Boluka and Appaneravanda Achayya hatched a plot to take advantage of the confusion in the entire coastal region to liberate their Raja. Periapatna was a bustling trading town with village fairs where merchants sold their wares. Disguised as oil vendors, they managed to slip into the fort. The disgruntled Hombale Nayaka also switched sides to assist the intruders. On the dark, moonless night of 14 December 1788, Hombale Nayaka threw a lavish dinner for the royal family. The guards too were invited to the feast where their food was mixed with sedatives. As the sturdy guards dozed, the royal family managed to sneak out of confinement with the support of the insiders of Mysore. Braving great difficulties and escaping the watchful eyes of the heavily guarded fortress, the royal family, comprising Virarajendra and several women and children, hurried their way through the woods and forests, suffering bruises and injuries. In two hours, they managed to reach the borders of Coorg.

Virarajendra slowly began regrouping his forces and led a valiant battle against the Mysorean armies. Leaving his family in a village called Kuruchi in southern Coorg, Virarajendra set off on an offensive. The young raja however naively believed that Palle Veeravarma, the Raja of Kote, in the neighbouring Waynad would ally with him in his efforts against Tipu. Once he crossed over to Veeravarma's domains, he realized that he was trapped there and was blackmailed to sign away large parts of southern Coorg to the Kote Raja to secure his own release. The Kote Raja had an old axe to grind, wanting to avenge his ancestor's killing by the Coorg Raja. With no option left by which to enable a passage back to his dominion, Virarajendra ended up losing territories to his neighbour. Fearing a hostile Kote Raja, Virarajendra quickly moved his principal wife Nanjammaji and daughter Rajammaji to a village in Nalaknad. Some of his minor wives and family members were still at Kuruchi. While Virarajendra was busy in his offensive against Mysore, the Kote Raja sent his armies to attack Kuruchi and burn down the residence where the royals were hiding. Virarajendra came back home, shocked to see his residence and all his family members in Kuruchi being reduced to a heap of ruins and ashes. The tragedy broke an already traumatized

Virarajendra. But putting this sorrow behind, he steadfastly focused on incursions into Mysore territories.

He ousted the Mysore armies from Bisli Ghat to Manantody and also led plundering attacks into Mysorean domains. To quell the irritant, Tipu dispatched Golam Ali to Coorg with a large force. Virarajendra was doomed, as he stared at yet another fatal failure. But this time, destiny seemed to favour him. Tipu's attention was diverted by the Malabar revolt and he ordered Golam Ali to divert his armies to the western coast. On his way back, Golam Ali was fiercely attacked by the Kodavas and the Mysoreans suffered great losses. An alarmed Tipu sent a reinforcement under four captains, one of whom was a Frenchman. But this army, too, was looted of all its baggage and stores by the hill-men of Coorg. Burhan-ud-din was then sent with a large contingent to strengthen the forts of Kushalnagar, Madikeri, Beppunad and Bhagamandala. But even as he was making his way to Madikeri, Burhan-ud-din was badly attacked by the Kodavas and he beat a hasty retreat to Srirangapatna.

In June 1789, along with his trusted chief, Kuletira Ponnanna, Virarajendra managed to sack and burn down Tipu's fort at Kushalnagar. The Mysorean garrison was chased out and they attempted to swim the river to safety. But the valiant Kodava forces hotly pursued them even as they were swimming and 500 of the 700 members of the garrison were killed.[15] The head of Tipu's commander at that fort was brought to Virarajendra as a proud war-trophy.[16] Burhan-ud-din tried to throw in supplies to the aid of the Bhagamandala fort. But he was repeatedly ambushed on the march and had to yet again rush in fright to Srirangapatna.

In August 1789, Tipu's garrison at Armeri in Beppunad was captured, followed by Amara Sulya and finally the mighty fort of Bhagamandala. The Bhagandeshwara temple there had been converted into a fort by Tipu. The temple was thus freed and the idols that the priests had kept in hiding to save them from the wrath of Tipu were reconsecrated. Two copper tiles of the temple roof that had got blown away by the shelling were replaced by Virarajendra with silver tiles that are present even today.[17] Over a relentless expedition thereafter that carried on for a few years, Virarajendra managed to get back all that he had lost. By 1791, with the recovery of the important fort of Madikeri, he was able to liberate his kingdom from decades of occupation by Haidar Ali and later Tipu Sultan and re-establish the rule of the Haleri Rajas. He is hence justifiably considered a hero by the Coorgis and re-named as Dodda Virarajendra after his re-assumption of power. He later established the town of Virajapet. Here he invited and sheltered several of the persecuted Canara Christians who had suffered Tipu's atrocities, even building for them the St Anne's Church.

Numerous oral history accounts abound in Coorg to this day of the many atrocities that Tipu and his armies committed on the Kodavas during their several expeditions. Alongside are also tales of incredible chivalry and resistance which the warrior Kodavas managed to put up. Artefacts related to the attacks on their temples by Tipu or the valiant pushback are displayed with great pride even now. Coorg chronicler C.P. Belliappa recounts one such site in Palangala, a remote village where a shrine atop a hill named Malethirke is rich in such oral narratives. He recounts how the shrine was attacked by Tipu's soldiers and the outnumbered Kodavas had no other option but to hide in the forests and pray for divine intervention. 'Their prayers were answered,' he writes, 'and according to lore, swarms of rock-bees attacked the troops and chased them down the ghats. There is evidence of this attack in the form of an old sword which was abandoned by the soldiers [of Tipu].'[18] The shrine has several other miracles that the devout speak about. Belliappa mentions how when the St Anne's Church was being constructed at Virajapet, its spire kept collapsing each time and none, including the Italian architect, could figure out the reason for this strange occurrence. They were then advised to offer a bell to the Malethirke shrine and, to their surprise, the spire stood tall and firm thereafter. Even to this day, the devout take vows to hang their bells all around the shrine to fulfil their prayers. Another widespread oral narrative of Coorg is a near unanimous hatred for Tipu and what he did to their brave ancestors.

Crushing the Rebellion

Tipu was enraged to hear about the tumult that had struck the coasts yet again. More than Coorg, Malabar was his prime focus. Arshad Beg was ordered to be imprisoned as he had proved singularly incapable, in the Sultan's eyes, of imposing moral strictures or containing the Nairs. Beg died in prison, a frustrated and depressed man. Hussain Ali Khan was made the Foujdar of Calicut. By December 1788, Tipu dispatched a large force of 6000 native troops and 170 Europeans under Lally and Meer Hussain Ali Khan to vanquish Ravi Varma. They drove him out of Calicut but he still remained at large, in the open country. In a letter to the newly appointed Foujdar, Tipu wrote on 14 December 1788:

> Meer Husain Ali has been dispatched [to you] with two kushoons. With the assistance of Almighty God, and guided by the Divine grace, he will, with the [further] aid of the holy Prophet, [soon] join you. You must [then] in conjunction with the aforesaid Meer, make prisoners of, and slay the infidels [utterly]. Such of the males among them as may be under twenty years of age, are to be made prisoners. Of the remaining unbelievers, let five thousand be suspended to trees.[19]

On 31 December 1788, in similar directives to Shaikh Qutb who had captured eighty-two Mapillahs, Nairs and Brahmins, Tipu advised that males over the age of twenty be hung upon trees.[20] Though the Mapillahs were Muslims, he meted the same punishments on them as he did on the Nairs and Brahmins as they had collaborated with them in the uprising. Their rebellion however did not last too long and they made peace with Tipu in the larger interests of his being a co-religionist. The Company's Resident at Calicut Sir Francis Gordon too had confirmed reports that the forces under Lally and Khan had received 'orders to surround and extirpate the whole race of Nayars from Kottayam to Palghat.'[21]

Tipu Enters Malabar

On 20 January 1789, Tipu set off again towards Calicut. The reports of the arrival of the large army of nearly 60,000 and of Tipu's march into their land made the Nairs seek shelter, as always, in the woods and mountains. Tipu ordered his army to surround the woods and seize the chiefs of the faction. He also sent messages to Francis Gordon not to give protection to any of the Nairs who might flee to Tellicherry. Leaving a portion of his troops in Calicut, Tipu swooped northwards, signalling thereby to the Hindu chiefs there to flee. Before he left Calicut, Tipu ordered Muhammad Ali, the second Diwan of Calicut, on 28 February 1789 that the 242 captured Nairs were being sent to him as prisoners. 'Having circumcised them,' Tipu ordered, 'you must enroll them among the faithful [make them Musalmans] . . . if any of those should escape, you will come under our displeasure.'[22] Tipu makes his religious fervour clear in another letter to Badr-u-zaman Khan and others, dated 7 March 1789, where he outlined the entire problem in Calicut, his earlier warnings to them and how they had repeatedly risen as a country against his diktats. As a result, the holy war or *jihad* against them had led 'to the spontaneous profession of the true faith by great numbers of infidels and their families . . . the positive duty of all Musalmans to take up arms for the advancement of Islam; and by expatiating on the favour which they will by so doing, acquire with God, with his Prophet, and with the Muhammadan world at large.'[23] This was to be read out to the entire Muslim population when they gathered for their Friday prayers at public mosques to inspire them too in this 'holy crusade'.[24]

The Rajas of Kottayam and Kadathanad, along with their principal officers, had all fled for Tellicherry by then and, unopposed, taken a boat from there to Travancore. Tipu shot off angry letters to the chief of the factors in Tellicherry, demanding an explanation as to why the errant chiefs of north Malabar were offered free passage through their domain, and also allowed, according to him, to carry with them Rs 10 lakh each. From 10–11 March, he even sent officers to Tellicherry to search for the fugitive rajas.

By then Tipu's forces numbering between 20,000 to 30,000 regulars had completely surrounded Kuttipuram, the headquarters of the Kadathanad family. About 2000 Nairs with their families had holed up inside an old fort. They valiantly held out for some time, but were obviously no match to the large Mysorean army. They finally offered to surrender and were given an option of either a 'voluntary profession of the Mahommedan faith, or a forcible conversion, with deportation from their native land. The unhappy captives gave a forced assent, and on the next day, the rite of circumcision was performed on all the males, every individual of both sexes being compelled to close the ceremony by eating beef.'[25] The act of eating beef that led to a total and irrevocable loss of caste among the Hindus was used to make them inevitably embrace Islam thereafter as the only option. This was held out as a major achievement by Tipu that other army detachments too had to emulate. In fact, in his letters Tipu himself gave elaborate details on emulating this very model to deal with the Nairs who had retreated into several forts and other places for shelter. To Muhammad Ali, the Bakshi of Ahasham or the chief-of-staff of infantry, Tipu wrote on 12 March 1789 about encircling another group of 'infidels' who had taken shelter in a fort, falling upon them from all sides and taking them prisoners. He then ordered Bakshi to make a 'repast of rice and beef, [which] you must feed the whole of the prisoners on the same day, and afterwards incorporate them with the professors of Islam. They are then to be given in charge to the Muhammadies, with the directions for their being all forthwith circumcised. This being done, let them be reinstated in their possessions.'[26] William Logan in the *Malabar Manual* writes that: '*Pakal kaataaka raavu veetaaka* is a saying still current regarding the hardships endured by the Nayars at this time. It was only at night that they could with safety visit their houses; during the day time they had to conceal themselves in the jungles.'[27] It is believed that no less than 30,000 Brahmins with their families fled from their places in the Malabar to take refuge in Travancore.[28]

Alarmed by this brutal dance of death and destruction that was ravaging Malabar, the hitherto loyalist Chirakkal Raja sought the protection of the factors in Tellicherry, whom his predecessor had ironically antagonized. His sister and entire family, along with 10,000–15,000 Nairs, managed to get safe passage to Travancore.

But the British refused to support the Chirakkal Raja as they did not want to incur Tipu's wrath. The raja finally got an audience with Tipu who was furious with him for letting so many Nairs escape. He arrived with a suitable retinue and with several gifts that he offered to the Sultan, who received him with great respect and cordiality. On getting to know about Tipu's plans to desecrate and plunder the family temple, the raja offered Rs 4 lakh and plates of gold with which the temple was roofed on the condition that it be spared. Tipu haughtily replied that all the treasures of the earth and sea given to him could not ensure the safety of the temple.[29] He also boasted about 'the destruction in the course of this holy war of eight thousand idol temples, many of them roofed with gold, silver, or copper, and all containing treasures buried at the feet of the idol, the whole of which was royal plunder.'[30] Wilks however discounts the number quoted here of temples desecrated stating that 'when crimes are deemed to be virtues, we may infer that their amount is much exaggerated.'[31] While the claims by Tipu might be inflated, it is quite possible that a significant number of temples in the Malabar were destroyed during this dreadful march.

The raja was then told to depart. Before he could get back to his capital, Tipu declared that the treachery of the raja had been discovered and therefore detached two brigades to attack and slay him. The raja tried to flee but was hotly pursued and eventually killed. His corpse was thereafter treated by Tipu with the most severe inhumanities and was mutilated. He 'had it dragged by elephants through his camp and it was subsequently hung up on a tree along with seventeen of the followers of the prince who had been captured alive.'[32] With the elimination of the Chirakkal Raja, Tipu decided to mend his bridges with the Bibi of Cannanore and proceeded there to solemnize the marriage of one of his sons, Abdul Khaliq, with the Bibi's daughter. She was also offered a part of Chirakkal to govern. These were all tactical moves to bring the estranged Bibi back on his side and, through her influence, quell the Mapillahs who had risen in rebellion. Soon, their revolt fizzled out and they became loyal supporters of the Sultan. Even in the marriage of his son with the

Bibi's daughter, Tipu ordered that '40,000 captives, unhappy families of the Koorg country and other parts of the Mallabar Coast are to be circumcised [converted].'[33]

As March 1789 drew to a close, Tipu's campaign had ended in utter destruction and ruin for Malabar and the unfortunate Nairs. In his letter dated 22 March 1789 to Abdul Kadir, the Talukdar of Kotungeery, Tipu boasts: 'We have conferred the honour of Islamism on ten or twelve thousand infidels, of whom we have detained Lumboony Bhutmar [perhaps a generic name for the Nairs] and some of their principal men who were the instigators of the [late] sedition . . . you must communicate this to the unbelievers [in your quarter] and moreover, sending for them, make Musalmans of them, and then dismiss them to their homes.'[34]

Tipu's biographer, Kirmani, gloats about how Tipu 'appointed a detachment of his troops to ravage the country [Malabar] of his enemies, and they accordingly lighted up the fire of oppression in all the towns and villages in that neighbourhood.'[35] In an almost poetic flourish, Kirmani exults:

> When they marched into that country, they committed many cruel acts, they lighted up such a fire of plunder, that at once they burned up everything it contained. From the hoofs of their horses, the mountains and plains were all trodden to dust, and even the rocks, trees and stones, deep sighs arose and wailing. After the whole country had been swept by the bosom of devastation, and when a host of the refractory and rebellious has been carried away by the whirlwind of desolation, those who remained being subdued, placed the ring of servitude in their ear of their lives [the ear-ring that they were made to wear after circumcision and conversion], and with their hands tied together submitted.[36]

After thus ravaging Malabar and leaving behind a trail of death, disaster, destruction, barbarities and the wails of hapless victims, Tipu moved to Coimbatore by the time of the outbreak of the monsoons in June. He marched in slow stages along the coast to Chowghat to both impress and terrorize the local population among his military might. The military regime that he established in Kerala is known as Padayottam. Tipu left behind in Malabar six divisions consisting of two brigades each with distinct establishments of spiritual, civil and military officials. They were ordered three duties: of surveying the lands, numbering productive trees and seizing the rest of the Nairs who had escaped.

Paolino da San Bartolomeo, a Portuguese Roman Catholic missionary who stayed in Malabar for about twelve and a half years, from 1776 to 1789, had travelled widely in Kerala. He spoke several Indian languages, like Sanskrit, Tamil and Malayalam, and met the Rajas of Travancore and Cochin several times. He wrote extensively and, in his memoirs, commented that he was better acquainted with Kerala than he was with his own country. In the memoirs, published in Italian in 1796 and in English in 1800, he offers an intimate, first-hand account of the terror that gripped Kerala in the wake of the Padayottam. He writes:

> The manner in which he [Tipu] behaved to the inhabitants of Calicut was horrid. A great part of them, both male and female, were hung. He first tied up the mothers, and then suspended the children from their necks. The cruel tyrant caused several Christians and Heathens [Hindus] to be brought out naked, and made fast to the feet of his elephants, which were then obliged to drag them about till their limbs fell in pieces from their bodies. At the same time, he ordered all the churches and temples to be burned or pulled down or destroyed in some manner. Christian and pagan [Hindu] women were compelled to marry Mohammedans. The pagans were deprived of the token of their nobility, which is a lock of hair called *kudumi;* and every Christian, who appeared in the streets, must either submit to be circumcised, or be hanged on the spot. This happened in the year 1789, at which time I resided at Verapole [Varapali in Travancore]. I had then an opportunity of conversing with several Christians and Pagans, who had escaped from the fury of this merciless tyrant; and I assisted these fugitives

to procure a boat to enable them to cross the river which runs past that city. This persecution continued till the 15th of April 1790.[37]

During his extensive travels of South India, Francis Buchanan met one Mr Brown who was the Danish Resident in the French colony in Mahe. Brown gave him an exhaustive interview of the state of Malabar and its people, their customs and traditions and also their conditions before and during the rule of Haidar Ali and Tipu Sultan. He reveals to Buchanan:

> During the government of his father, the Hindus continued unmolested in the exercise of their religion; the customs and observances of which, in many essential points supply the place of laws . . . Tippoo, on the contrary, early undertook to render Islamism the sole religion of Malabar. In this cruel and impolite undertaking, he was warmly seconded by the Moplays [Mapillahs], men possessed of a strong zeal, and of a large share of that spirit of violence and depredation which appears to have invariably been an ingredient in the character of the professors of their religion, in every part of the world where it has spread. All the confidence of the Sultan was bestowed on Moplays, and in every place they became the officers and instruments of government. The Hindus were everywhere persecuted and plundered of their riches, of their women, and of their children. All such as could flee to other countries did so; those who could not escape took refuge in the forests, from where they waged a constant predatory war against their oppressors . . . the ancient government of this country was at last completely destroyed, and anarchy was introduced . . . During this period of total anarchy the number of Moplays was greatly increased, multitude of Hindus were circumcised by force, and many of the lower orders were converted . . . the population of the Hindus reduced to a very inconsiderable number.[38]

Tipu restored the Zamorin of Calicut to a part of his territories as a means of reconciling with him and also using him as an agent for his future aggression plans in the region. But having seen the terrible fate that had befallen a hitherto ally who had carried out his tasks,

the Kolathiri Raja, the Zamorin was diffident and sceptical. He also
detested the mass circumcision and conversions, along with plunders
of temples, that Tipu had undertaken in Calicut. He soon joined in
the general insurrection against Mysore's hegemony. Tipu was also
trying to elicit the support of the Raja of Cochin and ordered him
to present himself at his camp. The raja replied that he had been
paying his tributes regularly and hence he should be excused from
the appearance. Tipu sent another order through an envoy in August
1789 to the Raja of Cochin repeating the same, that he wished
to purchase the fort of Cochin from the Dutch and needed the
intercession of the raja to carry out the transaction. The raja refused
a second time to visit Tipu's court, making the Sultan furious. He
openly declared that 'if they did not attend the summons, he would
come and fetch them by force.'[39] But to attack Cochin, he would
have to pass through the wall of Travancore, the Lines, that had
always eluded him, as they did Haidar.

Tipu however made his ambitions clear on what he wanted to do
with Cochin and thereafter, Travancore. In his letter to Syed Abdullah
and three others of religious orders, he wrote on 18 January 1790:

> Through the divine favour and with the assistance of prophesy
> [Prophet Mohammad], the whole of the infidels inhabiting
> the districts of Farrukhi [Calicut] have received the honour of
> Islamism. There are only a few on this side of the country of
> Cochin who remain [to be converted]; and these also it is our firm
> determination to exalt and distinguish by bestowing upon them
> the happiness of the true faith. As this [then] is an affair of holy
> war [jihad], we write to you, among others who are conversant in
> sacred matters.[40]

The same strategy is revealed in Tipu's letter to his favourite and
loyal commander, Badr-uz-zaman Khan, on 19 January 1790 where
he states:

> Don't you know that I have achieved a great victory recently in
> Malabar and over four lakh Hindus have been converted to Islam?
> I am now determined to march against that cursed Raman Nair

without delay. Thinking that he and his subjects would be soon converted to Islam, I am overjoyed and hence abandoned the idea of returning to Shrirangapattanam. Assemble therefore all the priests and other heads of the Muhammadan church, within your jurisdiction, and instruct them to exhort all true Musalmans to join prayers to the throne of God for the success of the holy cause in which he was embarked.[41]

The Raman Nair that Tipu mentions in the letter above was none other than Dharma Raja Balarama Varma, the ruler of Travancore, who now became the object of Tipu's ire. This hostility was to cost Tipu dearly.

The Travancore Lines

The unfulfilled desire of Haidar and Tipu had been the possession of the principality of Travancore that they always coveted. Haidar, at the time of his Malabar invasions too, had realized the strategic importance of Travancore and had always wished to annex it. However, given the Dutch presence in Cranganore, he had deferred the plan. After having conquered the Malabar region in north Kerala, right up to Cochin, Tipu now began to eye Travancore. He thus opened a new southern front as well. Like his father, he too realized that possessing Travancore would give him the strategic advantage of commanding the entire western coast and greatly enhance his standing and prestige among the European powers whose factories dotted the region. But Travancore was a firm ally of the British and conquering it was not as easy as Malabar had been. The Raja of Travancore Dharma Raja Balarama Varma (1758–1799) had been recognized at various occasions as a trusted ally of the British, including the treaties of 1769 and 1784 that ended the two Anglo–Mysore wars. Tipu was desperately searching for a pretext to raise a dispute with Travancore. That pretext presented itself in the form of the most unexpected of things—a defence wall.

When attacked by the Zamorin of Calicut in 1759, the Raja of Cochin had sought the help of Travancore to repel this aggression. He also agreed to cede to Travancore portions of his territory that extended from the hills to the branch of an estuary that separated the narrow island of Vipeen from the Arabian Sea. On this strip of land, the Raja of Travancore had begun the construction of the 'Travancore Lines' or *Nedumkotta* as a northern boundary towards Calicut to protect both kingdoms from future attacks by Mysore or its allies. From 1761, it took him five years to construct this mighty wall. It was an impressive 40-mile rampart that was flanked by a 16-foot ditch and topped by an impenetrable bamboo hedge. In 1789, the raja also bought from the Dutch the forts of Ayacotta and Cranganore. Tipu had eyed these forts with a view to securing the flanking positions to the Travancore Lines. But even before Tipu could take the matter forward with the Dutch while he was in Palghat, the Dewan of Travancore Keshava Pillai finalized the deal with Dutch merchants David Rabbi and Ephraim Cohain on 31 July 1789, under the supervision of the raja and the Dutch Governor John Gerard van Anglebeck. Though these forts belonged to the Dutch Company, the fact that they were in the territory of the Cochin Raja, who was a feudatory of Mysore, became another sore point in Travancore's already embittered relations with Tipu.

Though the Treaty of Mangalore recognized the Raja of Travancore as an ally of the British and that Tipu would hence not attack him, the strategic importance of the Lines as an access point to both the sea on one end and to the Carnatic and Arcot on the other, bothered Tipu. In his negotiations with the Raja of Cochin in 1788, Tipu tried to reclaim through him the land on which the Lines were erected. Travancore promptly conveyed these fears to the then Governor of Madras Sir Archibald Campbell and conveyed Tipu's mal-intent to violate the terms of the Treaty of Mangalore. At that time, Tipu had allayed the fears of both the British and the Raja of Travancore by professing his desire to maintain status quo and amity amongst them. However, he knew that occupying Travancore was his best bet in the eventual face-off that he would have with the

British and that it would give him immense strategic advantages. While he wanted an amicable settlement with Travancore, he even contemplated a reduction of that state through the force of arms. It was with this in mind that he had restored the Zamorin of Calicut with reduced powers so that he could act as his agent in the region, put forward claims on Travancore which would then be supported militarily by Mysore. But the Zamorin refused to comply as he had been obliged to the Raja of Travancore who had stood by him in his days of trouble. Anticipating an invasion by Tipu, the Raja of Travancore sought from the Madras Government about two or three battalions of the Company's troops to be stationed in his kingdom at his cost.

About September 1789, Tipu commenced his march from his camp at Coimbatore towards Travancore, at the head of 20,000 regular infantry, 10,000 spearmen and matchlockmen, 5000 horse and twenty field guns, passing through the woods of Anamalai. Until December 1789, he sent several representations to Travancore and the British to settle the matter. Tipu claimed to have a legitimate grouse against the Raja of Travancore. Firstly, for giving asylum to several chiefs and the Nairs who had been rebellious. And secondly, the construction of the Lines being on the land of Cochin, which was a Mysore subsidiary and hence needed the suzerain's permission for construction. In an agreement earlier, the Dutch had agreed to pay rent to Sirdar Khan for the fort of Cranganore. Tipu argued that the Lines intersected the country of his tributary, was built on his property and that Travancore had no legal right to build such a wall on Mysorean domain.

Tipu tried every means that he could to convince the Raja of Travancore who proved to be stubborn, obdurate and shrewd. The new British Governor of Madras John Hollond had warned the Raja of Travancore that his purchase of the forts of Ayacotta and Cranganore were against their wishes and that it might inflame trouble with Mysore. The Raja of Travancore argued that these forts had left the hands of Cochin and passed over to Dutch control almost 135 years ago. Cochin had ceded these to the Dutch in lieu of their support to them against the Portuguese. Hence the claim of Tipu that they belonged to his feudatory, the Raja of Cochin, was itself a flawed one. As a sovereign state, Travancore had every right to conduct commercial transactions independently with the Dutch or any other powers without any fear of Mysore.

Eventually, when information reached Hollond about the purchase of the forts he was irked and wrote to the raja on 17 August 1789: 'I cannot approve of your having entered into a treaty with the Dutch for extension of territory without the consent of this Government. This very impolitic conduct makes you liable to a forfeiture of the Company's protection for you cannot expect that they will defend territory of which you were not in possession when their troops were sent to your country and which have been since obtained without their assent. I therefore think it necessary that you should at once give back to the Dutch the places which you have thus indiscreetly received from them and thereby establish your affairs precisely upon their former footing.'[42] More than any concern for the alleged violation of the rights of Mysore, the British were obviously insecure about the growing proximity between Travancore and the Dutch. The raja tried to deflect the situation by informing Hollond that the decision to purchase the forts had been taken with the consent and upon the suggestion of his predecessor, Sir Archibald Campbell. Hollond tried to verify with his predecessor and an exasperated Campbell wrote back that to the best of his knowledge and memory no such thing had happened. So, it was clear that the raja had acted of his own accord and was trying to wriggle out of a difficult situation. Tipu was fully aware of the objections that the Company in Madras had regarding the raja's conduct and thus he was talking to all the parties concerned to force the raja to give up the claims.

Even as negotiations went on with the British, too, as a party, Tipu sent an independent vakil to the Raja of Travancore in December 1789, demanding that the latter's troops in Cranganore be withdrawn, the Malabar chiefs who had been sheltered in his domain be surrendered to Mysore and that the Lines be demolished.

If these demands were not complied with, he threatened that there would be a military attack on Travancore. But the raja threw up his hands stating that he could take no decision without the concurrence of his steadfast allies, the British. In a polite, yet firm letter, the raja replied:

> God is my judge that I have never taken any pains to assist them [the Malabar Rajas whom he sheltered], or gave them evil counsel, nor have I ever raised my disturbances in the country of the Circar [Mysore] until this moment, nor did I until now ever know of any enquiry or examination on the part of the Circar with respect to their remaining here . . . I have given positive orders that those Rajas should leave the country. Prior to the time that the Cochin Raja became a dependent on your Circar, the Calicut Raja had possessed himself of all his country; at that period, I expended large sums of money to lend him assistance and restored him his country. He then granted me a place for the purpose of building the wall of my boundary in his country, by an irrevocable grant, in consequence whereof, the wall was completed there, at a very great expense, since which five and twenty years have now elapsed. This is the real state of the case; nor has there until this present time been any let or molestation whatever in this respect, nor there ever will be any trouble caused to the Raja of Cochin by me. At the time of the negotiations for peace between you and the English, my name was also included in the treaty; it was well-known to the servants of your Circar that this boundary was then in being. When I received the fort of Cranganore from the Dutch, they proved by particular writings and treaties that no persons whatever had at that time, or ever had, the smallest claim or connection with it, but that it was dependent entirely upon them; in consequence of which, I bought it of them. I have never given protection to thieves or rebels to the Circar . . . as I cannot act in anything without acquainting the English, I have written all these

occurrences to the Governor of Madras; immediately on receipt of
these orders I shall fully answer everything regarding.[43]

Tipu wrote several letters to the British in Madras keeping them
informed of his actions in the Malabar vis-à-vis Travancore. In a
letter dated 24 December 1789, Tipu narrated the entire chain of
events and also about his sending several delegations to Travancore
under people like Abdul Kadir and Mohammed Amer Chobdar, but
to no avail. He urged the Company to 'send positive orders to Ram
Raja [Travancore ruler] on these three important subjects, that he
should relinquish the improper ideas he entertains, and in future
that he should not engage in anything that is improper which will
impair the basis of the goodwill which is between us, and no trouble
will be given by my army to the country belonging to Ram Raja.'[44]

But neither Hollond nor Tipu actually foresaw the skilful and
shrewd diplomat that the Raja of Travancore was. He directly
addressed his concerns to the British Governor-General Lord
Charles Cornwallis who had been appointed to the position in 1786.
He apprised Cornwallis of Tipu's threatening stance and the non-
committal, and somewhat hostile, tone of the Madras Government
on the matter. Cornwallis was obviously aware of the details of the
case and did not want Tipu to gain a larger foothold or control in
Travancore and hence sought an explanation on the matter from
the Madras Government. His argument was that if Travancore
was able to prove the claim that the forts belonged to the Dutch,
who had taken them directly from the Portuguese, and Cochin had
no role to play in it, then the Raja of Travancore deserved to be
supported. If Tipu took those forts by force or undertook hostilities
against Travancore, it could then be viewed as a violation of the
Treaty of Mangalore, making it a just cause for the British to open
a vigorous war against him. Hollond kept these communiques that
he had received from Cornwallis concealed from both the Raja of
Travancore and obviously Tipu. He would rather have the drama be
enacted out in its natural course of events and then precipitate an

intervention from his side, though that was not what his Supreme Government in Calcutta had ordered him to do.

The Attack on Travancore

Tipu's patience was running thin and the obduracy of the Raja of Travancore in maintaining his position angered him. Refusing the Company's offers to mediate the matter to a peaceful settlement, he decided to dispossess the raja of the forts by force. By mid-December 1789, Tipu had encamped at a place about four miles away from the Lines and began erecting his batteries there. George Powney, the British Resident in the Travancore court, records the advance of Tipu's armies on 24 December 1789:

> An officer who was at Vedyacottah yesterday evening came out of the gateways on the lines has just acquainted me that he saw tents pitched about two or three miles from that place, but he could not distinguish so as to form any idea of the extent of the encampment. Several of his rocket men and about 50 horse came within musket [sic] shot where he was; there they appeared to be reconnoitering; for after having stayed a short time, they went off again. It is impossible to penetrate his designs; he is a most unaccountable fellow . . . I really believe he means to do some act to insult the Rajah of Travancore and provoke him to commence hostilities, but the old man is aware of his designs and will command himself as much as possible.[45]

Keeping the Madras Government informed of his moves, assuming thereby their neutrality, on 29 December 1789, Tipu attacked Travancore. He marched at the head of 14,000 infantry and 500 pioneers. Seated in his palanquin and proceeding with two risalas and 2000 regular horse, by night, Tipu entered the battle against the implacable Travancore. Before daybreak, he found himself in possession of a large extent of the rampart on the right flank of the Lines. Breaching a weak part of the Lines, he hoped to place his entire force there in one day. Filling the ditch with bales of cotton and earth for his cavalry to enter, Tipu made the attack with 7000 men. It was a hastily ordered, badly misunderstood and ill-executed operation. As Tipu's troops made their way along the ditch, a party of twenty Travancoreans hemmed them in from all sides, pouring heavy fire on the intruders. They were driven out amid great slaughter. The commanding officer of the Mysorean army, Zamal Beg, was killed, creating utter confusion amongst the ranks. Several of the Mysorean forces that fell into the ditch died or were trampled to death in this confusion. The ditch was filled with their bodies, numbering more than 1000. Several others were taken prisoners. About 200 casualties were reported on the Travancore side.

Tipu himself was thrown down from his palanquin and was grievously injured, and narrowly escaped death. In fact, the bearers of his palanquin were all trampled to death. Some of the steady and active chela brigade members showed presence of mind to immediately lift him up on their shoulders and ascend the counterscarp. In fact, on this occasion great courage and loyalty was shown by a Canara Christian—Manuel Mendez, whose forefathers were ironically tortured and converted by Tipu. Mendez, a part of the risala of converted chelas from Mangalore, was also Tipu's personal attendant. Noticing the imminent trouble, he donned Tipu's attire and took his master's place in the palanquin, allowing Tipu to escape. The Travancore army then seized Mendez and cut him into three pieces.[46] In the confusion that followed Mendez taking his place in the palanquin, Tipu in fact fell twice in his attempts to get out of the mess. In the process, he irretrievably damaged his foot, leading to a lameness that remained with him for the rest of his life. Tipu's state sword, pistols, signet ring and other personal ornaments fell into the hands of the Travancore army as prized trophies, as did his palanquin.[47] The ring was the one he always wore and it was 'so very small that the finger on which it was worn must have been delicate in the extreme.'[48] The trophies were presented triumphantly by Keshava Pillai to the Raja of Travancore, who conveyed the good news to the British and the Nawab of Arcot. The Nawab requested the raja to send Tipu's sword, shield, dagger, belt, palanquin and other items to him and this was duly complied with.[49]

The defeat at Nedumkotta was a huge blow to Tipu and his prestige. The bubble of his invincibility had burst. The disgrace of losing his precious items, in addition to his lame foot, kept rankling in his mind and he simply could not forget the ignominy of this defeat by Travancore. Burning with the fire of revenge and retaliation, he retreated towards the northern frontier, sending for reinforcements from Srirangapatna, along with battering rams, guns and stores. By then, not getting much help from Madras, Travancore managed to raise an army of 1,00,000 that was distributed along the Lines for its defence.

The Governor of Madras, Hollond, wrote to the Sultan on 1 January 1790, criticizing his unilateral aggression on their ally, Travancore, even as they had offered to mediate a peaceful settlement. 'The forts in question,' he wrote, 'are of no value to us; but we think it necessary to inform you that we shall consider any attempt to take them by force on the present footing of affairs as an act inconsistent with the fair and liberal sentiments of honour and friendship subsisting between us and tending to create hostilities between the two Governments . . . if you are desirous of settling the points in contest by the investigation of commissioners, we will appoint one or more to meet such persons as may be appointed by you at any convenient place on the borders of our respective countries, and you will then judge whether our intentions are fair.'[50] The letter reached Tipu just after his shameful defeat. Addressing the Company, he wrote back on 15 January 1790, antedating it and concealing the facts by stating that his troops were merely searching for the Malabar fugitives and the Travancore army opened fire without warning. In retaliation, his troops had attacked and carried the Lines but he had ordered them to stop and even retreated gracefully.

Historian Mohibbul Hasan however strongly contests the fact that Tipu was personally present during this attack or was wounded grievously. He attributes this to rumours spread by some *harcarahs* (messengers) who returned from Tipu's camp and also rubbishes away the claims of trophies of the Sultan being confiscated by the enemy.[51] But in the Governor-General's own minute dated 2 April 1790, he refers to the correspondence from George Powney, the British Resident in Travancore court. He mentions how they were at variance with Hollond's reports that echoed Tipu's excuse that 'the attack was made by accident and without any orders from him.' But Hollond certainly knew, states Cornwallis, through the reports sent by Powney and 'accounts through different channels, positively said that the attack was not only made by Tippoo's direct orders but that there was every reason to believe that he actually conducted it in person, and was himself wounded or bruised in the action.'[52]

This became an important bone of contention for both sides— Tipu's argument was that he never committed wilful aggression and that he was merely hunting down the rebel Malabar chiefs, that too not personally but through his troops, who were shot at unprovoked by Travancore. The British however state that Tipu indeed led the assault from the front and this was a clear violation of the Treaty of Mangalore, thus opening the doors for renewed hostilities between the two sides. Though historians like Hasan tend to veer in support of Tipu's argument to provide him cover-fire in this matter, British official letters like the one quoted above, of Cornwallis, clearly testify that it was a provoked aggression that Tipu led personally, in which he suffered a humiliating defeat. Even if that is discounted as bias on the part of Hasan, Tipu's own sympathetic biographer, Kirmani, who otherwise extols him all through his narrative, paints an eloquent picture of his Travancore debacle, which is in consonance with the British and Travancore accounts:

But although several of the Sultan's confidential servants, such as Turbeut Ali Khan, and others, took the liberty to represent that in front the road was bad and intersected by the beds of deep river, and that a night expedition was not safe, and God forbid that the enemy should gain an advantage and the *ghazies* [warriors of Islam] be defeated; still their advice was disregarded ... the Sultan getting into his *palki* with two *risalas*, and two thousand regular

horse, proceeded onwards forthwith, dark as it was . . . in this time
the enemy attacked the Sultan's troops on all sides with arrows and
musketry, and caused incalculable distress and confusion among
them, and however vigorously they strove to repel their infidel
assailants, it was of no avail and they were overwhelmed with all
kinds of evil and calamity, but notwithstanding all this, three or
four hundred brave horsemen of good families, gave substantial
proofs of their valour and were all killed and wounded in front
of the Sultan. At this time, Kumruddin Khan, who was present
with the Sultan, by adjurations and entreaties falling at his feet,
took him out of his *palki*, and by the strong exertion of loyalty
and fidelity, caused him to be carried through the water to the
opposite side of the river, and then constrained him to turn his
steps towards his camp. But of those present in that battle not
one man ever returned safe to the presence. The Sultan's *palki*
with its bed, the great seal of the exchequer and a dagger were
taken by the infidels. Some report that the Sultan's turban was in
the palki, but it is a great mistake, for the Sultan's turban at that
time was upon his fortunate head, and the coloured turban which
fell into the hands of the enemy belonged to one of his footmen,
who ran before the Palki and who was accidentally killed by an
arrow, or a musket ball, and his turban falling near the *palki*, the
benighted infidels thought it was the Sultan's and placed in the
palki. In short, the Sultan and Kumruddin Khan escaped out of
the whirlpool of their fortunes, and the rest of the Khans, such as
Turbeut Ali Khan, Muhammad Omr, Urzbegi and Sayeed Khan
the Darogah of the treasury etc., were never after heard of.[53]

The Prevarications of Madras

All along, the Raja of Travancore kept beseeching the Madras
Government for support, but their tardiness alarmed him. The
precarious situation seemed to be known to everyone, except a
prevaricating Hollond. In a private letter, Sir Thomas Munro, who
was an official in Madras then, wrote: 'A second attack [by Tipu] is

daily expected; and if the king [of Travancore] is left alone, all his exertions against a power so superior can delay but for a short time his ruin. The English battalions were behind the Lines, but not at the place attacked; and it is said that they have orders not to act, even on the defensive . . . the barrier once forced, orders for them to act will arrive too late. All their efforts will then avail but little against the numbers of their enemies, and will only serve to draw a heavier vengeance on themselves and the unfortunate Rajah.'[54]

When the news of the attack on the Lines by Tipu reached Calcutta, Cornwallis was enraged. By the end of January 1790, he wrote to Hollond expressing his hope that war had already been declared against Tipu for this unprovoked aggression and blatant disregard of the Treaty of Mangalore. But the callous indifference and procrastination of the Madras Government, despite his several directives earlier, angered him further, accusing them 'of a most criminal disobedience of the clear and explicit orders of the Government dated the 29th of August and 13th of November, by not considering themselves to be at war with Tippu from the moment they had heard of his attack [on the Lines].'[55] On 8 February 1790, he shot off another missive to Hollond: 'After having thus enumerated the parts of your late public conduct which have appeared to us in a disadvantageous light, we have to require that you will assign your reasons for withholding the information from the Resident at Travancore, and from the Raja himself that we should assist in maintaining and defending the forts of Cranganore and Jayacottah [Ayacottah] if it should be proved upon investigation that those forts had been independent Dutch possessions before the country of Cochin became tributary to the Mysore Government . . . you seem to have acted in disregard or contradiction of our repeated instructions by which you were directed to look upon Tippoo if he should commit hostilities against either of our allies, the Nabob of Arcot or the Raja of Travancore, as at war with the Company.'[56]

With his position having become increasingly untenable, in due course, Hollond was eased out of his responsibilities by early March 1790. In fact, so alarmed was the Supreme Government in Calcutta by Hollond's conduct that Cornwallis had actually contemplated proceeding to Madras and taking over the military and civil responsibilities himself by superseding Hollond.[57] But he gave up the idea when General William Medows, who was serving as Governor of Bombay and the Commander-in-Chief of the Bombay Army, was transferred to Madras as the new Governor and Commander-in-Chief of the Madras Army. Through Sir John Kennaway and Sir Charles Malet, the British Residents in Hyderabad and Poona respectively, Cornwallis kept the Nizam and the Peshwa informed of Tipu's transgression against their common ally, opening a window for possible future alliances. Major William Palmer, the Resident with Mahadji Sindhia, was tasked with sounding out Holkar and Sindhia about the rumblings in the south and soliciting future cooperation. In fact, Cornwallis administered a strong threat to Holkar and indirectly to Sindhia, through Palmer, that if they dared to be friendly with Tipu, they would risk enmity with the Company too.[58] These talks had been going on with the respective courts right from 1788. Malet had by then formed personal friendships with most of the Maratha gentry at Poona and was creating the ground for a favourable atmosphere for an alliance. Only Mahadji was not very enthusiastic about this prospect, more so given his strained relations with Nana Phadnis. Kennaway was Cornwallis's trusted agent and his appointment in Hyderabad was to ensure that the Nizam, the weakest link in most alliances in the past, fell in line without much ado. Cornwallis did not wish to leave anything to chance before launching an all-out attack.

Tipu Re-attacks Travancore

As was feared by everyone, Tipu, after his retreat, regrouped himself to attack Travancore again on 2 March 1790. Beginning with skirmishes outside the wall, by 6 March, he had ordered his artillery to work. Another battery was erected at Bagavady Kottah. As he had during the siege of Mangalore, Tipu constructed mortars from which his army threw showers of stones and large billets of wood.

The courageous resistance they had earlier provided and the confidence of that victory now gave way to fear for the Travancoreans. The sturdy Lines resisted the heavy firing for nearly a month, after which it finally gave in. A breach of about three quarter of a mile in length was effected by the Mysoreans. The Travancore army found it a futile exercise to resist and retreated. The Mysore army, under Tipu, then marched inside Travancore. By 18 April, Tipu was right before Cranganore, with his army under the command of Lally. Cranganore was being defended by the Raja's troops under Captain Flory but seeing the vast army rushing in, they abandoned the fort and fled. Tipu easily occupied the fort and ordered the demolition of the fortifications. Lally proceeded thence to the fort of Kuriapilly that was also abandoned by the alarmed Travancoreans. The entire Lines thus fell into the Sultan's hands along with 200 pieces of cannon of various sizes and metals, a vast stock of ammunition and warlike stores that were all confiscated and dispatched to Coimbatore. After 15 April 1790, his army was in possession of the Lines near Ayacotta and 6000 of his horsemen had opened hostilities. All along, the Company's forces that were subsidized by Travancore, the 10th and 13th Madras Battalions under Captain Knox, remained mute spectators as no clear orders had emerged from the Government of Madras.

With the changes in the power structure in Madras having been set into motion, finally, the British troops received orders to cooperate with the Travancore army. But the force they had was no match for that of the Sultan in terms of numbers and hence the commander deemed it prudent to not go on an all-out offensive and risk the lives of all his men. This delay on the part of the British further encouraged Tipu to march into the interior of Travancore, unleashing destruction on the way in the districts of Parur and Alangad in early May 1790. The Dewan too had retreated by then. The insult of the previous defeat being fresh in his mind, Tipu is supposed to have taken a pickaxe himself and set an example for the others in his army to emulate him in demolishing 'the contemptible wall,' stone by stone.[59] His armies then committed several atrocities in the villages,

laying waste to the country both by their sword and with fire. Many
fled for shelter to the hills of Kunnathnaud and others were taken
prisoners. Hindu temples and Christian churches were vandalized.[60]
Pagodas, palaces, the houses of rich people and the huts of the poor
alike were burnt to cinders and their cries of anguish rent the air. The
triumphant Sultan then marched southwards and reached Alwaye
before the end of May 1790.

Fortunately for the Travancoreans, where the British forces and
their own armies let them down and did not step up to face the
challenge, nature seemed to come to their timely rescue. The rain
clouds burst forth rather prematurely. It was an unusually severe
south-west monsoon season and the tiny stream that river Alwaye
normally was, was swollen to the brim and overflowed, causing
flooding and immense hardships for Tipu's army. All his ammunition
and accoutrements got damaged; the bare necessities of the army
were all washed away by the impetuous currents. Several of his
troops succumbed to diseases like cholera and smallpox. Tipu and
his army had not seen a monsoon fury as severe as the one in 1790
and were bewildered by the critical situation they found themselves
in suddenly, after charting a stupendous success. It was perhaps at
this time that Tipu regretted burning down the numerous temples,
palaces and churches, if not for the religious or humanitarian sanctity
that was defiled, for the lack of proper places of shelter for himself
and his army in the wake of these monstrous monsoons. The land of
Lord Padmanabha Swamy, to whom the Raja's ancestor, Martanda
Varma, had pledged the kingdom, was steadily proving to be Tipu's
Achilles heel.

On 30 March 1790, Cornwallis sent a letter to Medows, the new
Governor of Madras:

> So far am I from giving credit to the late Government for economy
> in not making the necessary preparations for war according to the
> positive orders of the Supreme Government, after having received
> the most gross insults that could be offered to any nation, I think
> it is very possible that every cash of that ill-judged saving may

cost the Company a crore of rupees, besides which I still more sincerely lament the disgraceful sacrifice which you have made by that delay, of the honour of your country by tamely suffering an insolent and cruel enemy to overwhelm the dominions of the Rajah of Travancore which we were bound by the most sacred ties of friendship and good faith to defend.[61]

The arrival of Lord Charles Cornwallis, the First Marquis Cornwallis, marked possibly the toughest challenge that Tipu faced in his life. Cornwallis was fiercely patriotic, upright, fair and just in his dealings, except war with his enemies, when he forgot all tenets of mercy. Born on 31 December 1738, Cornwallis attended the military academy at Turin, and rose to the position of a Lieutenant Colonel while serving in Germany during the Seven Years' War. On succeeding his father, Earn Cornwallis's title as the Second Earl in 1762, he became politically active with the Whigs and took his seat in the House of Lords, where his abilities and connections led to several high-profile appointments for himself. Although opposed to the measures that provoked the American Revolution, he accepted a position in North America as Major General and served with distinction during those troubled years. However, for all his successes against the American rebels, he could do little against the military talents of American Commander-in-Chief, George Washington. Choked with tears and shame, he had to surrender at Yorktown on 19 October 1781. Surrendering his country's flag to the enemy after being disgraced in war is any soldier's worst nightmare and Cornwallis went through this ignominy. As he sailed towards his next assignment in India, Cornwallis was deeply cognizant of the fact that he had a reputation to repair. Neither could he afford such mishaps in India, as he had in America. So, he was extra cautious about all the diplomatic moves that he undertook. By then, the British, having been humbled by Tipu in the Treaty of Mangalore, were also itching for revenge. With Cornwallis's arrival in 1786, the stage was being set for a major showdown with Mysore, and Tipu's Travancore invasion served as the perfect spark.

13

The Third Anglo–Mysore War

A Grand Alliance Brews

Even as tensions soared in the coast, for over two years, Lord Charles Cornwallis had made preparations for a grand alliance against Tipu. Malet in the Peshwa court and Kennaway at Hyderabad were negotiating with the respective powers on the contours of such a grouping. By an act of British Parliament, the India Act of 1784, the Governor-General was prohibited from entering into any new treaty without the express authority and concurrence from the Court of Directors. This was his reason for not being able to support the confederates during the peak of their war with Tipu. So, Cornwallis's first impediment was to forcefully convey and convince the Court of Directors about the exceptional situation that was caused due to Tipu's aggression on their ally, Travancore. There was widespread apprehension of a renewed invasion of the Carnatic by Tipu, with French aid. The British had been closely watching Tipu's embassies to Constantinople, and more specifically to France, with great caution and interest. Their intelligence reports of the time suggested that they knew that Tipu's vakils, who had showered Louis XVI with costly presents amounting to 3,00,000 pounds sterling and cancelled bonds amounting to Rs 19 lakh, meant to seek an alliance against the Marathas and also the British.[1] Cornwallis particularly wanted the Marathas to realize that in the event of a combined attack on Tipu, they could regain their lost territories and expect the greatest advantages from the British success.[2] The Company's finances,

---

* Please refer to the corresponding illustration in the appendix.

too, were in the doldrums and Cornwallis hoped for a speedy and profitable termination of the war, when declared, against Tipu.

Though the Marathas and the Nizam were desirous of Tipu's downfall, there had been a change in the course of Indian politics of the time, accentuated by the ever growing power of the British. The two Indian states were therefore not too enthusiastic about the prospect of putting Tipu down completely, as they saw him, along with his French allies, as the most effective and only credible bulwark against the rising British power. Even as they despised Tipu, they, especially Nana, no longer wished to openly associate with the British. However, Cornwallis's deft diplomacy, routed through the efforts of Malet and Kennaway, began to bear fruit. Palmer was negotiating with Tukoji Holkar and Mahadji Sindhia.

Tukoji was completely against a Maratha alliance with the British and favoured one with Tipu instead. He even tried to prevail upon the Nizam and the Peshwa to desist from joining such a combination. But they ignored his entreaties. Palmer however managed to get Mahadji Sindhia's assent for the alliance. Sindhia conveyed the justified resentment that many in the Peshwa court nursed against the British for their neutrality in the recently concluded Maratha–Nizam attack on Tipu and hoped that Malet would address and remedy those disgruntlements.[3] Sindhia however opined that Tipu 'had sufficient confidence in his own strength, abilities and resources to undertake a war against us [confederates] without auxiliary support.'[4] Sindhia offered to proceed to Poona to negotiate on behalf of the British, provided they protected his dominion in the north and persuaded the Rajas of Jaipur and Jodhpur to return to Maratha dependency. Cornwallis rejected these proposals, but luckily for him, he did not need Sindhia's intervention in Poona as his confidante Malet had already wormed his way.

In his several letters to Malet, Cornwallis literally coached him about various scenarios that might emerge with Nana and how he must sagaciously handle them all, to the maximum advantage of the British nation. Cornwallis directed Malet to warn Nana that 'we [British] have no doubt of our own strength being sufficient to bring the war to an honourable issue, but that if the burden of it shall be left entirely upon ourselves, we shall probably not think it incumbent upon us in the course of future negotiations to attend to the interests of those of our friends who have contented themselves with looking on a scene, in which the future peace and tranquility of India was so materially implicated with indifference.'[5]

Through his wit, ingenuity, persuasiveness and intimate understanding of Maratha politics and nature, Malet managed to exert quite an influence on Nana in a very short span of time since his appointment as Resident in Poona on 6 March 1786. Right from 1787, on the instructions of Cornwallis, he had begun weaving the web of an alliance with the Marathas. Malet knew that he was dealing with an ace diplomat himself—Nana Phadnis, who had weathered many a storm by then. A man of medium height, with his slender physique, his sunken cheeks and wrinkled face as he is depicted in the several portraits of the time, Nana was also a shrewd diplomat and wily statesman who could not be easily gamed.

Malet suggested to Nana that the young Peshwa, who had turned sixteen then, should lead the Maratha armies in a proposed confederate attack on Tipu as that would give him practical field experience. Nana, who was unenthusiastic about another war, dismissed this suggestion. Lots of discussions happened on the various terms of a proposed agreement with numerous drafts being circulated. But on Malet's insistence, a treaty of an offensive and defensive alliance of fourteen articles was finally signed on 1 June 1790. The Maratha army of 10,000 horse was to accompany British troops whose expenses were to be defrayed by Poona. Territories and forts conquered were to be divided among victorious allies. Nana asked the British to assign the holy city of Varanasi, where the sacred shrine of Lord Vishwanath had been demolished by Aurangzeb, to the Marathas. But Cornwallis rejected this term. However, to allay Maratha suspicions, Cornwallis even went to the extent of placing the Company's Bombay contingent under Maratha command.[6]

The Nizam however kept prevaricating. He understood that once Tipu was vanquished and the Marathas were freed of his menace, their attention would turn to him and there would be repeated aggressions against Hyderabad for the collection of Chauth arrears. He tried to bargain with Cornwallis a term in the treaty that guaranteed to him British protection against any future Maratha attacks on his domains. Obviously, the British could not accede to such a request without offending the Marathas and so this was struck down. Cornwallis offered instead to use his friendly offices with the Peshwa court to diffuse any tensions, should there arise such a situation in the future. The Nizam was in two minds, but his minister whom he trusted immensely, Meer Abdul Qasim, strongly advised him to choose the British side. But even as Qasim was in Calcutta to discuss these terms with Cornwallis, in his characteristic duplicity, Nizam Ali had sent another envoy, Hafiz Farid-ud-din, in October 1787 to Srirangapatna 'proposing a strict and indissoluble union between the Mahomedan states.'[7] Tipu was willing to consider this, but proposed matrimonial alliances between the two families by marrying his son to the Nizam's daughter, which the Nizam haughtily rejected, thereby terminating those negotiations.

After he surrendered the Guntur principality to the British in September 1788, the Nizam sent a few more emissaries to Tipu. Farid-ud-din approached Tipu in November 1788 when the latter was in Coimbatore. He suggested to him that since they were both Muslims, they should bury their differences and unite as friends against common foes. The Nizam even sent a splendid copy of the Quran to Tipu. Tipu responded favourably and offered to restore all territories back to him, in return for Guntur being made over to him on the same rent as he paid the British for it. He once again proposed the marriage of his son with the Nizam's daughter and also offered to stand by him in wars against the British. His own envoys, Qutub-ud-din and Ali Raza, were sent to Hyderabad with costly gifts for the Nizam and to take the talks forward. Wilks suggests that the Nizam's continued rebuff of the matrimonial alliance was because he considered himself of superior lineage when compared to the house of Haidar Ali and its ancestry. He writes: 'It seems extraordinary that so acute a courtier as Ali Reza should not have been able to ascertain Nizam Ali's intentions, and save his master the awkwardness of a public refusal. "We are desirous," said Ali Reza, "of partaking of the Sheker-Bhat," the dish of rice and sugar sent as the first preliminary ceremonial of marriage; to which intimation Nizam Ali made no sort of reply, and there the negotiation and the embassy terminated.'[8] Mohibbul Hasan however attributes the breakdown of talks to Tipu's ambassadors being totally outwitted by Kennaway in Hyderabad. The court politics of Hyderabad was where the writ of Prime Minister Mushir-ul-Mulk and minister Meer Abdul Qasim, who strongly advocated a British alliance, prevailed over that of Imtiaz-ud-daulah, the Nizam's nephew, and Shams-ul-umara, the Commander of the Household troops, who favoured friendship with Tipu.[9] In reality, the Nizam, never favoured any alliance with Mysore and had made these overtures only to make the British insecure and to elevate his own bargaining power with them. That achieved, he happily dumped Tipu's ambassadors.

Finally, by 4 July 1790, the Nizam also came on board with the British. A tripartite army of 25,000 horses each was to attack Tipu's northern possessions before the onset of the monsoon to reduce as much of the territory as possible. As per the treaty, all the ancient palegars and zamindars, who were dependent earlier on the Peshwa or Nizam and had been dispossessed by Haidar and Tipu, were to be reinstated.

The alliance was further expanded with other smaller players who were now willing to jump onto this big bandwagon. The Raja of Coorg Dodda Virarajendra, who had secured his kingdom after prolonged captivity, also sent in an expression of interest to ally with the British in any efforts that they undertook to subdue Tipu.[10] A treaty was signed with him and Robert Taylor, the British Chief of Tellicherry, on 26 October 1790 as per which the raja agreed to provide supplies to the British, along with commercial privileges in his domain. The troops that he could commit to the war barely numbered 4000. But he was burning with a strong sense of revenge against Tipu for all the atrocities that he had undergone. Major Dirom records: 'Bred in adversity and obliged to submit to the duties of a religion which was foreign to his cast[e], the Rajah's mind was enlarged beyond the prejudices which generally fetter the natives in India: he was desirous of seeing, and being instructed; went on-board the ships at Tellicherry; was fond of conversing with our officers; of making himself acquainted with our discipline; and on many occasions, particularly on horseback, adopted the English dress.'[11] He also committed to allow free and exclusive passage to the British through his kingdom and eschew any connections with other European forces on the coast. The British promised to protect the raja's interests and domains against any aggressive actions that Tipu might undertake in the future.

In Cannanore, about 8000 troops of Tipu had been stationed. Anticipating that this would be a problem, the British tried to prevail upon the Bibi of Cannanore to send them away, but she remained evasive. The British feared the prospect of her provoking the Mapillahs against them and wanted her to accede to their demands. But Robert Taylor eventually managed to convince the Bibi to come to their side, despite the matrimonial links her family had with Tipu. She agreed to allow the Company to garrison her fortress in Cannanore during the war and also offered her son-in-law and one of her ministers as hostages, a day before the British troops set out. This was to be as a security for their admission into her fort. She also agreed to free trade with the Company on pepper and other items that her kingdom produced.

The Rajas of Chirakkal, Kadathanad, Kottayam and the Zamorin of Calicut too promised to ally with the confederates in this mission, and several others in the Malabar, who had an axe to grind against Tipu, were expected to join in. The Raja of Cochin Rama Varma also fell in line with the British who offered to assist him in recovering his territories from Tipu, after which Cochin was to become their subsidiary and pay annual tributes.

The dispossessed matriarch of the Mysore royal family, Maharani Lakshmi Ammanni, and her Pradhans too saw an opportunity in this growing alliance against their usurper. The Pradhans met General Medows in Tanjore after his assumption of office as Governor of Madras and professed the goodwill and support of their Maharani. Guns were fired from the ramparts of Tanjore fort to welcome the emissary of the Maharani of Mysore. Medows was however non-committal about a firm treaty with her without consulting their allies, the Marathas and the Nizam. But he wrote a letter to the Maharani promising her his best assistance, which was to be handed over through the Pradhans. His letter dated May 1790 read as follows:

> Maharanee Lakshmammanny, Sovereign of the Territories of Mysore, The repeated greetings of General Medows, Governor of Channapatan [Madras]. Your letter was duly delivered by your ambassador Tirumala Rao and I understand the contents thereof. God knows when Tipu may die and leave the country. Victory is God's grace. If He will enable us to restore the Kingdom to the rightful rulers, we shall indeed be very happy. We cannot now discuss about the distribution of territories. As the Nizam and the Mahrattas are now our allies, we cannot settle the point ourselves. It is right that you should bear the cost of the war, and it is also very good that you promise to pay the prize money to the troops. If we can but succeed in restoring the country to you and set things right, we shall feel pleased that we have accomplished a good purpose. We will do our best and the Almighty God should crown our efforts with success. We cannot say more now.[12]

Satisfied by the assurances, the Pradhans agreed to serve under Medows in the campaign. They collected a force of 100 horse and 2000 foot and accompanied the general. They kept the British informed of every move of Tipu through their vast network of spies that had infiltrated Mysore. This is evidenced by how, in the midst of the war, in addition to providing details of the operations, Captain Macleod wrote to Tirumala Rao on 16 September 1790: 'I have received the two *harcars* [messengers/spies] you sent me and I am much obliged to you for them . . . if you can get better *harcars* and news-writers that will go to stay in Tippoo's camp or some of his garrisons, I will pay them well and be much obliged to you.'[13] In a letter to Cornwallis, Medows writes to him, on 7 January 1791:

> The three Governors, the Nizam, and the Peshwah should dine at Seringapatam, with the old Queen of Mysore [Rani Lakshmi Ammanni] sitting at the head of the table. One is just likely as the other, but is more than likely we may crush this disturber of the public peace [means Tipu], if it is not sounder politics only to cripple him; but for my own part, I freely confess I should prefer the dignity and justice of dethroning this cruel tyrant and usurper, and restoring the kingdom to the Hindoo family—the lawful owner—to the wiser policy perhaps of only clipping his wings so effectually that he could soar no more in our time.[14]

Thus, a grand alliance had been forged by Cornwallis through sheer dint of hard diplomacy and precision over several years. Cornwallis wrote to the Marquis of Lansdowne on 15 April 1790 about this grand alliance:

> Upon my inviting the Marattas and the Nizam to join us in the war, they most readily sent me propositions for an alliance, which I have approved, and returned for their ratification. Besides this formidable confederacy, the Nairs whom Tipoo has so cruelly persecuted, and all his discontented subjects and tributaries on the Malabar coast, are ready to revolt, and I think he cannot for some time at least expect any aid from France . . . present rupture with Tippoo is to me, I cannot help considering it as fortunate for the permanent prosperity of our affairs in India, for it appears to me almost impossible that the alliance which is now formed against him, should not very considerably reduce his power; and with his determined enmity towards us, he might have had an opportunity of seriously distressing us, if he had waited to take advantage either of our being engaged in a war with France, or of any ill humour breaking out between us and the Marattas.[15]

Tipu's Actions

Back in Travancore, Tipu had managed to take the Lines by 15 April 1790. Reporting this to Powney, the Raja of Travancore wrote on 20 April 1790 that Tipu had entered the Lines, made a desperate attack and killed and wounded 4000 of his people who were defending the fort. He lamented that it was his 'bad fortune that no opportunity presented for the Company's troops to come to my assistance.'[16] The fort of Cranganore, too, surrendered to Tipu by 8 May 1790 though a detachment of British troops from Madras, and a regiment from Bombay, under the command of Colonel Hartley sent from Tellicherry, had been rushed in for defence. The country was laid open for waste and devastation and the locals were hunted down in large numbers and sent to captivity or death.[17] Tipu ordered a total destruction of the Lines and following Tipu's personal example of striking the first stroke at it with a pickaxe, his army carried on with the act. Bankers, shopkeepers, followers were all marshalled in to assist the soldiers in this demolition act as a symbol of crushing Travancore's defiance. In six days, the mighty Lines was reduced to rubble. By then, his own army's misery at Alwaye due to the monsoon floods and the emerging intelligence of a tripartite alliance alarmed Tipu.

Unfortunately for Tipu, misfortunes ganged up on him. His allies, the French, had a tumultuous time back home with the breaking out of the French Revolution. The growing unpopularity of Queen Marie-Antoinette and the corrupt practices of the monarchy led to violent upsurges, leading to the destruction of the Bastille and a formal authority to the National Assembly. The Republican Party there, composed primarily of Jacobins and Girondins, vouched for constitutional reforms of a moderate kind. As events progressed, Louis XVI was deposed, arrested, tried and later, in 1793, publicly executed, as was the Queen. In the wake of such turbulent upheavals, the French could not be expected to stand by Tipu in his emerging hostility with the confederates in India. Further, the new French Governor of Pondicherry, Thomas Conway, who had assumed office in 1787 was inimical to Tipu unlike Cossigny. 'I will write civil letters to Tipu,' he confessed to French leader Anne-César de la Luzerne in a letter on 7 January 1789, 'but I will not supply him with a single man without orders, and such orders I will not receive.'[18] His successor, Camille Charles de Fresne, even withdrew French troops from Pondicherry and instructed all French factories in India to remain neutral in the event of any Anglo–Mysore skirmish. They had been subsisting in Pondicherry on English money and even when Tipu offered to defray those expenses, there was no favourable response as the French did not wish to antagonize the British. So, it was essentially a solo act for Tipu to now combat a grand alliance of all the major and minor powers around him and also from within Mysore.

Hemmed in from all sides, Tipu sent conciliatory letters to the British to avert any fresh outbreak of hostilities. He offered to send a vakil to Madras to clarify his position and dispel any doubts. Writing to General William Medows, the newly appointed Governor of Madras on 22 May 1790, Tipu stated that this was necessary as 'the dust which has obscured your [Medows'] upright mind may be removed . . . in a word, the wish of my heart is this, that agreeable to the articles of the treaty of peace [Mangalore], our friendship may daily increase, and that by the favour of the Almighty there may never be the smallest deviation therefrom.'[19] It was filled with a pacific tone that complained of the 'representations, contrary to fact, of certain short-sighted persons, which had caused armies to be assembled on both sides, an event improper among those who are mutually at friendship.'[20] This was a completely different Tipu compared to the haughty manner in which he had responded to Hollond's propositions of appointing commissioners to ascertain the facts regarding the Lines, when he had rebuffed him saying, 'that he had, himself, ascertained the facts; after this what was the use of commissioners? Nevertheless, if Mr. Hollond wished it, he might send commissioners to the presence [Tipu's court].'[21] But the British would have none of it. Medows replied that 'the English, equally incapable of offering an insult as of submitting to one, had always looked upon war as declared, from the moment he attacked their ally the king of Travancore.'[22] Realizing his own precarious situation and the war drums beating so close, Tipu abandoned the Travancore campaign and rushed back to Srirangapatna in May 1790.

By the end of May 1790, the British had declared a fresh war against Mysore and its Sultan.

Outbreak of the War: First Phase

Taking command of his forces from Tiruchirapalli, Medows set forth on 26 May 1790. He was to proceed towards Palghat, reduce the forts there and in Coimbatore and then ascend the pass of Gejjalahutti. By then, forces under Col Kelly, comprising mainly troops from Bengal, were to penetrate from the Coromandel into the Baramahal and the two forces were to then decide the course of operations. Medows easily occupied the fort of Karur by 15 June, as it had been abandoned by the Mysoreans. A string of weak forts like Aravakurichi and Dharapuram which was guarded by just thirty men, soon fell to Medows by mid-July. The attainment of these chain of posts that were closely connected to one another and extended from the Coromandel Coast to the foot of the Gejjalahutti pass was the British strategy of planning an invasion into the heart of Mysore, from the south of the pass. By the time Medows reached Coimbatore he was astonished to find the city virtually empty. The chieftain, his family and the subjects had all fled. Making Coimbatore his headquarters, Medows dispatched Col James Stuart to Dindigul, Lt Col Oldham to Erode and Col Floyd towards Mysore. When Medows heard that Sayyid Sahib had arrived at Danayakkanakottai, about forty miles from Coimbatore, he commanded Floyd to surprise the Mysoreans. Floyd succeeded in driving Sayyid Sahib across the Bhavani River and also decamp towards the Gejjalahutti pass. Erode surrendered to Oldham in the first week of August.

The Dindigul fort was a well-built and guarded one, with ample supplies, 600–700 fighting men and no scarcity of water, provisions or ammunition. Captain Oram, under Col Stuart, ordered the Killedar Haidar Abbas to surrender the fort, but he stoutly refused, threatening to blow from a cannon anyone who trespassed. The British attacked the fort thereafter and a bloody combat followed, with Abbas and his troops offering stiff resistance. With incessant British firing, several of the troops within had fled in fright. Eventually, by 22 August, Haidar Abbas fluttered a white flag on a breach that the British had managed to inflict on the fort, expressing his desire to surrender. Dindigul was taken and Captain Bowser took charge of the fort.

Stuart, who had earlier planned on taking Palghat, had to abandon the expedition due to the monsoons and divert to Dindigul. Now that Dindigul had been captured, Stuart moved towards Palghat. In less than two hours of operations, Palghat capitulated by 22 September. One of the conditions of surrender was the protection of the Nairs who had joined Colonel Stuart and were employed in the blockade. Col Floyd, who was to move towards Mysore, managed to capture, by end-August, a string of depots starting with Tanjore, Tiruchirapalli, Karur, Erode and Satyamangalam. The fall of Satyamangalam, in particular, was strategic as Tipu temporarily lost access to Coimbatore. Cornwallis exuded hope on the prospects that these successes could accrue to the British: 'I entertain great hopes that the late rapid successes of General Medows and the probability of his being able to invade the Mysore Country in the next month with an army that Tippoo cannot resist will hold out so tempting a prospect of conquest and work so forcibly on the avarice and ambitions of the Mahrattas as to stimulate them to exertions, which a regard to good faith and to the solemn engagements has not yet been able to produce.'[23] The British were peeved by the tardy movement of the Nizam and the procrastination on the Maratha front in commanding Parshuram Bhau to attack the northern frontiers of Tipu, even as they engaged him in the south. They hoped these successes would inspire their allies to become more proactive.

Even as places and forts in the extended territories of the Mysore domain kept falling like pins to the British might, Tipu was keeping a close watch. By September 1790, he made a descent into Coimbatore district through the Gejjalahutti pass at the head of 40,000 men and a large train of artillery, leaving his heavy stores and baggage with

Purnaiya. The descent was 'so sudden, so silent, and so skillful in all respects, that it instantly occasioned a very material change in the general aspect of affairs'[24] and took the British by complete surprise. Fierce action followed at Satyamangalam on 13 September 1790. The massive British troops were totally routed by Tipu. Suffering severe casualties of about 556 men being killed or wounded and losing most of his baggage, guns and drought oxen, Col Floyd was forced to beat a hasty retreat to Coimbatore, abandoning the post of Satyamangalam. On his retreat, when the Mysoreans attacked Floyd at Cheyur, about twenty miles south of Satyamangalam, the Colonel managed to fight the Mysoreans off in another pitched battle. Here, Tipu's trusted kinsman and brave soldier, Burhan-ud-din, was killed in action and the news was received by the Sultan with great grief. Floyd joined Medows and Stuart's division at Velladi by the end of September 1790 and the plan of invasion of Mysore was deferred. Floyd had managed to escape and join Medows due to his sheer courage and perseverance and also the topography of the region that prevented Tipu from giving hot pursuit.

Cornwallis was concerned that this setback would negatively influence his Indian allies as 'the advantages, which Tipu gained there [Satyamanagalam], will no doubt be related to our allies with the grossest exaggerations, which unless countered by Captain Kennaway's and your [Malet] representations may have the effect of rendering them more backward than ever in fulfilling their engagements.'[25] He also sought to assure Malet 'how little our force or our spirits are affected by the small loss that we have met with.'[26]

Tipu now decided to reconquer the posts in Coimbatore province that the British had annexed. Erode surrendered to him by 25 September 1790. He then hoped to proceed southward and capture Coimbatore and marched there rapidly. Tipu, amply supported by his agent Lakshman Rao Raste, spread rumours and confusion in the Peshwa court about British capitulation in Coimbatore. Malet had to strive hard to dispel these rumours. By the time Tipu got there, Coimbatore had already been reinforced by the troops sent by Colonel Hartley from Palghat. So, he swiftly marched to Dharapuram which surrendered to the Mysorean forces on 6 October.

By then, news arrived of an English invasion of Baramahal, forcing Tipu to abandon the Coimbatore operations, leaving a contingent there under Qamar-ud-din, and proceed northward. A central division of the British army from Bengal left Burhanpur and reached Kanchipuram by August 1790. The force had 9500 men, including three regiments of European infantry, one regiment of Indian cavalry and formidable artillery. The troops assembled at Arni under Col Kelly's command. The strategy was to make a frontal attack on Mysore by laying siege to Bangalore and capturing districts adjacent to it. But Kelly's untimely demise on 24 September foiled British plans. His successor Colonel Maxwell, of the Madras Establishment, joined Medows in the Baramahal invasion. Entering Baramahal on 24 October, Maxwell reduced Vaniyambadi, Sheagur, Tirupattur and other mud forts. Reporting about his success and the fertile, prosperous region Maxwell writes: 'The country is highly cultivated, and a rich crop is now on the ground, and nearly ripe. The inhabitants having received from me assurances of safety and protection, have returned to their villages, and promise to supply the army with rice, which they are now beating out.'[27] By 1 November, Maxwell arrived at the formidable hill fort of Krishnagiri, even as he made Kaveripatnam his headquarters. But Maxwell was foiled in his attempts to take Krishnagiri by Tipu who suddenly appeared in the neighbourhood with amazing speed and secrecy.

Realizing that he could not make much headway in attacking the combined forces of Medows and Maxwell, Tipu changed his tactics and decided to attack the Carnatic in order to divert the British from their plans of a frontal invasion of Mysore. In fact, both parties moved towards the Thopur pass—the British to invade Mysore, and Tipu the Carnatic, and they reached the head of the pass at the same time. The British mounted a vigorous attack on Tipu but he managed to pass through without any significant loss. His cavalry too matched the march of his infantry with great courage and skill. By the end of November 1790, Tipu reached Srirangam and plundered it. He made two attempts in vain to take the fort of Thiagar that was ably defended by Captain Flint, who had distinguished himself in the Second Anglo–Mysore War in the defence of Wandiwash.

By 23 January 1791, Tipu had managed to take Permacoil and reach Pondicherry, once again seeking French support in the war. He sought the aid of 6000 men from the French, offering to pay for their expenses through a letter he had sent to King Louis XVI, with several presents. With this assistance, he hoped to destroy the British army and settlements in India for good, and transfer their possession to France. But Louis XVI declined this assistance saying: 'This resembles the affair of America, which I never think of without regret. My youth was taken advantage of at that time, and we suffer for it now; the lesson is too severe to be forgotten.'[28] Wilks mentions that 'in the midst of his distresses, the King [Louis XVI] was amused with the shabby finery of Tippoo's miserable presents to himself and the Queen, "trumpery to dress up dolls," which he desired M. Bertrand to give to his little girls.'[29] Bertrand de Moleville was the Minister of Marine who carried Tipu's proposals and gifts to the King. Tipu was thus abandoned by the French to defend his kingdom all by himself.

Tipu's strategy was faulty here, because if he had not wasted time soliciting the French and had attacked Madras instead, and destroyed the English military establishments at Kanchipuram, the war would have taken a totally different turn. It would have been as significant a loss for the British, just as Haidar's attack on Madras in the First Anglo–Mysore War had been. But here, Tipu lost a golden opportunity, even though he had reclaimed successes in the Carnatic.

Even in the midst of the war, Tipu sent another olive branch of peace to Medows on 5 December through his vakils Mir Sadak, Ali Raza and Appaji Ram, suggesting a restoration of friendship with the British through Commissioners that the General could appoint. Medows sent a quick reply through his Aid–de–Camp Captain Auley that he would not mind entering into a treaty, but for that to happen the 'first Article will be the unequivocal release of every English officer, known to be still in existence, and in confinement in the Mysore country.'[30] The peace negotiations went nowhere thereafter.

Medows was planning an invasion of Mysore but was called for the relief of Tiruchirapalli and Srirangam that had been ravaged by

Tipu. He decided to give him hot pursuit in the process but by then, he received a communique that Cornwallis had arrived in Madras on 12 December 1790 and was recalling him. A month ago, in November, after watching the reverses that the army suffered after initial successes, Cornwallis decided to enter the fray himself. The war had thus far yielded no tangible benefits to them and Cornwallis was getting increasingly restless and irritated. He hoped that his own entry would change the course of war and also imbibe great confidence and seriousness in the allies. He knew that Tipu would try everything he could to weaken the alliance and lure away his partners, especially after his initial successes. 'My principal object,' he wrote, 'in taking the field in person, and in carrying such powerful reinforcements from this country, is to convince the public in general, and our allies in particular, how sincerely earnest I am in my wishes to circumscribe the dangerous power of Tippoo, and to bring the war to a speedy and happy conclusion . . . hope that the Peshwa . . . will follow my example.'[31] By 27 January 1791, Cornwallis assumed total command of the war operations from Medows. He did not want an incidence of the Yorktown debacle to George Washington repeating itself in India or lose his half-hearted allies. With Cornwallis's entry, the war entered its second phase.

On the coast, though, Tipu received several reverses. On 10 December 1790, his commander Hussain Ali Khan was badly defeated by Colonel Hartley at Tirungadi, near Calicut. More than 1000 Mysoreans were killed or wounded and 900 men were taken prisoners. Hussain Ali managed to flee through the Tamarasherri pass. Shortly before this, General Robert Abercromby, the Governor of Bombay, arrived at Tellicherry. To subjugate the Bibi of Cannanore who was still dallying with the idea of entertaining Tipu's troops in her fort, he attacked Cannanore and took it by 17 December 1790. With these victories, the British supremacy over the Malabar was now total and complete. Malabar had been completely liberated from Mysore's possession.

Despite these reverses, the first phase of war had ended with considerable success for Tipu. The reasons for his success were that Tipu's cavalry was superior to the British and his artillery too was more in numbers. With 1,40,000 oxen and 1200 mules at his disposal, he was able to transport these across terrains too easily.[32] 'By his [Tipu's] swift marches and counter-marches,' writes Mohibbul Hasan, 'he had baffled the English commanders who had toiled in vain to catch up with him. He had inflicted great loss on the English armies both in men and in material, and had not only foiled the plans of Medows for the invasion of Mysore, but had invaded the Carnatic, thus converting a defensive into an offensive war. He had definitely proved his superiority as a skilful general and as a tactician of the first rank. Even Cornwallis . . . acknowledged: "We have lost time and our adversary has gained reputation, which are two most valuable things in war".'[33]

Second Phase of War

Accompanied by a large army comprising infantry, experienced cavalry, battering train, artillery, cattle and stores, Lord Charles Cornwallis marched out of Vellout on 5 February 1791, moving westwards towards Vellore. At the same time, the grand alliance armies, too, were to march from different directions. The Nizam's cavalry under Raja Tejwant Baramal, proceeding from Hyderabad and the principal Maratha cavalry under Haripant from Poona, were to join Cornwallis as he made his way towards Mysore territories from a north-easterly direction. Cornwallis had not been supportive of Medows's strategy of attacking Mysore from the south and always preferred this route. General Abercromby was to move in from the vicinity of Tellicherry. A section of the Maratha cavalry under Parshuram Bhau, the Patwardhan Chief of Miraj, assisted by a British detachment from Bombay under Captain Little, was to join Abercromby after reducing Dharwar in the northern territories of Tipu's domain, and then move down towards Srirangapatna to choke Tipu's resources. Cornwallis's plans were shrouded in such secrecy that Tipu got no wind of his exact movements, except vague intelligence of a possible British invasion into Mysore. Tipu was also complacent that the allies would not attack his domain while

'Cornwallis taking the sons of Tipu Sultan away as hostages'
by Daniel Orme, London 1799.

'Tippoo Sultaun delivering to Gullum Alli Beg the Vakeel his two
sons who are taking leave of their brother previously to their departure
from Seringapatam' by Joseph Grozer, London 1799.

'The last effort of Tippoo Sultaun in defence of the fortress of
Seringapatam' by John Vendramini, London 1802.

'The Last Effort and Fall of Tippoo Sultaun' by Niccolo
Schiavonetti, 1802.

'Finding the Body of Tippoo Sultaun' by Samuel William Reynolds, London 1800.

'The Body of Tippoo Sultaun Received by his Family' by Luigi Schiavonetti, London 1801.

'The Surrender of the Sons of Tippoo Sultaun' by Anthony Cardon,
London 1802.

Maharani of Mysore Lakshmi Ammanni.

'Arthur Wellesley, Duke of Wellington' by Charles Turner, 1806.

Marquess Wellesley, Governor-General 1798 to 1805,
produced in 1802.

Charles Marquis Cornwallis (1738–1803) by George J. Stodart.

Nawab of Arcot Muhammad Ali Walajah by George Willison.

A plan of the Carnatic region and Mysore by Robert Home, 1792.

LIEUTENANT GENERAL SIR EYRE COOTE, K.B.
Commander in Chief in the East Indies
from 1770 and 1777 to 1783.
Born in 1726. Died 28th April 1783 at Madras.

Sir Eyre Coote (1726–83) by John Thomas Setan in 1783.

Haidar Ali in 1762 (wrongly referenced as Commander-in-Chief of the Mahrattas): French painting by Pierre Adrien Le Beau (1748–1804) published at the end of the Seven Years' War.

Another portrait of a clean-shaven Haidar Ali, possibly in his later life. *The History of Hyder Shah, Alias Hyder Ali Khan Bahadur and his son Tippoo Sultaun.* London: W. Thacker & Co., 1855.

A mural of the Battle of Polilur on the walls of the Daria Daulat Bagh
Palace in Srirangapatna.

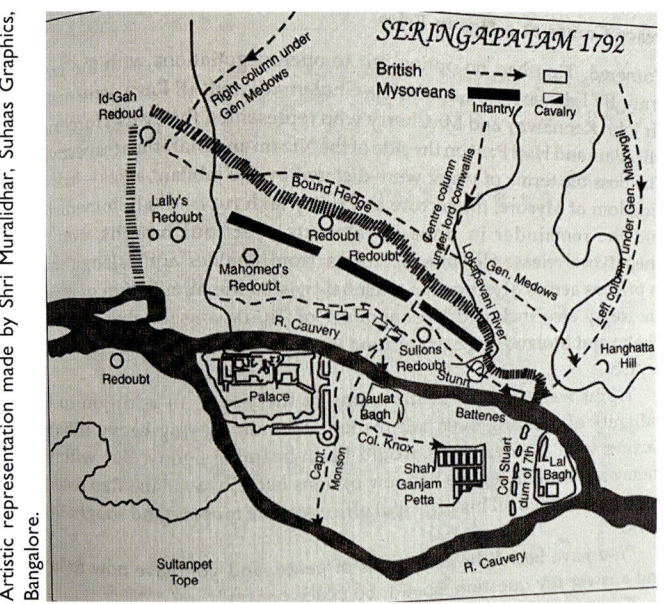

The allied attack on Mysore during the Third
Anglo–Mysore War.

Mysore after its partition post Third Anglo–Mysore War and division of territory among victorious allies.

The breach in the fort wall of Srirangapatna that welcomed the British in 1799.

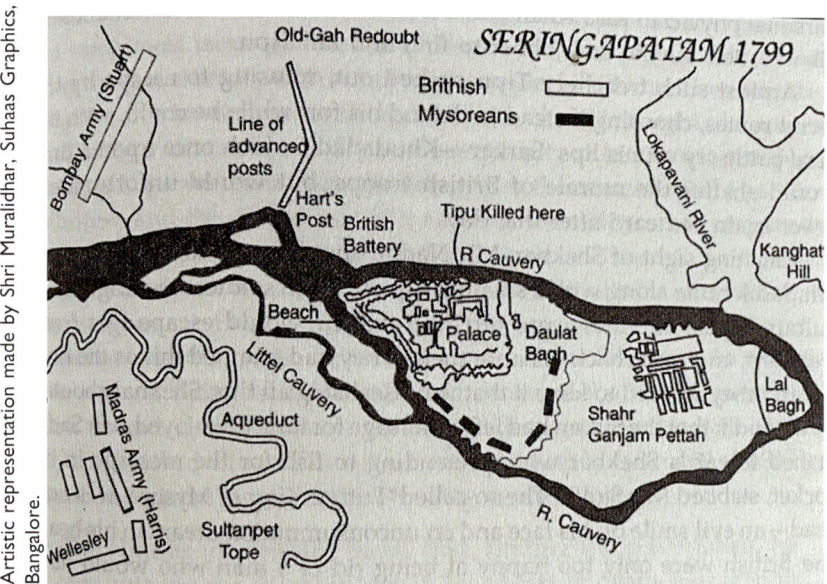

The final attack on the fort of Srirangapatna on 4 May 1799.

The Mackenzie inscription from Tipu's palace cursing the infidels.

Fateh Haidar

Abdul Khaliq

Muiz-ud-din

Moieuddin

The sons of Tipu Sultan.

Immadi Krishnaraja Wodeyar

Nanjaraja Wodeyar

Bettada Chamaraja Wodeyar VIII

Khasa Chamaraja Wodeyar IX

The Wodeyar rulers during the interregnum.

he was at large in the Carnatic and, in this miscalculation, allowed Cornwallis to steal a march over him.

When Tipu heard of the intent of the invasion into Mysore, even now not knowing the exact route, he hastily quit Pondicherry and made his way back through the passes of Changama and Palghat. He had assumed that Cornwallis's army would attack through the easier passes of Ambur or Baramahal. But here too, Cornwallis displayed his shrewdness. He tricked Tipu into believing that there was a movement along the Ambur pass, but in reality, fooled him and entered Mysore through a longer, tortuous route of Mugali pass. By the time Tipu realized where his enemies were and which route they were taking, Cornwallis had already entrenched himself firmly inside Mysore territories. Anticipating an attack on Bangalore, Tipu rushed there on 3 March 1791, dismissed and imprisoned its Commandant Sayyid Pir and another officer, Raja Ramachandra, on charges of treachery and intrigue. The faujdar of Krishnagiri, Bahaddur Khan, was made the new commandant in Bangalore with Muhammad Khan Bakhshi and Sayyid Hamid to assist him in defending the city and its fort.

Cornwallis marched towards Bangalore, and on the route places with no significant garrisons, like Kolar and Hoskote, were taken. By 5 March 1791, Cornwallis and his large army were within ten miles of Bangalore. A small cavalry of Tipu tried to resist but was no match for the British forces. Floyd began a reconnaissance of the east of the fort and had about 1000 horse of the Mysore side under Balaji Rao attack him. He had been ordered by Cornwallis not to get into any skirmish, but the situation led him to one. Floyd was wounded on his face and fell off his horse, and had to be carried away to safety. But for the darkness of the night which enabled many on the British side to escape, their losses might have been more severe. Tipu apprehended a night attack on his camp and left six miles west to Kengeri, leaving behind his garrison of 8000 men to defend the fort and 2000 regular infantry and 5000 peons for the defence of the *Peteh* or town.

Established by 'Naadaprabhu' Hiriya Kempegowda, a chieftain of the Vijayanagara dynasty of the Yelahanka Prabhu clan, in 1537, the mud fort of Bangalore was the nucleus of the city. Around it spread the Pete or town with a bustling population and trading community. Markets for grains (Tharagupete), bangles and musical instruments (Balepete), textiles (Nagarathpete and Chikkapete), oil extraction (Ballapurpete and Ganigarapete), flowers and horticulture (Tigalarapete) thrived in this area. Kempegowda is supposed to have witnessed a rare scene of a hare chasing a hunter dog, and also had dreams of the goddess of wealth Srilakshmi, which boded a good omen for him, to begin the construction of the mud-fort and the engulfing pete. The fort, with a moat surrounding it, had nine large gates. Under Haidar Ali and Tipu Sultan, the mud-fort was strengthened and rebuilt completely in stone. It was oval shaped with a circumference of over a mile and had a lofty rampart, twenty-six bastions to mount three guns a piece, five cavaliers and a deep ditch. It had two main gates called the Mysore Gate and the Delhi Gate, opposite the town. The town had wide, well-laid streets, and few other places in India could boast of better houses and richer inhabitants.[34]

The Fall of Bangalore

On 7 March 1791, Cornwallis who was encamped on the north-eastern part of Bangalore ordered an assault on the town with the 36th Regiment and a battalion of native infantry backed by six heavy guns.[35] The troops managed to push through a gateway on the north with hardly any resistance. However, the inner gates were more difficult to cross and were heavily barricaded with stones. They eventually scaled the ramparts and forced the Mysoreans to withdraw inside the fort. After an attack of over six hours, Gen. Medows managed to occupy the town. Through this, the British managed to procure rich stores of grain, military stores, bales of cotton and cloth, cannon pieces and gunpowder from a local factory. Grieved by the loss of the town, Tipu moved from Kengeri, with his entire force, to recover the pete. The main Mysorean force of 6000 infantry under Kumr-ud-din moved stealthily, to avoid being seen by the British from the pete. But Cornwallis understood this ploy and further reinforced the town. A fierce battle followed with the Mysoreans fighting valiantly to recover their town, but eventually failing and being driven out from every post they held, retreating back to the fort. In the process, severe casualties were suffered by Mysore with over 2000 men being killed, as per Wilks,[36] while only 131 losses of life were reported on the British side.

After taking and defending the town, the British armies now laid siege to the strong fort of Bangalore on 7 March 1791. Over the next fortnight, the fort was constantly attacked. Describing the siege, Wilks states:

> Few sieges have ever been conducted under parallel circumstances; a place not only not invested, but regularly relieved by fresh troops; a besieging army not only not undisturbed by field operations, but incessantly threatened by the whole of the enemy's force. No day or night elapsed without some new project for frustrating the operations of the siege; and during its continuance, the whole of the besieging army was accoutered, and the cavalry saddled, every night from sunset to sunrise.[37]

As the siege continued, the firing helped the British effect a breach by 18 March 1791, which was further widened over the next two days. Though they were the ones besieging the fort, the British were being exposed to the garrison from within and Tipu's army outside that was getting increasingly threatening. Kumr-ud-din had stationed himself in the neighbourhood of Basavanagudi, which was barely a mile and half from the Mysore Gate, to assist the beleaguered killedar. But the news of the battering down of the fort walls by British guns alarmed Tipu and he dispatched Toshikana Krishna Rao for assistance. The strategy was to have Lally defend the fort and the Mysorean forces, led by Kumr-ud-din and Sayyid Sahib, to launch an attack on the British. This entire operation was to be conducted in total secrecy with the British forces being taken by surprise. Krishna Rao is said to have fixed the time of the assault too. But Kirmani talks of Krishna Rao's treachery at this juncture and of his passing on hints to the British about these strategic plans. Krishna Rao, who knew the time of the assault, supposedly got the number of guards reduced at the breach, such that 'except a few sentinels, no one remained at their posts.'[38] However none of the other contemporary accounts substantiate these charges against Krishna Rao that Kirmani makes.

Tipu had decided to resume the defence by dawn. Having got wind of his plans, Cornwallis sought an early termination of the operations to their advantage with a night assault on 21 March 1791. Through the night, they climbed the ramparts of the fort, which was guarded by the French. Unfortunately for Tipu, the French betrayed him too and did not defend the fort well. The British breached the fort walls, entered and killed Killedar Bahaddur Khan. The Mysoreans were taken completely by surprise even as the British took a long, circuitous route to climb the main rampart at a place where there was least opposition. Tipu's reinforcements too reached very late. The Mysorean side lost more than 1000 men, while 131 of the British were killed or wounded. Writing about the siege and fall of Bangalore, Wilks records:

> It was a bright moonlight; eleven was the hour appointed, and a whisper along the ranks was the signal appointed for advancing in profound silence: the ladders were nearly planted, not only to ascend the faussebray, but the projecting work on the right, before the garrison took the alarm, and just as the serious struggle commenced on the breach, a narrow and circuitous way along a thin, shattered wall, had led a few men to the rampart, on the left flank of its defenders, where they coolly halted to accumulate their numbers, till sufficient to charge with the bayonet. The gallantry of the Killedar, who was in an instant at this post, protracted the obstinacy of resistance until he fell; but the energy of the assailants in front and flank at length prevailed. Once established on the ramparts, the flank companies proceeded as told off by alternate companies to the right and left, where the resistance was everywhere respectable, until they met over the Mysore Gate:

separate columns then descended into the body of the place; and at the expiration of an hour, all opposition had ceased.[39]

Thus fell the mighty fort of Bangalore which was a momentous event for the British as it brought the war right inside the heart of Tipu's domains and put them in control of probably the strongest and most important fortresses in Mysore. Bangalore was the gateway to Mysore and called *Dar-ul-Sultanat* or Capital of the Kingdom. Its collapse and capture meant that the very heart of Mysore was now threatened, sounding loud alarm bells for Tipu. He had to make haste if he did not want the situation to turn completely in British favour. Devanahalli, Chikkaballapura and Ambajidurga meekly surrendered to British might.

All through Cornwallis's march in the south, he had been assured by the Nizam that his troops under Raja Tejwant and Asad Ali Khan as second-in-command would join the British army as a powerful force multiplier. The Nizam had been urged numerous times to ensure that this large force from Hyderabad reached well on time for the siege of Bangalore. But in characteristic vacillation and procrastination, the Nizam's army was tardy in its forward movement. Right from the start of the operations in 1790, Cornwallis had been deeply disappointed by the dilatory tactics of the allies, especially the Nizam. Tejwant kept promising Cornwallis that they would reach on a particular date, but never kept his promise. By 12 March 1791, he reached Guramchirlah and marched at a snail's pace thereafter— marching a few miles every day and resting for the next five or six days thereafter. Bangalore was besieged and taken, but there was no sight of the Hyderabad force that was to have joined in this operation. Lt Col Thornton records: 'It would be hard to say which was most useless, the Commander Raja Teige Wunt Sing [Tejwant], or the rabble serving under him. There was neither organization nor was there any discipline. Every man was a law unto himself, both in what he did, and in the arms and equipment which he wore . . . In a last effort to extract some value from a contingent which was making such terrible inroads into his supplies, Lord Cornwallis agreed that

2000 of the Nizam's cavalry should undergo two weeks' instruction under a specially selected British officer . . . Captain Dallas.'[40]

Tejwant kept giving excuses to Cornwallis about Tipu's attempts to prevent the junction of the two armies, something which was so blatantly false that Cornwallis found it the 'most absurd and unfounded information.'[41] He began to assume that Tejwant had been bought over by Tipu and shared his apprehensions with Kennaway. Cornwallis added that he 'will not tamely submit either to evident breach of agreement, or to strong marks of deception, and that in the present case, unless, instead of receiving frivolous excuses, I shall soon see the most satisfactory grounds to expect the speedy junction of the above-mentioned body of cavalry, I shall not waste time in waiting for them, but proceed with the army to the execution of my own plan of operations, without placing any further dependence upon their assistance.'[42] It was finally by 13 April 1791 that the British army was finally united with Tejwant at Kottapalli, eighty-four miles north of Bangalore. A salute was fired in honour of the junction of the Nizam's cavalry with the British army. The convoy had brought along a vast amount of supplies and provisions, a reinforcement of 700 Europeans and 4500 Indian troops that included 450 cavalry. Tipu tried to strike the convoy but was unsuccessful. They made their way to Bangalore, which was the new base from where the allies planned a direct attack on Srirangapatna. But before one gets to the combined attack of the plan, we trace the movements and activities of the allied armies in other theatres of war up till this time.

The Movements of the Allies' Armies

Right from the time of the outbreak of the war, the attitude of the allies, the Marathas and the Nizam, was dilatory and circumspect. Their 'lukewarm and evasive conduct',[43] as Malet put it, was driven by several considerations. The campaign of Medows had not instilled much confidence in the allies. Realizing this, Cornwallis had come down himself to lead the war. The allies now waited to see how the operations progressed and if it was worth their while to plunge into the British design. They wanted to conserve their strength, even as they let the British and Tipu exhaust themselves in the war with each other, and knew that they could then enter the fray at the end, and tilt the successes to their advantage.[44] Cornwallis's repeated appeals to both courts and the efforts of Malet and Kennaway pushed the allies into some tardy action. But the allies soon began to fear the British wrath or a tactical disadvantage for them if the British concluded unilateral peace with Tipu. That way, they would have embittered both Tipu and the British and be left to the mercies of their retaliation. The Nizam and the Maratha side represented by Haripant hence met in mid-March 1791 at Pangal to thrash out their approach to the war. The impressive advance of Cornwallis by then also added to their decision to abide by the terms of their treaty with the British and be more proactive.

Right from the time of the commencement of the operations, in May 1790, the movements of the three allies were in different directions and at varied momentums. There were thus multiple theatres of war, and these side operations were happening even as the main army was consumed with a frontal attack on Mysore and on Tipu. It was only after the fall of Bangalore that they all converged.

The Nizam's Conquests

In May 1790, the Nizam's troops had been augmented by a British detachment under Major Montgomery and two battalions of native infantry. Even as Tipu was engaged in the Carnatic and Coimbatore in the first phase of the war, these troops entered the border districts of Tipu's domain without any fear of resistance. Proceeding from Raichur, they laid siege to Koppal on 28 October 1790. Another detachment of the same combined army moved from Koppal to capture Ganjikota, Sidhout and other places. While the Nizam's troops managed to take Koppal town, the strong fort was defended stoutly by its killedar Nanaji Rao Salonkhe, a native of Bellary. The artillery of the besiegers was so inferior and ammunitions in such short supply that in barely a week they were disabled by their own fire. The Nizam prevailed upon his minister too who favoured an abandonment of the siege to drop such thoughts due to initial failures. He even offered to lead the campaign by personally going to Koppal to annex it. Only by mid-January 1791 did new battering trains arrive from Raichur and Pangal that were engaged in continuous firing. All this helped the troops to finally effect a breach. The inmates provided such valiant opposition that the allied armies were left exasperated. By 8 March 1791, Kennaway was deflated enough to lament to Cornwallis that 'the chance of carrying Kopul [Koppal] by force is against us.'[45] It was only by 18 April that the fort finally fell after holding on so resolutely for months. The garrison was allowed to leave, carrying away their personal property. Bahadur Benda, Ganjikota, Sidhout and other places too fell in quick succession to the allies. By 19 September 1791, the Nizam and British army contingent moved to Gurramkonda and besieged it, and another unit was sent to capture Cudappah, Gutti and other places.

The Maratha Military Campaigns

On the Maratha side too, preparations began in March 1790. Nana had requested Parshuram Bhau to lead the campaign and he spent a couple of months in preparing for it militarily. After the treaty was signed between the Peshwa and the British, a contingent under Captain John Little was to join Bhau at Tasgaon; Bhau was leading a force of about 12,000 horse and 5000 infantry. By 15 August 1790, the combined armies had crossed the Krishna River, capturing Hubli, Mishrikota, Dodwad and other places, before reaching Dharwar by 18 September. Dharwar was important as the capital of the province between the rivers Krishna and Tungabhadra that Haidar Ali had conquered from the Marathas and was commanded by one of Tipu's most loyal commanders, Badr-uz-zaman Khan. Tipu had sent a further reinforcement under Sher Khan of 4000 men, in addition to the garrison of 10,000 men and fifteen guns that had already defended Dharwar. Even as the campaign for Dharwar was being planned, several detachments were simultaneously sent by Bhau between October 1790 and February 1791. These detachments conquered Gajendragadh, Savanur and Lakshmeshwar.

By the end of October 1790, the town of Dharwar was taken and the fort that had defences principally of mud was attacked. The Marathas randomly fired at the walls of the fort with no specific targets. They also followed 'an absurd practice not unusual with Mahrattas'[46] of dragging their guns back to their camps at night, giving the Mysorean side the opportunity to repair the little damages that their ineffective firing had caused. Most of the Maratha guns were old, clumsy, unserviceable and of inferior quality, often bursting from their own fire. Ammunition and supplies from Poona were also not sufficient for a long haul. Edward Moore, a member of Captain Little's detachment, has written an extensive eyewitness account of the entire campaign. He bitterly complained that with the tardy manner in which the Maratha campaign was being carried out, it might take them seven years to capture Dharwar. 'A gun is loaded,' writes Moore, 'and the whole of the people in the battery sit down, talk and smoke for half an hour, when it is fired, and if it knocks up a great dust, it is thought sufficient; it is reloaded, and the parties resume their smoking and conversation. During the two hours in the middle of the day, generally from one to three, a gun is seldom fired on either side, that time being, as it would appear by mutual consent, set apart for meals. In the night, the fire from guns is slackened, but musketry is increased on both sides, and shells are sparingly thrown into the fort, with tolerable precision.'[47]

The British side too did not have great battering trains, despite Captain Little's repeated remonstrances to the Bombay Government regarding the same. It was only by 28 December 1790 that a new battalion of Europeans and another of natives was sent to Dharwar under Lt Col Frederick who assumed charge of the British detachment.

Frederick wanted to steal a march over the Maratha forces who had sat there for months now and not taken Dharwar. He first sent a threatening letter to Badr-uz-zaman Khan to surrender but the latter kept prevaricating. Frederick then decided to launch an assault on the fort, being supremely confident of success. Parshuram Bhau advised him against the plan but eventually let him have his way.

On 27 February 1791, his troops advanced to the assault of the fort, but this ended in such a debacle for the British. The Mysorean side had set on fire the ditches that the British had filled with fascines in order to cross it. About forty were killed and over 100 wounded on the British side. The Marathas remained aloof and watched the discomfort of their complacent ally with perverse pleasure. So disappointed and demoralized was Frederick by this defeat that his health rapidly deteriorated thereafter and he eventually died on 13 March 1791. Major Sartorius then took command of the British army there.

Parshuram Bhau meanwhile kept writing to Poona for ammunition and guns which took the longest time to arrive. Once they did on 1 March, a fresh assault was mounted and after a siege of nearly twenty-nine weeks, the fort was finally breached. But the garrison continued to give very stiff resistance and inflicted great losses on the Marathas. But there was only that much that they could do to hold out. Their supplies, water and provisions were slowly drying out.

By then the news of the fall of Bangalore that came in totally demoralized the Mysorean forces. The initial garrison of 10,000 men had dwindled down to 3000 and Badr-uz-zaman Khan was finding it tough to resist further. By 30 March 1791, he agreed to surrender and the garrison was evacuated by 4 April, and he too was promised an honourable discharge. He was, according to Moore, 'a man of good appearance, of middle stature, about fifty or fifty-five years of age, has a handsome beard, and a scar, apparently from a wound, on his left cheek. He was very particular in returning the salutes of our gentlemen . . . his dress was white, quite plain, and vert neat; there was an interesting dejection in his countenance, which added to the esteem every soldier must feel for so gallant a brother, could not fail of exciting a sympathetic emotion for his distressing situation. He is related by marriage to Tippoo, and has the honour of his sovereign's unbounded confidence, which reflects equal credit on the merit of the one, and sagacity of the other.'[48] Though eventually vanquished, Badr-uz-zaman Khan had offered a great advantage to Tipu through his military operations. He had successfully managed to tire out the Maratha and British armies by holding them on for nearly six and a half months, during which time he had prevented their attempts to cut off supplies to Tipu and also managed to postpone their joining the main army that was focusing on an invasion of Srirangapatna.

Even though Badr-uz-zaman Khan was promised an honourable exit, while he was proceeding to the camp, the Marathas made fun of him and threw dust on his palanquin. Though Bhau advised Khan to pitch his tent closer to his own so that he might not be looted by the Maratha army irregulars, Khan took his camp about two miles away on the road to Shimoga. Violating the terms of the agreement, the Maratha army then looted Khan's camp and wounded him and several of his men lost their lives. They robbed him of everything he had, including seven guns that he had brought from Dharwar. Duff mentions that the reason for the Maratha outrage against Khan was the latter's destruction of the ammunition and stores within the Dharwar fort before he surrendered and left. Two thousand rifles too had been wilfully broken and several buried underground, lest they get into Maratha hands. When the Maratha army discovered this, they hurled the vilest abuses at him, as also Haidar and Tipu for being perpetual breakers of promises. This insult to himself and his masters is supposed to have incensed Khan so much that he drew out his sword and a scuffle followed, leading to the loot and murders that Khan's side suffered.[49] Bhau felt sorry for the misfortune that had befallen Khan. He received him with respect and even appointed a British surgeon to treat his wounds. The assaulters were punished. Reporting about this incident, Malet writes to Cornwallis on 18 April 1791:

Disputes had arisen between his [Khan's] people and the Marratta escort caused by Buddur's [Badr-uz-zaman] insisting on encamping at a greater distance from the Bhaou [Parshuram Bhau] than his escort thought proper. Blows ensued and Buddural Zuman Khan [sic] who had mounted his horse (as the Minister says to make his escape) received two severe wounds and was conducted in that condition to the Bhaou who received him kindly and has offered every assistance to be given him . . . everything that Buddural Zuman Khan had brought out of Dharwar was irrecoverably plundered and his people totally dispossessed. The minister added that though this fray had been accidental, Bhaou had intended coming to an explanation with Buddural Zuman Khan for abusing the articles of capitulation by bursting many of the guns of the fort and rendering all the guns unserviceable.[50]

But soon after Khan recovered, on the pretext of his violation of the terms of surrender, Bhau ordered the imprisonment of Khan and several others who were sent in irons to the Nargund fort. The accusation was that he was duty bound to surrender the fort in its actual condition and by his act of destroying the ammunitions and stores, lest they get into his opponents' hands, Khan had completely violated the agreement and deserved punishment.

The fall of Dharwar was as significant as the collapse of Bangalore. This led to the entire territory north of the Tungabhadra being freed from Mysorean forces and occupation. Bhau now wanted to march southwards towards Srirangapatna. They crossed the Tungabhadra in May 1791. On the way, he, along with Raghunath Rao Kurundwadkar, captured Ramagiri, Hosadurga, Sante Bidanur (present-day Santebennur in Davanagere), Mayakonda and Chengeri. If this army had joined Cornwallis immediately, after the reduction of Dharwar, instead of wasting 'precious time in reducing the northern districts of Mysore,' the war might have taken a different and better route for the allies. On their way southwards, the Maratha army unleashed loot, destruction and devastation on the hapless people of Mysore. Moore, who was part of the contingent, states: 'The route of the army is marked by ruin and devastation; every village and town being burned and razed with the ground, and the road strewed with horses and bullocks, from which issued a most intolerable stench. We have seen fifteen and twenty of these animals dead and dying, under one tree, where the poor creatures had creeped, to be out of the heat of the sun. In the distance of ten miles, perhaps as many destroyed villages will be seen, without an inhabitant to tell their names; such is the havoc this destructive army has caused on this fair country.'[51] They finally joined Lord Cornwallis on 28 May 1791 at Melukote.

The Shame at Sringeri

It was during this march towards Srirangapatna, somewhere around April 1791, that one of the most disgraceful episodes in Maratha history occurred. G.S. Sardesai states: 'Raghunathrao Patwardhan burning with the desire of revenge against Tipu, wantonly destroyed at this time the holy shrine of the Shankaracharya of Shringeri, an affront to Hindu religion by a brother Hindu, the sad memory of which long remained fresh in Maratha memory.'[52] That one of the holiest of shrines of the Hindus and among the four *mathas* (the residence for various religious scholars and ascetics within a Hindu sect, sometimes attached to a grand temple; a monastic order in Hinduism) that were believed to be established by Adi Shankaracharya was desecrated in this manner was truly a painful chapter in the matha's hoary history. The irregulars in the Maratha army, the *pindaris* and other similar marauders who accompanied the army, led by Raghunathrao Patwardhan, looted the temples and defiled the holy shrine of goddess Sharada.

A letter of this period from Raghunath Rao's father, Neelkanth Appa, to Balasaheb Patwardhan at Miraj mentions the episode of the Sringeri attack for the first time. On 14 May 1791, the letter of Trimbak Rao, Raghunath Rao's son, to his uncle Balasaheb Patwardhan at Miraj states: 'After the army crossed the Tungabhadra River, the *laamans* [a tribe] and *pindaris* reached Shivamoghe [Shimoga] and looted Sringeri, the Swami's [Shankaracharya] village. Swami's *danda* [staff], *kamandalu* [vessel] was also looted. Nothing was left. Even the women were assaulted and raped and some of them sacrificed their lives. The Swami's idol, the Dev Linga, was also looted. The elephant stable was emptied by the laamans. An anguished Swami undertook fasts for five days, thereby giving up his life.'[53] The detail of the Shankaracharya having fasted unto death, as mentioned in this letter, is of course untrue. The letter then goes on to say: 'When father [Raghunath Rao] heard of this loot, he dispatched the cavalry to arrest the laamans. The elephants were taken over. But the remaining stolen items were not be found.'[54]

The pindaris and laamans were plunderers who were employed in the armies as irregulars by both the Mughals and later the Marathas. Tipu's army, too, had irregulars of this nature, who were known as the *bayed*. The pindaris were mostly horsemen who were armed with spears and swords and tasked with unleashing terror on innocent people of the enemy domains and also passing on secret information that they would gather about the opponent. The etymology of their name too derives from the words implying 'those who took bundles of grass,' implying their addiction to drugs or other forms of addictions. They had no regular pay but subsisted on the loot they gathered during military campaigns. The majority of their leaders were Muslims, but they were recruited from all classes.[55] They had several groups called *durrahs* in which they organized and each had its own leaders and caste affiliations. It was this group of pindaris associated with the Maratha army that raided Sringeri to loot the treasures that the temple had. A.K. Shastry notes: 'Brahmin priests were killed in the affray, and the loot that was carried away was of the value of sixty lakhs of rupees.'[56]

The Shankaracharya's fast and also his anguished letters to the Peshwa were to draw the attention of the Maratha polity towards this shameful act. Nana Phadnis, too, was of the firm belief that even if the Patwardhans had to pay a lakh and fifty thousand rupees, they should do so readily in order to win back the Shankaracharya's favours and benediction. Nana wrote: 'Swami's math has been looted, and so Swami is on a fast. This does not augur well for our State. However, Dada [Raghunath Rao] should tell the brothers wherever he has a clue of the looters. He should act in a way that stern action is taken against the offenders, the Swami is consequently satisfied and his wrath disappears.'[57] But in his letter to the Peshwa on 30 December 1791, Raghunath Rao completely denied any participation or responsibility for the plunder. 'It was not merely our people who looted the mutt. The laamans of four other sardars too had gone, including ours. We do not know why the Swami is taking our name.'[58] He further demanded an enquiry into the matter. The Sringeri episode was thus clearly an aberration that was not part of Maratha state policy or battle strategy. The remorse and repentance, with an inclination to correct the wrongdoing is what these letters at the highest echelons of Maratha power demonstrate. Historian V.W. Khare who documented these correspondences states that while the resolution of this issue thereafter is not known, one does know for a fact that the Shankaracharya made a state visit to Poona the subsequent year.[59] So one may assume that by then his anger with the Marathas for what had inadvertently happened at the matha was assuaged.

But even before this reprehensible destruction, there seems to have been bonhomie and regular communication between Tipu and the Jagadguru Shankaracharya of Sringeri matha, Sri Sacchidananda Bharati III (1770–1814). In letters in Kannada to the Swamiji dated 3 April 1791 and 20 June 1791, Tipu seems to be updating him about the progress of the enemy troops within his kingdom and their assaults on the people. In both these letters he urges the Swamiji, whom he addresses as his guru, to offer prayers to Lord Ishwara to ensure the defeat and flight of the enemies and to bring succour, happiness and prosperity to the people of Mysore.[60]

The first correspondence between Tipu and the Swamiji about the desecration dates 6 July 1791. He writes to the Swamiji that he had heard of the horrors that the matha had faced where Maratha horsemen (*kudureyavaru*) had grievously attacked and harmed the Brahmins in Sringeri, pulled out and vandalized the idol of goddess Sharada and looted the place of all its possessions and treasures. The Swamiji had fled from the place to Karkala, along with four of his disciples, as Tipu's letter records. He unequivocally states in this correspondence that the idol of the goddess that had been consecrated and worshipped since times immemorial needs to be urgently reinstalled so that it lasts as long as the sun and moon exist. In his letter, Tipu quotes a Sanskrit proverb '*Hasadbhih kriyate karma roodadbhir anubhooyate'*—for the acts of foolishness committed in smiles but without any foresight, one often pays the price through tears and sufferings later. He hopes that similarly those who had unthinkingly destroyed a sacred place like the matha and committed, as per him, '*Guru Droha*' or treachery to the saint, were bound to have their karma catching up with them sooner than later, leading to all-round devastation, loss of wealth and ruin of family for the miscreants. He made a grant of 400 *rahatis* for the repair and restoration of the temple and the reinstallation of the idol.[61]

In a subsequent letter dated 18 July 1791, he requested the Swamiji to accept grains and cash from the *asaf* of Bidanur for the ceremonies related to the reinstallation. He also sent a palanquin and gifts to the Swamiji as a mark of respect. In all his letters, he makes an entreaty to him to pray and perform penances to ensure the total annihilation of his enemies, and welfare for himself, his government and the people of Mysore.[62] In an order to all his officers, killedars and amaldars, on 27 July 1791, Tipu directed them not to restrict the movements of Brahmins of the Sringeri matha to other places where their disciples resided.[63]

The Swamiji who had been outraged by the desecration had vowed to go on a hunger strike to end his life. But the letters and assurances of Tipu assuaged him and, being pleased, he sent back to the Sultan his benedictions in the form of sandal paste, coloured consecrated rice (*mantraakshate*) and a pair of shawls through Venkatachala Shastry of the matha. Acknowledging with gratitude the receipt of these blessings, Tipu sent back a saree and upper garment for the idol of the goddess that was to be reinstalled, along with hard cash and paddy for the ceremonies.[64] Since the looters had even taken away the temple elephant and palanquin, he ordered another elephant named Sallagesha to be gifted to the shrine.[65]

The news of this destruction and the anger of the Swamiji who wanted to go on a fast unto death reached the court in Poona, causing great anguish there. The Peshwa was deeply disturbed to hear about this horrific occurrence. A thorough enquiry into the incident was ordered and Parshuram Bhau was directed to compensate the matha and return all the looted treasures. Bhau, too, was extremely repentant about what had happened and informed the Peshwa that he would readily atone for what had happened in Sringeri. 'The Peshwa's letters,' writes A.K. Shastry, 'reveal his keen interest and sincerity in giving compensation to the matha. The positive reply from Parshuram Bhau to the Peshwa would lead to form an impression that the foolish plunder of Sringeri was not due to any deliberate intention on his part, but as a result of the predatory habits of the pindaris in his contingent.'[66]

Confederates at Srirangapatna

Tejwant and the Nizam's cavalry had belatedly already made a junction with Cornwallis. The main Maratha army under Haripant had left Poona on 1 January 1791 to join him as well. But this force too was slow in its progress. After he spent a few weeks at Pangal in April 1791, conferring with the Nizam on their joint strategy in the war, Haripant set off to join Cornwallis. The British plan was that Haripant move from there to Ganjikota and join the main army. However, Haripant, too, was tardy and decided to stay on in Kurnool to levy taxes from the Nawab Ranmast Khan. Malet expressed his utmost indignation to Nana about this prevaricating attitude of Haripant. In his defence though, Haripant mentioned that of his 13,000 horses, nearly 10,000 had already been dispatched to Ganjikota and he was waiting for a reinforcement to proceed himself. Malet once again strongly opposed this because as per the terms of the treaty, the Maratha side had to provide 25,000 horse and at this crucial juncture when Cornwallis was waiting for the allies to join, to claim shortage of troops was unpardonable, 'for all the breach and deficiency in the said cooperative engagements and for all the evils that have arisen or may arise therefrom to the Confederacy.'[67]

After his forces were reinforced, Haripant marched from Kurnool and was joined by his son Lakshman Rao in Sira. The place surrendered without any resistance. Balwant Suba Rao was also sent to siege Maddagiri, about twenty miles east of Sira and Haripant. After leaving a strong garrison at Sira, he marched south-west to join Cornwallis. By then, Bhau too was proceeding southwards.

After the fall of Bangalore and the intention of the allies to attack his capital, Tipu was alarmed and worried. So shaken was he that he considered evacuating his entire family, harem, treasures and all his officials with their families to safety in Chitradurga. But his mother prevailed upon him to suspend this plan as it would demoralize the troops and give a hint of his despondency. She also wrote a letter to the Nizam's favourite wife in which 'she supplicated compassion for an unfortunate Mussulman, her son, who in the pride and intoxication of youth had given offence to her family, which he [now] sincerely regretted.'[68]

Tipu also had frescoes and caricatures painted on the walls of all the houses in the main streets of Srirangapatna. In one there was a tiger seizing a trembling Englishman; another had a horseman cutting off two British heads in one blow; a third had Arcot Nawab Mohammad Ali, his old rival, being brought in chains and prostrating in front of a British officer who had placed his foot on his neck. These were Tipu's wishes that he hoped would be fulfilled. He also hoped that such public displays would boost the morale of the subjects and army. Perhaps again on the advice of his mother, he had these whitewashed soon after. Undoubtedly, Tipu seems to have been extremely tense and worried about what was going to unfold, given that the enemy had come so close to his gates. Among the large retinue of British prisoners in his captivity were about twenty good-looking and young boys who had been forced to sing and dance in the attire and style of a courtesan. Secret orders were passed to put all these unfortunate boys to death. Their corpses too were discarded outside the fort by the scavengers.

Tipu also became extremely wary of everyone who worked for him. Surveillance of everyone and everything that went in and out of government departments became the practice. He had completely lost his mental balance after the fall of Bangalore and ordered the indiscriminate execution of several of his officers against whom there was any whiff of suspicion of treachery. Among these were Jogaiya Pandit, the nephew of Achanna Pandit, and Raja Ramachandra Phadak, the Subadar of Arcot, as also the palegars of Rayadurga and Harpanahalli, at the mention of whose very names 'the fire of the Sultan's wrath burned fiercely'.[69] Tipu dispatched Krishna Rao from Bangalore to Srirangapatna to take charge of the capital and also organize money disbursements for the troops.

Even as he was facing such critical challenges in the battlefield, there were fresh attempts by the royalists within Mysore, who had been relentless in their efforts to reinstall the Wodeyar dynasty. Once again, none of the contemporary records are able to pointedly ascertain any exact knowledge or involvement of Maharani Lakshmi Ammanni in these fresh insurrections. Such was the surreptitious manner in which she seemed to operate. The British fanned these movements, especially among disconcerted palegars who had been dispossessed of their wealth. There was also widespread discontent regarding Tipu's exactions and religious frenzy that had manifested itself within and outside the domains of Mysore. Col Alexander Read, who commanded at Ambur, won over several of these discontented palegars, who kept a close connection with the harakaras or messengers in Tipu's camp, informing his enemies about his next move.

One such informant who was trying to leak information to the British in a letter written in Kannada was apprehended. The writer, a former Brahmin who had been forcibly circumcised and converted as Mohammad Abbas by Tipu, had allegedly carried this treason on the command of Sheshagiri Rao, the brother of Toshikhana's (Treasury) Krishna Rao. Saiyid Sahab was given the task of investigating the matter and Abbas was brought to the Sultan's presence. Abbas, being certain of his death, refused to implicate anyone else, no matter what tortures were inflicted on him. An enraged Tipu ordered Abbas to confess how long he had been a traitor for. He replied: 'From the period that you began to circumcise bramins [sic] and destroy their temples.'[70] Abbas was immediately put to death by being mercilessly dragged around the camp, tied to the foot of an elephant. But Saiyid

Sahib, who also had an old axe to grind against Krishna Rao for an old financial squabble while in Dindigul, connected the dots of the treason to lead up to Rao. Thereafter, Krishna Rao and his three brothers, including Sheshagiri Rao, were all tortured and executed. Krishna Rao was bodily lifted by *jetties* (wrestlers) and thrown into a boiling cauldron of oil, in which he eventually perished.[71]

Kirmani narrates this episode slightly differently. He mentions that after the discovery of the treason, when Saiyid Sahib sent orders to Krishna Rao to present himself to the durbar of the Sultan where his mother too was seated, the latter refused to comply. Saiyid Sahib used this as a confirmation of Rao's treachery, sent his soldiers to the latter's house, broke open the doors, put him to death and threw his body in the drain of the bazar. His house was thereafter plundered and all the property confiscated for the royal treasury. In the last moments before his death, Krishna Rao is said to have scoffed at the assailants saying: 'I have lighted up a fire, which as long as the Sultan lives will not be extinguished.'[72] Krishna Rao's beautiful, faithful and virtuous wife was 'tyrannically forced [by the Sultan] . . . to enter his seraglio, make a false charge and lying accusation'[73] against her own dead husband that he was indeed a traitor.

Tipu did not consider the fact that Krishna Rao, along with Purnaiya and several others, had been instrumental in keeping Haidar's death in the war camp secretive and also ensured a peaceful transition of power to him in those chaotic times of 1782–83. Krishna Rao, a Marathi Brahmin, was one of the ablest and wisest officers in the treasury and an expert in accounts and revenue matters. Quite uncharacteristic of his profession, Rao had also offered some sound advice on military matters in the past to both Haidar and Tipu. His wise counsel had in fact helped Tipu during the campaign against Medows. This 'execution of one of the most able and intelligent officers of the state'[74] was seen with horror by the rest of the officialdom and the people at large. Hayavadana Rao states: 'Whether Krishna Rao was in the attempt [of treachery] or not, it is clear that the moral basis—if any—of Tipu's administration had been sapped to its foundations by Tipu's own unbridled acts, and people were not only tired of him, but also actively against him.'[75]

While narrating the unfortunate fate that befell Krishna Rao, Wilks mentions that he tried to ascertain more details from Purnaiya, a close colleague and fellow caste-man. But he could never get Purnaiya to give his opinion and insights on this matter. Hayavadana Rao however writes: 'Later, but wholly untrustworthy, accounts have suggested that Purnaiya was jealous of Krishna Rao and left him to his fate without even putting a word of intercession on his behalf from entirely selfish motives, if he did not indeed connive at his unnatural dispatch.'[76] Hayavadana Rao however dismisses these insinuations as baseless and mere gossip because Purnaiya was at a higher level than Krishna Rao, both in position and also in the personal esteem and trust of Tipu and his mother whose word was followed with great respect by him.

The March to Srirangapatna

Meanwhile, Cornwallis was getting restive about the procrastination that his allies were inflicting on him. After the fall of Bangalore on 21 March, the allied forces had done precious little to convert that strategic success into mounting a frontal attack on Srirangapatna. On 3 May 1791, he decided to move his heavy guns from their base camp in Bangalore and move six to seven miles on the route to Srirangapatna. Tipu assumed that Cornwallis would take the main route to his capital that passed through Chennapatna and therefore destroyed all the grain and forage in his path. He had taken a strong position there, being supported by the hill forts of Ramagiri and Shivanagiri. But Cornwallis with his huge army—one regiment of European cavalry, five regiments of Indian cavalry, three battalions of artillery, seven regiments of European infantry, ten battalions of coast sepoys with seven other such from Bengal and 14,000 irregular horses, took a circuitous route to Srirangapatna. Giving Tipu a slip, they marched via Kankanahalli and Sultanpete. But even on this route, all the vegetation had been fully burnt and the troops could get neither grains nor a single informant who could guide or assist them. By then the onset of the monsoon, a month earlier than expected, had made matters worse. Roads were intersected by overflowing rivulets and ravines. Cattle and horses were dying for want of food. Major Dirom writes about the travails they faced in this campaign: 'The season of the year was unfavourable to the cattle; they were infected with an epidemic disorder which killed them in vast numbers, and rendered the greater part of what remained of little service. The scarcity of grain was such that the lower class of followers were reduced to the necessity of subsisting chiefly on the putrid flesh of the dead bullocks; and to add to the scene of distress, the small-pox unfortunately raged in the camp.'[77]

Facing the greatest hardships on the way, the exhausted grand army reached Arikere, about nine miles east of Srirangapatna on 13 May 1791. The plan was to cross the river Kaveri there and attack Srirangapatna. In his letter to Raja Tejwant, Cornwallis had explained his strategy:

> As Tippoo has on all occasions since the commencement of the war carefully avoided an action with the British armies of very inconsiderable numbers, and in particular could not venture to attack this army when a large part of it was employed in the siege of Bangalore, there is not the least probability that he will now hazard a battle with the strongest army that was ever brought in the field against him. It therefore falls to the share of the infantry to proceed with the artillery according to the plan which has been settled to attack Seringapatam and it is the duty of the cavalry to overrun the country, to cut off Tippoo's communication with his capital and to prevent the approach of his small detachments of light horse to disturb the troops that will be employed in the siege. To answer these purposes I desire that you will immediately detach a body of His Highness' [Nizam's] cavalry . . . to drive the enemy's small parties from the neighbourhood of the army and to intercept everything going to or coming out of Seringapatam . . . the detached corps should leave its heavy baggage with the army and move into the country as lightly equipped as possible which will enable it either to avoid with facility and detachments of the enemy that may be furnished with infantry and guns or to attack them with success if a favourable opportunity should offer.[78]

But luck was not on Cornwallis's side this time. The Kaveri River was swollen and overflowing with the early onset of the monsoons. Tipu, with 3000 cavalry and some infantry, had parked himself in a strong position about six miles in front of the allied army. Shrouded in utter secrecy, Cornwallis decided to conduct his army by a circuitous route on the night of 14 May 1791 through a ridge on the hills that were on Tipu's right and easy to cross. But the torrential rains spoilt his plans. He tried to draw Tipu into an action on ground other than the one which he was occupying. Taken totally by surprise and his troops busily drying their clothes after the storm, Tipu however decided to play ball. As Wilks states: 'The praise cannot in justice be denied to him [Tipu] on this occasion, of seeing his ground, and executing his movements with a degree of promptitude and judgement which would have been creditable to any officer.'[79]

Before the British could occupy the rocky ridges of the Karighatta hill, Tipu dispatched Kamr-ud-din to dominate there and open heavy fire on the enemy, leading to considerable losses. Col Maxwell however managed to capture the heights and drive away Tipu's infantry that was totally taken by surprise, and fled, leaving behind three guns. But the Mysore infantry regrouped and gave a stiff fight to the British troops. By then, the hitherto inert Nizam's cavalry, under Asad Ali Khan, woke up from its stupor and rushed to the aid of their beleaguered ally. But the action of the Nizam's contingent worked to the detriment of the allies. 'They surged in a disorderly mass,' writes Thornton, 'directly across the front of the British advance, effectually stopping all further progress, and allowing Tippoo to withdraw his shaken army in safety across the river to Seringapatam.'[80] Though Cornwallis attributed this to an error of judgement on the part of Tejwant, there was widespread belief was creeping in the British camp that Tejwant was Tipu's mole who had been bought over with the lure of gold, and that he was wilfully sabotaging the allied forces. This robbed Cornwallis of a massive victory that day which could have led to a complete annihilation of Tipu. Meanwhile, the Mysorean batteries, commanded by Sayyid Hamid, fired so incessantly that the allies were forced to withdraw.

Severe losses too were suffered with about 600 being killed and wounded on both sides.

Cornwallis's miseries were mounting. He had expected the Marathas and Abercromby too to join him by then, but they were delayed. Tipu's intelligence system was so efficient that they intercepted all the messages the Maratha armies of Haripant and Bhau or the British army, under Abercromby, were sending Cornwallis. He was entirely clueless about their movements and was panicking about the condition of his troops. Finally, Cornwallis decided to abandon the campaign in Srirangapatna for the moment and retreat to Bangalore, planning for a more concerted, future attack at a suitable time. On his way to join Cornwallis, Abercromby was attacked by Kamr-ud-din and Sayyid Sahib, his baggage destroyed or seized and his troops facing great slaughter. He too decided to withdraw back to the coast.

By 21 May 1791, the allied army had retreated out of Srirangapatna, towards Periapatna and Melukote. Here they were finally joined by the Maratha detachments whose arrival was greatly welcomed, as they had also brought with them immense amounts of provisions and supplies, gathered during their loot of Tipu's northern territories. Failing this, the British army might have died of starvation and Cornwallis might have had the most ignominious disaster after the shameful surrender at Yorktown.

An eyewitness Dirom wrote what he thought of the two Maratha chieftains who had finally joined them just then: 'Hurry Punt, about sixty years of age, a Brahmin of the first order and the personage of greatest consequence . . . third in the senate of the Mahratta state. His figure is venerable, of middle stature, and not corpulent; he is remarkably fair, his eyes grey, and his countenance of Roman form, full of thought and character. Purseram Bhow, aged about forty, stands high in military fame among the Mahrattas. He is an active man, of small stature, rather dark in his complexion, with black eyes and an open animated countenance . . . his antipathy to Tippoo is said to be extreme, for the Sultan had put one of his brothers to death in the most cruel manner; and Hyder's conquests to the northward fell chiefly upon the possessions of his family, which he lately recovered by the reduction of Dharwar.'[81] The Maratha troops were described as being remarkably plain, but neat in their appearance, mild in their aspect, polite and humane in disposition. But they made good bucks in this dire situation by selling their provisions at exorbitant rates to their own allies, the famished, starving British army. The Marathas who had just arrived on the scene were full of enthusiasm to resume the expedition against Srirangapatna. But Cornwallis was famished and so were his troops. He decided to hasten a return to Bangalore. Tipu had definitely won this round triumphantly by repulsing the enemy that had struck right at his gate. He sent an emissary of peace in the form of a white flag and fruit to Cornwallis on 27 May 1791, but the latter spurned the offer and did not wish to have 'even the appearance of friendly intercourse with the Sultan.'[82] On their retreat back to Bangalore, they took the fort of Huliyurdurga, but their attempts at Hutridurga and Savandurga were unsuccessful. The famished army finally reached Bangalore by 11 July 1791.

Cornwallis decided to defer his advance on Srirangapatna to a later month after they had recouped and also redrawn their strategies. Since the opening of the campaign, no less than 12,000 bullocks had perished on his side. The arrival of Captain Oldham's convoy helped partially address this concern.

Tipu's Conciliatory Moves

The war so far had brought several jolts to Tipu. The formation of such a large confederacy against him and the abandonment by the French, leaving him to defend his kingdom all by himself was his first big reality check. Right from the Marathas, Nizam and the British to virtually every small chieftain in his vicinity, be it in Coorg, Malabar, Cochin or Travancore, the deposed Mysore royal family and its loyalists, and even the Bibi of Cannanore, all had turned against him, wishing his downfall. He was isolated totally and had no one to fall back on. His embassies abroad had won him no tangible dividends. While the campaign against Medows had yielded the British precious little and Tipu had felt confident that this would help him wean away the allies, the confidence quickly dissipated into utter despondency when the most important city within his dominions, Bangalore, fell to the allied forces. The quick capitulation of Dharwar, Koppal and virtually the whole of the northern domains that his father had fought and won and later bargained hard with the Marathas to retain had all passed on to the enemy hands. The rudest jolt was the fact that the foe had reached his very gates at Srirangapatna. But for tactical mistakes and the ill luck of his opponents, such as the delayed meeting of the Maratha and British detachments, the sudden outbreak of the monsoon and starvation that afflicted the British, the fact that his position was so tenuous must have completely rattled Tipu. It perhaps seemed more necessary than ever for him at this juncture, whilst being pushed to the wall, to consolidate his position, try to mend fences with people and communities that he had alienated and not make fresh enemies. Gone was the hubris that the years of several successes after his ascension had bred in his mind.

Even as Cornwallis was packing up to leave his capital, on 26 May 1791, Tipu shot off a letter to the patels of Coorg, whom he had treated in the most miserable manner. 'It is well known to me,' he wrote, 'that you have for a long time experienced much trouble in your country and under this consideration I forgive everything which has happened—you may now fulfil your several duties as subjects and observe all the customs of your religion agreeably to ancient practices, and whatever you formally paid to your own Rajas, the same, I expect, you will now pay to this Circar.'[83] It was the same Tipu who, in his mindless bloodlust through Coorg, had devastated their shrines, forcibly converted many of them and also haughtily addressed them all as bastard children, given their social practice of polyandry. Suddenly, he seemed perfectly accommodative of all their 'ancient practices' and 'customs of religion.'

A similar conciliatory letter seemed to have been sent to Raja Virarajendra of Coorg through Mir Sadak, Krishna Rao and Kadar Khan, to which a polite rebuff was sent: 'I have received your letters and comprehend the purport of them,' wrote the raja, 'Whenever you write me your real sentiments, I will consider on them [sic] and reply to them—you now ask my friendship to which I will answer I have pledged my word to the English with whom I am in alliance. They have locked it up in a box which has been sealed and sent to Europe. How can I therefore give my word to you when the English chose to restore it to me again?'[84] In another reply, the raja wrote back: 'By similar fair speeches and promises, you have formerly deceived and ruined Coorg. God has given me one tongue, with which I have pledged fidelity to the English. I have not two tongues like you!'[85] Tipu realized that reconciling with the Kodavas or its raja after the innumerable tortures he had heaped on them was an impossible feat.

Tipu sent his emissaries, Appaji Ram and Srinivasa Rao, to negotiate peace with the Marathas. Parshuram Bhau refused to meet the envoys. In fact, as Major Dirom writes about Appaji: 'So little respected was this ambassador by the people of his own cast [sic] and nation among our allies, that he was openly insulted by the Mahrattas.'[86] The envoys then reached out to Haripant and conveyed their master's desire to 're-establish the old friendship between the two governments, which was marred of late only by the intervention of interested persons.'[87]

In his letters written in Marathi, Tipu beseeched Hari Pant, who was influential in the Peshwa durbar, to represent his case favourably with the Peshwa and Nana. 'The friendship has existed with the Peshwa since my father's time,' wrote Tipu, 'I am astonished that despite your residing with the Peshwa, the latter could labour ill-feeling against me, his friend. In respect of our mutual friendship, I am ready to conform to what you say.'[88] A few days later, on 6 June 1791 Hari Pant wrote back to Tipu: 'Your Majesty are wise and sagacious and can yourself find out who was the first to break up that friendship and unanimity. Had Your Highness remained firm in your sincerity and friendship, things would not have come to such a pass.'[89] Hari Pant insisted that since it was an alliance now, the Maratha side could not take any unilateral decision regarding this and he was sharing the letters and Tipu's intent with his allies, the British and the Nizam.

Even at the height of the war, Tipu had been reaching out to the Nizam to win him over using the co-religionist card. He sent his envoy, Mehdi Ali, with two jewels and two *khillats* to the Nizam and another to his minister, Azam-ul-Umara. Mehdi was to impress upon the duo that 'the Nawab's [Nizam] wishes, whatever they may be, shall be carried into execution and that his [Tipu's] fidelity and attachment shall daily increase thereby adding strength to their religion Islam.' He was to represent to the Nizam to help provide 'comfort to mankind and supporting the Muslim faith.'[90] Writing again to the Nizam through the latter's official, Muhammad Amin Arab, Tipu said:

> I entertain an earnest, sincere and lasting desire of cultivating the friendship of Nabob Nizam-ul-Dowlah Bahadur, who is a Mussulman Prince, notwithstanding which the said Nabob has without cause engaged in the destruction of the inhabitants of this country and in the assistance of strangers. I am at a loss in what manner to account for his resolution in undertaking to render mankind wretched and can conceive no other consequence that it will be attended with than obliging the lower class of them to forsake their homes . . . you are acquainted with all circumstances and feel for the honour of the faith, certainly must desire it, and I have no doubt wish in a becoming manner for a cessation of the present troubles and an increase in friendship between the two Governments.[91]

Amin refused to acquiesce to Tipu's request to send an ambassador to the Nizam without the concurrence of the allies. 'Whenever you are sincerely disposed to adjust differences,' he wrote, 'and make compensation for the injuries sustained from you by the three Sircars now and previous to your time and should be desirous of doing it in particular through His Highness [Nizam], there will be no objection.'[92] Tipu was asked to give in writing that he was willing to restore the rights of all three parties, the Nizam, Peshwa and the British, indemnify them for their losses and submit to the authority of the Nizam in a supplicant manner if he wished a forward movement in peace. Obviously, these negotiations went nowhere after that. Tipu tried to lure Tejwant away with money and succeeded too. But intelligence of this was quickly intercepted by the British who complained bitterly to the Nizam. The Nizam finally decided to recall Tejwant and send his son, Sikandar Jah, and his minister Mir Alam instead to represent Hyderabad in the war.[93]

The British were both critical and suspicious of Tipu's emissaries and their conversations with the allies. They expressed their thorough disapproval and annoyance about such moves and prevailed upon their allies not to entertain these communications with Tipu. They suspected that 'the whole affair of Mehed Ally Khan may have been the work of a separate intrigue, fabricated by the Nabob's [Nizam] ministry in concert with Hurry Punt . . . without the sanction of this court [Peshwa durbar].'[94] Such was the trust among the allies about one another and their commitment to this united cause.

Realizing that it was the British who controlled the Marathas and Nizam, Tipu also made overtures of peace to them, urging the three allies to restore status quo. In a letter to Cornwallis on 24 June 1791, Tipu wrote:

> In order to increase the friendship and good understanding with the English Company, the Nawab Asoph Jah [Nizam] and Seremunt Pundit Purdhan [Nana], Mapoje Ram is sent on the part of the Ahmudy Sircar [Mysore]. It is incumbent on our ancient intimacy that the three powers should admit him and act in such manner as shall add strength to the friendship and connection between the Sirkars above mentioned which will tend to the peace and happiness of mankind.[95]

Tipu dispatched his Minister Purnaiya to meet Cornwallis and secure peace, urging that 'the English should not sully their reputation for moderation and gentility. I am ready to face the worst, as I am not a ruler of standing and prestige. I might as easily lose what my father and I acquired through sheer strength of arms.'[96] But all his overtures were rebuffed by the allies, especially the British. 'I have uniformly resolved,' wrote Cornwallis to the Nizam, 'to receive any person whom Tippoo Sultaun might be desirous of deputing to me lest such a measure might bear the appearance of a deviation from our engagements.'[97] It was certain that Tipu's annihilation or reduction of stature was paramount for the allies.

It is on this wave of conciliation borne by political necessity and insecurities that we also find a transformed Tipu when it came to his religious policies towards other faiths. The letter to the Kodavas already demonstrated his openness to now accommodate their social, religious and cultural practices that he had hitherto found blasphemous and disgusting. Likewise, there is obviously quite a spurt of piety for Hindu shrines as, at this stage of being hemmed in from all quarters, he also risked alienating and antagonizing the majority populace of his kingdom, the Hindus. He visited the shrine of Kanchipuram where the work on the principal gate of the temple, that Haidar Ali had commissioned, lay incomplete. Tipu ordered this work to be finished at the earliest and generously offered to bear the entire cost for this. He also personally led a grand Hindu procession of the temple's holy chariot, and went to the extent of personally setting off profuse fireworks with his own hands on this occasion. He wanted to win the trust of the Hindus, both his subjects within Mysore and those outside.

Where realpolitik, diplomacy and military tactics failed him, he believed the supernatural could be his last resort. At Kanchipuram, after the completion of the gateway and the chariot festival, he commissioned several Brahmins to perform special rituals for his victory. They were to stand immersed in water for days on end and perform a certain penance that brought victory against all opponents. The Shankaracharya of Sringeri with whom he had established a cordial relationship was invited specially for the purpose of supervising this ritual in Kanchipuram. Forty thousand Brahmins were given alms and rations as charity, and a lot of wealth was spent to install gold idols in Hindu temples.

Tipu's letters to the Shankaracharya had constantly requested the latter, in the capacity of his guru, to perform penance and rituals to destroy his foes. His correspondence on 14 September 1791 thanks the Swamiji for the latter's undertaking of *Shata* (Hundred) *Chandi Japas* or chants to propitiate goddess Chandi and help him win against the enemies.[98] The Shankaracharya kept Tipu informed about the rituals that he was conducting for the latter's welfare and victory in the war. The rituals included *japas*, *homas* and *havanas* (fire-rituals) and so on.[99] By October 1791, the Swamiji also decided to undertake a more massive and potent *Sahasra* (thousand) *Chandi japa* for an entire *mandala* or cycle of forty-eight days and *havana* 'for the well-being of the people and the success of the government . . . destruction of enemies.'[100] In all the letters, Tipu expressed his deepest reverence and also gratitude to the Swamiji for undertaking these rituals and offered to reimburse all the expenses incurred in the process. Tipu also dispatched soldiers to guard the matha and ensure that miscreants did not create obstacles in the conduct of the rituals. After the rituals were completed, the Shankaracharya had planned to go to Poona on the invitation of the Peshwa who wished to atone for his sins and seek forgiveness. Tipu also sent for the Swamiji a grand palanquin that could carry him on this journey. He also advised the guru to seek a compensation of Rs 60 lakh from Parshuram Bhau for the desecration that was caused to the shrine.[101] In subsequent pilgrimages that the Swamiji undertook in December 1791 to Rameshwaram and so on, Tipu continued to generously organize the travel, stay and other comforts for him, as well as for the Brahmins, elephants, horses and camels that went along. About twenty soldiers were assigned to escort the Swamiji and his retinue safely to and from the pilgrimage sites.[102] Whether or not he was driven solely by the political constraints of the time, the correspondence between Tipu and the Shankaracharya continued over the next several years and gives a glimpse into his deep reverence and generosity towards the Swamiji.

Sardesai mentions that 'In short, he [Tipu] announced to the world how, though a Muslim, he served the interest of the Hindus in contrast to the spoilation practiced upon the Shankaracharya by the Hindu Patwardhans. In short, during these months of forced inactivity, Tipu moved heaven and earth to obtain peace from the allies.'[103]

Tipu faced a personal tragedy too during these difficult times. In 1792, his favourite wife, Ruqaiya Banu, the sister of Burhan-ud-din, whom he had wed in 1774, died. A few years after her death, Tipu married Khadija Zamani Begum in 1795, but she too passed away two years later. Around 1796, he married Sayyid Sahab's daughter.

The military inactivity following the retreat of Cornwallis from Srirangapatna was only a temporary calm before a much bigger and more catastrophic storm was to explode for Tipu in the months to come.

14

Towards a Costly Peace

Combing the Carnatic

Ever since Cornwallis had beat a hasty retreat from Srirangapatna to Bangalore, he had begun planning for the next more concerted campaign against Tipu's capital. Learning from the mistakes of the previous expedition, he desired better coordination among the allies and ready supplies for the troops when they planned their next attack on Srirangapatna. Among all the passes that led from the Carnatic into the tableland of Mysore, the Palghat Pass, being close to Bangalore, was the easiest route. It was through this pass that the Mysorean forces had invaded the Carnatic. The pass was commanded by several forts of which Hosur and Rayakottai were most strategically important. Cornwallis hence desired control over these so that unhindered communication with the Carnatic could then be established. On 15 July 1791, he marched to Hosur, which is about twenty-eight miles south-east of Bangalore. Mindful of its strategic importance, Tipu had tried to enhance its defences but they had remained largely incomplete. Major Gowdie's detachment managed to take the fort without much exertion. Inside the storehouses within the fort, the British detachment also found to their horror that three of their compatriots who had been imprisoned by Tipu were beheaded and buried and, upon excavation of their tombs, the remains confirmed their sad plight.[1]

Next at Rayakottai which was garrisoned by 800 men, the killedar tried to put up a defence but eventually gave up and, on

---

* Please refer to the corresponding illustration in the appendix.

22 July, surrendered on the promise of security and safe passage. The fort was amply supplied with guns, ammunition and provisions for its defence, which now fell into British hands. Two hundred French and English firelocks, that belonged to a regular infantry reinforcement, had also been sent in by Tipu earlier. The lofty and spacious fort had ample supply of water as well. The nearby hill forts of Anchetidurga, Neelgiri, Rutlengiri, Oodiadurg, Kenchillydurg too surrendered in quick succession. Thus, barring Krishnagiri, the capital of the Baramahal region, all the posts that were necessary to maintain regular and easy communication with the Carnatic fell to the British.

By 10 August 1791, a large convoy joined Cornwallis to strengthen his troops further. This convoy had 100 elephants, all loaded with treasure, 6000 bullocks with rice, 100 carts with arrack and several hundreds of coolies carrying other supplies. It was, as Dirom, states, 'a sight fit to have graced an eastern triumph'[2] with the lead elephant proudly carrying the British standard. Cornwallis knew it was a long haul and thus wished to take all possible precautions, especially after having burnt his fingers in the previous campaign.

Cornwallis now decided to capture the forts to the north and east of Bangalore that interrupted their communication with the Nizam's army stationed in Gurramkonda. After capturing the smaller forts, Major Gowdie reached the formidable fortress of Nandidurga by 22 September 1791. It was styled as '*Gurdun Shekoo*' or the Terror of the World, by Tipu. It was built on the summit of a mountain that was 1700 feet high and inaccessible on all sides, except for a narrow, rugged passage. In terms of strength and importance, it ranked very high within the Mysore domains, after Savanadurga, Chitradurga and Krishnagiri. After taking over the town, Gowdie commenced the siege on 27 September. It took the British army twenty-one days to effect two breaches in this intimidating fort.

By 18 October 1791, a storming party under General Medows was sent to storm the fort. Cornwallis was himself stationed just a few miles away from the fort. The garrison within the fort put up a stout resistance. The fort was illuminated in blue lights and a heavy fire of cannon, musketry and rockets opened from within, as also large boulders that were rolled down to attack the enemy. But the storming party soon mounted the breaches and entered the fort. A carnage followed of the hapless inhabitants. Kirmani states that 'thousands of women were . . . violated, some of them to preserve their virtue and religion threw themselves from the top of the hill down a precipice to the bottom, and thus sacrificed their lives to preserve their honour.'[3] Lutf Ali Beg, the Bakhshi, and Sultan Khan, the Commandant of the fort, along with all the fighting men were packed off as prisoners to Vellore. The women, Brahmins and others were conducted away by the troops to a small hill fort that was six miles away. Lutf Ali Beg had been in the service of Haidar and Tipu for over forty years by then and he had also been a member of that important embassy to Constantinople. During his conversation with the British, Lutf Ali, being the old retainer, told them that they can look forward to a very spirited defence in Srirangapatna, unlike the surprise attack that brought Bangalore down. The Sultan, according to him, was smug in the belief that the Company could ill afford another campaign. He revealed to them that 'Tippoo would never consent to a peace, unless he could conclude it with an honour to himself; and that we [British] mistook his character, if we imagined he would ever agree to give up his sovereignty, and solicit a pension to get fat, like an old woman, for the rest of his life.'[4] The fall of a fort as mighty as Nandidurga had a ripple effect. The neighbouring fort of Kamaldurga surrendered and the garrison in Gurramkonda that was besieged by the Nizam was thoroughly disheartened.

Coimbatore Campaign

Even as the British and the allies were consolidating their gains, Tipu resolved to win back the territories he had lost. In early June 1791, he sent Badr-uz-Zaman Khan's son, Baqar Saheb, with a contingent of 2000 regular infantry, eight guns and irregulars to recapture Coimbatore. Coimbatore was then under the command of Lt Chalmers who had a small force comprising Topasses (Indian Christians) and a contingent of Travancore sepoys under Migot da le Combe, a French officer in the service of the Raja of Travancore.

It was poorly defended and most of the heavy guns and stores had been moved to Palghat which was commanded by Major Cuppage. Baqar besieged the fort by 20 June 1791 and, after a protracted operation, only by 7 August, a breach was effected. But in the conflict that lasted for two hours, the Mysorean side was totally vanquished with the loss of 200 men. Cuppage, too, had rushed to the rescue of Chalmers whose position had been precarious. The Mysoreans were driven out beyond the Bhavani River.

Tipu meanwhile had moved northwards, towards Chitradurga, to stop the depredations of Parshuram Bhau who had been active in this region, and also to cut off the supplies that were coming in for the Marathas. But he did not wish to move too forward in the northerly direction and leave his capital susceptible. He only intended to cover a large convoy that he had expected from Bidanur, the only place from where supplies were assured for him. After the defeat of Baqar, Tipu once again sent Kumr-ud-din to try and seize Coimbatore, given its weak position under Chalmers. By 5 October, Kumr-ud-din had commenced a siege of the fort there and Chalmers was desperate once again for Cuppage's help from Palghat. Cuppage could not come this time himself, but sent his forces to relieve Chalmers. Since this was not helpful, it was only by 22 October that Cuppage left Palghat towards Coimbatore. No sooner than he departed from Palghat, Kumr-ud-din managed a dexterous movement to cut him off from Palghat and encircle him. This terrified Cuppage tried to flee back to Palghat, but was spiritedly attacked by Kumr-ud-din, inflicting heavy losses upon him and defeating him. Somehow, Cuppage managed to save himself and proceed to Palghat, leaving Chalmers and Coimbatore to their fate. The fort could not withstand the Mysorean siege and on 2 November 1791, Chalmers surrendered. The garrison was taken prisoner and packed off to Srirangapatna. This was seen by the British as another violation of the general terms of capitulation wherein the garrison on surrender was to be given free, unmolested pass, without being subjected to tortures thereafter. Chalmers was tricked into signing the terms of capitulation in multiple languages—English, Hindustani and Persian, the first two of which he understood, but not Persian. In that version, the release of the garrison and its security was made dependent on the pleasure of the Sultan and Chalmers had unwittingly signed his own imprisonment.

While Kumr-ud-din was busy reducing Coimbatore, Baqar Saheb was sent to reinforce the garrison in Krishnagiri and cut off the communications of the British army in Mysore with the Carnatic. By 31 October, an alarmed Cornwallis sent Colonel Maxwell towards the strong mud fort of Pennagaram, close to where Baqar was. Maxwell managed to easily take Pennagaram and other important places in the Baramahal, in and around Krishnagiri. He then proceeded to the mighty fort of Krishnagiri which was the only place of significance that Tipu now held in the Baramahal. By 7 November, he attempted a siege of the fort, carrying the town and the lower fort without much opposition. But as he proceeded upwards, the Mysorean attack became severe. Repeated attempts to use ladders to climb up and attack the inmates proved unsuccessful. Col Maxwell decided to cut his losses and retreat instead, after destroying the lower fort and setting the town on fire.

Route to Srirangapatna Cleared

The reverses that the British suffered in Coimbatore were soon compensated for by the main army of Cornwallis that was joined by Maxwell after his Baramahal expedition. The entire region between Bangalore and the Coromandel was now cleared for the access of supplies, though the route to Srirangapatna still had pockets of immense strength for Tipu to offer his resistance. Cornwallis now strategized the reduction of all the formidable forts that lay obstructing his pathway to Tipu's capital. His first target was the strong fort of Savanadurga that helped the Sultan to interrupt communications between Srirangapatna and Bangalore, and proved a major hurdle for the Governor-General. Situated about eighteen miles west of Bangalore, Savanadurga is a huge rock of granite that is about 4000 feet above sea level. The mountain from where it rose was about eight miles in circumference and a thick belt of bamboo surrounded it all over. High walls and barriers in the fort further made it impregnable. It had a garrison of 1500 men. It was often called the Rock of Death for its inhospitable terrain and climate. Tipu was very sure that the British would end up becoming a laughing stock as most of their troops would die of sickness and fatigue whilst trying to get to the steep hill. He had already begun congratulating his army in advance, waiting eagerly to see how the British end up inflicting misery on themselves.

On 10 December, Lt Col Stuart was tasked with leading the operations against this formidable fort, with Cornwallis camping about five miles away to support in case of need. Lt Col Cockerell, Captain Welch, Captain Alexander Read and others were all parked in and around the site of operation. Dragging the battery guns over rocks of considerable height, sometimes almost perpendicular, the British forces had to open an entire road amidst the dense bamboo vegetations. After the erecting of batteries that was meticulously planned by Chief Engineer Colonel Ross and the clearing of the forests, the assault was to begin on 21 December. Quite quickly a breach was managed, much to the alarm and shock of the Mysorean garrison. They had become so complacent about the natural strength of the hill-fort and Tipu's own over-confidence about an inevitable British disgrace that their guard was down. By the time the British ascended the breach, it was too late for the Mysoreans to offer any potent resistance. The troops entered the western citadel and even succeeded in capturing it without any loss to themselves. But about 200 men, including the commandant on the Mysorean side, were killed. Dirom states: 'Thus, in less than an hour, in open day, the stupendous and hitherto deemed impregnable fortress of Savendroog, was stormed without the loss of a man, only one private soldier having been wounded in the assault.'[5]

On 23 December 1791, Stuart marched against another strong and important hill fort of Hutridurga, about twelve miles west of Savanadurga. Feeble resistance was offered, but the British troops managed to storm it. The Mysorean side suffered huge losses of 110 men, while not a single man was killed on the British side. The Commandant and others were taken prisoners. Captain Welch meanwhile had managed to subjugate the other significant hill forts of Ramagiri and Shivanagiri. Tipu had reconquered Huliyurdurga that he had lost to Cornwallis on his retreat march. Colonel Maxwell was now sent to capture it back and without much exertion, the fort fell to them on 27 December.

In a justifiably congratulatory tone, Cornwallis wrote to the Bishop of Lichfield and Coventry on 29 December 1791: 'The speedy reduction of this place which has been considered all over India as impregnable, has struck great terror into the enemy's other garrisons, for in the three days subsequent to the assault on Savendroog, three other strong forts in its neighbourhood, each of them capable of making a good resistance, fell into our hands. By these successes, we have now a frontier line, to which our supplies may with ease be brought forward within 50 miles of the enemy's capital.'6

The Nizam's Progress

Elsewhere, the Nizam's main army had been engaged in an unproductive and wasted attempt to capture Gurramkonda. It was a strong hill fort that was nearly inaccessible, with two lines of fortifications surrounding the foot of the hill, known as the inner and outer forts. Muhammad Mehdi, a brave officer, commanded the garrison there which was no more than 700 men. The siege commenced on 15 September 1791 under Hafiz Farid-ud-din. No progress was made there in breaching the fort till November when the guns and a detachment of sepoys sent by Cornwallis from Nandidurga reached the place. Captain Andrew Read was to lead the operations. By 6 November 1791, Read managed to make a breach in the lower fort that was taken by assault. Several Mysoreans, including Mehdi, were killed in the ambush. The lower fort was captured and handed over to Hafiz Farid-ud-din. A large contingent of 25,000 men from

Hyderabad under the Nizam's second son, Sikandar Jah, attended by Mushir-ul-Mulk and Kennaway, joined Hafiz from Pangal. Leaving Hafiz with 5000 men and 900 horse to reduce the upper fort, they proceeded to join Cornwallis. Hardly had they moved some distance than they heard an alarming development.

Tipu had sent his eldest son, Fateh Haidar, who was about eighteen years of age then, with Ghazi Khan to assist him and reclaim Gurramkonda. This was completely a surprise appearance for Hafiz and his troops. Brimming with overconfidence and assuming the army to be no more than a few plunderers, he mounted his elephant, left behind his batteries and marched ahead with just about twenty horsemen to investigate the appearance of the Mysoreans. But no sooner had he advanced than he found himself surrounded from all sides by large numbers of Tipu's horsemen. An alarmed Hafiz tried to mount his elephant and flee back on his horse, during which time, he was captured by Fateh Haidar's forces. By 21 November, the lower fort was reoccupied by the Mysoreans.

The Mysore side had an old axe to grind with Hafiz Farid-ud-din. He had been the envoy from the Nizam's side to Tipu's court in 1789. It was with him and the Mysore envoy Ali Raza that issues related to the matrimonial alliance between the two rulers' families had been discussed and rebuffed by the Hyderabad side. With these old grudges still intact, Hafiz on his capture was therefore plundered to his last garment. Some generous jailor had taken pity on him and given him a patchwork quilt of sorts to cover his nakedness, as he sat ruing his confinement. In this state, Ali Raza, his diplomatic counterpart from Mysore, approached him and haughtily addressed him: 'You recollect the disrespectful language you employed towards my sovereign and me at Hyderabad on the occasion of the demanded marriage?' 'Perfectly well,' replied Hafiz, 'we were then serving our respective masters; that day is past. If you are here for the purpose of revenge, murder me at once, but do not dishonour me.' Ali Raza immediately ordered Hafiz to be led out to a concealed situation under cover of a rock and in his own presence to be cut into pieces in cold blood.[7] Kirmani however attributes Hafiz's death to Fateh

Haidar, who he states 'separated the head of Hafiz from his body and it was struck on a spear's head, and the whole of his followers, being totally defeated and dispersed, fled to Kirpa [Cudappah].'[8]

The expectation after this was that Fateh Haidar would march next to intercept the convoy coming from the Carnatic and unite with the main army that was planning a decisive attack on Srirangapatna. But since he did not have a large army, Fateh Haidar returned to the capital. The British forces under Read and the Nizam's army under Sikandar Jah were waiting for Fateh Haidar's departure, after which they once again attacked Gurramkonda and, by 25 December 1791, managed to take the lower fort back. Sikandar Jah was keen on joining the main army under Cornwallis. Hence, he left Asad Ali Khan to command Gurramkonda and proceeded southwards, reaching Bangalore and then joining Cornwallis at Magadi by 25 January 1792.

The Maratha Progress

After the aborted attack on Srirangapatna and the consequent retreat, the Maratha army under Parshuram Bhau moved back towards Sira by July 1791. Haripant continued with Cornwallis, but the bulk of his troops 'were dispersed on various pretexts, but in reality to occupy the [Mysorean] districts and to collect as much money as they could.'[9] The Marathas were in a strange dilemma. The string of British successes and the fall of several strong forts in Mysore awakened in the Poona durbar great consternation, envy and insecurity about the rising power of the British. Instead of playing second fiddle to their success, the Marathas now began strategizing on how best they could maximize their interests in this skirmish, by reconquering their earlier lost territories to Mysore and extending their sphere of influence. The more Charles Malet urged Bhau to proceed to Magadi to join Cornwallis's grand army, the more he receded westwards to conquer more Mysorean territories. Bhau was also seriously indisposed during this campaign, which was deemed serious and hence impeded his march. Parking at Doddaballapura, he left a corps under Balwant Rao to take Maddagiri. But Kumr-ud-din routed these troops who fled in alarm back to the base in Bangalore. Undaunted by these reverses, Bhau proceeded with a detachment under Captain Little, plundering territories on the way and setting several villages on fire. The plunder and devastation were so intense that it took several decades for these unfortunate places to resurrect themselves and shed their poverty and misery.[10] Moore who was part of the contingent writes:

> We counted ten villages in flames at the same time . . . It was by no means uncommon to see six or eight burning at once in several parts of this fine country . . . They [Marathas] can pour on an enemy's country an inundation of a thousand horse; and when we consider the ruin and devastation spread by such a host of locusts, we are inclined to think that the curse of God could not have fallen on Egypt in a more destructive form. The Mahrattas, although they, when impelled by the prospect of plunder, are deaf to the cries of distress, and callous to the calls of humanity, are not a sanguinary people; instances have seldom occurred . . . where lives have been wantonly sacrificed; the event in the end to be sure is the fame; the wretched inhabitants are driven in thousands naked from their habitations, to wander and starve in a country, everywhere equally destitute of the means of affording them relief.[11]

By September 1791, Bhau was around Chitradurga and took possession of Kanaguppe. He intended to invade the rich province of Bidanur that made more strategic sense to the Maratha power than aligning himself with the confederate goals. By 21 December 1791, Hole Honnur, which was on the banks of the Tunga and Bhadra, was taken by assault, followed by a massive loot and plunder of the fine town and torching of the houses there. Benkipur surrendered by the 24th. The ultimate aim of Bhau was to get possession of the much-coveted Bidanur that the Marathas had always eyed. He thought that the most opportune moment to fulfil this desire was now, when there was a British contingent with him to carry out the operations. Though this was certainly not on Cornwallis's agenda as he wanted to gather all the allied armies to make a renewed attack on Srirangapatna.

Shimoga was the next target where Bhau sent his son, Appa Saheb, along with Raghunath Rao Kurundwadkar, to combat Raza Saheb who led Tipu's forces to defend the place. In addition to the garrison under a commandant, Muin-ud-din Khan, there was a force consisting of 7000 infantry, 800 horse and ten guns under Raza Saheb, one of Tipu's relatives. Raza Saheb put up a very spirited defence and repulsed the Maratha attackers, inflicting much loss on them. But despite being in a position of strength, Raza Saheb's injudicious act of drawing off the guns from the centre in the midst of engagement and sending away elephants and valuables, betrayed a sense of insecurity that eventually demoralized his troops. It was Captain Little who led a valiant command of the allied troops against Raza Saheb thereafter and put them in a position of strength. 'The whole conduct of Captain Little on this occasion,' writes James Duff, 'was most exemplary. It reminds us of the generalship of Lawrence or of Clive . . . of the small number of British troops engaged, 60 were killed and wounded, and the loss would have been much greater, but for the judicious conduct of their commander, who exposed them as little as possible until he knew where their strength could be exerted with effect. The Mahrattas, though they contributed but little to the success of the day, lost about 500 men.'[12]

Shimoga fell by 3 January 1792 after a long, hard-fought battle where Raza Saheb was totally devastated. Several excellent guns and a large quantity of grains that were found in the Shimoga fort were confiscated by the victors. Muin-ud-din Khan surrendered on the condition that Captain Little was to guarantee his and his garrison's safe passage, especially after the experience of breach of faith in Dharwar and the fate that befell Badr-uz-zaman Khan. He was evacuated and kept in the British camp. But Bhau somehow managed to prevail upon Captain Little and secured their possession, going against the terms of capitulation and meting out a similar treatment as Badr-uz-zaman Khan had faced. This left Captain Little deeply humiliated and belittled.

Bhau then penetrated the woods and marched in the opposite direction to the allied armies, towards Bidanur, much to Cornwallis's utter disappointment and frustration. Cornwallis's strategy was a junction of Bhau's forces with those of Abercromby from Bombay, which were then to join the main grand army to Srirangapatna. But Bhau's own diversions into Bidanur would have meant a delay in the junction and upset all the plans of Cornwallis. He decided to take all necessary and 'further precaution to prevent the failure of the campaign.'[13] Their supplies stood the risk of exposure and the lack of provisions would have run the risk of yet another aborted and humiliating retreat from Srirangapatna. In a strongly worded letter to Bhau, Cornwallis wrote:

It has afforded me very great concern to learn by letter from Captain Little that you had marched from your camp at Changhurry to the westward. I recommended the position between Sera and Seringapatam to you as being the only means that occurred to me likely to prevent the enemy from getting in the rear of our respective forces, and to secure the constant supplies which my unremitting efforts have brought into train, and which are coming up for the general use of the armies during the siege of Seringapatam. From the situation in which you were when these advices left you, I am the more concerned that you did not immediately on the receipt of my letter, march to the position it pointed out, as I do not perceive how Hurry Punt and myself are to avail ourselves either of the great advantages we have obtained by the possession of Sawunterdroog [sic] and other hill forts lately taken, (since that part of the plan which was allotted to you has been neglected and the communication must be exposed from that quarter) or of the further assistance of your army in effecting the junction with General Abercrombie who agreeably to the orders he has received from me is arrived above the Ghauts, as you have been already informed. At all times well convinced of your zeal and attachment to the common cause, your march to the westward occasions me very great regret. I must consider any failure in the future operations of the alliance the result of your deviation from the arrangements concerted between us. I shall be compelled to expressed my undisguised sentiments to the Peshwa . . .[14]

Cornwallis and Malet also bitterly complained to Nana and Haripant to rein Bhau in. They were also threatened that if they did not wholeheartedly participate in the war with all their forces, they would be deprived of their share of Tipu's territory after they defeated him. Bhau was thereafter compelled by Poona to drop his Bidanur bravado and join Cornwallis as per the original plan. Also, alarmed by the imminent invasion of Bidanur that was one of the most important provinces of his kingdom, Tipu had sent Kumr-ud-din with a strong infantry force to trap Bhau and his cavalry in the woods. After being chided from all quarters, Bhau retreated from Bidanur, marched to Srirangapatna on 10 February 1792, reaching there only by 10 March.

Given Bhau's dilatory tactics, General Abercromby's plan of operations had been altered by Cornwallis. Instead of entering Mysore via Bidanur or the north-western route in conjunction with Bhau, he was to take up a position at Periapatna, about sixteen miles west of Srirangapatna. The Raja of Coorg was to assist him through his territories to make his way to Mysore. He moved towards Mysore on 22 January 1792 with an effective force of 8400 men. Around this time, the Nizam's armies too, under Sikandar Jah and Mir Alam, had joined Cornwallis at Magadi by 25 January. In view of Tipu's continuing overtures to end hostilities, Cornwallis shot off a letter to him on 16 January 1792:

It is well-known that after having made every conciliatory proposition in my power to prevent the war, I was forced by the dictates of honour and good faith to have recourse to arms to save one of the Company's allies [Travancore] from destruction, and I have been desirous to make peace as proper compensations can be received for the injuries and losses that have been sustained by the Company and by those allies with whom it is connected

in the strictest bonds of confederacy. But with what confidence
can a negotiation be carried on with a man who not only violates
treaties of peace but also disregards the faith of capitulations
during war. The garrison of Coimbatoor ought by the capitulation
to have been set at liberty upon certain conditions immediately
after its surrender, and I have just right to demand that the
agreement should be executed on the spot where it was made,
but being unwilling at this critical time to occasion any delay that
can be avoided in opening a negotiation, I shall not insist on a
literal performance of the original stipulations on account of the
length of time that the execution would require. Let therefore the
garrison of Coimbatoor be sent to this army, to be set at liberty
according to the conditions that were settled between Lieut.
Chalmers and Cummer-ud-Deen Khan, and I shall then be ready
in concert with the allies, to fix upon a place where Vakeels from
you may conveniently meet proper persons that will be deputed
on the part of the three Confederate powers for the purpose of
endevaouring to arrange the terms on which a general peace can
be re-established.[15]

In his reply, Tipu wrote back:

Your Lordship's letter arrived and I have understood the contents
. . . I sent Meer Cummer-ul-Dien to take the fort [of Coimbatore].
He arrived there and surrounded it; when assistance made its
appearance from towards Palicautcherry [Palghat] Cummer-ul-
Dien marching from Coimbetoor, attacked the force, defeated
it and then returned to the fort, and took the people that were
in it, prisoners; if engagements had taken place to release them,
how was it possible to act contrary thereto? Someone has reported
this falsely to your Lordship. Sometime ago when the troops of
the Ahmedy Sirkar [Mysore] besieged Darapooram the garrison
surrendered on capitulation, and were immediately furnished
with an escort and sent to your Lordship's army. God forbid, it
is not the practice of any state to confine those whose release may
have been stipulated by agreement. If with a view to the quiet

of mankind, it is your Lordship's pleasure to establish a peace between the four States, the confidential agents shall be sent to you from the Ahmedy Sirkar that the negotiation for peace may be entered into with your Lordship, with the Peshwa or with Nizam Ally Khan, that through your Lordship's means the peace and quiet of mankind may be effected.[16]

Tipu had a valid point there, as the breach of terms of capitulation had happened more on the allied front, especially the Marathas, at Dharwar and Shimoga among other places. But Cornwallis dismissed Tipu's defence and insisted that despite an agreement signed between Lt Chalmers and Kumr-ud-din Khan, the former and his garrison had been taken away in irons to Srirangapatna as captives. He curtly wrote back that 'it is impossible that I can have confidence in your sincerity whilst I remain in the belief that you have recently violated a capitulation and that you refuse to give the redress which I have a just right to demand.'[17] With no meeting ground, the stage was now set for a final allied army assault on Srirangapatna.

Major Dirom records: 'The Confederacy, which thus united the chief powers on the peninsula for the overthrow of a formidable and ambitious enemy, was also attended by an ambassador who arrived at this time, with a party of horse, from Madajee Bounselo [Bhosale], the Rajah of Berar. The Peshwa and the Nizam were themselves in the field, on their respective frontiers, and all India looked with anxious expectation to the event of this important campaign.'[18] That it took all his enemies and their combined strength to be united, despite their many contradictions and squabbles, just to defeat one man, spoke volumes of the terror that Tipu inspired in their hearts and the threat he posed to all of them.

An interesting contemporary account by Lt Roderick Mackenzie in the British army details what Tipu's men thought of him during this time:

Whilst the Sultaun by the erection of fortresses out of number, daily acquired internal strength, he invigorated his whole system by principles of sound government, and by an economical management of resources to which those of any neighbouring power, if state exigencies are considered, bore no comparison. However bigoted to the tenets of the Koran, the vast number of Hindoo temples recently decorated throughout his dominions authorizes an assertion, that his enthusiasm gave way to his ambition, and that his zeal to propagate the Mussulman faith, did not occasion so many instances of barbarity, as his rage for conquest and an innate cruel and revengeful disposition. Although parsimonious in a high degree, numbers of his confidential Hindoo servants, who during the war fell into our hands, acknowledged him a lenient and indulgent master; nor have we to boast of many instances where his people were induced by our flattering prospects of success, to throw off his yoke and shelter themselves under the benign influence of Christian rulers. On the contrary, with the exception of very few districts, the inhabitants of Mysore, have invariably laid waste their country. They destroyed their habitations, and flying in every direction, they drove their cattle into the most hidden recesses, burning their grain, although famine must have been the inevitable consequence. Checking the frauds of intermediate agents by severe and exemplary punishments, the Sultaun protected his ryuts [sic: ryots], who were chiefly of the Hindoo religion, from the enormities of black collectors; and wherever it became necessary to hold out an ostensible reason for the inhuman cruelties which he frequently committed, the cloak of religion was always spread to sanctify the transaction ... [Despite] the arrears due to his troops, yet their attachment to his cause, was such all along that they paid the most implicit obedience to his mandate in the worst of times.[19]

The Confederate Attack on Srirangapatna

With a large grand army that consisted of 22,033 men, a battering train of forty-two pieces and forty-four guns and an effective force in cavalry and infantry of 16,721 men, Cornwallis set off for the final attack on Srirangapatna on 25 January 1792. Passing through the jungles and hills on the way, several human dwellings were up in flames as the troops approached. By 3 February, they reached the mud fort of Keregodu and then ascended a high ground from which a full aerial view of Srirangapatna was visible, from behind what was called the French Rocks. Describing this grand alliance, Dirom writes: 'The Prince [Sikandar Jah], the Minister [Mushir-ul-mulk], Hurry Punt, and the tributary Nabobs of Cuddapa and Kanoul [Kurnool], who had accompanied Secunder Jaw [sic] from Hyderabad, were on elephants, richly caparisoned, attended by a numerous suite of their best horse, and preceded by their *chubdars*, who call out their titles; surrounded in short by an immense and noisy multitude. The Prince was in front, attended by Sir John Kennaway, on a howdered elephant, near enough to answer such questions as might be asked by His Highness respecting the troops.'[20]

On his part, Tipu, too, made every possible effort to strengthen the defences of his capital in the last six months, given that a re-attack by the allies, after an aborted attempt, was imminent. The Sultan had encamped at the north of Srirangapatna and was overlooking the enemy's movements. He had cleared the country of every bit of grass and green foliage within his enemy's reach. To disturb his opponents and to prevent them from having good sleep, he sent his party of people with rockets that were to be fired close to their camps at night. Particularly peeved and disturbed was the around-twenty-year-old Sikandar Jah, for whom it was the first military experience.

The island of Srirangapatna, that was formed by the two branches of the Kaveri River that separate and then reunite, was about three-and-a-half miles in length from east to west and a half mile broad at its widest point. In the western angle of the island was the strong fort and next to it, at a distance of about 500 yards, stood Tipu's Daria Daulat Bagh Palace. Right at the centre of the island, and about 1000 yards from the fort, was the pete or town that was surrounded by a lofty mud wall. On the eastern part of the island was the Lal Bagh Garden that was fortified towards the river by redoubts, batteries and a deep ditch. All around the island ran a bound hedge composed of bamboo and thorny plants, marking in a way, the boundaries of the capital city. The bound hedge on the north side of the river included an oblong space that was about three miles in length and half a mile broad. It was here that Tipu had encamped with 40,000 infantry and 100 guns in front, and 5000 cavalry in the rear end. He had taken a commanding position here and was well guarded not only by the hedge, but also by a large canal, rice fields and the winding Lokapavani River that emptied itself into the Kaveri. The Karighatta Hills on one side of his encampment, beyond the river, were fortified and commanded by Shaikh Ansar. Six large redoubts constructed again on commanding ground, added to the strength of his position. One of these was an Idgah in the north-west that was formidable and commanded by Sayyid Hamid. The corps of Europeans, and Lally's brigade, commanded by Monsiuer Vigie, supported the Mysore troops. Tipu had hoped to prolong the siege till the monsoon months, by which time the enemy would once again be humiliated enough to retreat in distress. Tipu had however lulled himself into thinking that nothing decisive would happen until the Bombay Army under Abercromby joined the main force. He hence diverted a lot of his efforts towards intercepting the reinforcements of Cornwallis and trying to prevent the junction with Abercromby.

But Cornwallis had other plans. He was determined to make a surprise night attack on the mighty fort of Srirangapatna. It was a calm and serene evening and the full moon that had just risen was promising to light up the path of success for the allies. At about half past eight on 6 February 1792, under the fully brilliant moonlit sky, three British columns marched in dead silence towards the Sultan's fortified encampments on the northern side of the Kaveri River, flanked by the defences of the Karighatta Hills. So secretive was the plan of this operation that even the allies—much to their consternation, got to know about this only after Cornwallis had marched ahead. They were alarmed to know that Cornwallis had ventured out with only part of his infantry, and without cannon, to attack all of Tipu's army in a fortified camp under the walls of his capital. They were fully confident that this foolhardy attempt of

Cornwallis would boomerang badly on them all 'and dreaded that the run of the allied armies might be involved in the attempt.'[21]

The Operations of 6 February 1792

The three divisions that had ventured out were under Major General Medows and Lt Col Stuart as his second-in-command on the right; the one in the centre under Lord Cornwallis himself and the left division under Lt Col Maxwell. The right division under Medows had 900 Europeans and 2400 Indians; the one in the centre under Cornwallis had 1400 Europeans and 2300 Indians, and the left under Maxwell had 500 Europeans and 1200 Indians. The total number of fighting men were thus about 2800 Europeans and 5900 Indians.[22] The right division under Medows entered the bound hedge at around 11.30 p.m. and quite contrary to the plan laid out, approached the Idgah redoubt and decided to seize it. Since it was a very strong post, Cornwallis had not favoured its attack. But owing to the mistake of the harcarahs or native guides, the column was led over to this post that was commanded by Sayyid Hamid. It had eleven guns and was well-fortified. A fierce combat followed. The British were initially repulsed by a gallant Mysorean defence, but eventually the redoubt was taken. Sayyid Hamid and nearly 400 of his men fell, while about eleven officers and eighty men on the British side were killed. The European corps under Monsieur Vigie, amounting to about 360, managed to escape. Medows retraced his steps after the firing ceased, in order to join Cornwallis at the foot of the hill, by daybreak.

Cornwallis, meanwhile, had divided his central division into three corps—the front corps under Lt Col Knox, the centre corps under Stuart and the rear under him as reserve. Between 10 p.m. and 11 p.m., the front corps had first marched ahead and come in contact with Tipu's cavalry that was then escorting the rocket men to disturb the enemy camps. They immediately rushed back to inform the Sultan about the attack, while he was supposedly in the midst of his dinner. The front corps managed to march ahead; one party under Captain Monson managed to reach the river first and this was followed by Knox. The troops under Knox managed to proceed towards Dariya Daulat Bagh Palace and then eastwards to the suburban Shahar Ganjam. They faced stiff opposition here from the Sultan's cavalry and infantry. There was constant firing at the river, too, as the British were trying to penetrate inside. As Dirom records: 'At the time of the firing of these guns, the Sultan was at the Mysore or southern gate of the fort, which he refused to enter. He was much enraged that the guns had opened without his orders, and sent immediately directions to cease firing, lest it be imagined in his camp that the fort itself was attacked and the panic among his troops in consequence become universal. To this order, wise as perhaps it was in its principle, may be attributed the little damage sustained by the troops, who crossed into the island, within reach of grape from the bastions of the fort.'[23]

The Mysorean side was definitely panic-stricken by the suddenness of this attack that was happening from so many sides. The town fell easily to Knox. The storming forces received intelligence of several Europeans who had been confined in Srirangapatna. Knox immediately sent a party to release 'twenty-seven half-starved wretches in heavy irons; among them was Mr Randal Cadman, a midshipman, taken ten years before by Suffrein, and by him delivered to Hyder.'[24]

Another party under Captain Hunter took post at Dariya Daulat, but given the precarious nature of his position there that would be discovered by his opponent by daybreak, he quit the island. Stuart and Maxwell, too, by then had managed to cross into the island. The corps under Cornwallis had been waiting for Medows to join, but he had been delayed. Sunrise was about two hours away and by then there was a sudden Mysorean attack on Cornwallis's contingent from the rear. Mackenzie too notes that the Mysoreans 'discovered no want either of discipline or valour.'[25] Fortunately for him, this was the same time that Hunter had quit the island and joined him, giving him timely cover. Heavy skirmishes followed but the Mysoreans were eventually repulsed. Cornwallis then retreated towards the Karighatta Hills, which is where he was joined by Medows.

The left division under Maxwell had also proceeded by 11 p.m. towards Karighatta, which was an important post, descended towards Tipu's camp, crossed the Lokapavani River and the bound hedge. But they managed to take the hill and the pagoda on top of it. Here the forces of Stuart joined them, and they had to cross the deep waters of the Kaveri to get to the island. Several men were drowned in the process, but the column still managed to cross with comparatively little losses.

On the whole, the night attack of the 6th of February had been successful for the British. They had established themselves on the eastern side of the island, and to the north they held the Idgah and Sultan's redoubts and the Karighatta Hill. The divisions under Cornwallis and Maxwell had achieved their tasks, though Medows had failed in what was assigned to him, he had managed to take the very important Idgah redoubt. The discipline and perseverance of the British and the stealth with which they operated, taking the Mysoreans by surprise, had won the night for the British side. Cornwallis had taken no small risk as well in these operations, leading from the front like a soldier. He was on horseback all night in the midst of heavy firing and skirmish, with a musket shot grazing past his left hand.

Tipu was having his evening meal when the news of the central British column entering the Sultan's redoubt reached him. Leaving his meal unfinished, he quickly mounted his horse and rushed for damage control. By then information started coming in of the nature of the attack and the complete penetration of the enemy into the camp. As this threatened his retreat, Tipu fled towards the fort which he felt was in danger. He took his position at the outwork of the fort that commanded the scene and remained there till morning, issuing orders and spending one of the most anxious nights of his life. In the confusion of the night, about 10,000 Kodavas, whom he had forcibly converted and incorporated into the Ahmadi Chelas corps, escaped to their province. A number of French and other Europeans

(Asad Ilahis) too made safe retreats. This included Monsieur Blevette, an old man who was the chief engineer, and Monsieur Lefolu, his French interpreter who had served in the Mysore army since the time of Haidar Ali. Thirty of these Europeans, headed by Joseph Pedro, a Portuguese, who was a captain in Tipu's army were all immediately absorbed into service by the Marathas. Some requested to go to the French settlements in India; others wished to return to Europe and a few joined the services of the allied forces.

Several of the deserters tried to cart away a large treasure from the camp that night which was the pay for the soldiers the following day. But Purnaiya who was ever alert ensured that these attempts were thwarted and all the treasure was sent back to the fort, laden on camels. By the time the day broke on the 7th, reports of killed, wounded and missing men on the Mysore side amounted to as much as 23,000. 'Have I no faithful servants to retrieve my honour?' the Sultan had exclaimed in grief and dismay.[26] A stirred cavalry responded with enthusiasm that they would work everything in their command to save their Sultan's life and prestige. His principal chiefs had thrown their turbans on the ground and sworn to either succeed or perish protecting their sovereign's honour.[27]

The Battle Continues

The dawn of 7 February was deceivingly calm. It concealed the immense operations that had happened all through the preceding night and put the allies in pole position, just outside their enemy's home. Tipu, too, decided to salvage all that was lost. Undoubtedly, posts on the island and redoubts had been captured by the allies, but he still held the fort and several other redoubts. With daylight, the Mysorean guns that had remained silent began firing to expel the British from the positions they had occupied. Advancing under cover of old houses and walls, Tipu's infantry first trained its fire against Stuart, who had come menacingly close to the Lal Bagh, facing the Shahar Ganjam. Stuart could barely return fire as most of their ammunition had been exhausted in the night or damaged while crossing the river. Cornwallis, who had perched himself at a pivotal position on the Karighatta Hill, noticed the precarious position of Stuart and sent a force to support him. On seeing this reinforcement coming, the Mysoreans retreated. They moved their attention to recovering the Sultan's important redoubt. But despite four attempts made all through the day, the Mysore side could not recapture it. The redoubt had become a gory scene, with several mangled corpses lying strewn around and the miserably wounded, imploring for urgent assistance.

Tipu then planned to dislodge the British from the island. Two columns of infantry entered the pete (town) and tried to attack the main position of Col Stuart. But they too were repulsed. In fact, insiders had leaked the information of a possible attack from Mysore to free the island and thus the British were well prepared to counter any such moves. All attempts of the Mysoreans to free the island and the Sultan's redoubt had failed miserably, despite their valorous attempts. By nightfall, they decided to quit all the posts north of the Kaveri. Major Dalrymple and Captain Brown's battalion was to keep the possession of the pete. This opened up the entire town with sufficient grains and provisions for the allied troops and forage to the north of the river.

The British troops destroyed Tipu's beautiful garden Lal Bagh to furnish materials for the siege. The garden, on the eastern side of the island, was shaded with large cypress trees and fruit trees of every description. It had trees 'bearing apples, oranges, guavas, grapes, plantains, cocoanuts, betelnuts; as also sandalwood, sugarcane, with cotton and indigo plants . . . paddy, raggy, choalum, . . . mulberry too from the extraordinary attention with which they were treated, [we] discovered that the Sultaun had set his mind on the manufacture of silk.'[28] Most of the trees were cut down to be made into fascines or used as firewood. The palace beside it was converted into a makeshift hospital for the wounded. Haidar Ali's tomb that stood beside was also under British control. The Sultan's army was broken and dispirited, that of the British was brimming with zeal and the joy of a hard-won success. The Sultan himself could naturally not be at peace to see his beautiful garden and other monuments in the possession of his sworn enemies. 'His anger,' writes Dirom, 'was expressed in a continual discharge of cannon from the fort, directed to the island, to the redoubts, and to every post, or party of ours within his reach. Some of his shot even ranged to the camp, and seemed aimed at headquarters; but the distance on every side was considerable, and his ineffectual cannonade served rather to proclaim the wrath of the sovereign, than to disturb or materially annoy his enemies.'[29] So horribly destroyed was the Lal Bagh that Dirom opines that 'the remaining years of his [Tipu's] ill-fated life would be unequal to renew the beauties of his terrestrial paradise.'[30]

By the morning of the 8th, the Mysoreans had completely withdrawn from the fortified camp. Pickets were sent into the redoubts and the British army was stationed out of the range of fire from the fort. Realizing that he had been hemmed in from all sides, Tipu made fresh overtures of peace. He was now willing to concede Cornwallis's earlier demand to release Lieutenants Chalmers and Nash, the officers he had taken prisoner in Coimbatore, violating the terms of capitulation.

Seated under the fly of a small tent pitched on the south glacis of the fort, in a desolate and shattered mood of utter dejection, and with only a few attendants serving him, Tipu summoned Chalmers and Nash to his presence. To Chalmers, he handed over two letters to give personally to Cornwallis, beseeching for peace. He strained to inform Chalmers that he had never intended to make war with the British and had always intended peace with them, requesting the latter's mediation. He presented them with two shawls and Rs 500 and ordered for horses and attendants to go with them to their camp. The duo, though detained, had not been ill-treated or put to irons and tortures like the earlier war prisoners had been. They were released on 12 February from captivity and sent to the British camp. Hence, Tipu decided to leverage their goodwill to prevail upon Cornwallis who seemed determined to crush him.

But if there was even an iota of a chance of peace, Tipu quashed it with his own utterly foolish and reckless intrigue. Even as he was suing for peace, he secretly dispatched a body of horsemen in disguise to penetrate the English camp and assassinate Cornwallis.[31]

The plot however unravelled on the 10th and if peace even stood a vague chance, that was obviously out of question now. Cornwallis was now even more resolved to continue with the siege.

Adding to Tipu's woes, the Bombay Army, under Abercromby, managed to circumvent the surveillance of Mysore, and making its way through Coorg and Siddheshwar Ghat, reached Srirangapatna around 19 February 1792. It had four European regiments, seven battalions of sepoys and were formed in three brigades. They could furnish about 2000 Europeans and 4000 native troops fit for battle. A considerable stock of provisions and materials, too, came in. Tipu made a feeble attempt to dislodge the general by sending Fateh Haidar to intercept him, but eventually gave it up. By now the allies had intensified the siege. Cornwallis was hoping with certainty to open the breaching batteries by 1 March.

The Final Siege

The fort of Srirangapatna that was located on the western end of the island was triangular in shape. It was embraced by the two branches of the Kaveri River on two sides and the base of the triangle faced the island and was the most liable portion for assault. Hence, the allied army decided to launch an attack on the fort from this direction, lodging at the Dariya Daulat Bagh. Colonel Ross, the chief engineer, on the advice and intelligence of the deserter Monsieur Blevette and other Europeans who had switched sides, decided to make the principal attack across the river against the northern face of the fort. The walls there were not as thick; there were no outworks and the flank defences, too, were limited. The ditch surrounding it, too, was dry and smaller in width and depth. The stone glacis built into the river was also broken at several parts due to the floods. Hence this seemed the weakest point for the fort.

Accordingly, on 18 February 1792, after dark, a contingent under Major Dalrymple quietly approached the camp of the Mysoreans without being noticed. A party under Captain Robertson marched inside, created chaos and killed several troopers and guards, raising a general alarm. The idea was to divert Mysorean attention towards this spot and free the northern side where a channel was being stealthily made by the British for an ambush. The fort was now a blaze of fire from all sides, illuminated from everywhere with blue lights, in anticipation of a general assault. On discovering the construction of the channel, Tipu had it bombarded. He also tried diverting the stream of the river by turning off the water from the large canal that was being cut at Kannambady to deprive and starve the enemy camp of water. But his attempts failed miserably. Tipu did not expect the enemy to cross the river with their guns and was alarmed to find them accomplish this feat and land at the southern side. He had come out in person at the head of his infantry, but the enemy had pretty much clambered in by then. The crisis had hit the doorstep of Tipu. Dirom narrates Tipu's actions during these crucial moments of his life:

> He [Tipu] was seen frequently every day on the ramparts particularly at the north face, viewing the English approaches, and giving directions to his own troops. He was constantly bringing guns to the works and cavaliers on that side, and had a multitude of people at work thickening the inner rampart, filling up the embrasures to strengthen the parapet where he could not have guns, and repairing such as had been blown and damaged by the firing of his cannon. He was at work day and night, making every preparation possible for a vigorous defence.[32]

Several people from Tipu's side deserted him at this stage, sensing the imminent danger that Srirangapatna and its Sultan faced. On 19 February, Abercromby managed to cross the river and invested the fort from the southern side. Tipu opened fire but this did not help much. The redoubt was occupied by the British after a spirited battle on the night of 21 February. They also seized the *tope* or grove situated between the redoubt and the fort. Here, too, the Mysoreans gave a very strong defence and tried to push the assailants back several times. But timely reinforcements came in for the British and they succeeded in pushing through. With every passing moment,

Tipu's position was becoming more and more perilous and critical. As Mackenzie writes:

> The critical stage at which his affairs had now arrived, evidently discovered to Tippoo Sultaun, that his suspension from total ruin could not be of long duration. Hemmed up on all sides by enemies flushed with victory, it was left him only to choose between a desperate defence against the storm, and a submissive compliance with the dictates of his opponents. Within doors, also, he was by no means secure from danger. However faithful their allegiance, it was natural to conceive that multitudes of peaceful people who had flocked to the capital could not relish a struggle of so little expectance, whilst their families and property remained at hazard on the issue. His favourite officer, with a large division of his best troops, continued still at a distance; nor was there aught of hope to cheer up the drooping spirits of his disconsolate garrison, or to dissuade them from surrendering his person as the best forfeit of his intemperate attack on Travancore.[33]

Throughout the Third Anglo–Mysore war, Tipu had led a lone battle against so many opponents. In the first phase, he had successfully repulsed Floyd, Medows and Maxwell. The arrival on the scene of Lord Cornwallis was a huge morale booster for the allies and added the heft of the Governor-General himself being on the battlefield. Previously, during the first attack of Cornwallis on Mysore, while the fall of Bangalore was grievous, the attack on Srirangapatna in May 1791 did end up with a loss of face for the allies. Fateh Haidar had shown promise by recapturing Gurramkonda and defeating Farid-ud-din. Kumr-ud-din had cut off a detachment of the Marathas in Maddagiri and reoccupied Coimbatore. Tipu's strategy delayed the advent of Abercromby to join the grand army.

But Tipu's fall began with the collapse of Bangalore that was more a psychological annihilation. The defences before Srirangapatna were not as well-organized and fortified as they should have been. The superiority of the British military technology and organization against the Mysorean one, which though it had been modernized on European lines considerably by both Haidar and Tipu, was no match for that of the allied army. His infantry and artillery, too, were inferior. Though he had rebuilt fortifications with the help of French engineers at great cost, they did not prove to be effective bulwarks against the allied onslaught. While the British cavalry was weak, the weakness was more than compensated by the cavalry of the allies. In those contests in the first phase that were primarily between Tipu and Medows, the British had no success. It was the combined forces that ensured that Tipu's power was reduced. Nonetheless, now hemmed in from all sides and with little options left, Tipu had to surrender and once again sue for peace, this time of course not on his terms, but on those of his victorious assailants.

Peace Negotiations

Even while fierce military operations and the siege were underway, the vakils from Tipu's side were constantly negotiating with the allied forces. The process had its ups and downs with the obdurate stands that the different players were adopting. Yet, the talks were going on. On 13 February 1792, Ghulam Ali Khan and Ali Raza Khan left the fort and met Kennaway who was representing the British. Mir Alam spoke on behalf of the Nizam and Govind Rao Kale and Bachaji Mahendale spoke for the Peshwa. The allies informed the vakils that Tipu must cede to them territories that yielded an annual revenue of Rs 3 crore. He was asked to pay Rs 8 crore towards defraying expenses of the war. Furthermore, a demand was placed that given his unreliable nature, Tipu was to surrender two of his sons as hostages till the first two conditions were met. The terms were of course maximalist and negotiations carried on from the Mysore side.

As the war proceeded, the bargaining power of the Mysorean negotiators was obviously decreasing with every military reverse they suffered. The issue of the hostages was a major stumbling block. After initially refusing this clause, Tipu offered to send one of his sons as hostage, instead of two, along with three officers. This proposal was rejected by the allies. Since his eldest son, Fateh Haidar, who was around eighteen years old then, was away in battle, it was decided to send as hostages his other sons, the second one aged eight named Abdul Khaliq and the third, aged five, named Muiz-ud-din. The other sons were too young to be sent as hostages.

By 23 February 1792, when all attempts to dislodge Abercromby had proved futile, Tipu assembled all his principal officers in the mosque and sought their advice. 'You have heard the conditions of peace, and you have now to hear and answer my question: shall it be peace or war?'[34] They all unanimously offered to lay down their lives to defend Srirangapatna, but hinted that the continued reverses had left the troops thoroughly demoralized. Hence, it was an implied suggestion to their Sultan that for now carrying on with the war might be an unprofitable venture and peace might be a better option. The terms of the preliminary treaty were signed and sealed the same day by Tipu and sent to the opponents. An armistice was thus signed and by 24 February the hostilities were halted.

The articles of the Preliminary Treaty of Srirangapatna concluded between the allies and Tipu Sultan were as follows:[35]

- Article 1: One half of the dominions of which Tippoo Sultan was in possession before the war to be ceded to the allies from the countries adjacent, according to their situation.
- Article 2: Three Crores and Thirty Lakhs of Rupees to be paid by Tippoo Sultan, either in gold mohurs, pagodas or bullion. One Crore and sixty-five lakhs to be paid immediately. One crore and sixty-five lakhs to be paid in three payments, not exceeding four months each.
- Article 3: All prisoners of the four powers, from the time of Hyder Ally, to be unequivocally restored.
- Article 4: Two of Tippoo Sultan's three eldest sons to be given as hostages for a due performance of the treaty.
- Article 5: When they shall arrive in camp, with the articles of this treaty, under the seal of the Sultan, a counterpart shall be sent from the three powers. Hostilities shall cease, and terms of a treaty of alliance and perpetual friendship shall be agreed upon.

Justifying these terms of peace, rather than a complete annihilation of Tipu, Cornwallis wrote to Sir Charles Oakeley, the new Governor of Madras, on 20 February 1792:

> I confess that an arrangement of this kind, which effectually destroys the dangerous power of Tippoo, will be more beneficial to the public than the capture of Seringapatam, and it will render the final settlement with our Allies, who seem very partial to it, much more easy. Those whose passions are heated, and who are not responsible for consequences, will probably exclaim against leaving the tyrant an inch of territory, but it is my duty to consult the real interest of the Company and the nation.[36]

A Painful Handover

While the terms of the treaty were absolutely humiliating for Tipu and sought to crush his power totally, the hardest clause to comply with was the handing over of his sons as hostages. By around the noon of 26 February 1792, the two young princes departed from the fort, even as twenty-one guns were fired in their salute as they made their faltering steps out. An obvious emotional scene preceded their departure where the members of the seraglio broke down while bidding farewell. Tipu was present at the ramparts of the fort, over the gateway, with a sombre, melancholic expression writ large on his face. The young boys were seated on a silver howdah atop a richly caparisoned elephant and the attendant vakils too were on elephants. The procession included several camel harcarahs (messengers) and seven standard bearers, who carried small green flags suspended from rockets. This was followed by a hundred pikemen with spears inlaid with silver. A guard of 200 sepoys and a horse party joined at the rear. In this order, the cavalcade marched forward to the headquarters where the battalion of Bengal sepoys, commanded by Captain Welch, received them. They were led towards Lord Cornwallis, attended by his staff and principal officers of the army, who stood at the door of his large tent, even as the young boys dismounted from their elephants. He gave them both a warm embrace and led them inside the tent, holding their hands. Once they were seated on either side of Cornwallis, Ghulam Ali, the vakil, told him: 'These children were this morning the sons of the Sultan, my master; their situation is now changed, their situation is now changed, and they must look up to your Lordship as their father.' Cornwallis had been gentle and compassionate with the young boys who were obviously in a state of disquiet and fear at being in unfamiliar surroundings, that too with their father's enemy. He assured the vakil that every attention and care would be shown to them and that they would be treated very well. At this, the faces of the young boys lit up and the fear that had consumed them so far eased up, both for them and the attendants.

The princes wore long, white muslin gowns and red turbans that had a string of pearls attached to them. Around their necks were several rows of large pearls, from which suspended big, bright emerald and ruby stones. Their genteel dignity, courtly manners and courteous behaviour at such a young age astonished everyone and won their hearts. Abdul Khaliq, the elder of the two, was rather dark in complexion, with thick lips, a small, flat nose and a thoughtful countenance. He was less admired than Muiz-ud-din, the younger son, who was bright, bonny and exceptionally fair-complexioned, a small, round face, large eyes and animated expressions. He was Tipu's favourite son and rumoured to be his father's choice for heir apparent. Tipu's vakils had told the British that Fateh Haidar, though positioned as the successor, was not a legitimate son and did not find much favour with his father due to his unpromising disposition. Dirom however contends that they were making up this story to shield Fateh Haidar from being demanded as a hostage by belittling his status.[37] Muiz-ud-din's mother, Ruqaiya Banu, the sister of Burhan-ud-din, had died of fright when Srirangapatna had been besieged and attacked. That at such a young age, the little boy having lost his mother so recently and his father's defeat having led him into the war camp of the opponents, obviously evoked more affection and sympathy for him. Cornwallis made some small talk with the boys and presented them with a large, gold watch, which

surprised them and pleased them immensely. As per the customs of
the Mysore durbar, betel nuts and rose incense were offered as a mark
of respect to the princes. Cornwallis hugged them warmly again and
escorted them to their suite, and the battalion to their tents.

The following day, on 27 February, Cornwallis paid a visit to
the tent in which the princes sat. It was within the mosque redoubt
and near a green wall that Tipu used during the war. Kennaway, Mir
Alam and the Maratha and Nizam's vakils were all seated thereafter
on chairs with Cornwallis siting between the two young boys. They
had already become more comfortable and less fearful of their
captors. Muiz-ud-din, who was everyone's darling, even chanted
some Arabic and Persian verses from the Koran, at the insistence of
Ghulam Ali, displaying some good education at a young age. They
presented Cornwallis a fine Persian sword and in return received
some firearms from the Governor-General. The tent was lined
with fine chintz and the floor covered with white cloth; attendants
occasionally kept coming in and spraying rose water, perfuming the
place constantly. As a diligent eyewitness who had recorded all these
minute details, Dirom states that 'there was a degree of state, order
and magnificence in every thing, much superior to what had been
seen amongst our allies. The guard of sepoys, drawn up without,
were clothed in uniform; and not only regularly and well armed, but,
compared to the rabble of infantry in the service of the other native
powers, appeared well-disciplined and in high order.'[38] Tipu fired
a royal salute from the fort on 28 February, to signify that he was
pleased with the cordial treatment and reception that was meted out
to his sons. By the night of the 29th, the payment of Rs 1 crore and
9 lakh was sent to the allied camp.

With hostilities having ceased for now, the sepoys and officers
were seen loitering around the vanquished capital. Some of the
sepoys of the allied armies tried to make communication with their
Mysorean counterparts, who spoke the same language or were of the
same caste. But they were rebuffed, and one of them is alleged to
have snapped: 'It is my orders not to speak to you; and I am besides,
not inclined to talk to people who come like thieves in the night, and

attack the enemy when unprepared for their defence!'[39] The British forces were particularly eager to see if they could locate any prisoners who had been kept concealed by Tipu and who might be discovered, as accidentally as some of them had been in the midst of the assault. The Mysore vakils feigned total ignorance and emphatically stated that no more prisoners were to be found. However, the British apprehended that in the dramatic events that followed the 6th of February, Tipu might have hastily put several of them to death. 'This system of cruelty,' stated Major Dirom, '. . . continued to brand the conduct of Tippoo's government.' Even during the siege and assault, some of the British soldiers who had fallen into their enemy's hands had been taken to the public bazaar and had their hands chopped off and then sent back. When shown these unfortunate souls, the vakils of Tipu again displayed total ignorance, claiming that they might have been caught stealing in the bazaar and hence punished by the locals, insisting that the Sultan never sanctioned such barbarity.

Tipu's Prevarications

After securing the safety of his hostage sons, Tipu began prevaricating on finalizing the terms of the final treaty. The earlier ones were only preliminary terms to ensure an end to hostilities. The devil was now in the thrashing out of the finer details on which there were many revisions. The territories to be ceded formed a lengthy part of the discussions. The extent of ceding them was to be based on their revenue generation and hence Kennaway demanded the revenue papers of the Mysore kingdom. Tipu's vakils, led by their chief negotiator in the revenue department, Subba Rao, tried to act smart by half by pretending that the revenue accounts of several of these provinces had been lost. Some were claimed to have been destroyed in the operations of the recent war. In one instance, they even gave statements overrating the districts claimed under the treaty to be ceded and underrating those that were left behind for their Sultan. On some instances, his coins were valued at double their value to bloat up the revenue figures. His gold and silver coins were arbitrarily given values according to the Sultan's pleasure. Added to the problem was the complexity of Tipu's new calendar and its usage in the calculation of revenue cycles, which further confused the evaluators.

The Maratha and Nizam vakils then brought in some revenue papers from their end, contending that they were the more authentic estimations of revenues of the Mysore kingdom. It was pegged annually at Rs 2 crore and 37 lakh. From this list, provinces were selected that yielded half this amount. Each of the three allied powers were to acquire an accession of territory equal to about Thirty-Nine and Half lakh rupees.

Tipu obstinately opposed ceding Baramahal and Salem districts and the forts of Gutti and Bellary. In particular, the claim of the British over Coorg incensed Tipu the most. The preliminary treaty had no mention of Coorg and only spoke of ceding adjacent provinces to those of the allies. It was later that Abercromby visited Cornwallis and pleaded on behalf of the Raja of Coorg who had proved to be a faithful ally. As per the promise given to the Raja, the British wanted to declare him as an independent sovereign under their protection. Tipu had every reason to consider the Raja of Coorg as being one of the principal troublemakers for him in this war and was filled with hatred and vengeance for him. His protest against the sudden inclusion of Coorg in the list of territories, in violation of the preliminary articles, was also justified. In fact, over the proposal of the British to take over Coorg, the peace treaty almost came to a breaking point as the terms had mentioned a surrender by Mysore of contiguous territories of the allied powers. Given that Coorg was contiguous to Srirangapatna, Tipu thundered: 'To which of the English possessions is Coorg adjacent? Why do they not ask for the key of Seringapatam? They know that I would sooner have died in the breach than consent to such a cession, and durst not bring it forward until they had treacherously obtained possession of my children and my treasure.'[40] But since he had agreed to the cession of Malabar, and Coorg was adjacent to it, the allied powers staked their claim for the province in that manner. Cornwallis had anticipated this dilly-dallying on the part of Tipu, as he wrote to Oakeley on 11 March 1792:

> I always expected that we should have a good deal of trouble in making Tippoo swallow so bitter a pill as the present treaty, and in that respect, I have not been disappointed, for he has practiced every species of chicane and every pretext for delay. It is, however, necessary for us on all accounts that the business should be brought to a speedy issue, and if he should not in two or three days comply with our positive requisitions, I shall think it necessary to have recourse to coercive measures. After giving up his two sons as hostages, and paying even by our account above eleven hundred thousand pounds, it is not easy to suppose that he can have an idea of renewing hostilities, yet he is a man that must not be trusted too far, especially, as besides all the difficulties he has started about the country and the money, he has notwithstanding my daily remonstrances and his repeated promises to desist, constantly employed great numbers of men in strengthening the wall opposite to our approaches.[41]

Even as the procrastination carried on with finalizing the terms of the treaty, the allies noticed by 10 March 1792, as mentioned by Cornwallis above, that contrary to the armistice, works of repair were going on in the fort. They strongly protested these measures and deemed them as suspicions for a sudden renewal of hostilities from Tipu's side, even as he kept the allies busy in evaluating revenue papers and debates around it. Strict orders were given to stop all such work. In his response, Tipu wrote to Cornwallis mentioning that 'His Lordship must have been misinformed; but for his satisfaction, if he desired it, he would throw down one of the bastions that he might see into the fort.'[42]

By now, even the troops of the allies had been exhausted and the few days of respite had already made them lazy enough to not want to pick up arms for a renewed ambush. The cypress trees they had felled from the Lal Bagh and used during the siege had all become dry, brittle and unusable. Six weeks of stay in Srirangapatna had left the place occupied by the allied troops, filthy and an outbreak of sickness was imminent. Vegetables and supplies were draining up steadily. Tipu, on the other hand, had managed some secret repairs and had received reinforced supplies from Bidanur that Kumr-ud-din had brought in. A resumption of hostilities might have worked well for Tipu this time. The British possibly knew this and hence wanted to conclude the treaty at the earliest and to their best advantage. As Mackenzie states: 'He [Tipu] was certain that in the event of being able to hold out but a few months, the myriads by whom he was surrounded, although they might possibly be provided against famine, must inevitably have yielded to the approaching monsoon. It was these impressions that actuated his conduct, from the first stage of negotiations.'[43]

With the aim of pressurizing the Sultan more and keeping him on tenterhooks, the allies now resolved to move his sons away from Srirangapatna to the Carnatic. On 16 March 1792, they were moved off to be transported to Bangalore. Seeing palanquins coming to escort them, the boys were alarmed and hesitated getting into them. They were cajoled and packed away, to halt midway before Bangalore, more as a pressure tactic to get Tipu to submit to the terms. The negotiators were informed that if the Sultan continued to prevaricate, they would recommence hostilities immediately.

Parshuram Bhau, who finally made his belated appearance at the theatre of war, was sent to guard the southern side of the fort along with Abercromby. Having appeared so late on the scene and also having indicated his severe antipathy for Tipu, Bhau began ravaging the capital and capturing several camels and cattle of Tipu's army. This was again a clear violation of the armistice, but Tipu had little option but to face this humiliation. Even Cornwallis knew of Bhau's violation. He had written to Malet that 'he [Bhau] will commit many irregularities upon his march [back from Srirangapatna], for his corps had hitherto paid very little respect to the treaty.'[44]

The pressure tactics had their desired effects. Tipu wrote to Cornwallis expressing his deep concerns for the misunderstandings that had cropped up and added that he was obliged to his Lordship for his kindness and indulgence. He requested that his sons may not be sent away to the distant Carnatic as he wanted the treaty to be finalized and handed over to Cornwallis through his sons. It would be a testimony not only of his own sincerity, but also of their participation in the whole process. Hence their presence at the site of negotiations was so important. He even sought an audience with Cornwallis, which the latter stoutly declined. Tipu presumptuously wrote to Cornwallis, rebuking Bhau for his excesses and demanding that Bhau be recalled and brought to account. Tipu further added that 'he should consider it a still greater favour if his Lordship would be pleased to permit him to go out and punish the Bhow himself!'[45] That Bhau was an ally of Cornwallis possibly missed his troubled mind.

The Definitive Treaty of Seringapatam, 1792

Finally, by 19 March 1792, with no options left and his strategy of delays to buy time till perhaps the monsoon failing, Tipu ratified the humiliating treaty. His Dewan Purnaiya was sent to execute the terms. The two princes with their escorts were brought to the camp by 10 a.m. to deliver the definitive treaty to the allies. Abdul Khaliq had by now gained a lot of composure and confidence in talking to the allies and handed over the parcels in triplicate of the treaty. Interestingly, Sikandar Jah and Haripant skipped this meeting. Even their representatives came in much later. Knowing fully well that the treaty had in it terms that crippled his father's powers, Khaliq handed them over with great and visible dissatisfaction. He even muttered some stern words to the Maratha vakil, which 'did great honour to the boy's manliness and spirit.'[46]

The treaty was based on the principle of equal partition to the three confederates. The British took possession of Malabar and Coorg, Dindigul, Shankaridurga, Baramahal and other places. The rentals of these were estimated to be 13,16,765 pagodas. The Maratha boundary was extended to the Krishna River which was their frontier in 1779, before the handover by Raghoba to Haidar. The cessions of the Doab, Dharwar and other places were valued at 13,16,666 pagodas. The Nizam was given back his possessions north of the Tungabhadra River and Cudappah to the south, again valued at a similar sum.[47] The Marathas and Nizam got back territories that once belonged to them. But the British managed to get new, lucrative provinces. Malabar and Coorg or the ports of the western coast, the spice trade routes and their maritime interests were all gained through the cession of these territories to them. With the loss of Baramahal, Palghat and Coorg, Mysore lost all the natural barriers that protected it, and made a future invasion into it a much easier task. Tipu's own invasions into the Carnatic were horribly hindered with the loss of Dindigul, Baramahal and Salem. He also lost fertile tracts in the Kaveri basin that provided immense grains to his armies. With the reduction of his territories by half and the huge indemnities he still owed the allies, the fiscal position of Mysore had been irreparably damaged and its ability to spend on its future defence, too, was limited.

The prize money for the allies that was realized from the sale of property captured during this war was £93,584. Cornwallis added a gratuity from the sum paid by Tipu and the Court of Directors, too, made a similar grant. But he and Medows renounced their gratuity and prize money. The share of a colonel was £1,161, of a sergeant was £29 and that of other ranks, £14. For the native Indian troops, a subadar got £27, a havaldar, £11 and other ranks £4.[48]

But the delicious irony of the whole matter was that the Raja of Travancore, whose noble cause the British were seemingly espousing, was left high and dry. The war began due to Tipu's alleged aggression on the Travancore Lines. Even as the raja celebrated the victory of the allied forces, he was shocked to have been slapped with a bill from the Government of Madras for expenses incurred by the Company in protecting Travancore. Though, this was part of the terms of the treaty that Travancore had signed in 1788 to enlist the Company's protection with troops maintained at their cost. The raja's coffers were drained and he somehow managed to cough up Rs

7 lakh. Sir Charles Oakeley further imposed Rs 10 lakh per annum as contribution towards expenses. Oakeley wrote to the raja: 'The war thus undertaken upon your account has been carried on with all the forces of the Company and at an enormous expense. Not only the revenues of this presidency [Madras], but those of Bengal and the greatest part of the resources of the Carnatic and Tanjore have been appropriated to this great undertaking, and on the ultimate success of our arms, Your Excellency must trust for all that is valuable to you, your territory, your honour, and even your personal safety.' The demands of the Company, he claimed, were 'calculated upon a fair and moderate estimate.'[49] The raja was aghast and wrote to his minister Kesava Pillay: 'I have not in any way bound myself to contribute to the expenses of the war; yet the Company presses for payment. I have raised loans and paid fourteen lakhs; yet they make further demands. My previous debts remain unpaid. I have raised money by doing what I ought not to do. I never was in such anxiety and distress before. The Company cares more for money than for their friend.'[50]

Tipu was perhaps among the few native powers who were aware of this British duplicity. When Haripant, who had cordial relations with Tipu and had also interceded on his behalf to Cornwallis to end the war earlier, paid a secret visit to Tipu before the allied armies vacated Srirangapatna, Tipu is said to have told him, rather prophetically: 'You must realize I am not at all your enemy. Your real enemy is the Englishman of whom you must beware.'[51]

Assessment of the Treaty

There was a mixed response to the treaty that Cornwallis had hastily signed with Tipu. Critics of the treaty mentioned that Tipu had been reduced to dire straits with the enemy reaching the very gates of his fort. To have refrained from annihilating him completely and to have given him a fresh lease of life was a tactical error on the part of Cornwallis—a criticism that he too was aware of and acknowledged, as seen earlier. But the prospect of acquiring

Srirangapatna and handling the many internal dissensions and the external jealousies overawed Cornwallis. He was found frequently exclaiming: 'Good God! What shall I do with this place?'[52] He was also being pressurized by the Board of Directors to conclude the war speedily, as the finances were running dry. Had the conflict carried on for another year, the Company would have found it thoroughly unsustainable and all the business firms of Bengal would have gone bankrupt. Already, for the past six months, the Bank of Calcutta had suspended its payments and its paper had lost 40 per cent in value.[53] In these circumstances, this seemed the most logical and advantageous conclusion for Cornwallis. Yet, there were justified misgivings. Writing about these criticisms, Mackenzie states:

> This glorious conclusion of the war was celebrated from the centre to the utmost extremities of the British Empire, with the most brilliant rejoicings; few indeed affected to disapprove of the treaty, and these were actuated by a desire of seeing the House of Hyder totally extirpated, without attending to the danger of throwing an addition of power into the hands of our northern allies . . . the peace was evidently calculated to ensure permanent as well as immediate advantages to the several European settlements in the east, for whilst the loss of half his [Tipu's] dominions would be fatal to his plan of conquest, the tranquility of India would, in all human probability, be out of danger from the restless disposition of Tippoo Sultan for many years. His resources crippled, his treasures exhausted, his troops dispersed, his artillery reduced to wreck, the most stern policy could not have demanded further reparation for the insult offered to the British nation, in the attack of her ancient and faithful ally, the inoffensive Prince of Travancore.[54]

Cornwallis had laboured under the misapprehension that he had effectually curbed Tipu's power for good. But future events were to show how mistaken he was and hence a lot of retrospective criticism of his policy comes about. As Lt Col L.H. Thornton notes:

> It will have been noted that Lord Cornwallis had held Tippoo in the hollow of his hand, and there were not wanting critics to say

that the Governor–General had been too lenient; that he should have crushed the Sultan completely and have erased the State of Mysore from the list of future possible belligerents. Apart from the fact that he was by nature inclined to moderation in all things, Lord Cornwallis had adopted a lenient attitude in dealing with Tippoo for two reasons. In the first place, the public at home was strongly opposed to further conquests in India. The terms enforced on Tippoo were in consequence accorded a favourable reception in Parliament, being in accordance with the public opinion. They none the less were opposed by a small and noisy group who denounced in one breath, the inception, conduct and termination of the war. Lord Porchester . . . declared that Lord Cornwallis had gone to war for reasons of avarice . . . the other reason which influenced Lord Cornwallis was his desire to maintain the balance of power in India. To Henry Dundas [President of the Board of Control] he wrote: 'We have effectually crippled our enemy without making our friends too formidable.' The Governor–General was afraid that if he completely destroyed the military power of Mysore, he would place the Mahrattas in a position of such preponderance that a conflict between them and the British for supremacy would be inevitable . . . this struggle was indeed inevitable, but it might have been undertaken without the expense of another war with Tippoo, had Lord Cornwallis adopted sterner measures in 1792. Few things, however, are easier than to be wise after the event.[55]

Sir Thomas Munro, who had served in the regiments that fought against Haidar in the Second Anglo–Mysore War and against Tipu in the third one, was among those disappointed with the turn of events. In a letter to his father, dated 28 April 1792, he had written:

Everything now is done by moderation and conciliation—at this rate, we shall be all quakers in twenty years more . . . if peace is so desirable an object, it would be wiser to have retained the power of preserving it in our hands, than to have left it to the caprice of Tippoo, who, though he has lost half his revenue, has by no means lost half his power. He requires no combination, like us, of an able

military governor, peace in Europe, and allies in the country, to
enable him to prosecute war successfully. He only wants to attack
them singly, when he will be more than a match for any of them
. . . when we have a General of less ability than Lord Cornwallis
at the head of Government, Tippoo may safely try, by the means
of Gooty, Chitteldroog and Biddanor, to recover the conquests
of the Mahrattas and the Nizam. If Lord Cornwallis himself
could not have reduced Tippoo without the assistance of the
Mahrattas,—for there is no doubt that without them he could
never, after falling back from Seringapatam in May, have advanced
again beyond Bangalore.[56]

In a later assessment, Munro however stressed the strategic need for
the British to have completely eliminated Tipu in this war. Till Tipu
was around, there was a tangible obstacle to the establishment of
British supremacy in India, he opined:

The dissensions and revolutions of the native governments will
point out the time when it is proper for us to become actors. It
can never arrive while Tippoo exists; while his power remains
unimpaired, we shall be perpetually in danger of losing what we
have. Why then not remove, while we can, so formidable an enemy?
But his system, if not broken, may in time be communicated to the
successors of the Nizam, or other Moorish [Muslim] people who
may hereafter appear in the Deccan. If once destroyed, there is
little danger of its being re-established; it would require what may
not appear in many ages—another Hyder; and even he would be
unequal to the task . . . let us then, while we can, make the most of
the superior stability of our own government; and if we are not, for
inconceivable reasons of state, to extirpate Tippoo, let us at least
humble him, by depriving him of the Malabar coast. When cut
off from all intercourse with Europeans, his political and military
systems may linger on during his reign, but will soon expire under
a successor.[57]

That there was so much discontent in the British army and pockets
back in England regarding the way the war was terminated was

thus obvious. In fact, around the time of the siege and before the peace negotiations, General Medows had attempted to kill himself. Returning to his tent, he loaded a pistol and fired it off on himself. The ball however did not wound him mortally, but passed through the skin of his abdomen. He had just taken another pistol, when Colonel Malcolm who heard the noise rushed in and saved him. Medows was rushed back to Madras for treatment and luckily for him, the wound was not too serious and he was saved. Medows had also favoured an overthrow of Tipu and a restoration of power to the displaced Hindu dynasty of the Wodeyars. He was thoroughly disappointed with what he thought were lost opportunities for the British. Instead of eliminating him once and for all, Cornwallis had given Tipu a chance to realign and recover from this shameful defeat. On top of this, when he was asked to receive Tipu's sons, an altercation had ensued between him and Cornwallis and it was in the heat of this moment that he had unsuccessfully attempted suicide.

But for all the reservations that people held out against him, Cornwallis had ably led from the front and by example, and had concluded a profitable war. Summarizing the benefits that accrued to the Company, he wrote to Sir Henry Dundas, President of the Board of Control, on 17 March 1792:

Our acquisitions on the Malabar coast are inaccessible to any enemy that does not come by sea, except on the north frontier, and I am assured that from the rivers and creeks with which that part of the country is intersected, it would be very difficult to attack us in that quarter. The possession of the Coorga country and of Palacatcherry [Palghat] effectually secure the two passes by which only Tippoo could possibly disturb us. The Rajahs on that coast are not independent, but now become our subjects, and if we can put them in some degree on the footing of the Bengal Zemindars and prevent their oppressing the people under them, the commerce of that country in pepper, spices etc. may become extremely advantageous to the Company. The net revenue amounts to about 25 lacs of rupees, which will be a great help at present to Bombay; and Cannanore will be a much better and safer

place of arms than Tellicherry. The revenues of the Coimbatore
country would have made our proportion too great, but if that had
not been the case, as it is an open defenceless country, I should
have preferred the districts I have chosen, viz. Barramaul, Salem,
and Dindigul, which form a strong barrier to the Carnatic and
to the southern provinces on the Coromandel Coast, and contain
several forts that no person in India can take from us.[58]

The myth of his invincibility broken after a string of successes, Tipu
Sultan was reduced and humiliated to such an extent that the fire of
revenge burnt relentlessly in his heart since the day he handed his
sons over as hostages and signed on the dotted line under duress.
The curtains were now slowly drawing up for what was to unfold as
yet another challenging chapter of his life. The final one, this time.

15

Between Two Wars

The victorious allies took their pound of flesh and marched out of Srirangapatna by the end of March 1792. Tipu was so deeply jolted by the humiliation of this crushing defeat that he brooded for several days and shut himself up in an agony of despair. Bowring states that after this humiliating defeat, 'Tipu always slept on coarse canvas instead of on a bed, and at his repasts listened to some religious book which was read out to him.[1]' He was filled a burning desire to avenge the insult heaped on him. But his first responsibility was to make good the arrears he owed to the allies, more so, to release his sons who were still held hostage and shifted away to Madras. It was decided that Rs 1.10 lakh crore would be paid from the treasury, and sixty lakh be contributed by the army. A sum of Rs 1.60 crore was to be brought in through the contributions of the civil officers and citizens of Mysore, taxed from them as a *nazarana* or forced gift.[2] The oppressive measures adopted to exact this money from people forced many, especially merchants, to flee to Baramahal and other provinces that had now come under the Company's control.[3] The destroyed fortifications in Srirangapatna were put to repair on a war footing and large numbers of people were employed for it. But these works remained largely unfinished for reasons unknown.

The terrible turn of events in the previous war had shaken Tipu completely and made him paranoid and sceptical of most people around him. Mir Sadak, whom he had displaced earlier for suspected treason, was reinstated as dewan. Tipu developed particular suspicion for the Hindus, especially the Brahmins, as Kirmani records:

As the Sultan had a great aversion to Brahmuns [sic], Hindus
and other tribes, he did not consider any but the people of Islam
his friends, and therefore, on all accounts his chief object was to
promote and provide for them. He accordingly selected a number
of Mussulmans who could scarcely read and write, and appointed
them Mirzas of the treasury departments and placed one over each
of the other accountants to the end that the accounts might be
submitted by them to him in the Persian language, and in the
extent of his dominions, in every Purgana by his orders was placed
an Asof [Magistrate] and in the towns yielding a revenue of five
thousands . . . pagodas, one Amil (collector), one Serishtadar, one
Ameen and one Mujmoodar, all Mussulmans.[4]

Tipu however decided to treat the Muslim officers in his service very
compassionately. He terminated the cruel punishments of beating,
flogging or displacing them. Instead, they all had to take a religious
oath of allegiance to the Sultanat. In his presence, they all assembled
at the mosque and after prayers, held the Quran on their head and
vowed solemnly to be faithful and loyal to the Sircar, not make
false charges or embezzle funds, or oppress the poor and peasantry,
dutifully do their daily chores and prayers, and abstain from forbidden
acts.[5] All those taking the oaths were given gifts and sent back. But
many of them broke these vows, especially those illiterate officers
who had now displaced the Brahmins—Deshmukhs, Deshpandes
and Kanungos who hitherto maintained accounts. The newly
appointed Asofs and Amils relied on the informal and secret help of
the displaced Brahmins to carry on with the revenue administration.
Though the Sultan perhaps heard of these through his spies, he
stuck to his resolve of not punishing his Muslim officers severely
henceforth.

Tipu built a mosque in every town and appointed a muazzim, a
malua and a kazi to each, and promoted the education and learning
of the Muslims. His attention was drawn more to prayers, reading
the Muslim scriptures and counting the beads of his rosary. The
old loyalists, both Hindu and Muslim, felt increasingly sidelined by

this new breed of 'low men and men without abilities [who] were raised to high offices and dignities . . . from this cause, however, it was that disorder and disaffection forced their way into the very foundations of the State, and at once the nobles and Khans, being alarmed and suspicious, became the instigators of treachery and rebellion.'[6] Mir Sadak was the principal nucleus of fanning discontent and inciting fraud and treason. With power concentrated in his hands, as the Sultan was still in his mode of brooding, Sadak began taking oppressive and violent measures that further caused seditious outbreaks. Kirmani states how Mir Sadak with his regular incantations, reading of spells and charms, prayers and rituals of burning pepper daily to supposedly ward off evil spirits, completely took charge of the dispirited Sultan's mind. If complaints against him were brought up to Tipu, he somehow managed to have his way through to dissuade his master and win back his trust. His pernicious grip over the administration embittered the few loyalists and admirers that Tipu had, and a general sense of discontent and disgruntlement simmered.

Tipu's bigotry around this time led him also to terminate worship in Hindu temples in the State, confiscate the funds of the temples being intended to balance the loss of revenue due to the tax levied on intoxicants.[7] This practice of slowly disenfranchising Hindu temples and the worship therein had gained momentum since the start of his reign, but gathered speed after the war. Throughout the extent of his kingdom, only two temples of Ranganathaswamy and Narasimha Swamy in the fort remained active, where pujas were permitted. His agents at Muscat had brought him news about the rising extremist form of Islam, the Wahhabi ideology, and how some of its adherents had assassinated the Turkish general in his camp, even as they served him as his corps.[8] 'This idea,' states Wilks, 'having once entered the Sultaun's imagination, he could speak of nothing but the tribes of Arabia, the *Eels* (tribes) of Persia, and the religious zeal, heroism, and devotion arising from such a bond of union and reciprocal attachment. He accordingly projected the establishment of a tribe, which should be as much devoted to his orders as the Wahabees to that of their chief.'[9] To this end, he decided to create a corps called Kebeela at first, and later renamed Zumra, to act as his bodyguards and also prescribed an appropriate dress for them. They had to be distinguished from the Brahmins and other Hindus, whom he distrusted, in their appearance too. Thus, we see that the disaster of the Third Anglo–Mysore War had a seriously deleterious effect on Tipu's psyche.

Tipu also fancied himself having face-reading powers and felt that he could assess the worth of an officer to be appointed by merely staring deeply into the man's eyes. Wilks narrates this interesting practice that Tipu followed: 'All candidates for every department were ordered to be admitted and drawn up in line before him, when looking steadfastly at them he would, as if actuated by inspiration, call out in a solemn voice: "Let the third from the left be Asoph of such a district; he with the yellow drawers understands naval affairs, let him be Meer-e-Yem, Lord of the Admiralty; he with the long beard and he with the red turban are but Aumils, let them be promoted" etc. There can be no question that he had studied his lesson for this fraudulent exhibition of oracular wisdom; but it failed in effect from the ludicrous blunders of the scene.'[10] Wilks talks about the absurd levels to which the Sultan's officers, on his advice, followed some of his regulations and strictures. Once, a husbandman had come running to the Amil of Kankanahalli to inform the latter about how a large field of sugarcane had accidentally caught fire. He sought the Amil's directives and help to douse it. With a pensive look, in total contrast to the gasping husbandman who was in urgency to save the field, the Amil said: 'Fetch the book of regulations; positively I can recollect nothing about a fire in a field of sugarcane.' The exasperated husbandman offered to give his suggestions if he were so permitted. He suggested that at the very earliest every man, woman and child of the town be sent with a pot of water to douse the fire. The Amil however was not at all convinced. The Sultan's regulation books did not mention this as a possible solution. So, the Amil, still displaying no sense of haste or urgency, opined that the rule book had no mention of what was to be done when a sugarcane field caught fire.

'The case is unprovided for, and must be reported and referred,' he wisely concluded. By then, obviously, the unfortunate field had burnt down completely. The matter of the Amil's costly prevarication was referred to the Sultan for his judgment. 'The Sultaun,' writes Wilks, 'heard the dispatch with a vacant stare, which sometimes preceded a laugh, and sometimes a wise reflection. The courtiers misinterpreted the look, and a competition ensured of wit and epigram, at the expense of the unhappy aumil [sic]. The royal stare continued for a time, and then dropped into philosophical preparative. "The man," said the Sultaun, "is a good and an obedient servant; prepare instantly an edict to be added to the regulations, prescribing what is to be done in the event of fire in sugar-fields."'[11]

On another occasion, when a case of embezzlement of funds was brought to Tipu's attention, the scribe who read the allegation implied by means of a metaphor that the accused had 'eaten' the money. In a deep, meditative position, after ruminating for a few minutes, Tipu adjudicated that since the accused was a Muslim, and that before eating he would be offering the same to the Almighty Allah with a 'bismillah' chant, even if the revenue was diminished, the praise of God was increased.[12] When ryots complained about extortion and oppression on account of the nazarana, Mir Sadak, who siphoned off some portions of it, intervened to inform the Sultan that this was all being done to cough up funds. Tipu immediately went silent as he was desperate to gather the money to be paid to his victors and release his sons. But Sadak somehow convinced the Sultan that the ryots were misrepresenting the case and in a fit of rage therefore, their chief spokesperson and an intelligent headman or Patel was ordered to be hanged on the spot.[13] The army too had not received more than seven months' pay and was in a state of terrible dissent and a brewing discontent. But Tipu started allotting jagirs in lieu of one half of the pay to corps, troops or companies, but not to individuals.

Through all these measures, Tipu kept paying the arrears regularly. By March 1794, the money that was due to the allies was fully paid and his two sons, who had been held hostage during this period, were finally liberated. With Captain Doveton, the princes made their way from Madras and joined their relieved father who greeted them at Devanahalli (renamed by Tipu as Yusufabad). On entering their father's tent, the young boys went close to the *masnad* where the Sultan sat, and placed their heads on his feet. Not displaying any emotions, Tipu, apparently unmoved, merely touched their necks with his hands. The boys arose and quietly took their seats beside him. In his conversation with Doveton, Tipu discussed various subjects of national and international relevance and declared that he deemed Lord Cornwallis as his best friend.

The Sultan threw a banquet to celebrate the occasion. The distinguished officers of his court who were invited to it were all elevated with the title of Mir Maran. Among them was Saiyid Gafar, Muhammad Raza (also known as *Benki* Nawab), the maternal uncle of Haidar and grandfather of the Sultan, Khan Jehan Khan and Purnaiya. Kirmani explains why Muhammad Raza got the name *Benki* Nawab—*benki*, in Kannada meant fire. During one of the Malabar conquests, Raza had been sent to quell the Nair revolts. 'Having brought the signs of the last day,' writes Kirmani, 'on these misguided people, and having taken many of them prisoners, he shut them with their wives and children up in a house and burned them alive. He was therefore, called by this name.'[14] On their return to Srirangapatna, the Mir Marans were presented dresses of gold embroidery and tassels, with jewels arranged in a certain order, and jewelled gorgets. The Sultan, who was on a renaming spree, changed the name of his army from *jysh* to *uskur*. The firearms were renamed from *bandook* or matchlock to *tofung;* a tope or cannon was to be now called a *duruksh* and a ban or rocket, a *shuhab* and so on.

During the war, taking advantage of Tipu's reverses, several palegars had declared their independence. After the war, once the allies departed leaving these palegars to Tipu's mercy, he decided to teach them all a lesson. These were the palegars of Maddagiri, Gudibanda, Harpanahalli, Punganoor and Uchangidurga. Early in 1793, Saiyid Gafar was sent against Basavappa Nayaka, who claimed to be a relative of the palegar of Harpanahalli and had seized the fort of Uchangidurga with a *bedar* force of 4000. Gafar was badly defeated and sent back. Thereafter, Tipu sent Kumr-ud-din with a large force and then another reinforcement under Khan Jehan Khan. Nayaka's garrison put up a very stiff resistance and held on for more than three months. Finally, the fort fell and Nayaka with 400 men were taken prisoners. The Sultan's forces ordered the fort to be razed. On the Sultan's orders, Kumr-ud-din wanted to make an example of the dissenters, and so the hands and feet of several prisoners were cut off and some of them were castrated to become eunuchs.[15] Saiyid Sahib had been sent to reduce the rebels who had taken control of Maddagiri, Rutlengiri and other places. After about three months, these places were recovered and the errant chiefs captured, their noses and ears cut off.[16]

The Allies after the War

Even after departing from Mysore, the Marathas continued to ravage the Mysore territories and the border districts. They refused to leave Soonda which was not assigned to them as per the treaty. The release of Badr-uz-Zuman Khan too was delayed and it was on Cornwallis's repeated requests that he was finally set free. Border disputes with both the Nizam and the Marathas continued for several months thereafter, because even though the treaty was signed, the actual lines on the ground had not been clearly drawn. Tipu complained to Cornwallis, but the latter coldly replied that 'these boundary arrangements should be settled [among the three Indian powers] in an amicable manner'.[17] Much of the normalization of the relationship with Tipu and the Marathas happened after the coming of Mahadji Sindhia to Poona in June 1792. He began to increasingly assert his position with the Peshwa, against his rival Nana and his loyalists like Haripant. Both parties wanted to wield control over the titular Peshwa whose position was becoming more that of a puppet than one of authority. Sindhia had even expressed his consent in 1790 to the British to become a part of the grand alliance if his northern possessions were protected by them and they aided him in reducing the Rajput states. Cornwallis had rejected this demand. Now that the war had ended favourably, Sindhia wanted to extract the maximum mileage for himself in Poona and not let Nana gain control. After a long hold over affairs of administration, Nana's hold seemed to be finally wearing off and he even wished to retire to the holy town of Banaras and spend the rest of his life there. Interestingly, until his death in 1794, Sindhia carried on friendly correspondence with Tipu.

Not being content with having subdued Tipu, Cornwallis was also keen that the latter be totally isolated from the allies, so that he could not regroup with them and try to recover his territories. Cornwallis's policy was to maintain the balance of power in South India, where he wanted Tipu to be crippled but not eliminated altogether so that he remained an effective bulwark against the Nizam, and more so against the Marathas. He intended to bind the allies into an explicit guarantee against future attacks by or on Tipu. In his letter to Malet dated 7 August 1792, Cornwallis stressed the need for such a clause among the allies:

> The Allies are bound to guarantee against Tippoo the territories that each of them might possess at the conclusion of the war; but it must always be adverted to, that the stipulation is merely defensive, and cannot operate unless Tippoo should attack either of them without just provocation. It must therefore be clearly expressed in the treaty of guarantee, that in case any difference should arise between one of the latter and Tippoo, the other Allies are to have a right to expect that the nature and circumstances of such difference shall be fully communicated to them, in order that they may give their opinion and advice, and endeavour to settle it by a temperate negotiation, and that they shall not be considered as bound to take up arms in his favour, until they are convinced that he had justice on his side, and all measures of conciliation shall have proved fruitless. Should a rupture become unavoidable, the interest and safety of the contracting powers will be so evidently, and deeply involved in the event, that it would be

highly injudicious in them to limit their exertions in endeavouring to bring it to a speedy and honourable conclusion.[18]

He framed a draft treaty and sent it to the courts of Hyderabad and Poona. While the Nizam was happy to commit to this, the Marathas saw no reason to curtail their future expansionist designs. Nana, in fact, wanted to make future claims of Chauth from Tipu, which both Cornwallis and the Nizam were opposed to. The Marathas knew that they had vanquished Tipu sufficiently and that he was no longer a threat to them. So, they now turned their attention, surprisingly, to their other ally, the Nizam. Nana was keener to ascertain his position against his rival, Mahadji, than to consider the guarantees given to the Nizam. The Marathas now began to press their claims of Chauth and Sardeshmukhi on him. This was the Nizam's biggest nightmare coming true. In his offensive and defensive alliance with the British in 1790, before entering the war with Tipu, he had made this an important prerequisite that the British support him against any possible Maratha aggression. Cornwallis tried his best to get Nana to sign a reasonable treaty of guarantee for the Nizam, but failed. Beyond verbal assurances, nothing concrete came from the Marathas, and the Nizam was left high and dry.

The discontent soon brewed into a fully fledged war between the two hitherto allies—the Nizam and the Marathas—by 1795. Rumours abounded that Tipu was allying with the Marathas against the Nizam, but they turned out to be untrue. The Nizam, abandoned by the British, even turned to French support and one of their talented officers, Monsieur Raymond, who had earlier served in Mysore under Haidar Ali, went over to his side to organize an efficient corps of infantry under European officers from Pondicherry. The main antagonism between Poona and Hyderabad was the clash of the personalities of the two ministers, Nana Phadnis and Mushir-ul-mulk. Mushir wanted to crush Maratha dominance with British support. The Nizam had deputed the milder minister and diplomat, Mir Alam, to Poona to negotiate terms, but these failed too. Cornwallis was unwilling to get into this squabble between his two hitherto allies, though Kennaway implored him to take sides. When the Chauth discussions ended in a stalemate, the Nizam decided to settle it in the war that broke out against the Marathas in 1793.

Tipu had his hand in increasing the Maratha–Nizam tensions. He kept warning Nana against playing into British hands and hated the Nizam bitterly. In the battle of Kharda that followed in March 1795, the Maratha alliance of the Peshwa, Sindhia (under Mahadji's nephew and successor, Daulat Rao) and Holkar emerged victorious. The Nizam had to submit to a disgraceful peace and Mushir-ul-Mulk was even kept in confinement for a year. His fortunes had reached their lowest ebb and the widespread discontent also manifested in the form of an internal rebellion in Hyderabad, led by the Nizam's son, Ali Jah. The Nizam even assigned to Raymond the principality of Cudappah to meet his expenses, arousing British suspicions. But the victory did not bring any significant, tangible benefits to the Marathas. Out of the 5 crore promised, only 30 lakh were realized, besides another territory that yielded 30 lakh.

While Tipu's relations with the Peshwa's durbar improved, those with the Nizam worsened after the Definitive Treaty of 1792. The stories of the Nizam trying to delay the release of Tipu's hostage sons made matters worse. Even as the Nizam–Maratha rivalry was brewing, another bone of contention between Mysore and Hyderabad was the principality of Kurnool. It had been a vassal province of the Nizam, but in 1765, Haidar had defeated its Nawab Ranmust Khan and forced him to pay tributes to Srirangapatna. The Nizam now raked up a claim to Kurnool, nearly three decades after the annexation, claiming that it had been his territory traditionally. Negotiations for this were to be held at Fort St George in Madras, though Cornwallis had strictly ordered the Madras Government to maintain complete neutrality in the affair. He believed that if the Nizam was allowed to have his way on the Kurnool matter, this would incite ambitions in the Marathas to make fresh claims on Mysore. Moreover, Ranmust Khan had hardly helped the allies in their war against Tipu, despite being told to, and hence Cornwallis had little consideration for his cause. Cornwallis opined that at some point of time the whole of southern India was the Nizam's territory, but with the conquests and victories of other players, the Nizam's hold had shrunk progressively. From the claims of Tipu and those of Ranmust Khan, it was clear that Kurnool had been a subsidiary of Mysore for nearly thirty years by then. Hence, the Nizam had no locus standi to claim Kurnool back. Even during the peace negotiations in Srirangapatna, the issue of Kurnool had come up. But Mir Alam and the Hyderabad side had been unable to produce evidence or vouchers bolstering their master's claims on the place. But so obsessed was the Nizam with reclaiming Kurnool that he tried to prevail upon Kennaway to negotiate his case with Cornwallis. The Nizam was willing to annex Kurnool and even pay the tribute that Ranmust Khan was paying to Tipu from the coffers of Hyderabad. Cornwallis found this preposterous and told him in his letter of 12 April 1793 that 'if you can submit to such degradation and enter into a private agreement with Tippoo, Kurnool can never be considered by the allies in the same light as other parts of your kingdom, and we cannot guarantee attacks on Kurnool against Tippoo.'[19]

Even as these talks were underway, a new situation developed in Kurnool with the death of Ranmust Khan by end-1792. A war of succession broke out between his two sons, Azim Khan and Alif Khan. On his deathbed, Ranmust Khan had appointed the younger son, Alif, as his successor and 'declared to him . . . that he should pay the balance of the *peeshcush* [tribute] due to the Ahamedy Sircar [Mysore] and in future be careful of his discharge of the peeshcush and of his obedience to the Sircar.'[20] So Tipu threw in his support for Alif Khan, while the Nizam sided with Azim Khan. When Alif Khan occupied Kurnool after his father's death, the Nizam decided to use the Company's troops against him in favour of Azim. But Kennaway sternly told him that the British were not inclined to get into this squabble. With no support coming his way, the Nizam tried to negotiate with Alif Khan but that too failed. Kurnool thereafter remained a tributary of Mysore with Alif as the vassal chieftain.

But even as Cornwallis tried to remain neutral regarding the claims that his allies made on Tipu, he very conveniently put forward the Company's claims on Mysore. The British occupied Waynad and other places, and also allowed the Raja of Coorg to occupy Amara and Sulya despite him not producing tangible documents of its earlier possession and Tipu having the same. Burning with revenge against the Coorg Raja, Tipu tried several intrigues to rekindle a succession war and a palace coup where Virarajendra was to be assassinated during the Shivaratri celebrations. But the raja got wind of the conspiracy and the protagonists of the plot in Coorg were all holed up and slain. Two of the would-be murderers were kept alive in chains as reminders of Tipu's duplicity, but each had one leg cut off to prevent their flight.[21]

Around this time, the term of Lord Cornwallis ended, and he was all set to sail back home. He had had an impressive tenure as Governor-General and the humbling of Tipu Sultan, the Company's biggest foe, was the crowning glory of his success. He had successfully redeemed himself from the disgrace of Yorktown and was going back a satisfied man. Cornwallis was succeeded by Sir John Shore, 1st Baron Teignmouth, on 28 October 1793. He had come to India in 1769 and had worked closely under Hastings. He had been appointed to the Court of Directors, to a seat on the Supreme Council. With his coming, the Residency in Hyderabad also saw a change, with Kennaway being replaced by William Kirkpatrick. Kirkpatrick had served as Resident to Mahadji Sindhia and was well versed with the intrigues and intricacies of Indian politics. He was also a Persian interpreter to Cornwallis during the Third Anglo–Mysore War. Shore, like Cornwallis, adopted a neutral stance in most of the clashes between the Indian powers. He did not even support the Nizam when the Marathas attacked him in 1795. The policy of non-intervention that Shore practised had only one beneficiary—Tipu, who steadily regained his strength and began to play his strategies with the rival contestant powers. He had been willing to support the Marathas in their war against the Nizam, but after the war, he was quite happy confabulating with the Nizam as well.

Burning with the humiliation of his defeat to the Marathas in 1795, the Nizam was becoming a votary of forming an alliance with Tipu to teach Poona a lesson. Tipu sent Sukharam Pandit and later

Khader Hussain Khan and Madina Shah as envoys to Hyderabad to discuss the contours of such a collaboration. The Nizam's nephew, Imtiaz-ud-daulah, too favoured such an alliance between Hyderabad and Mysore. But there were subtexts to Tipu's embassy to Hyderabad that played into the intrigues of that court. Khader Hussain Khan, who had come to Srirangapatna from Gulbarga, tried to fish in the troubled waters in Hyderabad. He tried to suggest that the rebelling prince, Ali Jah, seek Tipu's help to dethrone his father. In return, he was to cede territories south of the Tungabhadra and Krishna Rivers. Khader Hussain Khan was hence selected by Tipu to be a part of this embassy so that he could go to Hyderabad and confabulate with Ali Jah secretly. But as luck could have it, Raymond had managed to defeat the rebelling prince and taken him captive, just around the time the Mysorean embassy was to reach the Nizam's capital. Worried about his own life and the letters he carried for Ali Jah, Khader Hussain Khan destroyed and forged several of these letters. The other envoy, Madina Shah, was a saint from Kurnool, who was to use the religious angle to coax Hyderabad. The two envoys themselves came into conflict with each other in Hyderabad.

Both Shore and Kirkpatrick offered no encouragement to this idea of a Mysore–Hyderabad alliance as they did not want to offend the Marathas. They strongly felt that the Maratha empire, now embroiled in its own internal dissensions and trouble, was no longer a threat to the Nizam or other powers and they just needed to allow them time to self-combust. According to Wilks, the Nizam was more than willing to conclude an agreement with Tipu 'if the latter consented to exchange the pledge of a Koran,'[22] which the Sultan rejected. While no alliance materialized, Tipu continued to instigate intrigues in the troubled court of Hyderabad, till 1797, by playing one son against the father or using the Nizam's great niece in a matrimonial alliance with his family to spite him.

The Poona Potboiler

Poona meanwhile plunged into unending political crisis. The titular Peshwa Sawai Madhav Rao was feeling increasingly suffocated by the high-handedness of Nana and his desire to control him. Ever since Mahadji had come to Poona, he had counselled the Peshwa sufficiently to break free from Nana's shackles. Though never disrespectful of Nana, the Peshwa slowly began to assert himself more, and that came as quite a surprise to Nana to see his protégé develop a spine. But given his weak physical and emotional disposition, Sawai Madhav Rao often quickly took offence and felt hurt by Nana's high-handedness and strict supervision.[23] Finally, unable to bear the thrall in which he was placed and the repeated humiliations, the twenty-one-year-old Peshwa jumped off the high walls of the Shaniwar Wada Palace in Poona and ended his life on 27 October 1795.[24] Sardesai however states that 'whether the Peshwa died by an accidental fall from the balcony of his palace or whether he deliberately threw himself to the ground floor is a question which cannot be finally determined. Suicides cannot often be proved on unimpeachable evidence.'[25] The British Resident in his communication to the Governor-General about this unfortunate occurrence states that 'the Peshwa, in a temporary fit of delirium or derangement, jumped or fell from an upper gallery or terrace into a fountain below.'[26] Sardesai too attributes the Peshwa's sad death to an altercation that he had with Nana over the discovery of secret correspondence that was exchanged by the Peshwa with Bajirao II, the son of the deceased Raghoba. To prevent any turmoil and wars of claims and successions, Nana had imprisoned the three sons of Raghoba in Junnar, under the guardianship of Balavantrao Nagnath. It was Balvantrao who ferried messages between the Peshwa and Baji Rao II, which Nana discovered and was enraged about. The young man was thoroughly admonished by Nana for nurturing such dangerous relationships and this is said to have left the Peshwa deeply disturbed and possibly led him to the eventual act of ending his life.

Sawai Madhav Rao had no heirs and that complicated the succession issue in Poona. Daulat Rao Sindhia supported the cause of Baji Rao II, while Nana wanted to place another puppet, Chimnaji, younger brother of Baji Rao. These intrigues thoroughly divided the Maratha confederacy, right down the middle. Nana, desperate not to lose control, even made use of the Machiavellian Mushir-ul-mulk, who was a captive in Poona, to buttress his case. Chimnaji was briefly instated on the throne, and Baji Rao was kept prisoner. But the political tide in Poona kept changing rapidly and rival factions worked feverishly to outwit one another. As Sardesai rues: 'As the result of these intrigues and betrayals, a Maratha's word and promise came henceforth to be synonymous for falsehood and treachery throughout India and the race has not been able to work off the stain even in a century.'[27] After a year of disgusting squabbles and intrigues, eventually, Baji Rao II became the puppet Peshwa on 4 December 1796 with Nana as his Prime Minister. But given the immense distrust the two men had for each other, the administration came to a near halt as it was hostage to their gigantic egos. Things came to such a pass that Nana was even imprisoned by Daulatrao Sindhia in December 1797. Daulatrao himself was facing stiff internal resistance and a coup of sorts from the three widows of Mahadji—Lakshmibai, Yamunabai and Bhagiratibai—who detested him and wanted him out. Such was the troubled state of the polity in India in the last decade of the eighteenth century—a situation that was happily handed over to the British on a golden platter.

To make hay whilst the sun shone, Tipu dispatched one Balaji Rao as his envoy to meet the new Peshwa in Poona. The envoy met Baji Rao II and reminded him how his father, Raghoba, and Tipu's father Haidar had a long-standing relationship of amity and Haidar had helped Raghoba in his most troubled days. He also represented to the Peshwa that it was Nana Phadnis who had played an instrumental role in the misery that had befallen his father, had made the Marathas a stooge of the British, caused great anguish to Tipu too and that the Peshwa must consider Nana 'as a worm eating into the edifice of his government.'[28] The young Peshwa was quite carried away by this emotional rendition by Tipu's Marathi envoy. As Mushir-ul-Mulk was being sent back from captivity, Baji Rao II entertained hopes of being able to break free from the shackles of both Nana and Daulat Rao Sindhia. Tipu was willing to send his entire army to support his cause, and also to invade the Nizam's territories and subjugate him. He envisaged a lasting arrangement between the new Peshwa's regime and Mysore, by quelling all his opponents. However, the Sultan did not comprehend that even as he was negotiating favourably with both Mahadji and Daulat Rao, their ambitions came in direct conflict with this new project of emancipating the young Peshwa. Balaji Rao remained a secret agent from the Sultan's court in Poona and his antecedents were not discovered, even by Nana, till about April 1799.

Entreaties to the Muslim World

Around this time, owing to the opposition and enmity that he had faced in his father's court, the prince of Iran left his country, suffered several hardships on the way and eventually reached Srirangapatna. Tipu welcomed him with great honour, offered him costly gifts, a subsistence amount of Rs 2000 a month for his servants and made lavish arrangements for his stay, commensurate with his royal status, in the suburb of Ganjam. The Sultan's aim, as Kirmani states, was 'to join and act in concert with the kings of Islam.'[29] As illustrated in the sections below, Tipu aimed at creating a vast pan-Islamic alliance with powers outside India to consolidate and drive away all infidels—the British, Marathas, Rajputs and others—out of India and unfurl the flag of their faith on the subcontinent.

Once things cooled down in his home country, the grateful prince made a request to Tipu that he wished to depart in 1797. The Sultan asked the prince: 'After you have made your arrangements regarding the capital of the Sultanut of Persia, it is my wish that you and I in concert with Zuman Shah should endeavour to regulate and put in order, (divide between them seemingly), the countries of Hindostan, and the Dukhun.'[30] The prince agreed readily and offered to help Tipu with his missions in his part of the world. In fact, through his agents at Delhi, Tipu had opened correspondence with the ministers of Zaman Shah, son of Timur Shah and grandson of Ahmed Shah Abdali Durrani, the Amir (chief) of Kabul and of the Afghans.

In early 1796, Tipu had dispatched ambassadors, Meer Habibullah and Meer Mohammad Raza, to Zaman Shah with valuable presents, elephants and messages of friendship to pursue the common cause of 'carrying on the holy war against the infidels and freeing the region of Hindostan from the contamination of the enemies of our religion.'[31] Given the surveillance that he was under, Tipu asked his two envoys to move stealthily by way of Kutch on the pretext of commercial interests, proceed from there to Karachi again for ostensibly establishing a factory and finally Kabul with the excuse of going to Persia to make a religious pilgrimage to the holy tombs there. A detailed schedule of their travel and the people they needed to take assistance from was laid out in Tipu's secret letters to the envoys.

In his letter to Zaman Shah, Tipu stated that Delhi, which was the seat of Mohammedan power, had been reduced to a state of a ruin, since 'the infidels [Marathas] altogether prevail . . . it is incumbent upon the leaders of the faithful, to unite together and exterminate the infidels . . . the union of the followers of the faith [Islam] is necessary.'[32] The plans that Tipu suggested to Zaman Shah was that a joint operation was to be launched over two years. In the first year, Delhi was to be conquered, the Marathas expelled and the empire of Hindustan consolidated. Zaman Shah was requested to send a large army under a capable general to invade Delhi. The weak Mughal who 'had reduced the faith to this state of weakness'[33] was to be deposed and someone from the family anointed the new ruler. In that one year, Zaman Shah's general was to take complete control over the northern areas, subjugating the Rajputs and others. In the second year, the Afghan army was to invade the Maratha dominions in the Deccan from the north, while Tipu was to attack from the south, raising 'the standard of holy war and make the infidels bow under the sword of the faith.'[34] Once the Marathas were exterminated, the other infidels could be easily dispensed with, Tipu believed. The Deccan could then be mutually shared between the two as agreed upon.

Tipu, in his characteristic manner of overstating every directive that he gave to his officers to the very minute details, went on to dictate the plan and strategy to Zaman Shah too. He offered a second plan to him whereby if no competent general was found, Zaman Shah would himself be recommended to come to Delhi, conquer it and appoint a trusted vazir or minister there to carry on the military operations. A similar two-year plan was suggested to reduce the infidels. 'After their extirpation,' he pompously added, 'it will be proper to enjoin the Vizier acting on Your Majesty's part, to fix upon a place of rendezvous and there to meet me, that the proper means may be adopted for the settlement of the country.'[35] He wanted the envoys to get a written commitment, signed and sealed by Zaman Shah, for the fulfilment of these plans. He also wanted Zaman Shah to host two permanent agents from the Mysore court to reside in his court in Kabul to facilitate regular communication and better coordination. This proposal was accepted by the Shah.

All the exhortations that Tipu makes to Zaman Shah are of pan-Islamism and hatred for the infidels who did not belong to the faith. He extols Zaman Shah as 'the ornament of the throne, the promoter of religion, the destroyer of infidels and oppressors . . . employs your whole time and exerts every faculty, in the support of the enlightened religion, and is wholly devoted to its cause.'[36] He describes Mysore as that island of the faithful amidst the ocean of the infidels, 'in the midst of this land of infidels, the Almighty protects this tract of Mahomedan dominion like the Ark of Noah, and cuts short the extended arm of the abandoned infidel.'[37] This correspondence seems to have preceded the Third Anglo–Mysore War too, but gathered momentum after his defeat. Several letters of Tipu and Mullah Abdul Ghaffar Khan, a principal minister of Zaman Shah, and Ghulam Mohammad, the Shah's agent, on giving wheels to their plans, are extant.

In his letter dated 5 February 1797 to Zaman Shah, Tipu writes:

Agreeably to the Command of God and his Apostle [Prophet]
. . . we should unite in carrying on a holy war against the infidels,
and free the region of Hindustan from the contamination of the

enemies of our religion. The followers of the faith [Islam] in these territories, always assembling at a select time on Friday, offer up their prayers in the words: 'Oh God! Slay the infidels who have closed the way! Let their sins return upon their own heads, with the punishment that is due to them!'[38]

In his reply, Zaman Shah wrote:

> Your letter, replete with sentiments of friendship and regard, expressing your solicitude for the propagation of the faith, and the extirpation of the abandoned irreligious infidels; informing us that in the mosques, after the conclusion of public worship, supplications are made at the Throne of Grace for the increase of our dominion, and the success of our triumphant banners . . . arrived in a most auspicious season . . . as the object of your well-directed mind is the destruction of the infidels and the extension of the faith of the Prophet . . . we shall soon march with our conquering army to wage war with the infidels and polytheists, and to free those regions from the contamination of these shameless tribes with the edge of the sword; so that the inhabitants of those regions may be restored to comfort and repose; be therefore perfectly satisfied in this respect . . . continue to gratify us by communicating to us by letters, your situation and sentiments.[39]

To consolidate the Islamic world in his conquest against the British, Tipu also dispatched envoys with rich gifts to the Shah of Persia, Fath Ali Khan. Mir Abdur Rahman and Mir Ainullah Khan were sent from Mangalore on 20 March 1798, along with Mirza Karim Beg Tabrezi who was at Srirangapatna as an envoy of Rabia Khan, the maternal uncle of the Shah. They reached Muscat after a journey of forty days. By the end of July 1798, they approached Bushire, from whence they proceeded to Shiraz and finally Tehran. The entreaties sent to the Shah were similar to those sent to Zaman Shah about how the infidels had captured the land from the faithful and how, with Mughal power on the wane, Tipu was the only soldier of the true faith whose hands these Muslim monarchs must strengthen.

The Shah was requested for military aid and the exchange of ports. They were given a patient hearing by the Shah and sent back with gifts and assurances. Baba Khan and Fath Ali Khan were appointed by the Shah as his envoys to Srirangapatna to ascertain the whole situation. They left Tehran on 12 April 1799. By the time the Persian envoys neared Srirangapatna, the town had fallen, and the mission was aborted. As Denys Forest surmises: 'Ever since 1792, any power, whether inside the borders of India or beyond, must have received the overtures of Tipu Sultan as coming from a man who had been beaten in battle and stripped of half his territory—an even less attractive ally than in the days of the abortive 1786–87 missions to the Caliph and to France.'[40]

But hearing about Tipu's embassy to the Shah of Persia, the Company too sent their envoy, Mirza Mahdi Ali Khan, to counteract Tipu's diplomatic moves. The thrust of their moves was to persuade the Shah to attack Zaman Shah so that the latter was unable to join hands with Tipu to invade India. This embassy too came to Tehran around the same time as the one from Srirangapatna, but did not make much headway.

Tipu also sent an embassy to Turkey under Sayyid Ali Muhammad Qadri and with Madar-ud-din and Husain Ali Khan as members. But on reaching Basra, they realized that they could go no further as the British had intercepted their routes. By then Srirangapatna had fallen, and the agents were devastated. Yet, they insisted on going to Constantinople and handing over their Sultan's letters. Manesty, the British agent at Basra, was forcing the *Mutesellim* or high-official of the Ottoman Empire, Abdullah Agha, to dismiss the envoys and send them back to Bombay. Agha was unable to make up his mind and the envoys stayed in limbo for quite some time, before the British finally had them deported to Bombay on 28 November 1799 in the Company's boat, the *Antelope*.

The French Connection

The 1790s were tumultuous in Europe. The fire of the revolution that had broken out in France in 1789 had carried on for a decade, passing over several stages and, in the process, engulfing the whole European continent in conflict. The significant, radical catalyst of the Revolution in France was the Jacobin Club or the Society of the Friends of the Constitution. It comprised deputies to the Estates-General (later the National Assembly). They drew their name from the place where they had their meetings—Couvent des Jacobins on the Rue Saint-Jacques. They opposed the monarchy and advocated greater rights for the French people and supported a constitution in 1791. After the Revolution, the club aimed at consolidating the gains made and crushing down any aristocratic backlash. However, the Club split over the dispute on how Louis XVI should be treated and if he should be executed, with moderate deputies forming the rival club of the Feuillants. Maximilien Robespierre was among the few who stayed on and assumed a prominent position in the club.

With the establishment of the First Republic in September 1792, the Club too morphed into a more democratic Montagnard (Mountain) faction in the Assembly that favoured a republic. The moderate faction of the Girondins, who supported a constitutional monarchy, held greater power in the initial fledgling government. But soon Robespierre and the local Jacobin Clubs (numbering 8000 and some 5,00,000 members) unleashed what is called The Reign of Terror which was marked by terrible violence, massacres, trials and public executions of opponents for political crimes and treason. The Club was eventually held responsible for the violence and shut down in 1794 and Robespierre was executed. It was thus obviously a state of intense churn and flux in France. But the spirit of the Jacobins and Jacobinism survived even thereafter. An unstable Directory, led by unelected and corrupt Directors, took charge of the government in 1795—something that the Jacobin sympathizers viewed as a total betrayal of the Revolution. This period was marked once again by large-scale violence, repression and unrest.

With the execution of Louis XVI, France faced a new challenge of an inevitable confrontation with other monarchical kingdoms in Europe like Britain, Austria, Spain, Naples, Sicily, Netherlands, Portugal, Naples, the Holy Roman Empire, Russia, Prussia and others that watched with alarm how the French king was treated and eliminated. The ultimate goal of the revolution, to eliminate all monarchy, was obviously not something they wished to see gathering momentum. They formed the First Coalition against the alarming revolutionary trend and anarchy in France. Soon wars, known as the French Revolutionary Wars (the next phase being the Napoleonic Wars till 1815), broke out between the Coalition and France starting 1792. The newly formed United States of America preferred to remain neutral, despite British pressure. The impact was felt in India too with the British invading and capturing Pondicherry in August 1793. The French in India suddenly were on the precipice and had no native allies to fall back on. They made desperate moves towards their old ally, Mysore.

As mentioned earlier, France had betrayed Tipu in 1783 by unilaterally signing a peace treaty with Britain and therefore leaving him in the lurch in the midst of the siege of Mangalore. They had once again cited their treaty commitments as a reason for not entering into any fresh conflict with the British on Tipu's side during the Third Anglo–Mysore War. After the treaty, when Tipu tried to re-establish ties with the French, Governor Camille-Charles Le Clerc de Fresne remained evasive as he had no clear instructions from confusion-ridden Paris regarding how he was to deal with Tipu. But all that changed in 1793, when Britain invaded France. Suddenly the French discovered their old ally and reached out to Tipu, urging him to attack the British. The French believed that instability in India would weaken Britain's war resolve back home and they could get a reprieve. They lured him with the idea that this could be a great way for him to reclaim his territories after the humiliating Treaty of Srirangapatna of 1792. But Tipu was unwilling to bite the bait this time. He told them firmly that he could not trust them any longer, given their repeated betrayals. Tipu insisted that he would be open to signing such a treaty only if it was ratified by the National Convention at Paris, that he should be informed about any peace they might broker with the British midway and he be made a party to such a treaty. The response to his conditions was unsatisfactory and hence Tipu sat quietly and watched as Pondicherry fell. He did not even bother replying to the

French commander who had written to Srirangapatna soliciting their help.

However, by the end of 1794, the new Civil Commissioner of Pondicherry, Daniel Lescallier, made several friendly gestures towards Tipu. Two agents were sent to Srirangapatna to explain to the Sultan the details of the Revolution and the benefits that the changed government could bring to him and his quest of reclaiming his honour and lost territories. Tipu was again bitter about the past experiences, but he laid down clear conditions. He insisted in his correspondence of 16 October 1794 that a war should break out against the British with him as their ally and any peace made only with his concurrence and him as a party to it. He wanted the French to supply 10,000 men (that later reduced to 6000) with commensurate arms and ammunition. The conquests on the coasts were to go to the French, while those inlands, to Mysore.[41]

Lescallier conveyed these terms to Paris with his comments on how important it was to ally with Mysore and that the minute a French army invaded India and was joined by Tipu, all the other powers would ally with them to oust the British. Through Louis Monneron, the Deputy Extraordinary of the French Establishments in India, he conveyed hopeful messages to the Sultan that Paris had given a very positive reaction to these proposals. In reality, the Directory, embroiled in its own problems, had merely admired Lescallier's visionary project, but rejected it for immediate action. This was obviously never conveyed to Tipu and his failure was in not insisting on seeing the commitments in writing and in relying merely on the sweet talk of Lescallier and Monneron. The French in the Mysore army kept impressing upon Tipu the great ideals of the Revolution and how it had infused such superior energy and vision in the French nation, while of course withholding all the gory details about the utter anarchy that their country had descended into. As French historian Joseph Michaud writes:

> It did not matter to Tippoo Saheb that France was shaken by a popular revolution, provided he got from her the means to help him in his hatred towards the English. The French living at his court

did not fail to feed him on this hope. They told him often about the friendly intentions of the French nation. A watch-maker belonging to this nation and settled at Seringapatam, a man of no education, who hardly knew how to write, was the Secretary and Councillor for the Sultan of Mysore to look after his relations with France.[42]

Oblivious of what the official reaction from Paris was, Tipu, assuming that Lescallier and Monneron were indeed formally authorized, went ahead and even signed an offensive and defensive alliance with the French on 17 April 1796. War was to be declared against the British. In the event of peace, Tipu was to be made party to it and named as an ally of France and Holland. For every 1000 men set on the field by France, Tipu would have 5000 of his, and would additionally supply provisions. The French army was to land in the British factory of Tellicherry which they could occupy with his help. They would then occupy Pondicherry and Madras. Tipu was to annex the forts of Tiruchirapalli, Tanjore and Etrour and half of the Carnatic, while the rest would be annexed by the French. Bombay was to be handed over to the French, while Bengal was to be equally divided amongst the allies.[43] Tipu hoped that very soon an official ratification to this effect would arrive from the Directory in Paris. Sadly, for him, that never happened.

The Coming of Ripaud

In early 1797, Tipu's destiny was to take a decisive turn with the arrival in Mangalore of a French privateer, François Fidèle Ripaud de Montaudevert. Ripaud had sailed in from the Isle of France (Mauritius) and Bourbon. Born in North-western France's Saffré, Ripaud had enrolled as a sailor on the *La Palmier* at the age of eleven years. He was a *corsaire* or a government mandated pirate— one that has the authority of the government to attack pirate ships. At Mangalore, he was met by Ghulam Ali, the *Mir-e-Yam* or Lord of the Admiralty of the Sultan, who had, in the earlier embassy, gone to France as an envoy. The latter exerted his modest command of the French language to listen to Ripaud's story. Ripaud claimed that he was the Second-in-Command in Mauritius and had been authorized to discuss Mysorean cooperation with an army that had already been put together at Mauritius to oust the British. He was taken to Srirangapatna where he had long conversations with the Sultan himself. Though some suspicions had been initially aroused, Ripaud was a great talker who waxed eloquent about the growing friendship between the Republic of France and the Sultanat of Mysore. He merrily posed as an ambassador and representative of the French nation and its people. He offered Tipu the help of 10,000 men who had arrived from Europe under Rear-Admiral Sercey and General Magalon and were stationed in Mauritius. He wanted Tipu to send to Mauritius an embassy, with some trusted officials, which he would lead and officiate. Tipu imagined that the arrival of Ripaud was a consequence of the many representations that he had sent to France and that the Directory had merely forgotten to update him about this development. So consumed was Tipu by his hatred for the British and the desire to defeat them in war that he barely cross-verified if these were legitimate representations being made to him in an official capacity from the Government of France.

Tipu sought the advice of his Council of Ministers on how to deal with Ripaud and his offer of sending an embassy to Mauritius. The heads of the commercial department or *Malikut Tujjar* Shaikh Ahmed and Ahmed Ismail advised caution to the Sultan. 'This Ripaud that has come,' they told the Sultan, 'God knows what as it is; whence he comes and for what purpose. The evil and secret designs of those who are even inhabitants of this country, cannot be known all at once. For present however, it is advisable to retain him in the service of the *Sarkar*.'[44] Most others also recommended keeping him in service for a while and maintaining a watch on his conduct, even as Tipu once again wrote to 'the Rajah of the French'[45] to ascertain the authenticity of this mission. The summary of the council's assessment, dated 8 March 1797, written in the hand of Muhammad Raza, the 'Benki Nawab' is instructive, as the officers seem to have spoken their mind openly to their Sultan:

From first to last, the language of this man has been one of self-interest and falsehood, nothing has resulted from this business, and nothing else will come of it. From the erroneous statements of this scoundrel, the strongest doubts have arisen and even his request for permission to go a hunting to the distance of eight or ten *kaus*, is very suspicious. When so much chicane, covetousness of money, artifice and deceit are apparent in that short distance, what may not be expected in so long a voyage, with the *muallims*, (navigators or mates) his associates? The transacting of affairs of such vast importance through the medium of such a low fellow tends to throw discredit on the transaction. It is hoped that Your Highness will procure *muallims* of a better description, and that Your Highness, after procuring authentic intelligence of the state of the war etc. between the French and the English, will dispatch them at the first of the season. If these doubts and suspicions had not occurred in this business, nothing could have been better.[46]

But despite all the warnings, Tipu seems to have warmed up to Ripaud quickly, partly driven by his own severe hatred for the British and party due to Ripaud's way with words. Tipu had also sought the advice of the Council on the embassy. In a letter dated 25 March 1797 in his handwriting, he wrote to them asking them what negotiations such an embassy should do in Mauritius:

What occurs to my mind is this—to retain the Frenchman Ripaud as a *Wakil*—ostensibly as a servant—to purchase the ship which he has brought, load upon it black pepper and other articles of merchandize. To send two confidential persons, with letters from that Frenchman. There are two European navigators with Ripaud; to entertain them in the capacity of navigators; and entrusting to the verbal communications of these two reputable persons and the Frenchman what is intended to be communicated, satisfy the mind of the French Nation, and require Christian forces. The officers of each department to commit to writing their opinion separately. Ripaud has agreed to this . . . what negotiations and engagements shall be entered into with the French nation?[47]

The Council felt that the French troops should be under the command of the Sarkar. The joint forces must invade and destroy

Madras. The region from Pondicherry to Madras that yielded Rs 5 lakh to be handed over to the French, while the remainder of the Cuddalore district to be annexed by Mysore. The fort of Ginjee and Bombay to be settled for the French, while Mysore was to take over Goa. All the loot and plunder in the fort of Madras and the Black Town was to be kept by whoever acquired it. The Mysore armies were to also combine with the French in the conquest of Bengal and act together. An equal division of territories of Bengal was suggested between the French and Mysore.[48] Ghulam Ali and Mirza Baqir were appointed to proceed to Europe for the purpose of negotiation with the French nation, while Husain Ali and Mir Yusuf Ali were to accompany Ripaud to Mauritius, along with three of his associates.

The mission, however, got off to a disastrous start. The money, Rs 17,000, to purchase Ripaud's ship, was handed over to one Pernaud, who was to sail with Tipu's vakils and deliver that money to someone at Mauritius who had been nominated by Ripaud. In April 1797, the party arrived in Mangalore. The following night, Pernaud absconded with the loot and sailed away in another ship. Ripaud was deeply apologetic and offered to hand back the money. By then the south-west monsoon had set in and the Mangalore harbour was thrown totally out of action, necessitating therefore the postponement of the mission by a few months. Ripaud used this delay to his advantage.

After winning Tipu's trust and making use of the delay of the embassy, Ripaud formed a Jacobin Club in Srirangapatna 'in which,' writes Michaud, 'madness vied with ignorance'.[49] The ceremonials and the pomp, grandiose speeches and hyper-nationalism marked all their affairs. Denys Forest writes that 'this is the moment when the story of Tipu Sultan takes off into the highest reaches of the absurd and all touch with reality is lost . . . there is also pathos in the picture of a handful of exiles at a foreign despot's court deploying the whole ritual and jargon of the revolutionary epoch, oblivious of the fact that in their native land, the Revolution itself had already been devoured by its children.'[50] At first, this Club had fifty-nine members, all French officers and soldiers belonging to the party commanded by M. Dompard, with Ripaud as president and C. Vieniers as secretary. The first meeting was held on 5 May 1797 in the Parish Church.

Ripaud himself addressed the meeting and discussed the rights and duties of all the members. Excerpt from his inaugural address:

> Your separation from your Mother Country has deprived you till this day, of the knowledge of your rights as Free Citizens. You have begun to know them in striking the White Flag, which the nation held in execration, but which was the Idol of your errors. There still remains a duty for you to fulfil, that is, to hoist the National Colours; and to instruct yourselves in your rights . . . it is the duty of every Republican to instruct his Fellow Citizens from his own feeble lights, I present to you, the Rights of Man. It is from those rights that you will draw the Republican virtues which are to aid you in subduing the defects of your former habits, and to assist you in accomplishing this end, I shall submit to you some constitutional ideas.[51]

A president, two secretaries, two scrutators and two masters of ceremony were declared. Members were told to burn all the emblems of royalty and set up the national flag of France. Members had to swear to defend the Republican Constitution and to die with weapons in their hands, rather than see liberty perish. They addressed one another with the prefix of 'Citizen.' 'It was not enough,' says Michaud, 'for the obscure Ripaud to be raised all at once to the position of an Ambassador from a great nation. The title of Legislator was added to that of Ambassador, and the French, touched by his patriotism, begged him to make laws for them at once.'[52] He agreed.

In a meeting two days later, it was decreed that 'everything which related to royalty and to the ancient Government, should be burned on the day on which the National Flag should be displayed and the Oath to the Nation taken.'[53] The Club met for the third time on the 8th of May. Ripaud read the proceedings of the previous sittings. One of the 'citizens' of the Club rose to speak: 'Citizen Ripaud! We are filled with gratitude for the good instruction which you have given us, you have filled us with satisfaction, receive our acknowledgements, and administer to us the civic oaths which our brethren, the French

Republicans, have pronounced. You have enlightened us regarding our rights, but alas, we have promised nothing to our mother country, since the revolution, as our hearts are devoted to her, we wish to swear it.'[54] Choking with patriotic sentiments, all the citizens rose with acclamations and support to what they had just heard. Ripaud too was overwhelmed by this display of emotions and complimented the gathering. He then read out the oath they were to take under their National Flag: 'I swear, before the portion of the French people here assembled to support the Republican Constitution, to defend it, and my country, with all my strength and with all my powers, to submit to the laws decreed by the convention and to those which we shall frame, or to die in arms at my post, in the defence of the sacred right of a citizen, to live free, or perish!'[55] All the 'citizens' read this out in succession, individually, and committed themselves to the oath. Ripaud then read out twenty-two articles about the rules and conduct of members in consonance with the ideals of the French Revolution. These were all largely a long list of varying intensities of punishments, including death penalty, that would be handed out to 'citizens' if they erred. A Council of Discipline comprising seven 'citizens' was to monitor the conduct of the others. The meet ended with the singing of the song *'la hime a la patrie, en signe de joie.*[56]

On 15 May 1797, the French National Flag was unfurled at Srirangapatna. Several guns and muskets were then fired in honour. Ripaud, assuming the title of the Representative of the French Nation, went in procession to the court of Tipu. As the Sultan met him and some members, 500 salutes were fired in honour of the moment. Addressing Ripaud, Tipu said: 'Behold my acknowledgment of the Standard of your Country, which is dear to me, and to which I am allied, it shall be always supported in my Country, as it has been in that of the Republic, my Sister!'[57] After the exchange of pleasantries, a Tree of Liberty was planted with all honours in the parade ground. Citizen Ripaud made another stirring speech with dramatic flourish:

What horrors seize me! A religious sensibility overawes me! My knees fail me! My blood freezes! . . . I behold those victims of the ferocious English, sawn in pieces between planks. Women, the victims of their brutality, murdered in the same moment. Oh, extreme of horror! My hair bristles up! I see babes at the breast stained with the blood of their unfortunate mothers . . . perfidious and cruel English, remember there is God, the avenger of guilt![58]

After leading his audience to a crescendo, he questioned them, leading thereafter to an oath: 'Citizens, do you swear hatred towards all kings, with the exception of Tippoo Sultan, the Victorious, the ally of the Republic of France, to make war with tyrants and to love the motherland as well as the land of Citizen Tippoo.'[59] The members proclaimed their affirmation, swearing to 'live free or die!'[60] and took the oath individually. A salute of eighty-four cannons was fired. Legend has it that Tipu also donned a 'Cap of Equality', though there are no witnesses for the same.[61] The grand inauguration ended with the singing of hymns to France that were sung around the Tree of Liberty and the National Flag of France. A grand ball followed that night. There seems to have been two more documented sittings of the Club on 22 May and 4 June 1797, with no major developments noted in the proceedings beyond these six meetings.

Several authors such as Jean Boutier have argued that the entire episode of a Jacobian Club being established in Sriangapatna was a mere fiction of the British. It was a fabrication of documents by the British to justify their subsequent invasion of Mysore. Jean Boutier argues for instance that the original text did not have a subtitle. The subtitle was published only after the fall of Srirangapatna, and this subsequent subtitle of these being the proceedings of a Jacobian Club were meant to orient the reader and bias her understanding of Tipu.[62] The British are also accused in Boutier's paper of a massive propaganda drive by employing historians to write an unfavourable version of this episode and taint it as a Jacobian Club.[63] The argument is also that nowhere in the published proceedings is the word 'Jacobian' mentioned or talk of forming a society or a club. This was a straw man used by the British to discredit Tipu and accuse him of striving to spread the evils of the French Revolution in South

Indian French colonies, thereby justifying their invasion to put an end to it. Boutier argues that these meetings no doubt resembled a political association or club but were never termed that and hence should not be construed as a Jacobin Club that Tipu was patronizing.

But these arguments seem to be a case of extreme hair-splitting. The club might not have lasted too long, nor was it possibly called a Jacobin Club or the word included in the proceedings. But the tone and tenor of the speeches and the declarations made thereof, which even scholars like Boutier concede are authentic accounts, display an unabashed love for Republicanism and the values of the Revolution that were popular in France. That they did not explicitly name it so is hardly a credible defence to the fact that seeds of French Revolutionary thought were being sought to be sown in the virgin soil of Srirangapatna. That they failed to sprout is an altogether different issue. Also, the British hardly needed any justification for any of the invasions or attacks they made. In the subsequent chapter and the documents that emerge, there was enough and more damaging evidence that the British had carefully marshalled against Tipu and his hostile designs of sending embassies to France and other Middle Eastern powers in the hope of a grand offensive alliance against them. Those actions were in clear contravention to the terms of peace that all parties had signed in 1792. That therefore the British needed to *post-facto* fabricate a supposedly non-existent club to justify their invasion is stretching it a bit far. Nowhere in those justifications that are sought by the British to Tipu about his numerous embassies and the intrigues therein, have they even bothered questioning him about the existence of this Club, which was obviously too trivial a matter to precipitate a full-blown war.

Embassy to the Isle of France

The renewed attempt to send an embassy from Mysore to the Isle of France, seeking French support against the British, was made towards the end of the year. Tipu's vakils, Muhammad Ibrahim and Husain Ali Khan, were carrying letters from their masters to the French, posing all along as private merchants on a mercantile visit so that no suspicions were aroused in the enemy. Tipu's secret letter to the French Governor in Mauritius specifically asked them to supply about 10,000 French soldiers, 'and Negroes, as far 30,000 to be landed.'[64] Three thousand cavalry, 3000 infantry and 200 guns were also to be provided. Ships of war suitable for combat were requested to be made available till the conclusion of the war. Mysore would provide for the expenses of these troops, except for their liquor. Provisions and stores, bullocks for the artillery, camels, horses, palanquins, ammunition and powder were all to be provided by the Sarkar. After the victorious conquest and subsequent partition of the country, the French expenses, if any, were to be defrayed. The French troops were to be under the command of the Mysore forces. The French army was to land in the Mysorean territory of the Merjan fort, near Goa. Bombay was to be annexed and handed to the French. The joint forces were to then proceed from Goa, all the way to Madras and Masulipatnam, taking all places and forts on the way in a victorious march. Madras was to be reduced and handed to the French. The Marathas and Nizam Ali too were to then be crushed. From Masulipatnam, a combined army of 40,000 foot and 40,000 horse were to be sent to conquer Bengal. British possessions across India were to be reduced and all the forts, stores and territories across India, divided among the victorious allies. If either party formed unilateral treaties with the opponent, they would be liable for penal action. The enemies of one were to be the enemies of the other, and likewise for friends. Tipu's letters of negotiation also stressed that 'the sending of the four sardars of the *Khuda-dad Sarkar*, therefore on a deputation to the French nation, is my own act, and the publicity of this would be productive of disturbance.'[65] The French, if serious about the alliance, had to satisfy the Mysore envoys and also themselves through their oaths and commitments. A formal engagement and treaty had to be signed to emphasize all these aspects.

The embassy, thus tasked, sailed off Mangalore on 17 December 1797. To the shock of the Mysorean envoys, Ripaud's behaviour with them on-board was extremely rude and insolent. He demanded that the secret letters of the Sultan be shared with him so that he knew of its contents and they had nothing detrimental to his interests, which he would discover after reaching Mauritius. He snatched the papers, broke the seal and read the contents. He 'demanded money, threatened to take them to the coast of Bombay, where he said he had a number of prizes, and refused them even the water which was necessary for them.'[66] Braving all these insults and multiple hardships, the luckless embassy reached the Isle of France on 19 January 1798 to the harbour of Port Nord Ouest. The envoys had been clearly told by Tipu: 'You must profess yourselves to be merchants . . . They [French] must by no means pay you the compliment of going themselves, or of sending persons to meet you, nor show open marks of friendship towards the Khuda-dad Sarkar, nor outwardly show you any attention, in order that your mission may not become public.'[67] In fact, Tipu had even advised them to learn French but not tell the other side this but instead have an interpreter. But secretly they were to understand in the original 'their real sentiments, while they consult together upon the various subjects that come before them.'[68]

But despite multiple instructions by both Tipu and the envoys, Ripaud proudly boasted to the pilot who came aboard once the vessel landed, that he had brought with him the official ambassadors of Tipu Sultan. All the secrecy was thus thrown out of the window, placing the envoys in a difficult position and their Sultan's position becoming precarious and also fatal, as their identities were all exposed now. The port surgeon who arrived next to check the health of the guests gave an elaborate *salaam* to them all, as they were now an official, royal delegation of a friendly ruler and not sundry merchants from Mysore as they had posed. A highly ornamented boat came to lead them out; a guard of honour and a salute of 150 guns from the Governor-General of Mauritius Anne Joseph Hyppolite Malartic then awaited the embarrassed envoys.

Now that the damage had anyway been done due to the indiscreet behaviour of Ripaud, the envoys decided to make the best of the situation and have a detailed discussion with Malartic. They told

Malartic that 'the English tremble at the very name of our Sovereign and of the French, and will not be able to withstand the power of our Sovereign, supported by the aid of the French Republic, but will be defeated in every quarter.'[69] But to add to their woes, Malartic too gave full publicity to his engagements with them by a proclamation on 30 January 1798. It detailed how two ambassadors from the court of Tipu Sultan had reached him to firm up an offensive and defensive alliance with the French nation to flush the British out of India and what their points of discussion were broadly going to be. This 'Malartic Proclamation' read as follows:

> He [Tipu] desires to form an offensive and defensive Alliance with the French, and proposes to maintain, at his charge, as long as the War shall last in India, the Troops which may be sent to him. He promises to furnish every necessary for carrying on the war, wine and brandy excepted, with which he is wholly provided. He declares that he has made every preparation to receive the succours which may be sent to him and that on the arrival of the troops, the Commanders and Officers will find everything necessary for making a War, to which the Europeans are but little accustomed. In a word, he only awaits the moment when the French shall come to his assistance, to declare war against the English, whom he ardently desires to expel from India . . . we invite the Citizens, who may be disposed to enter as Volunteers, to enroll themselves in their respective Municipalities, and to serve under the banners of Tippoo. This Prince desires also to be assisted by the Free Citizens of colour; we therefore invite all such who are willing to serve under his flag, to enroll themselves. We can assure all Citizens who shall enroll themselves that Tippoo will allow them an advantageous rate of pay, the terms of which will be fixed by his Ambassadors, who will further engage in the name of their Sovereign that all Frenchmen who shall enter into his armies, shall never be detained after they shall have expressed a wish to return to their own country.[70]

The vakils were in for more surprises. Contrary to the high claims of a huge force of 10,000 people having been kept ready for combat,

Malartic broke the news to them that he hardly had 700 men in all, who were needed to defend the island. Admiral Sercey too promised just a few frigates. Malartic confessed that had they come a month ago, he might have managed at least 1000 men, but now they had all taken off to help the Dutch in Batavia. Malartic also conveyed to the envoys that Ripaud 'was merely a ship's officer, had not been sent by him to Mangalore, and had no status in the negotiations at all. In fact . . . Malartic regarded the vakils as having been dragged to Mauritius under false pretences.'[71] At best, he could call for volunteers from among the men he had there and arrange a ship to send them to Mysore in. Exactly ninety-nine men eventually turned up as volunteers to head to Mysore—so much for Ripaud's tall claims of a vast army that was in waiting. Chapuy, the General of the Land forces, Pierre Paul Dubuc, General of the Marine (of the rank of a Captain), and Desmoulins, Commandant of the Europeans, were the only significant officers dispatched. Dubuc was to be employed in due course by Tipu to send an embassy to France seeking a larger force.

The vakils were however shown fireworks displays and told fantastic fables about French invincibility and how they had pledged to reduce the British to distress and penury. The vakils believed most of these exaggerations and even noted them down faithfully in their memoirs that were to be submitted to their Sultan. They wrote in their memoirs for him about how 'the kings of Constantinople, America, Spain, Scotland, Denmark and Portugal had allied themselves with France and that their ambassadors or vakils were at Paris.'[72] Michaud laments about how 'many of the Chiefs of Hindustan knew so little of the politics of the European Nations that they hoped to conquer with the help of others.'[73]

Expectedly, the man who had instigated this embassy and its sovereign with the first set of fairy tales, Ripaud, had slipped away into obscurity once they reached Mauritius. The ambassadors were pleased and convinced that they had struck a good deal with a rising power that was on the threshold of global victory. The tragedy was that none of them realized how they had been so royally duped, nor did they mind such a small contingent of troops for now. If the

French were winning all over the world, surely men and material would come in aplenty later, they possibly surmised. They embarked on the *Preneuse* under Captain L'Hermite on 8 March 1798, and sailed back to Mangalore by 28 April.

What was equally tragic was that Tipu, too, did not see through this. The ninety-nine men received a hero's welcome. The envoys had brought along clove and nutmeg trees as per Tipu's orders, and he was only too overjoyed to see this. Palanquins and horses were sent to escort the officers and the envoys in a grand manner. In no accounts or correspondences of Tipu or of the envoys was there even a tinge of disappointment at what a disaster this had been and had opened up the fronts of a fatal combat with the British, who now had every legitimate reason to attack him as he had displayed aggressive plans.

'It is the most striking instance so far,' writes Denys Forest, '—there will be others to come—of the apathy or mental blindness which seems to have come over him [Tipu] in his last years.'[74]

16

And Then Came Wellesley

Richard Colley Wellesley was born on 20 June 1760 in a family of Irish landed gentry, but only recently ennobled. His father, Garret Wellesley, was second Baron Mornington, first Viscount Wellesley and first Earl of Mornington, and in addition, a happy composer of music. The musically inclined father even held a professorship in the University of Dublin, delivering annually a course of lectures on vocal and orchestral harmony.[1] Richard was sent to Harrow in 1770, where he is said to have even taken part in the riots that followed the Headmastership elections.[2] In his delightful biography of Wellesley, *The Marquess Wellesely, Architect of Empire*, W.M. Torrens paints a picture of his early years as a remarkably unambitious and spoilt son of a famous father. Richard Wellesley had two younger brothers, that included William Wellesley, famous in history as Arthur Wellesley and later as the Duke of Wellington. Richard Wellesley was appointed a member of the Board of Control in 1793 and he made it a point to acquire a keen knowledge of Indian states and their politics.

Sir John Shore was set to retire as the Governor-General of India in March 1798. Lord Hobart, the Governor of Madras, was to succeed him but fell out with the Directors. All through Shore's tenure, his procrastinations had cost the Company heavily. The Company's revenues too had steadily declined under Shore, and debts had mounted.[3] The Company's credit, too, was at its lowest ebb and money could not be borrowed in Bengal under 12 per cent.[4] 'Without active vitality of intelligence or energy,' writes

Torrens eloquently, 'like an elephant tied in a stall, Government had waxed fat and kicked, had grown unwieldy without developing even for self-assertion muscular power. The reins had been allowed to fall upon its neck, and it tramped on sluggishly and sulkily, praised by evil-doers and a terror to those that did well.'[5] Further, Shore's delay in implementing the military reforms that his predecessor Cornwallis had planned had already led to a tumultuous situation of a revolt brewing in the Indian Army, especially in Bengal. To handle such a situation, it was decided that Cornwallis was the only option who could avert this peril. He was sworn in as the new Governor-General on 1 February 1797. But right from the beginning it was unsure if Cornwallis would sail back to India for a second time. Even by 15 April, he was still very much in England, at Portsmouth, where fleet mutinies had broken out and a French attack seemed imminent. Cornwallis seemed keener to address the issues at home rather than get embroiled for a second time in the mess in India. He had been hustled off to Ireland to quell the threats that were rising there. Britain's position had been precarious in the Revolutionary Wars. One of her allies, Austria, had been defeated in Rivoli. The French Directory's strongman, Napoleon Bonaparte, had been leading many victories in Europe for his motherland.

Through a curious turn of events, the mantle fell on the Lord of Mornington the Marquis Wellesley i.e., Richard Wellesley. He arrived in Calcutta's Fort William on 17 May 1798 and took over as the Company's new Governor-General of India. Along with Clive and Hastings, Wellesley is regarded as one of the trio who helped secure for the British a mighty Indian empire. Even before setting out for India, he had announced his intention of conducting Indian affairs according to a 'resolution formed on principles which a long attention to the affairs of India had enabled him to fix with some degree of confidence.'[6] Wellesley (or Lord Mornington as was his official title) kept himself thoroughly briefed and updated about all the intrigues and politics that plagued several Indian states. As Lady Anne Bernard recounted of the few weeks he spent at the

Cape of Good Hope on the voyage to India to take over as the new Governor-General:

> He [Wellesley] has a levee every morning of yellow generals and captains from India with despatches for Government, who stop here, and finding His Excellency at the Cape, deliver up their official papers, which he opens, peruses and by such means will arrive instructed on the present position of affairs there, and will appear a prodigy of ability in being master of all so soon after his arrival.[7]

At the Cape of Good Hope, William Kirkpatrick was present on sick leave, as were Macartney and Lord Hobart on their way back to England. Wellesley held long, intense discussions with all these men to fully acquaint himself with what was to await him as he set sail from the Cape towards India. Even before he reached India, Wellesley had dispatched a detailed letter to Henry Dundas, the Chairman of the Board of Control, on 23 February 1798 and another on 28 February outlining his understanding of the Indian political scenario, especially with regard to Tipu:

> The most remarkable step which Tippoo has lately taken, is his communication with Zemaun Shah . . . if an invasion of Hindostan should ever seriously be attempted by Zemaun Shah, the diversion of our force, which would be occasioned by such an event, would offer the most favourable opportunity to an attack from Tippoo on our possessions in the Peninsula. No mode of carrying on war against us could be more vexatious or more distressing to our resources than a combined attack upon Oude [Oudh] and the Carnatic . . . Zemaun Shah has not abandoned his project of invading Hindostan, and that the safest means of rendering that project abortive will be to consider it as practicable, and to take the best precautions against it which the advantages of our situation and the interval of time can furnish . . . I wish to know from you, whether we ought to suffer, without animadversion and

spirited representation, such open acts of hostility on the part of Tippoo? My ideas on this subject are, that as on the one hand we ought never to use any high language towards Tippoo, nor ever attempt to deny him the smallest point of his just rights, so on the other, where we have distinct proofs of his machinations against us, we ought to let him know that his treachery does not escape our observation, and to make him feel that he is within the reach of our vigilance. At present it appears to me that he is permitted to excite ill will against us wherever he pleases, without the least attempt on our part to reprehend either him for the suggestion, or the Court, to whom he applies, for listening to it.[8]

This was perhaps the first time that Tipu was contending with a British Governor-General who was meeting him, being completely updated about all his plans, past and present, and was determined to tolerate no nonsense. Even Cornwallis had a certain brashness of military designs and a sluggishness inspired by his famed balance of power principle. But that was not the case with Wellesley, who had studied the problem well and knew what the quick solution had to be.

Barely had Wellesley taken over the office of Governor-General than on 8 June 1798, Calcutta newspapers were agog with copies of the Malartic proclamation and the peril at the southern end. In a letter to General Harris, Commander-in-Chief of the Madras Army, Wellesley wrote:

There seems to be so little doubt that the Proclamation was really published at the Mauritius, that it must become a matter of serious discussion between this Government and Tippoo. How such a discussion may terminate it is impossible to say. Perhaps the result of it may be to prove that M. Malartic has exaggerated, or wholly misrepresented the intentions of Tippoo; but on the other hand, if Tippoo should choose to avow the objects of his embassy, to have been such as are described in the Proclamation, the consequences may be very serious, and may ultimately involve us in the calamity of war. I wish you to be apprised of my apprehensions on this subject, and to prepare your mind for the possible event. You will therefore turn your attention to the means of collecting a force, if necessity should unfortunately require it; but it is not my desire that you should proceed to take any public steps towards the assembling of the army before you receive further intimation from me.[9]

Beyond what he saw in the press, Wellesley had also received official copies of the proclamation through Lord Macartney, who was at the Cape of Good Hope, and Sir Hugh Christian, Admiral commanding at the Cape. Though he had warned Harris to start preparing for the eventuality of a war, Wellesley maintained a steady communication with Tipu, without bringing the Malartic document or his French connections into the conversation. His first communique to Tipu was on 14 June 1798, as a response to Tipu's earlier letters to Sir John Shore on matters related to disputed territories with the Coorg Raja. 'Being anxious to afford you,' wrote Wellesley, 'every proof in my power of my sincere wish to maintain the good understanding which had so long subsisted between Your Highness and the Company . . . on my part, you will always meet with a religious adherence to every article of the treaties subsisting between us.'[10] The dispute at Waynad was also resolved to Tipu's advantage to lull him into a false sense of security with the new incumbent. But even as pleasantries were being exchanged with Tipu, and Harris could reply to his earlier letter, Wellesley was already writing to Harris a second time on 20 June 1798 stating that 'it is my positive resolution to assemble the army upon the coast.'[11] He was devising another direct march on Srirangapatna, of the kinds Cornwallis had made, with 'the object of striking a sudden blow against Tippoo before he can receive any foreign aid.'[12] He wanted to annex as many territories from Tipu between the western Ghats and the Malabar, so as to cut off his maritime communications with the French. Through such a combat, Wellesley hoped they could insulate the court of Srirangapatna from all possible French influence and instead force Tipu into admitting British representatives there.

But Harris and the entire Madras Government were in a tizzy about the prospect of a premature and ill-planned attack on Tipu when they were barely prepared. Josiah Webbe, the experienced Secretary of the Madras Council, exclaimed in horror: 'I can anticipate nothing but shocking disasters from a premature attack upon Tippoo in our present disabled condition, and the impeachment of Lord Mornington for his temerity.'[13] The general assessment of the British side was that while the policy of balance of power that Cornwallis had envisaged remained, things had changed drastically since the 1792 Treaty was signed. Tipu, though not advanced in strength, had gained a vantage ground on account of the discord between the allies, who had definitely receded from their power of strength as it stood in 1792. The Nizam's defeat by the Marathas in 1795, the war of succession in Hyderabad and the illness of the Nizam and the political chaos that Poona had plunged into after the Peshwa's death had all added relatively to Tipu's strength. Hence, reducing him was in the British interests, but the question was if the timing and military preparation were right.

Wellesley wanted to get the allies on-board and start preparing for what was increasingly seeming to be an inevitability. It was just that the allies had all drifted. Sir John Shore's non-committal attitude towards the Nizam in the wake of the Maratha aggression on Hyderabad had already broken the alliance and also sent the Nizam straight into the French lap, with Raymond stationed in Hyderabad as military commander. The bad condition of the fortifications since the Third Anglo–Mysore War and the costs that a future war might impose on the Company were other reality checks for the new Governor-General, in addition to the tatters in which their erstwhile alliance lay. After the initial bravado, Wellesley was more measured in his detailed letter of assessment of the dangers of the French connection that Tipu was flirting with posed to the Company, and the response to that in the form of an immediate attack on Mysore. He seemed to have gathered intelligence by himself, sitting in Bengal and without relying on the Madras Government. Lt Gen. Sir Alured Clarke, who was Commander-in-Chief since March 1798 and had served in that capacity in Madras, seems to have been his confidant on South Indian matters. Wellesley wrote as follows to Henry Dundas, the Chairman of the Board of Control, on 6 July 1798:

> The present state of our army in the opinion of all military men, leaves no doubt of the ultimate success of the plan which I have stated; and if its speedy accomplishment had appeared to me as certain as its ultimate success, I should not have hesitated one moment in ordering the movement of the troops for that purpose. But upon consulting the persons most conversant with military details, I found that the actual state of the frontier fortifications of the Carnatic, of the train of artillery, and of the stores of grain and other provisions, was such, as not to admit of any sudden movement of a large force, although it appeared certain that such a force might be collected within a very short space of time. I also found that the expense of making the necessary preparations would be very heavy, and that the result was likely to lead to a protracted and expensive, although, according to every opinion, a successful war. The present reduced state of the courts at Poonah and Hyderabad admitted no hope of immediate assistance from either of those powers . . . under all these circumstances, I felt with the utmost degree of pain and regret that the moment was unfavourable to the adoption of the only measure which promises effectual and permanent security to the territories committed to my charge . . .[14]

In this letter, Wellesley also conveyed to Dundas his intention to confront Tipu and call upon him to 'make a public disavowal of the proceedings of his ambassadors,' 'to declare distinctly the nature of his intentions towards us and our allies,' and explain 'the destination of the force raised by the Isle of France, and lately landed in Mangalore.'[15] The letter was however not sent to Tipu until much later. Wellesley had just assumed office and he wanted to be thorough in his military preparations and diplomatic dealings with his allies before opening up any confrontation with Tipu. He did not want Tipu to make promises and then get away, as Wellesley was clear in his mind that this was now to be a battle to the finish.

Mending Fences with Allies

Wellesley strategized that the first and more important step was to mend and consolidate estranged relations with his erstwhile allies. This was not going to be an easy task. In his dispatch from Fort St George on 6 July 1798, Wellesley wrote in exasperation: 'The dilatoriness, indecision and cowardice of our allies [Nizam and Marathas] are beyond belief to those who have not been eye-witness to these qualities in them, and there is a moral assurance that not one of them will take the field or be of the least use to us until we have secured a position to cover their advance or gained a decided advantage. The difficulties which press here are insuperable. The draught and cattle even for the defensive army cannot be collected to enable us to do more than merely reach Baramahal before the monsoon in October . . . a force capable of undertaking the siege of Seringapatam could not in all probability reach the place before February 1 [1799].'[16]

The French under Raymond had taken over the military set-up in Hyderabad, while under Mons. De Boigne, they had occupied the court of the Sindhia too. The troops in Hyderabad had, under Raymond, 'attained a degree of discipline superior in every respect to that of any native infantry in India, excepting the sepoys entertained in the English service.'[17] A large and well-organized train of field artillery, too, supplemented this. Raymond had also opened communications with Tipu, though these were discontinued after the arrival of the contingent from the Isle of France, due to the mutual rivalries and jealousies among the Frenchmen. The Jacobian and Republican principles, the Cap of Equality, the Tree of Liberty and all the other paraphernalia had been active in Hyderabad too, as they had been in Srirangapatna.

It demanded supreme tact and diplomacy on the part of Wellesley to wean the Nizam away from the French comfort that he had now secured. As per a Subsidiary Treaty (subsidy paid in exchange for military protection) in September 1798, the English force was to be augmented to six battalions with a formidable artillery, provided the Nizam dismissed the French corps under Raymond. These subsidiary alliances were all craftily designed by Wellesley where often, instead of cash subsidies, native powers ceded territories, which anyway served the Company well. The system of subsidiary alliances existed before his tenure, but he greatly enhanced its usage and added another element to it. When the subsidized force was not only permanent and stationed within the ally's territory, but also, instead of the protected ruler having to find a certain yearly sum from his general revenue for its upkeep, part of his territory was once and for all surrendered to the suzerain power.[18] This was the final and most developed kind of subsidiary alliance that Wellesley crafted and executed on many occasions.

Wellesley's stars seemed to have been extremely beneficial to him, as just around the time he was conceiving his mission in Hyderabad, Raymond died an untimely and sudden death. This put the French forces there under disarray, being without a strong leader, as an ineffectual man named Piron had succeeded Raymond. Without any loss of life or skirmish, the French forces, of 14,000 sepoys and mercenaries, organized by Raymond were completely disarmed and disbanded by October 1798. The Nizam was now completely at the mercy of the Company, which had stationed such a vast force in his court too. The British provided the Nizam a total of 6000 native troops, with 'firelocks and a due proportion of field pieces manned by Europeans, in return for a cash subsidy of 24 Lakhs, 17,100 rupees a year in silver of full currency.'[19] Captain Kirkpatrick, the British Resident and successor of Kennaway, was to now negotiate with an enfeebled Nizam the terms of a possible grand alliance against Mysore. 'I rely upon your ability,' wrote Wellesley to Kirkpatrick, 'and zeal for the public service to state the details of these important measures to Azim ul Omra [Nizam's minister] with every circumstance of advantage. Your communication should be unequivocal and unreserved; no part either of the principles or details of the arrangement requires any degree of concealment, my object being to unite all parties on the firm ground of their genuine interests.'[20]

The Malartic Proclamation was to be used as the main threat to all the powers that a French invasion, at Tipu's behest, as also one by Zaman Shah, was imminent and if they wished to protect their territories, allying with the British was their only hope. Wellesley willed to throw his lot with the cause of Sikandar Jah in the event of any war of succession at Hyderabad.

The Marathas were a tougher nut to crack for Wellesley. The young Peshwa Baji Rao II was as it is suffocated under the control of Daulat Rao Sindhia and had secretly solicited the help of the British on the one hand, and Tipu, on the other, to free himself. By October 1798, Nana did return from prison, but was a pale shadow of his former self. Nana favoured an alliance with the British and tried to get Parshuram Bhau and later his son, Appa Sahib, to join as they had done earlier. But Nana's efforts were all being thwarted by the young Peshwa. Under Sindhia's influence, the Peshwa was eluding all prospects of a subsidiary alliance with the British. The intrigues, rivalries and treachery that had consumed the Poona court into a cesspool made matters tougher for the British there.

As a signatory of the alliance in 1790, the British had every reason to expect direct communication with the Peshwa, sans any interference. Stripping him off his power over the Peshwa ran the risk of leaving the Sindhia to align with Tipu with whom he had a secret correspondence. But Sindhia's larger possessions across Hindustan were much bigger and under the threat of a British attack if he allied with Mysore. Wellesley played to these fears of Sindhia. Sindhia was also closely observing, with a certain degree of alarm, the manner in which Wellesley had his way in Hyderabad. He did not wish to incur a double risk to his territories, both in the north and the south, by angering the British.

One of the bones of contention with the Marathas was the 13th Article of the Treaty of 1790. To recapitulate, the 13th Article of that treaty mentioned that: 'If Tippoo should molest or attack either of the contracting parties, the others should join to punish him, the modes and conditions of which shall be hereafter settled by the three contracting parties.'[21] The Peshwa Durbar had further embellished this on 3 July 1793: 'If a breach of engagement occurs on the part of Tippoo with respect to either of the Allies, let that Ally advise the other Allies thereof, when having understood the said breach of engagement we will admonish him, and if he does not attend to the admonition, then let the States act agreeably to the treaties which have been formed.'[22] Thus, it was clearly binding on the Marathas that they could not wriggle out of. If Tipu showed an aggressive stance towards the British (and that was what was to be proved by them with all the proclamations and other invites of invasions), the Peshwa was treaty-bound to join the British in a military campaign against Mysore.

The Marathas tried to justify this initially as a personal commitment of the deceased Peshwa Sawai Madhava Rao. But Wellesley argued forcefully, as did William Palmer, the new Resident at Poona, that defensive treaties of this nature are not merely personal obligations of the reigning prince but permanent obligations that bind the state, irrespective of who ruled. Wellesley also wanted to steer clear of support to either the Peshwa or Sindhia for the moment. His singular foe was Tipu and his annihilation his one-point agenda. Sindhia could be easily threatened by the prospect of Zaman Shah's invasion and his support would be easy to obtain. To gain the young Peshwa's confidence, Wellesley even returned jewellery that his deceased father, Raghoba, had pawned with the British and which was worth about Rs 6 lakh and in their possession in Calcutta.[23]

Sindhia prevailed upon the young Peshwa not to give in to any demands of guarantees that were being sought as per the 13th Article of the Treaty of 1790. Wellesley was fine with a stance of neutrality at the present moment when it came to the Peshwa or other Maratha confederates, rather than having them move closer to Tipu. He was confident of being able to stitch them all together in a cogent alliance, driven by their self-interests that he would amplify to them in due course. For now, an English detachment, similar to the one formerly employed under Captain Little, was kept in readiness by Wellesley to join Bhau once war broke out with Mysore.

Tipu's Bungling Continues

It is unlikely that Tipu was not receiving intelligence about these tectonic shifts happening in his vicinity. He must have known that Wellesley had gathered wind of his ill-advised expedition to Mauritius and his entreaties to Afghanistan and Persia, but had stayed clear of confronting him directly. The French contingent that had come from Mauritius was insignificant militarily, but had roused British suspicions hugely. The possible prudent thing for Tipu to have done was to disband or send back this contingent and disown the Malartic Proclamation completely. That way, Wellesley would have had no leg to stand on when urging his allies to attack Mysore. But Tipu, as mentioned earlier, gave them a rousing welcome and gave them houses in a township built between Mysore and Srirangapatna. Dubuc drew a salary of Rs 2500 per month; lieutenants got Rs 250, midshipmen Rs 200, the Master of the port Rs 150 and the builder Rs 125 from the Mysore Sarkar.[24] In their representations, Dubuc and Chapuy gave several assurances to Tipu. Chapuy told Tipu that among the twenty soldiers of colour and of different nationalities, they were all trained in advanced artillery.[25] Dubuc mentioned that he had brought with him 'a port master and a ship-builder, both well qualified from their respective department,' and also 'a master carpenter and a marine cadet.'[26] Seemingly satisfied by such vague assurances, Tipu was very hopeful that this was just the beginning of a larger delegation from France that would come in once he exerted a bit more. So, as per the original plan, he intended to send another delegation, this time directly to the Directory in France itself to solicit more help.

Dubuc had not moved beyond Mangalore. On 8 July 1798, he was made the head of another embassy to the Government of France by Tipu. Shaikh Abdur Rahim and Muhammad Bismillah were to accompany Dubuc on this sojourn. As Tipu's principal ambassador, Dubuc was given wide discretion to negotiate terms, and also a Letter of Credit, though not mentioned on whom the ambassador might draw the hefty amount. 'Placing entire confidence in the fidelity of Citizen Dubuc,' read the Letter of Credit, 'Captain in the Navy of the French Republic . . . I authorize him, by this present Letter of Credit to procure either from the French Republic or from individuals such sums as he may require to fulfil the orders I have given him for different purchases, or to defray expenses which he may think urgent or necessary for the advantage of his mission. Being desirous that the said Letter of Credit, should have full power and value, I hereby bind myself to pay or cause to be paid all Bills of Exchange which Citizen Dubuc may draw upon on Sarkar.'[27]

Tipu's letter to the Directory, dated 20 July 1798, spoke of the long-lasting relationship between the French and Mysore since the time of his father Haidar Ali. He also lamented their betrayal of promise on the past few occasions. But hoped that 'the Republic will now repair the fault of their former Government by driving the English from their rich possessions in India.'[28] The proposals included sending 10,000–15,000 troops of all descriptions, infantry, cavalry and artillery. A naval force was to be stationed at the coast in case of necessity. The Sarkar was to provide military stores, provisions, horses, bullocks, carts and tents, along with all necessary items, except of course liquor which was banned in the Islamic kingdom of Mysore. The combined forces were to follow Tipu's orders on all marches. The French forces were to disembark at Porto Novo on the Coromandel Coast, where Tipu would join them (after twenty days advance notice of the contingent starting from France) and launch their joint operations in the 'heart of the enemy's country'[29] i.e., the Carnatic. The territories won were to be equally divided among the victorious allies. If the Republic was to enter into any peace treaty with England, Tipu and the Indian fight was to necessarily feature in the treaty. In addition, Tipu also sought for the Mysore royal service, four founders of brass and four founders of iron-cannon, four paper-makers, four glass-coaters, four glass-founders, four glass-cutters, two naval engineers and two good ship-builders.

Thus briefed, Dubuc along with his aide-de-camp, Major Filletay, and the Mysore vakil set off for their embarkation point, the Danish settlement of Tranquebar, which they reached by August 1798. They were to buy a vessel there and set sail. Upon reaching Tranquebar, Dubuc kept complaining to the Sultan that no convenient vessels were available or that he was short of funds. Several weeks and months were wasted in this manner. His letters to Tipu, requesting for money were all getting intercepted by the British, who were building a stronger, documented case of an intrigue that Tipu was plotting with their enemies, the French. Denys Forest mentions an unnamed informant who gives us a glimpse of Dubuc, as he lounged about Tranquebar, annoying the Danes: 'He bothers me most unmercifully with his gasconade, and how he has been *grandement reçu par le Nabob*. He has always been a great liar, and now he is a preposterous one.'[30] The Danish Governor, M. Anker, tried to resolve the British and Wellesley's enquiries about this man.

A letter from Dubuc to the Sultan, even as late as 16 December 1798 from Tranquebar, months after he landed there, talks about the same complaints and lack of money. He sought a year's advance of his pay and also wanted the bankers in Pondicherry, White and Mercier, to help arrange Rs 40,000 for the purchase of the vessel and for his expenses. This, despite Tipu having already advanced significant sums and the Letter of Credit too. To ingratiate himself with Tipu, Dubuc claimed to have access to great intelligence, as per which he apparently knew that Wellesley was expected to land on the Malabar coast by the end of that month. In his alarmist messages, he mentioned that this 'will be followed by a declaration of war; the object of which will be to take away your country and to dethrone you; substituting in your place and that of the heirs of your Crown, a Nawwab of their own creation; Your Majesty must perceive that nothing less than your kingdom is at stake. You must exert yourself and in particular endeavour to preserve it by negotiation, till the moment when (I flatter myself), I shall secure it for you and your august children forever.'[31] He advised Tipu to make immediate peace and treaties with the Marathas who could be the only bulwark for him against the expansionist designs of the British. There was of course merit to this counsel, though it was not Dubuc's place to sermonize on these issues and that too when his express mandate was to go to France to secure a large army.

An exasperated Tipu wrote back to Dubuc on 2 January 1799, urging Dubuc to 'make every exertion to depart with all possible expedition, for it is urgently necessary.'[32] The Letter of Credit for France was very much in his pocket, Tipu reminded and told him to make haste and leave for France without further delay. 'Your dispatches,' he cautioned Dubuc, 'have already been once intercepted and have furnished information of your destination which is much to be regretted. If you should write again, mention no names; we shall always understand each other: I have always written to you in that manner. You ask me send money from hence: how can this be done when letters pass with so much difficulty? I have sent envoys to Poona but it is your departure which most interests me and which is most pressing. Overcome all obstacles and proceed with speed . . . you need not doubt that you possess my entire confidence and that I consider you as one of my very good friends.'[33]

After so many repeated letters from Tipu, Dubuc finally left for the Isle of France on 7 February 1799, on the *Odensu,* flying the Danish flag. On reaching, instead of buying a new vessel with the money given to him by the Sultan and proceeding to France, he asked the authorities at Mauritius to provide him with one. They flatly refused as they had no such orders or written requests from Tipu. Dubuc somehow managed to gather more money from people there and purchased the *surprise,* which eventually sailed out to France only in early May 1799. Several weeks were aimlessly spent at various ports and places, till the boat was damaged beyond repair. The Mysore vakils were furious with this man for his lackadaisical attitude and had even contemplated beating him up.

The British had kept a close watch on the *surprise,* and wanted to intercept it several times, but had failed. Wellesley had himself kept a close eye on Dubuc's movements and had dispatched the *Osterley,* with a party of 28th Dragoons to intercept the vessel. Eventually, they captured it in the Isle of Seychelles. Dubuc managed to escape with all the loot he had gathered, including that of the fellow-envoys. The poor Mysore vakils were apprehended by the British and were also told of the fall of Srirangapatna. Unwilling to believe the news at first, they finally surrendered the jewellery and about Rs 2 crore that they were carrying as presents to the members of the Directory.[34]

Thus ended the tragic farce of Tipu's flirtations with the French and his numerous embassies to them under the most dubious and untrustworthy characters.

Wellesley Confronts Tipu

The charade of cordiality that existed between Tipu and Wellesley had to break at some point. The Governor-General, despite his earlier plans to confront Tipu about the French embassies and the Malartic Proclamation, had remained curiously silent on the matter for nearly five months since it had broken. Wellesley however was clear about what direction the British had to take vis-à-vis the Sultan. In a Minute of the Governor-General in the Secret Department, dated 12 August 1798, he gave an elaborate appraisal of the problem:

Having thus entered into offensive and defensive engagements with the enemy, having proceeded to collect in conjunction with the enemy, a force openly destined to act against the possessions of the Company, having avowed his preparations of war for the express purpose of attempting the entire subversion of the British Empire in India, and having declared that he only waits the effectual succour of the French to prosecute offensive operations; Tippoo Sultaun has violated the treaties of peace and friendship subsisting between him and the Company, and has committed an act of direct hostility against the British Government in India . . . The motive therefore of Tippoo Sultaun was no other than that avowed in his correspondence with the enemy, and published under the eyes of his own Ambassadors, 'an ardent desire to expel the British nation from India' . . . If the conduct of Tippoo

Sultaun had been of a nature which could be termed ambiguous or suspicious . . . it might be our duty to resort in the first instance to his construction of proceedings, which being of a doubtful character might admit of a satisfactory explanation. But when there is no doubt, there can be no matter for explanation . . . in the present the idea therefore of demanding explanation must be rejected, as being disgraceful in its principle and frivolous in its object . . .[35]

In the meanwhile, letters were merely being exchanged between Wellesley and Tipu on the handover of Waynad to Mysore and the latter seeking the resolution of a few other contested villages and so on. False shows of camaraderie and bonhomie were being made by both sides. As Tipu mentioned in his letter of 2 September 1798 to Wellesley in the context of the disputed territories: 'Mischief-makers, by starting empty disputes and altercations, hope to accomplish their own purposes, but by the favour of God, the fountains of union and harmony between the two states [Mysore and the British] possess too much purity and clearness to be sullied by the devices of self-interest persons.'[36] Wellesley too seemed to be getting perverse pleasure in informing Tipu about the defeats of French fleets at the Aboukir Bay. While writing about such reverses that his allies, the French, were facing, Wellesley appeared to be cocking a snook at Tipu: 'Confident from the union and attachment subsisting between us that this intelligence will afford you sincere satisfaction, I could not deny myself the pleasure of communicating it.'[37]

As mentioned earlier, Wellesely was keen on getting his act together and stitching up his ragtag allies into a cohesive fabric. He had also galvanized the defunct British army to some action and had got the siege train that was essential for any attack on Srirangapatna a bit closer to Vellore. Now that that task had been suitably completed, he decided to finally take the bull by its horns. There was also intelligence and rumours pouring in about a French expedition that had sailed from Toulon on 19 May 1798 for the invasion of Egypt and from there to India. If this happened and the expedition, inspired by Tipu, or otherwise, moved by way of the Red Sea or Basra, without being intercepted in the Mediterranean, an Indian front of the European Wars too could have opened up for the Company. Napoleon soon took possession of the Island of Malta and proceeded from there to Alexandria. One of the big motivations behind Napoleon Bonaparte's invasion of Egypt was to create a passage to India. This was evident in an undated letter that Napoleon wrote to Tipu Sultan, which was intercepted by the British:

> You have already been informed of my arrival on the borders of the Red Sea, with an innumerable and invincible Army, full of the desire of delivering you from the iron yoke of England. I eagerly embrace this opportunity of testifying to you the desire I have of being informed by you, by the way of Muscat and Mocha, as to your political situation. I would even wish you could send some intelligent person to Suez or Cairo, possessing your confidence, with whom I may confer. May the Almighty increase your power and destroy your enemies.[38]

Though the French navy was defeated at Aboukir Bay, Napoleon Bonaparte's campaign remained land-bound and his army managed to consolidate its hold over Egypt. This caused great consternation in the Ottoman Empire which had held sway over Egypt since 1517. Egypt had broken away from the Empire's direct control, but the Empire still held its influence over it. For the French, Egypt was viewed as the cradle of Western civilization and hence the intense desire to capture it at a time when it was trying to break away fully from the Ottomans. For the Ottomans and the Islamic world, Egypt was of great veneration, given its proximity to the city of Mecca, the Quiblah to which they faced to say their prayers and Medina where the sacred tomb of their Prophet was. The Ottomans also discovered several letters of the French design 'to divide Arabia into various republics; to attack the whole Mahommedan sect, in its religion and country; and by a gradual progression, to extirpate all Mussulmen from the face of the earth.'[39] Bonaparte positioned himself as a liberator of the people of Egypt from Ottoman and Mamluk oppression, even as he claimed friendship between France and the Ottoman Empire. It was Tipu's misfortune that he was caught in this crossfire between the two powers that he was courting against the British—the French and the Ottomans. Fishing in these troubled waters, the British prevailed upon the Ottoman 'Grand Signior' Sultan Selim III to urge Tipu, his ally, to break his ties with the French. Selim III accordingly sent a letter to Tipu, dated 20 September 1798, where he complained bitterly about the French and offered to mediate between Tipu and the British to resolve their differences:

> We take this opportunity to acquaint your Majesty. When the French Republic was engaged in a war with most of the powers of Europe . . . our Sublime Porte not only took no part against them, but regardful of the ancient amity existing with that nation, adopted a system of the strictest neutrality . . . they [French] all of a sudden have exhibited the unprovoked and treacherous proceedings . . . it is a standing law amongst all nations, not to encroach upon each other's territories, whilst they are supposed to be at peace . . . a conduct so audacious, so unprovoked, and so deceitfully sudden on their part, is an undeniable trait of the most extreme insult and treachery . . . now it being certain, that in addition to the general ties of religion, the bonds of amity and good understanding have ever been firm and permanent with your Majesty . . . we therefore sincerely hope . . . that you will not refuse entering into concert with us, and giving our Sublime Porte every possible assistance . . . a strict connection is expected between them [French] and your Majesty, for whose service they are to send over a corps of troops by the way of Egypt . . . they [French] are a nation whose deceitful intrigues and perfidious pursuits know no bounds. They are intent on nothing, but on depriving people of their lives and properties, and on persecuting religion, wherever their arms can reach . . . it is sincerely hoped that you will not refuse every needful exertion towards assisting your brethren Mussulmen, according

to the obligations of religion, and towards defending Hindostan itself, against the effect of French machinations. Should it be true, as we hear, that an intimate connection has taken place between your Court and that nation, we hope that by weighing present circumstances, as well as future inconvenience which would result from such a measure, your Majesty will beware against it, and in the event of your having harboured any idea of joining with them, or of moving against Great Britain, you will lay such resolution aside. We make it our special request that your Majesty will please to refrain from entering into any measures against the English, or lending any compliant ear to the French. Should there exist any subject of complaint with the former, please to communicate it, certain as you may be of the employment of every good office on our side, to compromise the same; we wish to see the connection above alluded to, exchanged in favour of Great Britain.[40]

Tipu's reply to this letter from Selim III was an 'incoherent rambling document' that ignored all the offers of mediation and stated that the British were the real and bitter enemies of Muslims all over the world.[41] Wellesley could not but conceal his glee at Tipu's discomfiture and made those snide remarks in his letters, conveying to him the news of the French naval defeats in the Nile by Nelson. But he finally broke the ice, and the gloves were off in his terse letter to Tipu, dated 8 November 1798:

It is impossible that you should suppose me to be ignorant of the intercourse which subsists between you and the French, whom you know to be inveterate enemies of the Company and to be now engaged in an unjust war with the British nation. You cannot imagine me to be indifferent to the transactions which have passed between you and the enemies of my country; nor does it appear necessary or proper that I should any longer conceal from you the surprise and concern with which I perceived you disposed to involve yourself in all the ruinous consequences of a connection, which threatens not only to subvert the foundations of friendship

between you and the Company, but to introduce into the heart of
your kingdom the principles of anarchy and confusion, to shake
your own authority, to weaken the obedience of your subjects and
to destroy the religion which you revere . . . in all your letters
you constantly professed a disposition to strengthen the bonds of
sincere attachment and the foundations of harmony and concord
established between you and the Honourable Company . . . the
Peishwah and His Highness the Nizam concur with me in the
observation which I have offered to you in this letter . . . I propose
to depute to you . . . Major Doveton, who is well known to you, and
who will explain to you more fully and particularly the sole means
which appear to myself, and to the allies of the Company, to be
effectual for the salutary purpose of removing all existing distrust
and suspicion, and of establishing peace and good understanding
on the most durable foundations . . . I shall expect your answer
to this letter, with an earnest hope that it may correspond with
the pacific views and wishes of the allies; and that you may be
convinced that you cannot in any manner better consult your true
interests than by meeting, with cordiality, the present friendly and
moderate advance to a satisfactory and amicable settlement of all
points of which any doubt or anxiety may have arisen in the minds
either of yourself or of the allies.[42]

Wellesley's brother, Arthur, had for several months been insisting
that an attempt be made to subjugate Tipu through a subsidiary
alliance, if that were possible. Now Wellesley, through this mission
by Doveton, hoped to extract three main concessions from Tipu:
have an allied Resident at his court in Srirangapatna, retrench all
Frenchmen in his service and cede to the Company the coastal
territories below the Ghats. Of these, the third was of course a
prospect that they knew Tipu would never agree to.

Tipu received the letter and the proposal of hosting Doveton
with a sense of total nonchalance. He desisted from even replying
to the hard-hitting letter from Wellesley and his charges. Instead,
in a vague letter that he sent on 20 November 1798 (and received

by the British on 15 December), he lamented about the intelligence that he was receiving about military preparations against him being afoot. He however expressed the fullest confidence that such reports were mere rumours and that he had 'no other intention (or thought) than to give increase to friendship . . . to confirm and strengthen the foundations of harmony and union.'[43] Wellesley had to send a reminder to Tipu on 10 December 1798 that his specific points, especially to the Doveton proposals, had all gone unanswered. He had to remind Tipu 'to perceive the propriety and necessity of giving your earliest and most serious consideration . . . sensible of the advantages likely to result to all parties, from the conciliatory measure of my deputing Major Doveton to you.'[44]

Finally, Tipu's letter reached Wellesley in Madras when he landed there on Christmas Day. Tipu expressed great pleasure and satisfaction on hearing about the French defeats, 'more pleasure than can possibly be conveyed by writing.' He hoped that the British who were faithful adherents to 'sincerity, friendship and good faith . . . the well-wishers of mankind, will at all times be successful . . . and that the French, who are of a crooked disposition, faithless and the enemies of mankind, may be ever depressed and ruined.'[45] He brushed aside the embassy to the Isle of France as being simply the trip of some merchants who sold their rice and in return brought back some forty artificers. 'In this Sircar,' wrote Tipu, 'there is a mercantile tribe, who employ themselves in trading by sea and land. Their agents purchased a two-masted vehicle, and having loaded her with rice, departed with a view to traffic. It happened that she went to Mauritius, from where forty persons, French and of a dark colour, of whom ten or fifteen were artificers, and the rest servants, paying the hire of the ship, came in here in search of employment. Such as chose to take service were entertained, and the remainder departed beyond the confines of this Sircar.'[46] He alleged that this incident had been distorted by the French, 'who are full of vice and deceit . . . to put about reports with the view to ruffle the minds of both Sircars [Mysore and the British]'.[47] After coming out with such eloquent fiction, Tipu emphasized that he had never swerved from the path of friendship with the British and hoped to deepen those bonds further, showing willingness to host Doveton at a suitable and mutually convenient date and place. 'I have the strongest hope,' Tipu signed off, 'that the minds of the wise and intelligent, and particularly of the four states, will not be sullied by doubts and jealousies, but will consider me from my heart desirous of harmony and friendship.'[48]

Wellesley would have no more of this forked-tongue sweet talk that Tipu was indulging in. On 9 January 1799, he shot off a more direct message to Tipu, replete with all the proof that had been gathered regarding the embassy to the Isle of France and the subsequent Malartic Proclamation. He gave the minutest details of all those who had constituted that embassy, on which dates it had proceeded from Mysore, when it had reached its destination, the happenings in Mauritius and what the outcome was. He was unwilling to let Tipu wriggle away with an excuse as blatant and dishonest as saying that it was a mere mercantile expedition that had nothing to do with his government. Wellesley also mentioned in the letter that he was aware that Tipu 'had engaged with several powers of Asia in various negotiations of the most hostile tendency, towards the interests of the Company and its allies.'[49] He enclosed a Persian translation of the Malartic Proclamation for the Sultan's ready reference and asked him if this too were part of the mercantile team's actions. Wellesley argued that there was irrefutable evidence that Tipu's ambassadors had indeed concluded an offensive alliance with the French against the Company and its allies. He also underlined that the British were aware that he was merely waiting for larger troops to come in from France or Mauritius to aid him in an unprovoked and sudden war that he had been conspiring to wage against the allies, in total contravention of the 1792 Treaty. That the contingent from the Isle of France was given royal shelter and patronage in Srirangapatna and fresh attempts to send another embassy under Dubuc had not been lost on the Company's all-seeing eyes. Despite all this evidence mounting against him, Tipu had been fairly treated by the British in the Waynad case, according to Wellesley. The allies were still hopeful of maintaining peace and readjusting the terms of coexistence in the wake of these new developments that had come to light. 'A new arrangement is become indispensable,' maintained Wellesley, 'in consequence of Your Highness' new engagements with the common enemy of the allies,'[50] and signed off with a warning that 'dangerous consequences result from the delay of arduous affairs.'[51] He once again urged Tipu to give peace a chance and let Major Doveton meet him soon to discuss the new terms of engagement.

On 16 January 1799, Wellesley sent Tipu a copy of the Declaration of War by the Grand Signior Sultan Selim III, the Sultan of the Ottoman Empire at Constantinople, against the French, in consequence of the latter's invasion of Egypt. He brought to Tipu's attention the letter that Selim III had written to him in September 1798 to 'exhort you [Tipu] to manifest your zeal for the Mussulman faith by renouncing all intercourse with the common enemy [French] of every religion and the aggressor of the Mahomedan Church.'[52] Building a strong case for Tipu eschewing all French connection, Wellesley impressed upon him that if he read the Ottoman Sultan's letter again, he would be able to discern a few things. 'The maxims of public law, honour and religion are despised and profaned by the French nation; who consider all the thrones of the world, and every system of civil order and religious faith, as the sport and prey of their boundless ambition, insatiable rapine and indiscriminate sacrilege.'[53] Appealing to Tipu's religious sentiments, he reminded him that the French had attacked the head of the Islamic world, the Caliph Sultan of the Ottoman Empire, through an unprovoked war in the heart of a country that has some of the most sacred monuments of the Muslim faith. As a true Muslim, it was Tipu's duty too to rise to the occasion against those who have attacked his sacred shrines and more so, when the Ottoman Sultan had himself now got into an alliance with the British to oppose French excesses. He referred to the letter of Selim III to remind Tipu that after having come to know of the alliance between Mysore and the French, the Ottoman Sultan 'admonishes you not to flatter yourself with the vain hope of friendly aid from those, who . . . could never have reached you until they had profaned the tomb of your Prophet, and overthrown the foundation of your religion.' In conclusion, Wellesley hoped: 'May the admonition of the head of your Faith dispose your mind to the pacific propositions which I have repeatedly, but in vain submitted to your wisdom. And may you at length receive the ambassador [Doveton], who will be empowered to conclude the definite arrangement of all differences between you and the allies, and to secure the tranquility of India against the disturbers of the world.'[54]

Despite these appeals and threats, Tipu's reply to Wellesley, which was received on 13 February 1799, made little sense to the British side:

> I have been much gratified by the agreeable receipt of your Lordship's two friendly letters, the first brought by a camel-man, the last by *hircurrahs*, and understood their contents. The letter of the Prince, in station like Jumsheid; with angels as his guards; with troops numerous as the stars; the sun illumining the world of the heaven of empire and dominion; the luminary giving splendour to the universe of the firmament of glory and power; the Sultaun of the sea and the land; the King of Rome (i.e. the Grand Signior); be his empire and his power perpetual! Addressed to me, which reached you through the British Envoy, and which you transmitted, has arrived. Being frequently disposed to make excursions and hunt, I am accordingly proceeding upon a hunting excursion. You will be pleased to dispatch Major Doveton (about whose coming your friendly pen has repeatedly written) slightly attended (or unattended). Always continue to gratify me by friendly letters, notifying your welfare.[55]

The terse, flippant and casual tone and attitude of this ramble of a letter incensed Wellesley who called it 'tardy, reluctant, insidious' and a deliberate insult.[56] The Dubuc case was still active at this time and reports were coming in of how the idea of an embassy to the Directory was still actively being pursued by Tipu. Wilks however mentions that he had 'been assured by those who were near him [Tipu] that the abrupt dictation was the mere effect of chagrin at the necessity of humiliation; that he then really intended and earnestly wished to receive the British envoy.'[57]

Tipu's state of mind was one of immense incoherence and nervousness. He was getting restless and agitated on the entire suspense regarding the French support, and at the same time, he had messed up matters with the British by being so dilatory and insulting of all offers of mediation. Wilks gives an account of what was going on in Tipu's mind, based on sources (whom he never names) who were close to Tipu and eyewitness accounts:

> The Sultaun for some time after the receipt of the letter from Lord Mornington, dated the 9th of January [1799] had nearly made up his mind to throw himself unconditionally on his Lordship's compassion, and to receive the envoy; but notwithstanding the significant intreaty, to lose not a single day in his reply, he went on with the procrastination naturally belonging to an unpalatable resolve, hesitating from day to day to execute the determination of the last; and the lingering indecision of the fatalist, suggested the hope that, if at the last moment no favourable chance should arise, he might still be in time to submit to an alternative, short of absolute destruction.[58]

There is no way to ascertain if Wilks's assertion that Tipu wanted to surrender to Wellesley at this point is true. He seemed to be still hopeful of French support and had been in contact with the worthless Dubuc, urging him to make haste, as he knew the noose was tightening around his neck. Sadly for him, no one else shared his sense of urgency on a matter so acute. In the process, Tipu lost out on an important lifeline that Wellesley had thrown at him in the form of Doveton. That opportunity had almost passed, and Tipu knew that with each passing day, time was only slipping by very perilously fast. While one can only guess the despair and anxious state of mind the Sultan might have been in, P.E. Roberts surmises that by then Tipu 'was plunged into a hopeless and fatalistic despair.'[59] He describes Tipu as resembling a sullen and huddled figure, passively awaiting the coup de grace of a victorious enemy . . . the fate-laden atmosphere is almost that of a Greek tragedy.'[60] Wellesley stopped communicating further on sending Doveton to Srirangapatna and that raised Tipu's alarms and increased his anxiety. So far, he was the one procrastinating and Wellesley had been making the offer repeatedly. Now the tables had turned and the silence from the British side unnerved Tipu.

Around this time, an undated letter of Napoleon Bonaparte to the Sharif of Mecca, written in Arabic, was intercepted by the British in Jidda on 17 February 1799. It read:

> You will be fully informed by the *Nocqueda* (*Nakhuda*; captain) of this Dow, how tranquil and quiet everything is at Cairo and Suez and between those places; and of the tranquility which is established among the inhabitants. Not a single Mamluk oppressor remains in the country and the inhabitants without dread or fear employ themselves in weaving, cultivating the ground and in other trades as formerly and by the blessing of God this will be daily increasing and the duties on merchandize and the taxes will be lessened . . . the road (voyage) between Suez and Cairo is open and safe, therefore do assure the merchants of your country, that they may bring their goods to Suez and sell them without dread or apprehension and may purchase in exchange for them such articles as they may wish. I now send you a letter for your friend Tipu Sultan, oblige me by forwarding it to his kingdom.[61]

None of Napoleon's letters ever seem to have reached Tipu, as they had all been intercepted by British intelligence.

The Maratha Prevarication

Wellesley had hoped to eventually get the Marathas on-board, just before the outbreak of war with Tipu. Tipu's envoy, Balaji Rao, had been staying at Poona stealthily, as already mentioned. So much so, that even the astute Nana did not discover his antecedents till about April 1799. Despite sending several friendly letters and emissaries, it was Tipu's fatal mistake to have not clinched any firm deal with the Peshwa who had anyway been favourable towards him, as was Sindhia. It was only when reports of a military build-up on the British side began reaching him that he finally decided to woo the Peshwa seriously. But it was too late. The envoy he sent to Gwalior was welcomed by Sindhia warmly, but eventually had to be dismissed under the pressure of Colonel John Collins, the Company's Resident there.

But Ahmed Khan and Fakhr-ud-din arrived in Poona by the end of 1798 and were received cordially by the Peshwa on 10 January 1799. Palmer bitterly protested against this, but they stayed on. 'You will peremptorily insist,' wrote a peeved Wellesley to Palmer on 19 February 1799, 'on the dismission of Tippoo's vakeels. Under the present circumstances, their detention at Poonah is little short of an insult to the British Government . . . I cannot draw conclusions favourable to the cordial cooperation of the Peishwa, in the present contest with Tipu Sultaun. The whole conduct of the Peishwa has betrayed a systematic jealousy, suspicion and even insincerity.'[62] He flatly refused emergent ideas of the Peshwa becoming a mediator between him and Tipu, as according to Wellesley, being a member of the Triple Alliance, the Peshwa was already an aggrieved party and hence, duty-bound to join the attack on the Sultan.

After some initial movements towards Lahore with a menacing march to invade India, Zaman Shah had retreated. Still, Wellesley wanted to keep Sindhia on tenterhooks with the possibility of an invasion planned by Shah again. 'If he [Sindhia] should enter into any connection,' warned Wellesley, 'with Tippoo, of a nature dangerous to the British interests, the security of his dominions in Hindostan will be exposed to hazard.'[63]

Palmer then informed Wellesley that Tipu had managed to purchase the Peshwa's neutrality and this new offer of him mediating truce, by paying to Poona a sum of Rs 13 lakh. Daulat Rao Sindhia, too, was party to this transaction.[64] Palmer protested strongly against such counter-moves and sought Nana's intercession. But Nana was too anxious by then about his own role and safety that he left the matter of participating in the war against Tipu entirely to the discretion of the Peshwa. The only man capable of leading the Maratha troops was Parshuram Bhau, but he was away fighting his own existential battle in Kolhapur. Palmer gave an ultimatum to the Peshwa that if Tipu's vakils were not dismissed from Poona, he would quit the service. It was after this that the Peshwa finally ordered the dismissal of the Mysore vakils by 19 March 1799. But they proceeded so slowly that even by the end of April, they had barely crossed fifty miles from Poona.

The issue with Baji Rao II was that he was not at all a decisive man and kept prevaricating, assuring Palmer of all support when the eventuality came. But he and Sindhia, in concert with Tipu and Raghoji Bhonsle, had planned a secret attack on the weakest link of the alliance, the Nizam. Getting to know about this, Wellesley quickly weaned Raghoji away from any such clandestine attempts. Had Baji Rao II and Sindhia, who were favourably inclined towards Tipu, joined hands in this decisive war, history would have taken a completely different turn. But the timid and indecisive Baji Rao fully believed that, like the war led by Cornwallis, this one too would drag on for several months or years. Looking at the fortunes of both parties, he would then switch over to the winning side. This total lack of vision was to cost the Marathas heavily, after the British had dealt with Mysore and their top irritant, Tipu.

Despite his non-committal attitude, Wellesley had Palmer promise the Peshwa that the allies were determined to crush Tipu, with or without support from Poona. 'Notwithstanding,' he told Palmer, 'the perverse and forbidding policy of the court of Poonah, I shall not fail to secure for the Peishwa an equal participation with the other allies in any cessions which may be enforced from Tippoo Sultaun. I authorize you to make this declaration in the most unequivocal terms, to the Peishwa and to Nana. If even this declaration shall fail to excite the Peishwa to employ every practicable effort to fulfil his defensive engagements with the Company, I trust, it will at least serve to prove the disenchanted attachment of the British Government to every branch of the triple alliance.'[65] But as Wellesley had apprehended, the Peshwa never got to make up his mind till the very end, and by then Srirangapatna had fallen, even without his help or participation in the war.

The Last Strike of the Royalists

The hurricane of developments came as a beacon of hope for the unfortunate Mysore royal family of the Wodeyars. The titular ruler, Khasa Chamaraja Wodeyar IX, who had been hand-picked and installed by Haidar, died in 1796, apparently of smallpox. Tipu did not see any need to install another puppet king on the throne and totally ignored Maharani Lakshmi Ammanni's pleas to coronate Khasa Chamaraja's two-year-old son, Krishnaraja III, as the successor. He instead packed off the old queen and the little boy along with the entire royal family to 'a miserable hovel'[66] in Srirangapatna to wallow in poverty and misery, after confiscating all their personal belongings and ornaments. The little boy Krishnaraja III had cried bitterly when Tipu's men took away his golden bracelets.[67] As long as Khasa Chamaraja Wodeyar was alive, the customary Dasara celebrations and durbars were being held and that was the one occasion when the Raja, seated on the throne, showed himself to the people. These festivities too were discontinued by Tipu after Chamaraja's death. For the first time since 1399 when their dynasty was first established, the chain of succession was broken for the Wodeyars. This only further strengthened the Maharani's resolve to vanquish Tipu.

Given her dodgy behaviour against him, Tipu placed the Maharani under strict house arrest and surveillance. In the grimy and dingy apartments of the Nataka Shala where she was virtually imprisoned, she often strained to quietly pen her letters in the dead of the night and under the light of the flickering lamp that she lit so as to not alert the soldiers who guarded her closely. The only concession she ever got in the day was a visit to the Kille Venkataramana Swamy temple in the palace complex to offer prayers as she was an extremely religious woman. Often, these letters were hidden beneath the flowers and other items for puja and, upon reaching the temple, through sleight of hand, were hurriedly passed on to the Brahmin priest who was her confidant. This, even as guards stood watching over her every move. A twitch of the eye or other non-verbal communications ensured that the transaction was over, and the letter was in good hands. She would then head back to the apartments in her palanquin to endure another day of house arrest. It was quite a marvel how these letters managed to circumvent Haidar and Tipu's elaborate spy systems and made their way to Madras, to her Pradhans and from there to the British.[68]

In a Kannada letter written to her loyal Pradhan, Tirumala Rao, in 1796, the Maharani poured her heart out before signing off in her characteristic pseudonym 'Sree Ranga':

We have been writing to you of our affairs from time to time. It is twenty-two years since you left the province. We are daily being persecuted by Tippu. We cannot say at what moment he may send assassins and get us murdered. And for the restoration of our kingdom, you have been exerting your best, winning the sympathies of English Sirdars in our favour, entering into treaties with them etc. and at what an amount of sacrifice and suffering! For our sake, 700 families of your kith and kin have been allowed to be ruthlessly murdered [the pre-Diwali massacre of the Manydam Iyengars], all your immense wealth has been spent and you are a ruined person . . . for now we learn that the French vakeel at the court of Tippu has been strongly advising him to put us all to death, as we may possibly one day be the cause of his ruin. We have now sent along with this a copy of the treaty which Tippu has lately made with the French. If you show this to the Governor of Madras and get him to invade the country with a large army before the arrival of French assistance to Tippu, it will save not only us, but the English also. But if on the contrary there be any vacillation as on the two or three previous occasions, Tippu and the French will unite like fire and air, and the whole country will be ruined.

Please do tell the Governor and the English there that if they may
not care for us, at least in pure self-defence in order to preserve
their own safety, they must put down Tippu at once before he
gets French aid. Under the circumstances, you will see, our life is
quite uncertain, and even if we are no more, as you are the best
well-wisher of the state, you should keep exerting your best, see
Tippu destroyed, and get a member of the royal family placed on
the throne . . . if however, it should happen by God's grace that we
should also be alive, and the English conquer Tippu and restore us
our kingdom, we shall pay the expenses of the English army to the
extent of one crore of pagodas. And for this they must abide by the
terms of our old treaty with Sullivan and Macartney. You should
communicate all this to the English and get the army to march at
once. And it cannot be timed to arrive here at a more opportune
moment. For Tippu is acting here in the most foolish manner.
He does not know who are his best friends, and who his worst
enemies. And hence he has lost control even over his own army.
He has no good military officers. And everybody here is wishing
for his discomfiture, and he is very unpopular. By whatever way
the army may come, it can have ample supplies and water.[69]

The Pradhans had been helping the British even during the Third
Anglo–Mysore War and aided the British campaign in Coimbatore
then. Tipu had sent a spy named Singree to ascertain the presence of
the Pradhans whom he wished to eliminate at all costs. He even sent
forces to attack Tirumala Rao who was stationed in the Coimbatore
fort with 2200 men and a garrison of merely one officer, 100 troops
and some measly ammunition. This was their most vulnerable
moment, and they could have easily fallen prey to Tipu's large
army. But fortune had favoured them at the right moment. Heavy
intermittent rains prevented Tipu's forces from reaching there on
time. By then, British reinforcements had come under Colonel
Wahab and Colonel Knox. Tipu then retreated, dismissing this as a
wasteful and costly campaign to nail the Pradhans.

However, Tirumala Rao had his fair share of controversy too
as he was embroiled in charges of corruption by the British and

accused of misappropriating over 1 lakh pagodas from the treasury in Coimbatore.[70] He had been appointed to manage the treasury and revenues in Coimbatore on a fixed salary, and he soon established a *kutchery* or office there. In December 1790, when Corbett was appointed as the Collector of the province of Coimbatore and scrutinized the books, he found the evidence of pilferage and squarely faulted Tirumala Rao. Rao denied the charges and passed the blame on to Amildar Puttayya whom he had nominated there in his place when he moved out of Coimbatore with the British army. But he was arrested in June 1791. It was then left to his younger brother, Narayana Rao, to make entreaties to the Government of Madras to release his brother. Sensing the potential utility of the duo, the British finally decided to release Tirumala Rao, and he gained their trust back as the Maharani's envoy.

With the coming of Wellesley, fresh parleys began between the Maharani and the British Government through the agency of the Pradhans. In a letter dated 3 February 1799 to Wellesley and Lord Clive, the Governor of Madras, Maharani Lakshmi Ammanni reinforced the complete support of the royal family in the British war against Tipu. Giving a detailed background of the misery into which her family had fallen, the Maharani also traced the relationship between her family and the British government, right from 1760. She recounted, referring to the aborted palace coup after 1782, 'just on the eve of our capturing Tippu and recovering our kingdom, our object was disclosed to Tippu, and consequently he put to death 700 families from amongst our relations as well as those of Tirumal Row, including men, women and children.'[71] Praising Wellesley's 'great nobility of character and purity of heart,' she placed 'implicit faith' in him and his goodness and hoped that he 'should root out the enemy, and restore to us our kingdom, according to the conditions of our last treaty with you.' As war expenses, she promised to pay 1 crore pagodas. She implored him to use his sense of justice and fair play and hoped that her family's honour would be finally restored.[72] Josiah Webbe, on behalf of the Company, acknowledged her letters and promised full British support. She was addressed grandiosely by him as 'Maharanee Narapati Matoshri Rana Sahib.'[73]

The stage was thus firmly set for the final kill. Brick by brick, the edifice of the Sultanat-e-khudadad was being chipped away. Tipu was going to face the toughest challenge of his life, encountering innumerable foes, both within and outside his dominions in this decisive milestone.

17

The Last Anglo–Mysore War

After his repeated letters to Tipu, on welcoming Doveton as an ambassador to discuss modalities of reconciliation, were either ignored or answered flippantly, Wellesley decided that he had given Tipu sufficient chances. Time was slipping by for Wellesley. If he delayed the campaign against Srirangapatna further, he would have encountered the notorious monsoons, lost a lot of money, the confidence of the recalcitrant allies and also the momentum of his troops. He consulted his confidant, his brother Arthur, who maintained the same line in his letter of 16 February 1799, 'send Doveton to Tippoo immediately, and give him notice at the same time that you intend to march an army into his country to enforce the propositions which you will make to him.'[1] Wellesley rationalized that Tipu's attitude during the entire correspondence was one of prevarication and buying time, and it seemed no different now. If he were to send Doveton on a peace mission, the allies 'would no longer be cordial; and we could not properly avail ourselves of the defection of any of Tippoo's subjects.'

Wellesley, however, waited till 22 February 1799 to write his last letter to Tipu. This too was sent to General Harris with the order that it be dispatched to Srirangapatna on the day he crossed the Mysore frontier. So, in all likelihood, Tipu must have received the letter only by around 10 March 1799. The letter was terse and to the point:

* Please refer to the corresponding illustration in the appendix.

I lament most sincerely that the friendly intimation contained in my letter of the 9th January regarding the dangers of delay, produced no effect on your discerning mind, and that you deferred your reply to that letter to so late a period in the season. Your long silence on this important and pressing occasion, compelled me to adopt the resolution of ordering the British forces to advance in concert with the armies of the allied powers. You are not ignorant that the period of the season rendered the advance of the army absolutely necessary to the common security of the allies. This movement of the army is to be imputed entirely to your repeated rejection of my amicable proposal of sending an ambassador to your presence. Under the present circumstances, to send Major Doveton to you could not be attended with those advantages which would have resulted from his mission at a proper season.[2]

The Fourth Anglo–Mysore War Breaks Out

Preparations had begun right from November 1798 with Wellesley's repeated visits to Madras and Fort St George to ascertain the condition of the army, the fortifications and the Carnatic route. From the months of June to December every year, owing to the monsoons and other natural factors, it normally became impossible for any army to approach Srirangapatna. Tipu was fully cognizant of this unique and singular advantage that his fort had over every other fort in India and hence his tactic was normally to push things long enough till the rain gods stepped in to help him. The British were aware of this and hence the operations had to commence with little further delay. War was finally declared against Tipu Sultan and a grand army of nearly 21,000 men, who had been assembled at Vellore under the command of General Harris, marched towards the Mysore frontier on 14 February 1799. By the 20th, it was joined near Ambur by another 16,000 troops from Hyderabad under Colonel Arthur Wellesley and Mir Alam. Unlike the previous occasion when Cornwallis's forces had to wander around aimlessly, waiting for the Nizam's cavalry to join, this time the forces, largely comprising the subsidiary alliance and Raymond's former corps, made a timely junction. The Bombay Army of nearly 6420 men under General Stuart assembled at Cannanore, while a large force under Colonel Read and Colonel Brown assembled at Tiruchirapalli in order to march to Srirangapatna from the south. Such a mighty force to reduce a prince who had already been cut to half his size after the previous war and had diminished in importance. Though depleted after the previous war, Tipu possibly had up to 30,000 soldiers. Conspicuous by its absence, unlike the last war, was the Maratha army, as the Peshwa was still contemplating what course of action to take.

It was expected to be a much faster, easier march to Srirangapatna as most of the eastern fortifications in Hosur and Bangalore had been demolished by Tipu. The accession to Baramahal and Salem districts after the 1792 Treaty and a general awareness of the routes, the fortifications and defence systems in Mysore, and especially Srirangapatna, after the Third Anglo–Mysore War, made the British troops a lot more confident that it was not after all an invincible citadel. A swift and decisive confrontation with Tipu at Srirangapatna, or on the road to it, is what the grand army anticipated. The intelligence the British were receiving from Srirangapatna also mentioned that Tipu might take the field immediately at the head of the main body of his army, that he might try to obstruct further progress towards Srirangapatna either by force or through negotiations. Under both circumstances, Harris was ordered by Wellesley not to concede but to continue the march to make a frontal attack on Srirangapatna. 'No treaty can be safely concluded with Tippoo Sultaun,' advised Wellesley, 'until your army shall either be in actual possession of his capital, or shall command the effectual means of securing its reduction.'[3]

Harris mounted the Ghats and entered Mysore by 5 March through the road to Hosur, hoping to find Tipu and stop him somewhere at Maddur or Chennapatna, on the way to Srirangapatna. Tipu had been camping in and around that area with a force of 12,000, as late as 3 March. Several frontier fortresses, including Wodiyardurg, Ancheridurga, Ratanagiri and others, fell to Harris, without much resistance. This helped Lt Col Read to also forward supplies without much hassle. Brinjaries or nomadic tribes were to help the army reload the cattle with supplies and grains for transport. The British army had always been plagued by short supplies and things were only slightly different this time.

Tipu had left Purnaiya and Sayyid Sahib to prevent Harris's advance. But Mohibbul Hasan states that as both of them 'had entered into an understanding with the English, they remained inactive and allowed the enemy to march without any hindrance.'4 It was unfortunate for Tipu that even a man like Purnaiya, who had been his father's closest confidant, and his own too, right from the perilous times of the transition of power to him in 1782, had now turned against him. Kirmani states that when the *kuzzaks* or light cavalry under his command charged at the advanced guard of the British and killed several of them, instead of being praised, they were severely admonished for attacking so rashly. Actions like these by several leading officers made the army feel that the intent 'was to avoid fighting and consequently they displayed no more zeal or enterprise and more like an escort or safeguard, quietly preceded and followed the troops of the enemy as they marched along.'5 Harris steadily moved north-eastwards to Kelamangalam and then to Bangalore where he reached by 14 March 1799, and wanted to establish a post, as during the last war.

The Bombay Army of over 6000 men meanwhile marched from Cannanore on 21 February 1799. They beat the harsh South Indian summer and arrived at the top of the Poodicherrum Ghats by 2 March in order to take up battle positions close to the Mysore frontier. They were confident that as per intelligence, Tipu was on the other side of Srirangapatna.

The Battle of Siddheshwara

The region's topography was hostile, thickly forested and impregnable, making it a herculean task to maintain a regular defensive position. Stuart had to make several divisions in his troops so that they could help each other when the need arose. The Raja of

Coorg accompanied Stuart in this campaign to guide him through the region. Siddheshwara was a critical military post, within the Coorg frontier. By virtue of its altitude, it gave a bird's eye view of the signals established between the two armies—that of Stuart and the other one under Harris, which had entered from the eastern direction. Stuart was only too aware that capturing this post would be the key to the final capture of Srirangapatna. The British troops kept a close watch on and around the post on the movement of the troops of their opponent. Tipu was expected on the other side of Srirangapatna to combat Harris, while they were making a westerly attack. They were hoping to find Muhammad Raza 'Benki Nawab' (relative of Tipu, son of Haidar Ali's maternal uncle, Ibrahim Sahib) there in defence, near the ford of Kannambadi, with an army of about 5000 *piadas* or irregular infantry. But it so happened that a sudden outburst of rain on the side where Tipu had embarked made him change his mind. He saw the untimely rain as an 'auspicious omen.'[6]

On 5 March 1799, the very day on which Harris had crossed the Mysore frontier, the troops reported the pitching of some 300–400 green tents and an extensive encampment just before Periapatna. This caused a flutter in Stuart's mind about whether Tipu was anywhere near. Yet, he continued with the advance and also sent another battalion to a convenient position for the reinforcement of the brigade around Siddheshwara. The ground at Siddheshwara was occupied by a brigade of three native battalions under Lt Col John Montresor. On 6 March, the second-in-command, Major General Hartley, was sent to ascertain the exact location and the movement of the Mysore forces. But the dense forest cover made it very difficult for Hartley to figure out anything, though he did anticipate a kind of intense movement and an imminent attack from the Mysorean side.

Expectedly, between 9 a.m. and 10 a.m., Tipu's forces sprang a sudden attack on the British troops under Montresor, simultaneously from the front and rear ends. Two columns of Mysorean forces united at the rear from the right and the left, just when the frontal attack was launched. It was Tipu's strategy to strangle the marching armies at the very first frontier post towards Mysore in his typical guerilla attack. But having had an inclination about the attack due to Hartley's inputs, Stuart hastened to Montresor's assistance with the two flank companies of his Majesty's 75th Regiment and the whole of the 77th. Finding Montresor being reinforced, the Mysoreans retreated after a short ambush of musketry. Harris found Montresor and his men 'exhausted with fatigue, and their ammunition almost expended.'[7]

In the process, the 'Benki Nawab,' Tipu's confidant and relative who led this attack, was killed. Other men of distinction were either slain or taken prisoners by the British. Fifteen hundred Mysoreans were killed and wounded, while twenty-nine men of the Bombay Army were killed, ninety-eight wounded and sixteen went missing.[8] Tipu's army in this battle had 11,800 of his best troops which was divided into four columns—a right column of 3000 under Sayyid Ghafar, the centre column of 1800 under Benki Nawab, a left column of 3000 under Babbar Jung and a reserve of 4000 commanded by the Sultan himself. Recording this victory in glowing terms, the Raja of Coorg, who was on the line of action with Stuart, reported the operations in detail in a letter to Wellesley: 'Many of the enemy were slain, and many wounded; the remainder having thrown away their muskets and swords, and their turbans, and thinking it sufficient to save their lives, fled in the greatest confusion.'[9]

The Bombay Army was considerably smaller than the Mysorean force and to be dealt a defeat at the very first frontier, and by a considerably smaller force, must have been a dampener for the Sultan. A crucial post had been occupied right in the presence of the Sultan's main army and there could be no better morale booster for the British to kick-start a war as decisive as this one. Wellesley, too, complimented the Bombay Army for their conduct and success, which he opined 'has seldom been equalled and never surpassed in India.'[10]

But Stuart anticipated that Tipu was not going to give up on this aborted attempt, 'but might endeavour to penetrate by another direction to the southward, still more open than the passage of Seedasere [Siddheshwara] where he would only be opposed by

Coorgs.'[11] Tipu remained at Periapatna until 11 March, before returning to Srirangapatna to regroup. It was yet to be seen if he would now intercept Harris or await him at his capital. He tried the first, but was eventually led to the second option.

Battle of Malavalli

Meanwhile, Harris had three routes from Bangalore, just as Cornwallis had in the earlier war, towards Srirangapatna. The southern route via Kankanahalli that Cornwallis had opted for in their first attempt on the Sultan's capital in 1791, the northern route via Savanadurga that he employed in the second attempt in 1792 and the central route via Chennapatna, which was normally where Tipu stationed himself to keep a close watch on all three routes. Harris chose the first route and, to intercept him, Tipu rushed to Malavalli, and by 18 March, encamped on the Maddur River. Here he was joined by Purnaiya and Sayyid Sahib. He held a commanding position here and could have prevented Harris from crossing the river. But either on bad counsel or misjudging the situation, Tipu tactically erred here by preferring to fight in the open instead of on a woody terrain. The efficient state of the Mysore gun cattle and the relatively miserable condition of the Carnatic bullocks precluded all idea of a successful pursuit of Tipu's army and this gave him the supreme confidence to venture upon this experiment on the high land of Malavalli, of which it was said 'a finer field of action it would be difficult to find.'[12] But here Tipu was misled by his treacherous Dewan Mir Sadak who wrongly informed Tipu about Harris's intention to conquer Chandagal fort situated on the right side of the river. Upon arriving there, Tipu was terrified to see the British marching eastwards, heading straight towards Srirangapatna. The British had crossed the river without any difficulty and encamped about fifty miles east of Malavalli, while the Sultan was at a considerable distance to the west.

Misjudging the intentions of the Mysorean troops that were stationed so far, Harris tried to march on. But they were caught by surprise when, by about 10 a.m. on 27 March, the guns were opened from the Mysorean end on the British cavalry. Harris quickly ordered the advance of His Majesty's 25th Dragoons and the 2nd regiment of the native cavalry, the three brigades of infantry to form a line towards the left and the whole to make a frontal and left attack on Tipu's forces. Col Wellesley was to move towards the right flank of the Mysore troops.

The rapid advance of the Mysorean troops baffled the British. They made a resolute charge on the British brigade commanded by Major General Baird. This was intended to charge the British line and to 'try the bayonet with us, by particular orders from Poorniah who commanded.'[13] But they found it difficult to counter His Majesty's 12th and the Scotch Brigade that ensured considerable losses for the Mysore side. This force, perhaps led by the Sultan himself, had maintained a heavy musketry attack on His Majesty's 74th Regiment. The Sultan's troops tried to encircle the enemy.

But eventually their advance was broken by Major General Floyd who ended up creating considerable chaos among the Mysoreans. Kirmani talks here about yet another act of treachery. He mentions that when Kumr-ud-din Khan was ordered to charge the enemy with his cavalry, he too shamefully neglected his duty, 'fell upon a division of the Sultan's brave troops and put them all into disorder.'[14] The disenchantment with Tipu on the part of most of his principal officers who meekly surrendered or participated with nonchalance made it clear that this was a war that Tipu was fighting hard to lose. With no zeal or resistance on the part of the principal strategists, it was wishful thinking that the Mysorean side even stood a chance. The division of the army and the attack of its two ends baffled the Mysoreans and this, coupled with an acute shortage of water, left them with little choice but to draw off their cannons and retreat.

Recounting the details of this crucial battle at Malavalli, after the fall of Srirangapatna, several years after the operation, when Harris had an opportunity to discuss the events with Purnaiya who had led the charge, he writes:

> There can be no doubt that the failure of this attempt decided the battle in Tippoo's mind, as his army instantly retreated; but

Poorniah afterwards confirmed it to me, and explained his hope of breaking our line by these 300-devoted men, and then of pouring in his whole cavalry. What might have been the consequence had the attempt succeeded cannot be known; but it surely may be noted as a remarkable circumstance . . . that as Commander-in-Chief of the army, I should be the executive agent to defeat this best proof of soldiership that I saw in my antagonist.[15]

This also calls to question Mohibbul Hasan's contention, drawn largely from Kirmani's accounts, that Purnaiya had turned traitor. If he had indeed been at the head of a command that sought to destroy the British troops at this crucial juncture, one wonders what his supposed collusion with the enemy then was.

In his eyewitness account of the Malavalli battle, Arthur Wellesley writes:

In the action of the 27th of March, at Malavelly, his [Tipu's] troops behaved better than they have ever been known to behave. His infantry advanced, and almost stood at the charge of bayonets of the 33rd, and his cavalry rode at General Baird's European brigade. He did not support them as he ought, having drawn off his guns at the moment we made our attack, and even pushed forward these troops to cover the retreat of his guns. This is the cause of the total destruction of the troops he left behind him, without loss to us, and of the panic with which we have reason to believe all his troops are now affected. His light cavalry, looties, and others, are the best of the kind in the world. They have hung upon us, night and day, from the moment we entered his country to this. Some of them have always had sight of us, and have been prepared to cut off any persons venturing out of the reach of our camp guards. We came by a road so unfrequented that it was not possible to destroy all the forage, which would have distressed us much . . . if Tippoo had had sense and spirit sufficient to use his cavalry and infantry as he might have done, I have no hesitation in saying that we should not now be here, and probably should not be out of the jungles near Bangalore.[16]

Thus, bad judgment, bad counsel and treachery were doing Tipu in, bit by bit, hurtling him towards his final disaster. In this skirmish at Malavalli, almost 2000 men of Tipu's army were killed or wounded—some of the bravest men and his best officers. The British suffered a loss of only sixty-six men being killed. A deeply emotional Sultan assembled a council of his principal officers at Bannur, a village on the left side of the Kaveri River and about twelve miles south-east of Srirangapatna. Reflecting on the losses at Siddheshwara and Malavalli, he sunk into absolute despondency and addressed his officers thus: 'We have now arrived at our last stage, what is your determination?' 'To die along with you!' was the universal thundering reply.[17]

It was decided in the meeting that Tipu must hasten to the southern part of the island and position himself at the village of Chandagal and make a 'last and desperate effort, with no alternative but death or victory.'[18] Everyone attending was emotionally charged as they knew well that the endgame was near. How it would end was all that was left to be seen—death or surrender. One of the chiefs, while departing, prostrated himself at the Sultan's feet and embraced them. The Sultan broke down into inconsolable tears at this and soon everyone was sobbing. The meeting ended thus in a pool of tears, as if it were being convened for the last time. The events of the subsequent weeks saw to it that this had indeed been their last hurrah. Mir Sadak was dispatched to supervise the destruction of all the buildings on the esplanade, on the side of the expected attack, and those in Shehar Ganjam that had not yet been destroyed. The Sultan's two eldest sons who were present with the army were sent to Srirangapatna with the express orders that they make a proper defence of the capital in the event of their father's death.

Run-Up to the Final Assault

The plan that was decided in that sombre meeting was that Tipu would place himself to Harris's rear, on the assumption that Harris would be taking the same route that Cornwallis had followed in 1791 and get to Srirangapatna through Arakere and Karighat. But Harris took slow, yet cautious marches to thwart Tipu's plans and made a circuitous leftward turn, crossing the ford at a place called Sosale. The forage on the regular route had been destroyed, while this one had ample supply and also could be crossed relatively unopposed. The junction too could be easily formed from here with the Bombay Army that was rapidly progressing, as also the supplies from Coorg and Baramahal. As expected, they found ample grains, draught and carriage cattle, as well as slaughter cattle and sheep on this route and, by 31 March, they had crossed over completely.

Destiny once again provided Tipu a chance. By 1 April, once Harris's troops had left Sosale, their artillery had not yet arrived on account of bad roads. The most opportune day for him to strike and vanquish the intruders was 2 April. Tipu even contemplated it, but gave up the idea on account of the most trivial superstition that it was an inauspicious day. His obsession with astrology and adherence to various superstitions had led him in the past to make several wrong decisions. But this was an unpardonable blunder. Consequently, Harris advanced by easy marches and, by 7 April, was within barely two miles of the Sultan's capital. Harris congratulated his troops on their first sight of the Sultan's famed capital, the island town of Srirangapatna. 'A continuance of the same exertions,' he exhorted, to inspire his weary troops, 'will shortly put an end to their labours, and place the British colours in triumph on its walls.'[19]

Tipu now assumed that Harris would cross into the island and that is why he decided to prevent this from Chandagal. But again, Harris took a different route, taking a circuitous one to the left. He advanced very slowly, covering twenty-eight miles in five days. Yet, he hardly faced much resistance or attack from the Mysore horse in front of him. The British were slowly occupying a position of strength, though the Mysoreans still held a few prominent posts from where their rocket men kept firing. Between the camping place of the British and the walls of the fort was a vast area of broken ground that was interspersed with wild bushes, granite rocks and dilapidated hamlets. This offered excellent cover for the Mysoreans to annoy the British army with their incessant rocketry and firing.

At the extreme end of this and about a mile from the city was a vast grove of betel nuts called Sultanpet Tope ('Tope' in Kannada meaning grove), which served as a launch pad for the Mysore side to hurl their rockets. General David Baird was tasked on the night of 4 April to dislodge the men from this place. By 11 p.m. when Baird and his troops scoured the grove, they found that the Mysoreans had vacated the place. Feeling secure, they returned. Though of course, Baird lost his way in the dark and it was Lt Lambton, a celebrated surveyor and astronomer in his staff, who helped Baird find his way back safely by about 4 a.m. But by daybreak, the Mysoreans reoccupied the place and the firing resumed.

Harris was determined to occupy some of these frontier posts. He sent Colonel Shawe to attack one of the posts at the aqueduct, which in its winding course protected much of the British front. Another contingent, under Colonel Arthur Wellesley, was sent to occupy Sultanpet Tope. Marching by sunset, both these parties faced stiff resistance and pushback from the Mysoreans, with heavy firing from the fort, and were forced to retreat with considerable losses. A spent ball from the Mysorean side even injured Wellesley slightly in the knee. He got separated from his forces and spent some time wandering in the wilderness, only to report to his commander-in-chief's camp well past midnight, reporting his inability to capture the Tope.

But the next morning, on 6 April, a larger force of the Scotch Brigade and two battalions of sepoys were ordered to be sent again under Col Wellesley. When all were ready to commence, Harris became uneasy on noticing that Col Wellesley was absent from the line of command. Fearing that the opportune time might pass due to this delay, he ordered General Baird to take the command and commence the attack. But by then Col Wellesley came in and Baird was asked to pull back. There was some friction between these two men and the fact that Col Wellesley was the Governor-General's brother and was possibly getting away with many omissions peeved the other officers. Messages from Wellesley senior to Harris, saying, 'Do not allow Arthur to fatigue himself too much,'[20] were obviously not much appreciated by his peers.

Despite these minor ego clashes, this time the British succeeded in occupying the posts in less than twenty minutes. Hussain Ali Khan, a youthful officer and high-ranking nobleman, saw his men retreat from the tope and charged at the enemy with his adherents, only to be shot at after a minor success. The same post that had caused such anxiety and confusion for two nights had fallen so quickly to Col Wellesley. As a result, the British were now in control of strong positions within 1800 yards of the fort. The occupation of the tope in particular gave the Commander-in-Chief a line of posts that offered complete security to his camp. It was now possible to form a straight line that was about two miles long and barely 1000 yards within the southern battlements of Srirangapatna. In front of them however was both the main course of the Kaveri River and a smaller branch of it called the Little Kaveri. Between these two, the Mysoreans held quite a few important positions and it was not until 20 April that they were removed from there. The western and north-western sides of the citadel were the weakest, with unfinished fortifications, and Harris planned to launch an attack from there.

On 6 April, Major General Floyd, who was second-in-command now to Harris, had set off from Periapatna to meet Stuart and bring him to Srirangapatna. Tipu sent the traitor Kumr-ud-din to intercept this march and prevent their junction from happening. However, Kumr-ud-din, after reaching the spot, merely watched the armies join and remained a mute spectator. Consequently, Floyd succeeded in joining the Bombay Army of Stuart and easily reached Srirangapatna. Wellesley reported to the Court of Directors that 'it may be safely affirmed not to be in the power of Tippoo, even materially, to retard this junction, which when effected, must excite a serious alarm in the mind of the Sultaun for the safety of his capital, if not of his person.'[21] The army however faced the same problems that Cornwallis's forces had faced in their operations—the failure of the cattle provided for the service of the army. The cattle of the Carnatic region fared miserably in the climate of Mysore and Srirangapatna, and this remained a major complaint for Harris all through. The superiority of the Mysore cattle had enabled Haidar

and Tipu to defeat every attempt made by British commanders to
overtake them in the field.

But Stuart was running short of supplies and his arrival caused
more shortages for Harris. Rice was running in short supply and they
had provisions left for only eighteen days. 'Unless Colonel Read's
supplies arrive before the 6th of May,' noted Harris in despair on
16 April, 'the army will be without provision. There is plenty in the
Coorg country, but we have no means to convey or escort it hither.'[22]
There was a positive side to this shortage of supplies. It set a sense
of alarm and urgency and compelled Harris to expedite the attack
on the fort from its weak north-western angle. The British made
steady progress and despite the resistance offered by the Mysoreans,
by the night of 26 April, the posts were all attacked and occupied.
Just before this, Tipu made so violent an attack upon them from the
guns of the fort that it seemed tough for the British to sustain. But
the British were determined and egged on though nearly 307 of their
officers and men were killed, wounded or missing. Nonetheless, this
was a valuable acquisition as it provided Harris the ground on which
the breaching batteries could be erected.

Tipu Sues for Negotiations

Even as the British troops were circling him right in his citadel,
Tipu had brief exchanges with Harris. His note on 9 April 1799 was
as follows:

> The Governor-General, Lord Mornington Bahauder sent me a
> letter, copy of which is enclosed. You will understand it. I have
> adhered firmly to treaties; what then is the meaning of the advance
> of the English armies and the occurrence of hostilities. Inform me.
> What need I say more?[23]

In an equally brief reply, Harris replied on 10 April:

> Your letter enclosing copies of the Governor-General's letter
> has been received. For the advance of the English and the Allied

armies and for the actual hostilities, I refer you to the several letters of the Governor-General, which are sufficiently explanatory on the subject.[24]

There was a lull in communication thereafter till 20 April, the day when the north bank batteries opened fire and a successful operation against the Mysorean positions on the south was in progress. Tipu then sent another note to Harris:

> In the letter of Lord Mornington, it is written that the clearing up of the matter at issue is proper, and that therefore you having been empowered for the purpose, will appoint such persons as you judge proper for conducting a conference, and resuming the business of a treaty. You are the well-wisher of both Circars. In this matter what is your pleasure? Inform me, that a conference may take place.[25]

Harris forwarded the communication to Wellesley for his advice on how this was to be taken forward. As early as 22 February 1799 when Wellesley declared war and also authorized Harris to carry out any further communications with Tipu, he had provided him two sets of terms, should Tipu sue for peace—Draft A and Draft B, as they were meticulously named. Draft A was to be used if the approach came from Tipu before the siege had begun. Draft B was to be sent to him if he made no peace moves until the batteries had actually opened fire on Srirangapatna.[26] Both drafts necessitated that Tipu Sultan receive and station in his court permanent ambassadors from each of the allies, for as long a period as the allies wished. The allies, too, were to receive an ambassador from Tipu on similar terms. He was to dismiss without delay from his service and remove from his dominions all French officers, natives of the Isle of France and Bourbon, as also all Europeans who were at war with Britain. He had to cut off all ties with the French nation, offer no asylum or shelter to any citizens or officials from that country in his domains. The two drafts differed in Articles Four and Six. Draft 'A' stipulated that

Tipu had to cede territory from his coastal areas, the entire sea-coast of Malabar below the Ghats, to the Company. An equal amount of territory as ceded to the Company in the coastal area had to be relinquished in perpetuity to both the Nizam and the Peshwa for contiguous border areas. He was also to relinquish all his disputed claims with the Raja of Coorg on Amara, Sulya and Yelu Saavira Seeme. Mysore had to release unequivocally any prisoners of war of the allies that it might be housing. An amount of Rs 1½ crore was to be paid as indemnity—75 lakh of which was to be paid immediately and the rest within six months. Until this money was recovered, Tipu had to surrender two of his three oldest sons to Harris as hostages.

Draft 'B' was more drastic. It sought cession of one half of the territory, that was with Tipu at the commencement of this war, to the allies. This effectively snatched away from him another half of whatever was left post the treaty with Cornwallis. The indemnity was raised to Rs 2 crore, to be paid in instalments within six months.

Wellesley's secret letter to Harris on 22 February had details of the valuation of the territories too. As it stood in 1792, the Sultan's dominions yielded 35 lakh pagodas. Of these, 17,50,000 pagodas were to be divided among the three allies. The Marathas got their share, too, even without participating in the current war. Canara, Coimbatore, Dharapuram, Erode, Karur etc., yielding 5,84,000 pagodas, were to go to the Company. Gutti, Gurramkonda, Anegundi and Kurnool, yielding 6,09,641 pagodas, was the Nizam's share. The excess here was to be made up to Tipu by the Nizam from the yields of Gutty or Gurramkonda. Bidanur, Harpanahalli and Rayadurg that yielded 5,89,516 pagodas was the Peshwa's pie. The minor excess here too was to be made up to Mysore by Poona.[27]

Upon hearing of Tipu's desire to negotiate, Wellesley advised Harris to send him Draft B with any improvisations that he might please. Harris trimmed the articles further. He changed the number of hostages to four of his sons (named too as Sultan Padshaw, Futteh Hyder, Moyer-ud-din and Abdul Khalick) and four of his generals (Meer Kummer-ud-din, Meer Mahomed Sadik, Syed Goffar and Purnea).[28] Harris put in these extra hostages in lieu of certain fortresses that he was authorized to demand but which could not be occupied in time. Harris was also directed by Wellesley that it was 'desirable that Tippoo Sultaun's power and resources should be reduced to the lowest possible state, and even utterly destroyed, if the events of war should afford the opportunity.'[29] The treaty was supposed to only name the Company and the allies to be included in general terms in the following manner: 'Definitive Treaty etc. between the Honourable English Company and their *allies [italics mine]*, concluded by Lieut-General Harris on the part of the said Company and of their *allies*, by virtue of the powers from the Governor-General etc.'[30] The names of Mir Alam or the Nizam were specifically advised not to be mentioned as part of the treaty. If the Nizam protested, they were to inform him that this was done to preclude claims from his arch-rival, the Marathas, for an equal partition. For the Marathas, there was to be a clause that though they made no contribution to this war, the Company was allotting territories to the Peshwa on the condition that within two months of the treaty, a satisfactory adjustment would be made by Poona with the Nizam and the Company on the burdens and expenses of war. Failing this, the territories granted to the Peshwa were to be ceded to the Company and the Nizam, who were at liberty to divide this among themselves. It was thus a carefully crafted plan to deliver the maximum mileage and benefits to the British cause.

Tipu was justifiably shocked by Draft B that he received and on 28 April 1799, he wrote to Harris stating that he wished to send two ambassadors to explain and negotiate the terms. Harris wrote back the same day that there was no scope for any negotiations and that he was forbidden by his master to entertain any vakils from Mysore. So, it was essentially a take-it-or-leave-it proposition for Tipu, who was given time until 3 p.m. the following day to submit his view. On the Sultan's reaction to this non-negotiable reply from Harris, Wilks writes: 'After the Sultaun's perusal of this reply, mixed indications rather of grief than rage, finally subsided into a silent stupor, from which he seldom seemed to wake, except for the purpose of affecting a confidence, by which no one was deceived, that the capital could not be taken. But no trace was evinced of those active energies of mind and body, by which alone such a confidence could be reasonably supported . . . but it was all deliberation and no decision; this essential work was not attempted, and the Sultaun even relaxed in that personal inspection which he had hitherto practiced, as if desirous to hide from his own observation, the extent and imminence of his danger.'[31]

There were obviously no options left now and Tipu had to fight it out to the best of his ability and expect a miracle. Even as these negotiations were going on, the British had not halted the hostilities. So, Tipu understood clearly what they wanted. There was no communication thereafter; the twenty-four-hour deadline that Harris had served on Tipu passed, and now everyone waited with bated breath for the final leg of the war.

The Final Storming of Srirangapatna

From the batteries that began to be erected starting 28 April 1799, continuous firing carried on to effect a breach in the fort. By the morning of the 30th, the six-gun breaching battery commenced its firing on the north-western bastion and continued throughout the day. By evening, the main rampart and the faussebraye wall (defensive wall outside the main walls of fortification) were considerably shattered. That night, the Nizam's battery too was set to fire. Until 2 May 1799, the guns of the British side kept up their severe fire and by sunset that day, the fort was finally breached and incessant firing further enlarged it. After nearly a month of continuous fighting and hardships, the British troops finally saw a glimmer of hope on 3 May when the breach was widened. While they rejoiced at the prospect of the long-drawn war against Tipu seemingly reaching its final stage, they were aware that he was among the most unpredictable of Indian rulers who could spring a surprise on them even at the last moment. But they also knew that they could fully count on the looming treachery within the ill-fated fort of Srirangapatna to finally spell doom on its Sultan.

That evening, a great explosion took place in the fort, caused by the bursting of a shell in a magazine, and an immense column of smoke engulfed the place. Several thousand rockets flew in every direction, causing many Mysoreans to be killed and wounded. Meanwhile, Harris was wondering which portion of the Bombay Army under Stuart would finally storm the fort.

To make use of the breach and take possession of the fort, Harris sought the help of Tipu's treacherous Dewan, Mir Sadak. Like several other traitors among Tipu's principal officers, Mir Sadak too had been in regular correspondence with the British for a while, conspiring against his master. As the firing went on, Tipu called his close circle to confer on the course he should take. Chapuy, the French officer from Mauritius, advised him that given the precarious situation, the Sultan with his cavalry, infantry, treasures, women and children must quit the fort and retire to Sira or Chitradurga. He also suggested that he set aside a small detachment of the troops to fight the attackers or, if it made things easier for him, the Sultan was well within his rights to hand over the Frenchmen in his army to the British. On the final suggestion though Tipu emphatically told Chapuy: 'If on your account, you being strangers from a distant land, the whole of our kingdom should be plundered and laid waste, well and good; but you shall not be delivered up.'[32] He then turned to his treacherous Dewan, Mir Sadak, who he assumed was a trusted confidant, and sought his advice on whatever Chapuy had suggested. Sadak told him: 'It must be well known to your Highness that this people [French] never kept faith with anyone, and Your Highness may be well-assured, that if you give up the fort to their care and defence, that at that very moment, it will fall into the possession of the English, for both these people [English and French] consider themselves originally of the same tribe, and they are one in heart and language.'[33]

It was possibly the proceedings of this meeting that also found their way to the British. In his letter to Harris on 28 April 1799, Wellesley had surmised that there was intelligence gathered that Tipu might flee from Srirangapatna to Chitradurga or some other strong hill fort. 'To counteract this attempt,' advised Wellesley, 'you will employ the whole activity, skill and zeal of your army; and you will omit no effort to intercept the Sultaun, if he should move out of his capital for the purpose of effecting such an escape.'[34] Evidently, the details of these secret consultations were being assiduously passed on to the enemy camp.

With the intention of quitting the crumbling fort, Tipu had his treasure, valuables and his seraglio, as also some elephants, camels and carriages kept in readiness to move at the earliest warning. He held another council meeting where Budruzaman Khan Nayut told the Sultan that such a move would shatter the courage of his faithful servants and 'the bonds of union in the garrison of the capital will be broken asunder.'[35] On hearing this, Tipu looked to the skies in despair and sighed: 'I am entirely resigned now to the will of God, whatever it may be!' and abandoned the plan of escaping from the doomed fort. He was often seen to turn philosophical and renunciatory, saying things like, 'As a man could die only once, it was of little consequence when the period of his existence might terminate.'[36] Tipu had mentally resigned himself to the inevitable. The packed articles however still remained ready for removal.

The troops inside the fort, that were on duty, numbered about 13,750 and were regularly relieved and the general charge of the angle attacked had been committed to Sayyid Sahib, who was assisted by an ardent Tipu-loyalist, Sayyid Ghafar. Aged about sixty, Sayyid Sahib was a favourite officer of the Sultan and was well versed in revenue affairs. But as Beatson mentions, 'as a military commander, his character was held in no estimation.'[37] His daughter was married to the Sultan in around 1796. Chapuy meanwhile commanded the large cavalier behind the angle bastion. The Sultan's eldest son, Fateh Haidar, along with Purnaiya commanded a detached corps along with the entire cavalry and Silledar horse, numbering 4300, to combat the northern frontier and were encamped at Karighat. Tipu's second son commanded the Mysore gate at the southern side. Kumr-ud-din, the traitor, was absent, and was aiding General Floyd. He was given command of 4000 troops to cut off the supplies and reinforcements of the British.[38]

Around this time, due to the machinations of Mir Sadak, one of the most trusted and loyal officers of the irregular infantry and cavalry since Haidar's time and one of Tipu's early preceptors in warfare, Ghazi Khan was executed on false charges. By then, Tipu seemed to have gotten a whiff that some of his officers had turned against him. He created a handwritten list of some of these traitors and handed it to Mir Moinuddin to have them caught and executed at the earliest. Moinuddin however was indiscreet and opened the paper that his master had handed over to him in the durbar, whilst a palace sweeper happened to glance at the list from a distance. He saw there that Mir Sadak's name was on the top of the list of people whom the Sultan doubted and wanted arrested and hanged. He rushed to the Dewan, warning him of the catastrophe that could befall him and that he remain on the alert.

Fearing for his life, Mir Sadak possibly accelerated his contacts with the enemy, urging them to make haste. On 3 May, some British officers crossed over to the glacis, examined the breach and strategized on plans for storming the fort. Perhaps it was on this occasion that Mir Sadak confabulated with the British officers, suggesting to them that the appropriate time for the assault should be midday on 4 May. About 4386 men, of whom 2494 were Europeans and 1892 native sepoys, were to participate in the attack, and were waiting in the trenches, before daybreak. They were under the command of Major General David Baird, an old foe of the Sultan. Twenty years ago, he had been held captive by Tipu for forty-four months and had undergone great torture as a prisoner. He was now seeking his revenge and wanted to go down in history as a commander who, within an hour, brought down the famed fort of Srirangapatna and crushed its heroic Sultan. Lt Lalor made a survey on the night of the 3rd of the passage of the river adjacent to the breach. It was found to be about 280 yards in breadth. The bottom was very rocky and rugged, but there wasn't a huge volume of water, though it had some deep pools. Scaling ladders and materials were all kept ready for the next day's storming operations. Firing was to continue as normally as ever even on 4 May, so that no alarm was excited.

The plan was that Mir Sadak, through his trusted commandant, the killedar of the fort, Mir Nadim, was to withdraw the Mysorean troops stationed at and around the breach temporarily, at the designated time of the storming in, on the pretext of making their payments. Sadly, for Tipu, there was no one to protest against such treacherous moves. But he had only himself to blame for this sorry state of affairs. As Wilks states: 'Among his own personal staff and attendants . . . there was not one man of professional character. He fancied the attachment of men raised by his own favour, to be more genuine and sincere, than the support of persons possessing established character and high pretensions.'[39] Whenever reports of the alarming progress of the besiegers was sought to be conveyed to the Sultan, his sycophantic staff would make light of it, ascribing it to paranoia, and that no calamity could even touch their invincible ruler. Lulled by the comfort of such sweet talk, Tipu paid no keen attention to any of these treacherous motives or developments till it was too late.

One of the most loyal and trusted officers of the Sultan who could have overseen these omissions and given the Sultan some sane counsel was Sayyid Ghafar. He was an officer of a provincial corps of English sepoys who had been captured along with Colonel Brathwaite during the Second Anglo–Mysore War but subsequently entered the Sultan's army and became a zealous confidant. On an earlier occasion, though severely wounded in the hand, Sayyid Ghafar foresaw the disaster. In anguish he had cried: 'He [Tipu] is surrounded by boys and flatterers, who will not even let him see with his own eyes. I do not wish to survive the result. I am going about in search of death, and cannot find it.'[40]

On the forenoon of 4 May 1799, he saw that the trenches were all unusually crowded and knew that his worst nightmares were going to come true. A storming of the fort was inevitable now. But he was frantic that the Sultan, surrounded by his sycophants, remained so blissfully unaware of the breach and also of the enemy gathered in the trenches, waiting to storm in. Even on that ill-fated morning of 4 May 1799, when Ghafar sent a report on the possibility of a storming in the day, the Sultan made light of it by surmising that the

British normally conducted night assaults and if at all there were to be a storming, it would happen at night and not in the day. Ghafar, who knew that it would be matter of a few hours before the storming would commence, was filled with both rage and desperation and wanted to rush to the Sultan, shake him out of his reverie and give him a sound reality check. Exasperatedly he exclaimed: 'I will go and drag him to the breach, and make him see by what a set of wretches he is surrounded; I will compel him to exert himself at this last moment.'[41] As he was rushing towards the Sultan's apartments, he met a party of pioneers who were mending some stones that had fallen off the walls rather than attend to the wide, gaping breach. He had been looking for them for long, but in vain, to help cut off the approach by the southern rampart. He wanted to drag them all to the place and show them where their actual and urgent work was necessary. But propitiously for the British, just at the time whilst he was urging the pioneers to make haste, Ghafar was killed by a cannon shot. It was perhaps planned by the traitors, as immediately after Ghafar fell, they signalled from within the ramparts to the enemy who was anxiously waiting outside, by waving their white handkerchiefs. The earnest attempts of the loyal Ghafar were unfortunately utterly wasted.

4 May 1799

The fateful day of 4 May 1799 dawned like any other day. Ever since the British had appeared in his island capital, Tipu had remained fully encamped on the ramparts, varying his position depending on how the enemy moved. Initially, he had his tent pitched to the southern face; it was then moved to the western side and finally, when the British opened their batteries, he moved his headquarters to a small stone apartment in the inner partition of the Kalale-Diddi, a water-gate on the northern side that had been built decades ago by Dalavayi Devarajayya.[42] This was where he ate and slept and gave orders to his officers and troops. Near his apartment, small tents were pitched for his servants and baggage.[43]

As mentioned, the news of the breach had been concealed from him entirely. He had preferred to live in his cocoon of make-believe. That morning, he mounted his horse, left his apartment and inspected what was shown to him as the 'breach'. He was led to a place by the traitors where just a few stones had fallen and was reassured that this would be readily and easily fixed. The actual breach however stood gaping wide open at another end, waiting for the British troops to storm in.

The last few hours were crucial, but these were perilously lost as Ghafar had feared. Perhaps it was the inevitability of what the sunset would bring that caused Tipu to take refuge instead in the final option that he had—supernatural aid. A large contingent of Brahmin priests from Chennapatna were called in at an exorbitant cost of offerings to carry out a continuous *japam* or chanting for the safety and life of the Sultan. In his youth, Tipu had viewed astrology as a pseudoscience, but somewhere along the way, he had become an extreme believer. Perhaps, it was around the time of the wedding of his son to the daughter of the Bibi of Cannanore and his subsequent visit to Coimbatore in 1789 that Tipu picked up astrology and, with time, he became quite proficient in it himself.

That morning, he looked at his own horoscope along with a few Muslim and Brahmin astrologers. The general opinion among them was that the 4th of May 1799, being the last day of the lunar month, was particularly inauspicious. They deduced that as long as Mars remained within a particular circle, the fort would hold out. This celestial rotation of the planet had sadly ended the previous night and the astrologers fearfully revealed this to Tipu. At least, from midday to about seven hours thereafter was an extremely unpropitious time for him; they saw that 'a dark cloud overshadowed the fort during the period.'[44] To avert any mishaps, he was advised to stay guarded and with his army at all times through the day, till sunset, and also offer generous alms. They had prescribed some oblations and alms that he gave on the morning of the 4th to rid himself of the ill effects that were portended. These had all been kept ready from the night of the 3rd itself.

Tipu, accordingly, proceeded to the palace, bathed and got ready for the rituals. He was dressed in a light-coloured jacket, wide trousers of fine flowered chintz, a sash of dark red silky cloth and a turban with one or two distinguishing ornaments.[45] Meanwhile, the inner apartments of the Sultan's palace in Srirangapatna were deceptively cool. While the mercury soared outside in a typical South Indian summer, at its peak in the month of May, the rooms inside seemed to belong to some exotic island. Huge mats sprinkled with water and perfume hung from the walls and balconies, even as manual fans ran round the clock. In more ways than one, this illusion too seemed symbolic. The man in command was living in a similar world of make-believe, where he was made to believe that things were fine and in total control. The historic fort of Srirangapatna had seen trouble in the past, but this time treachery had permeated virtually every brick and stone of the fort.

Tipu got down to the business of offering alms to the holy men who had assembled. To the priest of Chennapatna, he gifted an elephant, a bag of black sesame seeds and Rs 200. To other Brahmins, 'he gave a black bullock, a milch buffalo, a male buffalo, a black she-goat, a jacket of coarse black cloth, a cap of the same material, ninety rupees and an iron pot filled with oil.'[46] Before giving this last item of an iron pot with oil, he had to peer into the pot. This was part of the ritual oblation that involved his face being reflected on the surface of the pot of incanted oil. It was believed that through this, the ill effects of that individual could be transformed into something favourable. Before noon, Tipu completed these rituals that were conducted elaborately by the main priest who was leading the proceedings.

After the rituals were completed, the priests blessed him and advised him to have a light meal that he then sat down for. Just then, when he had barely broken his bread to eat, he received the unfortunate news of the death of his closest confidant, Sayyid Ghafar. The news of death coming at a time when he sought to conquer it, did it portend a larger message for him? Though deeply agitated by the news of Ghafar's death, Tipu quickly composed himself, decided that the time for rituals, incantations and meals was over. By then soldiers came rushing in to inform him that the enemy had made a huge breach in the fort and had managed to get inside. Nothing seemed to make sense to Tipu as just that morning he had been shown a place where barely a few stones had been dislodged and that it would be rectified immediately. How then could such a big breach be effected in the fort when no news or noise of it had reached his ears. He had to rush to the spot to ascertain for himself about what had happened. Requesting the priests to continue with their chanting, he left his meal unfinished and stormed out of the inner apartments. Mounting his horse, he rushed towards the breach. But unbeknownst to him, by then the British troops had entered the fort and the Union Jack was proudly fluttering at the breach.

The Storming by the British Troops

Around 11 a.m. on 4 May 1799, General Baird asked his troops in the trenches to be ready to proceed at any time, as it was decided that the fort be stormed at or after 1 p.m., once a signal for the same was received from within the fort. Each European received a cheering dram of liquor and a biscuit before the arrangement for the formation of the attack was finalized and begun. Harris was tense and nervous as the decisive moment that they had been planning for, for months, neared. When Captain John Malcolm saw him lost in thoughts and sitting alone in his tent, he asked him: 'Why, my Lord, so thoughtful?' Harris snapped back sternly: 'Malcolm! This is no time for compliments. We have serious work on hand. Don't you see that the European sentry over my tent is so weak from want of food and exhaustion that a sepoy could push him down. We must take this fort or perish in the attempt. I have ordered General Baird to persevere in the attack to the last extremity. If he is beaten off, [Arthur] Wellesley is to proceed with the troops from the trenches. If he also should not succeed, I shall put myself at the head of the remainder of the army, for success is essential to our existence.'[47]

After Sayyid Ghafar fell, at around half past one, the traitors, at Mir Sadak's behest, signalled to the British troops waiting in the trenches to storm the fort through the breach. It was the hottest part of a summer day in May when the Mysore troops had either gone for a small refreshment or had been lured away by Mir Nadim on the pretext of salary payments. Baird stepped out of the trenches, drew his sword and gave out a war cry: 'Now, my brave fellows, follow me and prove yourselves worthy of the name of British soldiers.'[48] Under the cover of heavy firing from their side, the British troops hobbled out of their hideouts, stumbling and sliding across smooth boulders, crossed the river and reached the foot of the fort even as musketry and rocket firing from within it was being directed at them. In about six minutes, they managed to reach the summit of the 100-feet-wide breach. In no time, men in red coats had all crammed inside and jumped over to the fort. Without firing a single shot, they had captured it and Sergeant Graham of the Bombay Army proudly unfurled the British standard on it. Writing about his experience of this momentous occasion, Lt Richard Bayly states in his war diary:

> We experienced little loss, until we were floundering on the rocky bed of the river, when the men began to fall fast. All who were wounded were inevitably drowned in a second afterwards. One step the water scarcely covered the foot, the next we were plunged headlong into an abyss of fathoms deep. Thus, scrambling over, the column at length reached the ascent of the breach, where numerous flankers who had preceded us, were lying stretched on their backs, killed and wounded, some of the gallant officers waving their swords and cheering our men on. We dashed forward, and the top of the breach was soon crowned by our intrepid lads, and the British flag hoisted. But this was for a moment only. A sudden, sweeping fire from the inner wall came like a lightning blast, and exterminated the living mass. Others crowded from behind, and again the flag was planted. At this time, General Baird was discovered at the ramparts. On observing a deep, dry, rocky ditch of sixty feet deep, and an inner wall covered with the troops of the enemy, he exclaimed: 'Good God! I did not expect this!' His presence of mind did not desert him . . . and we soon charging to the right and left of the breach along the ramparts of the outer wall.[49]

The forces that came in later were under Majors Beatson, Dallas and Allan. They found near the breach about three men of consequence, and in Mysore uniform, lying dead. One of them showed some signs of life and movement and when they approached him, it happened to be Sayyid Sahib. He had meanwhile tumbled and was terribly wounded. Dallas recognized him from the days back in Mangalore in 1784 when they met and talked, at a time when he commanded the escort with the Commissioners. Sayyid Sahib raised Dallas's hand several times to his forehead and affectionately embraced his knee. He could barely speak and asked for water which he was offered. 'Syed Sahib,' recounts Beatson, 'observing how much we were interested in his behalf, shewed his sense of our attentions by silent expressions of gratitude that are indescribable.'[50] He refused a surgeon's support and insisted that he must die instead. The Majors asked him if the Sultan was there inside and Sayyid Sahib replied in the affirmative that he was in the palace. They could barely trust their ears and repeated their query to which he replied: 'The Sultaun and all his family were still there, and that he had left them but a short time before.'[51] By then, heavy musketry recommenced from the southern side and so, leaving Sayyid Sahib to the command of two sepoys, the Majors marched ahead. A palanquin was summoned to take him to the safety of a camp, but while trying to get up, he lost control, staggered and fell over the battlements into the deep ditch and died soon after.

Shortly after the British stormed in, eight or ten French officers, including Chapuy, the chief commandant of the French troops serving the Sultan, surrendered. After capturing the breach, the invading forces divided themselves into two columns. The right column was commanded by Colonel Sherbrooke with four Companies of European flankers from the Scotch Brigade, and Regiment de Meuron was directed to attack the southern rampart. The left column under Colonel Dunlop with six companies of European flankers from the Bombay Army proceeded to attack the northern rampart. The right column had a pretty easy way through as most of the Mysoreans fled in panic from the western ramparts that had by then been so heavily enfiladed, and thereafter along the southern face of the fort. Many surrendered or, while attempting to escape, were dashed to pieces on the rocky bottom of the ditch. Within less than an hour, this column had occupied the southern ramparts and arrived on the eastern face of the fort.

But the left one under Dunlop faced immense resistance from the Mysoreans, as this was the part of the fortifications where Tipu was present, leading the charge by example. Dunlop was disabled by a sword-cut on the wrist in personal combat with one of Tipu's officers. But his men, under Lt Lambton, however, succeeded in taking control over the north-west bastion. The Mysoreans vigorously resisted at a number of traverses of the western and northern ramparts. Several leading British officers were killed or disabled. The British losses would have mounted immensely had it not been for the light infantry and part of the battalions of His Majesty's 12th Regiment under Captain Goodall which had been sent in as reinforcement. Goodall managed to give them the slip and crossed the inner ditch with a plan and made way from the outer to the inner ramparts that ran parallel. Despite the steady success, as Lushington notes: 'Neither officers, nor men, knew when they could, with safety, arrest the hand of victory, for both had been taught by mournful experience, that there was no hope of mercy from Tippoo, or of peace with him, or those under his command whilst his power and life remained. The path of the soldiers was therefore destructive and sanguinary.'[52]

As Bayly mentioned above, Baird discovered a second ditch full of water within the outer wall and was initially flustered at the prospect of crossing it as it seemed insurmountable. As the column marched forward along the ramparts, a seemingly God-sent scaffolding was discovered. Baird used it to cross the inner ditch and, in less than an hour, reached the Bangalore Gate in the centre of the eastern face of the fort. He let his men catch their breath and have some refreshments there. Majors Allan, Beatson and Dallas joined Baird at the Bangalore Gate and conveyed to him the intelligence that they had received from Sayyid Sahib of the Sultan being in the palace.

By then, two fresh battalions of sepoys had arrived and since almost every post of the ramparts was under their control, Baird was fully convinced that the Sultan would make no defence as it was a losing battle now. He directed Major Allan to proceed with a flag of truce to the palace and offer protection to the Sultan and his family if he immediately and unconditionally surrendered. If he showed any resistance, the palace was to be immediately attacked and every man there put to death. Though they had blocked all roads of retreat and escape, the British suspected that Tipu might give them the slip.

In fact, they had heard intelligence and rumours that Tipu felt the greatest anxiety with regard to his family. In the last few days, he had been making veiled references to destroying certain important papers and putting to death his principal women, even as he wanted to die defending the palace.[53] Beatson surmises that this was perhaps driven by the fear that given the terrible inhumanities and tortures that he had meted out on the British prisoners, it was least likely that they would reciprocate with any kindness to him or his family.[54] In fact, just a few days before the siege, and even while farcical negotiations were underway between the two sides, thirteen European prisoners who were languishing in the dungeons of Srirangapatna had been brutally put to death 'by breaking their necks in twisting the head, while the body was held fast'.[55] These included some of the unfortunate men who had lost their way on 6 April during the initial attack on the fort. Their bodies were then rolled up in mats and buried outside the fort. So, in the case of a tragic outcome, he was sure that the British would square up with him and his family. Baird thus wanted to ascertain that the Sultan was alive and so was his family. The task fell on Major Alexander Allan, who was regarded as a considerate and humane person. Major Allan had trained in warfare and diplomacy under Medows and Cornwallis.

Armed with a battalion of sepoys, Allan then proceeded to the palace with a white cloth tied to a sergeant's pike. Upon reaching, he saw Major Shee drawn up on the outside of the palace and, on a front balcony, several of Tipu's family and officers had assembled, with fear and worry writ large on their faces. The killedar Mir Nadim stepped

out and took Allan inside the palace where he met a courtyard filled
with worried looking men. Allan tried to ascertain from the body
language and conduct of the inmates about the whereabouts of their
Sultan. In his account, Allan mentions: 'I particularly remarked,
that one person prostrated himself before he sat down; from which
circumstance I was led to conclude, that Tippoo, with such of his
officers who had escaped from the assault had taken shelter in
the palace.'[56]

Allan amply assured them all of complete protection. To assuage
their fears, he promised to stay on with them and even surrendered
his sword to Mir Nadim, which he accepted rather unwillingly. He
wanted to meet Tipu's sons who were reluctant to come out. Allan
told them that delays would be attended with fatal consequences for
them all. He noticed people hastily moving backwards and forwards
in the interior of the palace. Tipu's men on the terrace urged Allan
to hold the flag in a more conspicuous position to give confidence to
those in the palace. Growing restless by the delay, Allan sent another
word for the princes. They sent back a message that until a royal
carpet was spread to receive them by the British officers, they would
not come out.

Finally, the carpet was laid. The young princes, one of whom
was Muiz-ud-din, the young boy who had been sent as hostage to
Cornwallis, and another son whose name is unmentioned, finally
made their appearance. They were understandably in a state of panic.
For young Muiz-ud-din, it must have been a sense of déjà vu as
just a few years ago, he had similarly faced the British during his
captivity as a hostage. Allan recounts: 'The recollection of Mozadeen
[sic], who on a former occasion I had seen delivered up with his
brother, as hostage to Marquis Cornwallis, the sad reverse of their
fortunes, the thought that however much their father deserved our
resentment, they were blameless, their fears which notwithstanding
their struggles to conceal, was but too evident, excited the strongest
emotions of compassion in my mind.'[57] Allan gently led them by the
hand and made them sit down, assuring them of all safety. On being

questioned further about their father, they consistently maintained that he was not in the palace.

By then, Baird, too, reached the palace and Allan asked the permission of the young princes to have the gates of the palace opened for Baird. This alarmed them and their attendants immensely, but seeing that it was the only option available and seemingly convinced by Allan's assurances, they complied. But by then, Baird insisted that the princes come out to meet him. This was met with violent protests and objections by the adherents. But being a practical young man, Muiz-ud-din decided that compliance with the orders was the best recourse at such a critical juncture.

At that moment, perhaps driven by his own immense hatred for the Sultan for the tortures meted on him and his fellow prisoners and the report that reached him of Tipu's murder of the thirteen prisoners a few days ago, Baird lost his cool and violated Allan's promise to the princes. When they stuck to their repeated line that their father was not in the palace and they had no knowledge of his whereabouts, he yelled at them, threatening to search the innermost recesses of the palace if they did not spill the beans to him. However, he quickly gathered his composure and treated the princes warmly thereafter. Their earnest faces, fear-filled innocent eyes and solemn declarations convinced the British that they were indeed unaware of where their father had gone. The princes were then ushered away outside the fort before it became too dark, under the command of Lt Col Agnew and Captain Marriot. Under an escort, they were taken to the camp of the Commander-in-Chief.

Tipu's forces at the palace were ordered to be completely disarmed. Baird now proceeded to ransack the palace, along with Allan and Lt Col Barry Close, refraining however from entering the zenana or women's apartments. They however left a sufficient force outside the zenana to preclude any possibility of the Sultan running out of it, should he be hiding there. The question, paramount on the minds of everyone in the palace, be it Tipu's family or the British as they sullenly watched the sun set on a tumultuous day, was where was the Sultan?

What Happened to Tipu?

After leaving his meal unfinished, Tipu had mounted his horse and stormed out of his inner apartments with a war cry on his lips, and a few attendants, including his faithful physician Raja Khan and two or three eunuchs. He took his sword that was kept in a rich belt, slung over his right shoulder and a small cartridge bag hung to an embroidered belt, thrown over his left shoulder.[58] Tipu intended to proceed towards the breach; it had finally dawned on him that the breach was large enough to let the enemy inside. But by then, since the breach had been already occupied by the British and their columns had divided themselves to enter the fort, it is unlikely that Tipu would have marched even a few miles. He saw that several of his men had by then fled or lay dead. He fell back from traverse to traverse along the northern face of the fort. Within about 200 yards of the breach, he even fired seven or eight times with his own hand at assailants whom he saw nearby. Raja Khan had reported later that three or four Europeans were killed by this firing from the Sultan.[59] At one of these places, he complained of immense pain in his leg—the result of the fall he had experienced in Travancore at the attack of the Lines that had left him with a permanent limp. He asked for his favourite mare to be brought in and mounted her. Raja Khan dutifully clung to him on this last sortie.

Even at this late stage, his few confidants advised him that given the hopeless and perilous situation the fort found itself in, it was sensible to escape through the sallyport or water gate that was nearby. This strategy would have been just what his father Haidar Ali had done in the wake of the treachery of Khande Rao, by swimming across the river, escaping to Bangalore, regrouping himself and attacking the opponent.

Sensing the perilous condition, Tipu showed an inclination to do so. But unfortunately for him, the traitor, his Dewan, Mir Sadak, who had followed him to keep a watch on his movements, had got the water gate shut, knowing well that this would have been the last refuge for his escape. Beatson however states that the water gate 'was so much crowded that he [Tipu] could not make his way to the town.'[60] Mir Sadak then hurried away towards another gate towards the Shahar Ganjam which offered another route to escape. He wanted to have this gate shut too, when a man came forward to him and abused him in the vilest form: 'Thou accursed wretch! Thou hast delivered a righteous prince up to his enemies, and thou now saving thyself by flight? I will place the punishment of thy offence by thy side!'[61] Saying so, he charged at the shocked Dewan and, with one swift stroke of his sword, beheaded the traitor, Mir Sadak. As Kirmani states, 'his [Mir Sadak's] impure body was dragged into a place of filth and uncleanness and left there.'[62] It is said that for long, passers-by spat at the spot where Mir Sadak was killed and some also hurled their shoes there, cursing him with vile abuses for betraying the Sultan.[63] As Mohibbul Hasan records: 'They [Mysore soldiers] mangled his [Mir Sadak] body in a shocking manner. Even after he was buried, his body was dug up and for over two weeks it was treated with insult by men, women and children, who assembled around it and threw filth on it. Strong measures had to be taken by the English to put a stop to this. Even now, people who revere Tipu's memory, while visiting Seringapatam [sic], throw stones towards the spot where Mir Sadiq was killed.'[64]

Meanwhile, a slightly wounded Tipu, ordered the water gate to be opened. But none of them obeyed his command. His treacherous killedar, Mir Nadim, who stood on the roof of the gate, conveniently ignored his master's command and looked the other way.[65] The last opportunity of escape and survival too was thus lost to Tipu.

With few options left, Tipu decided to burst forth into the ramparts for the defence of the crumbling fort. He perhaps did not anticipate the quantum of the risks involved or the size of the intruding army. He possibly naively believed that his presence would enthuse the soldiers defending the fort and they could together drive the enemy out. Raja Khan, the only man who shadowed Tipu in those last moments of his life, declared later that he had no idea what the Sultan intended to do or where he was planning to rush to or escape. Tipu proceeded towards the gateway that led from the centre of the northern ramparts to the interior of the fortress. On arriving there, he was now exposed fully to the fire, not only of the assailants on the northern rampart, but also of Goodall's detachment.

Under this firing, the Sultan's mare was hit and fell dead. The Sultan himself received a deep wound on his chest, in addition to those that he had already received on his march there. He was even shot at on the left breast by a volley that was being exchanged. Raja Khan attempted to disengage Tipu from the saddle and place him in a palanquin that was there. But in the process, both master and physician fell over each other on a heap of dead bodies that lay strewn. Tipu's turban too fell to the ground. Half-fainting by then, Tipu's lower body was completely entangled amongst corpses. Raja Khan, who lay beside and had himself been badly shot in the foot, urged Tipu to make himself known to the enemy so that he would be protected. But Tipu stoutly turned down the offer.[66] 'Are you mad? Be silent!' he is said to have admonished Raja Khan.[67]

By then, all hell had broken loose and mayhem ensued. The British had taken complete control over the fort, and they turned all the guns from the outer and inner ramparts towards the Mysorean troops that were attempting to flee. These harried men were running towards the gateway where Tipu was and, in a state of utter fright, dropped from the broken walls or threw themselves into the ditch. The multitudes of innocent inhabitants of the Srirangapatna fort, too, were fleeing in utter terror and distress and, along with the Mysore troops that were escaping, they too came under the enemy fire. They were all indiscriminately slaughtered and the place was soon strewn with bodies, heaped one on top of the other. Sadly, the clothes of the dead caught fire from the paper of the cartridges of the British and this caused a gigantic inferno to ravage the place. This fire kept blazing for hours, consuming the gates and the mangled mass of the putrid bodies, consuming them all in one giant conflagration.

The Sultan was sitting amidst the corpses watching this dance of death unravel right in front of his eyes. He had barely been there for a few minutes, under an archway, than a group of British soldiers rushed there with their swords drawn. The gaze of one of these British grenadiers fell on the costly, bejewelled and glittering sword-belt that the Sultan was wearing and the gold buckle by which it was fastened. Not even realizing that it was Tipu Sultan of Mysore sitting there like a vanquished tiger amidst mangled corpses, the soldier tried to snatch the belt from this man. An enraged Sultan stretched out his right hand to grab a drawn sword that lay within his reach. He made a deep cut with the sword, inflicting a heavy wound on the grenadier's knee. He struck another soldier nearby and within reach of his assault. Writhing in pain and annoyed by this unknown man's insolence, the wounded grenadier promptly raised his musket and shot at the Sultan's temple. Other accounts say that at this moment, a musket ball lodged at his mouth, near his left cheek.[68]

The next instant, Tipu Sultan fell down dead, amidst the heap of bodies that lay strewn all around him.

As Beatson's account notes of the most sworn enemy of the British, with a word of caution for Tipu's biographers:

> Thus ended the life and the power of Tippoo Sultaun. It will require an able pen to delineate a character apparently so inconsistent; but he who attempts it must not decide hastily. Those who have served this campaign, victorious and brilliant as it has proved, will however I believe agree that the infantry of the Sultaun were not inferior to our own sepoys; and that had he been joined three or four months ago by four or five thousand French troops, which he had every reason to expect, the event might have been very different. What infinite credit then is due to the man who planned and saw the fit moment to execute measures which, perhaps, have saved us from ruin![69]

The Search Party

By the time the sun had set on the gloomy fort of Srirangapatna on that ill-fated day of 4 May 1799, the British were fully in command of all the major frontiers and posts. But the fear of the Sultan's whereabouts and his possible return still loomed large. Having fought him for decades, the British knew that he was a master at springing surprises and could burst forth from nowhere suddenly and launch an attack. They had to see him, dead or alive, to get rid of these apprehensions. General Baird was losing his patience and he finally threatened Mir Nadim of dire consequences if he did not cooperate with the search for the Sultan. At this, Mir Nadim swore on Allan's sword that was with him and told Baird that the Sultan was not in the palace and, when last heard of, he was wounded and lay near a gateway on the north face of the fort. He even offered to conduct the British search party to find the Sultan. Accordingly, a group of people were assembled, that included Baird, Col Wellesley and Allan, to search for their dreaded foe.

The journey of the search party through the ramparts of the fort was literally like one through the stairways of hell. Heaps and heaps of dead bodies lay rotting and half-burnt, one over another. Vultures had already begun to position themselves for their feast. The multitude of bodies and the pitch darkness made it difficult to distinguish one from the other. Holding a lantern, the party kept dragging bodies out and Mir Nadim and a few others were identifying them. This seemed like an endless exercise, but had to be endured to provide certainty to the status of the Sultan's life. During the search, they suddenly saw the Sultan's palanquin and a little behind it, was the dead body of his favourite mare. Beside it, they noticed some slight movement and an agonized moan and accosted the man. He was Raja Khan, still alive, though terribly wounded and fainting. They asked Raja Khan about the Sultan and he pointed in a certain direction.

Under the faint, glimmering light, the party then separated several corpses, beneath whom they finally saw a body that resembled Tipu's. Mir Nadim, on close examination, confirmed that it was indeed Tipu Sultan. The British were scared to even touch him as they were not sure if he was dead. His body was warm, his eyes wide open and his hands still firmly clasped the sword in a tight grip. As Allan recounts in his memoirs:

When Tippoo was brought from under the gateway, his eyes were open, and the body was so warm, that for a few moments, Colonel Wellesley and myself were doubtful whether he was not alive; on feeling his pulse and heart, the doubt was removed. He had four wounds, three in the body, and one in the temple; the ball having entered a little above the right ear, and lodged in the cheek. His dress consisted of a jacket of fine white linen, loose drawers of flowered chintz, with a crimson cloth of silk and cotton, round his waist; a handsome pouch with a red and green silk belt, hung across his shoulder; his head was uncovered, his turban being lost in the confusion of his fall; he had an amulet on his arm, but no ornament whatsoever. Tippoo was of low stature, corpulent, with high shoulders, and a short, thick neck, but his feet were remarkably small; his complexion was rather dark, his eyes large and prominent, with small arched eyebrows, and his nose aquiline: he had an appearance of dignity, or perhaps sternness, in his countenance, which distinguished him above the common order people.[70]

According to another eyewitness: 'The features were neither agitated by passion nor disfigured by the extinction of life—an uncommon degree of composure and serenity was spread over his face. The expression was gentle and contented. In fine, the countenance of the Sultan far from discovering any furious passions had a tranquil and courteous air for which he was distinguished when alive.'[71]

The relief and satisfaction and the quiet hurrah of the search party echoed through those ramparts that had seen so much death and destruction on that unfortunate day. The body was then placed in a palanquin and carried to the palace, where his officers and eunuchs crowded around, recognizing it as their master's, and loud wails and shrieks of grief and horror emanated. As Shama Rao laments: 'Thus terminated . . . the glory of a man who had left the palace in the morning as a powerful sovereign of an independent state, but who was brought back at night as a mere lump of clay, bereft of consciousness, his kingdom overthrown, his capital taken and his palace occupied by his enemies.'[72] It was an irony that Tipu's capital was taken by the same Baird whom he had tortured and imprisoned for four years at a place, scarcely 400 yards away from where his corpse was discovered.

With Tipu's death being now firmly established, General Baird ordered Major Beatson to communicate to the Commander-in-Chief that the storming party be relieved that night as they were thoroughly exhausted. General Harris then wrote triumphantly to Lord Mornington from his camp on the night of 4 May 1799:

> I have the pleasure to announce to you, that this day at one o'clock, a division of the army under my command assaulted Seringapatam, and that at half-past two, the place was entirely in our possession. Tippoo Sultaun fell in the assault. Two of his sons, the Sultan Padshah and Moize U' Deen, are prisoners, with many of the principal sirdars. Our loss is trifling, and our success has been complete. I will forward to your Lordship details thereafter.[73]

The Traitors and the Others

It must have astonished even the British that a fort considered so impregnable and strong fell to their storming in barely a few hours and with so few casualties on their side. As Lushington notes: 'There was nothing like that lengthened, awful and doubtful struggle for victory which had been anticipated in the storming of a fortress, whose works are, even in their ruin, still stupendous to look at, on whose walls were mounted 287 pieces of ordnance, whose arsenals were filled with every munition of war, and all the stores required for a protracted siege, whose available garrison was not less than 20,000 men, and whose leaders were men of known and desperate courage.'[74] One of the principal causes for the fall of Srirangapatna was undoubtedly the treachery and indifference of Tipu's principal officers and the easy pass they gave the British at many crucial places. The British accounts obviously do not dwell on this aspect much, as that takes away the sheen from their victory and gallantry, that they took a fort as celebrated as this through devious means.

It seems that these intrigues had been on for several years and many of the principal officers had been in touch with the British and other enemies of Tipu since 1797. While Mir Sadak's treachery was blatant, people like Purnaiya possibly operated more subtly, without leaving behind a trail. However, historian Mohibbul Hasan quotes British secret agents in Mysore to document that Purnaiya and Mir Sadak had been imprisoned by Tipu after their correspondence with the Nizam, the British and the Marathas was intercepted by him. He claims that they had then pledged to remain loyal thereafter and begged for his mercy and forgiveness, after which they were reinstated.[75] It is quite unlikely that Tipu would forgive treason and that too from such high-ranking, trusted officials. There are really no proven records of any of these alleged secret correspondences, especially of Purnaiya, though circumstantial evidence of their indifference at critical junctures of the siege and the storming, point to a degree of treachery. Kumr-ud-din's case was also quite blatant like that of Mir Sadak, as there are letters between him and the Nizam on sharing the spoils and territories in the event of a victory.[76] Shaikh Shehab-ud-din Khan, or Sady Behery as he was known, was an influential Mapillah and Tipu's revenue officer in Mangalore. He too had negotiated with the British to help their cause against his master, possibly because Tipu was planning to hand over the fort of Honnavar to the French, which was deeply resented.[77]

Despite British attempts to not overtly make much of these stories of treason on the part of Tipu's officers, in some of the official documents, one gets a hint of the active communication channels that existed between them and people in Srirangapatna. For instance, Wellesley alludes to this treachery and widespread discontent and ill will that existed in Tipu's establishment against him, in a secret letter he wrote to the Court of Directors on 13 February 1799: 'The whole tenor of my intelligence from Mysore induces me to believe, that there is a general aversion in Tippoo's councils and armies to his intimate connection with the French; and I have already received intimations from various parts of his dominions, and from some of his principal ministers and officers, which promise considerable advantage in the prosecution of hostilities against him.'[78] In his letter to Harris too, Wellesley stresses on this aspect of using the brewing discontent to their advantage:

> I have reason to believe that many of the tributaries, principal officers, and other subjects of Tippoo Sultaun, are inclined to throw off the authority of that Prince, and to place themselves under the protection of the Company and of our allies. The war in which we are again involved, by the treachery and violence of the Sultaun, renders it both just and expedient that we should avail ourselves, as much as possible, of the discontents and disaffection of his people. It is, therefore advisable to arrange a plan for the regular conduct of the negotiations connected with this object.[79]

Col Arthur Wellesley, in a letter to his brother Henry, writes on 31 October 1798 about Mir Sadak's communication with the Governor of Madras, Lord Clive, 'desiring leave to come into the Carnatic and to throw himself under the protection of the English.' In a dispassionate way, Col Wellesley rejects the proposal: 'I don't see what end it will answer to have Meer Saduck in our possession. Secondly, if he come, either we must give him up when we settle matters with Tippoo if he require it, or we must keep him contrary to his inclination, which is not unlikely to throw a great difficulty in the way of the negotiation. If he come for safety, without encouragement, he must expect to be given up if it suits our interests.'[80] Even in a letter to his brother, the Governor-General, as late as 16 February 1799, Col Wellesley talks about the overtures of Kumr-ud-din, 'the defection of Tippoo's subjects,' the repeated references to 'disaffected sect of Mussulmans' and how best to utilize these to their advantage.[81]

Interestingly, in 1942 during the Indian Historical Records Commission Proceedings, historian Dr K.N. Venkatasubba Sastri, a Fellow of UK's Royal Historical Society, presented a set of confidential papers belonging to William Petrie of the Madras Council. These were letters between 1790 and 1802 addressed to Henry Dundas and Lord Mornington. Sastri, in his paper, illustrates that among Petrie's various correspondences, the striking part was his analysis of the reasons for the British victory in both 1792 and 1799. After citing two reasons which are more military and strategic in nature, Petrie cites a third one, rather enigmatically:

> Of course, this is a theme on which I am silent here and on which I shall speak and write with great caution and reserve elsewhere. I am possessed of much information on this curious and edifying event [fall of Tipu in 1799], which is still lodged in my mind and from whence I may never have the leisure to extract it before many of the most important traces are erased from the tablets of my memory. But I can never forget on how many slender hairs and threads the fortunes of this great event has been suspended, almost any one of which breaking would have dangerously retarded, if not entirely frustrated, the grand object of the measure.[82]

Sastri surmises that this possibly points to a fifth-column activity within the capital before it fell, as was the popular belief in Mysore. He cites several folk songs or *lavanis* in Kannada that mention the conspiracy of some ministers of Tipu that led to his fall. He quotes Urdu poet, Sir Muhammad Iqbal, who had penned a poem on three Muslim traitors who conspired against Muslim power in India— Mir Jaffar, Mir Jumla and the third was Mir Sadak whose '"tomb" in Seringapatam is still spat at and beaten with shoes by every Muslim visitor.'[83] A Kannada biography of Purnaiya too was supposed to have featured around this time in Mysore where the author labours hard to disassociate his protagonist from any rumours of treachery. Sastri argues that unless there was a prevalent, conscious local tradition that suggested the same, there was no need for a refutation. He calls upon historians to investigate more into 'the dubious note in Petrie's tone and manner and decide whether he is after all suggesting something as awful and sinister in the character of those individuals on the side of the British who brought about the downfall of Tippu Sultan.'[84]

Denys Forest, however, dismisses some of these suggestions and does not attribute treachery as the principal reason for the fall of Srirangapatna and its Sultan. He argues that there is not the slightest allusion to such treachery in the several eyewitness accounts that wrote copiously about the wars. It is quite improbable that everyone down the order also conspired to keep such acts of collusion under wraps, he states. Moreover, the enemies of the British establishment would have made a big deal of it in the press and in the politics back home in England, or even in India, if these stories of collusion had gained ground and credence with time.[85] Undoubtedly, while there was widespread discontent and treachery against Tipu, his own bad leadership, terrible follies, missed opportunities and lack of strategic moves at critical points cost him dearly in this decisive battle.

Whatever be the reasons, the fall of Srirangapatna and its dreaded Sultan was a momentous event in the history of India. The General Orders of Wellesley, issued by 15 May 1799, clearly declared: 'The events of the 4th of May, while they have surpassed even the sanguine expectations of the Governor-General in Council, have raised the reputation of the British arms in India to a degree of splendour and glory unrivalled in the military history of this quarter of the globe, and seldom approached in any part of the world. The lustre of this victory can be equalled only by the substantial advantages which it promises to establish, by restoring the peace and safety of the British possessions in India on a durable foundation of genuine security.'[86]

With this, the curtains came down not only on the Fourth and Last Anglo–Mysore War, but also on one of the most important epochs in the history of modern India, one that led to the firm establishment of the British Empire as the paramount power in the country after the last major bastion of resistance against it was breached.

18

Sunset over Srirangapatna

The sunrise of 5 May 1799 deceptively concealed the mammoth destruction, plunder, loot and rape of Srirangapatna that had occurred all through the previous day, well into the wee hours of the night. There was seemingly a wilful allowance to the battle-weary British soldiers to plunder the helpless capital of their beaten foe.[1] Even Governor-General Wellesley rationalized: 'The army conceive that as the place was taken by storm, they are of right entitled to what was found in it.'[2] Each soldier was allowed to fill their coffers as best as they could. The unfortunate inhabitants of Srirangapatna—old men, women and children in their thousands, were allowed to leave the fort by night. They took shelter behind the old walls and hedges in the neighbourhood of the camp. Allan had stayed on in the fort till past midnight before he reached the General's tent. To his surprise, the princes were not there, but they joined shortly thereafter. They had apparently refused to use palanquins and had crossed the breach and river by foot, which took them such a long time to reach the camp. Mir Nadim and other principal officers were handed over by Allan to Captain Macleod's charge, before he retired for the day to 'ruminate on the events of the day even to the most extraordinary I had ever witnessed, and which so much more resembled fictions of the brain than reality, that it was impossible to form a calm and connected idea of them.'[3]

After an exhausting day, Baird decided to catch some rest on the verandah of the palace. But his sleep was interrupted when he heard that fires had broken out all over Srirangapatna, that camp followers had broken into the town on the pretext of bringing in refreshments for their masters and large-scale arson and looting had followed.[4] The inhabitants of the capital bore the brunt of innumerable atrocities. Many were beaten or threatened with death if they did not disclose their wealth and property. Women collected in the streets in vigil all night in several large groups to prevent any acts of possible dishonour. The houses of Tipu's principal officers and sirdars were pillaged. Though guards were placed at Tipu's treasury which housed an enormous amount of wealth and jewels, some of the troops even managed to break into this treasury through an unguarded entrance and officers were themselves found admonishing their men to stop looting and filling their pockets, caps and everything that they could catch hold of, in order to stuff the valuables that they had discovered.[5] Among the valuables that were taken away was a casket of jewels alone worth Rs 45,00,000.[6] Baird's efforts to restrain the plunder bore little fruit. As an eyewitness, Col Bayly recounts the horrific events of the night of 4 May 1799 in his diary:

> The fortress now became one wild scene of plunder and confusion, but poor Woodhall and his men were appointed to extinguish the flames of some burning houses in the vicinity of the grand magazine of gunpowder, which, had it ignited, would have blown the whole garrison, friends and foes, into the air. He performed this arduous duty effectually, and although first in the town, his company were the only part of the regiment who did not reap any pecuniary reward for such daring heroism. The rest of the troops had filled their muskets, caps, and pockets with zechins, pagodas, rupees and ingots of gold. One of our grenadiers, by name Platt, deposited in my hands, to the amount of fifteen hundred pounds' worth of the precious metals, which in six months afterwards he had dissipated in drinking, horse-racing, cock-fighting and gambling.[7]

The large-scale plunder, following Tipu's death, was also seen as a failure on the part of Baird, despite his attempts which had led to victory that day in Srirangapatna. It became a convenient way to castigate Baird and place Lord Mornington's favourite, his younger brother, in command, even as tranquillity was being slowly restored in the fort. Colonel Arthur Wellesley was sent in to restore order in the fort, much to 'the great dismay and indignation of General Baird.'[8] There had always been a simmering rivalry between the two men, but this act of superseding him after his stellar achievement was too much for Baird to take. Arthur Wellesley immediately took over the fort and introduced severe measures to curb the plunder, including hanging eighteen sepoys. Baird bitterly remonstrated against what he perceived as utter injustice to be shunted away in this manner after leading such a successful campaign. But it seemed General Harris had been briefed by the Governor-General that his brother should be placed in command of the place after it fell. Baird retired in disgust from the Army.

Numerous applications were made to the newly appointed caretaker of the fallen fort, Col Wellesley, 'for male guards, to protect those families, who to avoid the fury of our troops after the storm, had concealed themselves in different parts of the Fort.'[9] It was a humungous task that lay ahead of Col Wellesley to restore some semblance of order amidst the raging madness and mayhem. In his letter to his brother, the Governor-General, Col Arthur Wellesley records after taking charge of the fort:

> It was impossible to expect that after the labour which the troops had undergone in working up the place, and the various successes they had in six different affairs with Tippoo's troops, in all of which they had come to the bayonet with them, they should not have looked to the plunder of this place. Nothing therefore can have exceeded what was done on the night of the 4th. Scarcely a house in the town was left un-plundered, and I understand that in camp jewels of the greatest value, bars of gold etc. have been offered for sale in the bazaars of the army by our soldiers, sepoys, and followers. I came in to take the command on the morning of the 5th and by the greatest exertion, by hanging, flogging etc. in the

course of that day I restored order among the troops, and I hope I have gained the confidence of the people. They are returning to their houses and beginning again to follow their occupations, but the property of every one is gone.[10]

The Last Rites

By the morning of 5 May, Abdul Khaliq, the second son of Tipu, who was earlier a hostage of Cornwallis, surrendered to Baird. He had been commanding the southern face of the fort the previous day, but had managed to flee when the troops stormed inside. Colonel Dalrymple, who was posting guards at the Daria Dowlat Bagh, saw a small group of horsemen on the north bank of the river waving a white handkerchief at him. He sent Captain Geraud to enquire who these men were and what they wanted. They revealed to him that they were there on behalf of one of Tipu's sons who wished to surrender on the condition of personal protection and preservation of his life and dignity. When Geraud assured them this, they were led to a hideout where he met Abdul Khaliq. So terrified was Abdul Khaliq of the British soldiers that he 'exacted a promise from Captain Geraud, not to quit him till he reached the General's [Baird] tent.'[11] He was then led to Baird with every mark of respect and warmth and then led to call on General Harris who also gave him every assurance of life and honour. Relieved, Abdul Khaliq sat down for refreshments with Mir Alam. On his way to the fort, he was told about the sad fate that had befallen his father who had fallen in the assault. He was ushered to the palace and then allowed to see his father's body. Allan records that 'when the curtain of the palanquin was drawn aside and he beheld his father's corpse . . . he shewed no emotion, either of pity or grief, but turning with seeming indifference from a sight which affected even common beholders,'[12] he began speaking to Col Wellesely who stood beside. Abdul Khaliq requested an early and honourable burial for his deceased father, preferably beside his father, Haidar Ali, in the mausoleum in the Lal Bagh. The other two princes in Harris's camp, too, were then informed about the tragic fate that had befallen their father and sent back to the palace, where they were inconsolable.

General Harris requested Mir Alam to organize the burial as per Islamic rituals and befitting every honour for a deceased ruler. The head qazi was then summoned, and the body was covered with fine muslins and rich clothes and placed in a state palanquin. At half past four, the funeral procession started from Tipu's palace towards Lal Bagh. The bier was carried by the servants of the palace, and was preceded by two companies of British troops. Abdul Khaliq followed behind the bier on horseback, with the killedar and several Muslims on foot, with two companies in the rear. During this procession, the qazi chanted verses from the Quran, and several attendants joined the chanting. As the procession made its way through the streets, several inhabitants prostrated themselves as the body passed by and cried aloud, lamenting the fate that had befallen their Sultan. Mir Alam and other officers of the Nizam were with Captain Malcolm to receive the procession as it slowly wound its way to Lal Bagh. They paid their respects to the deceased and joined the procession. As the entourage reached the mausoleum, the British troops lined themselves on both sides and offered a gun salute and arms. A salute of minute guns, corresponding to the age of the dead Sultan, was also given. Abdul Khaliq had initially objected to the presence of troops or the firing of guns, but consented after being told that it was the British way of offering tributes to the departed Sultan.[13] The body was then laid to rest beside that of Haidar Ali and all the prayers and ceremonies were conducted. An inscription was placed on the tomb: 'The light of Islam and the faith left this world. Tippu became a martyr for the faith of Muhammad. The sword was lost. The offspring of Haidar was a great martyr.'[14] On behalf of Col Wellesley, Rs 5000 was distributed to the qazi who conducted the ceremonies and also to the fakirs and poor who had gathered there with tears streaming down their eyes.

Several elegiac verses were composed on the occasion in honour of Tipu, as the translated one below:

Tippu Sultan was slain expectedly. He shed his blood for the sake of the religion of the True God on Saturday the 28th Zikad. The

Day of Judgment manifested itself at the seventh hour from the morning. Blood flowed from every wall and door in the streets of Seringapatam. His heart was ever bent on religious warfare and at length he obtained the crown of martyrdom, even as he desired. Ah! At the destruction of this prince and of his kingdom, let the world shed tears of blood. For him the Sun and the Moon shared equally in grief. The heavens were turned upside down and the earth darkened. When I (the poet) saw the sorrow for him pervaded all, I asked Grief for the year of his death, and an angel (Hatif) replied: 'Let us mourn his loss with burning sighs and tears, for the light of the religion of Islam has departed from the world.'[15]

As the poet stated above, scarcely had Tipu's remains been laid to rest than the skies suddenly got overcast and a tremendous storm followed, accompanied by thunder, lightning and heavy rain for hours. In this surreal and almost supernatural occurrence, it almost felt that the skies had opened up to lament the tragedy that had struck the island capital. It seemed like Srirangapatna needed to be washed so thoroughly as to cleanse the bloodstains of the thousands who had died in the bloody war. Col Bayly recounts these horrifying incidents of 5 May 1799 in his diary:

About five o'clock a darkness of unusual obscurity came on, and volumes of huge clouds were hanging within a few yards of the earth, in a motionless state. Suddenly, a rushing wind, with irresistible force, raised pyramids of sand to an amazing height, and swept most of the tents and marquees in frightful eddies, far from their site. Ten Lascars, with my own exertions, clinging to the bamboos of the marquee scarcely preserved its fall. The thunder cracked in appalling peals close to our ears and the vivid lightning tore up the ground in long ridges all around. Such a sense of desolation can hardly be imagined; Lascars struck dead, as also an officer and his wife in a marquee a few yards from mine. Bullocks, elephants and camels broke loose and scampering in every direction over the plain; every hospital tent blown away, leaving the wounded exposed unsheltered to the elemental strife.

In one of these alone eighteen men who had suffered amputation had all the bandages saturated, and were found dead on the spot the ensuing morning. The funeral party escorting Tippoo's body to the mausoleum of his ancestors, situated in the Lal Bagh Garden . . . were overtaken at the commencement of this furious whirlwind, and the soldiers ever after were impressed with a firm persuasion that his Satanic majesty attended in person at the funeral procession. The flashes of lightning were not usual from far distant clouds, but proceeded from heavy vapours within a very few yards of the earth. No park of artillery could have vomited forth such incessant peals as the loud thunder that exploded close to our ears. Astonishment, dismay and prayers for its cessation was our solitary alternative. A fearful description of the Day of Judgment might have been depicted from the appalling storm of this awful night. I have experienced hurricanes, typhoons and gales of wind at sea, but never in the whole course of my existence had I seen anything comparable to this desolating visitation. Heaven and earth appeared absolutely to have come in collision, and no bounds set to the destruction. The roaring of winds strove in competition with the stunning explosions of the thunder, as if the universe was once more returning to chaos. In one of these wild sweeps of the hurricane, the poles of my tent were riven to atoms, and the canvas wafted forever from my sight. I escaped without injury, as also my exhausted Lascars, and casting myself in an agony of despair on the sands, I fully expected instant annihilation. My hour was not, however, come. Towards morning the storm subsided; the clouds became more elevated, the thunder and lightning ceased, and nature once more resumed a serene aspect. But never shall I forget that dreadful night to the latest day of my existence. All language is inadequate to describe its horrors. Rather than be exposed to such another scene, I would prefer the front of a hundred battles.[16]

Had this giant storm broken out twenty-four hours earlier when the storming of the fort had commenced, the course of the last Anglo–Mysore War, and of Indian history itself, might have been different.

In the war between 4 April and 4 May, on the British front, twenty-two officers were killed and forty-five wounded, 181 non-commissioned rank and file European officers were killed, 622 wounded and twenty-two missing. A total of 119 natives in their army were killed, 420 wounded and 100 went missing. In all, 1531 men were affected, of whom 322 were killed, 1087 wounded and 122 were missing.[17] There were no clear numbers on the casualties suffered by the Mysoreans, especially during the storming operations. However, Allan records the numbers in Tipu's army at the commencement of the war. There were 47,470 fighting men excluding lascars and pioneers, 3503 stable horse, 9392 Silledar or irregular horse, 23,483 regular infantry, 6209 armed militia, 4747 Ashaam or peons, 101 Bakshis or Brigadiers, nine Meer Subdurs or Generals—overall about 94,537 men, whose upkeep and maintenance cost 2,92,349 Canteroi Pagodas or 2,43,624 Star Pagodas.[18]

The Treasures of Srirangapatna

The property that was seized on the fall of Srirangapatna was estimated at 40,30,300 Star Pagodas, equivalent to £1,600,000. The jewels were later estimated at Rs 36 lakh or £360,000.[19] The military stores seized were valued at Rs 10 lakh. The total number of ordnance captured was 929, including guns, mortars and howitzers, 176 of which were twelve-pounders and over.[20] In the palace, the British seized a bejewelled throne, a dazzling howdah, matchlocks and swords, plates of solid gold and silver, costly carpets and Chinaware, ivory chairs and abundant precious gems.

The idea was to consolidate all the treasures and apportion some of it as the 'Seringapatam Prize Fund' to award gallantry displayed in this crucial war. A board of officers, under Gen. Floyd as the President, was constituted to evaluate, make an inventory of all the captured property and treasures, and suggest distribution of the same. They found an astonishing amount of wealth in the form of lakhs of specie (money as coins), gold and silver plates, jewels, rich and valuable materials, precious stones and other costly and antique articles. Several of these belonged to the dispossessed Hindu royal family or the submissions from other rulers and palegars who had been won in war. The jewels were found in large dark rooms that were strongly secured and were deposited in boxes closed under the seal of Tipu or of Haidar.[21] Rich furniture, costly and ornate palanquins, carpets, the finest muslins and silks, and exquisite garments too were discovered. The fine garments alone were reckoned to be the quantity of 500 camel-loads.[22] There were also telescopes and optical glasses, pictures and paintings, chinaware and glassware that was sufficient to form a large mercantile warehouse.

The Committee also found twenty granaries and seven godowns with immense quantities of paddy, ragi, salt, pepper and horse-gram stored in the eventuality of a long siege. The oldest paddy stocked in was almost eleven years old and in good condition. Between 4000 and 5000 draught and carriage bullocks and some of the finest stallions and mares were also found. Several of the iron ordnance and all the fifty-one brass six-pounders were of British manufacture and the others cast in Tipu's own foundry were seen to be as perfect.

The total value of the specie, jewels, military and other stores spared by the pillagers of Srirangapatna seems to have been about £2,000,000.[23] How much of this was to be apportioned to the Nizam was to be determined by the percentage of his troops present during the final siege and storming operations.[24] But much was found that never made its way to this fund. As Henry Dodwell details for instance: 'A soldier of the 74th [Regiment] was related to have found Tipu's armlets, set with great diamonds; he passed them on to a Company's surgeon for 1,500 rupees; and the surgeon, after carrying them about round his waist for two years, sold them for a sum that brought him in £2,000 a year, of which he not ungenerously allowed £200 to the private. The prize fund itself was reckoned at 5,000,000 pagodas or £2,000,000; and such was the difficulty of disposing of the jewels at a fair price that many officers received their share in jewels.'[25]

As the Commander-in-Chief of the victorious campaign, Gen. Harris received about one-eighth of the total prize fund that was pegged at £2,000,000, i.e., £142,902.[26] A gorgeous emerald necklace, that was initially valued at £20,000, was also allotted to him. Harris however had lots of issues with the necklace that he complained as being 'full of flaws' and challenged the Prize agents and secured alternative baubles.[27] Price recounts how 'Sir David Baird made his appearance at the Prize table, exhibiting with anger, ill-suppressed, a large ruby ring, which he said was allotted to him at the value of 1,000 sultaunies, but which, on being taken out of the setting, proved to be nothing more than a lump of coloured glass, not worth even as many cowries.'[28] Numerous such complaints continued pouring in from even the senior-most officers, more than 1000 commissioned officers, who received a share in the fund.[29] Mir Alam was given a lakh of pagodas to be distributed among 6000 of Hyderabad cavalry. But both he and the Nizam felt that this was a very paltry sum, compared to the services they had rendered, and were consequently very irked and discontented.[30]

Major Price gives us an interesting first-person account of how he, along with six other Prize agents, had their task cut out. On the first day that they took charge of the specie, they sat down to count the coins and found no less than 12 lakh sultani pagodas. At Rs 4 to the sultani pagoda, this was about Rs 48 lakh or nearly half a million sterling. This was despite a night of pillage and loot that had taken place on 4–5 May 1799, with coins strewn all over the place on the western verandah that led to the Toshakhana or treasury. Some of the most exquisite pearls found their way to the bazars where soldiers had traded them for bottles of spirits.[31] After counting the remaining coins, the Prize Committee sealed them up in bags of 1000 each and congratulated one another for having become richer by 10,000 than they were in the morning at the start of this exercise. The Prize Committee even searched the apartments of the zenana, lest there should be any treasures and properties concealed there.[32]

The newly assembled throne of Tipu that he had never mounted was dismantled and parts of it sent to different places in Britain. The gilded tiger's head and the Humma bird were sent to adorn the treasures of Windsor Castle. A lot of the gold in the throne was removed and distributed too. A diamond star and ornaments were gifted to Marquess Wellesley for his gallant stewardship in this war. Wellesley later regretted this decision of breaking up such a magnificent throne which could have instead been gifted to the King of England. Attempts were made to retrieve it, but by then a lot of the gold had been melted away and distributed. Wellesley also took charge of several items of Tipu's clothing to prevent them from being appropriated by potential rebels as sacred relics of their martyred Sultan. This included '84 turbans, 50 pocket handkerchiefs, 26 caps and two green war helmets dipped in the fountain of Zum-Zum and deemed to be invulnerable.'[33] Three of his hunting cheetahs were sent as gifts to King George III.

Tipu's turban, one of his swords and a sword of Murar Rao of Gutti were sent as presents to Lord Cornwallis who was instrumental in first reducing Tipu's strength. A sword found in Tipu's bedroom was publicly presented by General Harris to the sulking General Baird for his having led the storming party to success on 4 May. The main sword of Tipu that he always used was presented in a public ceremony at Madras by Major Allan to Governor-General Wellesley on 30 May 1799. Allan was made the Aid-de-Camp of the Governor-General in recognition of his services. On the handle of the sword was the following inscription:

> My victorious sabre is lightning for the destruction of the unbelievers. Haidar, the Lord of the Faith, is victorious for my advantage. And, moreover, he destroyed the wicked race who were unbelievers. Praise be to him, who is the Lord of the Worlds! Thou are our Lord, support us against the people who are unbelievers. He to whom the Lord giveth victory prevails over all (mankind). Oh Lord, make him victorious, who promoteth [sic] the faith of Muhammad. Confound him, who refuseth [sic] the faith of Muhammad; and withhold us from those who are so inclined. The Lord is predominant over his own works. Victory and conquest are from the Almighty. Bring happy tidings, Oh Muhammad, to the faithful; for God is the kind protector and is the most merciful

of the merciful. If God assists thee, thou wilt prosper. May the Lord God assist thee, Oh Muhammad, with mighty victory.[34]

On several of his *furzees* or blunderbusses, the following inscription in Persian was found: 'This incomparable piece, belonging to the Sultan of the East, which has no equal, but in the most vivid lightning, will annihilate the enemy that it strikes, although Fate should otherwise have ordained him to live.'[35] On some gold medals, on one side was written in Persian: 'Of God, the bestower of Blessings!' and on the other side, 'Victory and conquest are from the Almighty.'[36] These were all struck perhaps in commemoration of the victories of the 1780s.

The British also found a stone inscription in the palace. Perhaps it was kept ready after Tipu's humiliating defeat in 1792. Meant to be put up at a prominent position on the fort walls in Srirangapatna, it read:

Oh! Almighty God! Dispose the whole body of infidels! Scatter their tribe, cause their feet to stagger! Overthrow their councils! Change their State! Destroy their very root! Cause death to be near them, cut off from them the means of sustenance! Shorten their days! Be their bodies the constant object of their cares (i.e. infest them with diseases), deprive their eyes of sight, make black their faces (i.e. bring shame and disgrace on them), destroy in them the organs of speech! Slay them as Shedaud (i.e. the Prince who presumptuously aimed at establishing a paradise for himself and was slain by command of God); drown them as Pharoah was drowned, and visit them with the severity of thy wrath. Oh Avenger! Oh! Universal Father! I am depressed and overpowered, grant me thy assistance.[37]

An equal treasure of a different kind was Tipu's vast, fine library. Initially it was decided to gift the valuables in the library to the Court of Directors, to establish a foundation for Eastern Literature. Later, they were shifted to the newly founded College at Fort William in

Calcutta. Only a very ornate and beautiful Quran, written in elegant styles and ornamentations, was shipped back to London to be placed in the library of Windsor Castle. This Quran was believed to have belonged to Aurangzeb and cost Rs 9000.[38] Tipu's library had a wide-ranging, eclectic collection of over 2000 volumes in several branches of Asiatic literature, with theology as the favoured area of interest. There were manuscripts and volumes in Persian, Arabic, Urdu and Hindi that dealt with prose and poetry in Hindi, Urdu, Dekhani, Persian and other languages, mathematics, jurisprudence, history, Sufism, physics, lexicography, medicine, *Hadis* and several other topics. It was believed that several of these were possessions of the Sultans of Bijapur and Golconda, but a majority of them had been acquired during the conquest of Chittoor, Savanur and Cudappah. There was also a curious Persian manuscript on magic which the prize agents read with much amusement and interest. These books and manuscripts were all, however, badly maintained and dumped in a dark room in the south-eastern angle of the upper verandah of the palace's inner quadrangle. Price writes that 'they were heaped together in hampers, covered with leather; to consult which it was necessary to discharge the whole contents on the floor.'[39] One of the princes who had been permitted to sit there as Price and other agents rummaged through the heap of books and manuscripts was overheard one day, whispering softly to one of his attendants: 'Only see how these hogs are allowed to contaminate my father's books!'[40]

Additionally, the library was a treasure trove of several state papers, secret correspondences of Tipu with political players within and outside India, Tipu's own journals, diaries and an account of his dreams that he maintained, the papers of Haidar Ali right from the time of his usurpation of Mysore, the proceedings with the French including the Jacobin Club—all of which opened to the British a new window to the mind of the man who had haunted them for decades and was an enigma. With the greatest zeal, these papers were gathered, catalogued and translated. Col William Kirkpatrick, with his vast knowledge of oriental languages, including Persian, and the political situation in various Indian courts, was assigned the supervision of these records and their translation. All these records found in the palace were passed into the control of Marquis Wellesley. In his note to the Governor-General, Kirkpatrick summarized: 'All the foregoing papers relate, more or less to the hostile designs of the Sultaun against the British power in India. Besides these papers, there have been found other documents of a miscellaneous nature, and illustrative of the character and genius of Tippoo Sultaun's government, of the constitution of his military force, and of the resources of his dominions.'[41] The correspondence between Tipu and Raymond in the Hyderabad army and the various interactions with Ripaud, the French Directory and the Isle of France, as also with Zaman Shah, the Shah of Persia, the Poona Darbar and Daulat Rao Sindhia were of particular interest to the British to understand what intrigues other contemporary players were planning against their authority. Through his agents in Delhi, Tipu had even opened communication with such distant courts as those of 'Rajahs of Joadpoor and Jynaggur, but even the more remote and obscure Rajah of Napaul [Nepal?].'[42] In the presence of Munshi Habibullah, the Sultan's principal secretary, Kirkpatrick discovered the handwritten journal of Tipu's dreams that were found in a secret escritoire. Habibullah knew of the existence of such a journal but had no knowledge of where it might be found as 'the Sultaun always manifested peculiar anxiety to conceal it from the view of any who happened to approach, while he was reading, or writing in it.'[43]

The Surrender Continues

Restoring order, disposing off the dead and settling issues relating to the surrender of Tipu's family and government were the principal tasks that confronted Col Wellesely after he took command of the vanquished fort. This was in addition to of course cataloguing the vast treasures and making a seemingly just and equitable distribution of the loot. Equally unpleasant was the task of disposing of the large number of tigers that were chained in Tipu's palace, most of whom had been hungry and starving for days and had consequently turned violent. Mir Alam was asked if he would take care of the beasts, but on his refusal, they were all shot dead.[44] Despite these stern measures, the plunder and loot of Srirangapatna and its inhabitants continued for quite a while. To assure the locals, peace flag marches were conducted. Only when the public execution of errant soldiers began did it instil some fear among the arsonists and things came slightly under control.

The abrupt disappearance of Tipu's government and its functionaries badly hit day-to-day administrative functions as well. Disposing of the dead was another huge task. Close to 11,000 dead bodies—including men, women and children of all ages, lay scattered in the ramparts or floating in the moat, several of them decaying by then and posing huge risks of an epidemic outbreak. As Allan recounts: 'What shocking sights, did every part of the works, the houses near the ramparts, and even the mosque exhibit, strewed with the dead and wounded.'[45] Most importantly, a political settlement and plan of succession to the jolted kingdom of Mysore was the urgent requirement that completely occupied Lord Mornington's focus and attention. He was planning to proceed to Srirangapatna via Royakottah and, in the meantime, he directed Henry Wellesley, his other brother and private secretary, and Lt Col Kirkpatrick, his Military Secretary, to proceed to Tipu's capital immediately.

Mons. Chapuy, along with most of the French officers (about twenty) and troops not exceeding 120, had already been taken prisoners. Karim Sahib, Tipu's younger brother, had already sought shelter from Mir Alam.[46] On 6 May, letters were sent to Fateh Haidar, Kumr-ud-din and Purnaiya to surrender and help in the setting up of a new administration, in lieu of protection. On 8 May, Kumr-ud-din (his father and Tipu's mother were siblings), who commanded 4000 horse, sent Ali Raza, one of Tipu's earlier vakils to Cornwallis, to General Harris. It was important for the British that this force that he commanded was not summarily dismissed, leading them to pillage the countryside; they would have to be assured that they would be taken into regular service.

Kumr-ud-din, who despite being Tipu's cousin had surreptitiously assisted the British and had been in touch with them, had sent his message through Ali Raza that he had no conditions to seek for his surrender, but would be happy if the jagir of Gurramkonda was given to him in lieu of his services. This, he claimed, 'would bind him forever to British interests.'[47] If this were not possible, he would like to retire with his family to Hyderabad and wanted British permission to do so. In fact, Kumr-ud-din's loyalty was bought by the British with the enticement of the Nawabship of Cudappah.[48] Harris gave him assurances of his just demands being met. Accordingly, on 10 May, he visited Srirangapatna from the French Rocks, near the island town, where he had been stationed and met Gen. Harris. Describing his appearance, Allan writes: 'Cummer-a-deen is of a remarkably robust frame of body and very corpulent; he is much marked with the smallpox, his complexion is dark and his countenance, which has nothing of character in it, is far from agreeable. He is much respected, not less for his military talents, than for his honour and justice—he came on horseback and we are told that he never goes into a palanquin.'[49]

In his letter to Harris dated 15 May 1799, Wellesley had written: 'I authorize you to assure Cummur-ud-Deen Khan that I receive with great satisfaction his unconditional submission to the generosity of the British power; and that he may rely with confidence on my countenance and protection; you will add that, in concert with His Highness the Nizam, I will readily take into consideration Meer Cummur-ud-Deen's claim to the Jaghire of Gurrumconda, but it would be premature at present to enter into any specific agreement on that head. However, I empower you to declare to Meer Cummur-ud-Deen immediately in my name, that if I shall be satisfied with his services in the restoration of tranquility, I will make an ample and liberal provision for him, fully equal to whatever may appear to be his just claims.'[50] Recommending Kumr-ud-din's case to his brother, Arthur Wellesley, too, wrote on 13 May 1799, making it amply clear that his loyalty to them had helped the British immensely to secure victory:

He [Kumr-ud-deen] has behaved so well and by coming in so
early has rendered us a great service, that *coute qui coute*, we ought
to give him what he wishes for. If he had remained in arms,
we never could have settled this country unless we incurred the
enormous expense of keeping our army in the field and even then,
the operations to be carried on would be liable to all the hazard
of protracted military operations. He has saved us this at least,
and has thereby rendered us a service almost as great as any of
those rendered by His Highness the Nizam. But the Nizam may
be satisfied by another part of the territory, and in that case, there
can be no doubt of the propriety of rewarding Cummer u Deen.[51]

All the other principal officers and sirdars of Tipu's regime were to
be informed that the degree of favour and protection that they could
seek to receive would depend on the fidelity with which they would
assist in a peaceful transition and also in submitting the details of
the properties they held, including stable horse, draught and carriage
cattle, arms, ordnance stores etc.

On 11 May, Purnaiya sent a message to General Harris, expressing
his desire to meet him and regretting the delay that was caused due
to the rising of the river that prevented him from moving out. The
following day, on the 12th, Purnaiya paid his visit and had a long
conversation with him about the settlement of Mysore, post the war.
Through the agency of Purnaiya, the disbanding of the Sultan's army
was completed. The Silledar horse returned of their own accord to
their lands. Some discussion took place with regard to the disposal
of the Bargeer or stable horse, which too were concluded at length
on 18 May, again with the intercession of Purnaiya. Trying to prove
himself useful to the British during this crucial period, Purnaiya also
made a very strange case. He suggested a plan to Harris that one of
the family members of Tipu should be instated in his place on the
throne of Mysore if law and tranquillity were to be restored in the
kingdom. This successor was to pay the British a tribute as would be
mutually agreed upon. The British troops should garrison such forts
as they deem necessary for the security of the kingdom. Purnaiya

strongly made a case for the succession of Tipu's eldest son, Fateh Haidar, and at the same time, for himself to be appointed as the new Dewan of Mysore as he was well versed with administrative and revenue matters that he could handle ably. If he wasn't made the next Dewan, he wished to retire to the holy town of Rameswaram.

Purnaiya's rationale was that unless a member of Tipu's family was installed, the troops that had not yet been disbanded would become 'lawless banditti'[52] that would go around pillaging the country. In his conversations, when Harris suggested the possibility of 'the establishment of a Hindu government in favour of the ancient family of Mysore [Wodeyars], but Purnaiya cautiously evaded entertaining this idea in the slightest degree.'[53] Harris's reasoning of this evasion was: 'The Muhammadan interest is so intimately blended with every Department of the State in this country [Mysore], that no plan by which it is set aside in favour of a Hindu prince would produce the very desirable effect of restoring tranquility, and reconciling the troops and most powerful class of the inhabitants to the change of Government.'[54] Col Wellesley was however quick to notice that these plans of Purnaiya 'were all framed with a view of his own interest, and the future management of the revenues of the country to be restored by himself.'[55] He did not believe that Mysore could not be settled in tranquillity if any of Tipu's family members were not placed on the throne or that the undisbanded army would rise in rebellion on account of this. It was also found that there was really no great influence exerted by the Muslim officials and they would all be satisfied if their personal interests and safety was guaranteed. As Lt Barry Close summarized:

> That Tippoo loaded the departments of his Government with dronish Mussalmans cannot be denied, but the characteristic of his domination was to reserve all power to himself and allow no hereditary claims or fixed offices that might in any shape oppose the dictates of his will. Individuals holding the principal offices of the State doubtless exercised authority and from such cause possessed some influence, but of these how many remain? Burhanuddin

was killed at Seringapatam, the Benki Nawab fell at Siddeswar, and Syed Sahib, Mir Sadak and Syed Gaffar at the storming of Seringapatam. Purnaiya is forthcoming and rests upon our will. Kamruddin rests upon our generosity and is perfectly at our devotion. Where then is the Mahomedan influence to embarrass us or to give a turn to our politics? Tippu's infantry are discharged, his Silledar horse are dissolved, his killedars pay us obeisance, his Asophs, if so disposes have not the means to resist us, the stable horse remain and look to our pleasure for subsistence and at best they are but so many loose individuals connected by no head and kept apart by separate interests. They are ours for actual service at a nod.[56]

Governor-General Wellesley too was completely against placing the reins of Mysore in the hands of any family that had a hand in establishing a French alliance. Therefore, on 20 May 1799, he desired to make enquiries of 'the state of the family of the ancient Rajahs of Mysore, and the character and disposition of the persons composing it.'[57] These decisions and opinions were obviously not conveyed to Purnaiya or Tipu's family as the British were keen on securing all their submissions first.

Purnaiya's agent showed Captain Malcolm a letter from Kumr-ud-deen to Fateh Haidar, urging the prince not to enter into any negotiations with the British. This, at a time, when he himself was negotiating with them through Ali Raza, with no provisions for his nephew. 'This gross duplicity,' states Allan, 'was meant to hurt the interests of the Princes; and probably was partly the cause, why Futty Hyder [sic] has so long delayed coming in.'[58]

But Fateh Haidar was perhaps enticed to surrender by Purnaiya's intercession and his advocating his cause for succession. On 13 May, he visited the British camp from the north bank of the river, beyond the French Rocks, where he had taken shelter since the time of the fall of the fort. Captain Malcolm first went to meet Fateh Haidar who was seated in a tent with about fifty to sixty Sirdars who were attending to him. General Harris met him with every mark of respect. Fateh

Haidar was naturally very depressed and melancholic by the sudden change of his and his family's fortunes. All the Sirdars, Chiefs of Regular horse and others greeted Fateh Haidar and Purnaiya. They were all seated on the floor on a carpet, except for Fateh Haidar who sat on a chair. A fine-looking Sirdar, Ameed Khan, then rose and in a loud, yet respectful voice addressed General Harris: 'You have been successful,' he said, and then pointing to the prince, said, 'behave in such a manner that your fame for justice, may go as far as your fame for victory; the whole world acknowledge that the English are brave, shew that you are equally generous.'[59] Something about the tone, tenor and manner of the rendition of this speech left a great impact on all the English officers. They assured Fateh Haidar of all support and justice for his cause, presented him gifts and departed. Kirmani is bitter about this submission of Fateh Haidar: 'He [Fateh Haidar] saw the symptoms of fear, distress, and despair, prevailing among his followers, and at the same time, heard the consolatory and conciliatory language used by the English General and other of his officers; included in which were hints or hopes held out of his being placed on the throne.'[60] Kirmani states that several of Fateh Haidar's bravest officers, including Malik Jehan Khan (actually Dhondoji or Dhoondia Wagh who had been forcibly converted to Islam), Mir Maran Syed Nasir Ali and other Asofs, urged him to live up to the legacy and bravery of his father and give a fight, possibly at a later date. They promised him every gallant support from their side. But Kirmani records that Purnaiya's advice and influence were too strong a bait for Fateh Haidar to refuse and he 'was deceived, and acted in conformity to their [the traitors'] wishes, at once rejected the prayers of his well-wishers and consequently, washing his hands off kingly power and dominion, he proceeded to meet and confer with General Harris.'[61]

Thus, by 14 May, Fateh Haidar and all of Tipu's children, numbering thirteen sons and thirteen daughters, along with all the principal surviving commanders of the deceased Sultan's army, had surrendered along with the Mysorean troops. His zenana had more than 600 women, consisting of both Haidar's and Tipu's families.

Tipu's eldest son, Fateh Haidar, was about twenty-six years old, while the youngest son, Sandy Sahib, was just eight months old. His eldest daughter, Padshah Begum, had died two years ago at the age of twenty-three. Allan lists the children's names and ages: Fateh Haidar (twenty-six years), Abdul Khaliq (twenty-one years), Mahomed Sultan Muiz-ud-din (fifteen-and-a-half years), Maoloz-ud-din [Moieuddin] (fifteen years, four months), Yaseen Sahib (twelve years), Subhaun Sahib (eleven years), Shuk-un-Ullah (nine years), Sarour-ud-deen (six years), Jamel-ud-deen (five years), Munawwar-ud-din (two-and-a-half years), Golam Mohammad (two years), Golam Ahommed (eighteen months) and Sandy Sahib (eight months).[62] The daughters were as follows: Baby Begum (fifteen years), Asmat Ulnissa Begum (twelve years), Noor Ulnissa Begum (ten years), Ameena Begum (ten years), Fateema Begum (eight years), Hollim Sahib Begum (five years), Buddoor Ulnissa Begum (five years), Ahommudy Begum (four years), Umdut Begum (four years), Kerim Unnissa (four years), Noor Jahan Begum (two years), Hussain Begum (eighteen months) and Sud Begum (eighteen months).

Simultaneously, the British also took measures to ensure that Tipu's important forts and possessions across and around Mysore were also captured. Letters were sent to the killedars of all the forts within the territories to surrender unconditionally and most of them did so without a whimper. On 13 May, the Bombay Army under Lt Gen. Stuart marched to Malabar via Coorg, to take full control of the coastal regions. The principal forts in Canara were all brought under their suzerainty. By 22 May, this operation was completed, and the army reached Cannanore.

In his letter to the Court of Directors in London on 11 May, Wellesley expressed his deep satisfaction at the annihilation of Tipu, their worst enemy in India and the only one to whom the French could have turned to, for assistance and alliance. All of this having been achieved within four months of his arrival in Madras and the commencement of hostilities was a sure feather in Wellesley's already decorated cap. The note mentioned triumphantly and with satisfaction, how with the fall of Tipu, the whole of the Mysore kingdom and its resources were now under British control. He ended his letter on a note of warning to other Indian princes:

> The dreadful fate of Tippoo Sultaun cannot be contemplated without emotions of pain and regret; but I trust it will serve as a salutary lesson to the native Princes of India, and will prove the danger of violating public engagements, and inviting foreign invasion for the prosecution of schemes of ambition and hatred against the British power.[63]

Tipu's Family Resettled

After having firmly made up his mind against the succession of Tipu's son to the throne of Mysore, the question was of what was to be done with his vast family. Before any communication was opened with the dispossessed Hindu royal family, it was considered appropriate to settle this issue. The Nizam had offered his dominions as a home for a part of Tipu's family, but Wellesley turned this down. He chose Vellore in the Company's territories as a place of residence and appointed Lt Col Doveton as the commander of the fort there. They were to be provided all stately honours, escorts, attendants and so on to maintain a modicum of nobility. A sum of 2,40,000 Canteroi Pagodas (1 CP=Rs 3) was allowed as annual maintenance for the family.

It was decided that the first four elder sons were to be moved as there weren't sufficient carriages to get the whole entourage out of the city. Col Wellesley accordingly met Fateh Haidar on 16 June and explained to him the Company's decision in this regard. Given his voluntary submission, the British decided to give him a liberal allowance of Rs 7 lakh per annum. Col Wellesley explained to him that in order to spare him the embarrassment or humiliation of his feelings at witnessing his father's kingdom (albeit, a usurped one) pass into someone else's hands, the Company felt it apt that they should be moved out before any such arrangement was made. Fateh Haidar expressed shock at this decision, especially when he had voluntarily surrendered himself. He mentioned that in the cases of Tanjore and Oudh, a natural succession plan had been followed. He protested against moving away from the place of his birth and also where the tombs of his father and grandfather lay. Who would look after them in his absence, he wondered.

It was an obviously difficult conversation that Col Wellesley had with him. But in a cool and matter-of-fact manner, he told Fateh Haidar that nowhere in the conversations had with him on his surrender, had his succession been assured to him. As Col Wellesely records:

> I admitted that the British Government had shown generosity in the instances to which he had alluded, but in the present case such generosity was not compatible with its interests, especially when Tippu and his family were intimately connected in politics with the irreconcilable enemies of the British with the sole object of driving the British out of India. Further, I observed, that there was no intention of separating him from the families of his father and grandfather longer than was necessary to procure conveyances for the latter to the Carnatic and that, in the meantime, they would be under my protection and that they had not suffered and he had no reason to fear that they would suffer from his absence upon the present occasion. I then told him that what had been proposed was for his sake as well as for the ease of the government of the country, that he must be aware that he would be an object of suspicion at all times and that he must expect that the smallest indiscretion on his part would occasion the detention of his person . . . he then said that he would consult some of his friends upon the subject and I told him that what I had said to him was the Commander-in-Chief's order which it was my duty to see obeyed and that I would send Captain Marriot to him in an hour to take his directions respecting the carriage of his baggage and family.[64]

A similar, direct conversation was then had with Abdul Khaliq, Muiz-ud-din and Moieuddin. All the princes kept negotiating for more members of their families to be included, as also for dhoolies, camels, elephants and so on. But they were told sternly that the conveyance availability as of then was limited and hence the entourage could be shifted only in instalments, in due course. Realizing that they had few options but to comply, the princes submitted.

On 18 June, the four princes and their attendants, along with Captain Marriot, were escorted out of Srirangapatna to Vellore, with troops numbering about 1500. On the journey to Vellore, Fateh Haidar was supposed to have expressed indignation at the reduced position and allowance and hoped to have a jagir assigned to himself. Abdul Khaliq, in a manner quite unbecoming of his royal stature, was focused more on the differential in the prices of rice in the bazaars in Vellore and Srirangapatna.[65] The other two princes made polite, engaging conversations with the British escorts, before all of them finally reached the fort of Vellore.

Meanwhile, Tipu's principal officers were all categorized into classes, depending on their seniority and importance. In addition to Sayyid Saheb, Mir Sadak and Benki Nawab, twenty-eight of Tipu's principal officers had been killed. The Mir Meerans or Principal Lords who survived were all given a pension of 3000 pagodas a year for life, while the second class of officers got 500 pagodas. These measures were influenced by what Beatson describes as 'the policy of securing, by a liberal provision, the attachment of so many persons of rank, and influence, to the interest and welfare of the British Government in India.'[66]

Wellesley Turns to the Wodeyar Family

It was only after Tipu's four elder sons had moved out of Srirangapatna that communication was opened by the British with the Wodeyar household. The lingering royal family of Mysore was put up at a miserable stable of sorts with a few sheds attached to it where they struggled for their upkeep. The family was led by the ninety-six-year-old grandmother, Devajammanni, the adopted mother of the deceased Immadi Krishnaraja Wodeyar. It included the fifty-eight-year-old, more prominent Maharani Lakshmi Ammanni, the widow of Immadi Krishnaraja, the daughter-in-law of the aged matriarch and the adoptive mother of the deceased Khasa Chamaraja Wodeyar, Krishnaraja who was five years old. Other members included the infant scion's maternal grandfather, Nandiraja, the five widows of the late Maharaja, and the deceased king's mother who was Immadi Krishnaraja's mistress.[67]

Maharani Lakshmi Ammanni, who had for long negotiated with the British, heartily thanked them for saving her family from the utter misery that they had been pushed into by eliminating the usurper of their throne. She was waiting in the wings for matters to settle after the storming of Srirangapatna and quickly sent feelers to the Company officials to not forget their long-standing friendship. Rumours were rife that the British wanted to annex the whole kingdom for themselves as it was such a long-drawn and hard-won campaign. The suggestions of Purnaiya to install Fateh Haidar as the successor must have come as an additional alarm to the Maharani who did not wish to jinx decades of her strenuous efforts for the restoration of power to her family. Luckily for her, Wellesley refused to elevate any of Tipu's lineage to the throne of Mysore. He decided in favour of a partition of Mysore among the victorious allies and restoring a substantial part of it back to the Wodeyars, but under British supervision. A Commission consisting of Gen. Harris, Col Wellesley, Henry Wellesley, Col Kirkpatrick and Lt Col Barry Close was put in place, along with Captains Malcolm and Thomas Munro as Joint Secretaries, to decide the contours of such a partition and restoration plan. The Commissioners assembled at Srirangapatna on 8 June 1799, bound themselves by the oath of secrecy and started their work.

Since Wellesley was particularly averse to handing over the throne of Mysore to the progeny of Tipu Sultan, the natural choice was therefore the displaced royal family that had suffered such indignities and humiliation under the four-decade long interregnum by Haidar Ali and his son. The British knew that the new sovereign would be ever indebted and grateful to the British power for delivering them from their wretched state and, therefore, would make a perfect and subservient ally. This would be so unlike Tipu or, as they apprehended, any of his sons who perhaps would feel the same rancour and ill will for the British.

The Commissioners deliberated on the partition clauses. The Nizam had so far just received a lakh of pagodas as prize money and his troops were not a part of the pillage party either. To assuage their seething ally who was feeling shortchanged, he had to be given suitable territory. He was to receive territories worth 600,000 pagodas centred on Gutti and Gurramkonda, along with a tract bordering on the line of Chitradurga, Sira, Nandidurga and Kolar. This was to exclude, however, the fortresses on the south that formed the frontier of the new kingdom of Mysore. Gurramkonda itself was given to Kamr-ud-din, as desired by him. He accordingly marched out of Srirangapatna, toward Gurramkonda on 19 June 1799.

The British were to take all of Tipu's coastal areas below the Western Ghats, the entire Malabar region and also Waynad, Dharapuram and Coimbatore. They also laid claims on all the important passes into Mysore from the east and south, including the citadel and the island of Srirangapatna which was to become a British garrison town. The military power of Mysore was to be fully dismantled; all the Frenchmen in the Sultan's service were taken to Madras as prisoners. The army had already been disbanded; the horses and the Silledars had returned under Purnaiya's supervision. Wellesley feared that an equal division of territories between the British and the Nizam would excite feelings of jealousy and insecurity in the Marathas and also augment the Nizam's powers. Hence, the Nizam was handed over just as much as was deemed fit and the lion's share went to the British.

Wellesley cleverly tried to insert a proviso in the partition agreements regarding their erstwhile allies, the Marathas. One of the biggest losers on the allies' side in this war were the Marathas. They were shocked by the speed and alacrity with which Wellesley had concluded the war in barely two months and destroyed Tipu's power and slain him. They had perhaps expected a long-drawn conflict like it had been under Cornwallis, where slowly they could enter the scene with varying bargaining powers. But the abrupt and sudden death of Tipu in the war spoilt all these calculations. That their bitter rival, the Nizam, had been on the victorious side and a faithful ally did not portend good tidings either. Wellesley argued that since the Marathas had not participated in the war, they had no claims on the spoils. But as a long-standing ally, the British were happy to cede to them territories worth 2,63,000 pagodas from Tipu's domains. These territories included Harpanahalli, Soonda and Anegundi, with parts of the districts of Chitradurga and Bidanur above the Ghats. This was subject to Poona satisfying the demands of both the British and the Nizam. In short, this actually meant that Wellesley was asking the Peshwa to contract a subsidiary treaty with the British. The Peshwa had to provide help if the British were to get into conflict with the French. In the case of a dispute between Poona and Hyderabad, the former was to obey the British mediation and settlement terms. Also, the Peshwa was to forfeit all claims of Chauth on the new Maharaja of Mysore.

The astute Nana saw through the trap and advised the indecisive Peshwa against accepting the agreement. For once, Baji Rao agreed with Nana's counsel and rejected the proposals. Nana prophetically advised the young Peshwa: 'Tipu is finished; the British power has increased; the whole of east India is already theirs; Poona will now be the next victim. Evil days seem to be ahead. There seems to be no escape from destiny.'[68] But neither Baji Rao nor Daulat Rao Sindhia seemed to grasp the enormity of the situation. They made vague plans for attacking the Nizam, which when conveyed to the British, caused them to assure Hyderabad that in the case of any aggression from the Maratha side, the British would stand by them like a rock. This assurance of Wellesley to the Nizam dissipated all the bravado that the young Peshwa was attempting. He continued with other mindless acts of trying to stitch a confederacy of Indian rulers and had hoped to join Tipu if he had held out for longer. All these intrigues were being duly noted by the British and slowly a case was being built against the Peshwa too, just as they had once done against Tipu.

Since the Marathas refused the offer, the territories that were promised to them were distributed between the British and the Nizam. However, it must be mentioned, that by 1800, the Nizam was forced to cede to the British all the territories that he had acquired in Mysore, both in the 1792 and 1799 wars in return for a force of British troops to be permanently stationed in Hyderabad.[69] Thus, the Nizam's supposed advantages vanished in just about a year after the conclusion of this victorious war.

On 22 June 1799, the Treaty was signed with the British and the Nizam as the main signatories and the Peshwa's name included conditionally. Through this treaty, the Company's revenues were augmented by about 7 lakh Star Pagodas (1Star Pagoda=Rs 3½) and that of the Nizam by about 5 lakh Star Pagodas. The revenue of the territory allotted to the new kingdom of Mysore was 25 lakh Star Pagodas and that apportioned conditionally for the Marathas was 3 lakh Star Pagodas.[70]

Restoration of the Wodeyar Family

On 24 June, the Commissioners proceeded to the apartment where the young Krishnaraja Wodeyar lived. It was on the northern side of the fort, next to the house of Mohiuddin, the fourth son of Tipu. It was considered appropriate to take Purnaiya along for this meeting. They found the prince and the royal family living in a condition of extreme poverty and humiliation, which 'excited the strongest compassion' in the Commissioners.[71] A curtain was drawn behind which sat Maharani Lakshmi Ammanni and the other female members of the household. The Commissioners were received with joy and gratitude by Nandiraja, the only male member of the household. They then informed the royal family about the broad plan that the Governor-General had made for the settlement of the province. From behind the curtain, the Maharani expressed her gratitude, through one of her attendants, to the British government for 'the clemency of the British nation, which had now raised her and her family from the abyss of human misery, to that station, of which they had been so long deprived by tyranny and usurpation.'

At length, she dwelt upon all the persecution that they had been forced to undergo for nearly four decades under the reign of Haidar and Tipu. Now that her grandson had been chosen to be the successor to the throne of Mysore, she hoped to spend her last days in comfort and peace. The young prince, about five years old, was seen to be extremely fair, with a lively and expressive countenance, but of 'delicate habit, and apparently of timid disposition.'[72] He showed signs of alarm on seeing all the Commissioners enter his home, but soon regained his composure. However Scottish historian James Mill describes the young prince rather disparagingly: 'The Raja was a species of screen put up to hide, at once from Indian and European eyes, the actual aggrandizement which the British territory had achieved.'[73]

Interestingly, despite his advocacy favouring Fateh Haidar's succession, Purnaiya was to be appointed as the Dewan of the new kingdom. It was remarkable how he had made himself relevant to every dispensation, even the one whose cause he had never supported. But with this were also rudely dashed all the hopes and promises that were made to the unfortunate Tirumala Rao, the Pradhan of the Maharani, who had laboured for decades as her emissary under adverse circumstances.

Tirumala Rao was in Madras on the fateful day of 4 May 1799 and had welcomed the news of Tipu's death by beating drums and distributing cartloads of sugar to people there.[74] His personal interactions with Lord Clive, the Governor of Madras, had kept his hopes alive of his being finally rewarded for his sacrifices and being made the dewan of the new dispensation. Clive asked him to proceed to Krishnagiri and wait on Governor-General Wellesley who had initially planned to visit Srirangapatna for the settlement. From Krishnagiri, he dispatched a letter to his patron, the Maharani, informing her of the British decision to appoint him as the new Dewan.

By then, as news of a possible restoration of the throne to her family was being made known to her, the Maharani sent a letter to Tirumala Rao on 3 June 1799 after receiving his communication from Krishnagiri:

Respects to our Tirumalachar,

By the blessing of God and the Brahmins, we have been doing quite well up to date. Please keep us informed about your welfare from time to time. We have understood everything from your letter that you sent with Jatavallabha Singri Iyengar. Your efforts so far, living in a foreign land for 24 years and suffering so much on our account, all for the sake of justice and patriotism, have now borne fruit. To such a wise man and great friend of ours, as you are, what more can we say in a letter like this? . . . the great good that you have done to the state now has brought you everlasting fame, which will last as long as the sun and moon endure. And in future, we shall fully abide by your acts, and shall have nothing to say against them. It is impossible for us to express the fullness of our gratitude for your invaluable services, by means of any letter. It can only be after we meet personally and talk to each other, that we shall be fully pleased and you yourself made to understand everything completely.[75]

Whilst he was at Krishnagiri, Tirumala Rao heard that Wellesley had abandoned the plan to go personally to Srirangapatna and had instead appointed Commissioners for the settlement of Mysore. He was asked to proceed to Srirangapatna to meet the Commissioners. He presented himself and his case, as also the Maharani's promises to him for several years about his appointment as the Dewan. By then, Purnaiya had been lobbying hard for his own case and had even helped the British in disbanding Tipu's army and horse, ingratiating himself with them thereby. Tirumala Rao received a rude jolt when, after assessing the situation, the Commissioners sent him a letter, informing him that 'having been long absent from the Mysore country, he [Tirumala Rao] might not possess that thorough and practical knowledge of the present state of its local resources and other minute particulars, which Purniah had been presumed to command in consequence of his long and unremitting residence in the country, and having held offices of importance under Tipu Sultan and his father; that the disorganized and unsettled condition of the country then newly conquered rendered the knowledge, though otherwise of secondary consequence, an indispensable qualification in anyone who should be placed at the head of its affairs at that crisis.'[76]

Tirumala Rao read this letter with utter disbelief. A man who had recommended the end of the Hindu dynasty was being promoted to a post of eminence, while he, who had for twenty-five years served with single-minded focus on the objective of reinstating them, and for which his entire community had paid a heavy price, was being relegated to oblivion. He wanted answers and wanted to meet his patron, Maharani Lakshmi Ammanni. But when he rushed to her apartments, he was curtly stopped and told that as per the directives of the British officials, he did not have the requisite permissions to meet the Maharani. He was told to leave Srirangapatna once and for all and settle down in Madras with an allowance being given to him. He could simply not believe his ears, if what was being ordered to him was indeed true. Shattered, disillusioned and crestfallen, Tirumala Rao made his way back to the city he had lived in for decades as a refugee, saving his life from the wrath of Haidar and Tipu.

The Maharani perhaps learnt of the treatment meted out to her loyalist and was keen to let him know that this did not have her sanction. While he was in Madras, he received a copy of her letter to Lord Mornington and Lord Clive, dated 25 June 1799, where she passionately made a case for Tirumala Rao's appointment as the Dewan. 'We had in the very beginning,' she wrote, 'promised to confer the Ministership [sic] upon our Tirumal Row, and on the faith of this, our promise, he put forth his strenuous exertions with the Company for the past 24 years as is very well-known to you . . . we have already promised our Tirumal Row to appoint him and his heirs as Ministers in hereditary succession, to grant him 10 per cent of the revenues of the state, and also to pay up all his expenses. It is therefore our request that you will be pleased to permit us to keep up our promise.'[77] The Maharani made several attempts thereafter too to influence the British to have her way with the Dewanship. But given that her own position was one of a supplicant to the Company, she was merely satisfied that at least the claims of her family had not been ignored. It was also an indication of how the new dispensation in Mysore was to function—completely under British diktats and with no autonomy on any important matters. Tirumala Rao was rewarded though for his services by being given an allowance on the same lines as the Mir Meerans of Tipu who had been pensioned off as part of the settlement. But his long-held dreams of securing the position of the Mysore Dewan for himself and his family heirs was dashed to the ground and they would merely be known to history as the 'Mysore Pradhans' of the Maharani.

Maharani Lakshmi Ammanni and the maternal aunt of the prince, Devajammanni, sent a formal letter to the British on 27 June 1799:

> Your having conferred on our child, the government of Mysore, Nuggur and Chitteldroog, with their dependencies; and appointed Purneah to be the Dewan, has afforded us the greatest happiness. Forty years have elapsed since our government ceased. Now, you have favoured our boy with the government of this country, and nominated Purneah to be his Dewan; we shall, while the sun and moon continue, commit no offence against your government. We shall, at all times, consider ourselves as under your protection and orders. Your having established us must forever be fresh in the memory of our posterity, from one generation to another. Our offspring can never forget an attachment to your government, on whose support we shall depend.[78]

The royal family consulted the Brahmin astrologers who suggested 30 June 1799 as an auspicious date to install Krishnaraja Wodeyar on the throne of Mysore. Srirangapatna was in such ruins that it was decided that the new government should be sworn in in the old city of Mysore. In addition to the plunder after its fall, Srirangapatna had also borne under Tipu a regime where every trace of the Hindu magnificence of the erstwhile royal family had been torn down. The royal family, and even the British, were averse to having the coronation in the Mohammedan palace of Tipu, where a large part of his family and the zenana were still present. Bangalore was considered as another option, but the idea was abandoned as it was in a corner of the territory assigned to the new Raja. So, finally old Mysore city was chosen as the place to have the ceremony. But even here not a single house of eminence was standing as Tipu had demolished most of the old buildings. In the new Mysore that he had constructed, there were hardly any good buildings and water came in from the Nazarbad fort that was a distance of more than half a mile.

Despite these shortcomings even in Mysore city, it was selected as the new capital for the kingdom. On the morning of 30 June 1799, the Commissioners, along with Mir Alam and an escort of European regiment, ushered the young prince to a makeshift pavilion that had been specially constructed near the Lakshmiramana Swamy temple, inside the old fort. Both Gen. Harris and Mir Alam held the little boy by his hands and placed him on the throne. Harris handed over the seal and signet of the kingdom to the prince and announced the appointment of Purnaiya as the new Dewan of the kingdom. Purnaiya was to serve as the regent to the king till he attained his majority. Barry Close was to be the British Resident in the court of the new ruler. The entire ceremony took place in an open pandal and Harris mentioned how large numbers of spectators were present to witness the momentous occasion and that joy was visible on their countenances.[79] Ghulam Ali Khan, Ali Raza, Badr-uz-Zuman Khan, Syed Muhammad Khan and other high-ranking officers of Tipu's regime too spontaneously attended the ceremony. Thus, the new prince, now named as Mummadi (the third) Krishnaraja Wodeyar, was installed as the ruler of a partitioned and emasculated Mysore, under the subservience of the British power.

A few days later, on 8 July 1799, the Subsidiary Treaty of Srirangapatna was signed between the British and the minor Raja, on whose behalf Maharani Lakshmi Ammanni and Purnaiya officiated. Spread over sixteen articles, this treaty formalized all the terms of the partition and the subsequent settlement. An annual subsidy of 7 lakh Star Pagodas was payable to the Company for the permanent station of their troops at the capital for the Raja's defence. In the event of the failure to pay up, it was left to the discretion of the Governor-General to assume direct charge over parts of the kingdom to procure the required funds. The Raja had no right of appeal if the Company chose to take over his territories for the above-mentioned reasons. He could not induct Europeans into his service or make or break alliances at his will; everything had to have the Company's approval. The Governor-General had full liberty to garrison or repair any fortress in Mysore with British troops and officers in times of peace or war, with the Raja bearing half the expenses. For the British garrison that had been stationed at Srirangapatna, all provisions and articles were to be made available free of any duty, tax or impediment. The Raja was also bound to heed any advice the Company gave him in good faith regarding the state of the kingdom's economy, finances, administration, justice system, trade, commerce, agriculture, industry and any other subject they deemed fit.

End of an Era

With this, in just two months after a bloody war and hard-contested victory, the British managed to settle the province and also its allies. The year 1799 was a milestone year, not only in the history of Mysore, but that of India as well. A new kingdom was born out of blood and strife, and the clock had turned back in favour of the Wodeyar family once again, after four decades of misery and misfortune that befell it. The worthlessness of its earlier rulers had cost them their kingdom. Destiny was giving them a second chance now. Whether they proved their mettle this time, albeit under the tight iron fetters of the English East India Company, was something that only time would tell.

The new settlement also gave a fresh opportunity to the master survivor Purnaiya. While other traitors met with ignoble ends, Purnaiya reinvented himself to serve his new masters. Shrewd and diplomatic, he switched sides with alacrity and convenience. The master tactician that he was, he transformed even adverse conditions to advantageous and profitable opportunities for himself. As Dewan, he drew a handsome salary of 6000 pagodas per annum, plus a 1-per cent commission on the revenue, which brought in another 19,000 pagodas or so.[80] A victory over his competitor to the post, Tirumala Rao, must have felt even sweeter to Purnaiya as Tirumala was related to Anche Shamaiya, the same man who had implicated him in false cases and almost brought him to the threshold of death. He was initially fearful of the royal family as he knew they viewed him with suspicion as a remnant of the old establishment, who had championed the cause of Tipu's son and who was not the Maharani's choice for the post. Since the Raja was a young boy and the Maharani was not adept in day-to-day affairs of administration, Purnaiya knew that he could become the de facto ruler and with his fiercely ambitious nature and networking skills, develop close friendship with the British Residents who were to be in Mysore over the next few years—Barry Close, Josiah Webbe, John Malcolm Wilks and A.H. Cole. In this arrangement that the British had plotted so strategically was, hence, sown the seeds of a future conflict between the ruler and his Dewan, in which obviously they would play arbiter. It was a harbinger of what was to unfold in Mysore over time.

With this, the curtains fell on the family and administration of Haidar Ali and Tipu Sultan who had held Mysore under their thumb for over four decades. From rags to riches, and then from glory to a grievous fall, the house of Haidar had seen it all. As the century turned, Mysore's history and, in effect, Indian history too had seen one of its most tumultuous convulsions and the future did not bode well for either. Wilks, in his magisterial account of the history of Mysore, aptly summarizes this episode that almost resembles in its fall a classical Greek tragedy:

> Thus terminated a dynasty composed only of two Sovereigns, the first of whom had risen from obscurity to imperial power, and the last, educated as a prince had fallen in the defence of a hereditary crown; resembling in some of the circumstances of its close, the fate of the Roman capital of the Eastern empire; substituting like that catastrophe, in place of the fallen dynasty, not only the power of a new Sovereign, but the influence of a new race; yet exhibiting the marked contrast, of kindling, not quenching in its fall, the lights of science and civilization.[81]

19

Affairs of State

Tipu Sultan's reign endured for merely seventeen years and was totally beset with bloody conflicts and battles. Amidst these tumultuous years, he, however, managed to find the time and interest to leave behind his imprint on the administration of Mysore. Unlike his father, Tipu did not wish to merely continue the set-up that was received by his family from the Wodeyars. As mentioned earlier, the administration was renamed Sarkar-e-Khudadad, the God-given Government. The army was augmented to include the Asad Ilahi and the Ahmadi corps—the former being the chelas from Malabar and the latter the Portuguese Nazarenes and Canara Christians. His trusted accomplice, theologian and ideologue, Zain-ul-abidin Shoostri, was marshalled to come up with numerous innovations in the military and administrative set-up. From the calendar to weights, measures, coins, commercial regulations, fiscal policies, banking and finance, agriculture and industry, police and judiciary, sociocultural life to even the names of places, Tipu wanted to leave his indelible mark on every aspect of a Mysorean's life, obliterating all the past traces of the Hindu Wodeyar rule.

Tipu's was a highly centralized system of government. Describing it to his father in a letter dated 17 January 1790, Sir Thomas Munro called it 'the most simple and despotic monarchy in the world, in which every department, civil and military, possesses the regularity and system communicated to it by the genius of Hyder, and in which all pretensions derived from high birth being discouraged, all independent chiefs and Zemindars subjected or extirpated, justice

665

severely and impartially administered to every class of people, a numerous and well-disciplined army kept up, and almost every department of trust or consequence conferred on men raised from obscurity, gives to the government a vigour hitherto unexampled in India.'[1] Even his sworn enemies, the British, and some of their chroniclers, had charitable things to say about how organized and galvanized the administration and army of Mysore was. Edward Moore, who was part of Captain Little's detachment during the Third Anglo–Mysore War, states: 'When a person travelling through a strange country finds it well-cultivated, populous with industrious inhabitants, cities newly founded, commerce extending, towns increasing, and everything flourishing so as to indicate happiness, he will naturally conclude it to be under a form of government congenial to the minds of the people. This is a picture of Tippoo's country, and our conclusion respecting its government.'[2]

Structure of Administration

The records found in the palace after the fall of Srirangapatna indicated a well-structured administrative set-up, divided into departments called *kutcheris* under heads who were responsible for them, working with the help of a board of officials. Tipu is said to have kept a keen watch on the functioning of all these important departments and to have met the heads of departments often for counsel. There were nine major centralized administrative departments in Mysore under him: Revenue and Finance (*Mir Asaf Kutcheri*), Military (*Mir Miran Kutcheri*), Ordnance and Garrison (*Mir Sadar Kutcheri*), Zumra (*Mir Miran Kutcheri*) that looked after army-men born in Mysore and known as *zumra*, Commerce (*Malik-ut-Tujjar Kutcheri*), Marine (*Mir Yam Kutcheri)* and the Treasury and Mint (*Mir Khazain Kutcheri*).

The head of the Mir Asaf or Revenue Department was called *diwan, huzur diwan* (principal diwan) or *mir asaf* and was among the leading officials of the kingdom. With five subordinates under him, he led the Central Board of Revenue and Finance. Each of these officials had a team of *shirastedars* (Chief Accountants) and *mutsaddis* (clerks) who kept the records for the department in Persian, Kannada and Marathi. Mir Sadak headed this department and was the huzur diwan of Tipu's administration—the most important official of the government.

The Mir Miran or Military Department too had a Board, headed by Purnaiya, who operated with fifteen officers working under him. Purnaiya was also a member of the Mir Asaf department. The Zumra department, within the Mir Miran, was created by Tipu in 1793 and had an army composed of men born in Mysore. Muhammad Raza headed this department.

The Mir Sadar or Ordnance and Garrison Department looked into the stores and manufacture of arms and ammunition, the defence of forts, supply of troops, provisions and materials during war. Ghulam Ali Khan was the head of this department, with eight officials called *bakshis*, who operated under him.

The Malik-ut-Tujjar or Commerce Department, which looked after trade and industry, was also handling naval establishments until 1796, when it was bifurcated into a separate unit. Ahmed Khan managed this department with nine officers working under him. The Mir Yam or Naval department, hived out of the parent body in 1796, had Hafiz Muhammad in charge with a team of seven officers.

Mir Khazain or Treasury and Mint had seven officers or *daroghas* under the supervision of Sayyid Amin. Each darogha had assistants and clerks supporting them. The *toshakhana* or treasury housed all the valuables, the jewellery, important papers of state, the seal of the Sultan and so on. The toshakhana was of two types—*naqdi* where bullion and money were housed; and *jinsi* that had costly wardrobes, silks, valuables and documents. Srirangapatna had five mints. One of these minted gold coins and was housed within the palace itself. The mints were managed by the daroghas of the Treasury Department. The Chief Darogha supplied the raw materials to the mints and once the coins were made, they were collected and deposited in the treasury. The *hukumnamahs* or regulations to the treasury were about prized items such as *zari*, a significant portion on firearms and muskets, timely payments of remunerations and allowances, running of mints, shops, bazaars and factories.[3]

The coins of Tipu Sultan were more varied than those of his father. They were issued in gold, silver and copper from no less than twelve mints across the kingdom. These places were also of political and military importance, and several of them were renamed with fanciful Islamic names by Tipu: Pattan (Srirangapatna), Nagar, Faiz Hisar (Gooty), Bengalur (Bangalore), Farrukh-yab Hisar (Chitradurga), Kalikut (Calicut), Farrukhi (Feroke), Salamabad (Satyamangalam), Khaliqabad (Dindigul), Zafarabad (Gurramkonda), Khwurshed-sawad (Dharwar) and Nazarbar (Mysore).[4] The name of Mughal Emperor Shah Alam II disappeared from the coins, as Tipu declared his independent sovereignty. Gold coins were named after Khalifas and silver coins after Imams. Ahmadi, Sadiqi, Faruqi, Haidari, Imami, Abidi, Baqiri, Jafari, Kazimi, Khizri, Mushtari are some of the names of these coins.

In addition to these principal departments, there was another important unit of Post and Intelligence under a darogha stationed at Srirangapatna. His team of officers were spread out across the kingdom, in different cities and towns, and they passed on important information and espionage to the capital, collected constantly through a large proliferation of spies. The letters were carried back and forth between places on horseback by harcarahs. The department of animal husbandry and cattle, started by Chikkadevaraja Wodeyar in the seventeenth century as *Benneya Chavadi*, was renamed Amrit Mahal by Tipu. The cows, sheep and buffaloes were all looked after by this department. Both Haidar and Tipu took considerable interest in also developing a sturdy breed of horses, as compared to the 'small, ill-shaped, vicious poney' that was common in India. They did not succeed and their cavalry remained 'extremely ill-mounted.'[5]

With the conclusion of the Treaty of Mangalore in 1784, Tipu initially divided his entire kingdom into seven provinces or *asafi tukris*. He soon increased them to nine and two years later to seventeen. By the end of the Third Anglo–Mysore War, their number and the provincial boundaries were further changed to thirty-seven asafi tukris. Such constant changes hampered the smooth functioning of the provincial administration. Each province had an Asaf or civil governor (almost always a Muslim) and a *Faujdar* or military governor—the former being in charge of revenue and the latter for maintenance of law and order. Their functions, jurisdiction and powers were strictly kept mutually exclusive so that neither encroached upon the other's turf, nor became too powerful and instead held the other in check. Some provinces had a senior and junior asaf too. Under the asafs were their deputies, the naibs, the mutsaddis, shirastedars, peons and copyists.

The provinces had several districts or *taluks* called *amildari tukris*. Each province had anywhere between twenty to thirty districts. By 1794 when there were thirty-seven asafi tukris, they had under them a total of around 1024 amildari tukris. Each district came under the Amildar, who was an officer of justice, police and revenue. Under him came a *tarafdar*, shirastedar (accountants also called *parupathyagaras* in Kannada), clerks and peons. The Amildar was to look after the villages that came under his jurisdiction, the welfare of the peasants, promote agricultural measures and produce and also supply provisions to the military stores and palace granaries. They reported to respective kutcheris in Srirangapatna. On the avaricious nature and corruption of these Asafs and Amildars, Buchanan records:

> Muslim Asophs [asaf] or Lord Lieutenants . . . superintend large divisions of the country; and this greatly increased the evil; for these men, entirely sunk in indolence, voluptuousness and ignorance, confident of favour from the bigotry of their sovereign, and destitute of principle, universally took bribes to supply their wants; and the delinquencies of the Brahmans were doubled, to make good the new demands of the Asophs, over and above their former profits. Owing to this system, although the Sultan had laid on many new taxes, the actual receipts of the treasury never equaled those in the time of his father. The Amildars, under various pretexts of unavoidable emergency, reported prodigious outstanding balances; while they received, as bribes from the

cultivators, a part of the deductions so made. Although the taxes actually paid by the people to government were thus much lighter than they had been in the administration of Hyder, the industrious cultivator was by no means in so good a condition, as formerly. The most frivolous pretexts were received, as sufficient cause for commencing a criminal prosecution against any person supposed to be rich; and nothing but a bribe could prevent an accused individual from ruin.[6]

As during the Wodeyar rule, each district had some thirty to forty villages under it that were managed by Patels/Gowdas and Shanbhogas (accountants). Patels/Gowdas administered justice in the villages with the help of panchayats and were the representative of the Amildar. Buchanan noted that Amildars, Parupathyagaras and Shanbhogas were 'almost universally Brahmans.'[7]

Appeals could go up to the district level to the office of the Amildar and Tarafdar, or up to the province to the Asaf and Faujdar. A High Court at Srirangapatna was another higher appellate authority, with the ultimate court of justice being the Sultan himself. Orders from the capital flowed down to all the subordinate administrative units, up to the village level.

Revenue Regulations

A detailed document in Persian, containing the revenue regulations of Tipu Sultan, had fallen into the hands of a British army officer, Colonel John Murray, during the Third Anglo–Mysore War. The royal seal on it bore the registration date of 5 March 1786. This was translated into English in Calcutta by Burrish Crisp around 1792. Parts of this translation were also incorporated into a book titled *British India Analyzed*, in 1795. These give us first-hand insights into how the revenues were administered during Tipu's reign.

Both Haidar and Tipu had been deeply suspicious of the palegars, who were virtual feudal lords with great political ambitions and shifting loyalties and acted as middlemen in the revenue collection system. Even Chikkadevaraja Wodeyar, being cognizant of this malaise, had started clipping their wings in the districts of Mandya, Mysore and parts of Bangalore. Haidar and Tipu further extended this over the other districts of Shimoga, Dakshina Kannada, Uttara Kannada, Chitradurga, Raichur, Bellary, Dharwad, Tumkur and Kolar too. Haidar was the one who gave serious thought to this and felt that the state could collect more revenues if the middleman was eliminated. A professional revenue collector would be more cost-effective and hopefully an apolitical entity, when compared to the palegar, and would also serve his interests well. Haidar therefore began replacing several palegars with a more systematic tax-collection regime. This was also another reason for the several mutinies that these disgruntled and dispossessed palegars stoked. Several of these palegars had been imprisoned and thrown into the dungeons in Srirangapatna. In their place, the Amildars were appointed as professional tax collectors. The main principle of their land tenure system was that a tenant and his heirs occupied the land as long as they cultivated it and paid rent. But if they did not meet these conditions, the government was free to transfer the land to other tenants. Tipu further tried to put an end to the intermediaries and created a framework for direct interaction of the state and peasants. In the process, however, there was extreme dependency on the government servants to ensure the model's success—a scheme fraught with the danger of them becoming the new, corrupt intermediaries who replaced the old, feudal order.

The revenue regulations document mentions that the Amildar was to go to the districts with these rules of the State, the seal of office and other paraphernalia and conduct a session with the ryots (peasants), Patels and others in the district, and encourage the peasants to cultivate more. Right at the beginning of the year, in these sessions, the Amildar was to give a *cowle* or security to the peasants to encourage more cultivation. To enable ryots who were needy and to purchase extra ploughs and seeds to enhance their arable lands, he was to provide advances of money in the form of *Takkavi* loans, at the rate of three or four pagodas for every plough, taking a security for their repayment. These were interest-free or non-usurious agricultural loans provided by the government to the peasantry. This Takkavi loan amount was to be recovered from them in one or two years in instalments. This scheme protected the peasants from moneylenders and local officers.

There were four kinds of land in the Mysore kingdom—wet, dry, *ijara* and *hissa*. The dry lands were irrigated by rain, while the wetlands were irrigated by tanks and rivers. Hissa lands were those where the produce was equally distributed between the state and the peasant, and the cultivator did not pay a tax (like the *bhagra* lands in Bengal). The ijara lands, like the *theka* land in Bengal, were leased to peasants at a fixed rate. The ijara system of revenue farming was introduced by Mughal Emperor Jahandar Shah and his minister Zulfiqar Khan in 1712. Under this system, lands were farmed out to third parties when peasants did not have sufficient means to cultivate their lands. Thus, the government began to contract with revenue farmers and middlemen to pay to the treasury a fixed amount of money while they were free to collect whatever they could from the peasants. The grain seeds sown on ijara land were more than hissa, but equal proportions of all four categories of land were to be distributed among old and new peasants. The clear categorization of the land, its proper assessment and a fixation of its rent, all with the intention of increasing the produce and the land under cultivation, were the main features of Tipu Sultan's revenue regulations.

The cultivators of dry lands paid a fixed rent that was calculated as being equal to one-third of the crop. Those who cultivated wetlands paid about one-half of the crop in kind. This was normally discharged in money at the average rates of that particular district. In Mysore, the land was measured and estimated by the quantity of grains/seed required to sow it and the term used was 'candy.' A candy consisted of twenty *kudus* and each kudu was of ten *seers*. These measures and weights differed from district to district, and also from grain to grain. Hence, one candy of land meant one candy of seed grain sown in that land. Wetlands were assessed at two to twelve pagodas per candy, and dry lands from two and a half to thirty pagodas per candy. Wetlands needed four times the seed to be sown than dry lands. Hence, dry land was considered to be equal to four times as large as a candy of wetland. Tipu introduced the system of collecting rent in cash. A farmer cultivated both dry and wetlands and on an average paid 40 per cent of his income to the state.[8]

An account of the increase and the deficiency of the produce was to be made every year. According to the cowle, the revenue was to be taken in cash or, if the custom otherwise prevailed, half of the produce was given to the peasant and the other half retained as the sovereign's share. The hissa land was to be well-manured and the peasant was to be compelled to cultivate the full proportion allotted. Cultivation of sugarcane was to be encouraged. If the patels and shanbhogas failed to do so, a double tax was to be imposed on them, calculated upon the quantity of sugarcane which may have been produced in some other village. Sugarcane was taxed from sixteen to seventy-two pagodas per candy in Bangalore and Maddagiri.

Patels were to plough their lands themselves, and not employ peasants to do so. If they did so, the whole of the produce so cultivated was to be taken by the government. By denying farming rights to the principal government officers, there was greater devolution of power to the peasants. No single person was allowed to have more than one *mauza* or estate as his own farm. Before farming out this estate, 'an accurate list of all the old and new inhabitants and an account of the gross receipts, shall be made out, according to which the lease shall be granted and a *mochulka* (security bond) be taken.'[9] In cases of revenue shortfall, the Amildar was to bridge the gap by bringing in more peasants, grant them takkavi loans and new ploughs to enable an enhancement of cultivation. Land rent was to be collected in three instalments. If harsh measures were taken by the Amildar to collect the revenue, he was to be fined twenty pagodas if the victim was a rich peasant and ten pagodas if he was a poor peasant. To prevent the exploitation of the peasants by the revenue farmers, the regulations stipulated:

> If a farmer, neglecting the cultivation of his farm, and suffering the lands to lie waste, shall impose fines upon the *reyuts* [ryots], and make undue exactions from them to enable him to fulfil his own

engagements, he shall be made to pay to Government the amount of such undue exactions, over and above the stipulated rent. Measures must also in future be adopted to prevent any person from levying oppressive fines from the reyuts; and defaulters in this respect shall be made to pay the amount of such exactions, and be moreover fined themselves.[10]

Measures were also taken to enhance the pie of farm land and enhance cultivation. Land which was lying fallow for years was to be assessed by the Amildar and given to the peasant for cultivation upon a cowle. The first year was exempted from any revenue payment and the second year entailed only half of the customary assessment. But third year onwards, the full amount of revenue was to be collected. Similar slabs were made for barren, mountainous and rocky lands. They were exempted in the first year, in the second year one-fourth of the customary assessment was paid, one-half in the third year, and the full rate by the fourth year. Waste lands, too, were rent-free in year one with one-fourth assessment in the second year. From the third year onwards, they were fully charged. The cultivators of dry land paid a fixed rent that was calculated at one-third the crop. Wetlands were assessed at higher rents, amounting to half the value of the crop collected in cash and not in kind. However, writing about Baramahal in 1800, Sir Thomas Munro stated that the rents there as 'in every other part of India, are too high,' and that Tipu's deficiency of receipts arose 'from the peculations of an [sic] host of revenue-officers.'[11]

Incentives were to be given for cultivating certain varieties of pulses, wheat, barley, mangoes, betel nut, coconut, pine, teak, sal and fruit trees. Cash crops like cashew, cardamom, cinnamon and vegetables were exempted from taxation. Keen to develop the silk industry in Mysore, Tipu encouraged mulberry plantation. In the nurseries of the Lal Bagh gardens in Bangalore and the one in Srirangapatna, seeds and saplings from various countries were procured and planted. Given the strict Islamic injunction against intoxication, growing cannabis that was used to make the drink of *bhang*, was firmly prohibited. Heavy fines were to be imposed on those hoodwinking the government in this regard. Special government permission was needed to fell sandal, teakwood and acacia trees. Sandal, in particular, widely found in Mysore and popular for its perfume, was to be encouraged, and anyone illegally felling it was to be fined Rs 500.[12] Arecanut got tax exemptions for the first five years and was assessed at only half the usual rate from the sixth year. The cultivators of betel leaves also enjoyed concessions that those growing coconut did.

Closely linked to the expansion of agriculture and codifying the revenue systems around it was an impetus that had to be given for irrigation. Incentives were given to those who aided the state in building tanks, wells and reservoirs.

Tipu's income from revenue, until the Treaty of Srirangapatna of 1792, was 68,89,893 pagodas (over Rs 2 crore), including the tribute of 66,666 pagodas from Kurnool.[13] After the Treaty, since his dominions shrunk by half, his income too was reduced to about 35–40 lakh pagodas. To make up for this reduction, he increased the assessment by 37.5 per cent (30 per cent on produce and 7.5 per cent as excise duty) in 1795. Though this did not help him reach the earlier numbers, at the time of the fall of Srirangapatna, his treasury was found to be brimming.

However, along with these beneficial measures for the peasants, differential treatment for people of various faiths was inherently embedded in Tipu's revenue regulations. Clause 63 of the regulations stated: 'The *Deostan* [Hindu temple] lands are all to be resumed throughout your district; and after ascertaining to what *simpts* [sub-divisions] they formerly appertained, you shall re-annex them, and include them in the *jummabundy* [revenue assessment] of those *simpts*.'[14] This meant that the grants given to the temple establishments had to be cancelled and confiscated by the government. That the Amildar was a Brahmin and had to do this to temples of his own faith would have been a hugely discomforting act for him. However, clause 69 offered special incentives to Muslims: 'The Qazis and other respectable Mahomedans, and such as follow the possession of arms, shall be exempted throughout your district from the payment of any house tax, or tax upon grain and other things which they may bring from the country for their food.'[15]

Tipu's special ire was reserved for the Christians in his kingdom too, as clause 70 states:

> You shall seize all the Padres and *Cullistauns* [Christians] that are to be found within your district, and send them under a guard to the *Huzzoor* [our Presence]—and you shall enquire and ascertain what zindigie [property], grain, cattle, land, and plantations they possess, and shall sequester the whole thereof for Government; and you shall deliver over the lands and plantations to other *reyuts* [ryots], whom you shall encourage to cultivate them, as, in case they are not cultivated, you will be required to make good, what they should have produced. In future, any person of the caste of *Cullistains* shall take up abode in your district, you shall seize him, with his family and children and send him and them to the *Huzzoor*.[16]

In contrast to Hindu temple lands being confiscated and Christian properties taken over, Clause Seventy-two laid out numerous benefits to mullahs and others:

> Wherever there are no mosques in your district, there are *qazis, mullahs* and *muezzins*. You shall transmit a statement of the allowances given to those persons, and the *inam* lands held by them under yours and the killedar's seals, to the kacheri; and continue them according to their *sannads* . . . wherever there is no mosque, a mosque shall be built and a mullah entertained at a monthly allowance of ten fanams and quantity of ground yielding ten fanams shall be granted for the purpose. The Patel shall also furnish a daily quantity of oil weighing two *fulooces* [pice] to light the mosque; and land for the support of the expense of the oil shall likewise be appropriated.[17]

Encouraging conversion to Islam, clause 73 states:

> Every person who shall become a convert to the Mahomedan faith, if he be a *reyut* [ryot], shall only pay half the usual assessment and shall be exempted from the payment of house tax; and if he is dealer in merchandize, his goods shall pass duty-free.[18]

Trade and Commerce

Commerce and industry seemed to attract a lot of Tipu's interest. Mysore was blessed with fertile soil and was rich in commercial crops. Its long coastline, whose control often made it the theatre of bloody wars for both father and son, offered facilities for exports and imports. Pepper, cardamom, silk, sandalwood, arecanut, ivory, coconut, betel leaves, muslin, flowers, fruits and vegetables, and pearls from the state were widely in demand in western markets. Tipu did not want control of the trade in these items to fall into the hands of traders or European companies. Instead he wanted the state to become the biggest importer and exporter and beneficiary of these goods. Through this state capitalism, the kingdom began to gain complete control over trade, commerce and industries. Tipu's mercantile fleet facilitated maritime trade in a structured manner. Commercial factories were established and agents stationed in faraway lands to create a market for Mysorean products. Government shops were opened at Jeddah, Muscat and Karachi to sell these articles. Commercial relationships were fostered with several kingdoms abroad—the Ottoman Empire, China, Muscat, Pegu, Armenia, Jeddah, Ormuz and Basra. As seen in the earlier chapters, his political diplomacy and embassies to these countries were also coupled with a trade and commercial element.

Mirroring the manner in which European companies had established their hold over factories for trade, Tipu too had two factories in Kutch in 1789—one at Mundhi and another at Mundra.

With seven daroghas and some 150 sepoys managing and guarding them, these factories facilitated brisk trade activities. The factory at Ormuz purchased pearls primarily. Efforts to establish factories at Aden, Bushire and Basra were unsuccessful.

However, the factory in Muscat became an important conduit for trade and commercial activities in the Persian Gulf in 1785, with over fifty products of Mysore being put up there for sale. Tipu's interest in the Gulf area was driven by the fact that from 1719 onwards, Muscat had begun to emerge as an important regional commercial centre. From 1728 onwards, Lahej and Aden had become important supply depots when Zaidi Yemen lost its control over the region. Nadir Shah had by 1750 managed to unify Persia to reduce the foreign influence in the region. Kuwait and Bahrain slowly began to emerge as other major commercial centres. The Wahhabi movement that was gaining ground also sought to create a purist Islamic state. Muscat was also on friendly terms with the French, Tipu's allies. In view of all these developments there, Tipu was desirous of taking advantage of the situation to advance his and his kingdom's interests. A permanent trade commissioner was also appointed in Muscat to establish friendly relations with the Imam there. Rice was one of the important goods from Mysore that was sold in Muscat on the condition that it should not be resold to any European powers, including the British and Portuguese, without Tipu's permission. This indicated that these commercial activities and interests were closely yoked to his political orientations and prejudices. In return for the exclusive purchase of rice that Mysore facilitated, the Imam gave preferential treatment to Tipu's trade in Muscat. While the Europeans paid a duty of 5 per cent, the rest of India 8 per cent, the Arabs and Persians 6.5 per cent, the merchants from Mysore paid only 4 per cent.[19] Similar reciprocal privileges were offered to the Imam and his subjects in Mysorean ports.

Imports of saffron-seeds, silkworms, horses, pistachio nuts, raisins, rock salt, pearls, sulphur, copper, dates and chinaware were undertaken. Tipu was proactive in attracting foreign merchants to his state, offering them concessions to open trade. This active solicitation of foreign trade also brought him further into the cross hairs of European competitors, especially the British, who had established their factories on the western coast of India. For instance, in a letter dated 11 January 1787 to Yakoob and other Armenian merchants, Tipu writes:

> The duties upon [such] goods [as you may import into our dominions] are, without exception, [hereby] remitted. Bring, therefore, with entire confidence to our ports, and into our kingdom, either by sea or by land [as you may think proper], your silk stuffs and [other] merchandize, and there [freely] buy and sell. Wheresoever you may [choose to] bring your goods, there a place shall be assigned for your residence: and if you should, at any time, be in want of workmen or labourers, the same shall be furnished [to] you, on hire, by our *Taalukdars*.[20]

His letters of 1785 to his darogha or Commercial Consul at Muscat, Meer Kazim, demonstrate the minute detail that he went into when instructing the latter about such specifics as loading and unloading the vessels. Meer Kazim was expected to report on a daily basis on the progress in the sale of the goods and also directed about what to procure for imports to Mysore. Tipu also advised Kazim not to be in a haste to sell the goods, but to keep them till they procured a good price and sufficient profits. In several cases, sitting in Srirangapatna, Tipu also fixed a suitable price at which Kazim must attempt to sell these in distant Gulf markets. He also advised him in some letters to purchase pearls from Bahrain as they were cheaper there. This indicated how deeply entrenched Tipu was in these minute details of the trade—all this, even while he was immersed in bloody military campaigns. These letters also indicate that Tipu seemed very eager to establish a pearl fishery on the Malabar coast, as also silkworm culture in his dominions. He wanted Kazim to procure silkworms and their eggs and also send five or six men who were well versed in rearing them. But he failed in both these attempts.[21]

There is an interesting case of his letter, dated 27 September 1786 to Burhanudeen and Kustury Runga, whom he had sent to Bengal with detailed instructions on procuring silkworms, how they need to be stored and where they need to be maintained. While translating the letter, William Kirkpatrick could not contain his amazement that these instructions were given whilst the Sultan was in the midst of a bloody conflict. In his annotation to the translation, Kirkpatrick states:

> When the peculiar circumstances under which the foregoing letter was written, are adverted to, it will, no doubt, be allowed to furnish a striking proof, of both the coolness and the activity of the Sultan's mind. He was at the date of it, not only deliberating on the measure to be pursued with respect to Shanoor [Savanur] in planning the future operations of the war on which he was engaged; and in providing for the safety of Burhanudeen's army; but he was in fact, on the eve of a general engagement with the Mahrattas. Yet, all these important and urgent considerations united, were not capable of diverting his attention from any of the minor objects of his interest. Thus, in the bustle of the camp, and in the face of an enemy, he could find leisure, and was sufficiently composed, to meditate on the rearing of silk worms.[22]

A Persian manuscript titled *Hukumnamaha-i-Tipu Sultan* or the 'Orders of Tipu Sultan' was recovered from the palace of Srirangapatna, after its fall, by Major Samuel Ogg of the Madras Establishment of the East India Company. William Kirkpatrick, who had translated and annotated select letters of the Sultan, also included these regulations in the Appendix of his work. They had been issued in two sets: one on 25 March 1793 and the other on 2 April 1794. With half his dominion lost to the allies after the Third Anglo–Mysore War, Tipu had to buck up to shore up the commercial prospects of his kingdom to make up for the deficits of the revenue yields. The new commercial regulations demonstrate a personal and centralized control of the trading activities that the Sultan wished to exercise. While several ideas seemed to occupy his mind, he did not have much time to experiment on these, as events caught up with him faster than he expected, leading to the fall of Srirangapatna in 1799.

The commercial regulations were executed even as his diplomatic missions were being sent to various countries to solicit military assistance. The Malik-ut-Tujjar Kutcheri was set up as a permanent board for trade promotion. The members met periodically, assessed import–export, sent invitations to foreign merchants and maintained minutes of their meetings that were forwarded for the Sultan's perusal. The new regulations undoubtedly helped promote and encourage maritime trade, but were not oblivious to the obvious benefits of inland commerce. The following were the stated objectives and tasks of this nine-member Board:[23]

1. They were to see that the various articles required for commercial purposes, such as silken stuffs, sandal-wood, pepper, cardamoms, coconuts, rice, sulphur, etc. were duly provided [according to the nature of the commodity] as well as for importation as for exportation.

2. They were to draw merchants to Mysore, by transmitting to them for that purpose the most solid and encouraging assurances [of favour and protection].

3. They were to seek out and engage in the service [of the state] trustworthy and economical *Mutsaddis* and able and experienced *Gumastehs*, skilled in accounts and commercial affairs, and of approved integrity and disinterestedness: and having procured such, were to employ them in the several *Kohties*, or factories [whether at home or abroad].

4. They were to pay the most minute attention to all the concerns of their department; to investigate the various accounts thereof, in the most rigorous manner; and to be careful, that no frauds, or embezzlements, were committed by any of those employed under them, whether in the foreign factories or in the home depots.

5. The heads of the departments as well as the various officers under them were to pledge themselves in the most solemn manner, according to the forms of their respective religions, to discharge the duties of their several stations, with the utmost diligence, concord and fidelity.

6. If any of the principal officers of the department should violate, or in any instance swerve from the duties of his station, all the rest were to unite in exposing the offender to shame and disgrace, and in representing his conduct to the Presence, in order that he might be signally punished for the same, and a useful example be thereby afforded to others.

7. If any of the inferior persons, attached to the different *Kohties,* or factories, should be guilty of fraud, or other misdemeanors, they were to be punished for the same, agreeably to the law of God.

8. In all cases of difficulty, or of particular importance, the heads of the department were to sit and deliberate together on the same; each person writing down, in a book to be provided for this purpose, his opinion on the point under consideration, and subscribing his name thereto. The book, containing these minutes or consultations, was to be deposited in a box, which was to remain under the seal [of the office] till there might be occasion to refer to it, for the justifications or explanation of the proceedings, or resolutions, of the meeting; which, in case of any difference of opinion, were to be determined by the majority of voices.

9. They were to report their proceedings fully and regularly to the Sultan, whose pleasure on the occasion would be signified in writing, at the back, or at the bottom of the said report.

10. In any transaction relating to large pecuniary advances, or being of such importance as to require particular secrecy, the written documents, necessary to be submitted on the occasion, were to written in the hand-writing of some member of the board, or one of the heads of the department, and delivered to the Sultan by such member himself; when a written answer, duly authenticated by the Sultan's own signature, would, in like manner, be secretly returned to him.

11. *Nubby Malik* [The Prophet is Lord!]. All *Hukm-namehs,* and other papers bearing the seal and signature of the Presence, must be deposited in a box, to which the seal [of

the department] is to be affixed. This box shall be lodged in the treasury at the seat of the empire [Srirangapatna], where it will be taken charge of by the Meer Meeran.

12. Care was to be taken, that all the Mahommedan officers of the department such as the *Mirzaey Duftur* etc. should be selected from the tribe of *Koreish* and the sect of *Siyuds*, following the tenets of *Hunifah*, to the end that they might agree the better together.

The Naval Department that was part of this, until it was hived off to become the Mir Yam, was tasked in 1793 with building 100 ships (called *Khizri* and *Ilyasi*). Ten of these, completely manned and equipped with warlike stores, were kept under the command of the head of the department. Merchants building these ships in Mangalore and other places were allowed to lade them with rice, coconuts and other articles that were not exclusively traded by the government. Iron, timber, ropes etc. that went into the building of the ships were to be locally procured, to boost inland commerce. Timber was sent from Calicut to Mangalore where the shipbuilding yard was set up. In addition, ships were built at Sadashivgarh and Bascoarji. Eventually about forty ships of war were manufactured, and they were stationed in three ports: Calicut, Mangalore and Sadashivgarh. About 10,000 men manned a variety of ships. The Board of Admiralty that he organized controlled a navy of twenty-two lines of battleships and twenty large frigates with seventy-two and sixty-two guns respectively, besides a fleet of merchant ships.

The factories of Muscat and Kutch were placed under the Malik-ut-Tujjar department. Sulphur that was imported from Muscat was to be delivered by him to the Asofs of Mangalore and Nagar to manufacture gunpowder. The employees of these factories were to be changed every three years. Profits from the sales of specific export items such as sandalwood, cardamom, coconuts, betel, rice, wax and honey were to be reported to the Sultan on a regular basis. Any reports of fraud and embezzlement were to be strictly penalized. Tipu had renamed the currency, Canteroi Pagoda, comprising ten fanams, as Rahiti. A sum of 4 lakh Rahitis was committed to the head of the department to purchase gold and silver bullion, expensive clothes and elephants that were to be kept ready for use.

The new commercial regulations reorganized and expanded the scope of inland trade. For this trade and commerce within the kingdom, commercial depots or marts and provincial factories were set up, with suitable duties assigned to them. The commercial head was asked to purchase and sell any items, except a few like sandalwood, spices, silver and gold on which the state had exclusive control. A wholesale trade policy was followed by the government in many articles, though private traders were not prohibited at subsequent levels of trade after the Commercial Board had sold the commodities to them. The normal trade activity that met the needs of the consumers had significant participation of local retailers, even as the government maintained strict controls. Through these measures, Tipu tried to keep away European traders from both inland and maritime trade and increase the government's control and participation in it. This also helped Tipu to monetarily keep his state treasury comfortable, despite the frequent wars and several defeats that he faced.

Thirty factories (*kothis*) were established at Srirangapatna, Bangalore, Mangalore, Kolar, Karur, Chitradurga, Karwar, Mulbagal, Bhatkal, Madanapalli, Calicut, Nandidurga, Banavasi, Gutti, Satyamangalam and so on. These factories employed European and Indian workmen and manufactured broad cloth, paper, scissors, hourglasses, pocketknives, guns, muskets, watches and cutlery. A French artist had prepared an engine, driven by water, for boring cannon. A big paper mill had come up within the fort of Srirangapatna. Glassware, fine sugar and steel wires for musical instruments were manufactured at Channapatna. Superior-quality sugar and sugar candy were made at Chikkaballapura and Devanahalli. The Chinese were invited to these places to help in the manufacture of sugar.

Silkworms brought in from Bengal and Muscat were cultivated to promote the silk industry in Mysore. There are several letters of Tipu, giving instructions on how to select the silkworms and bring them back safely to Mysore, even in the midst of bloody wars. Silk rearing was carried out in twenty-one centres across Mysore. The Patwegar and Khatri communities exclusively wove the silk cloth. While efforts seem to have been made to establish a vibrant silk industry, it did not come to fruition during Tipu's rule as the political events and the eventual fall followed in quick succession. Writing about the silk industry in Mysore as it existed shortly after the fall of Tipu, Buchanan records:

> The silk manufacture seems especially favourable for a country so far from the sea, and from navigable rivers: as long carriage on such a valuable article, is of little importance. At present, all the raw material is imported. But I see no reason why it might not be raised in Mysore to great advantage. Tippoo had commenced a trial, but his arbitrary measures were little calculated to ensure success. Some of the mulberry trees, however, that remain in his gardens, show how well the plant agrees with this climate.[24]

The textile industry, too, was promoted by Tipu. Fine muslin was produced in Mysore by Muslim weavers of the Patwegar community. Francis Buchanan noted how the 'weavers of Bangalore seem . . . to be a very ingenious class of men, and with encouragement, to be capable of making very rich, fine, elegant cloths of any kind that may be in demand.'[25] A special variety of cloth called *Sada Shillay* was manufactured at Sidlghatta, near Srirangapatna. Gubbi was known for its saris. Sathyamangalam and Coimbatore had several looms and were noted centres for textile manufacture, as were Salem and Harihara. The weavers too were advanced loans to manage their businesses.

Cutting of stones into various sizes and shapes was also an activity that Mysoreans took to. Iron smelting and casting was done at several places such as Madhugiri, Channarayadurga, Hagalvadi and Devarayadurga. Iron factories, named *Taramandal*, were located at Srirangapatna, Bangalore, Chitradurga and Bidanur. However, Francis Buchanan concludes that manufacturing several of these European items was 'done with a view of showing his subjects, that, if he chose, he was capable of doing whatever Europeans could perform.'[26] The processes of manufacturing these items were all kept top secret.

In a unique blend of state control and market capitalism, in order to inspire a commercial interest among his subjects, Tipu established a trading company that was open for the purchase of shares. Anyone who deposited Rs 5 to Rs 500 in it, was entitled to a profit of 50 per cent at the end of the year.[27] For those who deposited between Rs 500 to Rs 5000, the profit was 25 per cent; and for over Rs 5000, it was 12 per cent. Higher dividends to those investing smaller amounts were made possible to encourage small investors. If a shareholder wished to sell off his shares, he was to be given back his principal amount, along with the profits.

Distinctive skills and techniques were used to manufacture guns, muskets and daggers, many of which were made as per French designs. Monsieur Lafoli was the chief designer and had served Haidar as well. Even in his letter dated 2 April 1797 to the diplomatic mission sent to France, Tipu instructs:

> Ten cannon founders, ten ship builders, ten manufactures of Chinaware, ten glass and mirror makers, ten makers of ship clocks and wheels for raising water, and other kinds of wheel-work and workmen versed in fine gold plating are required in the Khoodadaud Sircar. You will state to the French sirdars that they are to consider the desire to manufacture these articles, as arising from the friendship and attachment of the Khoodadaud Sircar, and as means of promoting their interests and to request that they will therefore send ten artificers of each sort. After obtaining these people, you will fix suitable wages for them before you leave the place.[28]

The industrial policy of Tipu Sultan was thus a modern and progressive one that aimed to develop his state and make it self-sufficient. His Board of Admiralty, his Department of Commerce and his Bureau of Manufactories created employment opportunities for several people, beyond traditional agriculture alone. The construction work undertaken or the building of bridges, canals, tanks, forts and buildings generated jobs for many. Several of his measures, however, did not find sufficient time to yield results, as his rule was cut short by the final war. His measures however led to an over-concentration of power in the State that became absolutist. This government domination and interference, coupled with the corrupt and treacherous officers, obstructed economic activity in many cases. Restrictions and the secretive nature in several cases, as mentioned, did not lead to these industries becoming agents of mass production.

The Fighting Forces of the Sultanat

Tipu maintained a regular, standing army that was better equipped and disciplined than that of other contemporary Indian powers. As mentioned earlier, Tipu's military activity was largely based on the recommendations of the Persian treatise *Fathul Mujahideen* or the 'Victory of the Holy Warriors of Jihad', written in 1783 by his courtier, Zain-ul-abidin Shoostri. The book had eight chapters. The first chapter had general points on the Muslim creed, ablution, prayers, about Jihad or Holy war, the prohibition of tobacco, on disloyalty and on bequest. The second spoke about the newly fixed names for arithmetical divisions, weights and measures, computations and some theological verses. The third chapter dealt with military strategy. The fourth contained some commands issued by the paymaster-general or Commander-in-Chief. The fifth chapter described the appointments of military officers. The last three chapters dealt with practices related to the artillery, cavalry and infantry respectively.[29]

As described in the above treatise, Tipu divided his infantry (*jaish*) into kushoons or brigades, under a sipahadar who had a bakhshi and mutsaddis attached to each unit. In each kushoon, there were four *Risalas* or regiments of infantry and one of cavalry under a *risaladar* or colonel. He commanded over ten *jowkdars* or captains, the heads of a group of hundred men that formed a *jowk*.

Every jowk or company included two *sur kheils*, ten *jemadars* and ten *duffadars*. In those regiments of troop or regular horse that were modelled on European lines, the Major was called *teepadar* or *youzdar;* while the adjutant was the *soubadar* or *nakib*.[30] The sipahadar inspected the firelocks and arms preparedness, and also reported regularly on the unit, while the bakhshi assisted him in salary statements for the troops. The risaladar held a parade of the troops every day of the week, except on Thursday, which was a holiday.

Tipu reorganized the army in 1793 after the debacle in the Third Anglo–Mysore War. The army was divided into infantry and artillery on one side and cavalry on the other. The regular troops and the peons/irregulars made up the infantry. The regular infantry was further divided into five kutcheris and composed of twenty-seven *kushans*—the first two kutcheris had six kushans each, and the remaining three had five kushans under them. Each kushan was placed under a sipahdar with two field pieces attached to it. It consisted of four *tips* each under a *tipdar*. The strength of one *yaz* was eighty-seven men, of a *tip* was 348 and a kushan 1392. The kushun had with it one jowk of thirty-nine rocketmen, two jowks of 112 matchlockmen, two jowks of *khulasies* or lascars of 122 men and others amounting to a total of 360 men. The total number of men in each kushan was thus 1752 and in the regular infantry of twenty-seven kushans, this meant a total of 47,304 men.

In this new organization, the bakhshi's role became most important, and well beyond just being the salary disburser of the unit. In the cavalry, the regular horse (*aksar*) was divided into four brigades or kutcheries. Each of these four were further divided into five *mokums* or regiments. The number in each unit and subunit was not fixed. The kutcheri was headed by the bakhshi and the mokum under a mokumdar. The mokum was further subdivided into four risalas or squadrons, each under a risaladar or commander. The risala was then divided again into yaz (troops) under a yazakdar or captain, with sur kheils, havaldars and sepoys assisting him. The irregular horse consisted of the *silhadar* (about 4000) and predatory horse called *kuzuk* (about 8000). The irregular horse was not formed into definite corps and each officer who commanded a party made the arrangements as he deemed fit. Tipu seems to have made further changes and reorganizations in the army units around 1798. On the eve of the last and final Anglo–Mysore War, Tipu had 3502 regular horse, 9392 irregular horse, 23,483 regular infantry, 6209 regular militia and 4747 matchlockmen and peons.[31]

The Mysore Rockets

An important element of the military activity of Mysore was the extensive use of rocketry. Undoubtedly, mentions of rockets or 'fire-arrows' (*Agni-Baana/Agneyaastra*) have been found in several ancient Indian texts, including the epics. The first documented use is however attributed to the Chinese in the eleventh century CE. Interestingly, similar looking weapons are also found in the Hoysala architecture of the same period in Karnataka at the Halebidu temple. It was reported that in 1232 CE, after the death of Genghis Khan, Chinese rockets repulsed Mongolian attacks on the city of Kaifeng on the Yellow River. This invention possibly then found its way to Europe as well. Scholar Iqtidar Alam Khan writes that 'The increasing use of firearms from the middle of the fifteenth century in different parts of the world is often seen as a crucial factor in the rise of centralized monarchical states.'[32] The artillery of the Mughals, too, right from Babar's wars in Panipat (1526) and Kanwah (1527), speak of experimentation with firearms. It was in the Deccan though, right from the Vijayanagara times down to the Bahamanis, the Nizam Shahis and the Marathas, that the use of artillery and gunpowder in warfare seems to have become a norm. This technology seems to have naturally passed on to the Wodeyar rulers in Mysore too. It has been mentioned earlier that in 1726, when Peshwa Baji Rao I attacked Srirangapatna, he was surprised by the heavy firing from the magazines of the fort and sustained considerable loss of men in his army. He is said to have remarked that 'it was a sheer impossibility to withstand the matchlockmen of Seringapatam which appeared to be nothing short of a city of cannons (*firangi-pattana*).'[33]

These rockets re-emerged in their new avatar during the reign of Haidar Ali and Tipu Sultan. Haidar's father himself had been at the head of a unit of troops that included fifty *juzail-burdar* (rocketmen) in the Arcot service. As seen in the preceding chapters, during several of his attacks, Haidar Ali made extensive use of these rockets in his military campaigns. Be it the campaign in Mysore by Gopal Rao Patwardhan in 1764, in the First Anglo–Mysore War at the Changama clash with Smith or in the battle of Chinkurli in 1771, there was the ever-looming presence of the Mysore rockets in all these attacks. There was a regular rocket corps in the Mysore army. From about 1200 men in Haidar's time, this number rose to nearly 5000 in Tipu's time. Baanadars (that still retained the old nomenclature of a *baana* or arrow) were tasked with the rockets in his army.

The iron-cased rockets of Mysore alarmed the British. That this was something new that they were encountering becomes evident in the British chronicles, like those of Innes Munro who gives an account of how these rockets operated:

> Hyder Ally also employs some thousands of men for throwing rockets. This is a missive weapon, and made in the same form as those used by schoolboys, with this difference, that the stalk is a thick bamboo, eight or ten feet long, which has a tube of iron, from six to twelve pounds weight, fixed to the end of it, in which the fuse and powder are placed. In wet weather, or marshy grounds, these are set off flying in the air, and will reach to the distance of a mile and a half; but upon dry grounds they are pointed horizontally, and bound in a very uncertain direction, often creating great damage, particularly amongst cavalry and ammunition tumbrils. Hyder's train of artillery is chiefly composed of French and Danish guns of different calibers, but most commonly heavy metal, which are doubly yoked with trained bullocks; and are as well and expeditiously served as ours.[34]

During the Second Anglo–Mysore War at the Battle of Polilur in 1780, the surrender of Colonel Baillie was accentuated when an entire ammunition tumbril was set on fire by the rocket shots from the Mysore side. This episode, as mentioned earlier, is depicted in a painting on the western wall of the Daria Dowlat Bagh palace in Srirangapatna with the entire British side going ablaze.

Tipu Sultan, having a restless, innovator's mind, was already fascinated with several European inventions such as barometers and thermometers. He decided to redesign and redeploy these rockets with greater strength in his army as he realized their devastating power. During the Third Anglo–Mysore War, we saw how Lt Col Knox was attacked by rockets on the night of 6 February 1792 while trying to cross the Kaveri River from the northern side in Srirangapatna. Purnaiya and Kumr-ud-din commanded two rocket units during the Third Anglo–Mysore War. The Sultan's rocket attacks came in the kushoons or brigades of his army. The large artillery devices were built on wheeled carts and could fire at varied ranges, shoot multiple payloads and sometimes deploy a dozen rockets at the same time.

In the final Anglo–Mysore War, on 5 April 1799, at Sultanpet Tope, Colonel Arthur Wellesley was attacked and forced to flee by the attack of the Mysorean rockets. Denys Forest writes:

> At this point there was a large tope, or grove, which gave shelter to Tipu's rocket men and had obviously to be cleaned out before the siege could be pressed closer to Seringapatam island. The commander chosen for this operation was Colonel Wellesley, but advancing towards the tope after dark on the 5th, he was set up with rockets and musket-fire, lost his way, and as Beatson politely puts it, had to 'postpone the attack . . . until a more favourable opportunity should offer' . . . Wellesley's failure [was] glossed over by Beatson and other chroniclers, but the next morning he failed to report when a force was being paraded to renew the attack.[35]

This had been a major source of grievance between Col Wellesley and Gen Baird as earlier noted. The Sultanpet incident seemed to have left a deep and traumatic imprint on Col Wellesley (later the

Duke of Wellington). His biographer, Philip Guedalla, mentions that Wellesley would come back to this event much later in his life too, with many explanations of what happened on that fateful night. This incident 'might have been responsible for the indulgent view that Wellington often took of "shell-shocked" soldiers, for one of whom he pleaded sympathy noting, "Many a brave man, and I believe some very great men, have been found a little terrified by such a battle as [Waterloo], and have behaved afterwards remarkably well"—just as (presumably) Wellesley himself did after Seringapatam.'[36]

Once again, on 22 April 1799, there is an account of the use of rockets on the British troops under Col Stuart, encircling the fortress:

> On 22 April [1799], twelve days before the main battle, rocketeers worked their way around to the rear of the British encampment, then 'threw a great number of rockets at the same instant' to signal the beginning of an assault of 6000 Indian infantry and a corps of Frenchmen, all directed by Mir Golam Hussain and Mohomed Hulleen Mir Mirans. The rockets had a range of about 1000 yards. Some burst in the air like shells. Others called ground rockets, on striking the ground, would rise again and bound along in a serpentine motion until their force was spent.[37]

An eyewitness of these incidents in Srirangapatna in April 1799, Col Bayly, records in his diary:

> The rockets and musketry from upwards of 20,000 of the enemy were incessant. No hail could be thicker. Every illumination of blue lights was accompanied by a shower of rockets, some of which entered the head of the column, passing through to its rear, causing death, wounds and dreadful lacerations from the long bamboos of twenty or thirty feet, which are invariably attached to them. The instant a rocket passes through a man's body it resumes its original impetus of force, and will thus destroy ten or twenty until the combustible matter with which it is charged becomes expended. The shrieks of our men from these unusual weapons was terrific: thighs, legs, and arms left fleshless with bones protruding in a

shattered state from every part of the body, were the sad effects of these diabolical engines of destruction.[38]

In fact, even hours before the fort of Srirangapatna fell and Tipu was shot down on 4 May 1799, Gen. Baird and his troops met with furious musket and rocket fire.

From these accounts, it becomes clear that the British were totally caught unawares by the assault that the Mysorean rockets unleashed on them. That they were both petrified by it and also impressed by the technology employed becomes evident with the events that followed after the fort of Srirangapatna was captured. Back in England, engineer Col William Congreve had been researching, since the later decades of the eighteenth century, the technology of rockets at the Royal Laboratory at Woolwich Arsenal, with his father who was the Comptroller of the Laboratory. He was told that 'the British at Seringapatam had suffered more from them [the rockets] than from the shells or any other weapon used by the enemy.'[39] By 1801–02, the rockets that were developed in England had a range of about 500–600 yards, which was less than half of that of the Mysore rockets.[40]

Several thousands of rockets that were seized in Srirangaptana were sent to England to the Royal Artillery Museum for an in-depth study. A rocket research programme began in 1801. There is however no documented proof that under this programme, Congreve studied Mysorean craftsmanship and technology. He published his thesis *A Concise Account of the Origin and Progress of the Rocket System* in 1804. These new rockets were ironically to become known as 'Congreve Rockets'. In another delicious irony, these very rockets were used in the battle at Waterloo against Napoleon by the same Duke of Wellington Arthur Wellesley, who had run away in fright in Srirangapatna!

While the Mysore rockets vanished from the country of their origin, except three in the Government Museum of Bangalore, they surprisingly made a reappearance by chance in 2002. Over a 100 of these rockets were accidentally found in a well in Nagara in Shivamogga. This was possibly not too surprising as the contemporary British account of Captain Little, who came along with the Maratha army under Parshuram Bhau during the Third Anglo–Mysore War, had written that during their operations near Shimoga, they had come across the 'fort of Toorkhunhooly, commonly called Trookanelly,[41] a place famous for making rockets.'[42] So Shimoga and its neighbouring areas that were part of the erstwhile Bidanur or Nagar was where most of Tipu's rockets seem to have been manufactured. Shejeshwara Nayak, the assistant director and curator of the Government Museum in Shivamogga, elaborated: 'Rockets have been used in battles for over 700 years. But it was only in Mysore, under Hyder Ali, that iron casings were first used. Before that, rockets had wooden or paper casings. The iron casings drastically improved their efficiency and range. Mysore rockets were the most advanced ones during the second half of the eighteenth century.'[43]

The main contribution of Haidar Ali, and more so that of Tipu Sultan, in this field was the innovation made to the existing technology. As Nayak mentions above, the Mysore rockets were made of metal cylinders that had the combustible propellant material that was then strapped to a long bamboo pole, which was sometimes even 30 feet long. They had the highest range of about 1 kilometre. The use of iron which was of a much better quality in India then than in Europe increased the bursting pressures. This allowed the propellant, i.e., the gunpowder to be densely packed, giving thereby a higher thrust and longer range to the Mysore rockets.

A multidisciplinary study was undertaken on the excavated remains of the rockets and they yielded fascinating results. In an extremely illuminating and informative lecture on the subject, historian Nidhin George Olikara, who was part of the team that undertook the study, explains how clay was used as a refractory boundary layer inside the iron casings. This helped to keep the heat that was developed in the combustion chamber under control and from affecting the metal cylinder. Detailed laboratory studies revealed that the carbon content of the iron casing was kept extremely low, at 0.02–0.3 per cent. This low carbon content helped in rolling it and drawing the tube. This too was a manufacturing innovation in Mysore—to vary the carbon content in the manufacture of steel. The Mysoreans had also mastered the art of the radial burning of the rocket, as also the end-burning. Gunpowder was manufactured too in various parts of Mysore and the fuse was made of cotton or silk.[44]

Thus, while the technology for building rockets might have already been extant in India, it was Haidar Ali and later more so, Tipu Sultan, who understood the importance of this technology, used it to their most optimum advantage, undertook capacity building measures around its suitable deployment in the army, trained people in its usage and innovated new means of production. There is no documented evidence thus far of any other contemporary Indian powers having made modifications to the existing technology. And until any such discovery of similar usage by other contemporaries in India comes out, we can assume that Mysore, under Haidar and Tipu, led this innovation. All the coughing up of steady revenues that we saw in the preceding section and the rapid industrialization that was undertaken thus fed in seamlessly into the military economy under Tipu Sultan.

Renowned scientist Dr Roddam Narasimha, who has researched Mysorean rockets extensively, writes:

> First, in the 18th century there were still certain products, of which the rocket was one, where Indian technology was superior to the British and was so recognized by them. Secondly, following this recognition, the British effort to understand and master the technology already had the sophistication that we have come to associate with research and development in this age: scientific principles were applied, appropriate designs were made, and suitable products developed, tested and systematically evaluated. This whole process was something about which Indians of the 18th century had no clue whatever . . . Iron made in India was of a high quality too, even though Indian furnaces were operated inefficiently as compared with those of Europe. Samples of Indian

iron were sent to Sheffield, because it was 'excellently adapted for
the purpose of fine cutlery', and it was difficult to obtain such good
iron in England, except through imports from Sweden. There are
reports that in the 1790s the British started importing [Indian
iron] to reduce their dependence on Swedish iron.[45]

Tipu's Library

When Srirangapatna fell on 4 May 1799, Tipu's library was preserved
and the contents presented to the Asiatic Society of Bengal, to the
Universities of Oxford and Cambridge and the East India Company.
Captain David Price and Major Samuel Ogg, the Prize Agents of the
Bombay and Madras armies respectively, were tasked with assessing
the library collections. In his earliest notes on what he found in the
library, David Price writes:

> The library and depôt of manuscripts, was a dark room, in the
> S.E. angle of the upper virandah [sic] of the interior quadrangle
> of the palace. Instead of being beautifully arranged, as in the
> Bodleian, the books were heaped together in hampers, covered with
> leather; to consult which, it was necessary to discharge the whole
> contents on the floor. The selection, which we completed, with
> all the care and discrimination in our care to bestow, extended, in
> the whole, to the number of 300, and something over, all of them
> manuscripts of the choicest description; whether for matter, beauty
> of penmanship, or richness of decoration . . . We did not take
> any account of the remainder, or bulk, of this princely library.
> But I should conceive that it must have contained, altogether,
> from 3 to 4,000 volumes, or about ten times the number of
> our selection.[46]

Price and Ogg completed their selection by December 1799. Their
two lists consisted of 288 manuscripts selected for the Court of
Directors and sixty-one books dispatched to the Asiatic Society
of Bengal in Calcutta.[47] These included works that had beautiful
paintings, Hindustani poems, sciences and magic and so on.

All the Mysore manuscripts were transferred to the Fort William College that was founded in 1800 for the oriental scholars of the Company to study and decode. This was where a first serious attempt was made to classify and catalogue these manuscripts and books by Charles Stewart, the Assistant Professor of Persian at Fort William College, in collaboration with Maulavi Hussain Ali. Thirty-six per cent of the collection was in Arabic and 60 per cent in Persian. *A Descriptive Catalogue of the Oriental Library of the Late Tippoo Sultan of Mysore* was published by Stewart in 1809. In the preface, Stewart writes:

> The Library consisted of nearly 2000 volumes of Arabic, Persian and Hindy (or Hindustany) manuscripts, in all the various branches of Mohammedan literature. Many of these were beautifully written and highly ornamented; but a great portion were in a bad condition; and several having lost both the first and last pages, it was extremely difficult to discover the Author, or the period in which they were composed. Very few of these books had been purchased either by Tipoo or his father. They were part of the plunder brought from Sanoor [Savanur], Cudappah, and the Carnatic. Some of them had formerly belonged to the Mohammedan Kings of Bijapore and Golcondah; and the greater number had been the property of the Nabob Nesir Addowleh al Vahib Khan, brother of Mohammed Aly of the Carnatic, and were taken by Hyder in the fort of Chitore, during the year 1780. All the volumes that had been rebound at Seringapatam have the names of God, Mohammed, his daughter Fatimah and her sons, Hassen and Hussein . . . the names of the Four first Khalifs . . . on the four corners. At the top is 'Sirkari Khodadad' and at the bottom, Allah Kafy (God is Sufficient) . . . the topics of these were, in general theology or sufyism, which were his favourite studies. But the Sultan was ambitious of being an Author; and although we have not discovered any complete work of his composition, not less than forty-five books, in different subjects, were either composed, or translated from other languages, under his immediate patronage

or inspection. In most of these, his intolerance and aversion to all Christians and Hindus are strongly marked.[48]

Among the books that Tipu had commissioned was a compilation of the art of dyeing cloth and blending perfumes (*Mujuma al Senayi*), a work on medicine (*Bahr al-Manafi*), a Persian grammar book (*Kitab Amukhtan*), a compendium of Theology, Law and the art of government (*Fakhr ash-Shiukh*), and so on. There were 118 books on History, 115 books on Sufism, twenty-four books on ethics, 190 books on poetry, nineteen books on arts and sciences, seven books on Arithmetic and Mathematics, twenty books on astronomy, sixty-two books on Physics, forty-five books on philology, twenty-nine lexicographies, forty-six books on theology, ninety-five books on jurisprudence and forty-four Qurans.[49] Several theological texts on the Quran, the Hadith, Muslim Theology and Law were found in the library. Being fascinated by calligraphy, a Persian treatise titled *Risala dar Khatt-i-Tarz-i-Muhammadi* was composed with rules of calligraphy believed to have been invented by him.[50] A book on astrology, called *Zabarjad* is also credited to him.[51] Unlike Haidar who remained illiterate all his life, Tipu was a well-read man and the library collections, though part of the loot from other principalities, demonstrated the same.

His interest in science and technology was also born out of his immense curiosity. It is said that when he was around eighteen years old, when he raided Madras during the First Anglo–Mysore War, a microscope that belonged to one of Haidar's friends, had caught his attention there. Haidar Ali had it sent to Tipu as a gift through an English merchant, Mr Debonnaire.[52] Thus, in the plunder of the palace, the British found 'telescopes, and optical glasses of every size and sight, with looking glasses and pictures in unbounded profusion; while of china and glass ware there was sufficient to form a large mercantile magazine.'[53] Even when his sons were being released as hostages by the East India Company, Tipu had asked an Englishman, William Smith, to demonstrate some scientific experiments to him. Smith had recounted these in a letter to Dr Andrew Bell on 8 April 1794:

I exhibited the following experiments, viz. head and wig, dancing images, electric stool, cotton fired, small receiver and stand, hemispheres, Archimedes's screw, siphon, Tantalus's cup, water-pump, condensing engine etc., & Captain Doveton was present, and explained, as I went on, to the Sultaun, who was giving an instance of his being acquainted with some of these experiments. He has shewn [sic] us a condensing engine made by himself, which spouted water higher than ours. He desired me to teach two men, his *aruz-begs*[54] . . . on the 7th I was again sent for, and the following were exhibited: tumbler and balls, sealing-wax, twelve men shocked, among whom were several khans and *vackeels* . . . . Electric stool—a man of eminent rank stood, and the Sultaun applied his hand about the man to receive shocks . . . Pneumatic bell; microscope; mechanical powers . . . the Sultaun walked round the instruments, and handled several apparatus.[55]

But as mentioned in the preface by Stewart, there are several books of radical extremism and bigotry, a call for jihad against all infidels. *Muaiyid al-Mujahidin* or a Booster for Jihadists, for instance, is a collection of 104 Friday sermons that end with a call for jihad against all infidels in the kingdom, compiled by Tipu 'to rouse the zeal of his Mohammedan subjects against the Hindus and Christians.'[56] These were read out Friday after Friday in thousands of mosques wherever Tipu's writ ran.[57] Another titled *Fatawa-i-Muhammadi* is, according to the *Descriptive Catalogue*, a book that 'commences with the Sultan's favourite subject, war against infidels; and various extracts from the Quran, and Traditions [Hadis] are quoted to rouse the zeal of his Musalman subjects against the Hindus and Christians.'[58] The *Zad-al-Mujahidin* was a 'work . . . specially on the duties of a Musalman with regard to Holy War [Jihad] against infidels.'[59] It was 'an incitement to fanaticism or persecution of the Hindus, many of whom were compelled to become Mussulmans.'[60] In the *Aroos-i-Arifan*, there are 'the excellencies of the Mohammedan Religion, written for the conversion of the Hindus by some fanatic at Seringapatam, and dedicated to Tippoo Sultan.'[61] The preface to this book, written by Mahmud Bahri, clearly states that 'Tipu Sultan converted about ten lakhs of people to Islam and built 2227 mosques for saying prayers, and for the sake of Moslems, this new book was composed.'[62] Similar provocative incitements against Hindus and Christians were also seen in the *Vaaz al-Mujahidin*. It states that this was 'compiled by the order of Tippoo Sultan, whose mind appears to have been occupied Day and Night with this subject.'[63]

Historian Dr Suryanath Kamath mentions that a multi-storeyed library in the palace of Srirangapatna that housed several ancient manuscripts and treatises that belonged to the Wodeyar household attracted Tipu's ire. These holdings were perhaps in Kannada, Sanskrit and other classical languages. Kamath asserts that Tipu had these collections sent to the horse stables to be used to boil the grams for the horses there. This destruction of ancient treatises in the local language and also Tipu's over-dependence on Persian that came to replace the primacy of Kannada are seen as evidences of his antipathy for Kannada and its usage.[64]

The Dreams of Tipu Sultan

During the search of Tipu's inner apartments after the fall of the fort, Kirkpatrick discovered a curious manuscript in his escritoire, written ostensibly in the Sultan's own handwriting, as a register of his dreams. The Sultan's principal secretary, Habibullah, was present when this manuscript was found. Habibullah knew that such a register existed but was unaware of the contents, as the Sultan 'always manifested peculiar anxiety to conceal it from the view of any who happened to approach, while he was either reading, or writing on it.'[65] Later, on 23 April 1800, this little diary was presented in the name of the Marquis Wellesley to Hugh Inglis, the Chairman of the Court of Directors of the East India Company by Major Alexander Beatson. The diary is now in the collection of the India Office Library at the British Library in London.

Tipu seems to have had this penchant to jot down his dreams in Persian, as and when he saw them vividly enough to recall them. The preface to the book has him declaring 'the dreams I have had and am having are being written (in this register)'. The first of these thirty-seven recorded dreams dates back to 1785 and the last to 1798—covering thereby, almost the entire period of his reign. The majority of these dreams deal with wars and battles, with him defeating the infidels (on several occasions addressed as Nazarenes) and cutting them down to size. Some point to his reverence for the Prophet, and other Islamic saints and Sufis who keep appearing to shower their benedictions on him. In some, clearly, he records them immediately after he has woken up, as the entry ends with phrases like 'at this point, I woke up and wrote this down' and so on. Tipu himself has also interpreted these dreams in some cases, naturally in a manner that was favourable to him in the battle or a difficult situation that he was currently facing at that time. For instance, in Dream Twenty-eight, where he saw three silver trays filled with dates that were 'fresh and full of juice.' He interpreted this dream as the dominions of his three principal enemies—the Marathas, the British and the Nizam, which he hoped would all fall into his hands.[66]

Dream Thirteen talks of him prattling with a handsome young man who, after walking a few steps away from him, untied his hair from beneath his turban, and revealed himself to actually be a beautiful woman. When he woke up and discussed this curious dream, he was made to interpret it as an allusion to the Marathas who 'have put on the clothes of men, but in fact they will prove to be women.' At this point, he was, in fact, in conflict with Hari Pant, whose side he later defeated. The register thus concludes that true to this vision in his slumber, the Marathas 'all fled like women.'[67]

While being involved in the Malabar expedition against 'Raman Nair' (none other than Dharma Raja Balarama Varma, the ruler of Travancore), he had invoked Allah in his prayers before sleep, beseeching that 'in the hills the unbelievers of the land of the enemy have forbidden fasting and prayer; convert them all to Islam, so that the religion of Thy messenger may gain in strength.'[68] In his dream (Dream Seven), he saw a strange and hideous cow with its calf, looking like a big striped tiger in its countenance, face, teeth and so on. Its forelegs were those of a cow, and it had no hind legs as it came wobbling towards him. Tipu announces in his dream: 'God-willing, on arriving near this cow which looks like a tiger, I shall with my own hand cut it along with its calf into pieces.'[69] At this point, he woke up and then interpreted the dream to mean that 'the Nazarenes of the hills are like the cow with its calf with the appearance of tigers; and by the favour of God and through the felicity and aid of the Prophet, the place mentioned will be reduced with ease and all the irreligious Nazarenes will be slain . . . the absence of hinder-legs indicated that no one would afford them any help and that no Muslim would receive any injury at their hands.'[70]

In another dream (Dream Twelve), he goes to a big temple where there were several large idols. The idols suddenly take on a human countenance and the eyes begin to move, as though they were living beings. In the last row, there were two female idols draped in a sari that was drawn from between their two knees. He then indulges in some conversation with them. There are dreams of his visiting the Holy Kaaba at Mecca where some saint appears (and in one case Prophet Muhammad himself)[71] and confers a golden turban on him as a gift from God himself. Another where an assembly of fifty to sixty Muslim saints welcome him into their midst and bless his victory against infidels and his enemies.

Take, for instance, this dream (Dream Fourteen) of destroying the infidels:

On the 8th of the month Ja'fari, of the year Shata, 1218, from the birth of Muhammad, at Patan, the Capital, in the Darya Bagh, I had a dream: It seemed to me as if a battle had taken place near a wood with the Nazarenes and all the army of the Nazarenes had dispersed and fled, and by the favour of God, the army of the Sarkar-i-Ahmadi had been victorious. The officer of the unbelievers, with a few Nazarenes, retreated into a large house and closed the door. I asked my people as to what was to be done. They advised me to break open the door, in order that the house which was ornamented might suffer no damage. I said to them that the house was built of bricks and mortar, and therefore, we should set fire and burn down the gate and destroy all the Nazarenes within with our muskets. At this juncture, the morning dawned and I awoke. By the favour of God, it shall thus happen.[72]

Psychologically speaking, it is by analysing one's dreams that one gets to know the common themes and worries that preoccupy one's mind. Neurologist and psychoanalyst Sigmund Freud has suggested that dreams represent wish fulfilment, unconscious desires and conflicts. These repressed wishes are the wants and needs that have been denied, and they thus become part of the unconscious mind. They contain both manifest as well as latent content. The former is illustrated through visible images and remembered narratives that play out in the dream itself. The latter are the meanings and interpretations of the dreams. In Tipu's case, both these seem to form part of his dreams' diary. The dreams emanate from the subconscious mind of an individual. As per the Gestalt therapy of dream interpretation, every part of the dream, including other people and inanimate objects, relates to a part of the dreamer. Clearly, in Tipu's dreams, the battle scenes, the infidels, cows, his principal enemies and his wish to see them emasculated or them becoming feminine (implying powerless) seem to have occupied his subconscious mind all the time. Of course, an important drawback of dream analysis is that the person often self-reports and may not remember major details. In Tipu's register too, in several cases, he confessed that he completed the dream and its interpretation once he awoke. Hence, naturally a bias does creep in, influencing the manner in which the dream was recorded and analysed.

In more recent times, philosophers of consciousness and dreaming—Antti Revonsuo, Thomas Metzinger and Jennifer Windt have developed theories of consciousness whereby the concept of dreaming and the results of dream research play a crucial role. They all hypothesize that dreaming is a virtual reality or a realistic world-simulation constructed inside the brain. Other researchers such as Calvin S. Hall, George Lakoff, Rosalind Cartwright, Professor G. William Domhoff, William Dement and others too have several varied theories about dreams, its integration with the cognition process and with daily life and its challenges and experiences. Some dreams could also be premonitory and we do have an instance or two of that kind in Tipu's small register. Those who report remembering their dreams are said to operate from a region of their brain that causes them to wake up at the slightest of sounds. In Tipu's case too, his own description seems to indicate that he often woke up in starts, often obsessed to jot down all that he had seen in his sleep, before the dream evanesced.[73]

Historian Kate Brittlebank however also extrapolates these with the larger Islamic belief of the existence of an unseen realm (*alam ul-ghalib*) of which the imaginal world (*alam ul-mithal*) was an aspect. Mysticism and prophecies came from this realm and those adept at it were often hailed as great saints, who could portend the future or predict through their visions. She hence considers this dream register an important document in the long Islamic tradition of recording one's dreams and also imparting to them (and the dreamer) a paranormal or supranormal halo. In the midst of the uncertainties and struggles he was facing, Tipu seemingly tried to find both meaning as well as guidance through the medium of his dreams. Brittlebank thus concludes:

> It would clearly be a mistake to regard Tipu Sultan's dream book as an oddity or a document without historical usefulness. Considering the manuscript in its entirety, rather than merely focusing on the dreams, reveals the logic behind its construction as well as its place within the wider range of literature produced at the Mysore court. Above all, it provides an insight into how Tipu responded to the difficulties that he faced during the final years of his reign. Increasingly isolated and well aware of the threat posed by the rising power of the British, the Mysore ruler turned to the recognized methods of divination—astrology, bibliomancy and dream interpretation—in an attempt not only to understand but also deal with the situation. A man of considerable curiosity and resourcefulness, not to mention courage and self-belief, it may

well be that he looked to the past so as to influence the course of his future.[74]

A Day in the Life of the Sultan

What would a typical day in the life of Tipu Sultan be like, when he was not busy heading military expeditions or violently crushing rebellions? Many contemporary chroniclers—both British and Indian, have documented these details. He usually rose early, with the sun, and after being shampooed and rubbed, he proceeded for a wash. This was followed by a reading of the Quran for nearly an hour. He then held brief meetings with his principal officers and any others who sought his audience. This would be followed by a quick inspection of the Jamdar Khana, that housed jewellery, plates, fruits and valuables. A breakfast of nuts, almonds, jelly and milk would thereafter be served, which he would have with a munshi (secretary) and his three youngest children. His inner circle, consisting of Mir Sadak, the Benki Nawab, Purnaiya, Syed Mohammad Asif, Ghulam Ali, Ahmad Khan and his principal secretary Habibullah, sometimes joined in for breakfast and deliberations. There would be animated discussions that focused more on flattering the Sultan, about his chivalrous days on the warfront and so on. This was when the scribes would come in to take notes or have letters dictated or read out to him.

The breakfast and gossip would be followed by another royal durbar for which he would clothe himself in rich garments. On most other occasions, his attire would generally be plain and coarse—a typical, rugged military uniform. New recruits were inspected in the durbar and every detail of their caste, principality, extent of their religious knowledge and so on was personally ascertained. Only then was a decision taken regarding hiring someone or increasing the pay of deserving candidates. Those found wanting would be packed off to a qazi or Muslim scholar to be trained in Islamic studies. These examinations lasted for hours.

After a brief siesta, the evening saw the Sultan inspecting on horseback the army's war preparedness. Fortifications and repair work were looked into. His mind constantly thought of war and military preparations. Upon his return to the palace, details of arsenals, manufactories, and classified news from the espionage cell would be shared with him. He normally passed the evening in the company of his three elder sons, or one of his principal officers and heads of the various departments of the state, a qazi and Habibullah. They all usually sat together for supper. Habibullah had mentioned to Alexander Beatson later that these conversations were 'remarkably lively, entertaining and instructive.'[75] During the meal, he was fond of reciting passages from his most admired poets and historians; and sometimes 'he amused himself with sarcasms upon the *Caufer* [kafir] or infidels and enemies of the Circar and often discoursed upon learned and religious subjects'[76] with the Qazi and Munshi. After this, all of them were dismissed and he took a walk or a light exercise, and when he was tired enough, would lie down on his couch and read a book on religion or history, before he fell asleep.

From the principal front of his palace, which also served as a revenue office, he sometimes showed himself up to the cheering public. The entry into the private square was however through a strong, narrow passage, where there were four, tamed chained tigers always found. His private apartments had a large, lofty hall that opened up in the front and on the other three sides was fully shut off from ventilation. In this, he was 'wont to sit, and write much; for he was a wonderful projector, and was constantly forming new systems for the management of his dominions.'[77] Very few, except the likes of Mir Sadak, were admitted into this chamber. Behind this room was his bedchamber, which communicated with the hall by a door and two windows. The door was strongly shut from inside and an iron grating defended the windows. The Sultan, 'lest any person should fire upon him while in bed, slept in a hammock, which was suspended from the roof by chains, in such a situation as to be invisible through the windows. In the hammock were found a sword and a pair of loaded pistols.'[78] There was only one passage from this room that led to the women's apartments or zenana.

His harem consisted of numerous servants, eunuchs and 333 women. In fact, there were 601 women, that included 268 wives and concubines of Haidar and the rest of Tipu. Buchanan writes:

> The only other passage from the private square was into the zenana, or women's apartments. This has remained perfectly inviolate under the usual guard of eunuchs, and contains about six hundred women, belonging to the Sultan and his late father. A great part of these are slaves, or attendants on the ladies; but they are kept in equally strict confinement with their mistresses. The ladies of the Sultan are about eighty in number. Many of them are from Hindustan Proper, and many are daughters of Brahmans or Hindu Princes, taken by force from their parents. They have all been shut up in the zenana when they were young; and have been carefully brought up to a zealous belief in the religion of Mahomet. I have sufficient reason to think that none of them are desirous of leaving their confinement; being wholly ignorant of any other manner of living, and having no acquaintance whatever beyond the walls of their prison.[79]

Among the eighty superior women in his harem, were the two sisters of the Coorg royal family, three members of the Mysore royal family and also alarmingly, the niece of Purnaiya.[80] Whether this was the reason for Purnaiya's alleged treason, one would never know. The women of the families of Anche Shamayya and Krishna Rao who had dared to raise a rebellion also found their way to the harem. The married daughter of the Nargund commander too had been packed off to the harem. Denys Forest quotes Captain Marriott, who had been tasked with chronicling the Mahal after the fall of Srirangapatna, as stating that 'the majority of the women were originally Hindus, from families whom the Sultan had put to death or held in confinement.'[81] Tipu also seemed to fancy young, castrated boys. In his instructions to his embassy sent to Constantinople in 1785, he asked them to purchase 'twelve eunuchs of nine or ten years, of the Abyssinian race or any other' and added that the expenditures incurred 'should be paid out of the Government money.'[82]

Describing Tipu's physical appearance and personality, and the contrast with his father, Wilks writes, albeit with a lot of colonial disdain:

In person, he [Tipu] was neither so tall nor so robust as his father, and had a short pursy neck; the large limbs, small eyes, aquiline nose, and fair complexion of Hyder, marked the Arabic character derived from his mother. Tippoo's singularly small and delicate hands and feet, his large and full eyes, a nose, less prominent, and a much darker complexion were all national characteristics of the Indian form. There was in the first view of his countenance, an appearance of dignity which wore off on farther observation; and his subjects did not feel that it inspired the terror or respect, which in common with his father, he desired to command. Hyder's lapse from dignity into low and vulgar scolding, was among the few points of imitation or resemblance, but in one it inspired fear, in the other ridicule. In most instances exhibiting a contrast to the character and manners of his father, he spoke in a loud and unharmonious tone of voice; he was extremely garrulous, and on superficial subjects, delivered his sentiments with plausibility. In exterior appearance, he affected the soldier; in his toilet, the distinctive habits of the Mussulman; he thought hardiness to be indicated by a plain unincumbered attire, which he equally exacted from those around him, and the long robe and trailing drawers were banished from his court . . . of the vernacular languages, he spoke no other than Hindostanee and Canarese; but from a smattering in Persian literature, he considered himself as the first philosopher of the age. He spoke that language with fluency; but although the pen was forever in his hand, he never attained either elegance or accuracy of style. The leading features of his character were vanity and arrogance; no human being was ever so handsome, so wise, so learned, or so brave as himself. Resting on the shallow instructions of his scanty reading, he neglected the practical study of mankind. No man had ever less penetration into character; and accordingly, no prince was ever so ill served; the army alone remained faithful, in spite of all his efforts for the subversion of discipline and allegiance. Hyder delegated to his instruments a large portion of his own power, as the best means of its preservation. Tippoo seemed to feel every exercise of delegated authority as an [sic] usurpation of his own . . . from constitutional or incidental causes, he was less addicted than his father to the pleasures of the harem, which, however, contained at his death about one hundred persons . . . he could neither be truly characterized as liberal or parsimonious; as tyrannical or benevolent; as a man of talents, or as destitute of parts. By turns, he assumed the character of each. In one object alone he appeared to be consistent, having perpetually on his tongue the projects of jehad—holy war. The most intelligent and sincere well-wishers of the house concurred in the opinion of his father, that his heart and head were both defective, however covered by a plausible and imposing flow of words; and they were not always without suspicions of mental aberration . . . Tippoo was intoxicated with success, and desponding in adversity. His mental energy failed with the decline of fortune; but it were unjust to question his physical courage. He fell in the defence of his capital; but he fell, performing the duties of a common soldier, not of a general.[83]

Bowring mentions that unlike Haidar, Tipu retained his eyebrows, eyelashes and moustache. He is said to be modest and bashful that 'no one ever saw any part of his person, save his feet, ankles and wrists; while in the bath he always covered himself from head to foot.'[84] He dressed very simply, unlike Haidar. On long journeys, though, he wore a coat of gold cloth with a red tiger-streak embroidered on it. He normally wrapped a white handkerchief over his turban and under his chin. The colour of the turban became green in the later years of his life. He was not known to indulge in ribald conversations like his father did, but loved to philosophize on every subject under the sun. Given to extreme flattery, he was constantly surrounded by sycophants who praised every word that came out of his mouth. He evinced great distrust towards even his ablest servants, thereby slowly embittering them all against him. Bowring asserts that many who knew Tipu in the later years of his life discovered that 'his understanding was at times clouded over in a way that betrayed symptoms of mental aberration.'[85]

Drawing a rather harsh assessment of his legacy that was marred by his bigotry and despotism, Bowring states: 'He [Tipu] rivalled Mahmud of Ghazni, Nadir Shah, and Ala-ud-din the Pathan Emperor of Delhi surnamed the *Khuni* or the Bloody, all of whom were famous for the number of infidels slaughtered by their orders. For this very zeal for the faith, notwithstanding the cruelties which attended his persecutions, the name of Tipu Sultan was long held in reverence by his co-religionists in Southern India—a proof how readily crimes that cry to Heaven are condoned when the perpetrator of them is supposed to have been animated by a sincere desire to propagate the faith which he professed.'[86]

Quite evidently, a definitive conclusion on Tipu's legacy and his administrative achievements is extremely hard to come by, as it is a mixed bag that contains several elements of his innate bigotry. A fair estimate is provided by Kaveh Yazdani thus:

Tipu had clear pre-modern characteristics. He was a patriarch who possessed a harem with servants, eunuchs, and 333 women. He showed prejudice against the children of prostitutes and ran an Islamic theocracy that discriminated against non-Muslims in the administration, army, and taxation. He prohibited drinking alcohol and smoking tobacco or cannabis. Tipu neglected to modernise Mysore's traditional education system. He established no universities, military and engineering schools during his reign. He was neither interested nor capable of modernising the political and judicial system according to principles such as equality before the law, the rule of law, principles of democracy and citizens' rights. At the same time, he was very aware of the need to modernise the military, economic and technological structure of the country. He successfully continued his father's proto-modernisation of the military establishment along European lines . . . All this suggests that Tipu Sultan was neither pre-modern nor modern, but a person who, like his father Haidar, reflected the contradictions of a society in transition.[87]

20

A Bloodied Legacy

I seemed to be reciting the names of God on almonds amidst which I had mixed '*salgram*' stones,[1] *salgram* being an object of worship by the unbelievers. My motive in doing so was that like their idols who were embracing Islam, the unbelievers also would enter the fold of Islam. On concluding my recitation, I stated that all the idols of the unbelievers had embraced Islam and I ordered the stones to be picked out and replaced by almonds. My interpretation is that by the grace of God, all unbelievers would embrace Islam and the country would pass into the hands of the *Sarkar-i-Khudadad*.[2]

Thus had dreamt Tipu once, which he dutifully and proudly recorded in his dream register. But this was not a one-off exception to his innate desire to suppress the faiths of non-Muslims. The leitmotif of his rule and its bloodstained legacy are testimony to this, and to this horrifying aspect of his life we shall turn to now. There are multiple opinions about this complex and controversial aspect of Tipu's legacy. We must evaluate his actions both within and outside the borders of his kingdom to arrive at a semblance of a conclusion.

Tipu's Religious Policy within the Kingdom of Mysore

While analysing this, what one must evaluate is whether the monarch had:

711

1. An intent or inherent ill will against those who were not part of his faith.
2. Evidence of iconoclasm or destruction of places of worship of other faiths.
3. Discriminatory policies towards non-Muslims.
4. Whether symbols, rituals, festivals of other faiths were allowed to be continued.

The Intent

In the manifesto that Tipu Sultan brought out on 3 May 1786 as an article of faith for his Sarkar-e-Khudadad, he leaves no room for ambiguity:

> It is our constant object and sincere intention, that those worthless and stiff-necked infidels, who have turned aside their heads from obedience to the true-believers, and openly raised the standards of infidelity, should be chastised by the hands of the faithful, or made either to acknowledge the true religion or to pay tribute, particularly at this time, when owing to the imbecility of the princes of Hind, that insolent race having conceived the futile opinion, that the true believers are become weak, mean and contemptible; and not satisfied even with this, but preparing for war, have over-run and laid waste the territories of the Moslems, and extended the hand of violence and injustice on the property and honour of the faithful.[3]

From the letters, the books in his library and his own dream register entries and writings, it is amply clear that innately Tipu had immense antipathy for non-Muslims and considered it his bounden, religious duty to inflict a holy war (jihad) against them. The mode of undertaking this holy war and what it sought to achieve too has been well documented in the literature produced in his time. It is a different matter whether he could fully manifest what he deeply desired or whether the practical feasibilities and harsh realities made him compromise with this wish.

Within the kingdom of Mysore, like Haidar, Tipu too realized that his subjects who comprised a Hindu majority still had an unstinted reverence and soft corner for the Wodeyar family that his father had displaced. If he had indulged in any overt iconoclastic attempts within Mysore, he knew that the simmering anger among his subjects could well boil over into a full-scale rebellion—something that he could ill afford while being engaged in bloody battles with his many enemies and crushing revolts in other places. But his thoughts, his writing and his dreams do portray the innate animosity for those who did not subscribe to his faith and belief systems and how crushing them, even violently, was constantly on his mind. As discussed earlier, among other things the following lines were engraved on the handle of his sword: 'My victorious sabre is lightning for the destruction of the unbelievers. Haidar, the Lord of the Faith, is victorious for my advantage. And, moreover, he destroyed the wicked race who were unbelievers.'[4]

The eternal search for the legitimacy of his rule and to not be perceived as a usurper of someone else's throne remained a constant narrative in Tipu's short, yet stormy reign. The declaration of his independence from the Mughal emperor, and his many emissaries to the rest of the world, especially the Islamic nations, to seek for himself the sanction to rule Mysore, are testimonies to this burning desire within him. To achieve this, he made deliberate efforts to try and obliterate the memory and influences of the erstwhile Hindu Maharajas of Mysore on the populace. For this purpose, as Lewis Rice states, 'even the fine irrigation works, centuries old, of the Hindu Rajas were to be destroyed and reconstructed in his own name.'[5] Possibly, Tipu sought a more phased and gradual Islamization of the Mysore kingdom that was predominantly Hindu. Right from coining an Islamic name '*Sarkar-e-Khudadad*' for the kingdom itself, to introducing Persian in the court and to renaming existing cities and towns with Persian- and Islamic-sounding names, these can be seen as steps towards this direction. A blanket conversion of a kingdom as seeped in Hindu heritage as Mysore was an impossibility, as he came to realize.

The Dichotomy between Grants and Iconoclasm

The *Annual Report of the Mysore Archaeological Department* of 1935 states the following:

> Close to the eastern or Bangalore gate stood formerly a Hindu temple with a *prakara* wall and a verandah running around. It was very probably a structure of the early eighteenth century and was not of great architectural importance. It is said to have been dedicated to Hanuman or Anjaneya. Near it, in the field, Tipu is said to have played in his younger days when his father was yet a rising young officer in the Mysore army. One day a Fakir told the boy that he would some day become very prosperous and directed him to convert the temple into a mosque when he became a great man. When he became king, Tipu compelled the Hindus to remove the image from the temple, filled up the ground floor and on the top of the temple got erected the Jumma Masjid, the hall of which has numerous foil arches and a Mihrab on the west in the form of a small room. On the walls of the hall are found stone inscriptions with quotations from the Quran, etc. One of them gives the date of its construction corresponding to 1787 A.D. The main points of interest in the mosque are its two great and beautiful *minars* which combine majesty with grace. Their shafts are ornamented with cornices and floral bands while near the top are narrow terraces with ornamental parapets. From there a visitor gets a panoramic view of the neighbourhood. At the crown of the *minars* are large masonry *kalashas* placed upon flowers and fully ornamented. Above are small metallic *kalashas* of the Hindu type.[6]

In recent times, this has become a site of intense conflict and contestations with thousands of Hindu activists demanding permission to perform their prayers to Lord Hanuman inside the Jama Masjid Mosque in Srirangapatna.[7]

Tipu is said to have demolished the temple of Varahaswami—the boar avatar of Sri Mahavishnu, in Srirangapatna.[8] This was perhaps due to the disdain with which the animal is held in Islam.

After the fall of Tipu and the shifting of the capital to Mysore, the Wodeyars reconsecrated it as the Shweta Varahaswami temple in the palace complex.

During his visit to Coimbatore during 29–30 October 1800, Francis Buchanan records:

> I visited a celebrated temple at Peruru, which is two miles from Coimbatore. It is dedicated to Iswara, and called Mail [high] Chitumbra [Chidambaram],[9] in order to distinguish it from another Chitumbra, that is near Pondicherry . . . the Brahmans in the time of Haidar had very large endowments in lands; but these were entirely reassumed by Tipu, who also plundered the temple of its gold and jewels. He was obliged, however to respect it more than many others in his dominions; as when he issued a general order for the destruction of all idolatrous buildings, he excepted only this, and the temples of Seringapatam and Melukote. This order was never enforced and a few of the temples were injured, except those which were demolished by the Sultan in person who delighted in this work of zeal . . . even in the reign of the Sultan an allowance was clandestinely given, so that the puja, or worship, never was entirely stopped, as happened in many less celebrated places.[10]

As mentioned in the previous chapter, Tipu was highly superstitious and relied on several forms of divination, including astrology and his own dreams, to make sense of the chaos around him and the constant challenges that life was throwing at him. We have seen how, even on the last day of his life, he had summoned Brahmin priests and astrologers to conduct japam (chants) and pujas for him, as also to look minutely at his own horoscope for clues on what he should be doing. Octogenarian scholar Melukote Araiyar Sri Rama Sharma narrates an interesting anecdote: 'Given his predisposition towards superstition, it is widely believed that Tipu was told once by some wiseman that he should leave three types of stones (meaning idols) in Mysore unmolested: "*Yeddha Kallu* (standing stone), *Biddha Kallu* (Fallen stone), *Gundu Kallu* (round stone)." If he ever mistakenly attempted to desecrate these three, the end of his regime would usher in. The *Yeddha Kallu* here was the standing idol of Cheluvanarayanaswamy in Melukote, the *Biddha Kallu* was the supine idol of Ranganathaswamy in Srirangapatna, and the Gundu Kallu was the round Shivalinga of Srikantheshwara Swamy in Nanjanagud. Particularly, the astrologers and Brahmin priests seem to have induced this belief very strongly in Tipu's mind, along with a kind of manic fear for the very word "Ranga" or "Ranganatha" in his mind. The Chamundeshwari idol too was attempted to be destroyed during Haidar's time, but the priests got wind of this sinister plan. They hastily and cleverly concealed the original one and had a duplicate one installed, which bore the brunt of the attack. This mutilated idol is still housed in the Chamundeshwari temple in Mysore.'[11]

The fear in his mind for the word 'Ranga' seems quite plausible when one sees the plethora of temples in southern Karnataka, all part of erstwhile royal Mysore state, bearing the name of 'Ranga.' Several of them are not even shrines of Ranganathaswamy, the lying image of Sri Mahavishnu on the serpent. For instance, in Magadi, a small hamlet near Bangalore, which was the home of the chieftain who built the city and its original mud fort, Kempegowda, there is a temple of 'Magadi Ranga' that is believed to have been constructed during Chola times. The principal deity here, however, is a standing Venkateshwara, and behind somewhere is tucked in a small, innocuous idol of a supine Ranganatha. This deity has been named as Beleyo Ranga or the growing Ranga, with the belief that this small idol will grow someday into a large one as we normally see in Ranganatha shrines. The local folklore and tales from the priest confirm that the temple itself was hastily renamed so that it could be saved from the wrath of Tipu or his marauding armies. There seems to have been a standing instruction not to molest any temple that had 'Ranga' in its name. We thus have several such temples: Kalyana 'Ranga' in Hemagiri (which too is actually the temple of Venkateshwara), Biligiri Ranga atop the B.R. Hills in

Chamarajanagara (again a standing image of Ranganathaswamy), Guddada Hole 'Ranga' at Navile in Maddur (standing deity) and numerous others. So, it is quite likely that to save the deities and the temples, this innovative method was used by the Hindus of the time to quickly install a Ranganatha idol or rename their deity with a 'Ranga' suffix to ensure that they survived the sword of the Sultan. In fact, Maharani Lakshmi Ammanni too wrote her letters to her Pradhans or the British Government in Madras using the nom de plume or pen name 'Sri Ranga' possibly with this in mind that anything with that nomenclature would remain safe and unmolested.

The superstition instilled against the desecration of the three important shrines in Melukote, Srirangapatna and Nanjangud could also possibly explain why Tipu placated these with gifts, shawls, vessels and elephants. Here, too, Araiyar Sri Rama Sharma states: 'There were several costly necklaces of the nine gems (*navaratna*) that were gifted to the Shri Cheluvanarayanaswamy deity by the past Maharajas of Mysore, right from the times of Raja Wodeyar to Chikkadevaraja Wodeyar. One of these precious necklaces had been stealthily taken away by the priest to be hidden for safekeeping in a tank at Gowdagere. Hence that necklace still remains and is kept in the Mandya Treasury and brought to the temple for the annual Brahmotsava and other festivals. The rest of the ornaments were confiscated by Tipu Sultan. He donated a large war drum and elephants to the temple though. For the upkeep of the elephants, he appointed two Muslim families that had come from Andhra and Kerala, as the first ever Muslim settlers in Tirunarayanapura (Melukote). The "*Deevatige Salam*" practice was started by Haidar Ali. Two torches or Deevatige are lit in front of the temple tower (*rajagopura*) during the *Maha Mangalarathi* every evening, and the arati was renamed with an Urdu name "*Salam*", which continued even in Tipu's time.'[12] The donation of the two elephants and a kettledrum (nagara) to the Melukote temple is much talked about, though the confiscation of the jewellery or the reason for the stationing of the elephants is glossed over. The kettledrum has a Persian inscription on it that states the donation details: 'Second *qit'a naqara* Year 1215

(Mauludi corresponding to c. 1786 CE) by Mohammad Fazn Baksh, a servant of Sarkar-e-Haidari.'[13]

Tipu did present gifts to some temples. Seven silver cups and a silver camphor burner in the Sri Ranganathaswamy temple in Srirangapatna bear an inscription stating that they were 'gifts of Tippu Sultana Paachchha.'[14] But interestingly, three of these cups and the camphor burner also bear additional inscriptions on them stating that those articles were presented to the deity by one Kalale Kanthaiya who was mostly a contemporary of Chikkadevaraja Wodeyar—implying that these were donated several decades preceding Tipu. From this we might conclude that they were presented initially by Kalale Kanthaiya, carried away by Tipu later, and then regranted to the temple 'at the prayer of the devotees of the temple with his inscriptions newly engraved.'[15]

A 'jeweled silver cup in the Srikantheshwara temple of Nanjangud bears an inscription stating that it was a present from Tipu Sultan Padasha.'[16] Next to the Devi Parvathi shrine at the Nanjangud temple is a greenish jade *linga* or 'Padsha Linga' which is said to have been installed at the orders of Tipu Sultan.[17] According to folklore, Haidar's favourite elephant had fallen sick with an eye ailment, and it was by the blessings of the deity of Nanjangud that it regained its health. He was hence eulogized as 'Hakim Nanjunda'— the Divine Doctor.[18]

Writing in *The Proceedings of the Indian History Congress* in 1944, A. Subbaraya Chetty, a teacher from Madras, lists a series of endowments and grants that Tipu made. These are as follows:[19]

1782:

1. An order directing Haridasayya, the Amildar of the Baramahal territory to resume for the Sarkar, all the lands and franchises, except *Devadayam* and *Brahmadayam* (temple and Brahmin endowments).

2. The grant of Kothanuthala, a village in the present Cudappah district to one Ramachar, son of Komachar, for the puja of the Anjaneyaswami temple of Gandikota.

3. A Maharatta [Marathi] *Sanad* issued to his Amildar Konappa directing him to allow the Swamiji of Pushpagiri Mutt to enjoy the revenues of Thongapalli and Golapalli.

4. A *Sanad* ordering the continuation of usual worship of Venkatachalapali temple and restoration of the discontinued worship of Anjaneyaswami temple at Pulivendla in the Cudappah district.

5. Grant of Gattupet Agraharam as '*Sarva Manyam*' [tax-free land] for expenses of Narasimhaswami temple at a lesser rate than in his predecessor's time.

1783:

1. An *Agraharam* grant to Himakuntala Lakshminarasimha Somayyaji and five others in the south of the village of Potladurthi, Kamalapuram Taluq.

1784:

1. A *Sanad* granting Ventampalli Agraharam to Venkatachala Shastri and a number of Brahmins to dedicate their time praying for a length of his life and prosperity.

2. On Baba Budangiri [in Chickmagalur district], there is what is called Dattatreya Peetah. An inscription referring to Tipu's restoration of twenty villages given originally by the kings of Anegondi to the Peetah.

1785:

1. Grant to Narasimhaswami temple of Melkota [Melukote] of twelve elephants sent through the Naik Srinivasachar.

1786:

1. Grant of kettledrum to temple of Narasimhaswami of Melkota.
2. A Sanskrit verse in Canarese script recording the grant of lands to temples and Brahmins on the banks of Tungabhadra.
3. Grant of village of Ramakrishnam Botlupalli as shotryam to Ramakrishnam Botlu.

1787:

1. Grant of permission for the construction of a mosque on the side of a Hindu temple got from the Brahmins with their goodwill [the Anjaneya temple on which the Jama Masjid was built in Srirangapatna].

1788:

1. A Maharatta [Marathi] inscription ordering Asuf Mohamed to continue the enjoyment of the villages of Oballapet and Koppolu to Rangacharlu and Sumati Srinivasacharlu together with other allowances.
2. Continuance of all *Manyams* [land grants] to Chennakeswaraswami temple of Machunur.
3. A *Sanad* of Tippu granting hereditary annual pension of ten pagodas to Narasimhajoshi, a *panchangi* [astrologer].
4. Continuation of grant of life pension to Rama Pandit, a physician.

1789:

1. Grant of pension to Venkannachari and Srinivasa Moorthi Achari.

1790:

1. A Canarese inscription recording Tippu's grant of Inam of Kamalapuram to Lakshmikantachari.

2. An order of Tippu to Haridasayya, Amildar of Baramahal, directing the restoration of the land attached to the *Devasthanam* [temple] of Chandramowlishwara in the village of Kaveripatti village . . . on the representation of the fact by Sankarayya Pujari of Salem District, with all the produce that may have been collected from it in the interim, agreeable to established custom.

Between 1782 and 1792:

1. Directing that 1/64 of the grant made to Anandabhatt Gopalabhat of Anayam Pettah must be used for the maintenance of Lakshminarasimha Pagoda [temple] of that village.
2. Presentation of a Dutch-bell (carried from Christian churches of Malabar) to Venkataramana temple of Nagar.
3. Presentation of a jewelled cup (silver) to Sri Kanteshwara Temple at Nanjangud.
4. A proverb in vogue in Kanakala of South Canara district of '*Tippu Sultan Ale Ruppe*' in referring to the silver jewels Tippu presented to Veera Hanuman temple of Kanakala.
5. Babayya Durga [Dargah] at Penukonda and the Durga [Dargah] of Syed Salar Masul Sahib near Tonnur.
6. Pervali Kyfit—During the rule of Tippu, the temple of Sri Ranga of that village all the daily, annual and other periodical pujas, festivals, processions, worships, with all the facilities and privileges provided for everyone connected with that temple according to all traditions and all the court officials personally supported all the performances of the pujas.
7. In Tipu's time, the idol was installed in the Prasanna Venkateshwara temple in Uratur in Kommaditima and provision was made for the expenses of the daily worship and inam lands were granted to Archakas [priests] and other servants of the temple.
8. Tipu's *Sanad* for an annual allowance of 85 chakras to the two temples of Lakshminarayana and Somasundaraswami of Doulatabad.

When one analyses the entries provided by Chetty, a few things emerge. The sources of several of these entries are merely stated as 'L.R. (local records)' by Chetty, without giving sufficient details of what these are. Conspicuously, the number of annual grants were quite high in 1782 which was when Haidar Ali was still ruling; he died only in December that year. From 1783 onwards, which was when Tipu Sultan assumed power, the number of annual grants does see a dip. Chetty has added to the list sundry grants of life pension and so on to individuals (astrologers and physicians), as grants to temples. Curiously, even the case of the Anjaneya temple of Srirangapatna being converted to the Jama Masjid has been cited as a grant by Tipu! Some entries are actually of grants made to a dargah at Penukonda and Tonnur, and these two are cited as Hindu endowments. Some are appellate entries, as in redressal of a possible unfair confiscation of lands which, when contested by the affected party, was then restored to the original grantee. These, too, have been taken up as grants made by Tipu. Many grants are not borne out of any great love or respect for the Hindu religion but driven by fear and the insecurity of retaining his throne, instilled in him by the astrologers whom he wholly depended on.

Also, interestingly, the entries almost end after 1792, which marked the conclusion of the disastrous Third Anglo–Mysore War. This seems to suggest that after the war and the manner in which there was large-scale internal sabotage, Tipu gave up hope of being able to win over the trust of the Hindus. With his revenues coming down after the treaty signed in 1792, with half his dominions gone, he issued his new commercial regulations that called for a takeover of temple land grants. Temples in Mysore would have thereby lost their source of sustenance and daily worship after this state takeover of their grant lands. But to balance this out and placate the Hindu subjects, it is around this time that we find Tipu's letters to the Shankaracharya of Sringeri that have been discussed earlier. There does seem to have been a genuine reverence for the Shankaracharya both on the part of Haidar Ali and Tipu Sultan, as evidenced in the letters they had been writing to him earlier, which has been stated in preceding chapters. In the shameful episode of the destruction of the

Sharada temple by the pindaries in the Maratha army, along with a genuine concern for the Swamiji, there also seems to be realpolitik kicking in where Tipu wanted to capitalize on the situation to score a major point over his bitter foes, the Marathas. That these grants and offers of help were also followed by requests to pray for his victory and long life also show how by then he had come fully under the control of astrologers and others in the wake of the uncertainties of war and the reverses he faced. It was quite ironic that around the time he had confiscated the land grants made to temples and Brahmins, he was also requesting the Shankaracharya to employ the very same community of Brahmins to perform incantations, penances and other rituals for his longevity. As Wilks observes:

> This is nearly the form of the *jebbum* [Japam] which is always performed during a drought in Mysoor, for procuring rain. That Hyder, himself, half a Hindoo, should sanction these ceremonies, is in the ordinary course of human action; but that Tippoo, the most bigoted of Mahommedans, professing an open abhorrence and contempt for the Hindoo religion, and the bramins its teachers, destroying their temples, and polluting their sanctuaries, should never fail to enjoin the performance of the jebbum when alarmed by imminent danger, is, indeed, an extraordinary combination of arrogant bigotry and trembling superstition; of general intolerance mingled with occasional respect for the object of persecution.[20]

Discriminatory Practices

Another important factor to consider a sovereign's impartiality, or the lack thereof, is the manner in which subjects belonging to various faiths, other than his own, were treated. Were there systemic mechanisms and policies that disadvantaged one vis-à-vis another, did special benefits accrue to the members of the king's faith? About this, renowned scholar M.H. Gopal writes:

> He [Tipu] had great aversion to non-Muslims and this feeling became stronger by the ungrateful attitude of the Brahman revenue officials. After 1792, therefore, he placed the faithful Muslims in

more of the important offices like the *asofdaries* and *amildaries*.
Of the diwans or provincial revenue heads in 1792 only one was a
Hindu. Of 65 *asofs* and deputy *asofs* in 1797–98 not one was a non-
Muslim and almost all the principal *mustaddis* even were Muslim,
whole of the 26 Mysore civil and military officers captured by
the British in 1792 and demanded back by Tipu, six only were
Hindus and even they were petty clerks. The communalization of
offices in the *Khodadad Sirkar* began much earlier than 1792 but
was intensified after the third Anglo–Mysore War . . . Strangely,
the result was . . . the diminution of revenue . . . The officials so
appointed to posts requiring deep knowledge and great patience .
. . could scarcely read and write . . . the candidates were seldom
chosen for any other reason than their being Mohamedans . . . he
would promote a *tipdar* (commander of a hundred men) or a petty
amildar to be a Meer Meeran (the highest military rank); and raise
a *risaldar* to the honours of a Meer Asof (a member of the Board
of Revenue) or a wretched Killedar . . . to those of a Meer Suddm
(superintendent general of forts) . . . another change was the
introduction of Persian as the medium of accounts in the revenue
department. It was so far the practice in Mysore for the *tarafdars*
to make out the revenue accounts in Kannada, fair copies of which
were communicated to the *amildars* who had them translated
into Marathi. Copies in both languages were kept under separate
and independent officers meant as a reciprocal check . . . Tipu
ordered the accounts to be submitted in Persian probably to help
his Muslim officers and perhaps to Persianise [sic] Mysore . . . this
change must have resulted in widening the gulf between the higher
officials who were Muslims and their Hindu subordinates.[21]

Further, regarding the differential taxation systems between Muslims
and non-Muslims, M.H. Gopal writes:

Even in the Revenue Code . . . Tipu exhibited his communal
tendencies. Mussulmans were exempted from paying the house-
tax and taxes on grains and other goods meant for their personal

use and not for trade. Christians were seized and deported to the capital, and their property confiscated. Converts to Islam were given concessions such as exemption from taxes. Special attention was given to the education of Muslim children.[22]

The humiliating defeat in the Third Anglo–Mysore War seems to have been an inflection point in the reign of Tipu Sultan regarding his attitude towards the Hindus of his kingdom, whom he suspected increasingly of conspiring against him. Hence, reducing their participation in government, confiscating the lands and revenues of temples and Brahmins, and differential taxation systems seem to have gained momentum after this period.

Allowance of Visual Manifestations of Other Faiths

Recently, a lot of discussion was initiated around a heavy golden oval ring, weighing 41.2 gm, with the name of 'Ram' engraved inside it in Devanagari script, surrounded fully by floral buds. It was auctioned in London by Christie's in 2014 for £1,45,000.[23] After the fall of Srirangapatna, the ring had found its way to Arthur Wellesley, who gave it to his niece, Emily Wellesley-Pole (later Lady FitzRoy Somerset). She gave it thereafter to her husband Lord FitzRoy Somerset. It was deposited with the Royal United Service Institution by Lt Col George Somerset in 1895. The catalogue of this Royal United Service Museum that dates to 1908 describes this ring as: 'Ring which belonged to the famous Tippoo Sahib, Sultan of Mysore, who was killed at the Capture of Seringapatam, 1799, taken from his finger by Colonel Honourable A. Wellesley (Duke of Wellington), and given by him to his niece, Lady FitzRoy Somerset.'[24] This catalogue entry, made 200 years after his death and with the ring having passed through many hands, seems to have assumed that he always wore the ring. This has led several people to conclude that the ring was recovered from the corpse of Tipu Sultan when the British discovered it on that fateful day of 4 May 1799. But the eyewitness account of Major Allan, who was part of the search party that went looking for Tipu, that we have seen earlier clearly states: 'His [Tipu's] dress consisted of a jacket of fine white linen, loose drawers of flowered chintz, with a crimson cloth of silk and cotton, round his waist; a handsome pouch with a red and green silk belt, hung across his shoulder; his head was uncovered, his turban being lost in the confusion of his fall; he had an amulet on his arm, but **no ornament whatsoever** [*emphasis mine*].'[25] Such a heavy and prominent ring would not have missed the attention of a chronicler who was narrating every minor detail of the appearance of Tipu's corpse and the dress he wore. The ring nevertheless was in his treasury and could well have been a part of the loot plunder or a gift given to him (by, some say, the Shankaracharya of Sringeri, but there is absolutely no evidence of that) that he kept, but ascribing 'secular credentials' to Tipu, and of his wearing this ring always and it being found on his corpse, are merely fantastic tales. In fact, the auction listing by Christie's itself states: 'It is surprising that a ring bearing the name of a Hindu god would have been worn by the great Muslim warrior. It is perhaps more likely that the ring was taken from Tipu Sultan's collection.'[26]

References are often made to Seebi, a small town in Tumkur, that is home to a famous Narasimhaswami Temple.[27] It was constructed in the late eighteenth century by three brothers Lakshminarasappa, Puttanna and Nallappa in the memory of their father Kacheri Karnik Krishnappa who had served in the Wodeyar court and their mother Alamelu who burnt herself as sati on her husband's pyre. The brothers were revenue collectors in Tipu's time. The entrance to the temple has some stunning murals made of organic dyes that are still extant. The murals even while drawing from epics of Hindu gods and goddesses, also has scenes of Haidar Ali's darbar and of Tipu Sultan heroically fighting a tiger with a sword in one hand and in the other devouring a wild boar with a spear. Adding to his chivalry Tipu is crushing a cobra with his feet. All this in the midst of a forest with lush greenery and bees hovering around flowers, almost as joyful witnesses to this raw heroism. Haidar Ali had patronized one of the brothers, Nallappa and made him a foujdar, and as an obvious expression of gratitude and supplication, Nallappa had authored the *Haidar Nama*, a biography of Haidar Ali in Kannada. Often this attempt by the Karnik brothers to ingratiate themselves to their masters by having their portraits painted in the temple they had built is held up as a shining example of Tipu Sultan's syncretism, munificence and generosity towards Hindu shrines. A closer examination of the history and the possible circumstances under which this might have been commissioned by the brothers makes things clearer.

A letter by an anonymous British prisoner of war, holed up in the dungeons at Srirangapatna, dated 23 September 1783, was written during the time of the much-awaited and pompously celebrated festival of Dasara in Mysore. The reigning deity of the Wodeyar family was Chamundeshwari Devi, and the Mysore royal family had been celebrating Dasara with pomp each year over the ten days, just as their predecessors in Vijayanagara had. The letter states:

> The annual Gentoo [Hindu] feast commenced this evening, which was continued according to tradition for 9 days. The King of Mysore [the Wodeyar] made his appearance in front of his palace about 7 o'clock. It is only on the occasion of this anniversary that he is visible to his nominal subjects. This young prince in whose name the family of Haidar Ali who assume only the title of Regent carry on the administration of Government is allowed for himself and his family an annual pension. He is treated with all those marks of homage that are paid to crowned heads. In his name proclamation is made of war or of peace and the trophies of victory are laid at his feet. Like kings, too, he has his guards. But these are appointed and commanded by the usurper of his throne whose authority and safety depend on the prince's confinement. Yet such is the reverence that is paid by the people of Mysore to the blood of their ancient kings and so formidable are they rendered in their present state of subjection to the most vigorous character as well as powerful prince in the peninsula of Hindusthan, that it is thought by the present Government of Mysore not to cut off the hereditary

prince of Mysore according to the usual policy of despots but to
adorn with the pageantry of a crown.[28]

This report of the Dasara being held as a public event, as it was
during the time of Haidar, dates back to the first year of Tipu's
reign. We do not have documented evidence to show if the festival
was indeed commemorated as a grand public spectacle during the
rest of Tipu's rule, or if it was merely relegated to the inner confines
of the palace for the imprisoned Wodeyar family to conduct as a
private affair.

However, an interesting *sannad* of Tipu Sultan is in the
possession of the famed Parakala Matha of Mysore, with a seal in
Persian characters and dated to approximately 15 September 1783. It
is addressed to Kuppaiya, the manager of the department of temples
in the State (*devasthanadha seeme parupathyagara*). There seems to
have been a dispute that had erupted in the Melukote temple about
the invocatory verses that had to be used at the start of prayers.
The two sects within the Sri Vaishnava tradition—Vadakalai and
Tenkalai Iyengars hotly contested one another's claims of having
verses of their sect as the only invocatory mode. The inscription states
that Anche Shamaiya (a Sri Vaishnava himself) had created some
trouble by violating the old usage of introductory verses and this had
caused heartburn between the two sects. Tipu ordered Kuppaiya that
thenceforth, both forms of invocations should be employed in the
prayers. He was told to be fair to both sects. Further, an idol of Pillai
Lokachar, a saint of the Tenkalai sect, was ordered to be removed and
relocated to its original location in Melukote. A procession of the
principal deity of the Keshavaswamy Mantapa and other mantapas,
accompanied by the distribution of *tirtha* (sacred water) and *prasada*
(consecrated offerings) during the occasion of the Tirunakshatra
festivities, was ordered to be conducted with pomp and zeal. Tipu
Sultan, in the early part of his reign i.e., 1783, is thus also seen as an
arbiter between warring sects and also someone who permitted the
procession and festivities at Melukote with pomp.[29] Interestingly,
this was barely a month or two before committing the cruellest

atrocity on the same Sri Vaishanava community by massacring 700 families of the Mandyam Iyengars, who shared the same *gotra* of Bharadwaja with that of the Mysore Pradhans who were acting on Maharani Lakshmi Ammanni's behalf.[30]

Tipu outside Mysore Frontiers

Whatever constraints bound him within Mysore from expressing his innate hatred towards people not belonging to his faith, Tipu was free of those constraints in the places he invaded and occupied through brute force. Hence, the preceding chapters have amply demonstrated how in the blood-filled campaigns in Malabar, Coorg and Mangalore, the communities of Nairs and Thiyyas in Kerala, Kodavas in Coorg, Konkanis and Canara Christians near Mangalore suffered the worst of cruelties at the hands of Tipu Sultan. In Coorg, Tipu's invasions brought a halt to the important annual festivities that the Kodava people followed of worshipping the river Kaveri at its source Talakaveri. Several of their festivals and rituals that followed the seasons and also the agricultural cycles of sowing and harvest were also rudely interrupted by the constant fear of the Mysorean invasions. The famed Bhagandeshwara temple of Bhagamandala was also a victim of the Mysorean attacks. It is said that a Brahmin transported the Shiva linga of Bhagandeshwara to a safe place in the forest and ran away before the troops of Tipu could attack. Having heard about this, a nobleman named Utthayya, who had managed to save himself during the invasions, would go out each day to the forest with a Brahmin boy on his shoulders. The hidden linga and the river Kaveri would be secretly worshipped by them in a symbolic fashion, so that the rituals carried on uninterrupted. He would also bring some rice from his house and cook an offering to the deity. It was after Tipu's exit from Coorg and the return of the royal family that Bhagandeshwara was reconsecrated at Bhagamandala and the aborted rituals continued thereafter.[31]

As early as 13 February 1786, just three years into his rule, Tipu Sultan had already congratulated Badr-u-zaman Khan, who was then the Fauzdar of Nagar: 'Your two letters, with the enclosed memorandum of the Nair captives have been received. You did right in causing a hundred and five of them to be circumcised, and in putting eleven of the youngest of these into the Asad Ilahi class and the remaining ninety-four into the Ahmadi troop.'[32] This was obviously a continuation of the practice that Haidar Ali too had followed during his conquests outside Mysore.

Over the first decade of Tipu's rule, the Nairs and the people of Malabar continued to suffer the worst of tortures. As noted in earlier chapters, most of these are boastful letters exchanged between Tipu and his officers themselves, congratulating one another for killing, converting, circumcising, breaking temples or defiling them by feeding them beef. The mockery of the matriarchal system of Kerala or that of polyandry in Coorg was also seen earlier where Tipu assumed a mantle of a social reformer for these communities, abusing them with the worst of expletives. It is sufficient here to merely recall the earlier stated writings of Paolino da San Bartolomeo, a Portuguese Roman Catholic missionary who stayed in Malabar for about twelve and a half years, from 1776 to 1789:

> The manner in which he [Tipu] behaved to the inhabitants of Calicut was horrid. A great part of them, both male and female, were hung. He first tied up the mothers, and then suspended the children from their necks. The cruel tyrant caused several Christians and Heathens [Hindus] to be brought out naked, and made fast to the feet of his elephants, which were then obliged to drag them about till their limbs fell in pieces from their bodies. At the same time, he ordered all the churches and temples to be burned or pulled down or destroyed in some manner. Christian and pagan [Hindu] women were compelled to marry Mohammedans. The pagans were deprived of the token of their nobility, which is a lock of hair called *kudumi*; and every Christian, who appeared in the streets, must either submit to be circumcised, or be hanged on the spot. This happened in the year 1789, at which time I resided at Verapole [Varapali in Travancore]. I had then an opportunity of conversing with several Christians and Pagans, who had escaped

from the fury of this merciless tyrant; and I assisted these fugitives to procure a boat to enable them to cross the river which runs past that city. This persecution continued till the 15th of April 1790.[33]

The *Padayottakalam*

The terrifying and heart-wrenching military regime of Tipu Sultan in the Malabar has been written about in several works of literature in Kerala where it is termed as the bloody era called the '*Padayottakalam*.' It had a far-reaching impact on Kerala's sociocultural and economic order for generations to come. Summarizing these, A. Sreedhara Menon writes:

The brutalities committed by the Mysorean troops led to large scale migration from Malabar of people belonging to all strata of society. The hardworking peasants took refuge in the forests and jungles. Consequently, agriculture was ruined. What was once a fertile and flourishing country now assumed the appearance of a cheerless desert. The Nair gentry was dispossessed and shorn of its military and political power. The decline in agriculture resulted in their economic impoverishment also . . . moreover, many a flourishing town had been laid waste by the Mysore troops. Trade and commerce also declined steadily. The cultivation of pepper on which depended the economic prosperity of the country was suspended over large areas and Kerala's once prosperous pepper trade practically came to a standstill. The once flourishing sea ports of Kerala now presented a deserted look. Gold and silver which the country had amassed by centuries of trade with foreign countries virtually disappeared from the land. Extensive fields lay uncultivated, houses of nobles and landlords were in ruins and daily worship in many important temples was suspended. The economic depression that set in was so severe that the common people were on the verge of famine and starvation. To add to the economic distress of the times, the Mysorean invasions created a cleavage between the Mappilas and the Hindus and destroyed social harmony. The former had helped the Mysore Sultans in their campaigns in Kerala and aroused the active hostility of the Hindu population. With the expulsion of Tipu, the Mappilas who had enjoyed political power for more than 30 years lost their privileged status. They were unable to reconcile themselves to this discomfiture and were thereafter in a state of general revolt against established authority. The Mappila outbreaks of the 19th Century were thus in a way a legacy of the Mysore invasions.[34]

The one partially positive side effect of Tipu's invasion was his construction of a large network of roads in the Malabar. An extensive chain of roads connected the remotest parts of Malabar, including the wild forested areas, with most of these roads terminating at Srirangapatna.[35] These roads were built only for his army to march their way to the Malabar, carrying all their heavy artillery and guns. In fact, they came to be popularly known as 'Tipu's Gun Roads'. But due to the lack of attention to repair work, these hastily built roads were neither well-made nor properly drained, and soon fell into utter disrepair.[36]

Iconoclasm and the destruction of temples and churches were an integral part of his Malabar campaign. During his 1789 invasion, when the Chirakkal Raja tried to prevent Tipu, from desecrating his family temple by offering him Rs 4 lakh and plates of gold with which the temple was roofed in return for its safety, Tipu is said to have laughed it off. He haughtily replied that all the treasures of the earth and sea given to him could not ensure the safety of the temple.[37] He also boasted about 'the destruction in the course of this holy war of eight thousand idol temples, many of them roofed with gold, silver, or copper, and all containing treasures buried at the feet of the idol, the whole of which was royal plunder.'[38] However, Wilks himself discounts the number quoted here of temples desecrated stating that 'when crimes are deemed to be virtues, we may infer that their amount is much exaggerated.'[39] While the claims that Tipu himself made here to the Chirakkal Raja might be inflated, a significant number of temples in the Malabar were destroyed during his repeated invasions.

Noted scholar Vadakkankoor Raja Raja Varma bemoans the dance of destruction that Kerala faced during this time, in his *Kerala Samskrita Sahitya Charitram* (*History of Sanskrit Literature in Kerala*):

> There was no limit as to the loss the Hindu temples suffered due to the military operations of Tipu Sultan. Burning down the temples, destruction of the idols installed therein and also cutting the heads of cattle over the temple deities were the cruel entertainments of Tipu Sultan and his equally cruel army. It was heartrending even to imagine the destruction caused by Tipu Sultan in the famous ancient temples of Thalipparampu and Thrichambaram. The devastation caused by this new Ravana's barbarous activities have not yet been fully rectified.[40]

Writing about the temples destroyed in the Vettum region of Malappuram, the late P.C.N. Raja, a senior member of the Zamorin family, writes:

> The devastation caused by Tipu Sultan to the ancient and holy temples of Keraladheeswaram, Thrikkandiyoor and Thriprangatu in Vettum region was terrible. The Zamorin renovated these temples to some extent. The famous and ancient Thirunavaya Temple, known throughout the country as an ancient teaching-centre of the Vedas, revered by the devotees of Vishnu from Tamil Nadu, and existing before the advent of Christ, was also plundered and destroyed by Tipu's army. After dismantling and destroying the idol, Tipu converted the Thrikkavu Temple into an ammunition depot in Ponnani. It was the Zamorin who repaired the temple later. Kotikkunnu, Thrithala, Panniyoor and other family temples of the Zamorin were plundered and destroyed. The famous Sukapuram Temple was also desecrated. Damage done to the Perumparampu Temple and Maranelira Temple of Azhvancherry Thamprakkal (titular head of all Namboodiri Brahmins) in Edappadu, can be seen even today. Vengari Temple and Thrikkulam Temple in Eranadu, Azhinjillam Temple in

Ramanattukara, Indyannur Temple, Mannur Temple and many
other temples were defiled and damaged extensively during the
military regime.[41]

In more recent times, journalist Tirur Dinesh documents in great
detail the evidence of the destruction of several temples in Malabar,
especially the Malappuram district, during the Padayottakalam
of Tipu. In his book *Destroyed Temples of Kerala*, he gives a list of
these shrines, along with detailed documentary and photographic
evidence, as well as oral history accounts to buttress his claims.
Legend has it that an ancient Shiva temple existed at Thirunavaya,
believed to have been consecrated by Parashurama and among the
108 major shrines for Lord Shiva in Kerala. But pilgrims are unable
to find this temple at Thirunavaya. A Shiva Linga and pedestal were
excavated from a location there in 2003, but were hastily buried
again, claims Dinesh.[42] After its destruction and subsequent neglect
over time, the site was used by the British to establish a tile factory.
The ancient Shiva temple however remains buried and anonymous
in this important site.

At Thrikkandiyur Mahadeva temple, Tipu and his armies broke
down the *gopurams*, outer walls, lamp posts and so on. Legend has it
that they attempted to uproot the linga from the *sreekovil* (sanctum)
but failed. Then an axe was used to smash it, but that attempt too
failed. An exasperated army left the idol there, but unleashed their
wrath on the Nandi bull that sat outside and beheaded it with an
axe. Dinesh states that the Shivalinga there still bears marks of the
attacks of Tipu's forces.[43] Though normally in Hindu tradition an
idol once defiled is not worshipped, in this case, after the return of
the Zamorin who got the temple partially repaired, an *Ashtamangala
Deva Prashna* (a divination technique to seek answers) was conducted
and the guidance received was not to reinstall another linga but to
continue with the same. The headless idol of Nandi still sits outside
the sanctum as a grim reminder of the horrors that this shrine faced.

Dinesh reports that while they were on their way to find details
about the Athaadi Shiva temple that was believed to have been
destroyed by Tipu, they were shown more than thirty places en

route where temples had been ruined during the Mysorean invasion. In 1921, when Kerala saw the bloody Moplah riots, some of these temple spots, including the Athaadi Shiva temple, were forcibly taken over and mosques were built over them.[44] The Ambalakunathu Sreeparvathy temple at Nadakavungal became another victim of Tipu's violence and was lost to people, till about 2008 when it was revived. Accidentally, a perfect and untouched Shivalinga was discovered under the soil while digging the land for some other purpose. The linga was then put back in what is now a decrepit remnant of the old sanctum. The Narikottiri Narasimha temple too languishes in a pathetic state, amidst hopes of believers that someday it might get renovated and worship might resume. The Kundukuli Mahavishnu temple in the area too was a case where Tipu's armies had broken the deity into seven pieces.[45] The *dwarapalas* or sentinels were found in a well in the complex. The list is endless; these are tales of sorrow and horror, but also of resilience, where centuries after this wanton and heartless destruction, the theists are still gathering the pieces together to rebuild what was ruthlessly smashed.

The temples of Chenthala Vishnu, Chamravottam Kannannor Pisharath of Shiva and Vishnu belonging to the Pisharodis, Chokkoor Sreerama, Kulikapra Siva, Kuzhikalattu Siva, Pongattur Subrahmanya, Thanaloor Narasimha, Pakara Siva, Thirunavaya Navamukunda, Kalad Vamanamoorthy, Thavanoor Brahma, Thrippaloor Narasimha, Malaparambu Mattummal Narasimhamoorthy and Variyath Parambil Cholakkara Durga Bhagawathy are a few of the shrines in just the Malappuram district that Dinesh documents painstakingly in his book. They faced the attacks of Haidar Ali and Tipu Sultan during the invasions and later in 1921 during the Moplah riots. Several of them are still in a dilapidated condition, while in a few others, partial renovation has either been completed or is underway. The devout still keep their flicker of faith and hope alive that someday these shrines that meant so much to their ancestors will come back to life as bustling centres of their devotion.

About the famed Guruvayur temple of Lord Krishna, P.C.N. Raja states that Tipu Sultan reached the place after destroying Mammiyoor temple and the Palayur Christian Church. Having got wind of his nefarious plans and fearing the wrath of Tipu's army, the priests hurriedly moved the idol to a safer location at Ambalapuzha in Travancore, where it was kept in safety and regularly worshipped, till the end of Tipu's military regime. P.C.N. Raja attributes the relative lack of destruction of the Guruvayur temple to the timely intervention of Hydrose Kutty Moopan, an army general from Haidar Ali's times who had been converted to Islam by the latter during his Malabar invasion. Kutty supposedly prevailed upon Tipu to continue the land-tax exemptions that Haidar had made to the temple and also carried out repairs of the destruction caused by the Mysore army.[46] Even now, pujas are conducted at the Ambalapuzha shrine where the deity of Guruvayurappan had found temporary refuge.

Kozhikode (Calicut) faced the brunt of Tipu's wrath. He shifted the capital of his Malabar jurisdiction to a place near Calicut, on the banks of the Beypore river, renamed Feroke, where a fortress was built in 1788. The inhabitants of Calicut were all forced to leave their homes and settle down in Feroke. But after his defeat and exit from Malabar, the inhabitants returned to Calicut.[47] Thus, the grandiose project of building a new capital ended in failure. Thali, Thiruvannur, Varackal, Puthur, Govindapuram, Thalikkunnu and other important temples in Kozhikode and also those nearby were completely destroyed. Some of them were reconstructed by the Zamorin once he returned to power with British intervention, post the defeat of Tipu in the Third Anglo–Mysore War.[48]

The Roman Catholic church dedicated to *Madre de Deos* (Mother of God), possibly built in the first quarter of the eighteenth century, also bore the brunt of the Mysore invasions in 1788. The vicar and clergymen fled from there and sought sanctuary in Tellicherry and returned only in 1792 when Tipu was pushed out of the Malabar by the British after his defeat.[49] About the Latin liturgy in Malabar, William Logan writes in the Malabar Manual: 'Tippu Sultan in his proselytizing zeal carried away many Christians from Canara to Mysore and in 1793 and 1795, 87 families of these returned'; they were relocated by the East India Company in the district of Randatara in Chirakkal district, where lands were assigned to them and money advances made to help them rebuild their lives.[50]

Eminent historian of Kerala, Elamkulam Kunjan Pillai, recorded the atrocities committed by Tipu, especially in Kozhikode:

> Kozhikode was then a centre of Brahmins. There were around 7000 Namboodiri houses of which more than 2000 houses were destroyed by Tipu Sultan in Kozhikode alone. Sultan did not spare even children and women. Menfolk escaped to forests and neighbouring principalities. Mappilas increased many fold [sic] (due to forcible conversion). During the military regime of Tipu Sultan, Hindus were forcibly circumcised and converted to Muhammadan faith. As a result, the number of Nairs and Brahmins declined substantially.[51]

Sultan Battery in South Waynad was once noted for its ancient temples and the place was named Ganpathivattam, literally meaning the circle of the Lord Ganapathi.[52] This name was changed to Sultan Battery when Tipu built a fort there. The Ganapathi temple there, one of the old and important ones belonging to the Kottayam Rajas, was destroyed by Tipu and the idol and a few monolithic stones are all that are left there now.[53]

At Taliparamba, in north Malabar's Kannur district, is an ancient and important Rajarajeshwara temple dedicated to Lord Shiva. The shrine was regarded as one among the 108 important Shiva temples of ancient Kerala. It was a 'magnificent structure covered with brass plates and surrounded by a high laterite wall.' It had two large seven-storey gopurams or towers which were nearly 130 feet. The temple had many beautiful sculptures, and 'some fine *gopurams* (towers).'[54] Unlike Tamil Nadu, Kerala temples seldom had *rajagopurams* or royal towers. But this one had one such majestic tower that was partially destroyed by Tipu Sultan. The upper levels made of soft laterite were possibly blown by artillery, while the lower layers of granite and laterite are still standing. The debris lies there around the western and eastern entrances even today, as silent sentinels of the violence that was unleashed on them.

In November 1789, Tipu, at the head of a large army, made a steady march to the present Trichur district. On the way to Trichur,

Hindu temples and Christian churches were plundered and desecrated, and had their roofs blown off. Houses and bazaars were set ablaze; fruit trees and pepper vines were cut down. Reaching Trichur by 14 December 1789, Tipu made it the headquarters of a new collectorate over his entire Malabar jurisdiction. In Trichur was the Vadakkanathan temple of Lord Shiva that was among the 108 major shrines of Shiva in Kerala and believed to have been established by Parashurama. Tipu converted this ancient temple into his office and the Brahmin Mutts in Trichur into quarters for his officers. The memories of the wounds inflicted remained with the inhabitants for long. Thousands are said to have died here during his stay due to sheer hunger and starvation, if not by the persecution of the sword. After the Sultan's exit from Malabar, the survivors who had fled came back to start their lives afresh. But unfortunately for them, the place was completely ravaged by then. As an outcome of the large-scale destruction of crops and agriculture there, a severe famine raged. This was accompanied by epidemics like cholera and smallpox that caused the death of several of the survivors who had come back with hope to rebuild their lives. It took several years for normalcy to be restored.[55]

In January 1801, when Francis Buchanan visited Malabar and reached Tamarasseri, he found that all the lands there had come into the hands of the Mapillah mortgagees. Emboldened by the military regime of Tipu, the Mapillahs had flexed their strength beyond measure. Owing to the persecution of the Hindus by Tipu Sultan and these warlike activities and tactics of the Mapillahs, Buchanan found that one-fourth of the rice land of Kurumbranad was lying waste and overgrown with forest trees.[56] In the same Kurumbranad District, William Logan records a famed temple being destroyed: 'In Ponmeri *amsham*, 5 miles from Badagara, is a Siva temple which is 124½ feet by 87 feet. It is sculptured. The roof of the shrine is covered with copper. There is a granite slab at the eastern entrance . . . the temple is very old and was destroyed by Tippu's soldiers.'[57]

When Kuttipuram, near Badagara, which was the headquarters of the Kadathanad Rajas, was besieged by Tipu in 1789, the garrison there of 2000 Nairs and their families were offered a choice between 'a voluntary profession of the Muhammadan faith and a forcible conversion with deportation from their native lands.' They chose the former, and the next day the men were all circumcised and everyone forcibly made to eat beef.[58] Kuttipuram fort was one of the last places in Malabar to hold out against Tipu.

However, there are unverified claims of entries in the *inam* registers in Kozhikode archives that mention land grants made to some temples there. The source of these claims is the dissertation of C.K. Kareem, submitted in 1968 to the Aligarh Muslim University. Quoting Kareem,[59] Mohibbul Hasan writes about seven such instances where land grants were made: to the Mannur temple in Chelambra Amsom (Ernad), Thiruvanchikulam Siva temple in Vailattur Amsom (Ponnani), Guruvayur temple, Trikkandiyur Samooham temple in Trikkandiyoor Amsom (Ponnani), Naduvilmadathil Tirumumbu in Trichur and a private grant to a Namboodiri Brahmin.[60] One is not sure if these were the earlier grants from the times of Haidar that had continued, or if they had continued on the intervention of someone (quite like Hydrose Kutty who protected the Guruvayur temple). If these had indeed been grants made directly by Tipu Sultan they are likely to have been widely publicized, quite like his much-discussed letters to the Shankaracharya of Sringeri.

However, despite staggering evidence to the contrary and of the violent kinds stated in this chapter, there are several apologists for Tipu's excesses, who either deny or justify these barbarities. Mohibbul Hasan writes:

It is difficult to say how many inhabitants of Coorg and Malabar were forcibly made Muslims. The English versions cannot be regarded as authentic because they were, for the most part, intended to malign Tipu and serve as propaganda against him. Nor should any reliance be placed on Muslim accounts which, in their anxiety to represent the Sultan as a champion of Islam, also have a tendency to exaggerate, distort, and falsify. They are intended to create effect, to surround Tipu with a religious halo and exalt him to the position of a religious halo . . . it is usually forgotten while assessing Tipu's religious policy that some of the conversions were voluntary . . . Similarly, there were other rebels who changed their religion to please the Sultan. The latter welcomed their conversion hoping that in the way they would lose their influence over their followers, and thus cease to be dangerous. It is not unlikely that he might have even offered them inducements to become Muslims. But this is quite different from the traditional picture of Tipu painted by some writers in which he is represented as being perpetually engaged in making wholesale conversions of Hindus, and massacring those who refused to accept Islam.[61]

The logical loopholes in such arguments are evident to any sensible reader. If neither contemporary or later British accounts nor those of his courtiers and Muslim chroniclers are to be considered authentic, where else should one look for sources to understand Tipu? While there are bound to be exaggerations and biases in several sources, they do point towards a semblance of the truth. We have seen in an earlier chapter how in various letters, the number of converts from Coorg varied. Yet, it is possible to draw to a consensual number that can emerge from among all these varying figures. Tipu's own dream registers, his own *firmans* and letters to his officials, his and his officers' boastful claims of mass conversions, circumcisions, slaughter of cows, destruction of temples are well documented with absolutely no ambiguity. These, coupled with oral narratives and intergenerational memories that have stayed on over two centuries later, cannot all be brushed aside saying these were all perpetuated with a nefarious agenda. Are we to negate even Tipu's own words as being inauthentic, but deem contemporary assessments and extrapolations by today's historians as being more credible than the protagonist's own accounts? Also, Hasan's claim above that the Muslim chroniclers exaggerated these instances to depict him as a hero of Islam implies that there were expectations and theological sanctions for such acts by rulers for them to be considered a true Muslim. That in itself becomes both revealing, as well as deeply problematic.

Summing up this complex and difficult aspect of Tipu Sultan's legacy and rule, Hayavadana Rao's comments seem appropriate:

The causes of Tipu Sultan's fall have been dealt with in some detail . . . among these causes all of which contributed to his fall, we may justly set down his hatred towards the worship of images which left a deep impression on the populace . . . the destruction by Tipu of Brahmapuri near Seringapatam and the raising of a mosque on the razed temple was such as cannot be forgotten by the generality of the Hindus . . . it may be said generally of Haidar that his religious faith as a Shiah—if the deduction drawn as to that is well founded—helped to alter his outlook. His Muslim troops proved, however different. A number of temples in South India invaded by them bear witness today of mutilated images. Tipu however, moved away from his father's religious and political convictions, veering round more and more to the Sunni cult, which is more zealous in its views, particularly in the matter of the worship of images. However that may be and whatever the real causes, the fact cannot be gainsaid that Tipu proved a zealot and wrought incalculable injury to himself. He forgot that the worship of images was not merely a question of deep popular belief among the masses of the country but also one hallowed by ages of practice. He repeated the mistake of that other zealot Aurangzib [sic], of which he was guilty during his time.[62]

Epilogue

The Afterlife of Tipu Sultan and His Many Representations

As the sun set on the once mighty and invincible fort of Srirangapatna during that fateful summer of 1799, the house of Haidar Ali and Tipu Sultan was evicted from the Mysore kingdom by the British before the erstwhile royal family restored to the throne. The initial British fears that a dispossession of Tipu's family might anger the Muslims of Mysore, who they thought had a deep entrenched influence in the affairs of the state by virtue of their vast numbers in the administration, were also assuaged. Wellesley recounted that despite several Muslims occupying most of the influential positions in the government at the time of the Sultan's fall, the latter's dictatorial attitude to 'destroy every vestige of hereditary right . . . and to concentrate not only the whole authority of the State, but the whole administration of the Government in his own person' had stripped off most of the top-ranking, surviving Muslim officers of 'any individual weight, or collective force',[1] potent enough to jeopardize the British interests in Mysore. Hence, the restoration of power to the Hindu royal family was considered the safest option. The Nizam's proposal to host the family within his dominions was vetoed by the British as it was feared that this could arouse common feelings of bitterness for the East India Company. In his letter dated 4 June 1799 to Lt Gen. Harris, Col Arthur Wellesley, Henry Wellesley, William Kirkpatrick and Barry Close, the Earl of Mornington detailed his elaborate plans for the family of the slain Sultan:

Lieut. Colonel Doveton . . . has been directed to make every possible preparation for their accommodation at Vellore, which is destined for the future residence of the Sultaun's family. After their arrival, no reasonable expense will be spared to render their habitation suitable to their former rank and expectations; and it is my intention to give them a liberal pecuniary allowance. Colonel Wellesley will judge whether it may be necessary to give, either to the whole or to any branch of the family any specific assurance of the exact amount of the sums to be allotted to them respectively, if any such particular explanation should appear necessary for their satisfaction, I authorize you to make the allotment of stipend to each of them, as well as for the establishment of the Zenana, provided that the total sum for the maintenance of the family be not stated at more than three, or at the utmost, four lacs of pagodas. The sons of the late Sultaun may be accompanied by such attendants as they may select, provided the number be not so great as to endanger the public tranquility, or to form a point of union for the adherents of the late Sultaun. It might be desirable that Alli Reza should accompany the Princes, as he appears to be attached to the interests of the Company, and at the same time to entertain considerable affection for the Princes. The females and children of the several families must follow the Princes as speedily as possible. Colonel Wellesley, in my name, will give the most unequivocal assurances of protection and indulgence to every branch of the family . . . my most anxious expectation that the utmost degree of care will be taken to secure the personal property of the Princes, and of the women, when the period of their removal shall arrive.[2]

The four elder princes and their entourage, attended by Captain Marriott and escorted by a detachment under Lt Col Coke, departed from Srirangapatna on 18 June 1799, on their way to Vellore. As they passed through the streets of their capital, large crowds gathered to catch a final glimpse of their princes. But the British records mention that barring a few Muslim women, who shed copious tears for these unfortunate young men, there were no 'popular tokens of sorrow or regret at parting' and in the course of other districts, 'the inhabitants, as they passed, would not even make their *salams*, although repeatedly desired to do so by the escort.'[3] Fateh Haidar, who was about twenty-six years of age then, travelled with his wives and children. Tragically, two of the children died along the way, causing deep grief and anxiety to his parents, and worries over funeral rituals that could not be conducted. Fateh Haidar was described as being reserved and sullen, and filled with personal apprehensions. Abdul Khaliq and Muiz-ud-din, who had earlier spent time with British forces as hostages of their father, seemed more at ease with European forms and manners. Moieuddin was seen as a timid teenager of about fifteen years of age, and had just come out of the influence of the caretaker women of the zenana.

The princes, on reaching Vellore, seemed satisfied with the accommodation and arrangements, though they had their special demands. Fateh Haidar, described as 'restless, and jealous of his family privileges', demanded to have a village or *jagir* for himself to procure additional allowance in order to sustain his large family and also 'his mother and other female relatives with him, who belonged properly to his father's establishment'.[4] Abdul Khaliq, described as 'careless . . . unprincely. . . and extremely avaricious . . . only begged that the great difference in the prices of rice might be considered between the bazars of Seringapatam and Vellore'[5] while fixing his allowance. Moieuddin seemed 'amiable, engaging and attentive to everything which constitutes true politeness' while Muiz-ud-din seemed 'passionately attached to his amusements, particularly his horses and to the society of the English, and heedless of everything else'.[6] Though caricatured stereotypes are what these British pen-pictures are of Tipu's sons, they give a glimpse into the minds of these young boys, whose destiny suddenly took such an abrupt and rude turn.

But this translocation of Tipu's family was completed in stages. The four senior princes were packed off in the first installment by mid-June 1799. In May 1800, a year after the fall of Tipu when Francis Buchanan visited Srirangapatna, he still found the five younger sons of the deceased Sultan occupying the three sides of the square in the palace that were formerly used as warehouses. He found them to be 'well looking boys,' who were 'permitted to ride, and exercise themselves in the square, when they are desirous to do so ... allowed to view the parade, and to hear the bands of music belonging to the troops in garrison.'[7] Eventually, the entire family of the house of Haidar were shifted out to the ancient palace of the Nawabs of Arcot in Vellore Fort, with all the concubines, servants, hangers-on and other paraphernalia. It is said that Fateh Haidar, the eldest son of Tipu, had eight sons and sixteen daughters.[8] In all, nearly 3000 of these Mysoreans in exile were forced to make Vellore their new home. The senior princes were given a handsome allowance of Rs 50,000 a year that enabled them to maintain some semblance of nostalgic luxury and royalty that they had been used to, back in Srirangapatna. Their idle and worthless dependents were irritants in the social life of Vellore and even acted as pimps to get some unfortunate girls into the harems, on the promise of marriage to one or the other sons of the deceased Sultan.[9] With time, the princes who had initially shown some air of regality and wisdom, are said to have had a gradual degradation of their moral character, given their idleness in the midst of enough and more money to squander.[10]

Tumultuous South

The British were smug about having achieved a fait accompli in South India by vanquishing the long-standing thorn in their flesh. But little did they know that discontent against them kept brewing in South India, despite their spectacular success in the annihilation of Mysore and its Sultan. Dhondia Wagh/Dhondoji Wagh was a Maratha sardar who was born in Chennagiri (in Shimoga district) and joined Haidar Ali's army in 1780. During the campaign of Lord Cornwallis, he is said to have deserted the army and escaped to Dharwar, only to re-enter the Mysorean forces with his 200 horsemen. Tipu had tried to forcibly convert him to Islam, and on his refusal, he was chained and imprisoned in the dungeons of

Srirangapatna, being renamed as Sheikh Ahmed first, and then Malik Jehan Khan.[11] A Muslim teacher was also appointed to make him change his mind and influence his thoughts towards the tenets of that faith, as Tipu knew the military value and daring of Wagh. On the day Srirangapatna fell, Dhondoji was found 'chained to the wall of his prison like a wild beast'[12] and was released by a British soldier. Regrouping several of his former military aides, he began to assemble a militia against the British, establishing himself in Shimoga and styling himself as Ubhaya Lokadheeshwara or the Lord of the two worlds. His attempts to liberate areas in Bidanur and Gutti and intelligence of wanting to kidnap Colonel Wellesley and murder Purnaiya, alarmed the British. In a span of a few months, he managed to hold possession of a territory spanning Shimoga, Chitradurga, Dharwar and Bellary. From a slender force of 5000 men, he soon managed to muster a cavalry force of 5000 men and an army of 80,000 men, threatening to re-enter Mysore. The princes of Ramdurg, Sholapur, Kolhapur, Anegundi and Gwalior, as also some of the vanquished soldiers of Srirangapatna, expressed their tacit support to him,

On Dhondoji's taking of Chitradurga in July 1799, British regiments under Colonel Dalrymple were dispatched to curb this brewing uprising. Dhondoji managed to escape to the frontiers of the Maratha dominions by August 1799. He kept escaping from one place to the other, eluding and fatiguing his pursuers, and giving a slip to the British who were in hot pursuit. The guerilla warfare that was conducted in typical Maratha style alarmed the British who had newly occupied the province and were not as accustomed to its terrain as Dhondoji was. He even killed Dhondoji Pant Gokhla, the Maratha commander of 10,000 horse, 5000 foot and eight guns, in the vicinity of Kittur. This was to fulfil an old vow, and he dyed his moustache with the heart-blood of his enemy.[13] As his power and menace kept rising to alarming levels, the British pursued him determinedly. Colonel Arthur Wellesley overtook him at Konagal, in the Nizam's territories of Raichur, and slew him on 10 September 1800.

Between 1799 and 1802, unrest marked the western frontiers of Mysore that were under the Company's jurisdiction. The feudal lords of the Kanara region, who had escaped to Travancore fearing Tipu's anarchy, had hoped for a reinstatement after his fall. That being dashed with the Company taking full control of their erstwhile provinces fuelled their anger and discontent. Domba Hegde of Vittla openly defied British authority and assumed independent charge on 15 December 1799. He was assisted by Timma Naik, an officer in the Mysore army at Kasargod, who formed an alliance for Hegde with Subba Rao, the former shirastedar of Coimbatore. Rao had served in Tipu's army for years and was well versed in warfare. Subba Rao's accomplice, Mahtab Khan, the former treasury officer under Haidar and Tipu, could impersonate Fateh Haidar. Their plan was to galvanize the soldiers by showing that the entire movement of rebellion had royal sanction from Tipu's family. The confederacy was formed at Puttur, from where on 7 May 1800, they marched to occupy Jamalabad, raided Uppinangadi and Buntwal, which was a hub of commercial trade in South Kanara. The regions were all plundered and the loot transferred to their headquarters. The British used several devious methods to crush this hill revolt. Through deception, Timma Naik was slain and the others, including Subba Rao and Domba Hegde, were all neutralized by July 1800. Hegde and his two nephews, brother-in-law, a rebellious Shanbhougue and Jamadar, were all executed in full public view on 25 August 1800 to instil fear in the minds of any other mischief makers. The palegar of Aigur, Venkatadri Nayaka, who had given shelter to Dhondoji Wagh and supported his heroics, was captured in February 1802 and executed a few days later. Nearly 300 families, suspected of being sympathetic to the palegar's cause, were detained and Amildars were instructed not to allow trees and hedges to grow in so dense a manner that they might facilitate escape routes for potential rebels.

The revolts of the ruler of Balam (present day Aigur, near Sakleshapura) in 1800–02, the Waynad revolt in 1802, the Munkasira revolt in 1804 and the revolt of the palegar of Chitradurga in 1805 kept rocking the smug overconfidence of the British. During the time of the Second Anglo–Mysore War, the queen of Sivaganga, Velu

Nachiyar, had successfully torched a rebellion against the Company and even regained her kingdom from the control of the British and the Nawab of Arcot. The spirit of resistance against the British that Velu Nachiyar had instigated outlived her in the region she ruled over. Her erstwhile commanders, the Marudhu brothers, Vellai or Periya (elder) and Chinna (younger) Marudhu, were to become potent symbols of British resistance in South India in the aftermath of the fall of Srirangapatna.

The subsequent Poligar Wars (1799–1805) rocked southern India for a while. Protesting British exactions of tax revenues, the palegars revolted immediately after the capture of Mysore in 1799. The Marudhu brothers were at the centre of these revolts and the palace of Sivaganga became the theatre of heavy intrigues. It sheltered some of the fiercest rebels from different parts of Tamil Nadu. The Marudhus also extended their support to another legendary heroic character Veerapandiya Kattabomman (r. 1760–1799), the chieftain of Panjalamkurichi, who raised the bugle of revolt against the British. The rebels, surviving on large stores of grain and firearms in the jungles of the Sivaganga principality, stormed British strongholds and tried to reclaim several forts, including Melur and Natham near Madurai, and Palamaneri and Thiruchuzhi in Ramnad, and establishing total control over the coast, forcing the Company to redirect supplies to Ceylon.

On 16 June 1801, the Marudhus issued their famous rebel proclamation that was found plastered at several places including the Arcot Nawab's palace in the Tiruchirapalli Fort and one was addressed to the temple town of Srirangam. It was a unique and inspiring document that was unparalleled in the history of the freedom struggle in India. Calling himself an 'implacable enemy of the European low wretches', Marudhu censured the Nawab of Arcot for allowing the British to trample over the country's sovereignty and exhorted people to unite against them and overthrow the British from all of India:

> . . . in the island of Jamboo in the peninsula of Jamboo Dweepa this
> notice is given . . . the Europeans violating their faith have deceitfully

made the kingdom their own and considering the inhabitants as dogs, accordingly exercise authority over them . . . in these countries now governed by these low wretches, the inhabitants have become poor . . . there existing no unity and friendship amongst you the above castes . . . therefore you Brahmins, Kshatriyas, Vysyas, Sudras and Musselmen, all who wear whiskers, whether civil or military, serving in the field or elsewhere, and you subedars, jamedars, havildars, nayaks and sepoys in the service of the low wretches and all capable of bearing arms, let them in the first place display their bravery as follows. Wherever you find any of the low wretches destroy them and continue to do so until they are extirpated.[14]

It took the British a long time to subjugate the rebellions of these palegars, but eventually their military might triumphed. Kattabomman was hanged on 16 October 1799 and the Marudhu brothers were publicly executed on 24 October 1801, along with their sons and grandsons. A raging Chinna Marudhu was apparently carried and chained in a cage to his hanging.[15] A growing alliance of the Marudhus with Kattabomman's brother Oomaithurai and his general Sundaralinga Kudumbanar, and Kerala Varma Pazhassi Raja, the de facto head of the Kottayam kingdom in the Malabar, was also neutralized by the British. Thus, almost six years after the fall of Mysore, tumultuous rebellions rocked all of South India, and by 1805, the British managed to quell all the rebellions and bring them all under their thumb, finally abolishing the age-old palegar system.

The Vellore Revolt and Thereafter

The displaced family of Tipu Sultan, being right in the midst of all this tumult, in the Carnatic region, could obviously not remain unaffected by these sweeping winds of rebellion. Fortuitously for them, discontent was already brewing in the Vellore regiment when the sepoys there, to appear smart, were asked by the newly appointed Commander-in-Chief Sir John Craddock to sport a new form of turban that resembled the European hat. The new rules totally forbade the display of caste marks, beards or moustaches, earrings and turbans—a move that greatly disaffected both the Hindu and the Muslim sepoys of the regiment. The hat also had a leather cockade that was assumed to have been of cow or pig skin that outraged both communities. A turnscrew that the sepoys had to keep to load muskets, which they had to keep with them at all times, was in the shape of a cross. All of this caused sufficient consternation and discontent in the Vellore regiment, as it was seen as a direct affront to their faiths and an attempt to Christianize them. The scene in South India thus was a perfect trailer of what was to unfold at a much larger scale in 1857.

Several British officers foresaw the risks that such an impudent move could bring about in an already tenuous region. 'Beards and whiskers,' wrote Thomas Munro to his father, 'are not now such weighty matters in Europe as formerly; but even now, an order to shave the heads of all the troops in Britain, leaving them only a lock on the crown like Hindoos, or to make all the presbyterian soldiers wear the image of the Pope or St. Anthony, instead of a cockade, would, I suspect, occasion some expressions, if not acts, of disloyalty.'[16] But these strictures aroused more than mere acts of disloyalty. On 10 July 1806, parties of armed sepoys seized the magazine in the Vellore Fort and attacked the European garrison and the English officers. The colonels of the sixty-ninth and twenty-third Native Infantry were 'murdered, along with eleven other officers and eighty-two N.C.O.s and privates.'[17] A terrible disaster for the British in Vellore was averted however with the timely arrival of Colonel Gillespie, with his galloping guns, from Arcot that was about nine miles away.

The needle of British suspicion fell on the sons of Tipu, who were inside the Vellore Fort. Around the same time as this revolt broke out, in early July 1806, there were celebrations inside the fort. Seven years had passed since the death of their patriarch and their own displacement from Srirangapatna. The family of Tipu Sultan was finally preparing for joy after a long time. The occasion was the solemnizing of the marriage of one of Tipu's daughters. On this occasion, the Union Jack that fluttered on the ramparts of the fort had been pulled down and replaced with the red-coloured royal flag of the erstwhile Mysore Sultanat, with the sun at the centre and bearing green tiger stripes all around. It was believed that this flag had been in the possession of Prince Muiz-ud-din. And as the kingpin of the rebellion, it was he who had instigated the sepoys and made them bring down the British flag. Some witnesses deposed that the rebels had looted it from the prince's chambers and that he had no direct role in instigating this. According to some conspiracy theorists, it was from Gurramkonda that had been gifted as jagir to Tipu's cousin Kamr-ud-din that Muiz-ud-din had promised to marshal together a force of 10,000 men if only the Vellore mutineers could hold out for about eight days.

Thomas Munro immediately ordered a search for intrigues stretching beyond Vellore, to Chitradurga, Nandidurga, Srirangapatna and Gurramkonda, but found no such designs. The panic and mania about Tipu still haunted the British, as is evident in the letters of the times, with their trying to cover every vestige of possible disaffection and revolt. Lord William Bentinck, the Governor of Madras, whose successful tenure of quashing rebellions in South India was interrupted by the Vellore Mutiny, wrote to Thomas Munro on 2 August 1806:

> We have every reason to believe, indeed undoubtedly to know, that the emissaries and adherents of the sons of Tippoo Sultan have been most active below the Ghauts, and it is said that the same intrigues have been carrying on above the Ghauts. Great reliance is said to have been placed upon the Gurrumcondah poligars, by the princes. I recommend you to use the utmost vigilance and precaution; and you are hereby authorized, upon any symptom or appearance of insurrection, to take such measures as you may deem necessary. Let me advise you not to place too much dependance on any of the native troops. It is impossible at this moment to say how far both native infantry and cavalry may stand by us in case of need. It has been ingeniously worked up into a question of religion. The minds of the soldiery have been inflamed to the highest state of discontent and disaffection, and upon this feeling has been built the re-establishment of the Mussulman government, under one of

the sons of Tippoo Sultan. It is hardly credible that such progress could have been made in so short a time, and without knowledge of any of us. But, believe me, the conspiracy has extended beyond all belief, and has reached the most remote parts of our Army; and the intrigue has appeared to have been everywhere most successfully carried on. The capture of Vellore, and other decided measures in contemplation, accompanied by extreme vigilance on all parts, will, I trust, still prevent a great explosion.[18]

But despite Bentinck's certitude about the connivance of Tipu's sons in the revolt, and several committees of inquiries being established to join the dots, very little emerged to indicate their direct involvement. Either it was merely British paranoia about Tipu that lingered on, even seven years after his death, or the princes were so astute to have carried out this coup in such alarming and impeccable stealth. Even Munro rationalized this paranoia later:

The restoration of the Sultan [family] never could alone have been the motive for such a conspiracy. Such an event could have been desirable to none of the Hindoos who form the bulk of the native troops, and to only a part of the Mussulmans . . . the extensive range of the late conspiracy can only be accounted for by the General Orders having been converted into an attack upon religious ceremonies; and though the regulations had undoubtedly no such object, it must be confessed that the prohibition of the marks of castes was well calculated to enable artful leaders to inflame the minds of the ignorant, for there is nothing so absurd but that they will believe when made a question of religion . . . the general opinion of the most intelligent natives in this part of the country is, that it was intended to make the sepoys Christians.[19]

After having restored a semblance of peace in South India by quelling many rebellions in the aftermath of the fall of Mysore, the British were in no mood to take a chance. They had spent nearly a quarter of a century establishing their authority here and the last thing they wanted to see now was the captive descendants of their sworn enemy whom they had slain in battle, stirring up the cauldron. The British Government decided that irrespective of whether they were found to be guilty or not, this 'little Mysore' in the Carnatic had to now be dismantled for good. On 9 August 1806, Colonel Harcourt wrote to the Madras Council that in the first lot, about forty-two persons of this household need to be transported out to Vellore. This included all the male issue of Tipu, including his twelve sons and twenty-four grandsons, one or two of his nephews, and 'his unfortunate brother Karim, whose senses were somewhat deranged at intervals and whom Tipu had always kept under a gentle restraint'.[20] It was decided that they all be packed off from Vellore to Calcutta, right under the nose of the Supreme Government and the Governor-General, so that no mischief could go unnoticed.

Accordingly, by 20 August, around fifty people of the family left Madras by sea for Calcutta. Large crowds had gathered to watch the erstwhile royals being packed off this way, but there was no cheering or demonstrations from anyone. They were to be settled in the southern marshy, malarial suburbs of Calcutta, in close confinement, on the premises of a certain Mr Andrews at Russapuglah (around the present Tollygunge Club) that was used earlier to house the Persian Ambassador. The long journey to Calcutta and the trauma of repeated dislocation led to the sudden death of Abdul Khaliq on 12 September 1806—ironically, on the very day that the entourage set its foot at Sandheads, just before Calcutta. It was an ominous portend of what was to befall the unfortunate household thereafter. Tipu's eldest son and heir Fateh Haidar was declared illegitimate. Prince Muiz-ud-din was imprisoned for his alleged involvement in the Vellore Mutiny and his family deprived of all financial support. The sad and filthy condition of his prison in Calcutta ensured that it snuffed his life out soon. He died in misery in 1809. Another prince Moieuddin is said to have taken his own life. In a short span of thirty years, ten of the twelve sons succumbed to the unhealthy climate of Calcutta or died of natural and unnatural causes. Others in the family were, however, allowed to spread over Calcutta.

The generous Wellesley pensions ensured that they managed to lead a fairly decent and sometimes profligate life. Lord Minto's Minutes of 1807 had laid down that, 'they shall not quit their habitation in order to make visits without permission. They shall not attend processions or public ceremonies of religious festivals or domestic events'.[21] The security was tight enough, though not sufficient to warrant calling it an imprisonment. They were free to spend their pensions as they pleased and lead their lives without too much public involvement.

The two younger princes, Jamel-ud-deen (who was about ten during the time of the Vellore Mutiny) and his brother Golam Mohammad, lived on. Golam Mohammad was given permission to marry his first cousin, the daughter of his uncle Karim in 1814. The two surviving princes were even said to have embarked on a trip to Europe when they grew up. Quite predictably, they were quite a spectacle of interest and curiosity in the high society of London that had heard tales of their dreaded Mysore foe. Jamel-ud-deen is said to have been grumpy and not too endearing. He died in 1842. Golam Mohammad, however, charmed the British society and nobility and is said to have even enjoyed the friendship of Queen Victoria.[22] In a letter dated 6 April 1859 to her daughter, the Crown Princess of Prussia, the Queen wrote: 'You will also get a pair of screens from poor old Prince Gholam Mohammad, who has brought them for you. He and his son and grandson have just arrived—they were at the levee and dine with us tonight.'[23] The Queen also made him the Knight of the Order of the Star of India, K.C.S.I., shortly before his death due to dengue fever, on 11 August 1872. Obituary columns in London newspapers extolled the virtues and gentleness of the prince. He was earning a pension of £3788 per annum by then. One of his grandsons and a great grandson were in turn sheriffs of Calcutta in 1891 and 1913 respectively.[24] Through savings and other wise investments from his pension, Golam Mohammad had created a fairly vast estate in Calcutta. Before his death, he had set up the second wealthiest Muslim Trust in undivided Bengal as a symbol of his lineage. The long list of his properties included 'the Tollygunge

Club, part of the grounds of the Royal Calcutta Golf Club, the land upon which Shaw Wallace & Co. built their imposing office, Mysore House in Chetla now in ruins, an Imambara and Shahi Mosque in Tollygunge and the Tipu Sultan Mosque beside the Statesman House on Dharamtala Street.'[25] Several members of the house of Haidar Ali and Tipu Sultan continue to live in relative anonymity in Calcutta, bringing the curtains down on a dynasty that had an accidental tryst with royalty and history, in the nearly four decades of interregnum in Mysore.

The Tipu Persona in Britain

The constant news and dispatches from India about the Company's bloody skirmishes with Mysore and its ferocious and tyrannical ruler left a deep imprint on the psyche of the average British citizen. While there was applause and rejoicing at his total and complete annihilation at the fall of Srirangapatna in 1799, there was also increased curiosity and a kind of oriental exoticism associated with the man, described as the Tiger of Mysore. As new revelations of his letters, his dream registers, exquisite jewellery and ornaments, costumes, throne and so on became visible to the common public of Britain, the interest and curiosity further peaked. Rapid translations from Persian and other languages ensued of the letters, manuscripts, recorded minutes and secret correspondences, and other memorabilia found in his possession. The British were desperate to get a peep into the mind of the man whom they so deeply feared and hated. A lot of what they found was new discovery; a lot of what they produced also ensured a confirmation bias.

In popular art, scenes from his life, be it the surrender of his sons as hostages to Lord Cornwallis, the final storming of the Srirangapatna fort, his last attack and his body being discovered by Sir David Baird and others became inspirations for wall paintings on displays. By the end of the eighteenth and the start of the nineteenth centuries, panoramas were a popular form of entertainment in England with artists vying with one another to depict the truer to life and gigantic spectacles for a discerning audience.

An American artist, Mather Brown, who was living in England, wrote to the East India Company on 8 August 1792 expressing his desire to represent on canvas the episode of Tipu's defeat in the Third Anglo–Mysore War and more so of the surrender of his sons as hostages. *The Delivery of the Definitive Treaty by the Hostage Princes to Lord Cornwallis* was the art that was then created by Brown. A version of this, of 44.5x52 cm dimensions, is seen at the Bowes Museum, Barnard Castle. Cornwallis is seen looking down affectionately at the two boys, the younger of whom seems quite peppy and pulling his brother's hand (perhaps being unaware of what was happening), while the elder one looks a bit distraught. There is shock and gloom alike on the faces of Tipu's party, while the British entourage behind Cornwallis sport a smug, victorious look. The work was exhibited at the Morland Gallery in November 1792, with a pamphlet narrating the details. Brown made several versions of this historical event, with Cornwallis being shown more affectionately, looking down and holding the hands of the boys. Sean Willock argues that 'Brown showed the cross-cultural recognition of Cornwallis's paternity to have particular implications for imperialism . . . the supposedly benign treatment of the hostages is thereby registered as a spectacle of British benevolence, while the paternal relationship of Cornwallis to his captives is thought of as precursory to the political ties necessary for the maintenance of empire'.[26] He was seen leading them to a British (read civilized) way of life and etiquette, it seemed to convey, and thereby he was actually doing the boys a great favour. The boys leave behind billows of smoke, crestfallen but savage-looking natives, elephants and clasping the hands of their benefactor, they move on to a better life.

The work of Francesco Bartolozzi, titled *The Departure of the Sons of Tippoo from the Zenana,* that came thereafter in around 1794, had an imaginary scene as compared to Brown's. It depicts the scene in the zenana of Tipu where the several female members of the family are seen giving the boys a tearful farewell. Menfolk and two howdah-bearing elephants wait in the vicinity to usher the boys away. Obviously neither the men (nor of course the British) were given access to the most private of chambers, namely the zenana. Numerous known and anonymous artists began depicting the scene in their own imagination, showing how potent the symbolism and the myth surrounding Tipu Sultan and the significance of his annihilation was for the empire—all this, even when he was still alive and fighting the British. The return of the sons, too, is depicted in a few paintings around and after 1796.

After the death of the Sultan, Sir Robert Ker Porter (1777–1842) was among the earliest artists who invited subscriptions for his new artwork on the fall of Srirangapatna, which began appearing in newspapers from early October 1799 itself—barely six months after the storming back in Mysore. Although he had never visited India, Porter made this painting in a short span of barely six weeks, based entirely on inputs from the Company and its correspondences. His famous painting—*The Storming of Seringapatam*—was first exhibited to the public on 29 March 1800 at the Lyceum and was a large 120-feet long and 21-feet high canvas painting, covering in all 2550 square feet of canvas.[27] Several prominent British officers involved in the ambush were featured in it. It froze that moment of time when the fort was breached at two places and the Company officers were advancing inside, with fire, smoke, canons, guns seen all around, with the gopuram of presumably the Ranganathaswamy temple looming over all the anarchy from a distance. The exhibition was widely attended with people paying an admission fee of a shilling. Those seeking more historical background could pay an additional two shillings to pick up an elaborate booklet titled *Narrative Sketches of the Conquest of Mysore*, running into nearly 120 pages, to aid the art, 'on a scale and magnitude hitherto unattempted [sic] in this country.'[28] The booklet is said to have become so popular that it was reprinted four times in two editions between 1800 and 1804 with thousands of copies being picked. It had graphic details of Tipu's atrocities against the British prisoners and was possibly aimed into directing public opinion in Britain on the appropriateness of the war and the justified murder of a tyrant. The sheer size, spectacle and storytelling that came along through this gigantic art made the spectator feel as though they were one with the officers on that fateful day in May at Srirangapatna. Porter's work greatly enhanced the military prestige of the Company as a harbinger of justice and national pride that 'patriotically advanced and enhanced the government's full-blown vision of empire as a historical spectacle of glory in which all amongst the British populace could participate.'[29]

The booklet ends with a triumphant and self-congratulatory note:

> Thus have the wisdom and energy of British councils, and the steady bravery of British soldiers, united to overthrow one of the most powerful tyrants of the east; to accomplish as complete and as just a revolution, as can be found on the records of history; and to produce such an increase of revenue, resource, commercial advantage, and military strength to the British establishment in India, as must for years to come ensure a prosperous and happy tranquility, not only to the Company's possessions, but to the native principalities, and to millions of inhabitants on the fertile plains of Hindostan.[30]

But Porter was not satisfied with just one painting on a theme that had brought him so much popularity. He made another painting, this time of the *Finding the Body of Tippoo Sultan*, where through the dark, hellish ramparts of the fort, the search party finally discovers his corpse. The light shimmering from the lanterns and torches in their hands was almost symbolic of how it was the British power that was lighting up the darkness of a squalid India. Arthur William Devis picked up the cue from Porter in his work, *Major-General Baird and Col Arthur Wellesley Discovering the Body of Tippoo Sultaun at Seringapatam.*

The popularity that Porter's masterpiece brought about gave rise to several others attempting similar themes. Alexander Allan's *The Assault on Seringapatam,* Joseph Mallord William Turner's *The Siege of Seringapatam,* Thomas Stothard's *The Storming of Seringapatam* and others were examples of the surfeit of paintings depicting the proud victory of British troops in the last Anglo–

Mysore War. Earlier Henry Singleton had painted the events of
1792 that terminated the Third Anglo–Mysore War, including the
handover of Tipu's sons as hostages to Lord Cornwallis. He too
produced four oil sketches on the assault of the fort and the discovery
of Tipu's corpse. This was titled as *The Last Effort and Fall of Tippoo
Sultaun*. Tipu is seen fighting with his sword and turbanless, while a
British officer near him has his sight at his jewel, for which he was
anyway shot eventually. Henry Singleton and Anthony Cardon also
made paintings of *The Surrender of Two Sons of Tippoo Sultaun in
1799*, after the fort was captured by the British. Luigi Shiavonetti's
The Body of Tippoo Sultaun Recognized by his Family has an element of
Greek tragedy painted all over it. His young sons are shown clasping
the corpse or sobbing on the ground, as are his officers, some of whom
are in deep, somber conversation, while a womanly figure (looking
like a European lady) is seen grieving with her hands outstretched
dramatically—almost exhorting destiny or God or so for the ill-luck
that befell their family. Weapons laid down on the ground indicate
a surrender by the Mysore side. Notably several of these art works
emerged before the end of 1800, just a year after Tipu met his end.

From the canvas success, the natural next step was the theatre
stage. Plays on Tipu and his life were quite popular in London,
even while he was alive. *Tippoo Saib, or British Valour in India* was
staged at Covent Garden on 1 June 1791, at the heights of the Third
Anglo–Mysore War. *Tippoo Sultan, or The Siege of Bangalore* followed
thereafter on 9 April 1792 at Astley. Dennys Forest extracts a rare
review of this staging that appeared in the *Madras Courier* on 13
December 1792 that makes for delightful reading and gives a peep
into how the British viewed the Mysore court and its ruler:

> Had Astley resided all his life in Mysore and its neighbouring
> countries, he could not be better informed than he is respecting
> the manners, customs etc., of Tippoo Saib, his court and subjects.
> Tippoo in the first act, is discovered seated at a table, surrounded
> by his nobility dressed in the Turkish manner, but instead of
> turbans they all appear in Armenian caps enriched with plumes

of feathers. His guards, who are seen at a distance, are clothed in Tyger's [sic] skins and armed with halberds, resembling very much the Beef Eaters in the Tower. In the second Act the manners and customs of the people are introduced. The High Priest of the Sun, who comes forward attended by numbers of priests of various orders, having made his invocation, he retires to commence the sacrifices of the day, the victims for which are seen bound, with wreaths of flowers round their necks, and consist of Hares, Rams and Hogs. In the back part of the stage there are a number of people wrestling and others running races, a party of beautiful virgins urging them to victory and to the prize. Others are dancing, leaping, skating etc. etc.[31]

After the fall of Srirangapatna, several other plays began to be staged. *Tippoo Saib, or the Storming of Seringapatam* by J.H. Amherst was produced at the Royal Coburg on 20 January 1823. Since enough time had passed since the incident and more resources were made available of the episode, this seemed to be a little more authentic in its design and content. *The Storming of Seringapatam, or The Death of Tippoo Saib* was readied at Astley's Royal Amphitheatre for the Easter of 1829. It had 'the entire ragbag of pseudo-Orientalism and pseudo-history . . . emptied on stage and overflowed into the arena'[32]—with even scenes of the Ganga by moonlight fitted into a Mysorean geography! Being a circus company, it brought to the production a rare military spectacle that had seldom been seen before. Acrobatics, large animals and drilling in formation combined to provide the viewers a dazzling experience. The reviews though were splendid and Mr Cartlitch as Tipu, 'looked very fierce and roared as loud as any of the tigers of that royal sultan ever did'.[33] These plays further cemented the views and opinions of the Company and its senior management about Tipu, which had already begun with the art works and their exhibitions. These were timely too as Britain was still engaged in wars against revolutionary France, and Napoleon was yet to be vanquished. In such a scenario, the artwork and plays galvanized British public opinion, stuffing them with national pride and esteem, to forge an identity driven by common national purpose. That a trusted oriental ally of their biggest enemy, the French—with whom they were engaged in a bitter war at that moment—had been so totally and completely vanquished necessitated a more dramatic underscoring of the victory.

Tipu Sultan made generous appearances in English literature, as well as in plays and paintings. In 1805 Dr John Leyden, Surgeon to the Mysore Survey, translated a sorrowful *Dirge on Tippoo Sultan* from the Kanara, from popular local Kannada songs and references to his supporters and betrayers at the last stages of his life. It emphasized that neither Tipu's military strength or valour, nor his faith in Islam were sufficient to save him, as he failed to secure the grace of the local presiding deity of Srirangapatna (i.e., Ranganathaswamy). It ends philosophically, stating only the lotus feet of Lord Vishnu were permanent and everything else ephemeral and transient. Some stanzas of this went thus:

> How quickly fled our Sultan's state!
> How soon his pomp has pass'd away!
> How swiftly sped Seringa's fate
> From wealth and power to dire decay!

> How proud his conquering banners flew!
> How stately march'd his dread array!
> Soon as the King of earth withdrew
> His favouring smile, they pass'd away.
>
> :
>
> :

> The noon-tide came with baleful light,
> The Sultan's corpse in silence lay;
> His kingdom, like a dream of night,
> In silence vanish'd quite away.

> But say, to fence the falling state,
> Who foremost trod the ranks of fame?
> Great Kummer, chief of soul elate,
> And stern Sher Khan of deathless name.

Meer Saduk too, of high renown,
With him what chieftain could compare?
While Mira Hussen virgins own
As flowery-bow'd Munmoden fair.

:

:

Pournia [Purnaiya] sprung from Brahma's line,
Intrepid in the martial fray,
Alike in council formed to shine:---
How could our Sultan's power decay?

:

:

Vain was each prayer and high behest,
When Runga doom'd thy fatal day;
How small a bullet pierc'd thy breast!
How soon thy kingdom past away!

Amid his queens of royal race,
Of princely form the monarch trod;
Amid his sons of martial grace,
The warrior mov'd an earthly God.

:

:

Where were the chiefs in combat bred,
The hosts, in battle's dreadful day?
Ah! Soon as Crishna's favour fled,
Our prince, our kingdom pass'd away.

How vain is every mortal boast,
How empty earthly pomp and power!
Proud bulwarks crumble down to dust,
If o'er them adverse fortune lower.

In Vishnu's lotus-foot alone
Confide! His power shall ne'er decay,
When tumbles every earthly throne,
And mortal glory fades away.[34]

Bernard Wycliffe published the poem *The Mussulman's Lament over the Body of Tipu Sultan, Written on the Spot where he Fell* in 1823. Narrative accounts of the war from several eyewitness accounts, documenting every little detail of the several wars fought against Tipu till the last one, started getting published and widely read. The accounts of the prisoners of Srirangapatna and their woes too created a stir in the minds of the faint-hearted.

Walter Scott's novel *The Surgeon's Daughter* is set in the mid-to-late 1770s between the two Anglo–Mysore Wars. It revolves around the love story between a young Menie Gray and Richard Middlemans. Quite curiously, Tippoo is shown as a lecherous monster who lusts for the young lady and by a strange turn of events, with the help of Haidar Ali, Menie is rescued.[35] The racy, detective novel *Moonstone* by Wilkie Collins, first published in 1868, has the story of a large, yellow diamond that changed several hands, before it reaches the possession of Tipu Sultan, who places it as an ornament in the handle of a dagger, and commanded it to be kept among the choicest treasures of his armoury. The novel opens with a graphic account of the storming of the fort, the rape and pillage of Srirangapatna that followed Tipu's fall and the discovery of this mythical diamond.[36] Philip Meadows Taylor's *Tippoo Sultaun: A Tale of the Mysore War* in 1840 qualifies to be termed as a historical novel. It goes into the mind and emotions, and his persona looms large throughout the narrative. Graphic scenes of violence and excesses and the atrocities heaped on victims of war and prisoners are vividly portrayed. George Alfred Henty's *Tiger of Mysore: A Story of the War with Tippoo Saib* came nearly a century after Tipu's death, in 1895. There are more details on the war than on Tipu who is an antagonist here. By the time it was written, since the British Raj had well-entrenched and stabilized itself in India, the novel is on predictable lines of justifying the rule and the wars.

And thus continued the oriental fascination of British art, theatre, poetry, prose and literature in the stormy life and times of one of their most dreaded enemies in distant India.

Post-colonial Representations of Tipu Sultan

If the colonial representation came with its fair share of bias against Tipu, who is portrayed as a despotic tyrant and bigot while supporting British imperialism, conquest and plunder, then the post-colonial revisionism of his story presents its own share of problems. From 1999 onwards, a new mythology, as scholarship, has been replacing narratives around the Mysore ruler. In a counter-hegemonic version, this school labours to portray Tipu as a man of the masses for whom he strove, a darling of the subaltern, a modernizer and innovator, a patriot and a fallen nationalist freedom fighter. Ironically, the same school often derides nationalism itself and concludes that there was no sense of nationhood or a nation-state called India till the British Raj set in firmly. What nation then was Tipu the freedom fighter of? In his long encounters with foreigners, we have seen that he was not averse to dealing with or even allying with them. His alternative idea of the Indian nation would have been no less colonial and imperialistic than the British, as he had the French as his allies and to whom, till the very end, he kept sending emissaries and solicitations. His open invitations to the Caliph of Turkey or the Afghans to invade India and establish a religious, pan-Islamist supremacy, positing himself as the true torchbearer of the faith was no majorly egalitarian view of how India might have turned out to be, had by a twist of fate Tipu Sultan been victorious. Straddling between French colonialism and orthodox Islamism of the virulent kind, India would have shaped into something totally unrecognizable and toxic.

Post-colonial studies debunk most of the colonial accounts and writers, from Mark Wilks to Francis Buchanan, Lewin Bowring, or eye-witness accounts by British army officers such as Alexander Beatson, Roderick Mackenzie, Alexander Allan, or prisoners like James Scurry or James Bristow. They have mostly been brushed aside as being biased to buttress the oriental despot image of Tipu Sultan. Though, selectively many of these accounts are quoted too, when they make charitable references to the man. Or accounts of a contemporary of these chroniclers, such as Edward Moor is considered favourably as he does not portray as negative an image of the Sultan as the others.

In his doctoral thesis, academic Michael Soracoe argues that the construction of the despotic image of Tipu Sultan and his portrayal as a tyrant was a strategy deployed by the East India Company to divert the attention of the British Parliament and people from the atrocities and excesses committed in the colonies and to justify the spread of the empire for a larger good. Pride in British rule and the Company's military successes had to be evoked among the masses back in England. Hence, argues Soracoe, the British were to be seen as invading 'Mysore not as conquerors but as liberators of the mass of the population from the tyranny of Tipu Sultan.'[37] He avers that expansionist and corrupt Governor-Generals consciously tarred the image of Tipu Sultan to make their own aggressive actions palatable to British audiences at home. The Company itself was undergoing several changes through the eighteenth century. It was being run by a Council of Directors who sat in London and were appointees of the proprietors who owned the Company's stocks. Between Calcutta, Madras and Bombay Presidencies, they carried out the trade, military and later administrative functions. The Regulating Act of 1773 stamped the authority of the British Parliament over the Company and the territories it had, including in India, paving the way for the creation of the position of a Governor-General. The India Bill of 1784 created a Board of Control that included the Chancellor of the Exchequer, the Secretary of State, and four Privy Councillors, stamping the authority of the British government over the Company. It is in this backdrop that scholars such as Soracoe argue that the Company, too, wanted to make the maximum of its success in Mysore against a longstanding foe and deflect any criticism of maleficence and corruption of its own high-ranking officials. While there might be some truth in this argument, the colonial accounts of Haidar Ali are vastly complimentary and appreciative of his tact, strategy and even religious policy. Ironically, it was under Haidar's stewardship that the British suffered the maximum losses in the first two Anglo–Mysore Wars. Yet, the colonial chroniclers did not seem to 'demonize' him in the manner they are accused of having painted Tipu, while with the former they would have had a natural grouse and axe to grind. As the adage goes, there certainly could not be smoke without some fire somewhere.

The Persian accounts, be they of Kirmani or Zain-ul-abidin Shoostri or Tipu's own letters translated by Kirkpatrick, are deemed to be essays of exaggeration by the protagonist and his sycophantic courtiers. Kate Telstcher points out that the translation of the letters has been 'framed to conform to expectations of despotism.'[38] Critiquing such narratives, scholar Narasingha Sil mentions that whatever might be the negative opinions of a man like Kirkpatrick about the Sultan, from the preface to his translated works 'his scheme of translation, his hermeneutical methods, and his scholarly introspection and circumspection in respect of his literary enterprise'[39] appear to be extremely sound. Sil, thus, concludes that despite the surfeit of epithets that Kirkpatrick hurls at Tipu, portraying him as cruel, oppressive, harsh and tyrannical, the translation of the letters bear fidelity to the scholarly process and is not doctored in a manner as to vent his own personal disdain for the Sultan.

Narasingha Sil notices similar tendences in other works of post-colonial scholars such as Kate Telstcher (1995), Amal Chatterjee (1998), Ruchira Banerjee (2001), Constance McPhee (1998), Linda Colley (2000) and Janaki Nair (2006). While Amal Chatterjee views even the prisoner accounts as a bogeyman to posit Indian rulers as such as tyrannical, Ruchira Bannerjee 'in a footnote . . . lumps the works of Beatson (1800), Scurry and Oakes together as the products of propaganda in favour of a war against Tipu Sultan'.[40] Sil also denounces these post-colonial attempts of critiquing the Anglo–Mysore Wars and Tipu from a pictorial representation as an 'overkill' and dismisses attempts of those like Nair as suffering from 'logical asymmetry in its comparative analysis of the pictorial representations of Tipu Sultan and his British adversaries by the colonial and imperial painters.'[41]

When claims of exaggeration of violence are made against contemporary chroniclers, a question that begs an answer is why

would the need be felt to exaggerate the wanton cruelty, especially
against infidels, to embellish one's own royalty or legitimacy? That
violence is intrinsically linked with kingship and authority, especially
in the pre-modern era that Haidar Ali and Tipu Sultan operated in
is a fact. However, such violence coupled with theological sanctions
and desires to single out communities and groups based primarily
on identity pose a double whammy. The latest, modern definitions
of a genocide, as ratified by the United Nations Convention on the
Prevention and Punishment of the Crime of Genocide, in1948,
underscores 'intent' to destroy, either in whole or part, any ethnic,
racial, religious or national group as a necessary condition for using
the term.[42] Terming the treatment of the people of Malabar or Coorg
or the Mangalore Christians or Mandyam Iyengars by Tipu definitely
does fall in this definitional category, if we were to retrospect the
actions from a modern definition. All kings were violent, and all
wars were bloody is a flimsy, insufficient cover to show that some
were indeed especially more violent than the norms and manifested
a deep-seated theological intent to commit these acts.

Much is also made of the folk songs or *lavanis*—ballads that are
sung and performed in public spaces. These were folk songs that were
more common in the northern parts of Karnataka given a significant
Marathi influence. In comparison, the *powada* in Marathi poetry
is a more developed genre, right from the late seventeenth century
with eulogies to various popular historical figures or addressing
social issues. During the run up to the freedom struggle and the
attainment of freedom, several lavanis were composed in Kannada
with historical themes and great leaders of the past. The Karnataka
Janapada Parishat that promotes folklore has published a compilation
of such lavanis titled '*Swatantrya Samaradha Lavanigalu*' or Lavanis
of the Freedom Struggle, by S. Vishakantha Rao. Apart from Rani
Lakshmi Bai of Jhansi, Congress leaders Tyabji, Surendranath
Banerjee, Govind Ranade, Lokamanya Tilak, Aurobindo Ghose,
Gandhi, Bhagat Singh, Netaji Subhash Chandra Bose, Jawaharlal
Nehru and others, a popular lavani features Haidar Ali and Tipu

Sultan too. Another similar compilation is by B. Nilakanthayya. The lavani on the two Mysore rulers traces their history, right from the early days of Haidar Ali, his ancestry and rise in the Mysore polity, till the time of Tipu's death. The refrain is interesting too:

Beshak Tamasha Tiger Nishana Tipu Sultanana birudaythu
Masalath Maadidha Mir Sadakanige Desha Drohi
yembesaraaythu.[43]

Tipu Sultan's title and name was identified by the Tiger symbol,
But the evil doer Mir Sadak was immortalized in
history as a traitor.

Another variant is of the first line: *Mysuru Haidaraliya Keerthi Desha Videsha Meredoyithu* (The fame of Mysore's Haidar Ali spread all over the country and outside). The second line continues to invariably castigate Mir Sadak in all the variants. These songs seem to have been recorded on the gramophone too in the 1930s and 1940s.[44] They were also sung in *jatre* or village fairs in the early decades of the twentieth century. This lavani is often cited as an important marker of how Tipu was memorialized and celebrated by the subaltern, the masses and his memory kept alive for centuries after his death in these rustic, unsophisticated tunes and lyrics of the common people.

Countering this was Kannada literature's iconic figure and celebrated author and novelist Dr S.L. Bhyrappa, who in a series written for the Kannada newspaper *Vijaya Karnataka* in 2006, took on his ideological rival and fellow writer-playwright Girish Karnad. Karnad had, by then, written a popular play in 1997, *The Dreams of Tipu Sultan*, that sought to humanize the eighteenth-century monarch and his vision for Mysore. The two learned men had several ideological run-ins with each other on the matter of representation of Indian history and its characters. About the lavanis, Bhyrappa wrote in his essay titled 'It is Impossible to Build Nationalism on a Foundation based on Historical Falsehoods':

During the Indian freedom struggle, wandering bards, minstrels, and those who sang lavanis used to sing rustic songs that glorified Tipu at street corners, in marketplaces, and fairs. These semi-literate and illiterate people had no knowledge of history. They were patronized by Muslims, especially Muslim merchants and businessmen who gave them *bakshish*. In the same vein, some playwrights wrote plays glorifying Tipu as a great patriot based on the sole fact that he had fought against the British. Thus informed, the audience and general public began to believe that this was the true picture of the historical Tipu Sultan. Post-independence, our Marxists, vote bank politicians, and religiously-driven Muslim writers, artists, playwrights, and filmmakers portrayed Tipu as a patriot and a national hero. Real history died. The British were depicted as heartless villains for taking two sons of Tipu as hostages. Girish Karnad, who adheres to this tradition of painting Tipu as a national hero takes up this hostage episode in his play and makes Tipu mouth this highly revelatory dialogue of sociology: 'A new language has come to our land. A new culture. *Angreji*! A culture that takes children aged seven–eight as war hostages. However, taking war hostages was a tradition practiced by Muslim rulers who ruled India. Either Girish Karnad is ignorant of the fact that the British merely followed this existing tradition or he has deliberately suppressed it.[45]

The jury is thus still out on Tipu Sultan, his legacy, his characterization and his contributions—225 long years after his corpse was found on the night of 4 May 1799, amidst a heap of dead bodies, by the British search party in those dark ramparts of the Srirangapatna fort. He continues to excite passions, polarize people and is hotly contested in political and ideological standpoints. While the jury is still out on what kind of a man and ruler Tipu Sultan was, a semblance of a sober, factual assessment of the Sultan is by scholar Narasingha Sil:

All his measures including renaming his government as some kind of a divine endowment or reorganizing his army into *ilahi* or *Ahmadi* consisting of slaves or *chelas* were both military and Islamic in tone . . . Tipu basically belonged to that class of rulers who could be classified as feudal autocratic. To him, visible evidences of personal loyalty and security of his regional hegemony were extremely meaningful . . . we have reports of Tipu's wanton cruelty . . . Tipu was a regnant ruler keenly conscious of personal prestige and dignity, but could not command loyalty from his own officers . . . most probably, Tipu was more feared than respected or loved by his subjects . . . admittedly, Tipu appointed Hindus to positions of trust and responsibility as indeed did the Mughals and other regional Muslim rulers. It is however doubtful that appointment of Hindus to responsible posts followed any principle other than sheer common sense . . .

It is time we arrived at a reasonably realistic assessment of Tipu Sultan. If it is fair to maintain that Tipu was an energetic, assiduous, and industrious ruler and an immensely brave soldier, it is also reasonable to consider reports of his haughtiness and hubris. Despite many adulatory assessments, it is quite obvious on the basis of several eyewitness accounts that Tipu, fed by the flattery of his sycophants, came to believe that he was the greatest prince of Hindustan, if not of the world. This benighted narcissism rendered him deaf to any admonition from his well-wishers and led to his ultimate nemesis . . .

Yet, we must recognize with the benefit of hindsight the crucial role Tipu Sultan played in the history of English imperialism in the subcontinent. He proved himself to be a worthy adversary who for a short period of time made his formidable presence felt in the declining decades of Mughal India.[46]

Voltaire had famously said, 'History is the lie commonly agreed upon!'. In the case of Tipu Sultan, sadly, common agreement on even this lie eludes us.

Acknowledgements

There have been numerous individuals and institutions who have helped me in the research and the production of this book.

I am deeply thankful to the following institutions within India and outside: The National Archives of India (New Delhi), The National Library (Kolkata), The Karnataka State Archives (Bengaluru), the Kannada Sahitya Parishat (Bengaluru), The Mythic Society (Bengaluru), The Kozhikode District Archives, the Sringeri Matha, Samskriti Foundation (Melukote), the Diocese of Mangalore, The British Library India Office Library (London), The British Museum (London), The Victoria & Albert Museum (London), The Bharatiya Vidya Bhawan (London), The National Archives of the United Kingdom (Kew, London) and the Archives Nationales (Paris).

It is a blessing that the nonagenarian and literary legend of our times, Dr S.L. Bhyrappa, not only went through this manuscript in detail, but also penned the foreword to it. Eternally grateful to him for his generous affection and encouragement of my research and writing. I am immensely obliged to Dr Shashi Tharoor, Dr Bibek Debroy, Dr Swapan Dasgupta, Shri Yaduveer Krishnadatta Chamaraja Wadiyar, Smt. Sudha Murthy and Shri Sanjeev Sanyal for their endorsements of the book.

Mere words are insufficient to express my sincerest thanks to the following who helped me at various stages of my research journey:

- Mysuru: Shri Yaduveer Krishnadatta Chamaraja Wadiyar, the scion of the Mysore royal family, Prof. G.L. Shekhar, Shubha Sanjay Urs.

- Bengaluru: Shri C.T. Ravi, Smt Shobha Karandlaje, Shri Tejasvi Surya, Shri T.V. Mohandas Pai, Dr (Late) Suryanath U. Kamath, Shri Beluru Sudarshan, Shri M.P. Kumar, Dr T.S. Mohan, Dr Mandyam, D. Srinivas, Shri Sandeep Shetty, Shri Ashwath Narayann S. (Ajay), Prof. K.S. Kannan, Dr H.R. Meera, Dr Shyamala Vatsa, Shri Soham Jagtap, Shri V. Nagaraj, Shri M.R. Prasanna Kumar and Shri Jayasimha (all from the Mythic Society).
- To Shri Sravan Kumar for his timely and well-made illustrations of maps for the book.
- Mangaluru: Shri Gurdath Baliga.
- Kodagu: Shri C.P. Belliappa, Shri N.U. Nachappa.
- Melukote: Shri Araiyar Srirama Sharma, Prof. M.A. Alwar, Smt. Vidya Alwar.
- Thiruvanthapuram: Prof. M.G. Sashibhooshan, Shri Sreejith Panickar, Shri Gokul Yuvaraj.
- Kozhikode: Smt. Sulini Nair.
- Pune: Dr Uday Kulkarni, Dr Avinash Dharmadhikari, Dr Pushkar Lele, Rajesaheb of Miraj Shri Gangdadhar Rao Patwardhan, Gopalraje Patwardhan and Madhavraje Patwardhan.
- New Delhi: Prof. Heeraman Tiwari.
- London: Ms Leena Mitford, Dr Andrew S. Cook, Ms Ursula Williams-Sims (all at the British Library who helped me wade through the ocean of documents on this subject at the India Office there), Ms Manasi Paresh Kumar.
- Prof. Madhav Das Nalapat.
- My friends Smt. Alo Pal and Shri Kushal Mehra for reading the rough drafts of the manuscript and providing very valuable feedback.

I am deeply indebted to my publishers, Penguin Random House India, for their continued faith in me, especially my dear friend Premanka Goswami, and Rea Mukherjee, Gunjan Ahlawat, Vineet Gill and Cynthia Rodrigues for ideating on the content, refining it, meticulously reviewing several drafts of the manuscript, and designing the beautiful cover page. They are undoubtedly any writer's dream publishing team!

My parents, Smt. Nagamani Sampath and Shri Sampath Srinivasan, and my maternal grandmother, Smt. Kantha Bai, nurtured my childhood obsession with history, particularly the history of Mysore. My voyages of discovery became a family project of sorts in which all of them joined forces. This book has been a germination of that very interest that they planted and nurtured in me back then. The sacrifices they endured for me fills my heart with immense gratitude and love. I realize that whatever I am today is solely because of them.

Research and writing are solitary journeys, and in the course of it, one often feels isolated and disoriented. In all those trying times, as otherwise too, Sandeep Singh Chauhan has been a rock solid support and a patient sounding board. Despite not being a great history buff himself, he endured the torture of reading several portions of this manuscript and always gave sane advice on a diurnal basis for a wide range of matters, including helping me choose a title or the cover page for my books. I am blessed to have him as an integral part of my life.

My spiritual guru, Sadguru Sakshi Shree of the Siddha Sudarshan Sakshi Dhaam (Ghaziabad), has always been my anchor to ground me amid my myriad challenges. To Guruji I pay my respectful regards. To them all, as well as to my dear Leo for putting a smile on my weary face after exhausting nights of writing this book, I owe ton loads of gratitude. I am also thankful to several friends, family and well-wishers for keeping me grounded and motivated through the journey.

Last, but not the least, my obeisance unto the Divine, without whose inspiration and grace, not a word could have been written.

Bibliography

India Office Library (IOL), British Library, London

- L/P&S/1: Secret Court of Directors, and Secret Committee (1778 on).
  L/P&S/2: Board of Control Secret Minutes (1785 on).
  L/P&S/4: Board's Abstracts of Secret, Political and Foreign Letters and Despatches (1784 on).
  L/P&S/5: Secret Correspondence with India (1756 on)—Board's and Company's series together, often with enclosures.
  L/P&S/6: Political Correspondence with India (1792 on)—Board's and Company's series together.
- L/P&S/19: Political and Secret Miscellaneous Records (c.1750 on) Madras Military & Political Proceedings.
- MSS Eur E196 'Tipu Sultan Papers.'
- MSS Eur F228/40 'Copies of Correspondence of Tipu Sultan Seized at Seringapatam'.
- 39857–39858, Staunton's and Sadleir's journals as commissioners to Tipu Sultan in 1783 and 1784, & Associated Papers.
- Verelst Collection. MSS Eur F 218/18: 24 folios related to Madras and the 1st Mysore War 1767–69.
- Correspondence Tippu Sultan MSS- MSS Eur E196.
- MSS Eur F 198/1/14.
- MSS Eur F228/21: 1809–1811.
- MSS Eur F198/1/15.
- MSS Eur F 195/54.
- MSS Eur F198/1/16: 1790s.

- MSS Eur C639 Sir William Jones Papers
- MSS Eur C229.
- Richard Wellesley Correspondence & Papers: MSS 12564–13915, 37274–318, 37414–16, 49979–92, 51728.
- Wellesley Despatches & Minutes: MSS Eur D 623.

British Museum, London

- Wellesley Papers: MSS 12585–88, 12606, 12610, 13710, 13727–29, 37278–79.
- Macartney Papers: MSS 22, 452.
- Prints & Drawings Department.

Public Record Office, London

- Foreign Office Records—F.O. 78; 27/28/29/30: France, Turkey, Portugal, Switzerland & Denmark.
- Cornwallis Papers: 30/11/112-152.

Archives Nationales, Paris

- *Catalogues des Manuscripts Conserves aux Archives Nationales*: 2769 (T, 15267). *Memoire sur l'Inde,* 1788.
- Correspondance Consulaire, Baghdad (1776–86; 1787–91) Bassorah (1743–91), Constantinople (1787–90).

National Archives of India, New Delhi

- Original Records, 1783–1799.
- Secret Proceedings, 1780–1799.
- Political Proceedings, 1790–1799.

National Archives, Kew, United Kingdom

- Cowley Papers (FO 519)
- Charles Cornwallis Papers (PRO 30/11)

- Grant's Political Survey of the Northern Circars, 20 December 1784, PRO 30/11/57/b, National Archives of UK, Kew, London, n.d.

Published Books

A Handbook to the Records of the Government of India in the Imperial Record Department, 1748–1859. Calcutta: Government of India Central Publication Branch, 1925.

Aitchison, C.U. *A Collection of Treaties, Engagements & Sanads Relating to India & Neighbouring Countries*. Vol. 9. New Delhi: Mittal Publications, 1983.

Ali, Sheikh. *British Relations with Haidar Ali, 1760–1782*. Mysore: Rao and Raghavan, 1963.

———. *Tipu Sultan*. New Delhi: National Book Trust, 1972.

———. *Tipu Sultan: A Study in Diplomacy and Confrontation*. Mysore: Geetha Book House, 1982.

Allan, Alexander. *An Account of the Campaign in Mysore (1799)*. Edited by Nares Chandra Sinha. Calcutta: The University Printing & Publishing Co. Ltd., n.d.

Annual Report of the Mysore Archaeological Department for the Year 1918. Bangalore: Government Press, 1919.

Annual Report of the Mysore Archaeological Department for the Year 1935. Bangalore: Government Press, 1936.

Annual Report of the Mysore Archaeological Department for the Year 1938. Bangalore: Government Press, 1940.

Annual Report of the Mysore Archaeological Department for the Year 1940. Mysore: Government Branch Press, 1941.

Anonymous. *Islamic Culture*. Vol. XIV. Published under the Authority of H.E.H. the Nizam's Government, Hyderabad, 1940.

Anonymous. *Memoirs of the Late War in Asia*. Vol. 2. London: Murray, 1788.

Anonymous. *Narratives Sketches of the Conquest of the Mysore*. London 1800.

Anonymous. *The Life of General, the Right Honourable Sir David Baird, in Two Volumes*. London: Richard Bentley, 1832.

Anonymous Officer in the East India Service. *Authentic Memoirs of Tippoo Sultaun, Including His Cruel Treatment of English Prisoners, with a Preliminary Sketch of the Life and Character of Hyder Ally Cawn.* Calcutta: Mirror Press, 1819.

Anonymous Officer. *Memoir of the Life and the Character of the late Lieut.-Colonel John Campbell.* Edinburgh: N.p., 1836.

Arberry, A.J. *The Library of the India Office: A Historical Sketch.* London: Billing & Sons Ltd., 1938.

Archer, Mildred. *Tippoo's Tiger.* London: H.M. Stationery Off, 1959.

Asiatic Researches; or Transactions of the Society Instituted in Bengal for Inquiring into the History and Antiquities, the Arts, Sciences and Literature of Asia. Vol. 5. London: Allen & Co., 1799.

Ayyar, K.V. Krishna. *The Zamorins of Calicut: From the Earliest Times down to A.D. 1806.* Calicut: Norman Printing Bureau, 1938.

B. Nilakanthayya. *Swatantrya Sangramadha Lavanigalu.* Bangalore: Karnataka Janapada Parishat, 2008.

Balakrishna, Sandeep. *Tipu Sultan: The Tyrant of Mysore.* Chennai: Rare Publications, 2013.

Bartolomeo, Paolino da San. *A Voyage to the East Indies.* Translated by William Johnston. London: J. Davis, 1800.

Bayly, Col. *Diary of Col. Balyly: 1796–1830.* London: The Army & Navy Cooperative Society Ltd., 1896.

Beatson, Lt. Col. Alexander. *A View of the Origin and the Conduct of the War with Tipu Sultan.* London: W. Bulmer & Co., 1800.

Becher, Henry. *Remarks and Occurrences of Mr. Henry Becher, during his Imprisonment of Two Years and a Half in the Dominions of Tippoo Sultan, From Whence he Made his Escape.* Bombay: N.p., 1793.

Bell, Andrew. *The Madras School, or, Elements of Tuition.* London: J. Murray, 1808.

Belliappa, C.P. *Nuggets from Coorg History.* New Delhi: Rupa & Co., 2008.

Bowring, Lewin Bentham. *Haidar Ali and Tipu Sultan and the Struggle with the Musalman Powers of the South.* Dehradun: EBD Publishing & Distributing Co., 1893.

Bristow, James. *Narrative of the Sufferings of James Bristow*. London: J. Murray, 1793.

Brittlebank, Kate. *Tiger: The Life of Tipu Sultan*. New Delhi: Juggernaut, 2019.

Buchanan, Francis. *A Journey from Madras Through the Countries of Mysore, Canara, and Malabar*. Vol 1. London: W. Bulmer & Co., 1807.

———. *A Journey from Madras Through the Countries of Mysore, Canara, and Malabar*. Vol 2. London: W. Bulmer & Co., 1807.

———. *A Journey from Madras Through the Countries of Mysore, Canara, and Malabar*, Vol 3. London: W. Bulmer & Co., 1807.

Buddle, Anne. *The Tiger and the Thistle: Tipu Sultan and the Scots in India*. Edinburgh: Trustees of National Gallery of Scotland, 1999.

Byrant, G.J. *The Emergence of British Power in India, 1600–1784: A Grand Strategic Interpretation*. Suffolk, U.K.: Boydell Press, 2013.

Campbell, Richard Hamilton. *Tippoo Sultan: The Fall of Seringapatam and the Restoration of the Hindu Raj*. Bangalore: Govt. Press, 1919.

Chennabasappa, Ko, ed. *Apratima Deshabhakta Tippu Sultan*. Bangalore: Navakarnataka Publications Pvt. Ltd., 2013.

Clarke, Francis. L., and William Dunlap. *The Life of the Most Noble Arthur, Marquis and Earl of Wellington*. Parts. 1&2. New York: Van Winkle & Wiley, 1814.

Collins, Wilkie. *The Moonstone*. London: Tinsley Bros., 1868.

Dalton, Charles. *Memoir of Charles Dalton: Defender of Trichinopoly, 1752–1753*. London: W.H. Allen & Co., 1886.

Davies, Huw J. *The Wandering Army: Campaigns that Transformed the British Way of War*. Connecticut: Yale University Press, 2022.

De, Barun, ed. *Perspectives in Social Sciences*. Vol. 1: *Historical Dimensions*. Calcutta: Oxford University Press, 1977.

Desai, Walter Sadgun. *Bombay and the Marathas Upto 1774*. New Delhi: Munshiram Manoharlal, 1970.

Dinesh, Tirur. *Destroyed Temples of Kerala*. Vol. 1. Trivandrum: TrasaDasyu, 2020.

Dirom, Major. *A Narrative of the Campaign in India, which terminated the war with Tippoo Sultaun, in 1792*. London: Bulmer & Co., 1794.

Dodwell, Henry. *The Nabobs of Madras*. New Delhi: Asian Educational Services, 1986.

D'Souza, A.L.P. *History of the Catholic Community of South Kanara* Mangalore: Desco Publishers, 1983.

Duff, James Grant. *History of the Mahrattas*. Vol. 2. Calcutta: R. Cambray & Co., 1912.

———. *History of the Mahrattas*. Vol. 3. Calcutta: R. Cambray & Co., 1918.

Dompart, M. *Official Documents Relative to the Negotiations Carried on by Tippoo Sultaun with the French Nation and Other Foreign States*. Calcutta: Honourable Company Press, 1799.

Dubois, Abbe J.A. *Letters on the State of Christianity in India*. London: Longman, 1823.

Fernandes, Praxy. *Storm over Seringapatam: The Incredible Story of Hyder Ali and Tippu Sultan*. Bombay: Thackers, 1969.

Firth, Charles Harding. *The Marquis Wellesley*. Oxford: Thos. Shrimpton & Son, 1877.

Fisher, Michael H. *The Politics of the British Annexation of India, 1757–1857*. New Delhi: Oxford University Press, 1996.

Forest, Denys. *Tiger of Mysore: Life and Death of Tipu Sultan*. New Delhi: Allied Publishers Private Limited, 1970.

Forrest, George. W. *Selections from the Letters, Despatches and Other State Papers preserved in the Bombay Secretariat: Maratha Series*. Vol. 1, Parts 1 & 2. Bombay: Government Central Press, 1885.

Francis, W. *Madras District Gazetteer: Madura*. Vol. 1. Madras: Government Press, 1906.

Fullarton, William. *A View of the English Interests in India*. London: T. Cadell, 1787.

Garodia Gupta, Archana. *The Women Who Ruled India: Leaders, Warriors, Icons*. Gurugram: Hachette India, 2019.

Gleig, George Robert. *The Life of Major-General Sir Thomas Munro.* London: Henry Colborn & Richard Bentley, 1830.

Gidwani, Bhagwan. S. *The Sword of Tipu Sultan: A Historical Novel about the Life and Legend of Tipu Sultan of India.* Bombay: Allied Publishers, 1976.

Goel, Sita Ram, ed. *Tipu Sultan: Villain or Hero?* New Delhi: Voice of India, 1993.

Gopal, M.H. *Tipu Sultan's Mysore: An Economic Study.* Bombay: Popular Prakashan, 1971.

Grainger, John D. *The British Navy in Eastern Waters.* Suffolk, U.K: Boydell & Brewer, 2022.

Green, Charles Francis. *British India Analyzed.* Parts 1–3. London: R. Faulder, 1795.

Greville, Charles Francis. *British India Analyzed: The Provincial and Revenue Establishments of Tippoo Sultaun.* Part 1. London: R. Faulder, 1795.

Habib, Irfan, ed. *Resistance and Modernization under Haidar Ali & Tipu Sultan.* New Delhi: Tulika Books, 2019.

——— ed. *State & Diplomacy under Tipu Sultan.* New Delhi: Tulika Books, 2014.

Hasan, Mohibbul. *History of Tipu Sultan.* Delhi: Aakar Books, 1951.

Henderson, J.R. *The Coins of Haidar Ali and Tipu Sultan.* Madras: Government Press, 1921.

Hermoine de, Almedia, and George Gilpin. *Indian Renaissance: British Romantic Art and the Prospect of India.* Aldershot: Ashgate, 2005.

Home, Robert. *Select Views in Mysore, the Country of Tippoo Sultan.* London: Published by Mr Bowyer, 1794.

Hunter, James. *Picturesque Scenery in the Kingdom of Mysore.* London: W. Bulmer for E. Orme, 1805.

Husain, Mahmud. *The Dreams of Tipu Sultan (Translated from the Original Persian).* Karachi: Pakistan Historical Society Publications No. 7, n.d.

Indian Historical Records Commission: Proceedings of Meetings, Vol. XIX, Nineteenth Meeting held at Trivandrum, December 1942. New Delhi: Manager of Publications, 1943.

Innes, C.A. & F.B. Evans, ed. *Madras District Gazetteers: Malabar, Vol. 1.* Madras: Government Press, 1951.

Josyer, G.R. *History of Mysore and the Yadava Dynasty.* Mysore: Coronation Press, 1950.

Karyappa, Addanda. *Tippu Matthu Kodavaru: Bacchitta Sathya Bicchittaaga.* Kodagu: Rangabhumi Kodagu Prakashana, 2015.

Kausar, Kabir. *Secret Correspondence of Tipu Sultan.* New Delhi: Light & Life Publishers, 1980.

Khare, Vasudev Waman. *Aitihasik Lekh Sangrah.* (Marathi). Vol. 8. Pune: Aryabhushan, 1915.

———. *Aitihasik Lekh Sangrah.* (Marathi). Vol. 7. Pune: Aryabhushan, 1912.

———. *Aitihasik Lekh Sangrah.* (Marathi). Vol. 9. Pune: Aryabhushan, 1915.

Kincaid, C.A. & Rao Bahadur D.B. Parasnis. *A History of the Maratha People.* New Delhi: S. Chand & Co., n.d.

Kirkpatrick, William. *Select Letters of Tippoo Sultan.* Bombay: Asiatic Society, 1811.

Kirmani, Meer Hussain Ali Khan. *Nishan-i-Hydari,* Translated by Colonel W. Miles as *The History of Hydur Naik.* London: Oriental Translation Fund of Great Britain & Ireland, 1842.

———. Translated by Colonel W. Miles as *The History of The Reign of Tipu Sultan.* New Delhi: Abhijeet Publications, 2017.

Krishnayya, D.N. *Kodagina Itihasa.* Bangalore: Karnataka Sahitya Parishat, 2014.

Kulkarni, Uday S. *Solstice at Panipat.* Pune: Mula Mutha Publishers, 2011.

———. *The Extraordinary Epoch of Nanasaheb Peshwa.* Pune: Mula Mutha Publishers, 2020.

———. *The Mastery of Hindustan: Triumphs & Travails of Madhavrao Peshwa.* Pune: Mula Mutha Publishers, 2022.

Lawrence, A.W. *Captives of Tipu: Survivors' Narratives.* London: J. Cape, 1929.

Logan, William. *Malabar Manual.* 2 Vols. New Delhi: Asian Educational Services, 2010.

Lohuizen, Jan Van. *The Dutch East India Company and Mysore. 1762–1790.* Brill, 1961.

Low, Charles Rathbone. *History of the Indian Navy (1613–1863).* Vol. 1. New Delhi: Manas Publications, 1985.

Lindsay, John. *Lives of the Lindsays.* Vol. 3. London: John Murray, 1849.

———. *Lives of the Lindsays.* Vol. 4. London: Wigan, 1840.

Lushington, S.R. *Life and Services of Lord General Harris.* London: John. W. Parker, 1840.

MacAlister, Keith. *A Concise Statement of Facts Regarding the Negotiation between the East India Company and Tippoo Sultaun, Concluded at Mangalore, in the Year 1784.* Edinburgh: J. Ballantyne and Co., 1818.

Mackenzie, Roderick. *A Sketch of the War with Tippoo Sultaun.* Calcutta: N.p., 1799.

Malcolm, John. *Sketch of the Political History of India.* Vol. 1. London: James Moyes, 1811.

Malleson, Colonel George. B. *The Decisive Battles of India: From 1746 to 1849 Inclusive.* London: Reeves and Turner, 1888.

———. *Seringapatam; Past and Present. A Monograph.* Madras: Higginbotham, 1876.

Martin, Robert Montgomery, ed. *The Despatches, Minutes and Correspondence of the Marquess Wellesley. Volume 1.* London: John Murray, 1836.

———. *The Despatches, Minutes and Correspondence of the Marquess Wellesley, Volume 2.* London: John Murray, 1836.

Mehendale, Gajanan Bhaskar. *Tipu As He Really Was.* Pune: Swatantraveer Savarkar Adhyasan Kendra, 2018.

Menon, A. Sreedhara. *Kerala District Gazetteers: Kozhikode.* Trivandrum: Government Press, 1962.

————. *Kerala District Gazetteers: Trichur.* Trivandrum: Government of Kerala, 1962.

Menon, P. Shungoonny. *A History of Travancore from the Earliest Times.* New Delhi: Gyan Publishing House, 2020.

Michaud, Joseph. *Histoire des Progrès et de la Chute de l'Empire de Mysore, sous les Règnes d'Hyder-Aly et Tippoo-Saib. (History of Mysore under Hyder Ali and Tipu Sultan).* Paris: Giguet et cie., 1801. Translated by V.K. Raman Menon as *History of Mysore under Hyder Ali & Tippoo Sultan.* New Delhi: Asian Educational Services, 2003.

Middleton, Richard. *Cornwallis: Soldier & Statesman in a Revolutionary World.* Connecticut: Yale University Press, 2022.

Moienuddin, Mohammad. *Sunset at Srirangapatnam: After the Death of Tipu Sultan.* Hyderabad: Orient Longman, 2000.

Moor, Edward. *A Narrative of the Operations of Captain Little's Detachment.* London: J. Johnson, 1794.

Mortan, Rev. James. *The Poetical Remains of the Late Dr John Leyden, With Memoirs of His Life.* London: Longman, 1819.

Munro, Innes. *A Narrative of the Military Operations on the Coromandel Coast.* London: T. Bensley, 1789.

Murthy, M. Chidananda. *Moola Dakhalega Lalli Hudhugiddha Tippu.* Bangalore: Bharatha Vikasa Parishattu, 2013.

Muthanna, I. M. *Tipu Sultan X'Rayed.* Mysore: N.p., 1980.

Nandakumar, K.N., ed. *Bharathakke Tippu Koduge Yenu?* Gadag: Ladai Prakashana, 2020.

Narasimhachar R., ed. *Archaeological Survey of Mysore: Annual Report 1912.* Vol. 4. Dharwar: Karnatak University, 1977.

Narrative Sketches of the Conquest of the Mysore Effected by the British Troops and their Allies, in the Capture of Seringapatam and the Death of Tippoo Sultaun, 2nd ed. London: Printed by W. Justins, 1800.

Oakes, Captain Henry. *An Authentic Narrative of the Treatment of the English who were taken Prisoners on the Reduction of Bednore.* London: Clarsley, 1785.

Orme, Robert. *A History of the Military Transactions of the British Nation in Indostan. Vols. 1–2.* London: F. Wingrave, M. DCCC. III, n. d.

Owen, S.J. *A Selection from the Indian Despatches, Memoranda of the Duke of Wellington.* London: Henry Frowde, 1880.

Panikkar, Kavalam Madhava. *Malabar and the Mysore: Being the History of Expansion of Mysore in South.* New Delhi: Life Span Publishers and Distributors, 2020.

Peixoto, Eloy Joze Correa. 'Memoirs of Hyder Ally from the year 1758 to 1770'. In *Annual Report of the Mysore Archaeological Department.* Bangalore: Government Press, 1938.

Ponnappa, Lt. Col. K.C. *A Study of the Origins of Coorgs.* Kodagu: Self Published, 1997.

———. *The Cambridge Shorter History of India,* Part 3: *British India.* Cambridge: University Press, 1935.

———. *Calendar of the Madras Despatches, 1744–1755.* Madras: Madras Government Press, 1920.

———, ed. *The Diary of Ananda Ranga Pillai.* Vol. 7. Madras: Government Press, 1919

———. *Dupleix and Clive: The Beginning of Empire.* London: Methuen & Co., 1920.

Porter, Robert Ker. *Narrative Sketches of the Conquest of Mysore, Effected by the British Troops and their Allies in the Capture of Seringapatam, and the Death of Tippoo Sultaun.* London: N.p. 1800.

Prabhu, Alan Machado. *Sarasvati's Children: A History of the Mangalorean Christains.* Bangalore: I.J.A. Publications, 1999.

Price, David. *Memoirs of the Early Life and Service of a Field Officer.* London: W.H. Allen & Co., 1839.

Punganuri, Ramachandra Rao. *Memoirs of Hyder and Tippoo: Rulers of Seringapatam.* Translated by Charles Philip Brown. Madras: Simkins & Co., 1940.

Qadir, Abdul Khwaja. *Waqai-i-Manazil-i-Rum: Tipu Sultan's Mission to Constantinople.* Edited by Mohibbul Hasan. New Delhi: Aakar Books, 1968.

Ray, Aniruddha, ed. *Tipu Sultan and His Age: A Collection of Seminar Papers.* Calcutta: The Asiatic Society, 2002.

Rao, C. Hayavadana. *History of Mysore.* Volumes 1–3. Bangalore: Government Press, 1943–1946.

———, ed. *Mysore Gazetteer.* Vol. 1. Bangalore: Government Press, 1927.

———, ed. *Mysore Gazetteer.* Vol. 2. Bangalore: Government Press, 1928.

———, ed. *Mysore Gazetteer.* Vol. 3. Bangalore: Government Press, 1929.

———, ed. *Mysore Gazetteer.* Vol. 4. Bangalore: Government Press, 1929.

Rao, Shama M. *Modern Mysore: From the Beginning to 1868.* Bangalore: Higginbothams, 1936.

Rennell, James. *Marches of the British Army in India During the Campaigns of 1790 & 1791.* London: W. Bulmer & Company, 1792.

Richter, Georg. *Manual of Coorg: A Gazetteer of the Natural Features of the Country and the Social and Political Condition of its Inhabitants.* Mangalore: C. Stolz, 1870.

Rice, Lewis, B. *Mysore: A Gazetteer Compiled for the Government.* Vol. 1. London: Archibald Constable & Co., 1897.

———. *Mysore and Coorg.* Vol. 3. Bangalore: Mysore Government Press, 1878.

———. *Mysore and Coorg from the Inscriptions.* London: Archibald Constable & Co. Ltd., 1909.

Roberts, P.E. *India under Wellesley.* London: G. Bell & Sons Ltd., 1929.

Robson, Francis. *The Life of Hyder Ally.* London: S. Hooper, 1786.

Ross, Charles, ed. *Correspondence of Charles, First Marquis Cornwallis.* Vol. 1. London: John Murray, 1859.

———. *Correspondence of Charles, First Marquis Cornwallis,* Vol. 2. London: John Murray, 1859.

———. *Correspondence of Charles, First Marquis Cornwallis,* Vol. 3. London: John Murray, 1859.

S. J. Moore, J, ed. *The History of the Diocese of Mangalore*. Mangalore: Codialbail Press, 1905.

Saldanha, S.N. *The Captivity of Canara Christians under Tippu in 1784*. N.p, 1993.

Salmond, James. *A Review of the Origin, Progress and Result, of the Late Decisive War in Mysore, in a letter from an officer in India*. London: W. Davies, 1800.

Sampath, Vikram. *Splendours of Royal Mysore: The Untold Story of the Wodeyars*. New Delhi: Rupa & Co., 2008.

———. *Bravehearts of Bharat: Vignettes from Indian History*. Gurugram: Penguin Random House India, 2022.

Samuel, E. *The Asiatic Annual Register, Vol. XII, for the year 1810–11*. London: T. Cadell & W. Davies, 1812.

Sardesai, Govind Sakharam, ed. *Poona Residency Correspondence*, Vol. 2. Bombay: Government Central Press, 1936.

———. *New History of the Marathas*. Vol. 2. Bombay: Phoenix Publications, 1948.

———. *New History of the Marathas*. Vol. 3. Bombay: Phoenix Publications, 1948.

———. *Madhavrao Peshvanchya Karnatakatil Swarya*. Mumbai: N.p., 1935.

———. *Selections from the Peshwa Daftar: Affairs of Northern India: Peshwa Madhav Rao I, 1761–1772*. Bombay: Government Press, 1933.

Sarkar, Jadunath, ed. *The Allies War with Tipu Sultan: 1790–93*, Vol. 3. Bombay: Government Press, n.d.

———, ed. *Poona Residency Correspondence*. Vol. 1. Bombay: Government Central Press, 1936.

———. *English Records of Maratha History: Mahadji Sindhia and North Indian Affairs, 1785–1794*. Bombay: Government Central Press, 1936.

Sastri, Petrie Papers, Indian Historical Records Commission Proceedings of Meetings, Vol. XVIII, 1942.

Sattar, Abdul. P. *Nawab Haidar Ali*. Mysore: Kavyalaya Publishers, 2005.

Scott, Jonathan. *An Historical and Political View of the Decan*. London: J. Debrette, 1791, 1798.

Scurry, James. *The Captivity, Sufferings and Escape of James Scurry*. London: Henry Fisher, 1824.

Sharma, H.D. *The Real Tipu: A Brief History of Tipu Sultan*. Varanasi: Rishi Publications, 1991.

Shastry, A.K. *The Records of The Sringeri Dharmasamsthana*. Sringeri: Sringeri Matha, 2009.

Sen, Surendra Nath. *A Portuguese Account of Haidar Ali*. In 'Early Career of Kanhoji Angria and Other Papers'. Calcutta: University of Calcutta, 1941.

———. *Studies in Indian History*, Calcutta: University of Calcutta, 1936.

Simha. Prathap. *Tipu Sultan: Swatantrya Veerana?* Hubli: Sahitya Prakashana, 2013.

Sinha, Narendra Krishna. *Haidar Ali*. Calcutta: A. Mukherjee & Co. Pvt. Ltd., 1941.

Silva, Severine. *History of Christianity in Canara*. Vol. 1. Karwar: Self-Published, 1957.

Srinivasacharya, M.A., and M.A. Narayanaingar. *The Mysore Pradhans*. Self-Published, n.d.

Stewart, Charles. *A Descriptive Catalogue of the Oriental Library of the Late Tippoo Sultan of Mysore*. Cambridge: University Press, 1809.

Strandberg, S. *The Tiger of Mysore or To Fight Against Odds*. Stockholm: Samuel Travel, 1995.

Supplementary Despatches and Memoranda, Vol. 1. The Duke of Wellington. London: John Murray, 1858.

Taylor, Philip Meadows. *Tippoo Sultaun: A Tale of the Mysore War*, Vol. 1–3. London: K. Paul, Trench and Trübner, 1880.

Teignmouth, Lord. *Memoir of the Life and Correspondence of John Lord Teignmouth*. Volumes 1–2. London: Hatchard & Son, M DCC XLIII.

Teltscher, Kate. *India Inscribed: European and British Writing on India, 1600–1800*. New Delhi: Oxford University Press, 1995.

Thornton, Lt Col L.H. *Light and Shade in Bygone India.* London: John Murray, 1927.

The Asiatic Annual Register, or the View of Hindustan, and of the Politics, Commerce and Literature of Asia, For the Year 1799. 2nd Edition. London: J. Debrett, 1801.

The Beauties of the Late Right Hon. Edmund Burke, Selected from the Writings of that Extraordinary Man. Vol. 1. London: J.W. Myers, 1798.

Tour, Maistre de La (M.D.L.T.). *The History of Hyder Shah, Alias Hyder Ali Khan Bahadur and his son Tippoo Sultaun.* London: W. Thacker & Co., 1855.

Torrens, W.M. *The Marquess Wellesley, Architect of Empire: An Historical Portrait.* London: Chatto & Windus, 1880.

V. Nagam Aiya, *The Travancore State Manual.* Vol. 1. Trivandrum: Travancore Government Press, 1906.

Venkatesh, Suman, trans. *The Correspondence of the French during the Reign of Hyder Ali & Tipu Sultan.* Bangalore: Karnataka State Archives, 1997.

Waite, Rosamond. *Life of the Duke of Wellington.* London: Rivingtons, n.d.

Wilkin, Captain W.H. *The Life of Sir David Baird.* London: George Allen & Co. Ltd., 1912.

Wilks, Mark. *Historical Sketches of the South of India in an attempt to trace the History of Mysore.* Vol. 1. New Delhi: Asian Education Services, 1989.

———. *Historical Sketches of the South of India in an attempt to trace the History of Mysore.* Vol. 2. New Delhi: Asian Education Services, 1989.

Williams, L.F. Rushbrook. *Great Men of India.* The Home Library Club, n.d.

Wylly, Colonel H.C. *A Life of Lieutenant General Sir Eyre Coote.* Oxford: Clarendon Press, 1922.

Journal Papers and Articles

Ahmed, Sameer. 'Fall of a Tyrant, or Heroic Last Stand? Tipu Sultan and the Moral Undercurrent in Historiography'. *Rethinking History*, 26.2 (2022): pp. 207–31.

Ali, Sheikh. 'Land Tenure in Mysore Under Tipu Sultan'. *Proceedings of the Indian History Congress*, 19 (1956): pp. 368–71.

———. 'Mauritius Records on the French and the Third Mysore War'. *Proceedings of the Indian History Congress*, 18 (1955): pp. 265–67.

———. 'Nizam-Tipu Relations During 1787–1789'. *Proceedings of the Indian History Congress*, 17 (1954): pp. 364–68.

———. 'Tipu Sultan and Sir John Shore'. *Proceedings of the Indian History Congress*, 20 (1957): pp. 243–46.

———. 'Why did the Nizam Desert the English in the First Mysore War?'. *Proceedings of the Indian History Congress*, 24 (1961): pp. 202–05.

Azavedo, Marinho. 'The Cause of the Captivity of the Canara Christians under Tipu Sultan in 1784'. *Proceedings of the Indian History Congress*, June 1935, 1.2 (June 1935): pp. 62–65.

Barua, Pradeep P. 'Maritime Trade, Seapower, and the Anglo-Mysore Wars, 1767–1799'. *The Historian*, 73.1 (2011): pp. 22–40.

———. 'Military Developments in India, 1750–1850'. *The Journal of Military History*, 58. 4 (1994): pp. 599–616.

Bennell, A.S. 'Wellesley's Settlement of Mysore, 1799'. *The Journal of the Royal Asiatic Society of Great Britain and Ireland*, 3/4 (October 1952): pp. 124–32.

Bhatia, L. M. 'Behind the Myth of Tipu Saheb'. *Indo-British Review [India]*. 13.1(1987): pp. 47–50.

Boutier. Jean. *Les 'lettres de créances' du corsaire Ripaud. Un 'club jacobin' à Srirangapatnam(Inde), mai-juin 1797. Le monde créole: peuplement, sociétés et condition humaine XVIIe-XXe siècles: mélanges offerts à Hubert Gerbeau / sous la direction de Jacques Weber; avec le concours de Jean Benoist et Sudel Fuma, Les Indes Savantes*, 2005.

Brittlebank, Kate. 'Accessing the Unseen Realm: The Historical and Textual Contexts of Tipu Sultan's Dream Register'. *Journal of the Royal Asiatic Society*, Third Series, 21.2 (April 2011): pp. 159–75.

———. 'Among the Unbelievers: "Non-Muslim" elements in Tipu Sultan's Dreams'. *Journal of South Asian Studies*, 33.1 (April 2010): pp. 75–86.

———. 'Tales of Treachery: Rumour as the Source of Claims that Tipu Sultan was Betrayed'. *Modern Asian Studies*, 37.1 (February 2003): pp. 195–211.

Chakraborty, Ayusman. 'That Disgrace in Human Form: Tipu Sultan & the Politics of Representation in Three 19th Century English Novels'. *Rupkatha Journal on Interdisciplinary Studies in Humanities*, 5.1 (2013): pp. 55–66.

De, Barun. 'Some Socio-Political Implications of the Cognomen "Tipu Sultan"'. *Proceedings of the Indian History Congress*, 52 (1991): pp. 700–07.

Ehrlich, Joshua. 'Plunder and Prestige: Tipu Sultan's Library and the Making of British India'. *Journal of South Asian Studies*, 43.3 (2020): pp. 478–92.

George, Alex. 'Sultan & the Saffron'. *Economic & Political Weekly*, 25.52 (29 December 1990): pp. 2833–35.

Gupta, Bunny, & Jaya Chaliha. 'Exiles in Calcutta: The Descendants of Tipu Sultan'. *India International Centre Quarterly Journal*, SPRING 18.1 (1991).

K.M. Lokesh. 'The Captivity of the Canara Christians under Tipu Sultan: A Study in the Perceptions of the Catholic of Canara'. *Proceedings of the Indian History Congress*, 69 (2008): pp. 475–85.

Khan, Iftikhar. A. 'The Regulations of Tipu Sultan for his State Trading Enterprises'. *Proceedings of the Indian History Congress*, 53 (1992): pp. 225–35.

Khan, Iqtidar Alam. 'Gunpowder and Empire: Indian Case'. *Social Scientist*, 33, No. 3-4 (Mar–Apr 2005): pp. 54–65.

Kumar, Raj. 'The Mysore Navy under Hyder Ali & Tipu Sultan'. *Proceedings of the Indian History Congress*, 52 (1991): pp. 578–80.

Margerison, Kenneth. 'Visions of Empire: Contesting British in India After Seven Years War'. *The English Historical Review*, 130. 544 (June 2005): pp. 583–612.

Martin, Meredith. 'Tipu Sultan's Ambassadors at Saint-Cloud: Indomania & Anglophobia in Pre-Revolutionary Paris'. *A Journal of Decorative Arts, Design History and Material Culture*, 21.1 (Spring–Summer 2014): pp. 37–68.

Marshall, Peter. 'British Expansion in India in the Eighteenth Century: A Historical Revision'. *History*, 60.198 (1975): pp. 28–43.

McPhee, Constance. 'Tipu Sultan of Mysore and British medievalism in the paintings of Mather Brown'. *Orientalism Transposed: The Impact of the Colonies on British Culture*. (1998).

Moienuddin, Mohammad. 'Distortions of Indian History with Reference to Tipu Sultan'. *Proceedings of the Indian History Congress*, 61.1 (2000–2001): pp. 660–66.

More, J.B.P. 'Tipu Sultan and the Christians'. *Islam and Christian–Muslim Relations*, 14.3 (July 2003): pp. 313–324.

Nair, Janaki. 'Tipu Sultan: The Power of the Past and the Possibility of a Historical Temper'. *Journal of South Asian Studies*, 43.4 (2020): pp.581–97.

———. 'Tipu Sultan, History, Painting & the Battle for "Perspective"'. *Studies in History*, 22.1 (2006): pp. 97–143.

Oturkar, R.V. 'Dynamic Contents of Chauth and Sardeshmukhi'. *Proceedings of the Indian History Congress*. Vol. 2. (1959).

Rai K., Mohankrishna. 'Portuguese Hegemony over Mangalore'. *Proceedings of the Indian History Congress*, 64 (2003): pp. 614–21.

Roy, Madhabi. 'Hukumnama for the Treasury Department of Tipu Sultan'. *Proceedings of the Indian History Congress*, 77 (2016): pp. 324–32.

Sastri, K.N.V. 'Comparison of Haider Ali and Tipu Sultan with the Urartus'. *Proceedings of the Indian History Congress*, 9 (1946): pp. 349–50.

Sil, Narasingha. 'Tipu Sultan in History: Revisionism Revised'. *SAGE Open* April–June 2013: I–II.

———. 'An Anatomy of Colonial Penetration & Resistance in The Eighteenth Century: The Odyssey of Siraj-ud-Daula & Tipu Sultan'. *Journal of Asian History*, 39.1 (2005): pp. 44–91.

Sims-Williams, Ursula. 'Collections Within Collections: An Analysis of Tipu Sultan's Library'. *Journal of the British Institute of Persian Studies*, Iran, 59. 2 (2021): pp 287–307.

———. 'The Official & Personal Seals of Tipu Sultan of Mysore'. *Journal of the Royal Asiatic Society*, Series 3, 32.4 (2022): pp. 792–807.

Sinha, N.K. 'Peshwa Madhav Rao I and the First Anglo–Mysore War'. *Proceedings of the Indian History Congress*, 3(1939): pp 1334–39.

Soboul Albert. K. Antonova. *The Struggle of Tipu Sultan Against British Colonial Power* (New Archive Documents), Academie des sciences de l'U.R.S.S (1962).

Sridharan, M.P. 'Tipu's Letters to French Officials'. *Proceedings of the Indian History Congress*, 45 (1984): pp. 503–08.

Stein, Burton. *Thomas Munro: The Origins of the Colonial State and His Vision of Empire.* New Delhi: Oxford University Press, 1989.

The Proceedings of the Indian History Congress, 7th Session, 29, 30 & 31 December 1944. Madras: Madras University, 1945.

The Quarterly Journal of The Mythic Society: 1939–40. Bangalore: Daly Memorial Hall.

Varma, Birendra. 'Tipu Sultan's Embassy to the Court of Zaman Shah'. *Proceedings of the Indian History Congress*, 33 (1971): pp. 478–82.

Washbrook, David. 'Merchants, Markets & Commerce in Early Modern South India'. *Journal of the Economic and Social History of the Orient*, 53. 1–2 (2010): pp. 266–89.

Willock, Sean. 'A Neutered Beast?: Representations of the Sons of Tipu Sultan—"The Tiger of Mysore"—as Hostages in the 1790s'. *Journal for Eighteenth Century Studies*, 36.1 (2013).

Yadav, Bhupendra. 'Giving the "Devil" his Due'. *Economic & Political Weekly*, 25.52 (29 December 1990), pp. 2835–37.

Yazdani, Kaveh. *Haidar Ali and Tipu Sultan: Mysore's Eighteenth-Century Rulers in Transition.* Itinerario Volume XXXVIII, Issue 2 (2014).

————. 'Foreign Relations and Semi-modernization during the Reigns of Haidar Ali & Tipu Sultan'. *British Journal of Middle Eastern Studies*, 45.3 (2018): pp. 394–409.

Dissertations

Datta, Susil Kumar. 'The Downfall of Tipu Sultan: 1793–99'. PhD diss., School of Oriental Studies, 1924.

Kareem, C.K. 'Kerala Under Haidair Ali and Tipu Sultan'. PhD diss., Aligarh Muslim University, 1968.

Soracoe, Michael. 'Tyrant! Tipu Sultan and the Reconception of British Imperial Identity'. PhD diss., University of Maryland, 2013.

Notes

Prologue

1 An abridged version of a part of this Prologue appeared as an Op-Ed article by the author in the *Mint Lounge*, dated 1 February 2014, titled 'Why we Love to Hate Tipu Sultan', https://www.livemint.com/Leisure/bO9Ma9Sb2g4aUvIUT29fCP/Why-we-love-to-hate-Tipu-Sultan.html

2 Arberry, A.J. *The Library of the India Office: A Historical Sketch* (London: Billing & Sons Ltd., 1938), pp. 30–31

3 https://www.ndtv.com/india-news/tipu-sultan-tableau-on-republic-day-sparks-war-on-twitter-549002

4 https://www.firstpost.com/explainers/the-rich-history-of-tipu-sultans-sword-sold-for-rs-140-crore-12647942.html

5 https://www.daijiworld.com/news/newsDisplay?newsID=368413

6 https://www.telegraphindia.com/india/tipu-jayanti-runs-into-protests-again/cid/1513675

7 https://www.telegraphindia.com/india/tipu-jayanti-runs-into-protests-again/cid/1513675

8 https://101reporters.com/article/politics/Tipu_Sultan_Jayanti_Tempers_flare_in_Kodagu_as_Karnataka_govts_intent_puts_Congress_BJP_on_collision_course

9 https://101reporters.com/article/politics/Tipu_Sultan_Jayanti_Tempers_flare_in_Kodagu_as_Karnataka_govts_intent_puts_Congress_BJP_on_collision_course

10 https://indianexpress.com/article/cities/bangalore/girish-karnad-offers-apology-over-remarks-on-kempegowda/

11 https://indianexpress.com/article/cities/bangalore/girish-karnad-offers-apology-over-remarks-on-kempegowda/

12 https://www.deccanherald.com/india/karnataka/uri-gowda-nanje-gowda-not-fictional-c-t-ravi-1201745.html

13 https://www.thehindu.com/news/national/karnataka/vokkaligara-sangha-takes-exception-to-uri-gowda-and-nanje-gowda-characters/article66638852.ece

14 Goel, Sita Ram (ed.) *Tipu Sultan: Villain or Hero?* New Delhi: Voice of India, 1993, p. 70.

15 Goel, Sita Ram (ed.) *Tipu Sultan: Villain or Hero?* New Delhi: Voice of India, 1993, p. 62.

16 Goel, Sita Ram (ed.) *Tipu Sultan: Villain or Hero?* New Delhi: Voice of India, 1993, pp. vii–viii.

1. The Ancestry of Haidar Ali Khan

1 Kirmani, Meer Hussain Ali *Nishan-i-Hydari,* translated from the Persian as *The History of Hydur Naik* by Colonel W. Miles (London: Oriental Translation Fund of Great Britain & Ireland, 1842), p. 1.

2 Wilks, Mark, *Historical Sketches of the South of India in an Attempt to Trace the History of Mysore,* Volume 1 New Delhi: Asian Education Services, 1989, pp. 261–62.

3 Bowring, Lewin Bentham, *Haidar Ali and Tipu Sultan and the Struggle with the Musalman Powers of the South* (Dehradun: EBD Publishing & Distributing Co., 1893), p. 12.

4 Hasan, Mohibbul, *History of Tipu Sultan* (Delhi: Aakar Books, 1951), p. 1, n. 3.

5 Kirmani, pp. 6–7.

6 Wilks, Vol. 1, p. 263.

7 Ibid., p. 268.

8 Foot: foot soldiers, horse: mounted soldiers.

9 Wilks (Vol. 1) states that a Naik who was formerly a provincial governor was by then degraded to signify commander of anything from twenty to 200 or more peons or irregular soldiers, armed with matchlocks, pikes, swords and targets, p. 262, n. 3.

10 This prediction of astrologers and Fatteh Mohammad's refusal to kill the infant is from Kirmani, pp. 10–11.

11 Hayavadana Rao, however, states that Fatteh Mohammad was killed in 1730, and it was a battle against the chief of Chitradurga, Hiriya Madakari Nayaka near Gummanahalli. Rao, C. Hayavadana, *History of Mysore (1399–1799 AD)*, Volume 2 (Bangalore: Government Press, 1946), p. 205.

12 Kirmani, p. 16.

13 Ibid.

14 Wilks, Vol. 1, p. 269.

15 Bowring, p. 18.

16 Wilks, Vol. 1, pp. 269–70.

17 Bowring, p. 18.

18 Kirmani, p. 21.

19 Ibid., p. 22.

2. Cataclysmic Convulsions

1 Wilks, Vol. 1, p. 50. n.

2 See Buchanan, Francis, *A Journey from Madras through the Countries of Mysore, Canara, and Malabar*, Vol. 1 (London: W. Bulmer & Co., 1807), pp. 60–63, for more details on the geography, location and appearance of Srirangapatna during his travels from 1800.

3 Wilks, Mark, Vol. 1, p. 111.

4 Wilks, Vol. 1, p. 118.

5 Hayavadana Rao, Vol. 2, p. 26.

6 Sardesai, Govind Sakharam, *New History of the Marathas*, Vol. 2 (Bombay: Phoenix Publications, 1948), p. 54.

7 Ibid., p. 41.

8 Oturkar, R.V., 'Dynamic Contents of Chauth and Sardeshmukhi', *Proceedings of the Indian History Congress*, Vol. 2 (Indian History Congress, 1959), p. 290.

9 Wilks, Vol. 1. p. 241

10 Ibid., p. 257.

11 Wilks, Vol. 1, p. 257.

12 Kirmani, Meer Hussain Ali Khan, *Nishan-i-Hydari*, translated from the Persian as *The History of Hydur Naik* by Colonel W. Miles (London: Oriental Translation Fund of Great Britain & Ireland, 1842), p. 37.

13 A unit of a particular currency.

14 Hayavadana Rao, Vol. 2, p. 89.

15 Kulkarni, Uday S., *The Extraordinary Epoch of Nanasaheb Peshwa* (Pune: Mula Mutha Publishers, 2020), p. 31.

16 Forrest, G., *The Siege of Madras in 1746 and the Action of La Bourdonnais*, Transactions of the Royal Historical Society, 1908, 2, 189–234, n. 1, doi:10.2307/3678377, p. 200.

17 Kulkarni, p. 153.

18 Wilks, Vol. 1, p. 299.

19 Ibid.

20 Wilks, Vol. 1, p. 299.

21 Ibid., p. 300.

22 Ibid., p. 301.

23 Dodwell, H. (ed.), *The Diary of Ananda Ranga Pillai*, Vol. VII (Madras: Government Press, 1919), p. xxii.

24 Bowring, Lewin Bentham, *Haidar Ali and Tipu Sultan and the Struggle with the Musalman Powers of the South* (Dehradun: EBD Publishing & Distributing Co., 1893), p. 25.

25 Wilks, Vol. 1, p. 309.

26 Kirmani, p. 36.

27 Dodwell, Henry, *Calendar of the Madras Despatches, 1744–1755* (Madras: Madras Government Press, 1920), p. ix.

28 Kulkarni, Uday S., *The Extraordinary Epoch of Nanasaheb Peshwa* (Pune: Mula Mutha Publishers, 2020), p. 200.

29 Dalton, Charles, *Memoir of Charles Dalton: Defender of Trichinopoly, 1752–1753* (London: W.H. Allen & Co., 1886), pp. 143–44.

30 Rao, C. Hayavadana, *History of Mysore (1399–1799 AD)*, Volume 2 (Bangalore: Government Press, 1946), p. 137.

31 Dalton, Charles, *Memoir of Charles Dalton: Defender of Trichinopoly, 1752–1753* (London: W.H. Allen & Co., 1886), p. 126.

32 Wilks, Vol 1. p. 358.

33 Rao, C. Hayavadana, Vol. 2, pp. 150–51.

34 Ibid., p. 154.

35 Sinha, Narendra Krishna, *Haidar Ali* (Calcutta: A. Mukherjee & Co. Pvt. Ltd, 1941), p. 14.

36 Dodwell, Henry, *Calendar of the Madras Despatches, 1744–1755* (Madras: Madras Government Press, 1920), p. 173.

37 Wilks, Vol. 1, pp. 377–78.

38 Rao, C. Hayavadana, Vol. 2, p. 178.

39 Rao, C. Hayavadana, Vol. 2, p. 207.

3. Before the Usurpation

1 Rao, C. Hayavadana, *History of Mysore (1399–1799 AD)*, Volume 2 (Bangalore: Government Press, 1946), p. 207.

2 Wilks, Mark, *Historical Sketches of the South of India in an Attempt to Trace the History of Mysore*, Volume 1 (New Delhi: Asian Education Services, 1989), p. 409.

3 Rao, Shama M., *Modern Mysore: From the Beginning to 1868* (Bangalore: Higginbothams, 1936), p. 26.

4 Hayavadana Rao, p. 267.

5 Hayavadana Rao, p. 268.

6 Kirmani, Meer Hussain Ali Khan, *Nishan-i-Hydari*, translated from the Persian as *The History of Hydur Naik* by Colonel W. Miles (London: Oriental Translation Fund of Great Britain & Ireland, 1842), pp. 26–27.

7 Kirmani, p. 28.

8 Kirmani, p. 29.

9 In recent times, there have been some outlandish claims that Tipu was named after a Shaivite saint in Nayakanahatti village near Chitradurga, Thippe Rudra Swamy, whose shrine Haidar and his wife were allegedly devoted to. None of these claims have any historical basis or documentary evidence, and are just part of folklore; the claims are circulated more in recent times for political means to provide an exalted 'secular' image to both Haidar and his son, and to ingratiate caste groups

that revered this saint. https://www.notesonindianhistory. com/2022/07/how-tipu-sultan-got-his-name.html

10 https://toshkhana.wordpress.com/2020/12/21/a-re-examination-of-tipu-sultans-date-of-birth-as-per-the-date-specified-by-himself-and-presenting-an-online-mysorean-mauludi-calendar/

11 This date better matches the account of Wilks (Vol. 1), where he states that Tipu was nine years old when Khande Rao took the abandoned family captive in August 1760, p. 469.

12 Francis, W., *Madras District Gazetteer: Madura*, Vol. 1 (Madras: Government Press, 1906), p. 183.

13 Sinha, Narendra Krishna, *Haidar Ali* (Calcutta: A. Mukherjee & Co. Pvt. Ltd, 1941), p. 17.

14 Wilks, Vol. 1, pp. 390–91.

15 Wilks, Vol. 1, p. 393.

16 Ibid., p. 393.

17 Pannikkar, K.M., *Malabar and the Mysore*, p. 31.

18 Hayavadana Rao, Vol. 2, p. 194.

19 Wilks, Vol. 1, p. 396.

20 Sinha, Narendra Krishna, *Haidar Ali* (Calcutta: A. Mukherjee & Co. Pvt. Ltd., 1941), p. 20.

21 Peixoto, Eloy Joze Correa, 'Memoirs of Hyder Ally from the year 1758 to 1770' in *Annual Report of the Mysore Archaeological Department* (Bangalore: Government Press, 1938), p. 89.

22 Ibid.

23 Incident cited by Wilks (Vol. 1), p. 413.

24 Sinha, p. 21.

25 Hayavadana Rao, p. 211.

26 Sinha, p. 4.

27 Wilks, p. 409.

28 Sardesai, G.S., *Selections from the Peshwa Daftar*, Vol. 28, Letter No. 197.

29 SPD, Vol. 28, Letter No. 226.

30 Hayavadana Rao, p. 215.

31 Hayavadana Rao, p. 219.

32 Wilks, pp. 412–13.
33 Uday Kulkarni, p. 376.
34 Hayavadana Rao, p. 225.
35 Kirmani, p. 73.
36 Wilks, p. 417.
37 Sen, Surendra Nath *A Portuguese Account of Haidar Ali* in 'Early Career of Kanhoji Angria and Other Papers', Calcutta: University of Calcutta, 1941, p. 81.
38 Sen, p. 82.
39 Wilks, Vol. 1, p. 468.
40 Ibid., p. 469.
41 Wilks, Vol. 1, p. 471.
42 Ibid., p. 472.
43 Hayavadana Rao, p. 238
44 Sinha, p. 33.
45 Sen, *A Portuguese Account of Haidar Ali*, p. 83.
46 Sinha, p. 35; Kirmani, pp. 93–94.
47 Rao, Shama M., *Modern Mysore: From the Beginning to 1868* (Bangalore: Higginbothams, 1936), p. 42.
48 Robson, Francis, *The Life of Hyder Ally* (London: S. Hooper, 1786), p. 23.
49 Sinha, p. 28.

4. Haidar's Rule

1 Rao, C. Hayavadana. *History of Mysore (1399–1799 A.D.)*, Volume 2 (Bangalore: Government Press, 1946), pp. 290–91.
2 The entire episode cited by Hayavadana Rao, Vol. 2, p. 291.
3 Hayavadana Rao, Vol 2., pp. 291–92.
4 Ibid., pp. 292–93.
5 Wilks, Mark. *Historical Sketches of the South of India in an Attempt to Trace the History of Mysore*, Volume 1, New Delhi: Asian Education Services, 1989, p. 491.
6 Wilks, Vol. 1, p. 492.
7 MMDLT, p. 124, f.n.

8   Hayavadana Rao, Vol. 2, p. 387.

9   Wilks, Vol. 1, p. 493.

10 Kirmani, Meer Hussain Ali Khan. *Nishan-i-Hydari,* Translated from Persian as *The History of Hydur Naik* by Colonel W. Miles (London: Oriental Translation Fund of Great Britain & Ireland, 1842), p. 111.

11 Kirmani, p. 122.

12 Kirmani, p. 124.

13 Wilks, Vol. 1, p. 503.

14 Sinha, Narendra Krishna, *Haidar Ali* (Calcutta: A. Mukherjee & Co. Pvt. Ltd., 1941), p. 43.

15 Kirmani, pp. 126–27.

16 Sinha, p. 42.

17 Michaud, Joseph, *History of Mysore under Hyder Ali and Tippoo Sultan,* translated from French by V.K. Raman Menon (New Delhi: Asian Educational Services, 2003), p. 22.

18 J. Michaud, p. 22.

19 Rao, Shama M., *Modern Mysore: From the Beginning to 1868* (Bangalore: Higginbothams, 1936), p. 51.

20 Wilks, p. 508.

21 Tour, Maistre de La (MDLT.), *The History of Hyder Shah, Alias Hyder Ali Khan Bahadur and his Son Tippoo Sultaun* (London: W. Thacker & Co., 1855), p. 58.

22 Kirmani, p. 139.

23 MMDLT, p. 58.

24 Peixoto, Eloy Joze Correa, 'Memoirs of Hyder Ally from the year 1758 to 1770' in *Annual Report of the Mysore Archaeological Department.* (Bangalore: Government Press, 1938), p. 100. None of the other accounts of the history of Mysore have any mention of who this 'Uda Purssu' is or of this combat.

25 Hayavadana Rao, p. 472.

26 Wilks, Vol. 1, p. 512.

27 Sinha, p. 43.

28 Robson, Francis, *The Life of Hyder Ally* (London: S. Hooper, 1786), p. 31.

29 Francis Robson, p. 32.
30 Sinha, p. 45.
31 Peixoto, p. 101.
32 Peixoto, p. 101.
33 Hayavadana Rao, Vol 2, p. 554.
34 Wilks, Vol. 1, p. 525.
35 MDLT, p. 61.
36 Ibid.
37 MMDLT, p. 60.
38 Kulkarni, Uday, *The Mastery of Hindustan: Triumphs & Travails of Madhavrao Peshwa* (Pune: Mula Mutha Publishers, 2022), p. 130.
39 Sinha, p. 47.
40 Wilks, p. 519.
41 Sinha, pp. 48–49.
42 Desai, Walter Sadgun, *Bombay and the Marathas Upto 1774* (New Delhi: Munshiram Manoharlal, 1970), p. 184.
43 Ibid., p. 185.
44 Sinha, p. 52.
45 Wilks, p. 523.
46 Hayavadana Rao, Vol. 2, p. 547.
47 MDLT, p. 62
48 MDLT, p. 63
49 Ibid., p. 64.
50 Panikkar, Kavalam Madhava, *Malabar and the Mysore: Being the History of Expansion of Mysore in South* (New Delhi: Life Span Publishers and Distributors, 2020), p. 41.
51 Peixoto, p. 103.
52 Ibid.
53 Hayavadana Rao, Vol. 2, p. 575.
54 MDLT, p. 69.
55 K.M. Panikkar, pp. 43–44.
56 Wilks, Vol. 1, p. 533.
57 V. Nagam Aiya, *The Travancore State Manual*, Vol. 1 (Trivandrum: Travancore Government Press, 1906), p. 381.

58 MDLT, p. 73.
59 Hayavadana Rao, Vol. 2, p. 579.
60 MDLT, p. 79.
61 Piexoto, p. 104.
62 MDLT, p. 80.
63 MDLT, p. 80.
64 MDLT, p. 80.
65 Wilks, Vol. 1, p. 535.
66 Rao, C. Hayavadana, *History of Mysore (1766–1799 A.D.)* Volume 3 (Bangalore: Government Press, 1946), p. 12
67 Hayavadana Rao, Vol. 3, p. 13.
68 Hayavadana Rao, Vol. 3, pp. 16–17.
69 Wilks, Vol. 1, p. 550.
70 Sinha, p. 57.
71 Wilks, Vol. 1, p. 550.
72 Wilks, Vol. 1, p. 555.
73 Sinha, p. 58.
74 Michaud, p. 49.
75 Hayavadana Rao, Vol. 3, p. 520.
76 Hayavadana Rao, Vol. 2, p. 1054.
77 Kirmani, p. 478.
78 Rao, Ramachandra, *Memoirs of Hyder and Tippoo: Rulers of Seringapatam.* Translated from Marathi by Charles Philip Brown (Madras: Simkins & Co., 1940), p. 33.
79 Hasan, Mohibbul, *History of Tipu Sultan.* (Delhi: Aakar Books, 1951), pp. 7–8.
80 Kirmani, Meer Hussain Ali Khan, *Nishan-i-Hydari,* Translated from Persian as *The History of Hydur Naik* by Colonel W. Miles (London: Oriental Translation Fund of Great Britain & Ireland, 1842), p. 479.

5. The First Anglo–Mysore War

1   Peixoto, Eloy Joze Correa, 'Memoirs of Hyder Ally from the year 1758 to 1770' in *Annual Report of the Mysore Archaeological Department* (Bangalore: Government Press, 1938), p. 106.

2   Tour, Maistre de La (M.D.L.T.), *The History of Hyder Shah, Alias Hyder Ali Khan Bahadur and his son Tippoo Sultaun* (London: W. Thacker & Co., 1855), p. 134.

3   Kirmani, Meer Hussain Ali Khan, *Nishan-i-Hydari*, Translated from Persian as *The History of Hydur Naik* by Colonel W. Miles (London: Oriental Translation Fund of Great Britain & Ireland, 1842), p. 248.

4   MDLT, p. 140.

5   MDLT, pp. 153–54.

6   Wilks (Vol. 1) quotes Col Smith's letter to state the comparative strengths of the armies:
    Cavalry: 30,000 (Nizam) + 12,000 (Haidar) = 42,860; Infantry: 10,000 (Nizam) + 18,000 (Haidar) = 28,000; Guns: 60 (Nizam) + 49 (Haidar) = 109.
    The opposing side: Cavalry: 30 (European) + 1000 (Muhammad Ali) = 1030; Infantry: 800 (European) + 5000 (Native) = 5800 and 16 European Guns. A highly lopsided army balance, as is evident. Wilks, p. 569.

7   Robson, Francis, *The Life of Hyder Ally* (London: S. Hooper, 1786), p. 45.

8   Wilks, Vol. 1, p. 584.

9   Kirmani, p. 252.

10 Kirmani, pp. 253–54.

11 Wilks, Vol. 1, pp. 586–87.

12 Peixoto, p. 107.

13 Kirmani, p. 255.

14 MDLT, p. 202.

15 MDLT, p. 202.

16 MDLT, p. 206.

17 Hayavadana Rao, Vol. 3, pp. 59–60.

18 Kirmani, p. 256.

19 Wilks, Vol. 1, p. 592.

20 Kirmani, p. 260.

21 Wilks, Vol. 1, p. 600.

22 MDLT, pp. 228–29.

23 Francis Robson, p. 64.

24 MDLT, p. 235.

25 MDLT, p. 236.

26 Rao, Shama M., *Modern Mysore: From the Beginning to 1868* (Bangalore: Higginbothams, 1936), p. 68.

27 Sinha, pp. 85–86.

28 Hayavadana Rao, Vol. 3, p. 77.

29 Malleson, Colonel G.B., *The Decisive Battles of India: From 1746 to 1849 Inclusive* (London: Reeves and Turner, 1888), p. 220.

30 Hayavadana Rao, Vol. 3, p. 86.

31 Robson, pp. 73–74.

32 Ibid., p. 76.

33 Ibid., p. 78.

34 Shama Rao, p. 71.

35 Wilks, Vol. 1, p. 654.

36 MDLT, p. 199.

37 De La Tour states that this was a new ship, finely painted and gilt, and had its cannon of brass, but the British ensured that this was built in such a manner that it was totally unfit for any war use and only worthy as a parade in a harbour! Tour, Maistre de La (M.D.L.T.), *The History of Hyder Shah, Alias Hyder Ali Khan Bahadur and his son Tippoo Sultaun* (London: W. Thacker & Co., 1855), p. 244.

38 Du Pré to Orme, quoted in Hayavadana Rao, Vol. 3, pp. 146–47.

39 Peixoto, p. 111.

40 He was someone who opposed the treaty.

41 MDLT, p. 246.

42 Sinha, p. 94.

43 Wilks, Vol. 1, p. 669.

44 Ibid.

45 Sinha, p. 94.

46 Michaud, Joseph, *History of Mysore under Hyder Ali & Tippoo Sultan*, translated from French by V.K. Raman Menon (New Delhi: Asian Educational Services, 2003), p. 30.

47 Wilks, Vol. 1, p. 681.
48 Ibid., p. 682.

6. Period of Unrest

1   Sinha, Narendra Krishna, *Haidar Ali* (Calcutta: A. Mukherjee & Co. Pvt. Ltd., 1941), p. 96.
2   G. Narayana Rao, *Quarterly Journal of the Mythic Society*, Vol. 39, no. 2 (Bangalore, 1948), p. 176.
3   Peixoto, p. 113.
4   Quoted in Sinha, p. 100.
5   Hayavadana Rao, Vol. 3, p. 164.
6   Quoted in Hayavadana Rao, Vol. 3, p. 168–69.
7   Peixoto, p. 118.
8   Wilks, Vol. 1, p. 705.
9   Hayavadana Rao, Vol. 3, p. 175–76.
10 Wilks, Vol. 1, p. 695.
11 Ibid. Kirmani, however, makes no mention of this episode.
12 Hayavadana Rao, p. 190 footnote.
13 Wilks, Vol. 1, p. 698.
14 Kirmani, p. 198.
15 Wilks, Vol. 1, p. 699.
16 Kirkpatrick, William, *Select Letters of Tippoo Sultan* (Bombay: Asiatic Society, 1811), pp. 4–5.
17 Kirkpatrick, p. 4.
18 Kirkpatrick, p. 6.
19 Kirmani, p. 202.
20 Kirmani, p. 206.
21 Sinha, p. 111.
22 Kirmani, p. 208.
23 Kirmani, p. 227.
24 Buchanan, Francis, *A Journey From Madras Through the Countries of Mysore, Canara, and Malabar*, Vol. 2 (London: W. Bulmer & Co., 1807), pp. 69–72.
25 Buchanan, Vol. 2, p. 68.

26 Buchanan, Vol. 2, p. 91.
27 Buchanan, Vol. 2, p. 165.
28 Sinha, p. 113.
29 Wilks, Vol. 1, p. 714.
30 Wilks, Vol. 1, pp. 726–27.
31 Sinha, p. 117.
32 Wilks, Vol. 1, p. 712.

7. Towards a New Churn

1 Hayavadana Rao, Vol. 3, p. 230.
2 Wilks, p. 717.
3 Kirmani, p. 341.
4 Hayavadana Rao, Vol. 3, p. 258.
5 Hayavadana Rao, Vol. 3, p. 251.
6 Kirmani, p. 349.
7 *Quarterly Journal of the Mythic Society*, Vol. XXXI, 1939–40, pp. 353–54.
8 Kirmani, p. 349.
9 Kirmani, p. 350.
10 Kirmani, p. 356.
11 Kirmani, pp. 359–60.
12 Hayavadana Rao, Vol. 3, p. 264.
13 Rao, Shama M., *Modern Mysore: From the Beginning to 1868* (Bangalore: Higginbothams, 1936), p. 97.
14 Shama Rao, p. 97.
15 Logan, William, *Malabar Manual*, Vol. 1 (New Delhi: Asian Education Services, 2010), p. 424.
16 Shama Rao, pp. 100–03.
17 Wilks, Vol. 1, p. 743.
18 Bowring, p. 75.
19 Shama Rao, p. 104.
20 Sinha, p. 165.
21 Hayavadana Rao, Vol. 3, p. 285.
22 Wilks, Vol. 1, p. 756.

23 Sen, Surendranath, *Studies in Indian History* (Calcutta: University of Calcutta, 1936), pp. 148–49.

24 Typically, *galivats* were smaller ships that normally did not exceed 70 tons and had two masts. They were basically rowboats with sails, with six or eight cannons that could fire pounder shells. *Ghurabs* were large frigates, the bigger naval ships that had two or three masts, ranging from 150 to 300 tons. *Palas, Manchwa* and *Shibars* were hybrid vessels, smaller than ghurabs but bigger than galivats.

25 Low, Charles Rathbone, *History of the Indian Navy (1613–1863)*, Volume 1 (New Delhi: Manas Publications, 1985), p. 153.

26 Munro, Innes, *A Narrative of the Military Operations on the Coromandel Coast* (London: T. Bensley, 1789), pp. 121–22.

27 See f.n. 22.

28 Sen, pp. 150–51.

29 Sen, p. 151.

30 Quoted in Sinha, p. 163.

31 Innes Munro, pp. 132.

32 Josyer, G.R., *History of Mysore and the Yadava Dynasty* (Mysore: Coronation Press, 1950), p. 56.

33 Sampath, Vikram, *Splendours of Royal Mysore: The Untold Story of the Wodeyars* (New Delhi: Rupa & Co., 2008), p. 197.

34 Rao seems to be a title symbolic of a higher status in society, though technically they were Mandyam Anandampillai Tirumala Iyengar and Mandyam Anandampillai Narayana Iyengar.

35 See Wilks, Vol. 1, p. 814 for more details on this.

36 Kirmani, p. 368.

8. The Second Anglo–Mysore War

1 Sinha, p. 180.

2 Shama Rao, p. 105.

3 Quoted in Sinha, p. 184.

4 Munro, Innes, *A Narrative of the Military Operations on the Coromandel Coast* (London: T. Bensley, 1789), pp. 133.

5 Kirmani, pp. 382–83.

6 Burke, Edmund, *The Beauties of the late Right Hon. Edmund Burke* (London: J.W. Myers, 1798), p. 58.

7 Munro, p. 135.

8 Munro, p. 147.

9 Ibid., p. 142.

10 Lindsay, John, *Lives of the Lindsays,* Volume IV (London: Wigan, 1840), p. 145.

11 Lindsay, p. 146.

12 Munro, p. 151.

13 Robson, Francis, *The Life of Hyder Ally* (London: S. Hooper, 1786), p. 116.

14 Wilks, Mark, *Historical Sketches of the South of India in an attempt to trace the History of Mysore,* Volume 2 New Delhi: Asian Education Services, 1989, p. 22.

15 Lindsay, p. 179.

16 Ibid., p. 178.

17 Bowring, Lewin Bentham, *Haidar Ali and Tipu Sultan and the Struggle with the Musalman Powers of the South* (Dehradun: EBD Publishing & Distributing Co., 1893), p. 92.

18 Wilks, Vol. 2, p. 22.

19 Munro, pp. 161–66.

20 Wilks, Vol. 2, p. 27.

21 Lindsay, p. 191.

22 Munro, p. 175.

23 Bowring, p. 92.

24 Sinha, pp. 190–91.

25 Sinha, p. 191.

26 Barua, Pradeep P., 'Maritime Trade, Seapower and the Anglo–Mysore Wars, 1767–1799', *The Historian,* Spring 2011, 73.1 (2011), p. 31.

27 Wilks, Vol. 2, p. 43.

28 Ibid., p. 55.

29 Robson, pp. 122–23.

30 Kirmani, pp. 418–20.

31 Munro, p. 231.

32 Robson, pp. 124–25.

33 Wilks, Vol. 2, p. 76.

34 Munro, p. 241.

35 Munro, p. 246.

36 Wylly, Colonel H.C., *A Life of Lieutenant General Sir Eyre Coote* (Oxford: Clarendon Press, 1922), p. 257.

37 Wylly, p. 254.

38 Wilks, Vol. 2., p. 94.

39 Wilks, Vol. 2, pp. 121–22.

40 Narrated in Hayavadana Rao, Vol. 3, pp. 367–68.

41 Sinha, p. 217.

42 Barua, p. 32.

43 'Letter Addressed to John Sullivan by Tirumal Row & Narayan Row' extracted in Srinivasacharya, M.A. & M.A. Narayanaingar, *The Mysore Pradhans* (Self-Published, n.d.), p. 22.

44 Translation of the original Persian and Marathi treaty, executed by Lord Macartney to the Pradhans, extracted in *The Mysore Pradhans*, p. 23.

45 Aitchison, C.U., *A Collection of Treaties, Engagements & Sanads Relating to India & Neighbouring Countries*, Vol. 9 (New Delhi: Mittal Publications, 1983), p. 224.

46 Aitchison, p. 223.

47 Aitchison, pp. 224–28.

48 'Translation from an original Persian and Marathi letter from Lord Macartney to Maharani Lakshmammanny', extracted in *The Mysore Pradhans*, p. 24.

49 Kirmani, p. 471.

50 Shama Rao, p. 117.

9. The Man and His Legacy

1 Hayavadana Rao, Vol. 3, p. 488.

2 Grant's Political Survey of the Northern Circars, 20 December 1784, PRO 30/11/57/b, National Archives of UK, Kew, London.

3   Shama Rao states that the revenue earlier was about 43 lakh
     Varahas and, under Haidar, this jumped to one crore, ten lakh
     Varahas, p. 121.
4   Sinha, p. 243.
5   Ibid.
6   For an extensive account on this, please see J.R. Henderson, *The
     Coins of Haidar Ali and Tipu Sultan* (Madras: Government Press,
     1921).
7   Hayavadana Rao, Vol. 3, p. 556.
8   Shama Rao, pp. 121–22.
9   Peixoto, p. 118.
10   Sinha, p. 274.
11   MDLT, p. 15.
12   Ibid.
13   MDLT, p. 18.
14   Kirmani, p. 491.
15   Wilks, Vol. 2, p. 756.
16   Kirmani, p. 486.
17   MDLT, p. 20.
18   Extracted from Kirmani as a supplement from the account of
     Mirza Ikbal's *Ahwali Hydur Naik*, p. 498.
19   Ibid.
20   Peixoto, p. 119.
21   MDLT, p. 26.
22   Wilks, Vol. 1, p. 695.
23   Wilks, Vol. 2, p. 756.
24   Extracted from Kirmani as a supplement from the account of
     Mirza Ikbal's *Ahwali Hydur Naik*, p. 497.
25   Ibid., pp. 497–98.
26   Extracted from Kirmani as a supplement from the account of
     Mirza Ikbal's *Ahwali Hydur Naik*, pp. 503–04.
27   Hayavadana Rao, Vol. 2, p. 275.
28   Wilks, Vol. 2, pp. 757–58.
29   Extracted from Kirmani as a supplement from the account of
     Mirza Ikbal's *Ahwali Hydur Naik*, p. 504.

30 Extracted from Kirmani as a supplement from the account of Mirza Ikbal's Ahwali Hydur Naik, p. 510–11.

31 Extracted from Kirmani as a supplement from the account of Mirza Ikbal's *Ahwali Hydur Naik*, p. 511–12.

32 Hayavadana Rao, Vol. 3, p. 407.

33 Extracted from Kirmani as a supplement from the account of Mirza Ikbal's *Ahwali Hydur Naik*, p. 500.

34 Ibid., pp. 499–500.

35 Peixoto, p. 114.

36 Ibid.

37 Hayavadana Rao, Vol. 3, p. 468.

38 Ibid.

39 Extracted from Kirmani as a supplement from the account of Mirza Ikbal's *Ahwali Hydur Naik*, p. 500.

40 Sampath, Vikram, *Splendours of Royal Mysore: The Untold Story of the Wodeyars* (New Delhi: Rupa & Co., 2008), p. 220.

41 Wilks, Vol. 2, pp. 758–59.

42 Shama Rao, p. 101.

43 Shama Rao, pp. 118–19.

44 Kirmani, p. 489.

45 Letter No. 81, Shastry, A.K., *The Records of The Sringeri Dharmasamsthana* (Sringeri: Sringeri Matha, 2009), p. 163.

46 Ibid.

47 Letter No. 82, A.K. Shastry, *The Records of The Sringeri Dharmasamsthana*, p. 163.

48 Letter No. 83, A.K. Shastry, *The Records of The Sringeri Dharmasamsthana*, pp. 164–65.

49 Letter No. 84, A.K. Shastry, *The Records of The Sringeri Dharmasamsthana*, p. 165.

50 Hayavadana Rao, Vol. 3, p. 412.

51 Ibid.

52 Kirmani, p. 483.

53 Kirmani, p. 484.

54 Ibid., p. 485.

55 Wilks, Vol. 1, p. 841.

56 Bowring, p. 113.

57 Sinha, pp. 271–72.
58 Hayavadana Rao, Vol. 3, pp. 475–76.

10. Passing on the Mantle

1 Wilks, Mark, *Historical Sketches of the South of India in an attempt to trace the History of Mysore,* Volume 2 (New Delhi: Asian Education Services, 1989), p. 172.

2 Bristow, James, *Narrative of the Sufferings of James Bristow* (London: J. Murray, 1793), p. 62.

3 Scurry, James, *The Captivity, Sufferings and Escape of James Scurry* (London: Henry Fisher, 1824), p. 302.

4 Rao, C. Hayavadana, *History of Mysore (1766–1799 A.D.),* Volume 3 (Bangalore: Government Press, 1946), p. 560.

5 Munro, Innes, *A Narrative of the Military Operations on the Coromandel Coast* (London: T. Bensley, 1789), p. 302.

6 Bristow, p. 62.

7 Hayavadana Rao, Vol. 3, p. 562.

8 Michaud, Joseph. *History of Mysore under Hyder Ali & Tippoo Sultan,* translated from French by V.K. Raman Menon (New Delhi: Asian Educational Services, 2003), pp. 49–50.

9 Kirmani, Meer Hussain Ali Khan. Translated from Persian as *The History of The Reign of Tipu Sultan* by Colonel W. Miles, Vol. 2 (New Delhi: Abhijeet Publications, 2017), p. 4. (hereinafter called as Kirmani Vol 2).

10 Michaud, pp. 47–48.

11 Quoted in Hayavadana Rao, Vol. 3, p. 568. In *Despatches* dated 29 January 1783; 29 December 1782.

12 Munro, p. 308.

13 Scurry, p. 300.

14 Scurry, p. 301.

15 Hayavadana Rao, Vol. 2, p. 573.

16 Anonymous officer in the East India Service, *Authentic Memoirs of Tippoo Sultaun* (Calcutta: Mirror Press, 1819), pp. 33–34.

17 Scurry, p. 98.

18 Wilks, Vol. 2, pp. 212–13.

19 Oakes, Captain Henry, *An Authentic Narrative of the Treatment of the English who were taken Prisoners on the Reduction of Bednore* (London: Clarsley, 1785), p. 84.

20 Scurry, pp. 306–07.

21 Prabhu, Alan Machado, *Sarasvati's Children: A History of the Mangalorean Christians* (Bangalore: I.J.A. Publications, 1999), p. 177.

22 Wilks, Vol. 2, pp. 219–20.

23 Anonymous Officer, *Memoir of the Life and the Character of the late Lieut. Colonel John Campbell* (Edinburgh: n.p., 1836), p. 51.

24 Hayavadana Rao, p. 586.

25 Irshad Hussain Baqai, 'Tipu Sultan and Brigadier-General Macleod' in *Resistance and Modernization under Haidar Ali & Tipu Sultan*, Irfan Habib ed. (New Delhi: Tulika Books, 2019), p. 56.

26 Hasan, Mohibbul, *History of Tipu Sultan* (Delhi: Aakar Books, 1951), p. 40.

27 *Memoir of John Campbell*, p. 57.

28 Ibid., p. 51

29 Prabhu, p. 178.

30 Munro, p. 350.

31 Hasan, p. 37.

32 Fullarton, William, *A View of the English Interests in India* (London: T. Cadell, 1787), p. 177.

33 *Memoirs of the Late War in Asia*, Vol. 2, p. 134.

34 Hayavadana Rao, Vol. 3, p. 628.

35 Wilks, Vol. 2, p. 241.

36 Wilks, Vol. 2, p. 250.

37 Hayavadana Rao, Vol. 3, p. 632.

38 Kirmani, Vol. 2, p. 9.

39 Wilks, Vol. 2, p. 251.

40 Narrated to the author in an interview with Dr M.A. Alwar, Professor in Maharaja Sanskrit College, Mysuru, and a descendant of the family that has passed on these oral narratives. A few other senior members of the families corroborated the story but refused permission to be named in the book or have

their identities released, making one wonder what the fear was now, after more than two centuries of the episode. The episode has also been recorded by Natampally Narasimhan, Former President of Mandyam Sri Vaishnava Sabha, in an article 'The Massacre of Mandyams 1783' published in 2021.

41 Hayavadana Rao, Vol. 2, p. 635.
42 Hayavadana Rao, Vol. 2, p. 639.
43 *Memoir of John Campbell*, p. 59.
44 Munro, p. 348.
45 Hayavadana Rao, Vol. 3, p. 651.
46 Memoirs of the Late War, Vol. 2, pp. 142–43.
47 Hasan, pp. 71–73.
48 Dodwell, H.H., *The Cambridge Shorter History of India, Part III: British India* (Cambridge: University Press, 1935), p. 592.
49 Sampath, Vikram, *Splendours of Royal Mysore: The Untold Story of the Wodeyars,* (New Delhi: Rupa & Co., 2008), p. 230.
50 Dodwell, *The Cambridge Shorter History of India*, p. 592.
51 Sampath, p. 229.
52 Munro, pp. 370–73.
53 Scurry, p. 75.
54 Rao, Shama M., *Modern Mysore: From the Beginning to 1868* (Bangalore: Higginbothams, 1936), p. 133.
55 Scurry, p. 62.
56 Ibid., p. 63.
57 Bristow, p. 48
58 Bristow, pp. 39–42.
59 Lives of the Lindsays, Vol. 3, pp. 285–86.
60 *Memoirs of the Late War in Asia*, Vol. 2, p. 55.
61 Ibid., p. 56.
62 Ibid., p. 74.
63 Ibid., Vol. 2, p. 79.
64 Bristow, pp. 55–56.
65 Bristow, pp. 65.
66 Ibid., pp. 65–66.
67 Oakes, p. 89.

68 Ibid.

69 Bristow, pp. 72–73.

70 Dodwell, p. 592.

71 Shama Rao, p. 136.

72 Moore, S.J. (ed.), *The History of the Diocese of Mangalore* (Mangalore: Codialbail Press, 1905), p. 18.

73 Moraes, George M., 'Muslim Rulers and Their Christian Subjects' in *Resistance and Modernization under Haidar Ali & Tipu Sultan,* Irfan Habib ed., p. 132.

74 Buchanan, Francis, *A Journey From Madras Through the Countries of Mysore, Canara, and Malabar,* Vol 3 (London: W. Bulmer & Co., 1807), p. 24.

75 Prabhu, p. 167.

76 Stated in the Letter of the Archbishop of Goa to the Governor of Goa, dated 17 November 1771 in Pissurlencar, *Antigualhas,* Fasciculo I, No. 30, p. 196.

77 Prabhu, p. 172.

78 Saldanha, S.N., *The Captivity of the Canara Christians under Tipu Sultan,* (N.p., 1993), p. 18. Footnote b.

79 J.P.B. Moore, *Tipu Sultan and the Christians,* p. 316.

80 Scurry, pp. 99–100.

81 Moraes, p. 135.

82 Pissulencar, *Antigualhas,* No. 75, p. 302, No. 81, p. 314.

83 Silva, Severine, *History of Christianity in Canara,* Vol. 1 (Karwar: Self-Published, 1957), p. 120.

84 Prabhu, p. 183.

85 *History of the Mangalore Diocese,* p. 39.

86 *Tarikh-i-Khudadadi,* in Kirkpatrick, William, *Select Letters of Tippoo Sultan* (Bombay: Asiatic Society, 1811), pp. 58–59.

87 Prabhu, p. 186.

88 Ibid.

89 Ibid., p. 187.

90 Silva, Severine, *History of Christianity in Canara,* Vol. 1 (Karwar: Self-Published, 1957), p. 126.

91 https://web.archive.org/web/20120321053956/http://www.daijiworld.com/chan/exclusive_arch.asp?ex_id=189

92 *History of the Mangalore Diocese*, pp. 40–41.
93 Saldanha, p. 11.
94 *History of the Mangalore Diocese*, p. 41.
95 Silva, p. 128, f.n. 1.
96 Ibid., p. 133.
97 *History of the Mangalore Diocese*, p. 45.
98 Saldanha, p. 12.
99 *History of the Mangalore Diocese*, p. 44.
100 Hasan, p. 366.
101 Scurry, pp. 102–05.
102 Dubois, Abbe J.A., *Letters on the State of Christianity in India* (London: Longman, 1823), pp. 73–75.
103 A.L.P. D'Souza, *History of the Catholic Community of South Kanara* (Mangalore: Desco Publishers, 1983), p. 40, and Farias, Kranti K., *The Christian Impact on South Kanara* (Mumbai: Church History Association of India, 1999), p. 77.
104 Saldanha, p. 6.

11. Sarkar-e-Khudadad

1 Hayavadana Rao, Vol. 3, p. 562, f.n. 3.
2 *Tarikh-i-Khudadad*, p. 202, In Kirkpatrick, William, *Select Letters of Tippoo Sultan* (Bombay: Asiatic Society, 1811).
3 *Tarikh-i-Khudadad*, p. 203, in *Select Letters*, Kirkpatrick.
4 Ibid.
5 Richter, Georg. *Manual of Coorg: A Gazetteer of the Natural Features of the Country and the Social and Political Condition of its Inhabitants* (Mangalore: C. Stolz, 1870), p. 246.
6 Hayavadana Rao, Vol. 3, p. 678, f.n. 3.
7 *Tarikh-i-Khudadad*, in *Select Letters*, p. 207.
8 Hayavadana Rao, Vol. 3, p. 679.
9 Kirmani, Vol. 2, p. 47.
10 Letter CXVII, Tipu Sultan to Meer Zynul Abideen, Kirkpatrick, William, *Select Letters of Tippoo Sultan* (Bombay: Asiatic Society, 1811), p. 150.
11 Kirmani, Vol. 2, pp. 21–22.

12 Kirmani, Vol. 2, p. 49.

13 Ponnappa, Lt Col K.C., *A Study of the Origins of Coorgs* (Kodagu: Self Published, 1997), p. 20.

14 Moegling, Hermann F., *Coorg Memoirs: An Account of Coorg and of the Coorg Mission* (Bangalore: Wesleyan Mission Press, 1855), p. 95.

15 Richter, p. 248.

16 https://swarajyamag.com/politics/kodavas-want-spotlight-on-genocide-inflicted-upon-them-by-tipu-sultan

17 Chidanandamurthy, M. *Moola, Dakhalegalalli Hudhugiddha Tippu* (Bangalore: Bharata Vikasa Parishat, 2013), p. 48.

18 https://swarajyamag.com/politics/kodavas-want-spotlight-on-genocide-inflicted-upon-them-by-tipu-sultan

19 Krishnayya, D.N., *Kodagina Itihasa* (Bangalore: Karnataka Sahitya Parishat, 2014), p. 192.

20 https://swarajyamag.com/politics/kodavas-want-spotlight-on-genocide-inflicted-upon-them-by-tipu-sultan

21 Krishnayya, p. 193.

22 Chidanandamurthy, p. 48.

23 Belliappa, C.P., *Nuggets from Coorg History* (New Delhi: Rupa & Co., 2008), pp. 46–47.

24 Belliappa, p. 47.

25 Letter CXCVI, Tipu to Ranmast Khan, *Select Letters*, pp. 228–29.

26 Letter CCII, Tipu to Meer Muinudeen, *Select Letters*, p. 236.

27 Kirmani, Vol. 2, p. 56.

28 Hayavadana Rao, Vol. 3, p. 683.

29 Richter, p. 248.

30 Wilks, Vol. 2, p. 283.

31 Ibid., p. 294.

32 Rice, Lewis, *Mysore and Coorg*, Volume III (Bangalore: Mysore Government Press, 1878), pp. 101–02, 132.

33 Hasan, p. 79, f.n. 4.

34 Mehendale, Gajanan Bhaskar, *Tipu As He Really Was* (Pune: Swatantraveer Savarkar Adhyasan Kendra, 2018), p. 36.

35 See Mehendale, pp. 36–38.

36 Wilks, Vol. 2, p. 294.

37 Wilks, Vol. 2, p. 295.

38 Grant Duff, James, *History of the Mahrattas*, Vol 2 (Calcutta: R. Cambray & Co., 1912), p. 468.

39 Duff, Vol. 2, p. 469.

40 Sardesai, Govind Sakharam, *New History of the Marathas*, Vol. 3 (Bombay: Phoenix Publications, 1948), p. 176.

41 Khare, Vasudev Waman, *Aitihasik Lekh Sangrah* (Marathi), Vol. 8 (Pune: Aryabhushan, 1915), p. 3840.

42 Hayavadana Rao, Vol. 3, p. 686.

43 Khare, Vol. 8, p. 3840.

44 Duff, Vol. 2, p. 473.

45 Khare, Vasudev Waman, *Aitihasik Lekh Sangrah (Marathi)*, Vol. 7 (Pune: Aryabhushan, 1912), #2668, p. 3691.

46 Grant Duff, James, *History of the Mahrattas*, Vol. 3 (Calcutta: R. Cambray & Co., 1918), p. 3.

47 Letter III, Tipu to Mahomed Ghyas, in Kirkpatrick, *Select Letters*, pp. 7–8.

48 Hayavadana Rao, Vol. 3, pp. 689–90.

49 Letter LXXIV, from Tipu to Kumr-ud-din, in Kirkpatrick, *Select Letters*, p. 102.

50 Kirkpatrick, *Select Letters*, p. 117.

51 Letter LXIX from Tipu to Kumr-ud-din, in Kirkpatrick, *Select Letters*, pp. 89–90.

52 Letter LXXXV from Tipu to Burhan-ud-din, in Kirkpatrick, *Select Letters*, p. 114.

53 Letter XCII from Tipu to Burhan-ud-din, in Kirkpatrick, *Select Letters*, p. 123.

54 Letter XCIII from Tipu to Kumr-ud-din, in Kirkpatrick, *Select Letters*, p. 124.

55 Duff, Vol. 3, p. 5.

56 Ibid.

57 Letter CCXVII from Tipu to Burhan-ud-din, in Kirkpatrick, *Select Letters*, p. 252.

58 Wilks, Vol. 2, pp. 288–90.

59 Sardesai, Vol. 3, p. 173.
60 Duff, Vol. 3, p. 19.
61 Hasan, p. 93.
62 Wilks, Vol. 2, p. 294, f.n. 1.
63 Letter XCI, Tipu to Mahommed Ghyas and Noor Mahommed Khan, in Kirkpatrick, *Select Letters*, p. 121.
64 Letter CIII, Tipu to Mahommed Ghyas and Noor Mahommed Khan, in Kirkpatrick, *Select Letters*, p. 136.
65 Letter CLXV, Tipu to Mahommed Ghyas and Noor Mahommed Khan, in Kirkpatrick, *Select Letters*, p. 193.
66 Letter CLXVII, Tipu to Mahommed Ghyas and Noor Mahommed Khan, in Kirkpatrick, *Select Letters*, p. 195.
67 Letter CCXX Tipu to Burhan-ud-din, in Kirkpatrick, *Select Letters*, pp. 253–54.
68 Chapter IX of the Quran.
69 Chapter LXI of the Quran.
70 Chapter II of the Quran.
71 Kirkpatrick, *Select Letters*, pp. 293–95.
72 *Tarikh-i-Khudadad*, in Kirkpatrick, *Select Letters*, pp. 330–31.
73 Duff, Vol. 3, pp. 13–14.
74 Sardesai, Vol. 3, p. 179.
75 Sardesai, Vol. 3, p. 179.
76 Kirmani, Vol. 2, pp. 82–83.
77 Wilks, Vol. 2, p. 304.
78 Ibid.
79 Ibid., p. 305.
80 Kirmani, Vol. 2, p. 89.
81 Ibid.
82 Ibid., p. 90.
83 Sardesai, Govind Sakharam (ed.), *Poona Residency Correspondence*, Vol. 2 (Bombay: Government Central Press, 1936), p. 80.
84 Sardesai, *Poona Residency Correspondence*, Vol. 2, pp. 80–81.
85 Ibid., p. 81.
86 Sardesai, Govind Sakharam, *New History of the Marathas*, Vol. 3, pp. 179–80.
87 Sardesai, *Poona Residency Correspondence*, Vol. 2, p. 93.

88   Wilks, Vol. 2, p. 306.

89   Ibid.

90   Hayavadana Rao, Vol. 3, p. 715.

91   *Tarikh-i-Khudadad*, in Kirkpatrick, *Select Letters*, p. 482.

92   Letter from Yvon to Malet, dated 14 March 1787, in Sardesai, *Poona Residency Correspondence*, Vol. 2, p. 104.

93   Extract of Charles Mallet journal, in Kirkpatrick, *Select Letters*, p. 490.

94   Brittlebank, Kate, *Tiger: The Life of Tipu Sultan* (New Delhi: Juggernaut, 2019), p. 49.

95   Letter LXXI, Tipu to the Badshah, in Kirkpatrick, *Select Letters*, p. 91.

96   Kirmani, Vol. 2, p. 97.

97   Brittlebank, p. 50.

98   Kirmani, Vol. 2, p. 94.

99   Kirmani, Vol. 2, p. 95.

100 Wilks, Vol. 2, p. 312.

101 Josyer, G.R., *History of Mysore and the Yadava Dynasty* (Mysore: Coronation Press, 1950), p. 67.

102 Hasan, p. 129.

103 Ibid.

104 'Statement of Instructions (*Hukumnama)* for Negotiations with the Khundkar of Rum', Iqbal Hussain, 'The Diplomatic Vision of Tipu Sultan' in *State & Diplomacy under Tipu Sultan,* Irfan Habib (ed.), pp. 40–42.

105 Iqbal Husain, 'The Diplomatic Vision of Tipu Sultan' in *State & Diplomacy under Tipu Sultan,* Irfan Habib (ed.) (New Delhi: Tulika Books, 2014), P. 20, 28.

106 Qadir, Abdul Khwaja, *Waqai-i-Manazil-i-Rum: Tipu Sultan's Mission to Constantinople,* edited by Mohibbul Hasan (New Delhi: Aakar Books, 1968), p. 14.

107 *Hukumnamahs* addressed to Sayyid Ghulam Ali Khan, Sayyid Nurullah Khan, Lutf Ali Khan and Jafar Khan, Iqbal Husain, 'The Diplomatic Vision of Tipu Sultan' in *State and Diplomacy under Tipu Sultan,* p. 29.

108   Iqbal Husain, p. 33.

109   Ibid., p. 42.

110   Ibid., p. 36.

111   Ibid., p. 53.

112   Ibid., p. 36.

113   *Select Letters*, p. 266.

114   Letter CCXXXIII, Tipu to Ghulam Ali Khan, Lutf Ali Khan and Shah Noorullah Khan, *Select Letters*, pp. 265–66.

115   Wilks, Vol. 2, pp. 363–64.

116   Hayavadana Rao, Vol. 3, p. 911.

117   Ibid.

118   Letter CCCC, Tipu to Ghulam Ali Khan & Co., in Kirkpatrick, *Select Letters*, pp. 448–49.

119   Qadir, *Waqai*, xii.

120   Hayavadana Rao, Vol. 3, p. 913.

121   Kirmani, Vol. 2, p. 98.

122   Hasan, *History of Tipu Sultan*, p. 114.

123   Meredith Martin, 'Tipu Sultan's Ambassadors at Saint-Cloud: Indomania and Anglophobia in Pre-Revolutionary Paris', *West 86th: A Journal of Decorative Arts, Design History, and Material Culture*, Vol. 21, No. 1 (Spring–Summer 2014), p. 47.

124   Hukumnamah for negotiations with the King of France, Iqbal Husain, in Irfan Habib (ed.) *State & Diplomacy under Tipu Sultan*, p. 48.

125   Iqbal Husain, pp. 48–49.

126   Meredith, p. 43.

127   Venkatesh, Suman, *The Correspondence of the French during the Reign of Hyder Ali & Tipu Sultan (Translation from French to English)* (Bangalore: Karnataka State Archives, 1997), pp. 96–97.

128   Hasan, p. 122.

129   Wilks, Vol. 2, p. 362.

130   Michaud, pp. 84–87.

131   Ibid., p. 87.

12. Southern Terror

1 Wilks, Vol. 2, p. 322.
2 Letter CCCCXXXI, Tipu to Meer Ibraheem, in Kirkpatrick, *Select Letters*, p. 471.
3 Letter CCLXXIV, Tipu to Urshud Baig Khan, in Kirkpatrick, *Select Letters*, p. 310.
4 Letter CCXCIII, Tipu to Abdul Kureem, in Kirkpatrick, *Select Letters*, pp. 315–16.
5 Letter CCCCXVIII, Tipu to Urshud Baig Khan, Foujdar of Calicut, in Kirkpatrick, *Select Letters*, p. 463.
6 Letter CCCCXIX, Tipu to the Dewans of Calicut, in Kirkpatrick, *Select Letters*, p. 464.
7 Kirkpatrick, *Select Letters*, p. 464.
8 Wilks, Vol. 2, pp. 313–14.
9 Ibid., p. 318.
10 Wilks, Vol. 2, p. 318.
11 Logan, William, *Malabar Manual*, Vol. 1 (New Delhi: Asian Educational Services, 2010), p. 452.
12 *Malabar Manual*, p. 452.
13 *Malabar Manual*, Vol. 1, p. 452.
14 One is not sure if this is the same man who had earlier collaborated with Arshad Beg to drive Kurukkal away. If he indeed was, perhaps that was done more due to the affable nature of Beg and the manner in which he had ingratiated himself with the chiefs of Malabar by his moderation.
15 Richter, p. 250.
16 Belliappa, p. 50.
17 Ibid.
18 Interview of author with C.P. Belliappa; author's article https://www.deccanherald.com/content/482335/miscellany-shrine-bells-anecdotes.html
19 Samuel, E., *The Asiatic Annual Register, Vol XII, for the year 1810–11* (London: T. Cadell & W. Davies, 1812), Letter No I pp. 385–86.
20 *The Asiatic Annual Register*, Vol. XII, Letter No. VII, p. 387.

21 *Malabar Manual*, Vol. 1, p. 453.

22 *The Asiatic Annual Register*, Vol. XII, Letter No. XIII, p. 389.

23 Ibid., Letter No. XIV, pp. 389–91.

24 Ibid.

25 Wilks, Vol. 2, pp. 323–24.

26 *The Asiatic Annual Register*, Vol. XII, Letter No. XV, p. 391.

27 *Malabar Manual*, p. 455.

28 Aiya, V. Nagam, *The Travancore State Manual*, Vol. 1 (Trivandrum: Travancore Government Press, 1906), p. 388.

29 K.M. Pannikkar, *Malabar and the Mysore*, p. 69.

30 Wilks, Vol. 2, pp. 331–32.

31 Ibid., p. 332.

32 *Malabar Manual*, Vol. 1, p. 456.

33 Sarkar, Jadunath (ed.), *The Allies War with Tipu Sultan: 1790–93*, Vol. 3 (Bombay: Government Press, n.d.), Letter #51. Yvon to Malet, dated 31 December 1789, p. 48.

34 *The Asiatic Annual Register*, Vol. XII, Letter No. XX, p. 393.

35 Kirmani, Vol. 2, p. 104.

36 Ibid.

37 Bartolomeo, Paolino da San, *A Voyage to the East Indies* translated from German by William Johnston (London: J. Davis, 1800), pp. 141–42.

38 Buchanan, Francis, *A Journey from Madras Through the Countries of Mysore, Canara, and Malabar*, Vol. 2 (London: W. Bulmer & Co., 1807), pp. 190–91.

39 Hayavadana Rao, Vol. 3, p. 724.

40 *The Asiatic Annual Register*, Vol. XII, p. 394.

41 *The Asiatic Annual Register*, Vol. XII, Letter XXVII, p. 396.

42 Panikkar, Kavalam Madhava, *Malabar and the Mysore: Being the History of expansion of Mysore in South* (New Delhi: Life Span Publishers and Distributors, 2020), p. 77.

43 Panikkar, p. 88.

44 Panikkar, p. 84.

45 *The Allies War with Tipu Sultan*, Letter #53, George Powney to Major Alexander Dow, p. 50.

46 Saldanha, S.N., *The Captivity of Canara Christians under Tippu in 1784* (N.p, 1993), p. 20.

47 Menon, P. Shungoonny, *A History of Travancore from the Earliest Times* (New Delhi: Gyan Publishing House, 2020), p. 228.

48 *Travancore Manual*, Vol. 1, p. 396.

49 Shungoonny Menon, p. 228.

50 Ibid., p. 229.

51 Hasan, pp. 164–65.

52 *Correspondence of Marquis Cornwallis*, Vol. 2, p. 11.

53 Kirmani, Vol. 2, pp. 105–07.

54 Gleig, George Robert, *The Life of Major–General Sir Thomas Munro* (London: Henry Colborn & Richard Bentley, 1830), p. 93.

55 *Travancore Manual*, Vol. 1, p. 397.

56 Ross, Charles (ed.), *Correspondence of Charles, First Marquis Cornwallis*, Vol. 1 (London: John Murray, 1859), pp. 479–80.

57 *Correspondence of Cornwallis*, Vol. 1, p. 464.

58 Cornwallis to Palmer, #93, dated 20 May 1790, *Poona Residency Correspondence* Volume 2, pp. 174–75.

59 Shungoonny Menon, p. 232.

60 Ibid., p. 233.

61 *Travancore Manual*, Vol. 1. p. 398.

13. The Third Anglo–Mysore War

1 See Letter #9 from Archibald Campbell to C.W. Malet, 22 July 1787, in Sircar, Jadunath, *The Allies' War with Tipu Sultan*, Vol. 3, pp. 7–8.

2 Letter #11, Cornwallis to Malet, dated 29 August 1787, *The Allies' War with Tipu Sultan*, p. 9.

3 #259. Palmer to Cornwallis, 21 February 1790, in Sarkar, Jadunath (ed.), *Poona Residency Correspondence*, Vol. 1 (Bombay: Government Central Press, 1936), pp. 363–64.

4 Ibid., p. 364.

5 Letter # 60, Cornwallis to Malet, 27 January 1790, *The Allies' War with Tipu Sultan*, pp. 54–56.

6 Sardesai, *New History of the Marathas,* Vol. 3, p. 184.

7 Duff, Vol. 3, p. 41.

8 Wilks, p. 335.

9 Hasan, p. 182.

10 Letter #109 Robert Taylor to Robert Abercromby, 17 May 1790, *The Allies' War with Tipu Sultan,* pp. 137–38.

11 Dirom, Major, *A Narrative of the Campaign in India, Which Terminated the War with Tippoo Sultaun, in 1792* (London: Bulmer & Co., 1794), p. 93.

12 Appendix F, Letter to Rani Lakshmammanni from Gen Medows, in Srinivasacharya, M.A. & M.A. Narayanaingar, *The Mysore Pradhans* (Self-Published, n.d.), p. 25.

13 Appendix G, *The Mysore Pradhans,* p. 26.

14 Letter of Medows to Cornwallis, in Ross, Charles (ed.), *Correspondence of Charles, First Marquis Cornwallis,* Vol. 2 (London: John Murray, 1859), p. 78.

15 Charles, pp. 20–21.

16 Letter #93, Raja of Travancore to Resident of Travancore, 20 April 1790, *The Allies' War with Tipu Sultan,* p. 113.

17 Hayavadana Rao, Vol. 3, p. 738.

18 Hasan, p. 183.

19 Letter #111, Tipu Sultan to William Medows, 22 May 1790, *The Allies' War with Tipu Sultan,* pp. 140–41

20 Ibid., p. 141.

21 Wilks, Vol. 2, pp. 382–83.

22 Ibid., p. 383.

23 Letter #151: Cornwallis to Palmer, 22 September 1790, *The Allies' War with Tipu Sultan,* pp. 205–06.

24 Hayavadana Rao, Vol. 3, p. 767.

25 Letter #159: Cornwallis to Malet, 11 October 1790, *The Allies' War,* p. 211–12.

26 Ibid.

27 Extract of a Letter from Lt. Col. Maxwell, 25 October 1790, *The Allies' War,* pp. 217–18.

28 Wilks, Vol. 2, p. 416.

29 Ibid.

30 Hayavadana Rao, Vol. 3, p. 780.

31 Letter #169: Cornwallis to Malet, 7 November 1790, *The Allies' War*, pp. 224–25.

32 Hasan, p. 195.

33 Hasan, p. 195.

34 Hasan, p. 199.

35 Thornton, Lt. Col. L.H., *Light and Shade in Bygone India* (London: John Murray, 1927), p. 158.

36 Wilks, Vol. 2, pp. 432–33.

37 Ibid., p. 434.

38 Kirmani, Vol. 2, p. 123.

39 Wilks, Vol. 2, pp. 435–36.

40 Thornton, *Light and Shade in Bygone India*, pp. 164–66.

41 Cornwallis to Kennaway, 2 April 1791, *Correspondences of Lord Cornwallis*, Vol. 2, p. 87.

42 Ibid., p. 88.

43 Letter #168, Malet to Cornwallis, 6 November 1790, *The Allies' War with Tipu Sultan*, p. 223.

44 Ibid., Malet's assessment.

45 Letter #241, Kennaway to Cornwallis, *The Allies' War*, pp. 336–37.

46 Duff, Vol. 3, p. 48.

47 Moore, Edward, *A Narrative of the Operations of Captain Little's Detachment* (London: J. Johnson, 1794), p. 30.

48 Moore, pp. 37–38.

49 Duff, Vol. 3, pp. 51–52.

50 Letter #297, Mallet to Cornwallis, *The Allies' War*, p. 393.

51 Moore, p. 52.

52 Sardesai, Govind Sakharam, *New History of the Marathas*, Vol. 3 (Bombay: Phoenix Publications, 1948), p. 189.

53 Khare, Vasudev Waman, *Aitihasik Lekh Sangrah (Marathi)*, Vol. 9 (Pune: Aryabhushan, 1915), p. 68.

54 Ibid.

55 https://www.britannica.com/topic/Pindari

56 Shastry, A.K., *The Records of The Sringeri Dharmasamsthana* (Sringeri: Sringeri Matha, 2009), p. 171.

57 Khare, p. 56.

58 Khare, pp. 56–57.

59 Ibid., p. 57.

60 Shastry, Letters # 86, 87, pp. 168–69.

61 Shastry, Letter #88, p. 171.

62 Ibid., p. 173.

63 Ibid., p. 174.

64 Shastry, Letter #91, p. 175.

65 Ibid., Letter #92, p. 176–177 & Letter #95, p. 181.

66 Ibid., p. 172.

67 Letter #304, Malet to Cornwallis, 29 April 1791, *The Allies' War*, pp. 402–04.

68 Wilks, Vol. 2, p. 448.

69 Kirmani, Vol. 2, p. 126.

70 Wilks, Vol. 2, p. 450.

71 Hayavadana Rao, Vol. 3, p. 892.

72 Kirmani, Vol. 2, p. 129.

73 Ibid.

74 Wilks, Vol. 2, p. 450.

75 Hayavadana Rao, Vol. 3, pp. 895–96.

76 Ibid., p. 891.

77 Dirom, p. 2.

78 Letter #311, Cornwallis to Tejwant, 8 May 1791, *The Allies' War*, pp. 412–13.

79 Wilks, Vol. 2, p. 456.

80 Thornton, p. 171.

81 Dirom, pp.7–8.

82 Ibid., p. 6.

83 Letter #319, Tipu to Patels of Coorg, *The Allies' War*, pp. 421–22.

84 Ibid., p. 422.

85 Richter, Georg, *Manual of Coorg: A Gazetteer of the Natural Features of the Country and the Social and Political Condition of Its Inhabitants* (Mangalore: C. Stolz, 1870), p. 256.

86   Dirom, p. 38.

87   Kausar, Kabir, + *Secret Correspondence of Tipu Sultan* (New Delhi: Light & Life Publishers, 1980), p. 11: Letter #1 from Tipu to Hari Pant Phadke dated 1 June 1791.

88   Letter #2, Tipu to Hari Pant, in *Secret Correspondence*, p. 11.

89   Letter #4, Hari Pant to Tipu, in *Secret Correspondence*, p. 12.

90   Letter #6, Tipu's instructions to Mehdi Ali Khan, March 1791, in *Secret Correspondence*, pp. 13–14.

91   Letter #292, Tipu to Muhammad Amin Arab, 15 April 1791, *The Allies' War*, p. 388.

92   Letter #309A, Muhammad Amin Arab to Tipu, 15 April 1791, *The Allies' War*, p. 411.

93   Letter #334, Kennaway to Cornwallis, 29 June 1791, *The Allies' War*, pp. 437–38.

94   Letter #324, Malet to Cornwallis, 30 May 1791, *The Allies' War*, pp. 424–25.

95   Letter #333, Tipu to Cornwallis, 24 June 1791, *The Allies' War*, p. 438.

96   Sardesai, *New History of the Marathas*, Vol. 3, p. 190.

97   Letter #350, Cornwallis to Nizam, 22 July 1791, *The Allies' War*, p. 467.

98   Shastry, Letter #96, p. 182.

99   Shastry, Letter #97, p. 183.

100 Ibid., Letter #98, p. 185.

101 Ibid., Letter #102, dated 22 November 1791, p. 190.

102 Ibid., Letter #104, dated 21 December 1791, p. 193.

103 Sardesai, *New History of the Marathas*, Vol. 3, p. 190.

14. Towards a Costly Peace

1   Dirom, Major, *A Narrative of the Campaign in India, which terminated the war with Tippoo Sultaun, in 1792* (London: Bulmer & Co., 1794), pp. 33–34.

2   Dirom, p. 36.

3   Kirmani, Vol. 2, p. 139.

4   Dirom, p. 50.

5   Dirom, p. 72.
6   Ross, Charles (ed.), *Correspondence of Charles, First Marquis Cornwallis*, Vol. 2 (London: John Murray, 1859), p. 132.
7   Wilks, Vol. 2, p. 516.
8   Kirmani, Vol. 2, p. 141.
9   Duff, Vol. 3, p. 60.
10 Hasan, p. 236.
11 Moore, pp. 141–42.
12 Duff, Vol. 3, p. 65.
13 Letter #408, Cornwallis to Robert Abercromby, 8 January 1792, *The Allies' War*, p. 551
14 Letter #411, Cornwallis to Parshuram Bhau, 9 January 1792, *The Allies' War*, pp. 553–54.
15 Letter #419, Cornwallis to Tipu Sultan, 16 January 1792, *The Allies' War*, p. 563.
16 Letter # 423, Tipu Sultan to Cornwallis, Received 24 January 1792, *The Allies' War*, p. 566.
17 Letter # 425, Cornwallis to Tipu Sultan, 21 January 1791, *The Allies' War*, p. 568.
18 Dirom, p. 116.
19 Mackenzie, Roderick, *A Sketch of the War with Tippoo Sultaun* (Calcutta: n.p., 1799), Vol. 2, pp. 72–73.
20 Dirom, p. 120.
21 Dirom, p. 142.
22 Ibid., p. 140.
23 Dirom, p. 155.
24 Ibid., p.157.
25 Mackenzie, Vol. 2, p. 202.
26 Wilks, Vol. 2, p. 540.
27 Dirom, p. 175.
28 Mackenzie, Vol. 2, pp. 215–16.
29 Dirom, pp. 188–89.
30 Dirom, p. 211.
31 Hayavadana Rao, Vol. 3, p. 868.
32 Dirom, p. 212.
33 Mackenzie, Vol. 2, p. 230.

34 Hayavadana Rao, Vol. 3, p. 878.

35 Dirom, pp. 225–26.

36 Ross, Charles (ed.), *Correspondence of Charles, First Marquis Cornwallis*, Vol. 3 (London: John Murray, 1859), p. 151.

37 Dirom, p. 232.

38 Dirom, p. 231.

39 Ibid., p. 234.

40 Hayavadana Rao, Vol. 3, p. 874.

41 Cornwallis to Charles Oakeley, *Correspondences of Cornwallis*, Vol. 2, p. 157.

42 Dirom, p. 236.

43 Mackenzie, Vol. 2, pp. 235–36.

44 Letter #449, Cornwallis to Malet, 28 March 1792, *The Allies' War*, p. 586.

45 Dirom, p. 246.

46 Dirom, p. 248.

47 Hayavadana Rao, Vol. 3, pp. 877–78.

48 Hayavadana Rao, Vol. 3, p. 878.

49 Shungoonny Menon, History of Travancore, pp. 239–40.

50 Ibid., p. 240.

51 Sardesai, Govind Sakharam, *New History of the Marathas*, Vol. 3 (Bombay: Phoenix Publications, 1948), p. 192.

52 Gleig, George Robert, *The Life of Major–General Sir Thomas Munro* (London: Henry Colborn & Richard Bentley, 1830), Vol. 1, p. 131.

53 Hasan, p. 266.

54 Mackenzie, Vol. 2, pp. 237–38.

55 Thornton, pp. 218–19.

56 Gleig, Vol. 1, pp. 131–32.

57 Ibid., pp. 123–24.

58 *Correspondences of Cornwallis*, Vol. 2, pp. 159–60.

15. Between Two Wars

1 Bowring, Lewin Bentham. *Haidar Ali and Tipu Sultan and the Struggle with the Musalman Powers of the South*. (Dehradun: EBD Publishing & Distributing Co., 1893), p. 224.

2   Hayavadana Rao, Vol. 3, p. 921.

3   Wilks, Vol. 2, p. 563.

4   Kirmani. Vol. 2, pp. 154–55.

5   Ibid., p. 154.

6   Kirmani, Vol. 2, p. 156.

7   Hayavadana Rao, Vol. 3, p. 925.

8   Wilks, Vol. 2, pp. 607–08.

9   Ibid., p. 608.

10 Wilks, Vol. 2, pp. 604–05.

11 Ibid., pp. 579–80.

12 Wilks, Vol. 2, p. 579.

13 Hayavadana Rao. Vol. 3, p. 927.

14 Kirmani, Vol. 2. p. 159.

15 Hasan, p. 271.

16 Kirmani, Vol. 2, p. 153.

17 Letter from Cornwallis to Tipu Sultan, 10 February 1793, *Correspondences of Cornwallis*, Vol. 2, p. 210.

18 Malcolm, John, *Sketch of the Political History of India*, Vol. 1 (London: James Moyes, 1811), pp. 139–40.

19 Hasan, p. 276.

20 Letter #494, Tipu to Ghulam Ali and Ali Raza, *The Allies' War*, p. 640.

21 Richter, Georg, *Manual of Coorg: A Gazetteer of the Natural Features of the Country and the Social and Political Condition of its Inhabitants* (Mangalore: C. Stolz, 1870), p. 260.

22 Wilks, Vol. 2, p. 630.

23 Sardesai, Govind Sakharam, *New History of the Marathas*, Vol. 3 (Bombay: Phoenix Publications, 1948), p. 306.

24 Hayavadana Rao, Vol. 3, p. 943.

25 Sardesai, Vol. 3, p. 304.

26 Ibid., p. 307.

27 Sardesai, Vol. 3, p. 323.

28 Hayavadana Rao, Vol. 3, p. 957.

29 Kirmani, Vol. 2, p. 161.

30 Kirmani, Vol. 2, p. 163.

31 Hayavadana Rao, Vol. 3, p. 947.

32 Dompart, M., *Official Documents Relative to the Negotiations Carried on by Tippoo Sultaun with the French Nation and Other Foreign States* (Calcutta: Honourable Company Press, 1799), Document #22, p. 62.

33 Ibid.

34 Ibid.

35 Ibid.

36 *Official Documents Relative to the Negotiations Carried on by Tippoo Sultaun with the French Nation and Other Foreign States,* Document #23, p. 63.

37 Ibid.

38 Ibid., Document #26, p. 66.

39 *Official Documents Relative to the Negotiations Carried on by Tippoo Sultaun with the French Nation and Other Foreign States,* Document #28, pp. 67–68.

40 Forest, Denys, *Tiger of Mysore: Life and Death of Tipu Sultan* (New Delhi: Allied Publishers Private Limited, 1970), pp. 244–45.

41 Hasan, p. 284.

42 J. Michaud, p. 107.

43 Soboul Albert and K. Antonova, *The Struggle of Tipu Sultan Against British Colonial Power* (New Archive Documents), Academie des sciences de l'U.R.S.S., 1962; une-brochure, 24 p. Documents No. 3, 4.

44 Kabir Kausar, Secret Correspondence of Tipu Sultan (New Delhi: Light and Life Publishers, 1980), No. 7, p. 59.

45 Ibid.

46 Ibid., No. 8, p. 61.

47 Kausar, Letter No. 1, p. 51.

48 Ibid., pp. 51–52.

49 Michaud, p. 108.

50 Forest, p. 250.

51 Salmond, James, *A Review of the Origin, Progress and Result, of the Late Decisive War in Mysore, in a Letter from an Officer in India* (London: W. Davies, 1800), Appendix (B).

52 Michaud, p. 108.

53 Salmond, Appendix (B).
54 Ibid.
55 Salmond, Appendix (B).
56 Hasan, p. 289.
57 Salmond, Appendix (B).
58 Salmond, Appendix (B).
59 Michaud, p. 109.
60 Salmond, Appendix (B).
61 Forest, p. 251.
62 Read: Boutier, Jean, *Les 'lettres de créances' du corsaire Ripaud. Un 'club jacobin' à Srirangapatnam (Inde), mai–juin 1797. Le monde créole: peuplement, sociétés et condition humaine XVIIe–XXe siècles: mélanges offerts à Hubert Gerbeau / sous la direction de Jacques Weber; avec le concours de Jean Benoist et Sudel Fuma, Les Indes Savantes*, 2005.
63 Boutier's French paper translated by Ms. Alo Pal.
64 Kausar, No. 8, p. 63.
65 Kausar, No. 8, p. 65.
66 Michaud, p. 111.
67 Kausar, No. 13, p. 73.
68 Ibid., p. 78.
69 Kausar, No. 18, pp. 103–04.
70 Forest, Appendix II, pp. 341–432.
71 Ibid., pp. 254.
72 Michaud, p. 113.
73 Ibid.
74 Forest, p. 256.

16. And Then Came Wellesley

1 Torrens, W.M., *The Marquess Wellesley: Architect of Empire, An Historical Portrait* (London: Chatto & Windus, 1880), p. 22.
2 Firth, Charles Harding, *The Marquis Wellesley* (Oxford: Thos. Shrimpton & Son, 1877), p. 1.
3 Torrens, p. 152.
4 Ibid.

5   Ibid.

6   Firth, p. 8.

7   Lindsay, John, *Lives of the Lindsays,* Vol. III (London: John Murray, 1849), p. 399.

8   Montgomery, Martin (ed.), *The Despatches, Minutes and Correspondence of the Marquess Wellesley,* Vol. 1 (London: John Murray, 1836 (hereinafter called *Wellesley's Despatches)*, No III, dated 28 February 1798, pp. 26–31.

9   *Wellesley's Despatches,* Volume 1, No XIII, dated 9 June 1798, p. 54.

10 *Wellesley's Despatches,* Volume 1, No XIV, dated 9 June 1798, pp. 59–61.

11 *Wellesley's Despatches,* Volume 1, No XVII, dated 20 June 1798, p. 64.

12 Ibid.

13 Torrens, p. 158.

14 *Wellesley's Despatches,* Volume 1, No XXII, dated 6 July 1798, pp 83–84.

15 *Ibid.,* p. 84.

16 Torrens, p. 158.

17 Hayavadana Rao, Vol. 3, p. 954.

18 Roberts, P.E., *India Under Wellesley* (London: G. Bell & Sons Ltd., 1929), p. 35.

19 Forest, p. 267.

20 *Wellesley's Despatches,* Vol. 1, No XXV, dated 8 July 1798, p. 100.

21 *Wellesley's Despatches,* Vol. 1, No XXII, dated 6 July 1798, p. 113.

22 *Wellesley's Despatches,* Vol. 1, No XXII, dated 6 July 1798, p. 113.

23 Sardesai, Govind Sakharam, *New History of the Marathas,* Vol. 3 (Bombay: Phoenix Publications, 1948), p. 352.

24 Kausar, Kabir, *Secret Correspondence of Tipu Sultan* (New Delhi: Light & Life Publishers, 1980), #20, p. 207.

25 Kausar, #17, Chappuis to Tipu, pp. 201–02.

26 Kausar, #18, Dubuc to Tipu, pp. 203–04.

27 Kausar, #23 (b), p. 213.

28 Kausar, #22, p. 209.

29 Kausar, #22, p. 211.

30 Forest, p. 269.

31 Kausar, #24, p. 216.

32 Ibid., #25, p. 218.

33 Ibid.

34 Hasan, pp. 300–01.

35 *Wellesley's Despatches*, Vol. 1, No XLVIII, pp. 159–208.

36 Letter LXXII, 2 September 1798, *Wellesley's Despatches*, Vol. 1, pp. 273–74.

37 Letter XCIII, 4 November 1798, *Wellesley's Despatches*, Vol. 1, p. 322.

38 Kausar, Letter #27, p. 222.

39 Letter from Ottoman Sultan Selim III to Tipu Sultan, dated 20 September 1798, *Wellesley's Despatches*, Vol. 1, p. 415.

40 Letter from Ottoman Sultan Selim III to Tipu Sultan, dated 20 September 1798, *Wellesley's Despatches*, Vol. 1, pp. 415–17.

41 Roberts, p. 49.

42 Letter XCVI. 8 November 1798, *Wellesley's Despatches*, Vol. 1, pp. 326–28.

43 Letter No. CIII, 20 November 1789, *Wellesley's Despatches*, Vol. 1, pp. 347–48.

44 Letter No. CVIII, 10 December 1789, *Wellesley's Despatches*, Vol. 1, p. 363.

45 Letter No. CXIV, 18 December 1789 and received on 25 December, *Wellesley's Despatches*, Vol. 1, p. 381.

46 Ibid., p. 382.

47 Ibid.

48 Ibid., p. 383.

49 Letter No. CXXI, 9 January 1799, *Wellesley's Despatches*, Vol. 1, pp. 394–400.

50 Ibid., p. 399.

51 Ibid., p. 400.

52 Letter No. CXXVI, 16 January 1799, *Wellesley's Despatches*, Vol. 1, pp. 413–15.

53 Ibid., p. 417.

54 Letter No. CXXVI, 16 January 1799, *Wellesley's Despatches*, Vol. 1, p. 418.

55 Letter No. CXXXVI, 13 February 1799, *Wellesley's Despatches,* Vol. 1, pp. 433–34.

56 Roberts, p. 50.

57 Wilks, Vol. 2, p. 685.

58 Wilks, Vol. 2, p. 679.

59 Roberts, p. 51.

60 Ibid. p. 51.

61 Kausar, Letter # 28, pp. 222–23.

62 No. CXXXVIII, Wellesley to Palmer, 19 February 1799, *Wellesley's Despatches*, Vol. 1, pp. 439–41.

63 Ibid., p. 441.

64 Sardesai, Vol. 3, p. 353.

65 No. CLXVI, Wellesley to Palmer, 3 April 1799, *Wellesley's Despatches,* Vol. 1, p. 513.

66 Wilks, Vol. 2, p. 605.

67 Ibid.

68 For more details, see Sampath, pp. 143–46.

69 Srinivasacharya, M.A., & M.A. Narayanaingar, *The Mysore Pradhans* (self-published, n.d.) Appendix J, pp. 29–30.

70 Sampath, p. 261.

71 Srinivasacharya and Narayanaingar, Appendix M, p. 35.

72 Ibid., pp. 34–36.

73 Ibid., Appendix N, p. 36.

17. The Last Anglo–Mysore War

1 *Supplementary Despatches and Memoranda*, The Duke of Wellington (ed.), Vol. 1 (London: John Murray, 1858), Arthur Wellesley to Lord Mornington, 16 February 1799, p. 193.

2 No. CXLI, *Wellesley's Despatches*, Vol. 1, 22 February 1799, p. 454.

3 No. CXLVII, Wellesley to Harris, 25 February 1799, *Wellesley's Despatches* Vol. 1, p. 473.

4 Hasan, pp. 307–08.

5 Kirmani, Vol. 2, p. 171.

6 Beatson, Lt Col Alexander, *A View of the Origin and the Conduct of the War with Tipu Sultan* (London: W. Bulmer & Co., 1800), p. 72.

7 Lushington, S.R., *Life and Services of Lord General Harris* (London: John. W. Parker, 1840), p. 269.

8 Beatson, p. 77.

9 Lushington, p. 271.

10 No. CLXXVII, Lord Mornington to the Court of Directors, 20 April 1799, *Wellesey's Despatches*, Vol. 1, p. 531.

11 No. CLIV, Stuart to Lord Mornington, 8 March 1799, *Wellesley's Despatches*, Vol. 1, pp. 483–87.

12 Lushington, p. 283.

13 Lushington, p. 278.

14 Kirmani, Vol. 2, p. 173.

15 Lushington, pp. 281–82.

16 Letter from Arthur Wellesley to Lord Mornington, 5 April 1799, Owen, *Wellesley's Despatches*, pp. 62–63.

17 Wilks, Vol. 2, p. 717.

18 Ibid.

19 Lushington, p. 288.

20 Lushington, Letter from Wellesley to Harris, 3 April 1799, p. 314.

21 No. CLXXVII, Lord Mornington to the Court of Directors, 20 April 1799, *Wellesley's Despatches*, Vol. 1, p. 534.

22 Lushington, p. 315.

23 No. CLXXII, Tippoo Sultaun to Gen. Harris, 9 April 1799, *Wellesley's Despatches*, Vol. 1, p. 522.

24 Ibid.

25 No. CLXXIX, Harris to Lord Mornington, 22 April 1799, *Wellesley's Despatches*, Vol. 1, p. 538.

26 See pp. 460–65 in *Wellesley's Despatches*, Vol. 1.

27 *Wellesley's Despatches*, Vol. 1, p. 465.

28 Forest, p. 286.

29 No. CLXXX, Lord Mornington to Harris, 23 April 1799, *Wellesley's Despatches*, Vol. 1, pp. 538–39.

30　Ibid., p. 539.

31　Wilks, Vol. 2, pp. 735–36.

32　Kirmani, Vol. 2, p. 176.

33　Ibid.

34　No. CLXXXVIII, Wellesley to Harris, 28 April 1799, *Wellesley's Despatches,* p. 561.

35　Kirmani, Vol. 2, p. 177.

36　Beatson, p. 162.

37　Ibid., p. 133.

38　Shama Rao, pp. 207–08.

39　Wilks. Vol. 2, pp. 738–39.

40　Ibid., p. 739.

41　Wilks, Vol. 2, p. 739.

42　Hayavadana Rao, Vol. 3, p. 991.

43　Beatson, p. 161.

44　Kirmani, Vol. 2, p. 178.

45　Appendix No. XXXIII, Beatson's account, p. ci.

46　Beatson, p. 162.

47　Lushington, pp. 332–33.

48　Ibid., p. 333.

49　Sampath, p. 278.

50　Beatson, p. 132.

51　Beatson, p. 133.

52　Lushington, pp. 335–36.

53　Wilks, Vol. 2, p. 746.

54　Beatson, pp. 165–66.

55　Ibid., 167.

56　Appendix XLII, Major Allan's account in Beatson, p. cxxvii.

57　Ibid., p. cxxix.

58　Appendix No. XXXIII, Major Allan's Account in Beatson, p. ci.

59　Beatson, p. 164.

60　Beatson, p. 164.

61　Kirmani, Vol. 2, p. 180.

62　Ibid.

63　Shama Rao, p. 211.

64　Hasan, p. 329.

65 Kirmani, Vol. 2, p. 150.

66 Wilks, Vol. 2, p. 747.

67 Beatson, p. 165.

68 Beatson, p. 137.

69 Appendix No. XXXIII, Beatson's account, p. civ.

70 Appendix XLII, Allan's account, Beatson, p. cxxxi.

71 Hasan, p. 318.

72 Shama Rao, p. 215.

73 Lushington, pp. 344–45.

74 Lushington, pp. 441–42.

75 Hasan, pp. 324–25.

76 Hasan, p. 325.

77 *Wellesley's Despatches*, Vol. 1, p. 443.

78 No. CXXXVII, Governor General to Secret Committee of Court of Directors, 13 February 1799, *Wellesley's Despatches*, Vol. 1, p. 437.

79 No. CXXXIX, Wellesley to Harris, 22 February 1799, *Wellesley's Despatches*, Vol. 1, p. 442.

80 Wellington, *Supplementary Despatches*, Vol. 1, p. 125–26.

81 Ibid., 193–94.

82 Venkatasubba Sastri, K.N., Petrie Papers, Indian Historical Records Commission Proceedings of Meetings, Vol, XVIII, 1942, p. 289.

83 Ibid.

84 Ibid., p. 290.

85 Forest, p. 296.

86 Lushington, p. 364.

18. Sunset over Srirangapatna

1 Forest, p. 293.

2 Dodwell, Henry, *The Nabobs of Madras* (New Delhi: Asian Educational Services, 1986*)*, p. 67.

3 Allan, Alexander, *An Account of the Campaign in Mysore (1799)*, Edited by Nares Chandra Sinha (Calcutta: The University Printing & Publishing Co. Ltd., n.d), p. 82.

4 Shama Rao, p. 216.
5 Ibid.
6 Hasan, p. 319.
7 Bayly, Col., *Diary of Col. Bayly: 1796–1830* (London: The Army & Navy Cooperative Society Ltd., 1896), p. 94.
8 *Diary of Col. Bayly*, p. 94.
9 Allan, p. 83.
10 Owen, S.J., *A Selection from the Indian Despatches, Memoranda of the Duke of Wellington* (London: Henry Frowde, 1880), Arthur Wellesley to Lord Mornington, 8 May 1799, p. 66.
11 Allan, p. 82.
12 Ibid., p. 83.
13 Allan, p. 84.
14 Shama Rao, p. 219.
15 Shama Rao, pp. 218–19.
16 Bayly, pp. 95–96
17 Allan, p. 92.
18 Ibid., p. 99.
19 Price, David., *Memoirs of the Early Life and Service of a Field Officer* (London: W.H. Allen & Co., 1839), p. 436.
20 Hayavadana Rao, Vol. 3, p. 1071.
21 Shama Rao, p. 252.
22 Ibid.
23 Forest, p. 299.
24 Lushington, p. 377.
25 Dodwell, p. 67.
26 Hasan, p. 320.
27 Forest, p. 300.
28 Price, p. 441.
29 Ibid., p. 442.
30 Hasan, p. 320.
31 Price, p. 436.
32 Shama Rao, p. 251.
33 Forest, p. 300.
34 Hayavadana Rao, Vol. 3, p. 1073.
35 Allan, p. 94.

36 Hayavadana Rao, Vol. 3, p. 1073.
37 Hayavadana Rao, Vol. 3, p. 1074.
38 Shama Rao, p. 254.
39 Price, p. 445.
40 Ibid., p. 446.
41 Beatson, p. 181.
42 Beatson, p. 194.
43 Ibid., p. 197.
44 Shama Rao, pp. 238–39.
45 Allan, p. 83.
46 *Wellesley's Despatches,* Vol. 1, p. 571.
47 Lushington, p. 350.
48 Hasan, p. 324.
49 Allan, p. 87.
50 Lushington, pp. 361–62.
51 Owen, p. 70.
52 Hayavadana Rao, Vol. 3, p. 1079.
53 Ibid.
54 Ibid.
55 Letter to Lord Mornington, 23 May 1799, Owen, *Despatches,* pp. 70–71.
56 Shama Rao, pp. 256–57.
57 Hayavadana Rao, Vol. 3, p. 1080.
58 Allan, p. 88.
59 Ibid., pp. 89–90.
60 Kirmani. Vol. 2, p. 183.
61 Kirmani, Vol. 2, p. 184.
62 Allan, p. 93.
63 Letter No. CXCVIII, Lord Mornington to Court of Directors, 11 May 1799, *Wellesley's Despatches,* p. 578.
64 Shama Rao, pp. 259–60.
65 Ibid., p. 261.
66 Beatson, p. 224.
67 Allan, p. 103.
68 Sardesai, Vol. 3, p. 354.
69 Shama Rao, p. 248.

70 Shama Rao, p. 249.
71 Beatson, p. 237.
72 Beatson, p. 238.
73 James Mill, *History of British India*, Vol. 6, p. 116.
74 Srinivasacharya, M.A., and Narayaniyengar, M.A., *The Mysore Pradhans*, p. 15.
75 Srinivasacharya and Narayaniyengar, p. 37.
76 Sampath, p. 373.
77 Appendix P., Srinivasacharya and Narayaniyengar, pp. 37–38.
78 Beatson, pp. 236–37.
79 Shama Rao, p. 267.
80 Forest, p. 305.
81 Wilks, Vol 2, pp. 753–54.

19. Affairs of State

1 Gleig, George Robert, *The Life of Major–General Sir Thomas Munro*, Vol. 1 (London: Henry Colborn & Richard Bentley, 1830), p. 84.
2 Moore, Edward, *A Narrative of the Operations of Captain Little's Detachment* (London: J. Johnson, 1794), p. 201.
3 For more, see Roy, Madhabi, 'Hukumnama for the Treasury Department of Tipu Sultan' in *Proceedings of the Indian History Congress*, 77 (2016), pp. 324–32.
4 Henderson, J.R., *The Coins of Haidar Ali and Tipu Sultan* (Madras: Government Press, 1921), p. 8.
5 Buchanan, Francis, *A Journey from Madras Through the Countries of Mysore, Canara, and Malabar*, Vol. 1 (London: W. Bulmer & Co., 1807), p. 121.
6 Buchanan, pp. 71–72.
7 Ibid., p. 82.
8 B. Sheik Ali, 'Developing Agriculture: Land Tenure under Tipu Sultan' in *Resistance and Modernization under Haidar Ali & Tipu Sultan*, Irfan Habib (ed.) (New Delhi: Tulika Books, 2019), p. 163.

9   Greville, Charles Francis, *British India Analyzed: The Provincial and Revenue Establishments of Tippoo Sultaun,* Part 1 (London: R. Faulder, 1795), p. 5.

10 Ibid., pp. 5–6.

11 Gleig, p. 204.

12 Greville, p. 14.

13 Hasan, Mohibbul, *History of Tipu Sultan* (Delhi: Aakar Books, 1951), p. 344.

14 Greville, p. 37.

15 Ibid., pp. 40–41.

16 Greville, p. 41.

17 Ibid., pp. 43–44.

18 Greville, p. 44.

19 Hasan, p. 345.

20 Letter CCCCXXV, Kirkpatrick, William, *Select Letters of Tippoo Sultan* (Bombay: Asiatic Society, 1811), p. 467.

21 See Letters CLIV, CLV, CLVI, CLIX, CLX, Kirkpatrick, *Select Letters* pp. 185–89.

22 Kirkpatrick, *Select Letters* pp. 418–19.

23 Appendix E, Kirkpatrick, *Select Letters* pp. xxxvi–xxxviii.

24 Buchanan, p. 222.

25 Buchanan, p. 221.

26 Ibid., p. 70.

27 Hasan, p. 348.

28 *The Asiatic Annual Register for the year 1799,* pp. 199–200.

29 *Islamic Culture,* Vol. XIV, April 1940, p. 146.

30 Kirmani, Meer Hussain Ali Khan, Translated from Persian as *The History of The Reign of Tipu Sultan* by Colonel W. Miles (New Delhi: Abhijeet Publications, 2017), pp. 21–22

31 Hasan, p. 354.

32 Alam Khan, Iqtidar, 'Gunpowder and Empire: Indian Case' in *Social Scientist,* 33 (3/4) (Mar–Apr 2005), p. 54.

33 Rao, C. Hayavadana, *History of Mysore (1399–1799 A.D.),* Vol. 2 (Bangalore: Government Press, 1946), p. 26.

34 Munro, Innes, *A Narrative of the Military Operations on the Coromandel Coast* (London: T. Bensley, 1789), p. 132.

35 Forest, Denys, *Tiger of Mysore: Life and Death of Tipu Sultan* (New Delhi: Allied Publishers Private Limited, 1970), p. 283.

36 Lecture titled, 'Rockets in Mysore and Britain, 1750-1850 A.D.' by Roddam Narasimha, on 2 April 1985 at the inauguration of the Centre for History and Philosophy of Science, Indian Institute of World Culture, Bangalore, pp. 9–10.

37 Narasimha, p. 10.

38 Bayly, Col. *Dairy of Col., Balyly: 1796-1830* (London: The Army & Navy Cooperative Society Ltd., 1896), pp. 82–83.

39 Narasimha, p. 12

40 Ibid.

41 Historian Nidhin George Olikara deduces this place to be today's Tadakanahalli village in Shivamogga district of Karnataka.

42 Moore, Edward, *A Narrative of the Operations of Captain Little's Detachment* (London: J. Johnson, 1794), p. 169.

43 https://bangaloremirror.indiatimes.com/bangalore/cover-story/over-100-missiles-of-tipu-sultan-found-in-a-shivamogga-well/articleshow/62575085.cms

44 For more details, please watch a fascinating lecture on this subject by Nidhin George Olikara: https://www.youtube.com/watch?v=9ZBhjlPp-mg or visit his blog article regarding this https://toshkhana.wordpress.com/2021/03/30/the-mysore-rocket/

45 Narasimha, pp. 19–21.

46 Price, David, *Memoirs of the Early Life and Service of a Field Officer* (London: W.H. Allen & Co., 1839), pp. 445–46.

47 Sims-Williams, Ursula, 'Collections Within Collections: An Analysis of Tipu Sultan's Library' in *Journal of the British Institute of Persian Studies*, Iran, 59. 2 (2021), p. 288.

48 Stewart, Charles, *A Descriptive Catalogue of the Oriental Library of the Late Tippoo Sultan of Mysore* (Cambridge: University Press, 1809), pp. v–vi.

49 Yazdani, Kaveh, *Haidar Ali and Tipu Sultan: Mysore's Eighteenth-Century Rulers in Transition*. Itinerario Volume XXXVIII, Issue 2, 2014, doi:10.1017/S0165115314000370, pp. 105–06.

50 Anonymous, *Islamic Culture*, Vol. XIV. Published under the Authority of H.E.H. the Nizam's Government, Hyderabad, 1940, p. 151.

51 Ibid., p. 152.

52 Tour, Maistre de La (M.D.L.T.). *The History of Hyder Shah, Alias Hyder Ali Khan Bahadur and his son Tippoo Sultaun* (London: W. Thacker & Co., 1855), p. 202.

53 Anonymous, *Narratives Sketches of the Conquest of the Mysore* (London, 1800), p. 98.

54 The men who hand over the people's petitions to the chief.

55 Bell, Andrew, *The Madras School, or, Elements of Tuition* (London: J. Murray, 1808), pp. 234–36.

56 Stewart, Ibid., p. 77.

57 Forest, p. 116.

58 Stewart, p. 157.

59 *Islamic Culture*, Vol. XIV, p. 147.

60 Stewart, p. 45.

61 Ibid.

62 *Islamic Culture*, Vol. XIV, p. 148.

63 Stewart, p. 45.

64 Quoted in Murthy, Dr M. Chidananda, *Moola DakhalegaLalli Hudhugiddha Tippu* (Bangalore: Bharatha Vikasa Parishattu, 2013), p. 9.

65 Beatson, p. 197.

66 Husain, Mahmud, *The Dreams of Tipu Sultan (Translated from the Original Persian)* (Karachi: Pakistan Historical Society Publications No. 7, n.d.), p. 87.

67 Ibid., p. 64.

68 Husain, p. 69.

69 Ibid., p. 70.

70 Ibid., p. 71.

71 Dream 31, Husain, p. 90.

72 Husain, p. 65.

73 For this analysis and insight into what dreams mean, I am deeply obliged to renowned psychiatrist in Bangalore, Dr Shyamala Vatsa.

74 Brittlebank, Kate, 'Accessing the Unseen Realm: The Historical and Textual Contexts of Tipu Sultan's Dream Register' in *Journal of the Royal Asiatic Society*, Third Series, 21.2 (April 2011), pp. 174–75.

75 Beatson, p. 161.

76 Beatson, p. 161.

77 Buchanan, p. 70.

78 Ibid. p. 73.

79 Buchanan, p. 74.

80 Forest, p. 211.

81 Ibid.

82 Hussain, Iqbal, 'The Diplomatic Vision of Tipu Sultan: Briefs for Embassies to Turkey and France', 1785–86 in Irfan Habib (ed.), *State & Diplomacy under Tipu Sultan* (New Delhi: Tulika Books, 2014), p. 35.

83 Wilks, Mark, *Historical Sketches of the South of India in an attempt to trace the History of Mysore*, Vol. 2 (New Delhi: Asian Education Services, 1989), pp. 760–65.

84 Bowring, Lewin Bentham, *Haidar Ali and Tipu Sultan and the Struggle with the Musalman Powers of the South* (Dehradun: EBD Publishing & Distributing Co., 1893), p. 222.

85 Bowring, Ibid., p. 226.

86 Ibid., pp. 226–27.

87 Yazdani, p. 111.

20. A Bloodied Legacy

1 Sacred stones for Hindus, especially Vaishnavas, who consider them a symbol of Lord Vishnu himself.

2 Husain, Mahmud, *The Dreams of Tipu Sultan (Translated from the Original Persian)* (Karachi: Pakistan Historical Society Publications No. 7, n.d.), pp. 92–93.

3 Kirkpatrick, William, *Select Letters of Tippoo Sultan* (Bombay: Asiatic Society, 1811), p. 293.

4   Rao, C. Hayavadana, *History of Mysore (1766–1799 A.D.),* Vol. 3 (Bangalore: Government Press, 1946), p. 1073.

5   Rice, B. Lewis, *Mysore: A Gazetteer Compiled for the Government,* Vol. 1 (London: Archibald Constable & Co., 1897), p. 409.

6   *Annual Report of the Mysore Archaeological Department for the Year 1935* (Bangalore: Government Press, 1936), p. 61.

7   https://www.timesnownews.com/india/karnataka-right-wing-group-demands-permission-to-hold-puja-in-jamia-masjid-calls-it-anjaneya-temple-article-91598714 and https://indianexpress.com/article/cities/bangalore/hindus-prayers-tipu-sultan-mosque-karantaka-srirangapatna-7919851/

8   Brittlebank, Kate, *Tiger: The Life of Tipu Sultan* (New Delhi: Juggernaut, 2019), p. 100.

9   Arulmigu Patteeswarar Swamy temple, also called Mel Chidambaram, at Coimbatore.

10   Buchanan, Francis, *A Journey from Madras Through the Countries of Mysore, Canara, and Malabar,* Vol. 2 (London: W. Bulmer & Co., 1807), p. 251.

11   Interview of Araiyar Sri Rama Sharmaji with the author.

12   Interview of Araiyar Sri Rama Sharmaji with the author.

13   Translated from original for the author by Persian scholar Nikhil Paranjape.

14   Narasimhachar R. (ed.), *Archaeological Survey of Mysore Annual Report 1912,* Vol. IV (Dharwar: Karnatak University, 1977), p. 105.

15   Ibid., pp. 105–06.

16   *Annual Report of the Mysore Archaeological Department for the Year 1918* (Bangalore: Government Press, 1919), p. 60.

17   *Annual Report of the Mysore Archaeological Department for the Year 1940* (Mysore: Government Branch Press, 1941), p. 26.

18   https://mysore.nic.in/en/tourist-place/srikanteshwaranandeswara-temple/

19   *The Proceedings of the Indian History Congress, Seventh Session* (Madras: Madras University, 29–31 December 1944), pp. 416–19.

20 Wilks, Mark, *Historical Sketches of the South of India in an Attempt to Trace the History of Mysore*, Vol. 1 (New Delhi: Asian Education Services, 1989), pp. 813–14, fn.

21 Gopal, M.H., *Tipu Sultan's Mysore: An Economic Study* (Bombay: Popular Prakashan, 1971), pp. 71–72.

22 Ibid., p. 68.

23 https://www.bbc.com/news/world-asia-india-27529905

24 https://toshkhana.wordpress.com/2012/03/25/tipu-sultan-and-the-ring-of-rama/

25 Appendix XLII, Allan's account in Beatson, Lt. Col. Alexander, *A View of the Origin and the Conduct of the War with Tipu Sultan* (London: W. Bulmer & Co., 1800), p. cxxxi.

26 https://www.bbc.com/news/world-asia-india-27529905

27 For more see https://www.newindianexpress.com/cities/bengaluru/2013/Apr/04/alluring-mural-paintings-of-seebi-464723.html

28 Rao, Shama M., *Modern Mysore: From the Beginning to 1868* (Bangalore: Higginbothams, 1936), pp. 268–69.

29 *Annual Report of the Mysore Archaeological Department for the Year 1938*, pp. 123–25.

30 See Chapter 10 for more details.

31 Karyappa, Addanda, *Tippu Matthu Kodavaru* (Kodagu: Rangabhumi Kodagu Prakashana, 2015), pp. 44–45.

32 Letter No. CCXXIV, Kirkpatrick, *Select Letters*, pp. 256–57.

33 Bartolomeo, Paolino da San, *A Voyage to the East Indies*, translated from German by William Johnston (London: J. Davis, 1800), pp. 141–42.

34 Menon, A. Sreedhara, *Kerala District Gazetteers: Kozhikode* (Trivandrum: Government Press, 1962), p. 162

35 Innes, C.A., and F.B. Evans (ed.), *Madras District Gazetteers: Malabar*, Vol. 1 (Madras: Government Press, 1951), p. 268.

36 Menon, *Kerala District Gazetteers: Kozhikode*, p. 408.

37 Panikkar, Kavalam Madhava, *Malabar and the Mysore: Being the History of Expansion of Mysore in South* (New Delhi: Life Span Publishers and Distributors, 2020), p. 69.

38 Wilks, Mark, *Historical Sketches of the South of India in an Attempt to Trace the History of Mysore*, Vol. 2 (New Delhi: Asian Education Services, 1989), pp. 331–32.

39 Wilks, p. 332.

40 Quoted in Raja, P.C.N., 'Religious Intolerance of Tipu Sultan' in Goel, Sita Ram (ed.), *Tipu Sultan: Villain or Hero?* (New Delhi: Voice of India, 1993), p. 11.

41 Raja, p. 13.

42 Dinesh, Tirur, *Destroyed Temples of Kerala*, Vol. 1 (Trivandrum: TrasaDasyu, 2020), p. 11.

43 Ibid., p. 20.

44 Ibid., p. 22.

45 Dinesh, p. 32.

46 Raja, p. 13.

47 Menon, *Kerala District Gazetteers: Kozhikode*, p. 759.

48 Raja, p. 13.

49 Menon, *Kerala District Gazetteers: Kozhikode*, p. 757.

50 Logan, *Malabar Manual*, Vol. 1, p. 214.

51 Korath V.M., 'The Sword of Tipu Sultan' in Goel, Sita Ram (ed.), *Tipu Sultan: Villain or Hero?* (New Delhi: Voice of India, 1993), p. 4.

52 Menon, *Kerala District Gazetteers: Kozhikode*, p. 769.

53 Menon, *Kerala District Gazetteers: Kozhikode*, p. 71.

54 Logan, *Malabar Manual*, Vol. 2, p. cclxviii.

55 This whole paragraph is drawn from Menon, A. Sreedhara, *Kerala District Gazetteers: Trichur* (Trivandrum: Government of Kerala, 1962), pp. 171–72.

56 Menon, *Kerala District Gazetteers: Kozhikode*, p. 465.

57 Logan, *Malabar Manual*, Vol. 2, p. cccxviii.

58 Menon, *Kerala District Gazetteers: Kozhikode*, p. 762.

59 Kareem, C.K., 'Kerala under Haidar Ali and Tipu Sultan', thesis submitted to the Aligarh Muslim University for the award of Doctor of Philosophy, 1968.

60 Hasan, Mohibbul, *History of Tipu Sultan* (Delhi: Aakar Books, 1951), p. 364.

61 Hasan, pp. 362–63.
62 Hayavadana Rao, Vol. 3, pp. 1252–53.

Epilogue

1   Earl of Mornington to Honourable Court of Directors, 3 August 1799, Montgomery, Martin (ed.). *The Despatches, Minutes and Correspondence of the Marquess Wellesley*, Vol. 2 (London: John Murray, 1836), p. 73.

2   Montgomery, *The Despatches, of the Marquess Wellesley*, Vol. 2, pp. 20–22.

3   *Narrative Sketches of the Conquest of the Mysore Effected by the British Troops and their Allies, in the Capture of Seringapatam and the Death of Tippoo Sultaun*, 2nd ed (London: Printed by W. Justins, 1800), p. 115, footnote.

4   Ibid., pp. 116–17, footnote.

5   *Narrative Sketches of the Conquest of the Mysore*, p. 117, footnote.

6   Ibid.

7   Buchanan, Francis, *A Journey From Madras Through the Countries of Mysore, Canara, and Malabar,* Vol 1 (London: W. Bulmer & Co., 1807), pp. 69–70.

8   Forest, Denys, *Tiger of Mysore: Life and Death of Tipu Sultan* (New Delhi: Allied Publishers Private Limited, 1970), p. 329.

9   Forest, p. 329.

10 Ibid.

11 Rao, Shama M. *Modern Mysore: From the Beginning to 1868* (Bangalore: Higginbothams, 1936), p. 345.

12 Shama Rao, p. 345.

13 Ibid., p 347.

14 Archana Garodia Gupta, *The Women Who Ruled India: Leaders, Warriors, Icons* (Gurugram: Hachette India, 2019), p. 218–19.

15 For more on Velu Nachiyar and the Marudhu brothers, see chapter 14 of Sampath, Vikram, *Bravehearts of Bharat: Vignettes from Indian History* (Gurugram: Penguin Random House India, 2022).

16 Gleig, George Robert *The Life of Major-General Sir Thomas Munro* (London: Henry Colborn & Richard Bentley, 1830), p. 367.

17 Forest, p. 330.

18 Gleig, p. 362.

19 Gleig, p. 364.

20 Forest, pp. 331–32.

21 Gupta, Bunny, & Chaliha, Jaya, 'Exiles in Calcutta: The Descendants of Tipu Sultan' in *India International Centre Quarterly Journal*, SPRING 18.1 (1991), p. 182.

22 Forest, p. 333.

23 Ibid.

24 Ibid.

25 Gupta and Chaliha, p. 183.

26 Willock, Sean. 'A Neutered Beast? Representations of the Sons of Tipu Sultan "The Tiger of Mysore"—as Hostages in the 1790s' in *Journal for Eighteenth Century Studies*, 36.1 (2013), pp. 127–28.

27 See more on https://www.storyltd.com/auction/item.aspx?eid=4051&lotno=71

28 *Narrative Sketches of the Conquest of the Mysore*, p. iii.

29 Hermione de Almedia and George Gilpin, *Indian Renaissance: British Romantic Art and the Prospect of India* (Aldershot: Ashgate, 2005), pp. 161–62.

30 *Narrative Sketches of the Conquest of the Mysore*, pp. 122–23.

31 Forest, pp. 317–18.

32 Ibid., p. 319.

33 Ibid. pp. 320–21.

34 Rev. James Mortan. *The Poetical Remains of the Late Dr John Leyden, With Memoirs of His Life* (London: Longman, 1819), pp. 277–85.

35 See more at: http://www.walterscott.lib.ed.ac.uk/works/novels/daughter.html#:~:text='The%20Surgeon's%20Daughter'%20is%20set,%2C%20Ebenezer%20Clarkson%20of%20Selkirk).

36 See more at https://www.encyclopedia.com/arts/culture-magazines/moonstone

37 Unpublished thesis 'Tyrant! Tipu Sultan and the Reconception of British Imperial Identity, 1780-1800,' University of Maryland, 2013, p. 12.

38 Teltscher, Kate, *India Inscribed: European and British Writing on India 1600–1800* (New Delhi: Oxford University Press, 1995), p. 237.

39 Narasingha Sil, 'Tipu Sultan in History: Revisionism Revised' in *SAGE Open* April–June 2013: I-II, p. 5

40 Ibid., p. 6

41 Ibid., pp. 6–7.

42 See more on https://www.un.org/en/genocideprevention/documents/atrocity-crimes/Doc.1_Convention%20on%20the%20Prevention%20and%20Punishment%20of%20the%20Crime%20of%20Genocide.pdf

43 B. Nilakanthayya. *Swatantrya Sangramadha LavanigaLu* (Bangalore: Karnataka Janapada Parishat, 2008), p. 4.

44 A gramophone recording of this can be heard on: https://www.youtube.com/watch?v=1WZVCRD6Z6w

45 *Vijaya Karnataka* 2006, a translation of the Kannada article, by Sandeep Balakrishna is on https://en.wikiquote.org/wiki/S._L._Bhyrappa

46 Narasingha Sil, pp. 1–9.

Index

Scan QR code to access the
Penguin Random House India website

Appendix

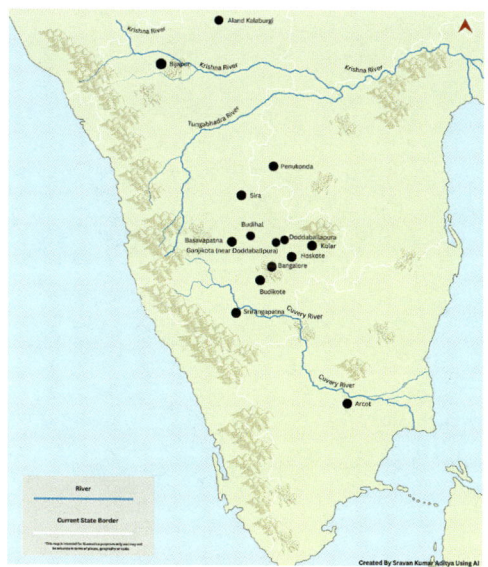

Chapter 1

Chapter 2

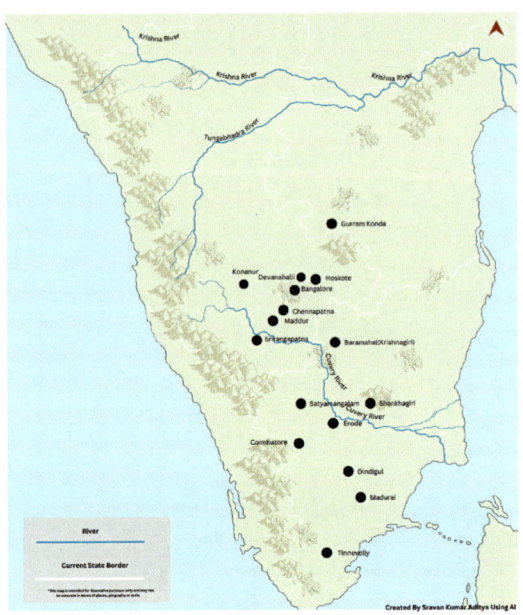

Chapter 3

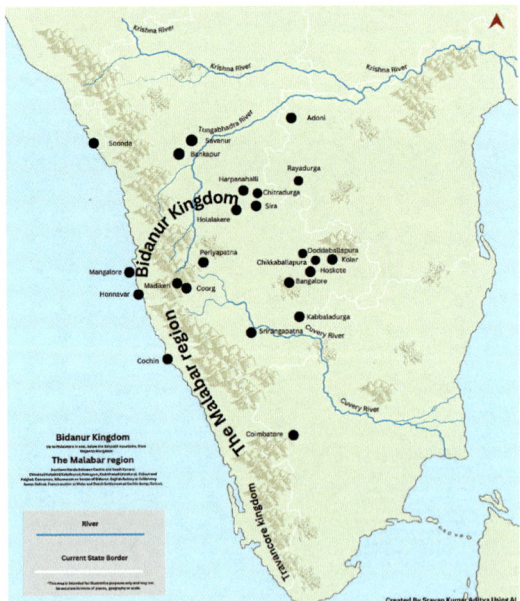

Chapter 4

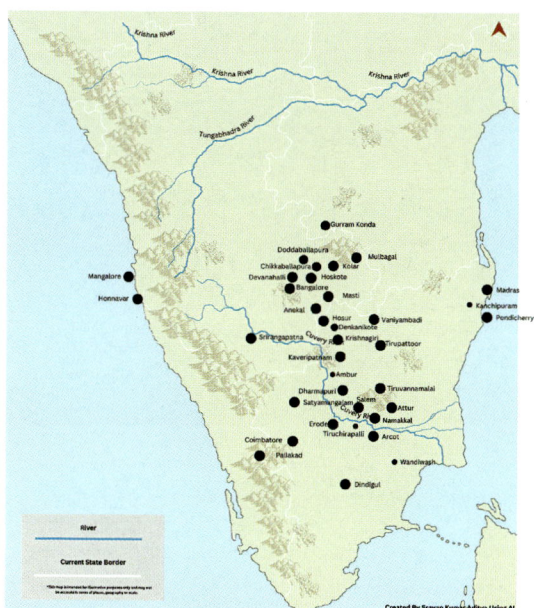

Chapter 5

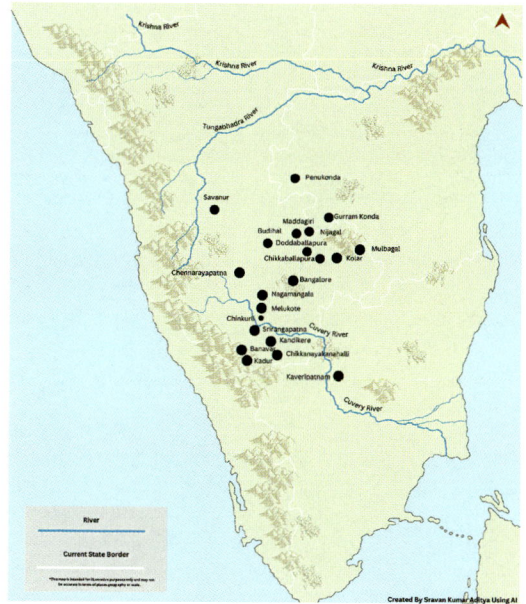

Chapter 6

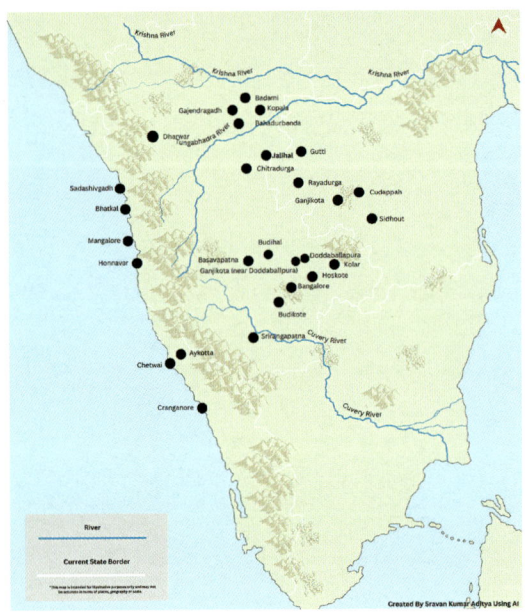

Chapter 7

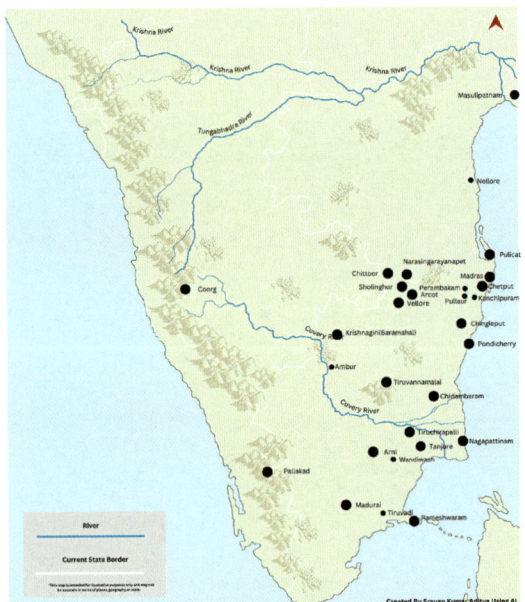

Chapter 8

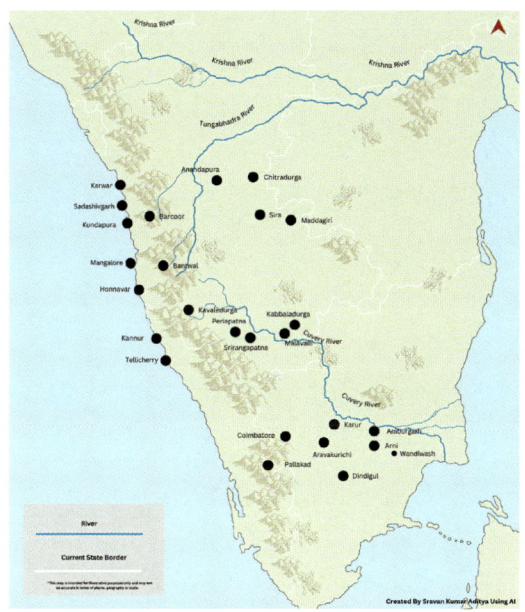

Chapter 10

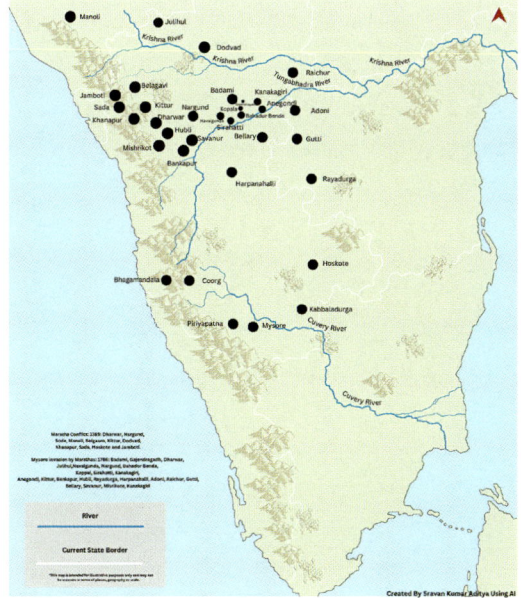

Chapter 11

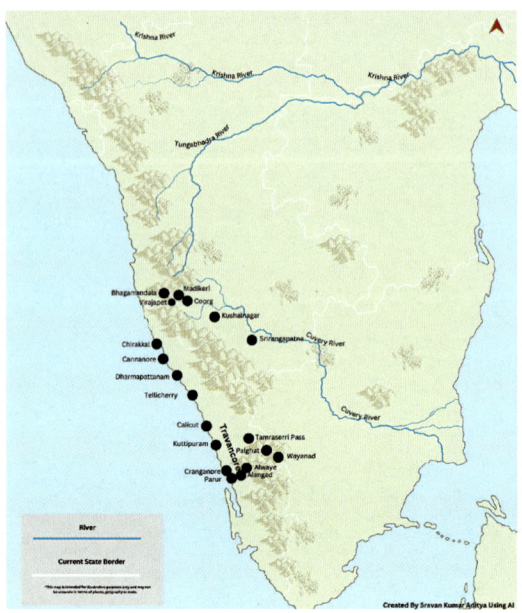

Chapter 12

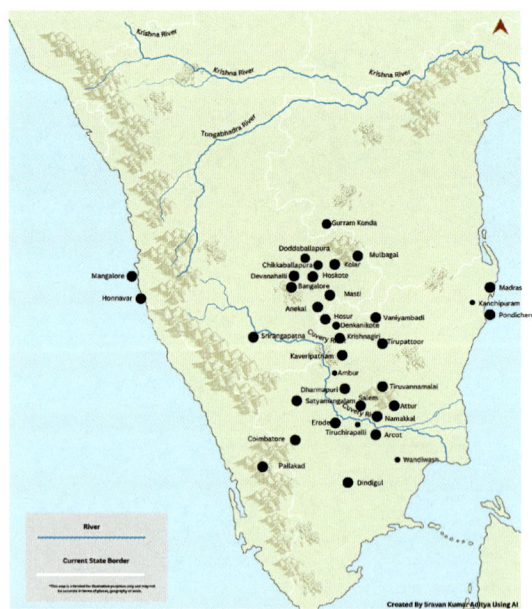

Chapter 13

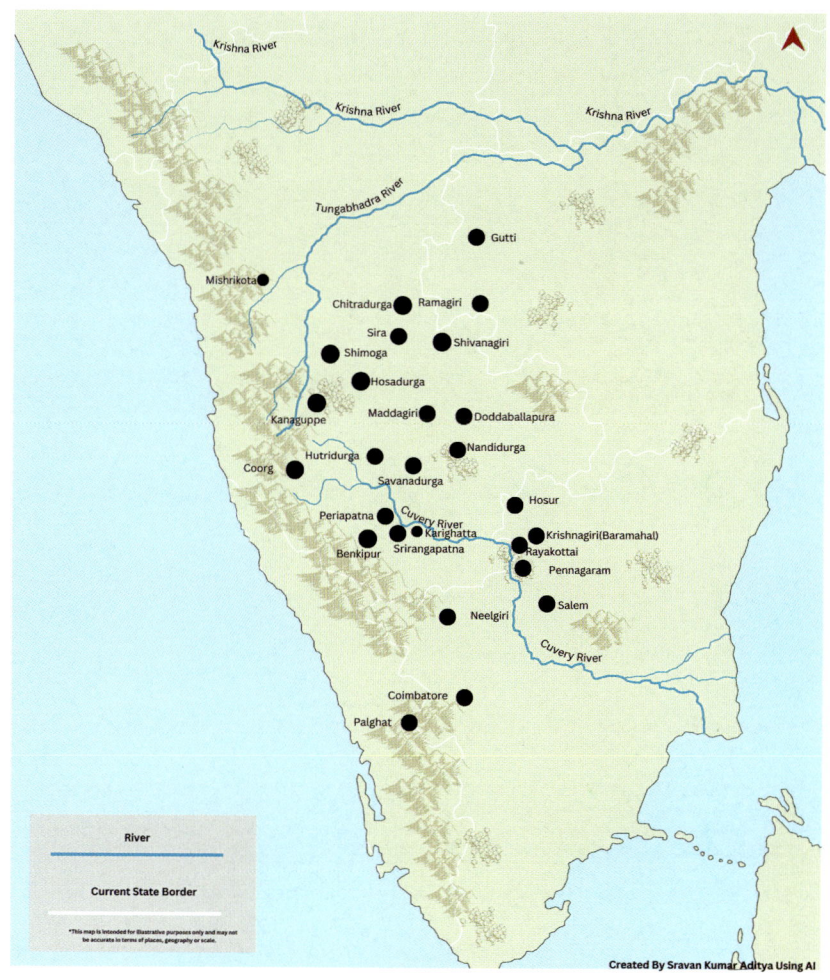

Chapter 14

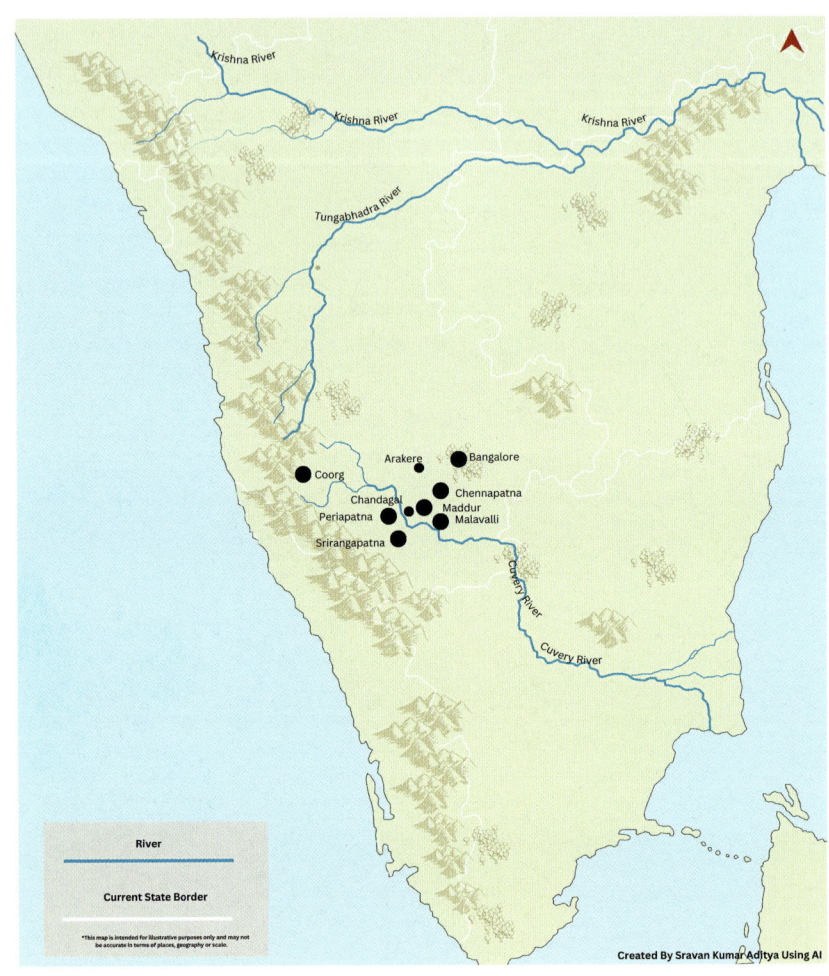

Chapter 17